VW VANAGON

1980-1982 INCLUDES DIESEL
SHOP MANUAL

By

ALFRED A. PEGAL

SYDNIE A. WAUSON
Editor

JEFF ROBINSON
Publisher

CLYMER PUBLICATIONS

World's largest publisher of books devoted exclusively to automobiles and motorcycles

12860 MUSCATINE STREET · P.O. BOX 20 · ARLETA, CALIFORNIA 91331

FIRST EDITION
First Printing June, 1982

SECOND EDITION
Revised by Kalton C. Lahue to include 1982 models
First Printing July, 1983

Printed in U.S.A.

ISBN: 0-89287-351-5

Production Coordinators, Linda Glover and Bessie Jacinto

Technical illustrations by Mitzi McCarthy and Manual Banuelos

COVER:
Photographed by Michael Brown Photographic Productions, Los Angeles, CA
Assisted by Tim Lunde, Liz Lawson
Vanagon courtesy of Volkswagon of America
Jacket and vest courtesy of Simpson
Safety equipment, Torrance, California
Special thanks to Gwen and Robbie Jones.

CONTENTS

VW
VANAGON
1980-1982 INCLUDES DIESEL
SHOP MANUAL

QUICK REFERENCE DATA

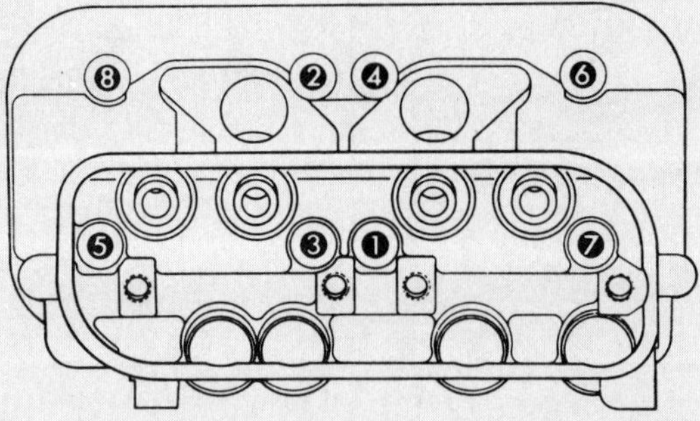

CYLINDER HEAD TORQUING

Hand tighten nuts to align components, then torque to 30 N•m (22 ft.-lb.) in sequence

BREAKER POINT DISTRIBUTOR

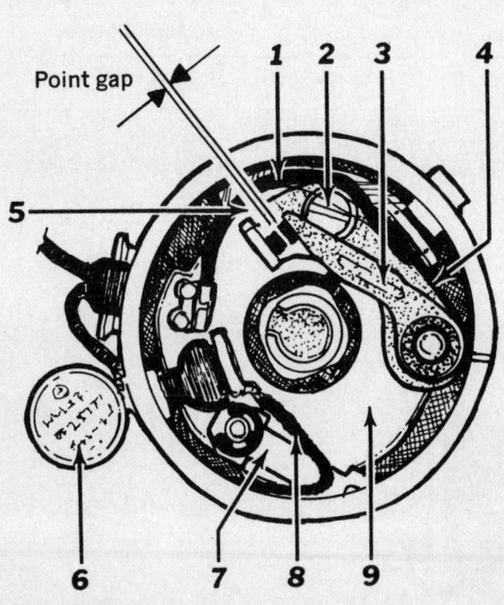

1. Low tension cable
2. Retaining screw
3. Breaker points
4. Breaker arm spring
5. Pins and adjusting slot
6. Condenser
7. Vacuum advance pull rod
8. Ground connection
9. Advance plate

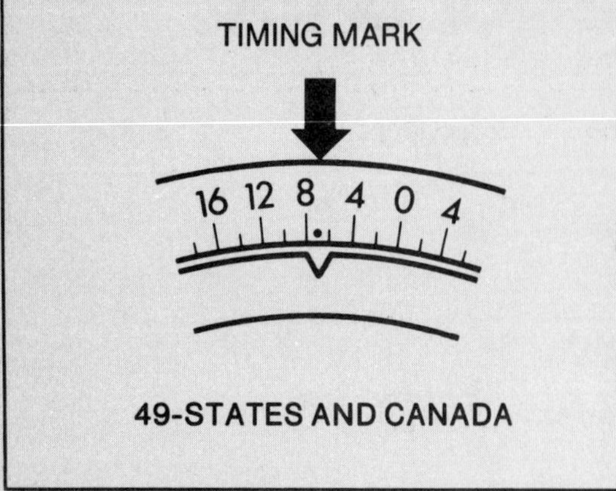

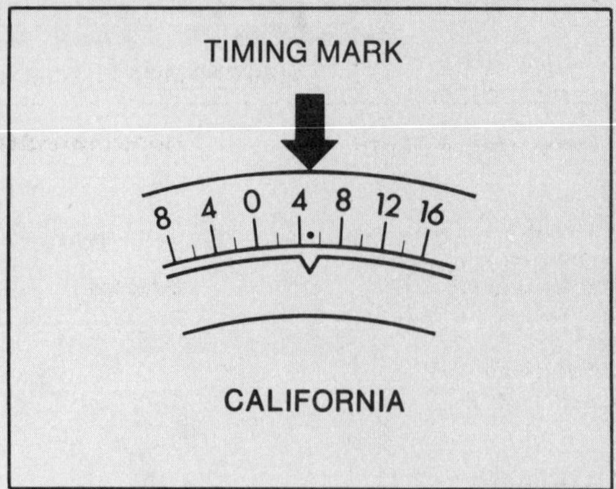

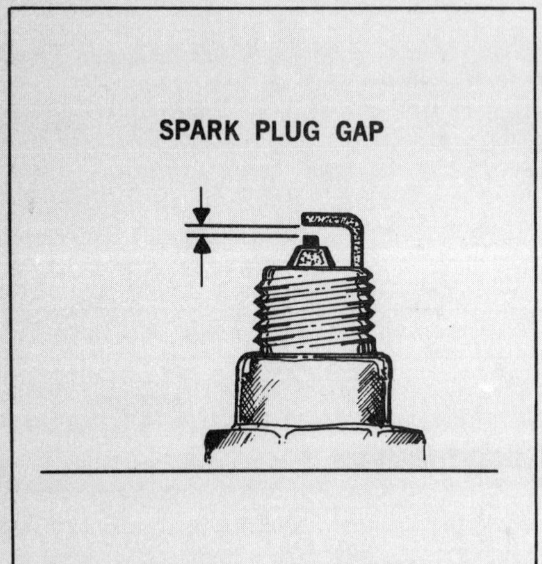

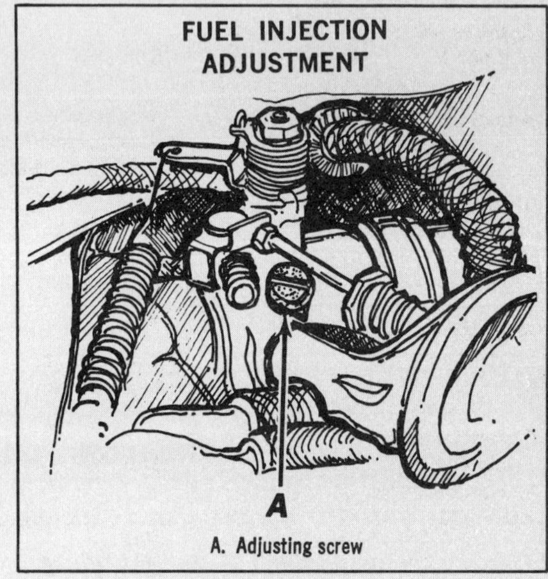

A. Adjusting screw

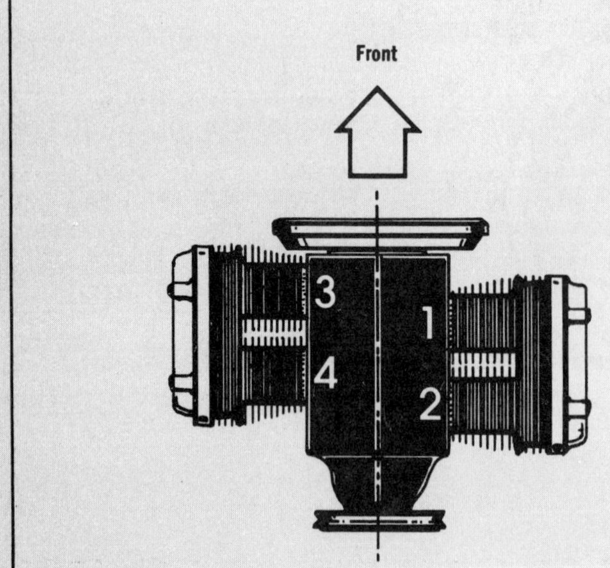

FIRING ORDER: 1 - 4 - 3 - 2

RECOMMENDED OILS, FLUIDS AND CAPACITIES

Temperature Range	Recommended Type	Capacity
Engine oil[1] (gasoline)		
Below -13° F	SAE 5W	3.2 U.S. qt. (3.0 L[2])
Between -13° F and +13° F	SAE 10W	3.7 U.S. qt. (3.5 L[3])
Between 5° F and 40° F	SAE 20-20W	
Between 40° F and 68° F	SAE 30W	
Above 68° F	SAE 40W	
Engine oil[4] (diesel)		
From +15° to +80° F	SAE 20W-40, SAE 20W-50	3.7 U.S. qt. (3.5 L[2])
From -5° to +50° F	SAE 10W-30, SAE 10W-40	4.2 U.S. qt. (4.0 L[3])
Consistently below -15° F	SAE 5W-20	
Manual transaxle		
Below -13° F	ATF (DEXRON)	3.7 U.S. qt. (3.5 L)
Between -13° F and 0° F	Gear oil SAE 80W	
Above 0° F	Gear oil SAE 90W	
Automatic transaxle		
All temperatures	ATF (DEXRON)	Dry fill: 6.4 U.S. qt. (6.0 L)
Automatic transaxle final drive		
Below -13° F	ATF (DEXRON)	3.7 U.S. qt. (3.5 L)
Between -13° F and 0° F	Gear oil SAE 80W	
Above 0° F	Gear oil SAE 90W	
Hydraulic brake/clutch fluid		
All temperatures	DOT 3 or DOT 4	Keep filled

1. Use oil rated for API service SE or SF.
2. Without filter change.
3. With filter change.
4. Use oil rated for API service SF/CC or SF/CD.

GASOLINE ENGINE TUNE-UP SPECIFICATIONS

SPARK PLUGS		
Plug Type		
Bosch	W145M2 or W8CO	
Beru	145/14/3L	
Champion	N288	
Plug Gap	0.023-0.028 in. (0.6-0.7 mm)	
Plug Torque	22 ft.-lb. (30 N•m)	
IGNITION SYSTEM		
Firing Order	1-4-3-2	
Distributor		
	California	**49-States and Canada**
Dwell	Electronic Ignition	44-50°
Point Gap	Electronic Ignition	0.016 in. (0.4 mm)
Ignition Timing		
49-States and Canada	7.5° BTDC	
California	5° ATDC	
Idle Speed		
	California	**49-States and Canada**
Manual Trans.	850-950 rpm	800-950 rpm
Automatic Trans.	850-950 rpm	850-1000 rpm
Vacuum Advance/Retard		
Hose/Hoses	ON	OFF
Valve Clearance	Adjustment not required (Hydraulic Lifters)	

CYLINDER HEAD NUT TORQUE

NOTE:	Torque in three stages
Stage 1	10 ft.-lb. (13.6 N•m)
Stage 2	16 ft.-lb. (21 N•m)
Stage 3	22 ft.-lb. (30 N•m)

INTRODUCTION

This detailed, comprehensive manual covers 1980-1982 Volkswagen Vanagons. The expert text gives complete information on maintenance, repair and overhaul. Hundreds of photos and drawings guide you through every step. The book includes all you need to know to keep your VW running right.

Chapters One through Eleven contain general information on all models and specific information on 1980-1981 models. The Supplement at the end of the book provides service information for 1982 models that differs from earlier years.

Where repairs are practical for the owner/mechanic, complete procedures are given. Equally important, difficult jobs are pointed out. Such operations are usually more economically performed by a dealer or independent garage.

A shop manual is a reference. You want to be able to find information fast. As in all Clymer books, this one is designed with this in mind. All chapters are thumb tabbed. Important items are indexed at the rear of the book. Finally, all the most frequently used specifications and capacities are summarized on the *Quick Reference* pages at the front of the book.

Keep the book handy. Carry it in your glove box. It will help you to better understand your VW, lower repair and maintenance costs, and generally improve your satisfaction with your vehicle.

CHAPTER ONE

GENERAL INFORMATION

The troubleshooting, tune-up, maintenance, and step-by-step repair procedures in this book are written for the owner and home mechanic. The text is accompanied by useful photos and diagrams to make the job as clear and correct as possible.

Troubleshooting, tune-up, maintenance, and repair are not difficult if you know what tools and equipment to use and what to do. Anyone not afraid to get their hands dirty, of average intelligence, and with some mechanical ability can perform most of the procedures in this book.

In some cases, a repair job may require tools or skills not reasonably expected of the home mechanic. These procedures are noted in each chapter and it is recommended that you take the job to your dealer, a competent mechanic, or machine shop.

MANUAL ORGANIZATION

This chapter provides general information and safety and service hints. Also included are lists of recommended shop and emergency tools as well as a brief description of troubleshooting and tune-up equipment.

Chapter Two provides methods and suggestions for quick and accurate diagnosis and repair of problems. Troubleshooting procedures discuss typical symptoms and logical methods to pinpoint the trouble.

Chapter Three explains all periodic lubrication and routine maintenance necessary to keep your vehicle running well. Chapter Three also includes recommended tune-up procedures, eliminating the need to constantly consult chapters on the various subassemblies.

Subsequent chapters cover specific systems such as the engine, transmission, and electrical systems. Each of these chapters provides disassembly, repair, and assembly procedures in a simple step-by-step format. If a repair requires special skills or tools, or is otherwise impractical for the home mechanic, it is so indicated. In these cases it is usually faster and less expensive to have the repairs made by a dealer or competent repair shop. Necessary specifications concerning a particular system are included at the end of the appropriate chapter.

When special tools are required to perform a procedure included in this manual, the tool is illustrated either in actual use or alone. It may be possible to rent or borrow these tools. The inventive mechanic may also be able to find a suitable substitute in his tool box, or to fabricate one.

The terms NOTE, CAUTION, and WARNING have specific meanings in this manual. A NOTE provides additional or explanatory information. A CAUTION is used to emphasize areas where equipment damage could result if proper precautions are not taken. A WARNING is used to stress those areas where personal injury or death could result from negligence, in addition to possible mechanical damage.

SERVICE HINTS

Observing the following practices will save time, effort, and frustration, as well as prevent possible injury.

Throughout this manual keep in mind two conventions. "Front" refers to the front of the vehicle. The front of any component, such as the transaxle, is that end which faces toward the front of the vehicle. The "left" and "right" sides of the vehicle refer to the orientation of a person sitting in the vehicle facing forward. For example, the steering wheel is on the left side. These rules are simple, but even experienced mechanics occasionally become disoriented.

Most of the service procedures covered are straightforward and can be performed by anyone reasonably handy with tools. It is suggested, however, that you consider your own capabilities carefully before attempting any operation involving major disassembly of the engine.

Some operations, for example, require the use of a press. It would be wiser to have these performed by a shop equipped for such work, rather than to try to do the job yourself with makeshift equipment. Other procedures require precision measurements. Unless you have the skills and equipment required, it would be better to have a qualified repair shop make the measurements for you.

Repairs go much faster and easier if the parts that will be worked on are clean before you begin. There are special cleaners for washing the engine and related parts. Brush or spray on the cleaning solution, let it stand, then rinse it away with a garden hose. Clean all oily or greasy parts with cleaning solvent as you remove them.

WARNING

Never use gasoline as a cleaning agent. It presents an extreme fire hazard. Be sure to work in a well-ventilated area when using cleaning solvent. Keep a fire extinguisher, rated for gasoline fires, handy in any case.

Much of the labor charge for repairs made by dealers is for the removal and disassembly of other parts to reach the defective unit. It is frequently possible to perform the preliminary operations yourself and then take the defective unit in to the dealer for repair, at considerable savings.

Once you have decided to tackle the job yourself, make sure you locate the appropriate section in this manual, and read it entirely. Study the illustrations and text until you have a good idea of what is involved in completing the job satisfactorily. If special tools are required, make arrangements to get them before you start. Also, purchase any known defective parts prior to starting on the procedure. It is frustrating and time-consuming to get partially into a job and then be unable to complete it.

Simple wiring checks can be easily made at home, but knowledge of electronics is almost a necessity for performing tests with complicated electronic testing gear.

During disassembly of parts keep a few general cautions in mind. Force is rarely needed to get things apart. If parts are a tight fit, like a bearing in a case, there is usually a tool designed to separate them. Never use a screwdriver to pry apart parts with machined surfaces such as cylinder head and valve cover. You will mar the surfaces and end up with leaks.

Make diagrams wherever similar-appearing parts are found. You may think you can remember where everything came from — but mistakes are costly. There is also the possibility you may get sidetracked and not return to work for days or even weeks — in which interval, carefully laid out parts may have become disturbed.

Tag all similar internal parts for location, and mark all mating parts for position. Record number and thickness of any shims as they are removed. Small parts such as bolts can be identified by placing them in plastic sandwich bags that are sealed and labeled with masking tape.

Wiring should be tagged with masking tape and marked as each wire is removed. Again, do not rely on memory alone.

When working under the vehicle, do not trust a hydraulic or mechanical jack to hold the vehicle up by itself. Always use jackstands. See **Figure 1**.

Disconnect battery ground cable before working near electrical connections and before disconnecting wires. Never run the engine with the battery disconnected; the alternator could be seriously damaged.

Protect finished surfaces from physical damage or corrosion. Keep gasoline and brake fluid off painted surfaces.

Frozen or very tight bolts and screws can often be loosened by soaking with penetrating oil like Liquid Wrench or WD-40, then sharply striking the bolt head a few times with a hammer and punch (or screwdriver for screws). Avoid heat unless absolutely necessary, since it may melt, warp, or remove the temper from many parts.

Avoid flames or sparks when working near a charging battery or flammable liquids, such as brake fluid or gasoline.

No parts, except those assembled with a press fit, require unusual force during assembly. If a part is hard to remove or install, find out why before proceeding.

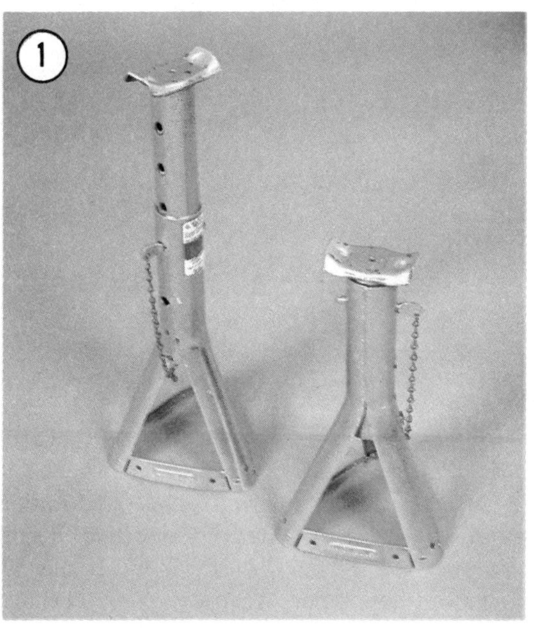

Cover all openings after removing parts to keep dirt, small tools, etc., from falling in.

When assembling two parts, start all fasteners, then tighten evenly.

The clutch plate, wiring connections, brake shoes, drums, pads, and discs should be kept clean and free of grease and oil.

When assembling parts, be sure all shims and washers are replaced exactly as they came out.

Whenever a rotating part butts against a stationary part, look for a shim or washer. Use new gaskets if there is any doubt about the condition of old ones. Generally, you should apply gasket cement to one mating surface only, so the parts may be easily disassembled in the future. A thin coat of oil on gaskets helps them seal effectively.

Heavy grease can be used to hold small parts in place if they tend to fall out during assembly. However, keep grease and oil away from electrical, clutch, and brake components.

High spots may be sanded off a piston with sandpaper, but emery cloth and oil do a much more professional job.

Carburetors are best cleaned by disassembling them and soaking the parts in a commercial carburetor cleaner. Never soak gaskets and rubber parts in these cleaners. Never use wire to clean out jets and air passages; they are easily damaged. Use compressed air to blow out the carburetor, but only if the float has been removed first.

Take your time and do the job right. Do not forget that a newly rebuilt engine must be broken in the same as a new one. Refer to your owner's manual for the proper break-in procedures.

SAFETY FIRST

Professional mechanics can work for years and never sustain a serious injury. If you observe a few rules of common sense and safety, you can enjoy many safe hours servicing your vehicle. You could hurt yourself or damage the vehicle if you ignore these rules.

1. Never use gasoline as a cleaning solvent.
2. Never smoke or use a torch in the vicinity of

flammable liquids such as cleaning solvent in open containers.

3. Never smoke or use a torch in an area where batteries are being charged. Highly explosive hydrogen gas is formed during the charging process.

4. Use the proper sized wrenches to avoid damage to nuts and injury to yourself.

5. When loosening a tight or stuck nut, be guided by what would happen if the wrench should slip. Protect yourself accordingly.

6. Keep your work area clean and uncluttered.

7. Wear safety goggles during all operations involving drilling, grinding, or use of a cold chisel.

8. Never use worn tools.

9. Keep a fire extinguisher handy and be sure it is rated for gasoline (Class B) and electrical (Class C) fires.

EXPENDABLE SUPPLIES

Certain expendable supplies are necessary. These include grease, oil, gasket cement, wiping rags, cleaning solvent, and distilled water. Also, special locking compounds, silicone lubricants, and engine cleaners may be useful. Cleaning solvent is available at most service stations and distilled water for the battery is available at most supermarkets.

SHOP TOOLS

For proper servicing, you will need an assortment of ordinary hand tools (**Figure 2**).

As a minimum, these include:

a. Combination wrenches
b. Sockets
c. Plastic mallet
d. Small hammer
e. Snap ring pliers
f. Gas pliers
g. Phillips screwdrivers
h. Slot (common) screwdrivers
i. Feeler gauges
j. Spark plug gauge
k. Spark plug wrench
l. Torque wrench

Special tools necessary are shown in the chapters covering the particular repair in which they are used.

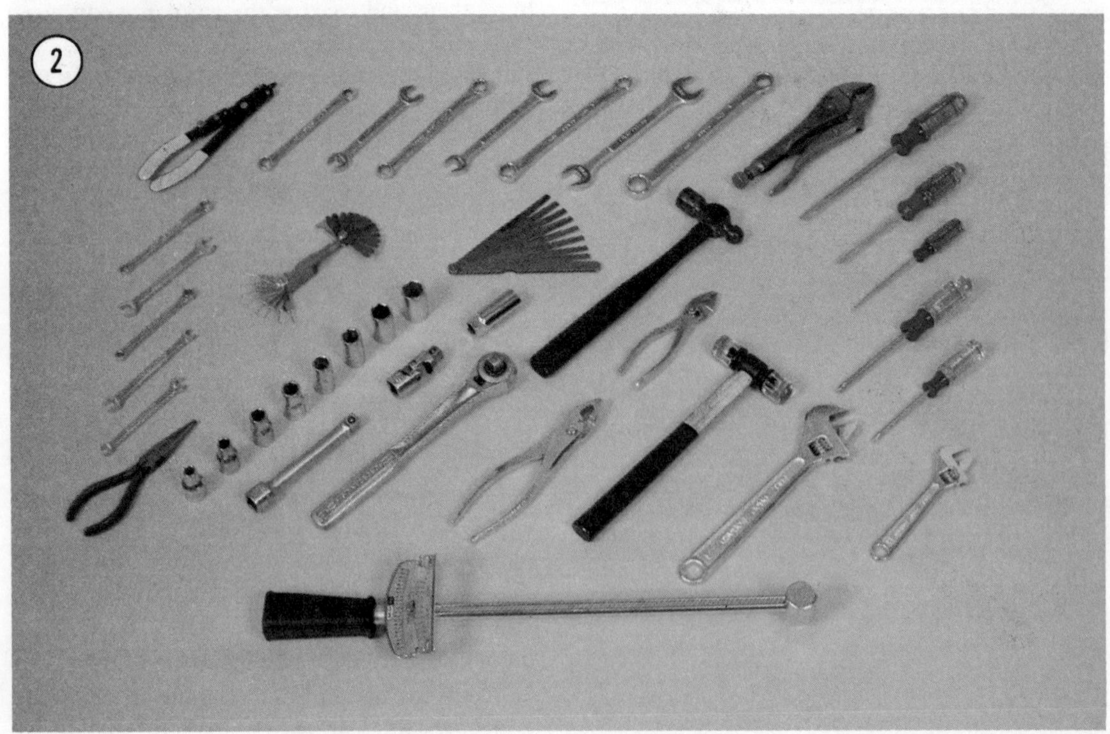

Engine tune-up and troubleshooting procedures require other special tools and equipment. These are described in detail in the following sections.

EMERGENCY TOOL KIT

A small emergency tool kit kept in the trunk is handy for road emergencies which otherwise could leave you stranded. The tools listed below and shown in **Figure 3** will let you handle most roadside repairs.

a. Combination wrenches
b. Crescent (adjustable) wrench
c. Screwdrivers — common and Phillips
d. Pliers — conventional (gas) and needle nose
e. Vise Grips
f. Hammer — plastic and metal
g. Small container of waterless hand cleaner
h. Rags for cleanup
i. Silver waterproof sealing tape (duct tape)
j. Flashlight
k. Emergency road flares — at least four
l. Spare drive belts (cooling fan, alternator, etc.)

TROUBLESHOOTING AND TUNE-UP EQUIPMENT

Voltmeter, Ohmmeter, and Ammeter

For testing the ignition or electrical system, a good voltmeter is required. For automotive use, an instrument covering 0-20 volts is satisfac-

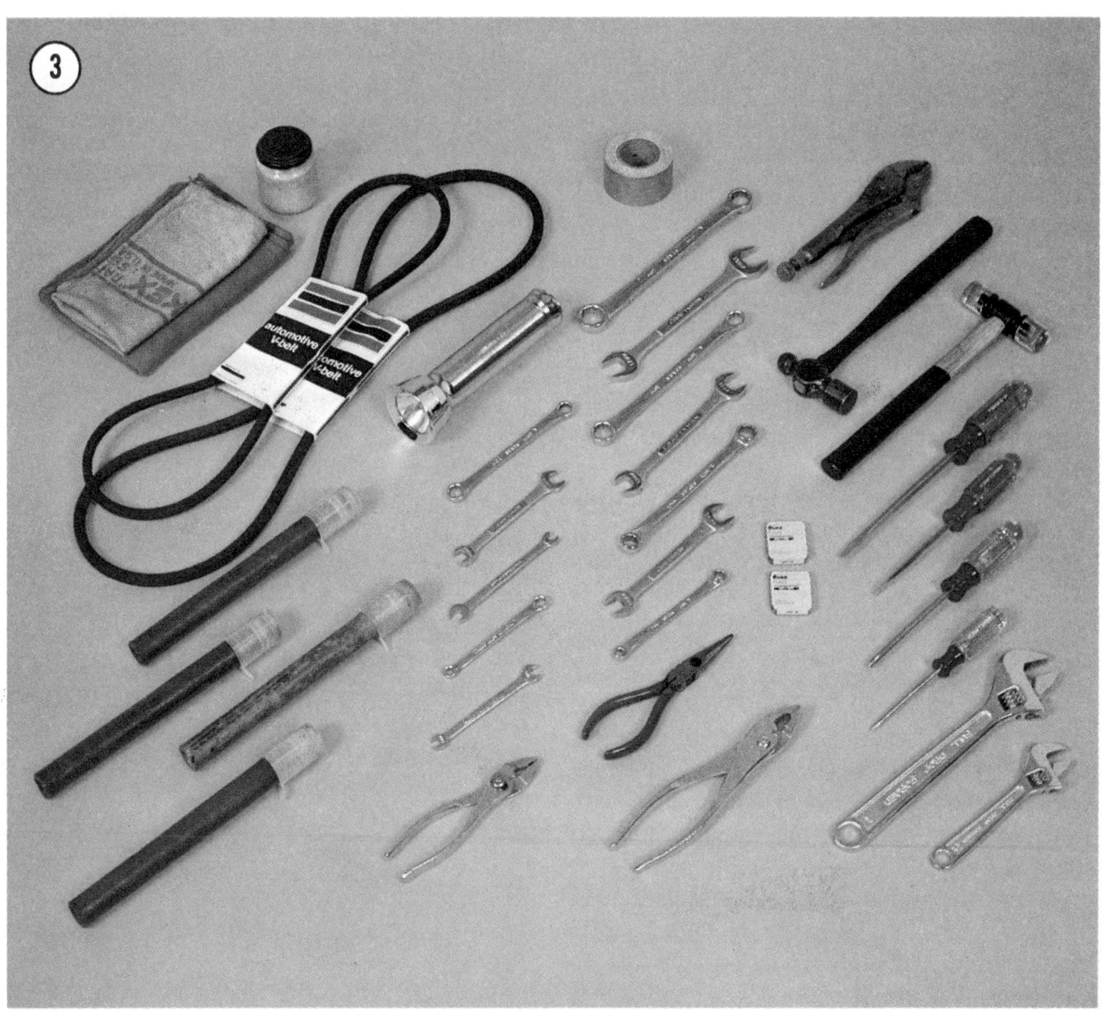

3

tory. One which also has a 0-2 volt scale is necessary for testing relays, points, or individual contacts where voltage drops are much smaller. Accuracy should be ± ½ volt.

An ohmmeter measures electrical resistance. This instrument is useful for checking continuity (open and short circuits), and testing fuses and lights.

The ammeter measures electrical current. Ammeters for automotive use should cover 0-50 amperes and 0-250 amperes. These are useful for checking battery charging and starting current.

Several inexpensive VOM's (volt-ohm-milliammeter) combine all three instruments into one which fits easily in any tool box. See **Figure 4**. However, the ammeter ranges are usually too small for automotive work.

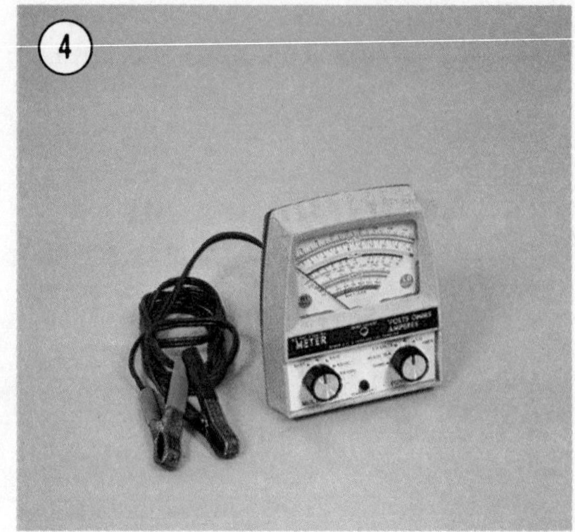

4

Hydrometer

The hydrometer gives a useful indication of battery condition and charge by measuring the specific gravity of the electrolyte in each cell. See **Figure 5**. Complete details on use and interpretation of readings are provided in the electrical chapter.

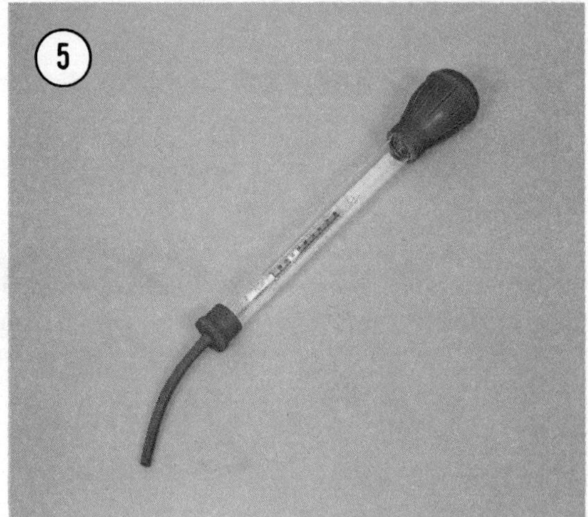

5

Compression Tester

The compression tester measures the compression pressure built up in each cylinder. The results, when properly interpreted, can indicate general cylinder and valve condition. See **Figure 6**.

Most compression testers have long flexible extensions built-in or as accessories. Such an extension is necessary since the spark plug holes are deep inside the metal air cooling covers.

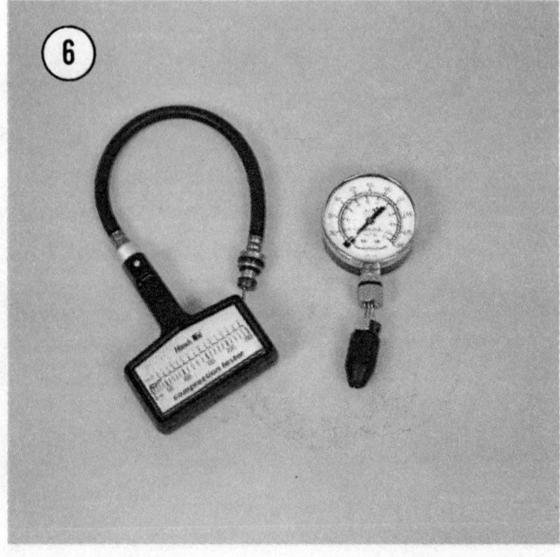

6

Vacuum Gauge

The vacuum gauge (**Figure 7**) is one of the easiest instruments to use, but one of the most difficult for the inexperienced mechanic to interpret. The results, when interpreted with other findings, can provide valuable clues to possible trouble.

To use the vacuum gauge, connect it to a vacuum hose that goes to the intake manifold. Attach it either directly to the hose or to a T-fitting installed into the hose.

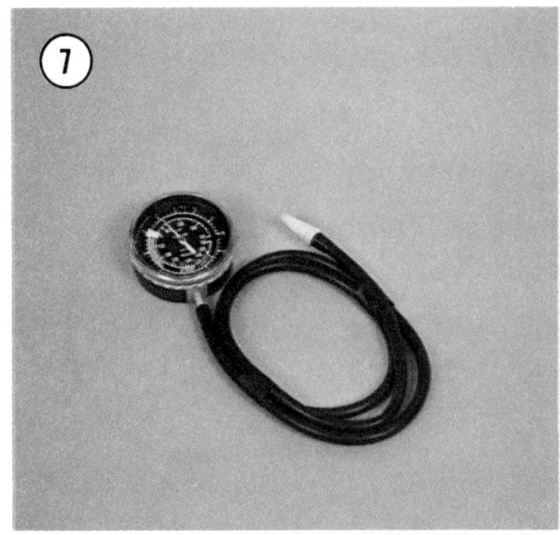
7

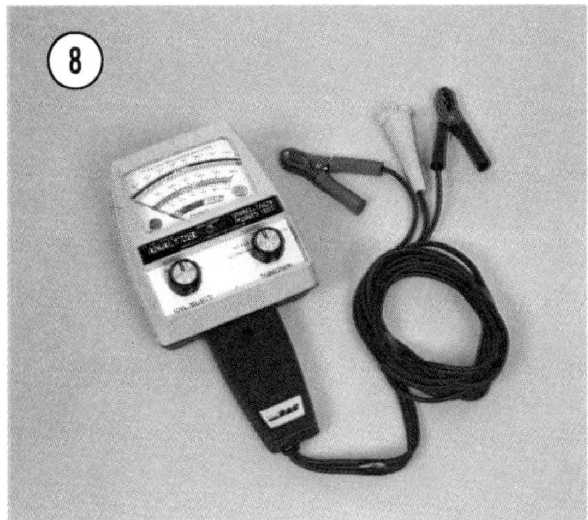
8

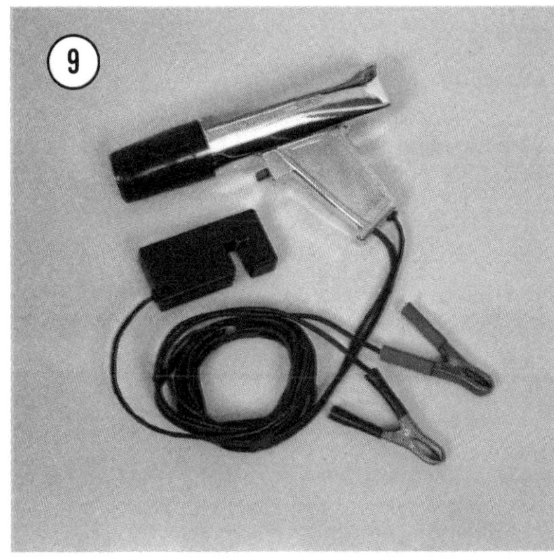
9

NOTE: *Subtract one inch from the reading for every 1,000 ft. elevation.*

Fuel Pressure Gauge

This instrument is invaluable for evaluating fuel pump performance. Fuel system troubleshooting procedures in this manual use a fuel pressure gauge. Usually a vacuum gauge and fuel pressure gauge are combined.

Dwell Meter (Contact Breaker Point Ignition Only)

A dwell meter measures the distance in degrees of cam rotation that the breaker points remain closed while the engine is running. Since this angle is determined by breaker point gap, dwell angle is an accurate indication of breaker point gap.

Many tachometers intended for tuning and testing incorporate a dwell meter as well. See **Figure 8**. Follow the manufacturer's instructions to measure dwell.

Tachometer

A tachometer is necessary for tuning. See **Figure 8**. Ignition timing and carburetor adjustments must be performed at the specified idle speed. The best instrument for this purpose is one with a low range of 0-1,000 or 0-2,000 rpm for setting idle, and a high range of 0-4,000 or more for setting ignition timing at 3,000 rpm. Extended range (0-6,000 or 0-8,000 rpm) instruments lack accuracy at lower speeds. The instrument should be capable of detecting changes of 25 rpm on the low range.

Strobe Timing Light

This instrument is necessary for tuning, as it permits very accurate ignition timing. The light flashes at precisely the same instant that No. 1 cylinder fires, at which time the timing marks on the engine should align. Refer to Chapter Three for exact location of the timing marks for your engine.

Suitable lights range from inexpensive neon bulb types ($2-3) to powerful xenon strobe lights ($20-40). See **Figure 9**. Neon timing lights are difficult to see and must be used in dimly lit areas. Xenon strobe timing lights can be used

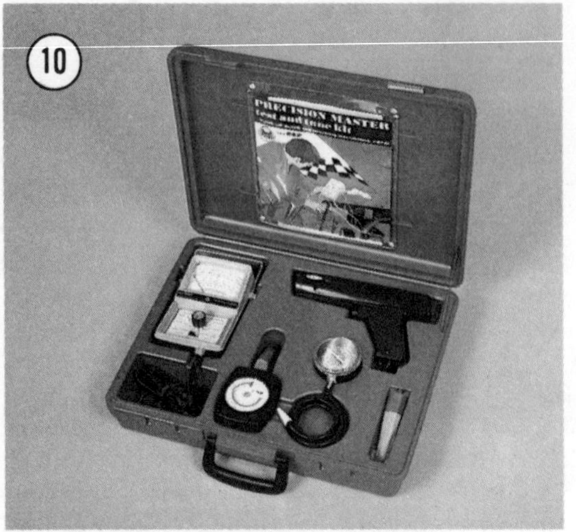

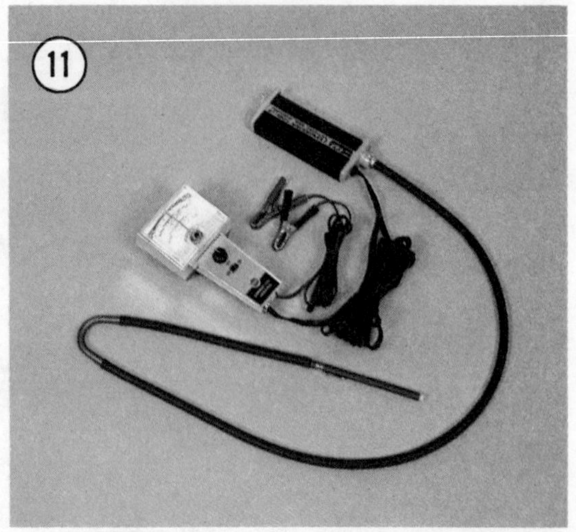

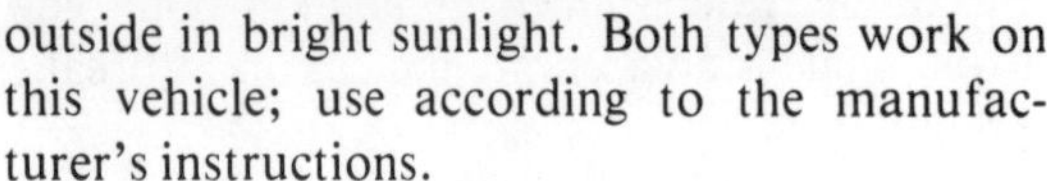

outside in bright sunlight. Both types work on this vehicle; use according to the manufacturer's instructions.

Tune-up Kits

Many manufacturers offer kits that combine several useful instruments. Some come in a convenient carry case and are usually less expensive than purchasing one instrument at a time. **Figure 10** shows one of the kits that is available. The prices vary with the number of instruments included in the kit.

Exhaust Gas Analyzer

Of all instruments described here, this is the least likely to be owned by a home mechanic. This instrument samples the exhaust gases from the tailpipe and measures the thermal conductivity of the exhaust gas. Since different gases conduct heat at varying rates, thermal conductivity of the exhaust is a good indication of gases present.

An exhaust gas analyzer is vital for accurately checking the effectiveness of exhaust emission control adjustments. They are relatively expensive to buy ($70 and up), but must be considered essential for the owner/mechanic to comply with today's emission laws. See **Figure 11**.

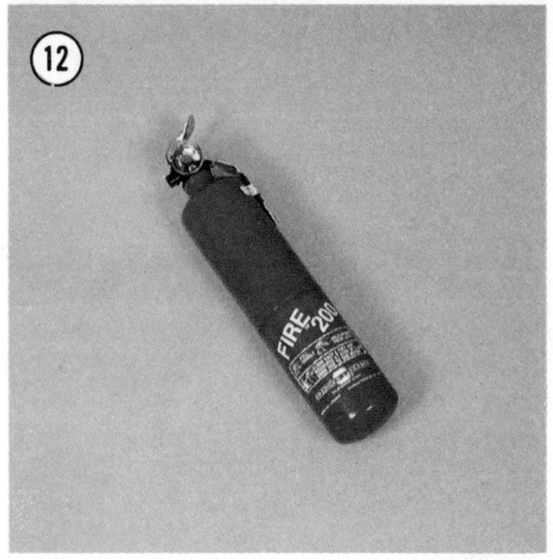

Fire Extinguisher

A fire extinguisher is a necessity when working on a vehicle. It should be rated for both *Class B* (flammable liquids — gasoline, oil, paint, etc.) and *Class C* (electrical — wiring, etc.) type fires. It should always be kept within reach. See **Figure 12**.

CHAPTER TWO

TROUBLESHOOTING

Troubleshooting can be a relatively simple matter if it is done logically. The first step in any troubleshooting procedure must be defining the symptoms as closely as possible. Subsequent steps involve testing and analyzing areas which could cause the symptoms. A haphazard approach may eventually find the trouble, but in terms of wasted time and unnecessary parts replacement, it can be very costly.

The troubleshooting procedures in this chapter analyze typical symptoms and show logical methods of isolation. These are not the only methods. There may be several approaches to a problem, but all methods must have one thing in common — a logical, systematic approach.

STARTING SYSTEM

The starting system consists of the starter motor and the starter solenoid. The ignition key controls the starter solenoid, which mechanically engages the starter with the engine flywheel, and supplies electrical current to turn the starter motor.

Starting system troubles are relatively easy to find. In most cases, the trouble is a loose or dirty electrical connection. **Figures 1 and 2** provide routines for finding the trouble.

CHARGING SYSTEM

The charging system consists of the alternator (or generator on older vehicles), voltage regulator, and battery. A drive belt driven by the engine crankshaft turns the alternator which produces electrical energy to charge the battery. As engine speed varies, the voltage from the alternator varies. A voltage regulator controls the charging current to the battery and maintains the voltage to the vehicle's electrical system at safe levels. A warning light or gauge on the instrument panel signals the driver when charging is not taking place. Refer to **Figure 3** for a typical charging system.

Complete troubleshooting of the charging system requires test equipment and skills which the average home mechanic does not possess. However, there are a few tests which can be done to pinpoint most troubles.

Charging system trouble may stem from a defective alternator (or generator), voltage regulator, battery, or drive belt. It may also be caused by something as simple as incorrect drive belt tension. The following are symptoms of typical problems you may encounter.

1. ***Battery dies frequently, even though the warning lamp indicates no discharge*** — This can be caused by a drive belt that is slightly too

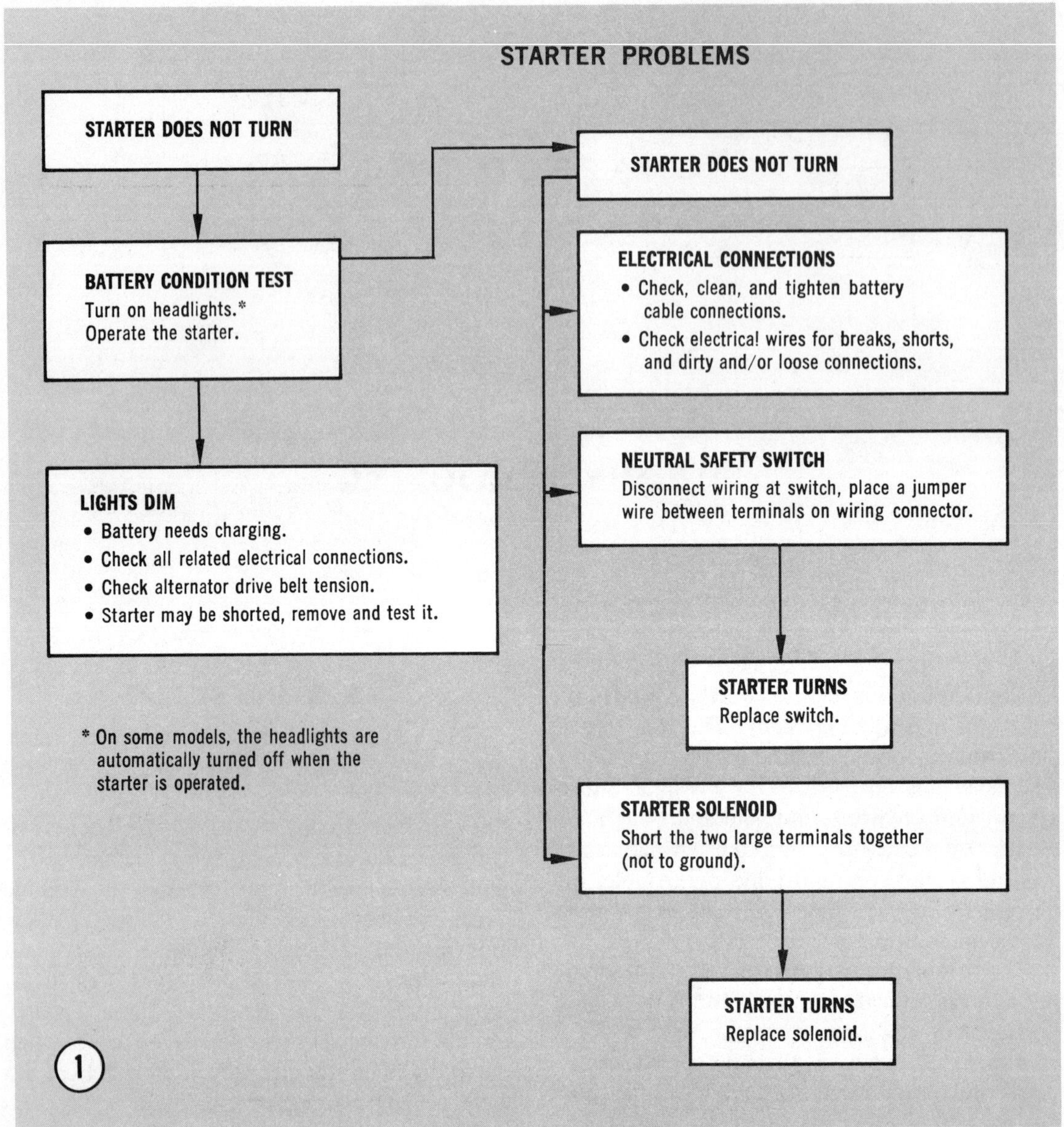

loose. Grasp the alternator (or generator) pulley and try to turn it. If the pulley can be turned without moving the belt, the drive belt is too loose. As a rule, keep the belt tight enough that it can be deflected about ½ in. under moderate thumb pressure between the pulleys (**Figure 4**). The battery may also be at fault; test the battery condition.

2. ***Charging system warning lamp does not come on when ignition switch is turned on*** — This may indicate a defective ignition switch, battery, voltage regulator, or lamp. First try to start the vehicle. If it doesn't start, check the ignition switch and battery. If the car starts, remove the warning lamp; test it for continuity with an ohmmeter or substitute a new lamp. If the lamp is good, locate the voltage regulator and make sure it is properly grounded (try tightening the mounting screws). Also, the alternator (or generator) brushes may not be making contact. Test the alternator (or generator) and voltage regulator.

3. ***Alternator (or generator) warning lamp comes on and stays on*** — This usually indicates

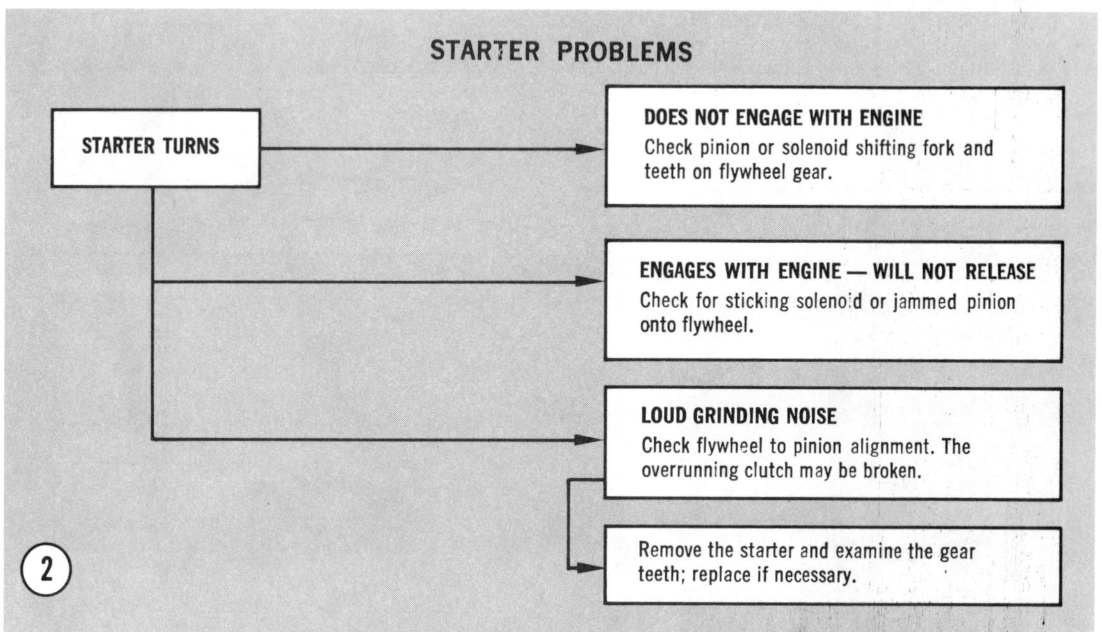

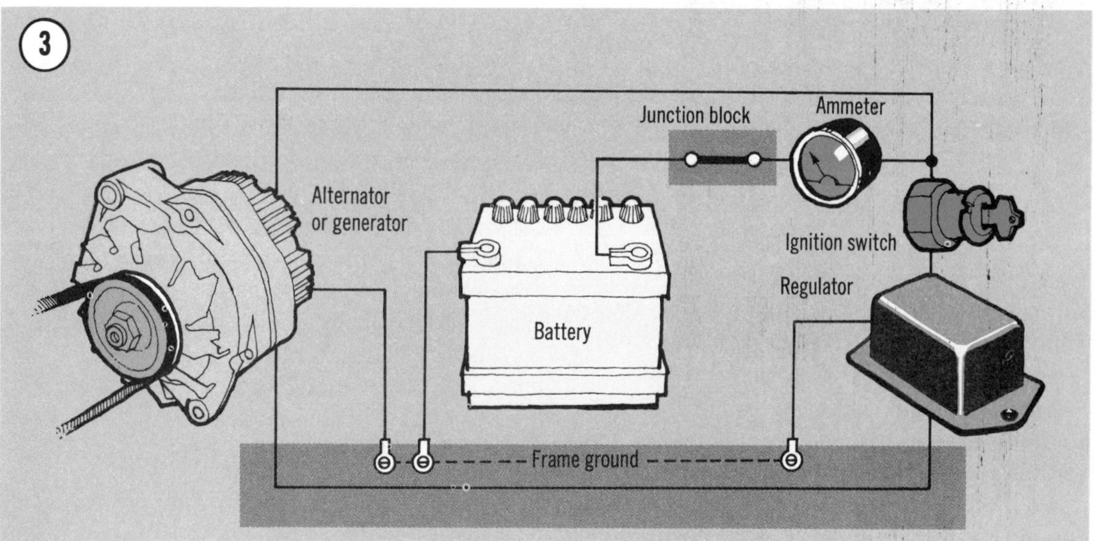

that no charging is taking place. First check drive belt tension (**Figure 4**). Then check battery condition, and check all wiring connections in the charging system. If this does not locate the trouble, check the alternator (or generator) and voltage regulator.

4. ***Charging system warning lamp flashes on and off intermittently*** — This usually indicates the charging system is working intermittently. Check the drive belt tension (**Figure 4**), and check all electrical connections in the charging system. Check the alternator (or generator). *On generators only*, check the condition of the commutator.

5. ***Battery requires frequent additions of water, or lamps require frequent replacement*** — The alternator (or generator) is probably overcharging the battery. The voltage regulator is probably at fault.

6. ***Excessive noise from the alternator (or generator)*** — Check for loose mounting brackets and bolts. The problem may also be

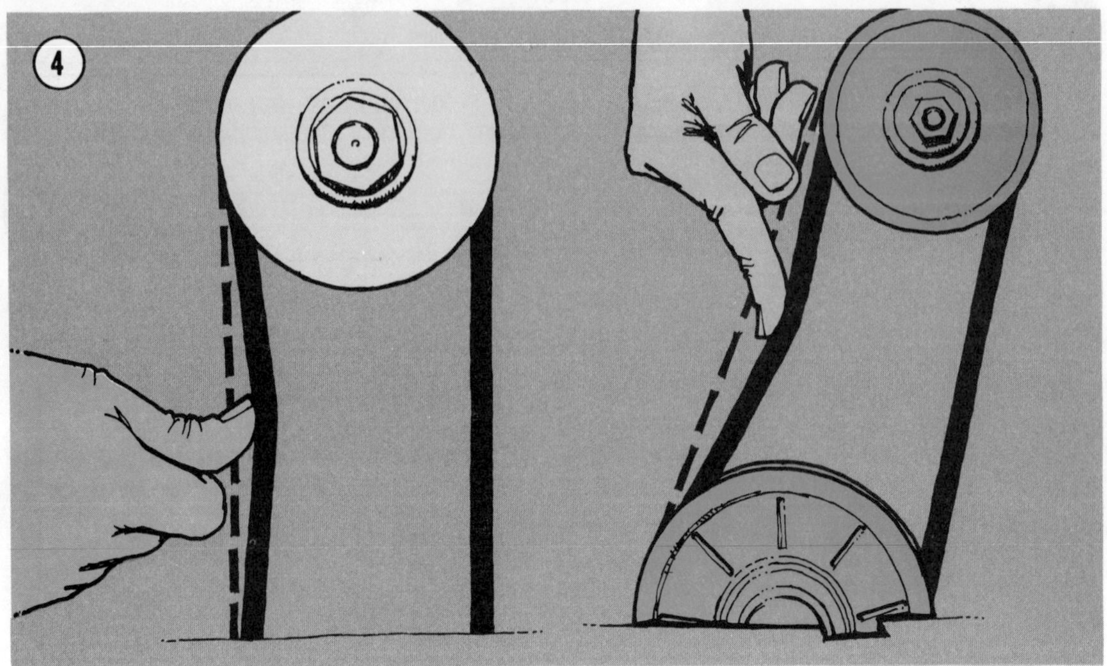

worn bearings or the need of lubrication in some cases. If an alternator whines, a shorted diode may be indicated.

IGNITION SYSTEM

The ignition system may be either a conventional contact breaker type or an electronic ignition. See electrical chapter to determine which type you have. **Figures 5 and 6** show simplified diagrams of each type.

Most problems involving failure to start, poor performance, or rough running stem from trouble in the ignition system, particularly in contact breaker systems. Many novice troubleshooters get into trouble when they assume that these symptoms point to the fuel system instead of the ignition system.

Ignition system troubles may be roughly divided between those affecting only one cylinder and those affecting all cylinders. If the trouble affects only one cylinder, it can only be in the spark plug, spark plug wire, or portion of the distributor associated with that cylinder. If the trouble affects all cylinders (weak spark or no spark), then the trouble is in the ignition coil, rotor, distributor, or associated wiring.

In order to get maximum spark, the ignition coil must be wired correctly. Make sure that the double wire from the battery is attached to terminal No. 15 on the ignition coil and that the single wire from the distributor is attached to terminal No. 1 on the ignition coil.

The troubleshooting procedures outlined in **Figure 7** (breaker point ignition) or **Figure 8** (electronic ignition) will help you isolate ignition problems fast. Of course, they assume that the battery is in good enough condition to crank the engine over at its normal rate.

ENGINE PERFORMANCE

A number of factors can make the engine difficult or impossible to start, or cause rough running, poor performance and so on. The majority of novice troubleshooters immediately suspect the carburetor or fuel injection system. In the majority of cases, though, the trouble exists in the ignition system.

The troubleshooting procedures outlined in **Figures 9 through 14** will help you solve the majority of engine starting troubles in a systematic manner.

Some tests of the ignition system require running the engine with a spark plug or ignition coil wire disconnected. The safest way to do this is to disconnect the wire with the engine

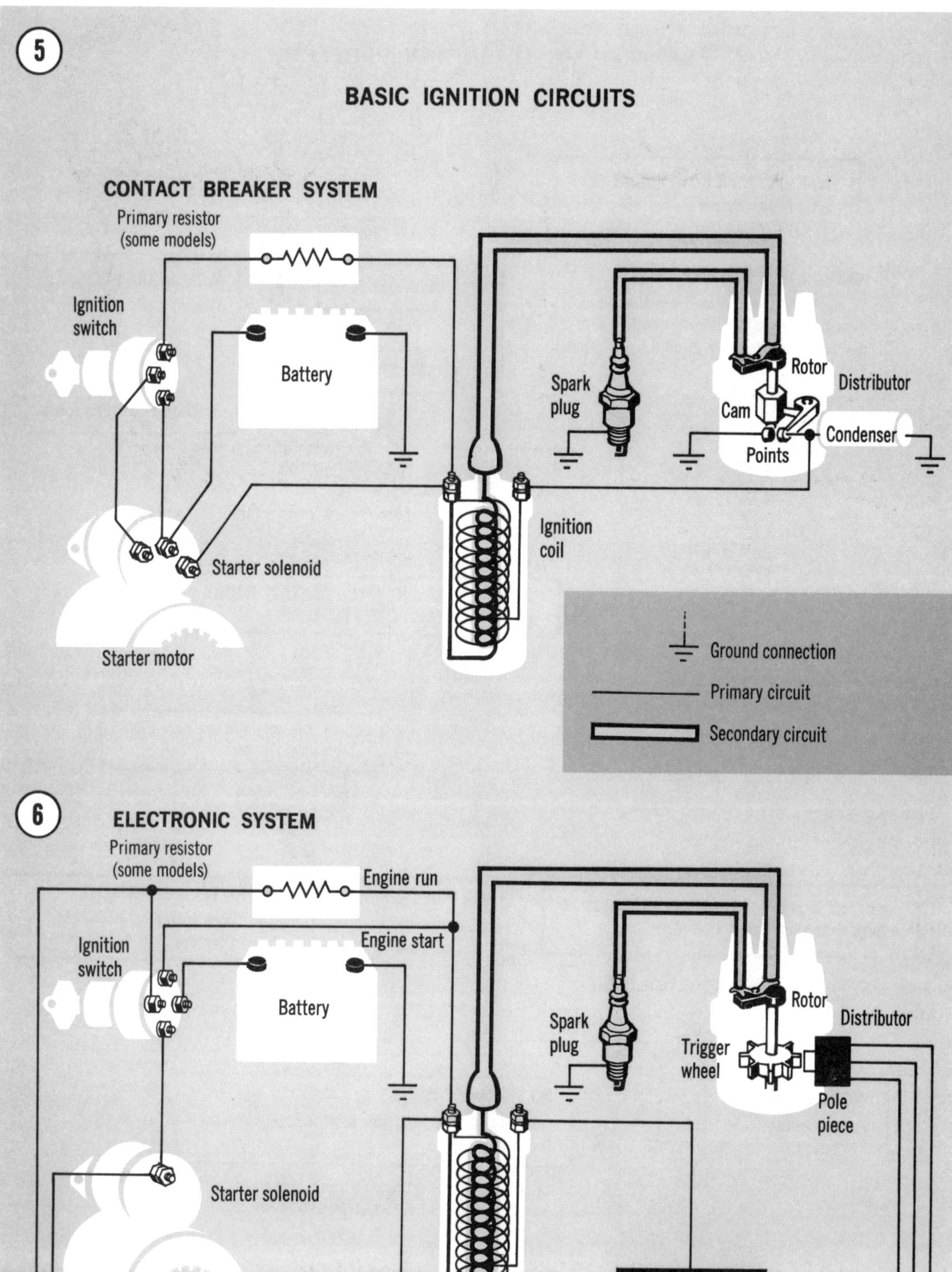
5
BASIC IGNITION CIRCUITS
CONTACT BREAKER SYSTEM
Primary resistor
(some models)
Ignition
switch
Battery
Spark
plug
Rotor
Distributor
Cam
Condenser
Points
Ignition
coil
Starter solenoid
Starter motor
Ground connection
Primary circuit
Secondary circuit
6
ELECTRONIC SYSTEM
Primary resistor
(some models)
Engine run
Engine start
Ignition
switch
Battery
Spark
plug
Rotor
Distributor
Trigger
wheel
Pole
piece
Starter solenoid
Starter motor
Electronic
module

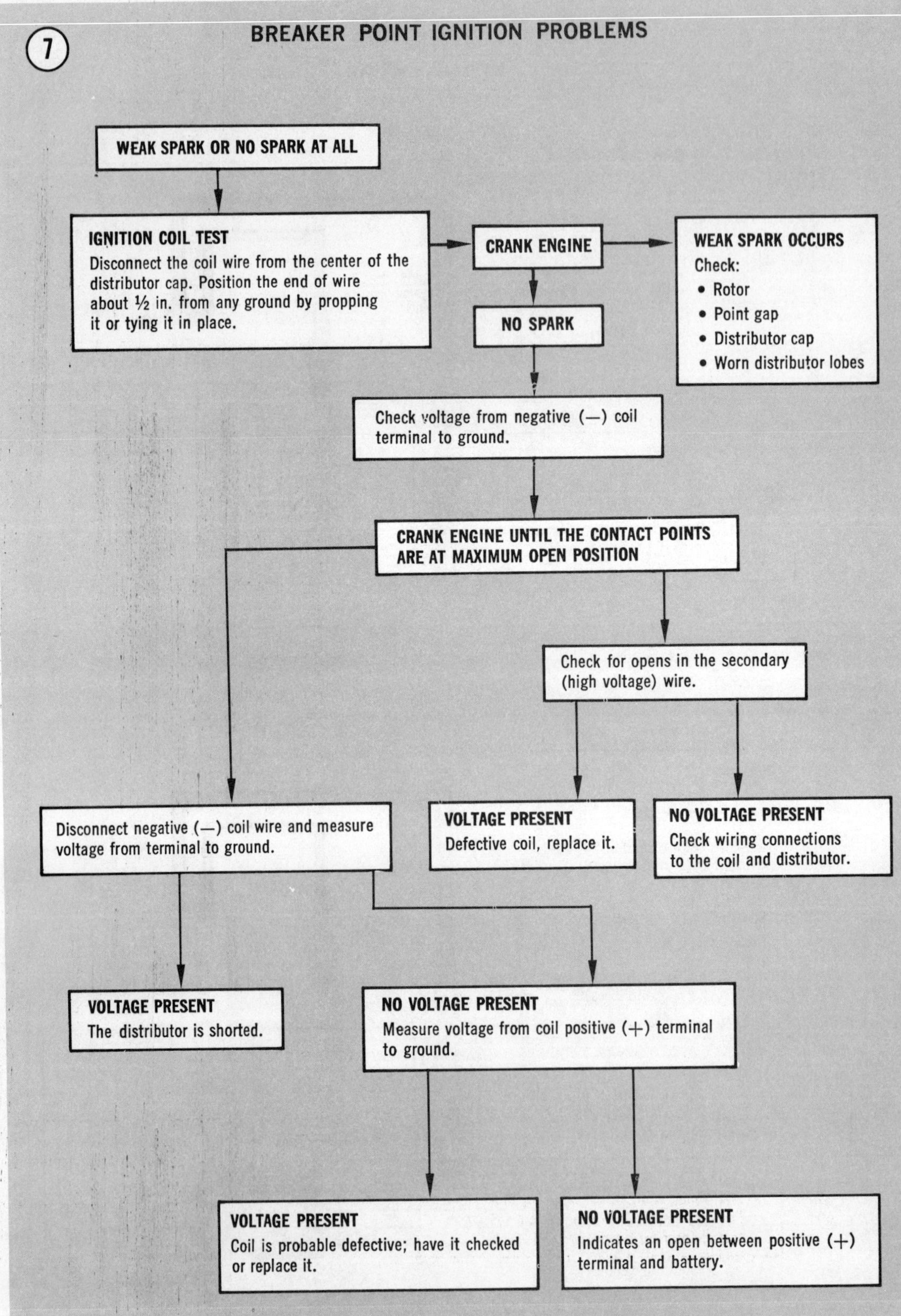
7
BREAKER POINT IGNITION PROBLEMS
WEAK SPARK OR NO SPARK AT ALL
IGNITION COIL TEST
Disconnect the coil wire from the center of the distributor cap. Position the end of wire about ½ in. from any ground by propping it or tying it in place.
CRANK ENGINE
WEAK SPARK OCCURS
Check:
• Rotor
• Point gap
• Distributor cap
• Worn distributor lobes
NO SPARK
Check voltage from negative (—) coil terminal to ground.
CRANK ENGINE UNTIL THE CONTACT POINTS ARE AT MAXIMUM OPEN POSITION
Check for opens in the secondary (high voltage) wire.
Disconnect negative (—) coil wire and measure voltage from terminal to ground.
VOLTAGE PRESENT
Defective coil, replace it.
NO VOLTAGE PRESENT
Check wiring connections to the coil and distributor.
VOLTAGE PRESENT
The distributor is shorted.
NO VOLTAGE PRESENT
Measure voltage from coil positive (+) terminal to ground.
VOLTAGE PRESENT
Coil is probable defective; have it checked or replace it.
NO VOLTAGE PRESENT
Indicates an open between positive (+) terminal and battery.

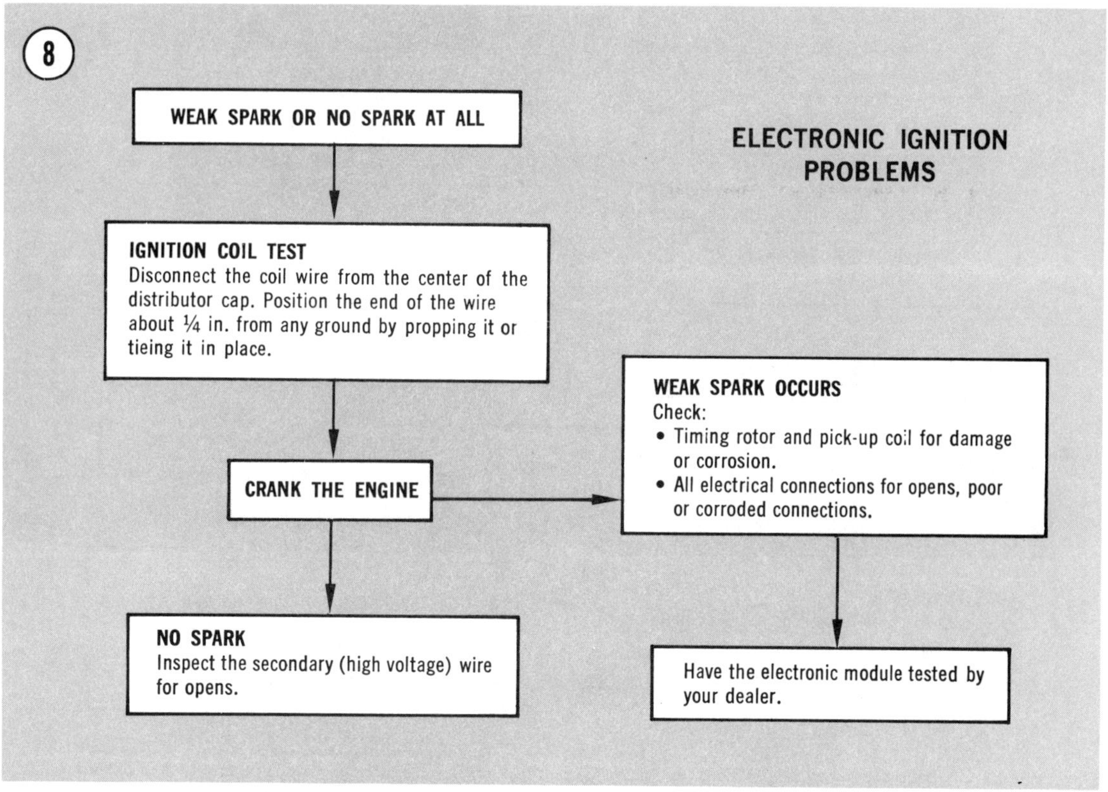

8

WEAK SPARK OR NO SPARK AT ALL

ELECTRONIC IGNITION PROBLEMS

IGNITION COIL TEST
Disconnect the coil wire from the center of the distributor cap. Position the end of the wire about ¼ in. from any ground by propping it or tieing it in place.

CRANK THE ENGINE

WEAK SPARK OCCURS
Check:
- Timing rotor and pick-up coil for damage or corrosion.
- All electrical connections for opens, poor or corroded connections.

Have the electronic module tested by your dealer.

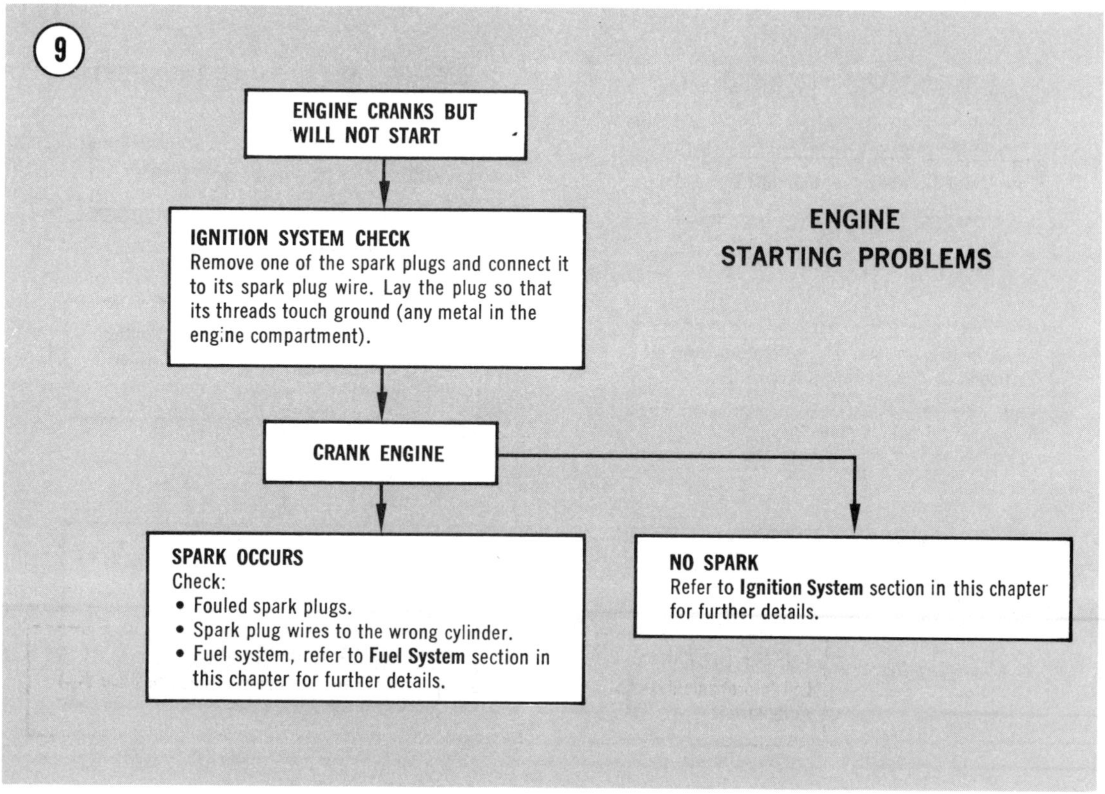

NO SPARK
Inspect the secondary (high voltage) wire for opens.

9

ENGINE CRANKS BUT WILL NOT START

ENGINE STARTING PROBLEMS

IGNITION SYSTEM CHECK
Remove one of the spark plugs and connect it to its spark plug wire. Lay the plug so that its threads touch ground (any metal in the engine compartment).

CRANK ENGINE

SPARK OCCURS
Check:
- Fouled spark plugs.
- Spark plug wires to the wrong cylinder.
- Fuel system, refer to **Fuel System** section in this chapter for further details.

NO SPARK
Refer to **Ignition System** section in this chapter for further details.

10
STEADY ENGINE MISS
ENGINE MISSES STEADILY
DISCONNECT ONE SPARK PLUG WIRE AT A TIME
START ENGINE AND LET IT IDLE
MISS REMAINS THE SAME
That cylinder is not operating correctly.
Check:
• Spark plug condition and gap.
• Spark plug wires for opens or cracks in the insulation.
• Distributor cap.
MISS INCREASES
That cylinder is operating correctly—continue to next cylinder.

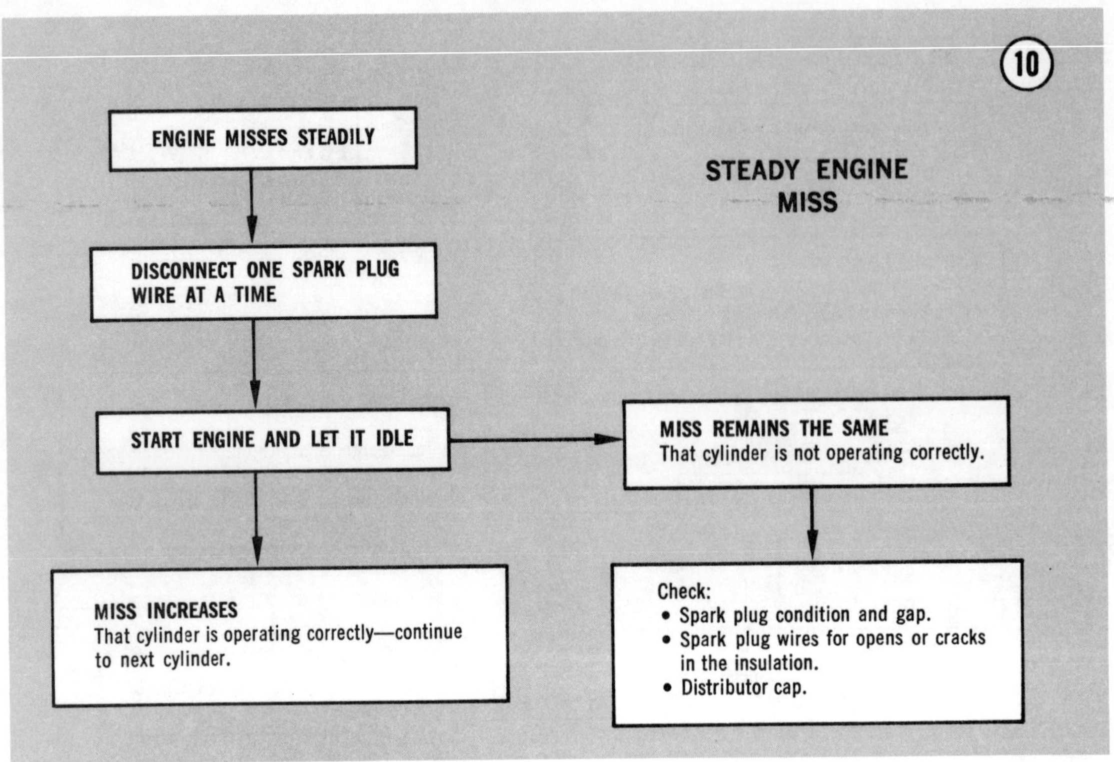

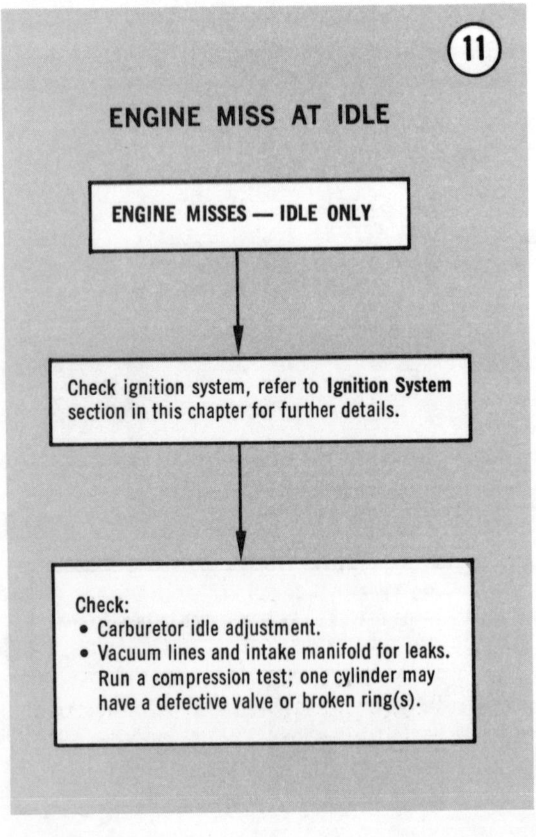

11
ENGINE MISS AT IDLE
ENGINE MISSES — IDLE ONLY
Check ignition system, refer to Ignition System section in this chapter for further details.
Check:
• Carburetor idle adjustment.
• Vacuum lines and intake manifold for leaks. Run a compression test; one cylinder may have a defective valve or broken ring(s).

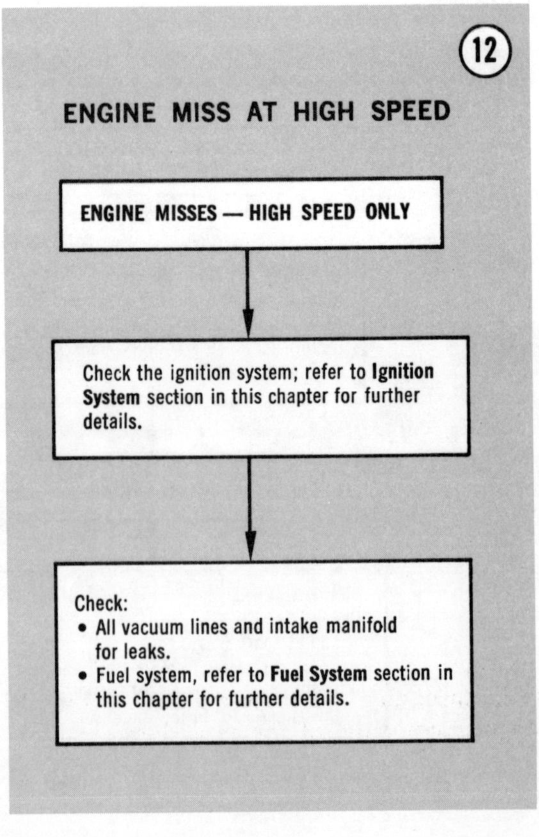

12
ENGINE MISS AT HIGH SPEED
ENGINE MISSES — HIGH SPEED ONLY
Check the ignition system; refer to Ignition System section in this chapter for further details.
Check:
• All vacuum lines and intake manifold for leaks.
• Fuel system, refer to Fuel System section in this chapter for further details.

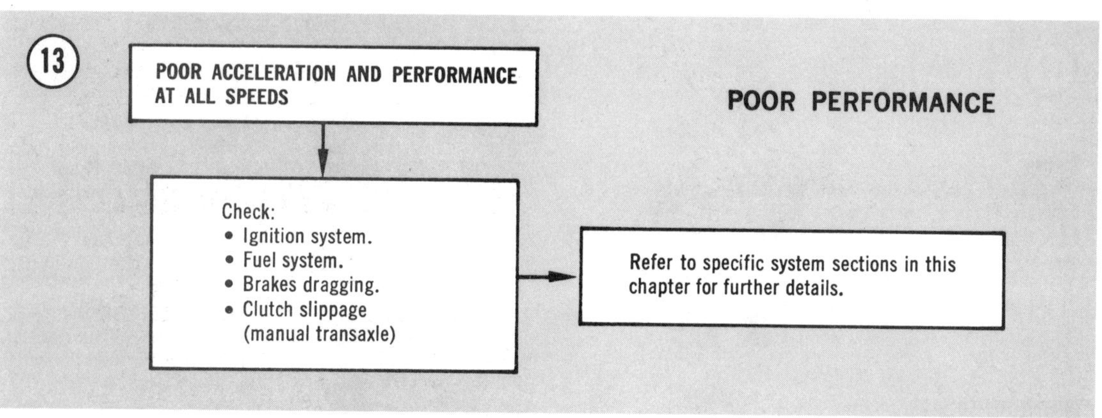

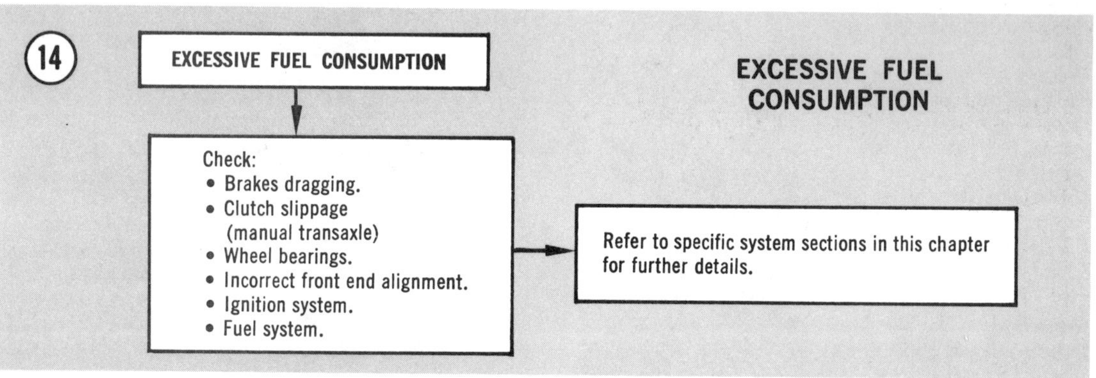

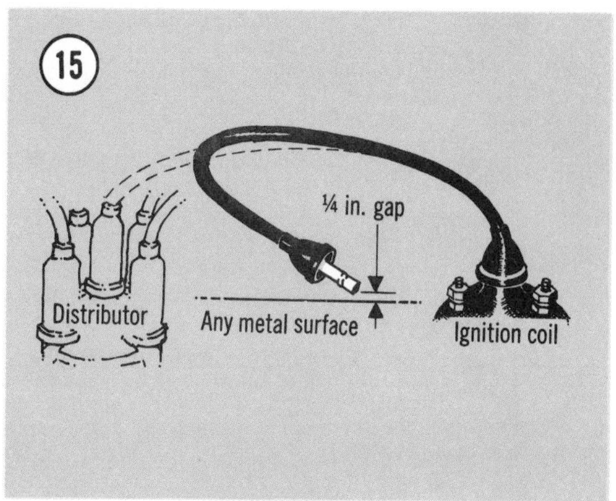

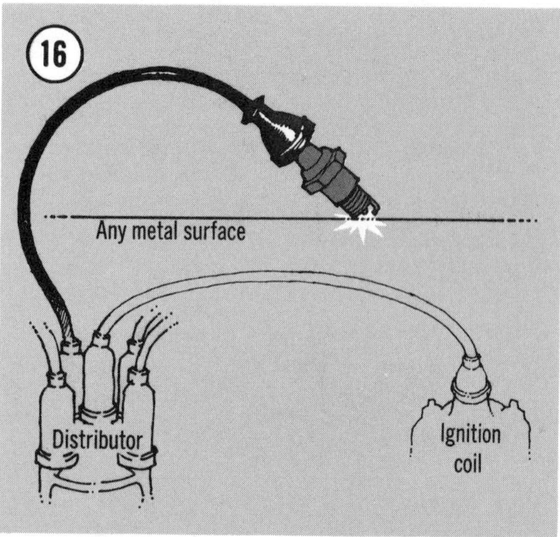

stopped, then prop the end of the wire next to a metal surface as shown in **Figures 15 and 16**.

WARNING

Never disconnect a spark plug or ignition coil wire while the engine is running. The high voltage in an ignition system, particularly the newer high-energy electronic ignition systems could cause serious injury or even death.

Spark plug condition is an important indication of engine performance. Spark plugs in a properly operating engine will have slightly pitted electrodes, and a light tan insulator tip. **Figure 17** shows a normal plug, and a number of others which indicate trouble in their respective cylinders.

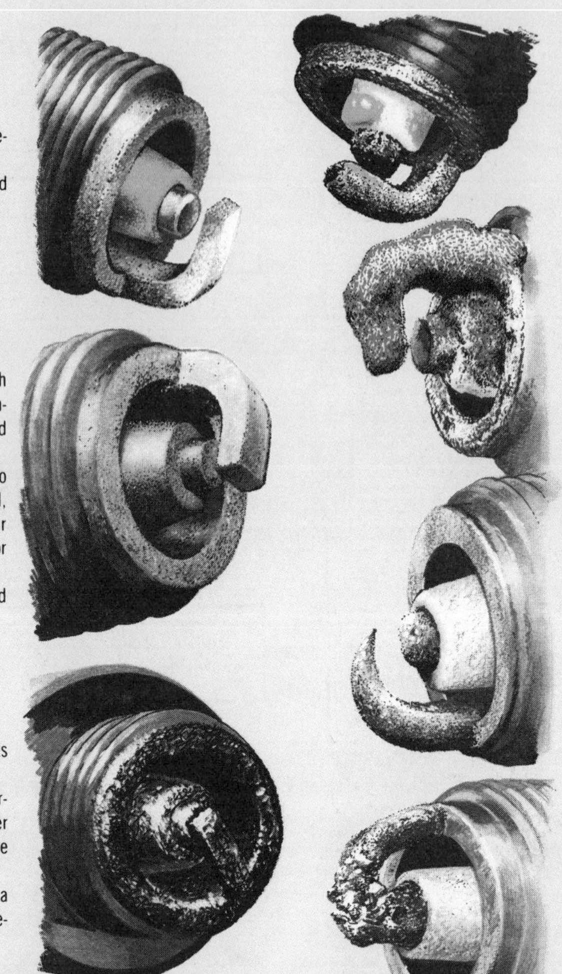

NORMAL

- Appearance—Firing tip has deposits of light gray to light tan.
- Can be cleaned, regapped and reused.

CARBON FOULED

- Appearance—Dull, dry black with fluffy carbon deposits on the insulator tip, electrode and exposed shell.
- Caused by—Fuel/air mixture too rich, plug heat range too cold, weak ignition system, dirty air cleaner, faulty automatic choke or excessive idling.
- Can be cleaned, regapped and reused.

OIL FOULED

- Appearance—Wet black deposits on insulator and exposed shell.
- Caused by—Excessive oil entering the combustion chamber through worn rings, pistons, valve guides or bearings.
- Replace with new plugs (use a hotter plug if engine is not repaired).

LEAD FOULED

- Appearance — Yellow insulator deposits (may sometimes be dark gray, black or tan in color) on the insulator tip.
- Caused by—Highly leaded gasoline.
- Replace with new plugs.

LEAD FOULED

- Appearance—Yellow glazed deposits indicating melted lead deposits due to hard acceleration.
- Caused by—Highly leaded gasoline.
- Replace with new plugs.

OIL AND LEAD FOULED

- Appearance—Glazed yellow deposits with a slight brownish tint on the insulator tip and ground electrode.
- Replace with new plugs.

FUEL ADDITIVE RESIDUE

- Appearance — Brown-colored, hardened ash deposits on the insulator tip and ground electrode.
- Caused by—Fuel and/or oil additives.
- Replace with new plugs.

WORN

- Appearance — Severely worn or eroded electrodes.
- Caused by—Normal wear or unusual oil and/or fuel additives.
- Replace with new plugs.

PREIGNITION

- Appearance — Melted ground electrode.
- Caused by—Overadvanced ignition timing, inoperative ignition advance mechanism, too low of a fuel octane rating, lean fuel/air mixture or carbon deposits in combustion chamber.

PREIGNITION

- Appearance—Melted center electrode.
- Caused by—Abnormal combustion due to overadvanced ignition timing or incorrect advance, too low of a fuel octane rating, lean fuel/air mixture, or carbon deposits in combustion chamber.
- Correct engine problem and replace with new plugs.

INCORRECT HEAT RANGE

- Appearance—Melted center electrode and white blistered insulator tip.
- Caused by—Incorrect plug heat range selection.
- Replace with new plugs.

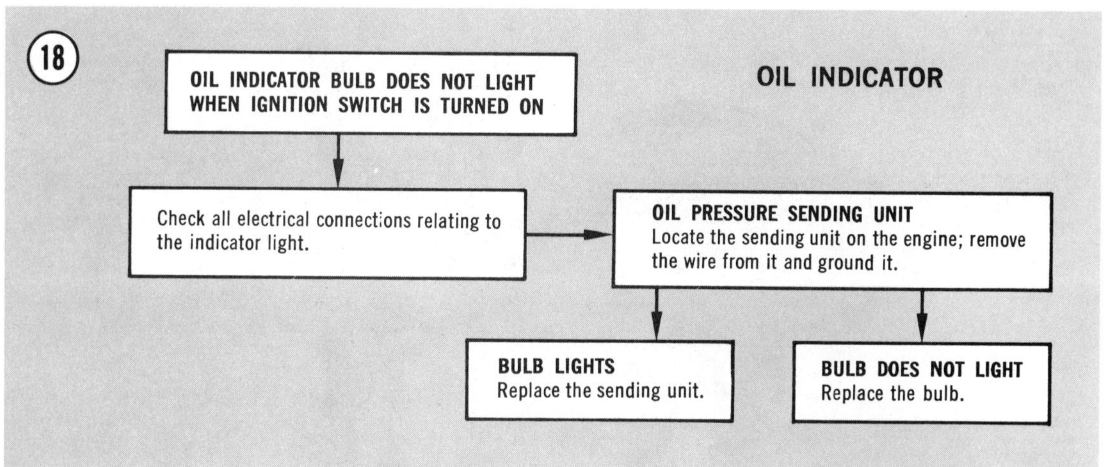

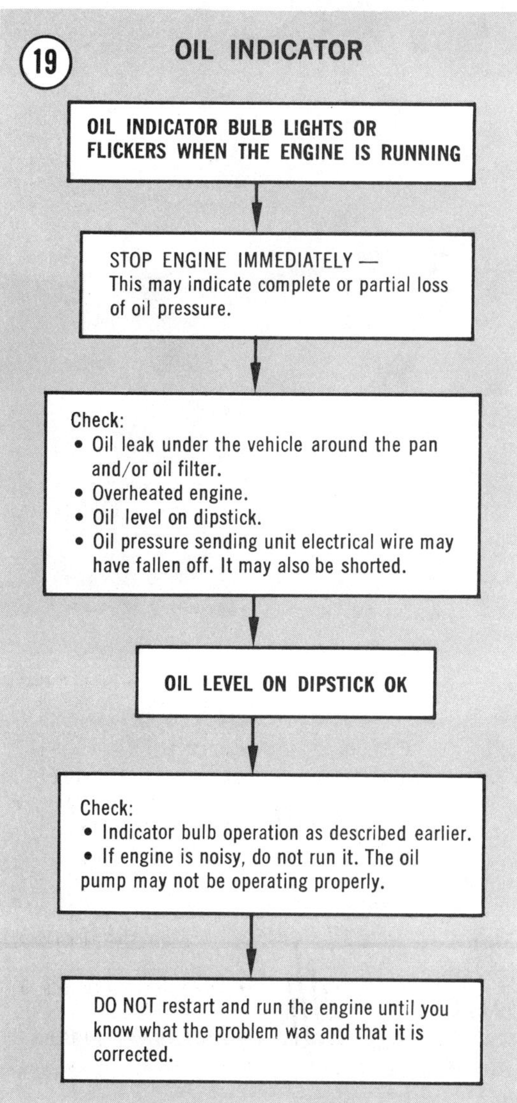

ENGINE OIL PRESSURE LIGHT

Proper oil pressure to the engine is vital. If oil pressure is insufficient, the engine can destroy itself in a comparatively short time.

The oil pressure warning circuit monitors oil pressure constantly. If pressure drops below a predetermined level, the light comes on.

Obviously, it is vital for the warning circuit to be working to signal low oil pressure. Each time you turn on the ignition, but before you start the vehicle, the warning light should come on. If it doesn't, there is trouble in the warning circuit, not the oil pressure system. See **Figure 18** to troubleshoot the warning circuit.

Once the engine is running, the warning light should stay off. If the warning light comes on or acts erratically while the engine is running there is trouble with the engine oil pressure system. *Stop the engine immediately*. Refer to **Figure 19** for possible causes of the problem.

FUEL SYSTEM (CARBURETTED)

Fuel system problems must be isolated to the fuel pump (mechanical or electric), fuel lines, fuel filter, or carburetor(s). These procedures assume the ignition system is working properly and is correctly adjusted.

1. ***Engine will not start*** — First make sure that fuel is being delivered to the carburetor. Remove the air cleaner, look into the carburetor throat, and operate the accelerator

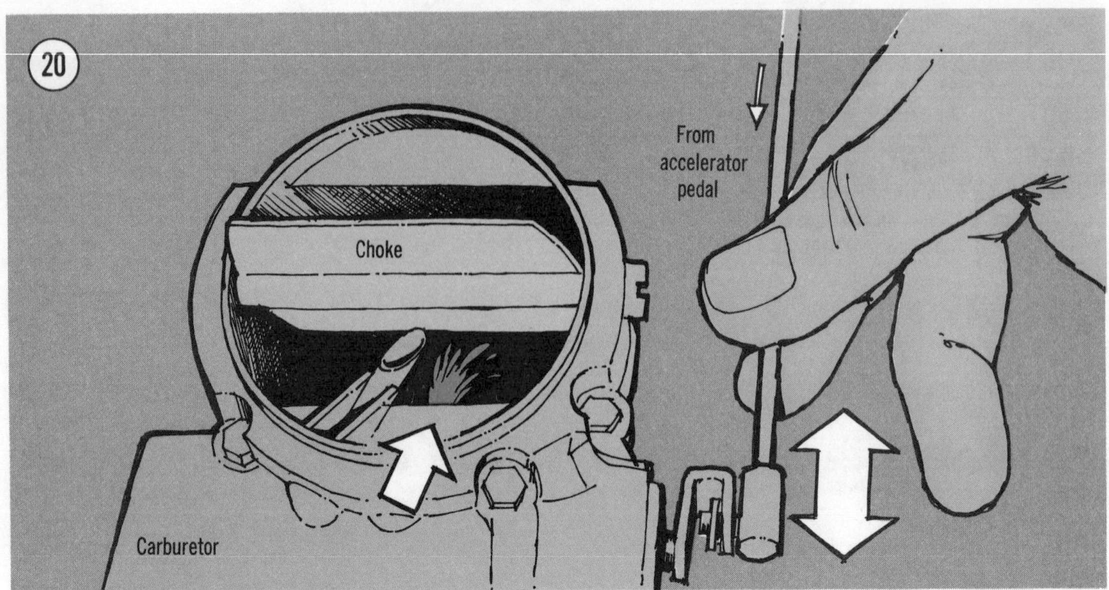

linkage several times. There should be a stream of fuel from the accelerator pump discharge tube each time the accelerator linkage is depressed (**Figure 20**). If not, check fuel pump delivery (described later), float valve, and float adjustment. If the engine will not start, check the automatic choke parts for sticking or damage. If necessary, rebuild or replace the carburetor.

2. ***Engine runs at fast idle*** — Usually this is caused by a defective automatic choke heater element. Ensure that the heater wire is connected and making good contact. Check the idle speed, idle mixture, and decel valve (if equipped) adjustment.

3. ***Rough idle or engine miss with frequent stalling*** — Check idle mixture and idle speed adjustments.

Poor idle may also be caused by a defective or dirty electromagnetic cutoff valve. Check that the electromagnetic cutoff valve wire is connected to the valve (on the carburetor) and making good contact. If it is, turn the ignition switch on, disconnect the wire and touch it to the valve terminal. If the valve is working, there should be a slight click heard each time the wire touches. If the valve is defective, turn the small setscrew on the end of the valve fully counterclockwise. This permanently opens the valve, permitting the car to idle properly until the valve can be cleaned or replaced.

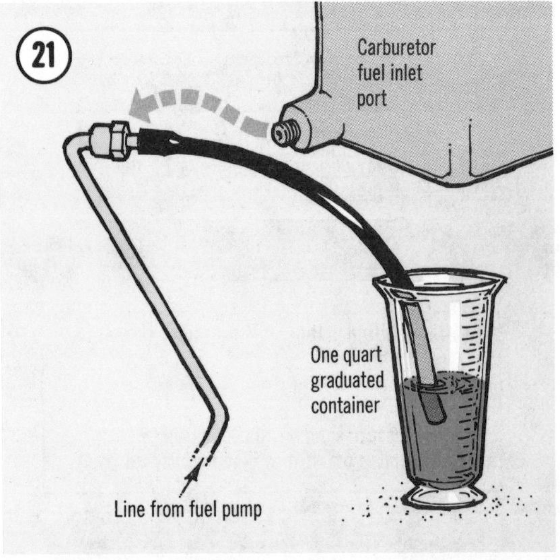

NOTE: *The engine may "diesel" in this condition. Replace the valve as soon as possible.*

4. ***Engine "diesels" (continues to run) when ignition is switched off*** — Check idle mixture (probably too rich), ignition timing, and idle speed (probably too fast). Check the throttle solenoid (if equipped) and electromagnetic cutoff valve for proper operation. Check for overheated engine.

5. *Stumbling when accelerating from idle* — Check the idle speed and mixture adjustments. Check the accelerator pump.

6. *Engine misses at high speed or lacks power* — This indicates possible fuel starvation. Check fuel pump pressure and capacity as described in this chapter. Check float needle valves. Check for a clogged fuel filter or air cleaner.

7. *Black exhaust smoke* — This indicates a badly overrich mixture. Check idle mixture and idle speed adjustment. Check choke setting. Check for excessive fuel pump pressure, leaky floats, or worn needle valves.

8. *Excessive fuel consumption* — Check for overrich mixture. Make sure choke mechanism works properly. Check idle mixture and idle speed. Check for excessive fuel pump pressure, leaky floats, or worn float needle valves.

FUEL SYSTEM (FUEL INJECTED)

Troubleshooting a fuel injection system requires more thought, experience, and know-how than any other part of the vehicle. A logical approach and proper test equipment are essential in order to successfully find and fix these troubles.

It is best to leave fuel injection troubles to your dealer. In order to isolate a problem to the injection system make sure that the fuel pump is operating properly. Check its performance as described later in this section. Also make sure that fuel filter and air cleaner are not clogged.

FUEL PUMP TEST (MECHANICAL AND ELECTRIC)

1. Disconnect the fuel inlet line where it enters the carburetor or fuel injection system.

2. Fit a rubber hose over the fuel line so fuel can be directed into a graduated container with about one quart capacity. See **Figure 21**.

3. To avoid accidental starting of the engine, disconnect the secondary coil wire from the coil.

4. Crank the engine for about 30 seconds.

5. If the fuel pump supplies the specified amount (refer to the fuel chapter later in this book), the trouble may be in the carburetor or fuel injection system. The fuel injection system should be tested by your dealer.

6. If there is no fuel present or the pump cannot supply the specified amount, either the fuel pump is defective or there is an obstruction in the fuel line. Replace the fuel pump and/or inspect the fuel lines for air leaks or obstructions.

7. Also pressure test the fuel pump by installing a T-fitting in the fuel line between the fuel pump and the carburetor. Connect a fuel pressure gauge to the fitting with a short tube (**Figure 22**).

8. Reconnect the primary coil wire, start the engine, and record the pressure. Refer to the fuel chapter later in this book for the correct pressure. If the pressure varies from that specified, the pump should be replaced.

9. Stop the engine. The pressure should drop off very slowly. If it drops off rapidly, the outlet valve in the pump is leaking and the pump should be replaced.

EMISSION CONTROL SYSTEMS

Major emission control systems used on nearly all U.S. models include the following:

a. Positive crankcase ventilation (PCV)
b. Thermostatic air cleaner
c. Air injection reaction (AIR)
d. Fuel evaporation control
e. Exhaust gas recirculation (EGR)

Emission control systems vary considerably from model to model. Individual models contain variations of the five systems described here. In addition, they may include other special systems. Use the index to find specific emission control components in other chapters.

Many of the systems and components are factory set and sealed. Without special expensive test equipment, it is impossible to adjust the systems to meet state and federal requirements.

Troubleshooting can also be difficult without special equipment. The procedures described below will help you find emission control parts which have failed, but repairs may have to be entrusted to a dealer or other properly equipped repair shop.

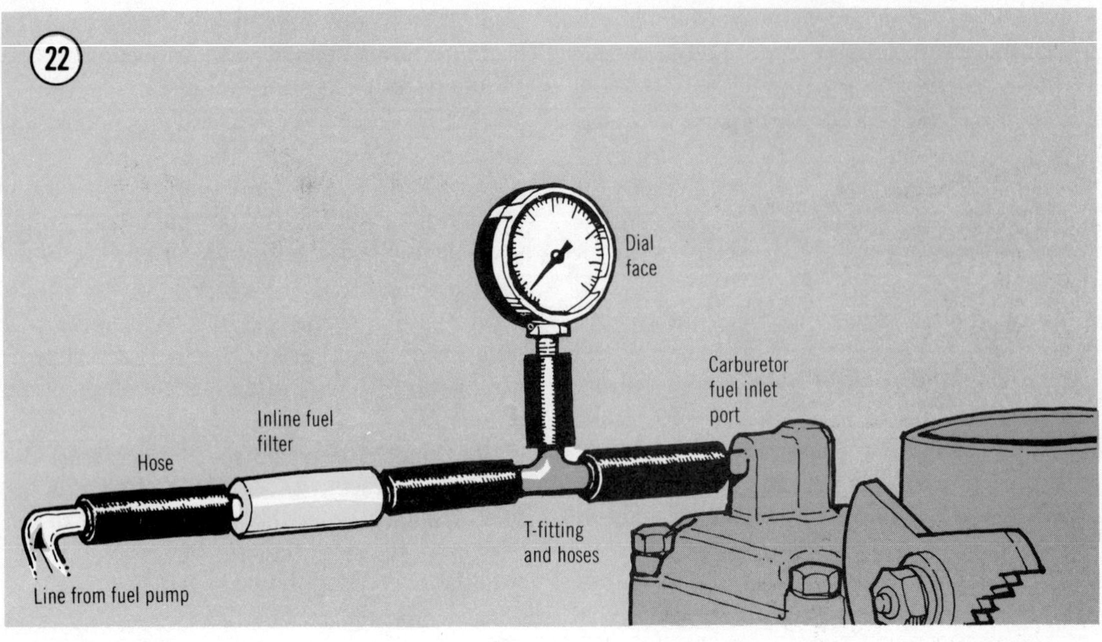

23

EXHAUST EMISSION PROBLEMS

CO CONTENT TOO LOW →

Check:
- Idle speed too low.
- Idle mixture adjustment (too lean).
- Carburetor jets and channels; clean and/or replace.
- Engine condition with a compression and vacuum test.

CO CONTENT TOO HIGH →

Check:
- Idle mixture adjustment (too rich).
- Defective automatic choke.
- Air filter warm air inlet door for sticking.
- Carburetor jets and channels; clean and/or replace.
- Engine condition with a compression and vacuum test.

HYDROCARBON LEVEL TOO HIGH →

Check:
- Throttle valve closes completely.
- Spark plug condition and gap.
- Ignition timing (too advanced) and breaker point gap (if so equipped).
- Intake manifold for leaks.
- Valve clearance (too small).
- Engine condition with a compression and vacuum test.

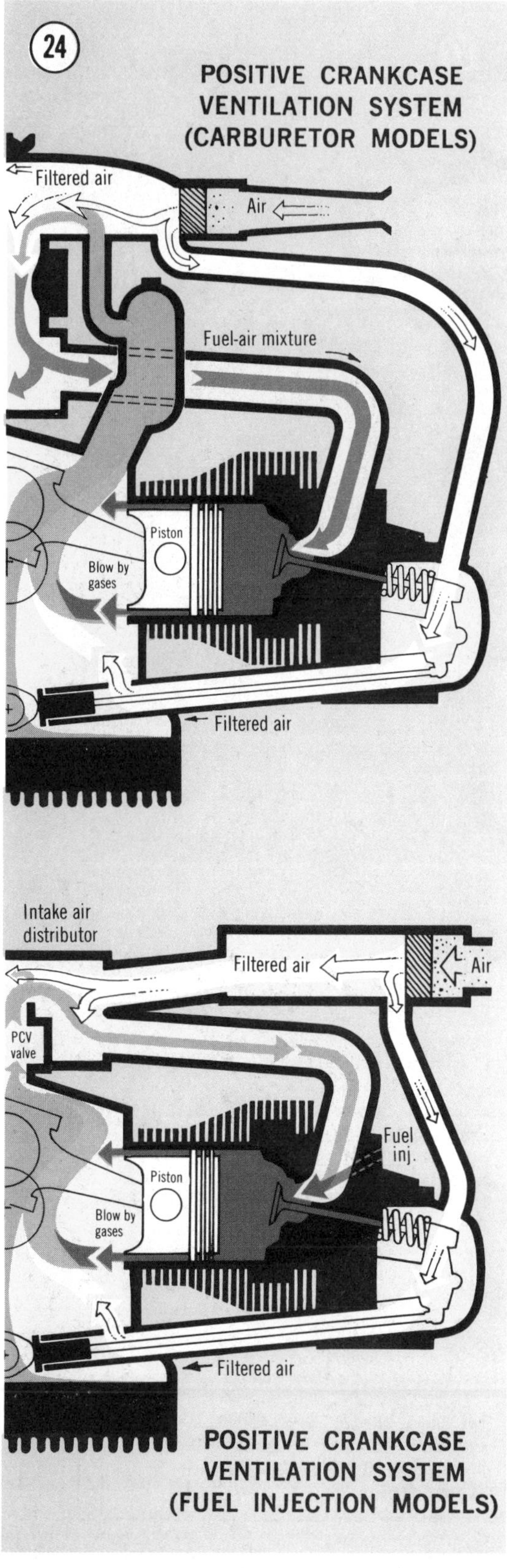

24

POSITIVE CRANKCASE VENTILATION SYSTEM (CARBURETOR MODELS)

POSITIVE CRANKCASE VENTILATION SYSTEM (FUEL INJECTION MODELS)

25

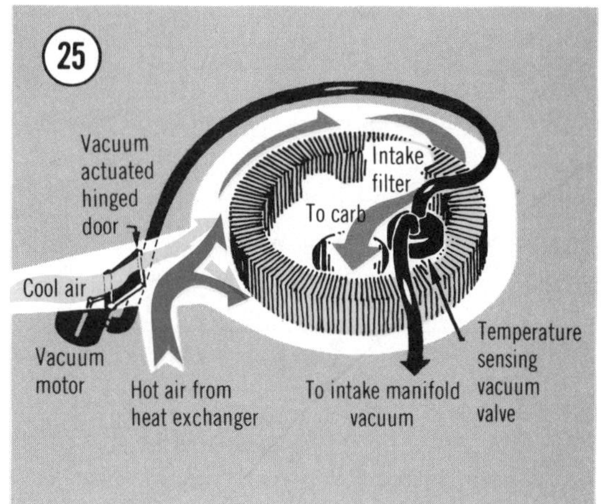

With the proper equipment, you can test the carbon monoxide and hydrocarbon levels. **Figure 23** provides some sources of trouble if the readings are not correct.

Positive Crankcase Ventilation

Fresh air drawn from the air cleaner housing scavenges emissions (e.g., piston blow-by) from the crankcase, then the intake manifold vacuum draws emissions into the intake manifold. They can then be reburned in the normal combustion process. **Figure 24** shows a typical system.

Thermostatic Air Cleaner

The thermostatically controlled air cleaner maintains incoming air to the engine at a predetermined level, usually about 100°F or higher. It mixes cold air with heated air from the exhaust manifold region. The air cleaner includes a temperature sensor, vacuum motor, and a hinged door. See **Figure 25**.

The system is comparatively easy to test. See **Figure 26** for the procedure.

Air Injection Reaction System

The air injection reaction system reduces air pollution by oxidizing hydrocarbons and carbon monoxide as they leave the combustion chamber. See **Figure 27**.

The air injection pump, driven by the engine, compresses filtered air and injects it at the exhaust port of each cylinder. The fresh air mixes with the unburned gases in the exhaust and pro-

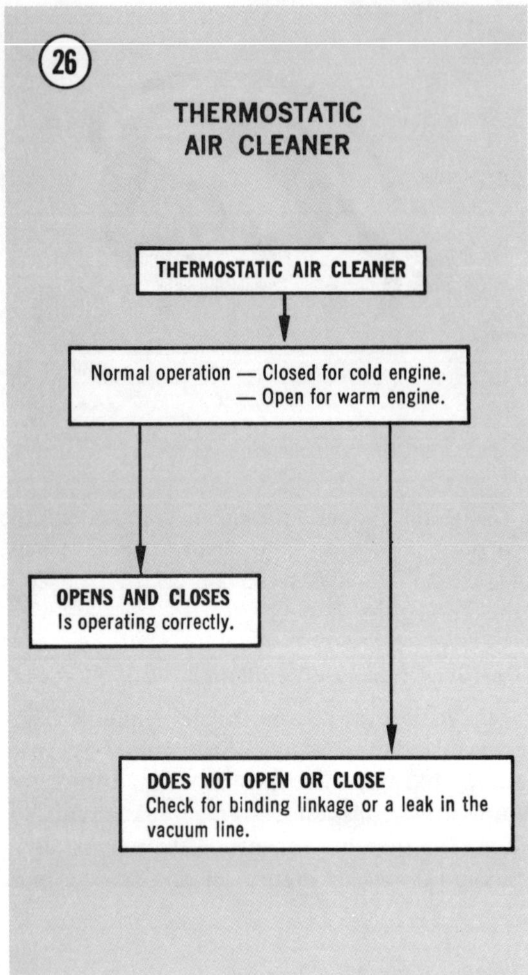
26
THERMOSTATIC
AIR CLEANER
THERMOSTATIC AIR CLEANER
Normal operation — Closed for cold engine.
— Open for warm engine.
OPENS AND CLOSES
Is operating correctly.
DOES NOT OPEN OR CLOSE
Check for binding linkage or a leak in the vacuum line.

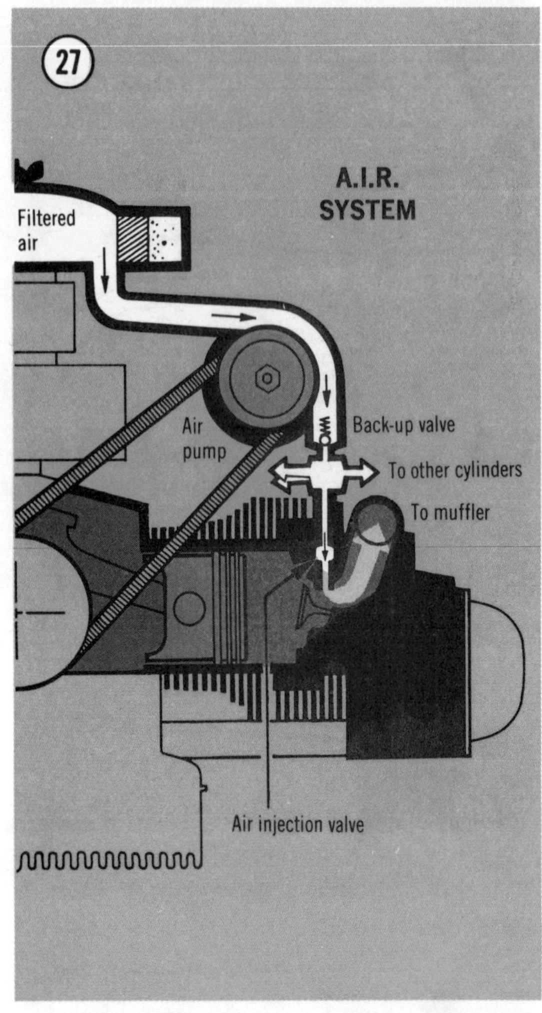
27
A.I.R.
SYSTEM
Filtered
air
Air
pump
Back-up valve
To other cylinders
To muffler
Air injection valve

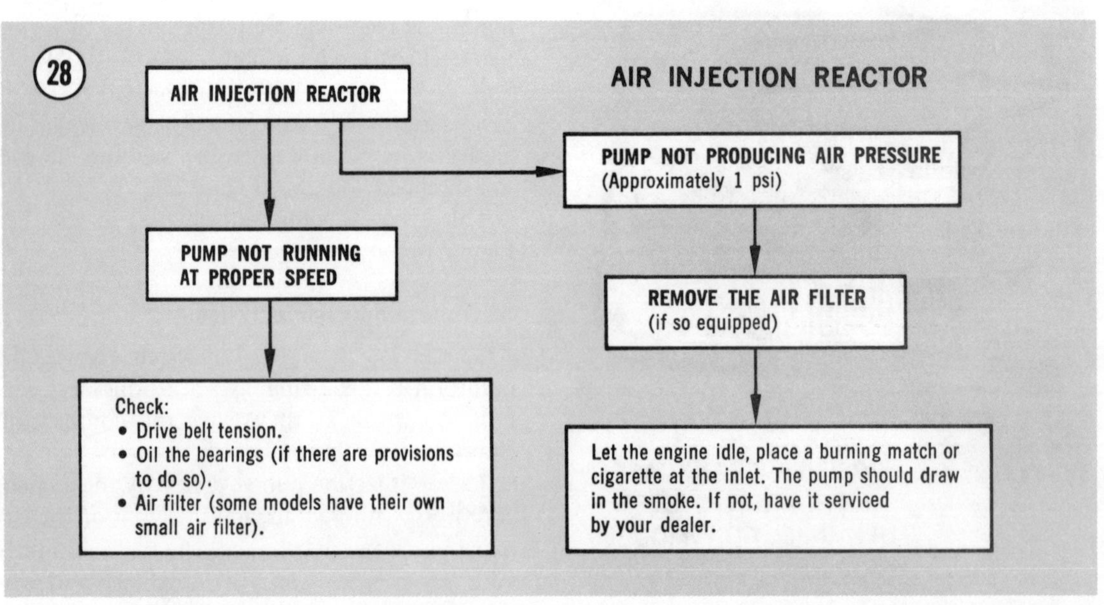
28
AIR INJECTION REACTOR
AIR INJECTION REACTOR
PUMP NOT RUNNING
AT PROPER SPEED
Check:
• Drive belt tension.
• Oil the bearings (if there are provisions to do so).
• Air filter (some models have their own small air filter).
PUMP NOT PRODUCING AIR PRESSURE
(Approximately 1 psi)
REMOVE THE AIR FILTER
(if so equipped)
Let the engine idle, place a burning match or cigarette at the inlet. The pump should draw in the smoke. If not, have it serviced by your dealer.

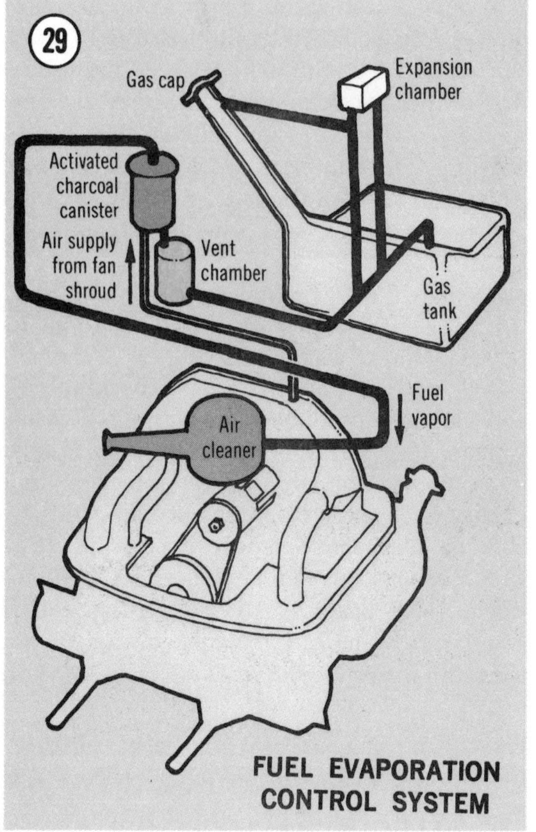

FUEL EVAPORATION CONTROL SYSTEM

motes further burning. A check valve prevents exhaust gases from entering and damaging the air pump if the pump becomes inoperative, e.g., from a drive belt failure.

Figure 28 explains the testing procedure for this system.

Fuel Evaporation Control

Fuel vapor from the fuel tank passes through the liquid/vapor separator to the carbon canister. See **Figure 29**. The carbon absorbs and stores the vapor when the engine is stopped. When the engine runs, manifold vacuum draws the vapor from the canister. Instead of being released into the atmosphere, the fuel vapor takes part in the normal combustion process.

Exhaust Gas Recirculation

The exhaust gas recirculation (EGR) system is used to reduce the emission of nitrogen oxides (NO_X). Relatively inert exhaust gases are introduced into the combustion process to slightly reduce peak temperatures. This reduction in temperature reduces the formation of NO_X.

Figure 30 provides a simple test of this system.

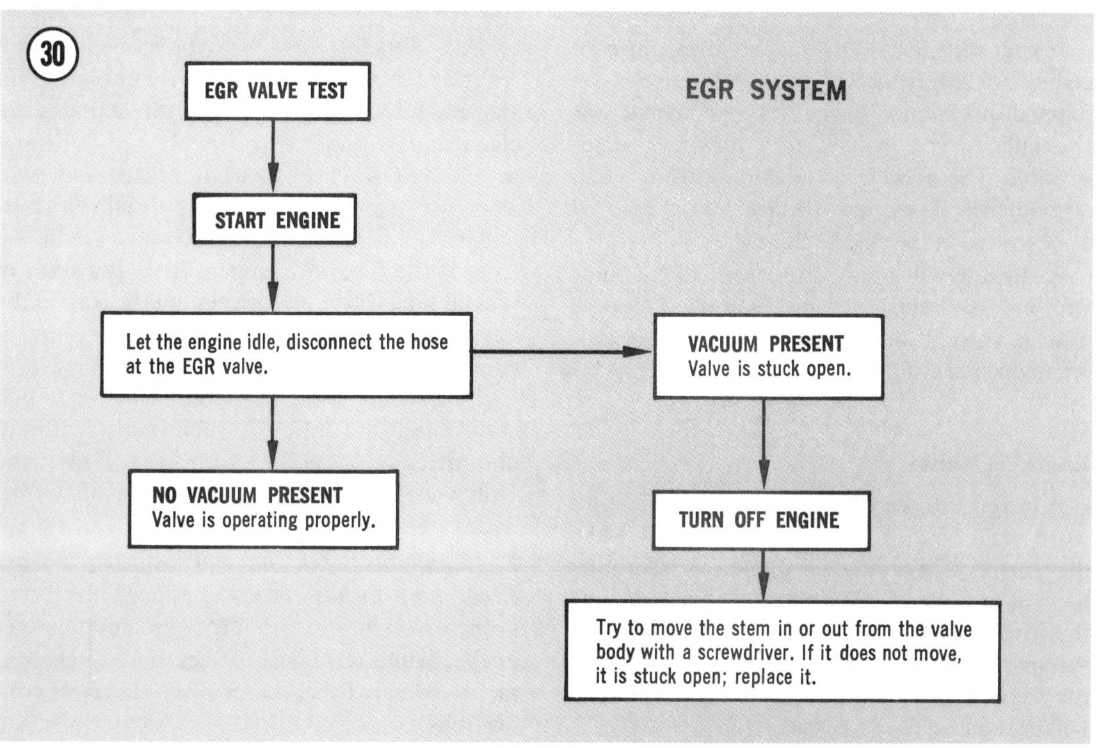

EGR SYSTEM

ENGINE NOISES

Often the first evidence of an internal engine trouble is a strange noise. That knocking, clicking, or tapping which you never heard before may be warning you of impending trouble.

While engine noises can indicate problems, they are sometimes difficult to interpret correctly; inexperienced mechanics can be seriously misled by them.

Professional mechanics often use a special stethoscope which looks similar to a doctor's stethoscope for isolating engine noises. You can do nearly as well with a "sounding stick" which can be an ordinary piece of doweling or a section of small hose. By placing one end in contact with the area to which you want to listen and the other end near your ear, you can hear sounds emanating from that area. The first time you do this, you may be horrified at the strange noises coming from even a normal engine. If you can, have an experienced friend or mechanic help you sort the noises out.

Clicking or Tapping Noises

Clicking or tapping noises usually come from the valve train, and indicate excessive valve clearance.

If your vehicle has adjustable valves, the procedure for adjusting the valve clearance is explained in Chapter Three. If your vehicle has hydraulic lifters, the clearance may not be adjustable. The noise may be coming from a collapsed lifter. These may be cleaned or replaced as described in the engine chapter.

A sticking valve may also sound like a valve with excessive clearance. In addition, excessive wear in valve train components can cause similar engine noises.

Knocking Noises

A heavy, dull knocking is usually caused by a worn main bearing. The noise is loudest when the engine is working hard, i.e., accelerating hard at low speed. You may be able to isolate the trouble to a single bearing by disconnecting the spark plugs one at a time. When you reach the spark plug nearest the bearing, the knock will be reduced or disappear.

Worn connecting rod bearings may also produce a knock, but the sound is usually more "metallic." As with a main bearing, the noise is worse when accelerating. It may even increase further just as you go from accelerating to coasting. Disconnecting spark plugs will help isolate this knock as well.

A double knock or clicking usually indicates a worn piston pin. Disconnecting spark plugs will isolate this to a particular piston, however, the noise will *increase* when you reach the affected piston.

A loose flywheel and excessive crankshaft end play also produce knocking noises. While similar to main bearing noises, these are usually intermittent, not constant, and they do not change when spark plugs are disconnected.

Some mechanics confuse piston pin noise with piston slap. The double knock will distinguish the piston pin noise. Piston slap is identified by the fact that it is always louder when the engine is cold.

ELECTRICAL ACCESSORIES

Lights and Switches (Interior and Exterior)

1. ***Bulb does not light*** — Remove the bulb and check for a broken element. Also check the inside of the socket; make sure the contacts are clean and free of corrosion. If the bulb and socket are OK, check to see if a fuse has blown. The fuse panel (**Figure 31**) is usually located under the instrument panel. Replace the blown fuse. If the fuse blows again, there is a short in that circuit. Check that circuit all the way to the battery. Look for worn wire insulation or burned wires.

If all the above are all right, check the switch controlling the bulb for continuity with an ohmmeter at the switch terminals. Check the switch contact terminals for loose or dirty electrical connections.

2. ***Headlights work but will not switch from either high or low beam*** — Check the beam selector switch for continuity with an ohmmeter at the switch terminals. Check the switch contact terminals for loose or dirty electrical connections.

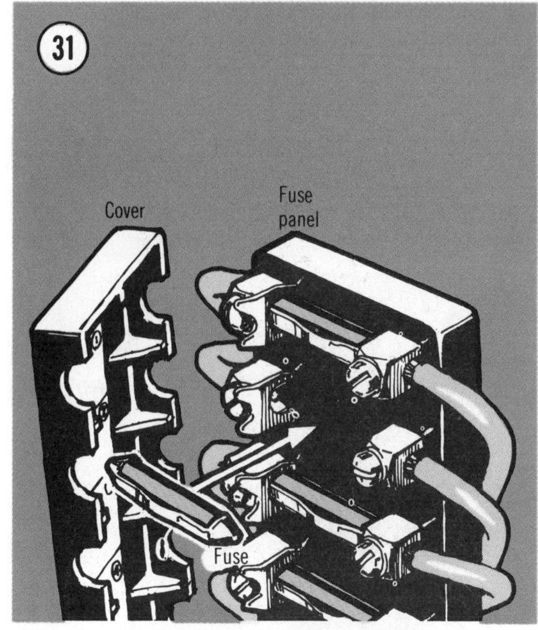

3. ***Brake light switch inoperative*** — On mechanically operated switches, usually mounted near the brake pedal arm, adjust the switch to achieve correct mechanical operation. Check the switch for continuity with an ohmmeter at the switch terminals. Check the switch contact terminals for loose or dirty electrical connections.

4. ***Back-up lights do not operate*** — Check light bulb as described earlier. Locate the switch, normally located near the shift lever. Adjust switch to achieve correct mechanical operation. Check the switch for continuity with an ohmmeter at the switch terminals. Bypass the switch with a jumper wire; if the lights work, replace the switch.

Directional Signals

1. ***Directional signals do not operate*** — If the indicator light on the instrument panel burns steadily instead of flashing, this usually indicates that one of the exterior lights is burned out. Check all lamps that normally flash. If all are all right, the flasher unit may be defective. Replace it with a good one.

2. ***Directional signal indicator light on instrument panel does not light up*** — Check the light bulbs as described earlier. Check all electrical connections and check the flasher unit.

3. ***Directional signals will not self-cancel*** — Check the self-cancelling mechanism located inside the steering column.

4. ***Directional signals flash slowly*** — Check the condition of the battery and the alternator (or generator) drive belt tension (**Figure 4**). Check the flasher unit and all related electrical connections.

Windshield Wipers

1. ***Wipers do not operate*** — Check for a blown fuse and replace it. Check all related terminals for loose or dirty electrical connections. Check continuity of the control switch with an ohmmeter at the switch terminals. Check the linkage and arms for loose, broken, or binding parts. Straighten out or replace where necessary.

2. ***Wiper motor hums but will not operate*** — The motor may be shorted out internally; check and/or replace the motor. Also check for broken or binding linkage and arms.

3. ***Wiper arms will not return to the stowed position when turned off*** — The motor has a special internal switch for this purpose. Have it inspected by your dealer. Do not attempt this yourself.

Interior Heater

1. ***Heater fan does not operate*** — Check for a blown fuse.. Check the switch for continuity with an ohmmeter at the switch terminals. Check the switch contact terminals for loose or dirty electrical connections.

2. ***Heat output is insufficient*** — Check that the heater door(s) and cable(s) are operating correctly and are in the open position. Inspect the heat ducts; make sure that they are not crimped or blocked.

3. ***Exhaust fumes in passenger compartment*** — Open all windows and inspect heat exchangers and heating system immediately.

WARNING

Do not continue to operate the vehicle with deadly carbon monoxide fumes present in the passenger compartment.

2

COOLING SYSTEM

Engine cooling is provided by an engine driven fan which draws in outside air for the cylinders and cylinder heads. Thermostatically controlled air flaps limit the amount of cold air when engine is cold to provide rapid warm up.

If the engine is running abnormally hot, check fan drive condition and tension, air control ring adjustment and/or air control thermostat.

If overheating is extreme, the engine will have to be removed and the cooling duct system removed and inspected.

CLUTCH

All clutch troubles except adjustments require removal of the engine/transaxle assembly to identify and cure the problem.

1. ***Slippage*** — This is most noticeable when accelerating in a high gear at relatively low speed. To check slippage, park the vehicle on a level surface with the handbrake set. Shift to 2nd gear and release the clutch as if driving off. If the clutch is good, the engine will slow and stall. If the clutch slips, continued engine speed will give it away.

Slippage results from insufficient clutch pedal free play, oil or grease on the clutch disc, worn pressure plate, or weak springs. Also check for binding in the clutch cable and lever arm which may prevent full engagement.

CAUTION

This is a severe test. Perform this test only when slippage is suspected, not periodically.

2. ***Drag or failure to release*** — This trouble usually causes difficult shifting and gear clash, especially when downshifting. The cause may be excessive clutch pedal free play, warped or bent pressure plate or clutch disc, excessive clutch cable guide sag, broken or loose linings, lack of lubrication in gland nut bearing or felt ring. Also check condition of main shaft splines.

3. ***Chatter or grabbing*** — A number of things can cause this trouble. Check tightness of engine mounts and engine-to-transmission mounting bolts. Check for worn or misaligned pressure plate and misaligned release plate, or excessive cable guide sag.

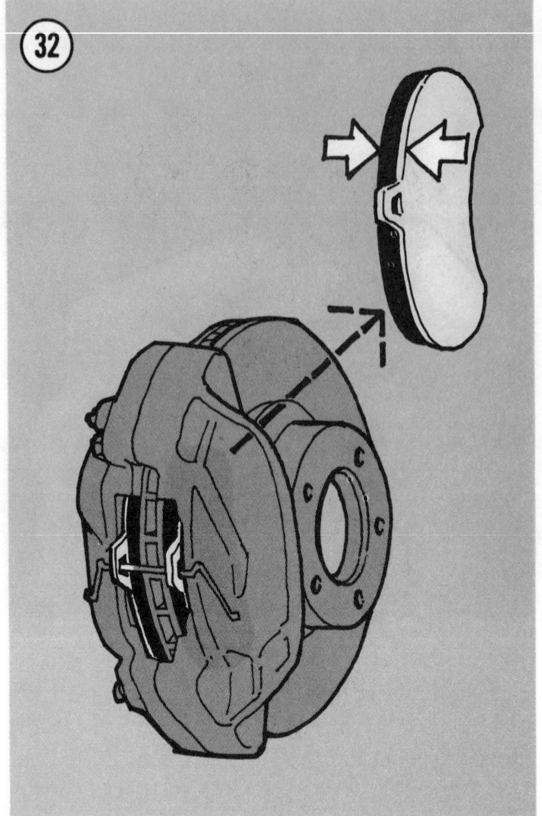

4. ***Other noises*** — Noise usually indicates a dry or defective release or pilot bearing. Check the bearings and replace if necessary. Also check all parts for misalignment and uneven wear.

MANUAL TRANSAXLE

Transaxle troubles are evident when one or more of the following symptoms appear:

a. Difficulty changing gears
b. Gears clash when downshifting
c. Slipping out of gear
d. Excessive noise in NEUTRAL
e. Excessive noise in gear
f. Oil leaks

Transaxle repairs, except for one oil seal, are not possible without expensive special tools.

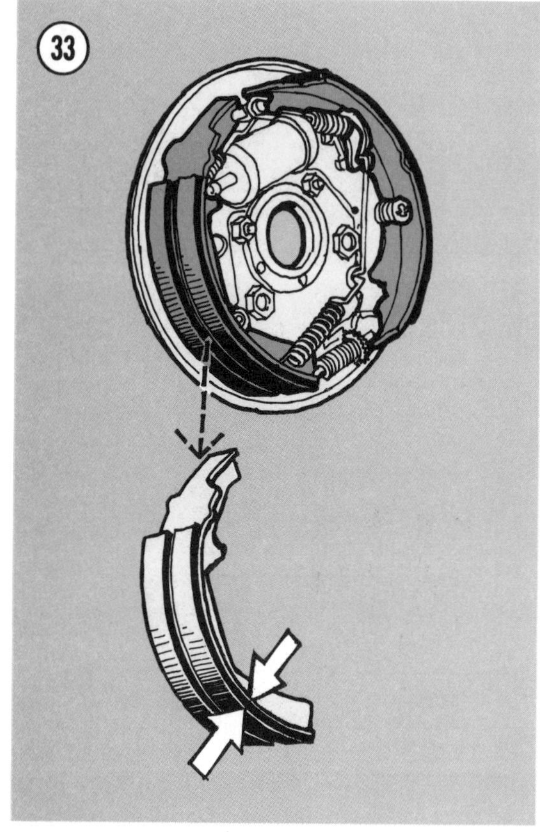

The main shaft oil seal, however, is easily replaced after removing the engine.

Transaxle troubles are sometimes difficult to distinguish from clutch troubles. Eliminate the clutch as a source of trouble before installing a new or rebuilt transaxle.

AUTOMATIC AND SEMI-AUTOMATIC TRANSAXLE

Most automatic and semi-automatic transaxle repairs require considerable specialized knowledge and tools. It is impractical for the home mechanic to invest in the tools, since they cost more than a properly rebuilt transmission.

Check fluid level and condition frequently to help prevent future problems. If the fluid is orange or black in color or smells like varnish, it is an indication of some type of damage or failure within the transmission. Have the transmission serviced by your dealer or competent automatic transmission service facility.

Refer to transaxle chapter for specific troubleshooting procedures.

BRAKES

Good brakes are vital to the safe operation of the vehicle. Performing the maintenance specified in Chapter Three will minimize problems with the brakes. Most importantly, check and maintain the level of fluid in the master cylinder, and check the thickness of the linings on the disc brake pads (**Figure 32**) or drum brake shoes (**Figure 33**).

If trouble develops, **Figures 34 through 36** will help you locate the problem. Refer to the brake chapter for actual repair procedures.

STEERING AND SUSPENSION

Trouble in the suspension or steering is evident when the following occur:

a. Steering is hard
b. Vehicle pulls to one side
c. Vehicle wanders or front wheels wobble
d. Steering has excessive play
e. Tire wear is abnormal

Unusual steering, pulling, or wandering is usually caused by bent or otherwise misaligned suspension parts. This is difficult to check without proper alignment equipment. Refer to the suspension chapter in this book for repairs that you can perform and those that must be left to a dealer or suspension specialist.

If your trouble seems to be excessive play, check wheel bearing adjustment first. This is the most frequent cause. Then check ball-joints as described below. Finally, check tie rod end ball-joints by shaking each tie rod. Also check steering gear, or rack-and-pinion assembly to see that it is securely bolted down.

TIRE WEAR ANALYSIS

Abnormal tire wear should be analyzed to determine its causes. The most common causes are the following:

a. Incorrect tire pressure
b. Improper driving
c. Overloading
d. Bad road surfaces
e. Incorrect wheel alignment

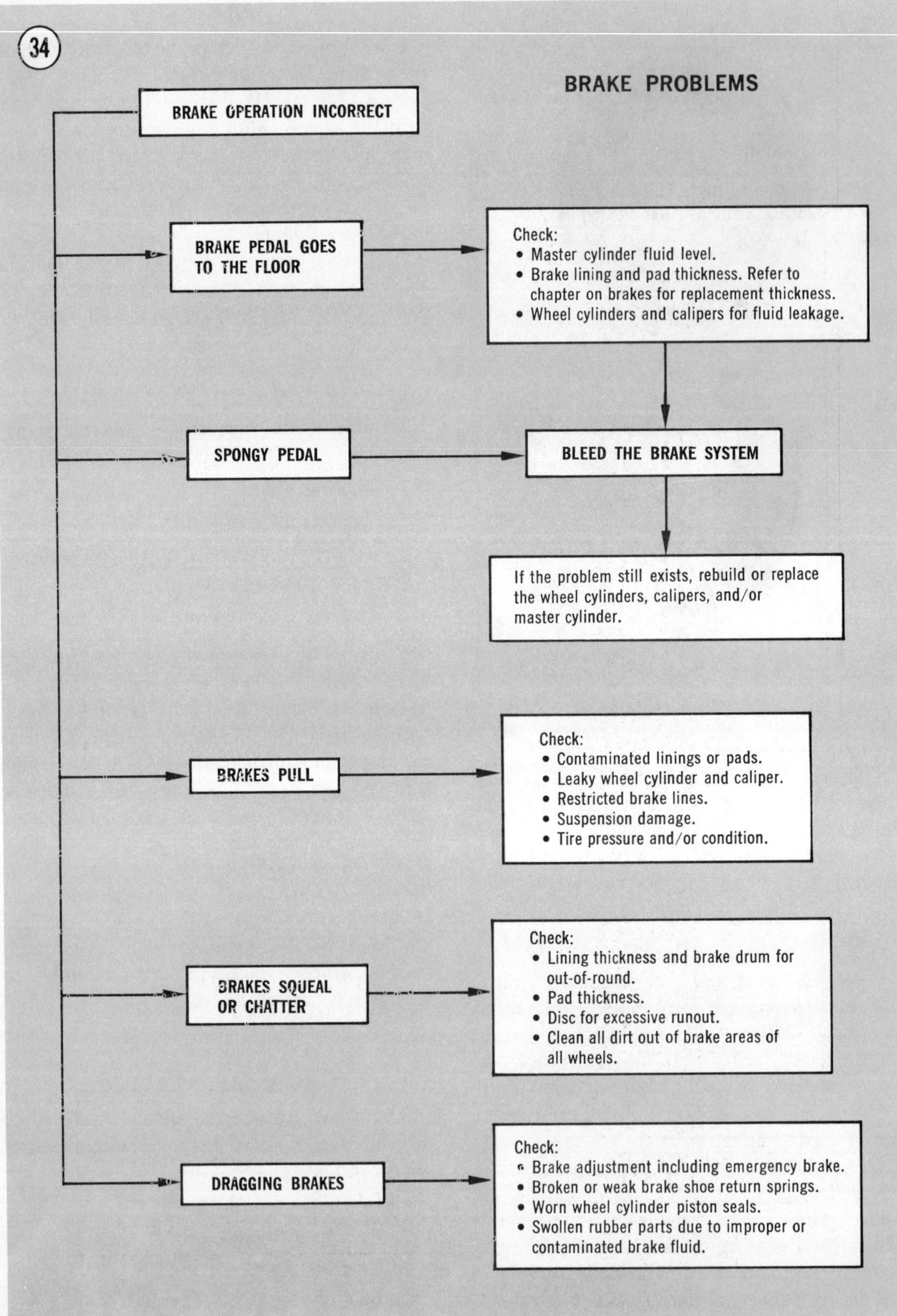
34
BRAKE PROBLEMS
BRAKE OPERATION INCORRECT
BRAKE PEDAL GOES TO THE FLOOR
Check:
• Master cylinder fluid level.
• Brake lining and pad thickness. Refer to chapter on brakes for replacement thickness.
• Wheel cylinders and calipers for fluid leakage.
SPONGY PEDAL
BLEED THE BRAKE SYSTEM
If the problem still exists, rebuild or replace the wheel cylinders, calipers, and/or master cylinder.
BRAKES PULL
Check:
• Contaminated linings or pads.
• Leaky wheel cylinder and caliper.
• Restricted brake lines.
• Suspension damage.
• Tire pressure and/or condition.
BRAKES SQUEAL OR CHATTER
Check:
• Lining thickness and brake drum for out-of-round.
• Pad thickness.
• Disc for excessive runout.
• Clean all dirt out of brake areas of all wheels.
DRAGGING BRAKES
Check:
• Brake adjustment including emergency brake.
• Broken or weak brake shoe return springs.
• Worn wheel cylinder piston seals.
• Swollen rubber parts due to improper or contaminated brake fluid.

35

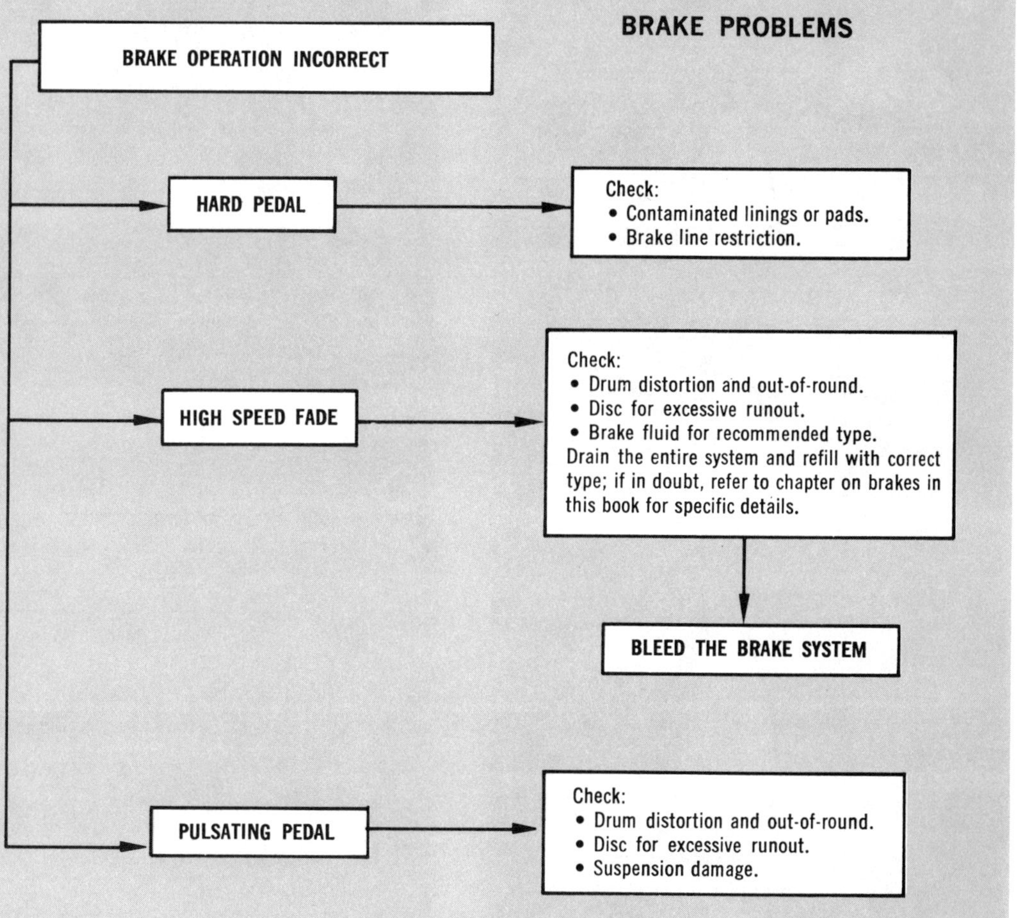

BRAKE PROBLEMS
BRAKE OPERATION INCORRECT
HARD PEDAL
Check:
• Contaminated linings or pads.
• Brake line restriction.
HIGH SPEED FADE
Check:
• Drum distortion and out-of-round.
• Disc for excessive runout.
• Brake fluid for recommended type.
Drain the entire system and refill with correct type; if in doubt, refer to chapter on brakes in this book for specific details.
BLEED THE BRAKE SYSTEM
PULSATING PEDAL
Check:
• Drum distortion and out-of-round.
• Disc for excessive runout.
• Suspension damage.

36

BRAKE PROBLEMS
BRAKE LIGHT ON INSTRUMENT PANEL COMES ON AND STAYS ON (1968 and later models)
PARTIAL OR COMPLETE BRAKE SYSTEM FAILURE
Check the entire brake system for signs of brake fluid leakage and/or damage. Thoroughly inspect the master cylinder, wheel cylinders, calipers, brake lines, and flexible hoses.
DO NOT drive the vehicle until you know what the problem was and that it is corrected.

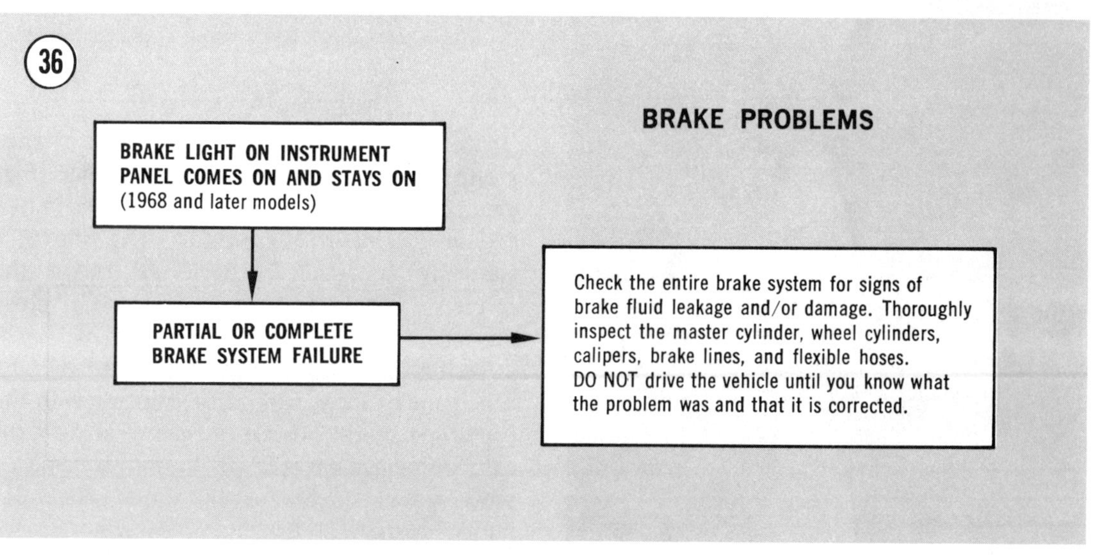

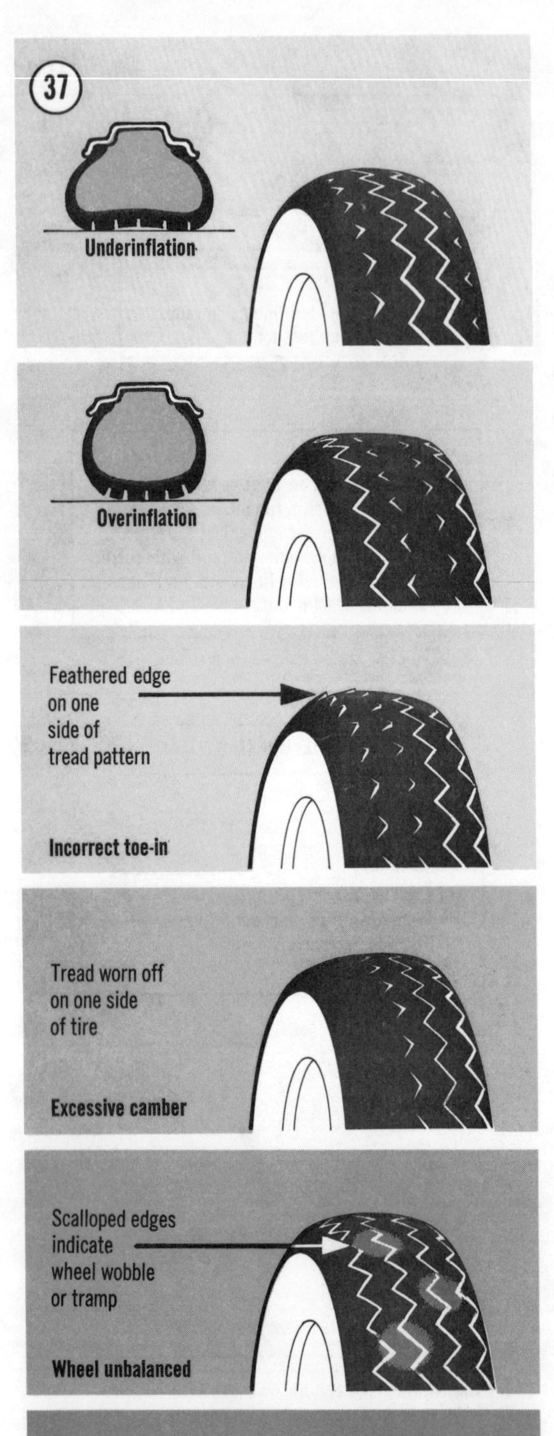

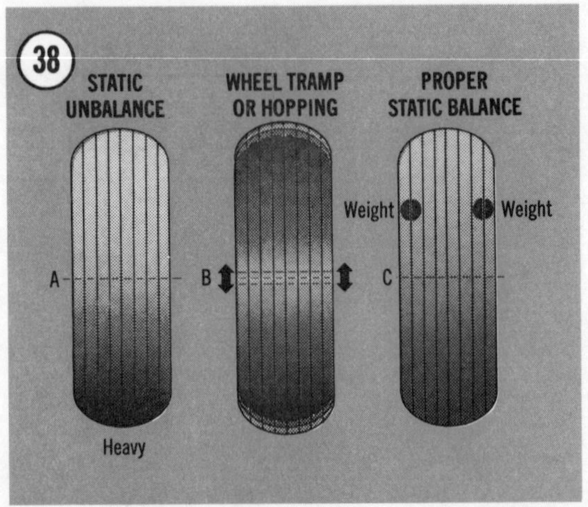

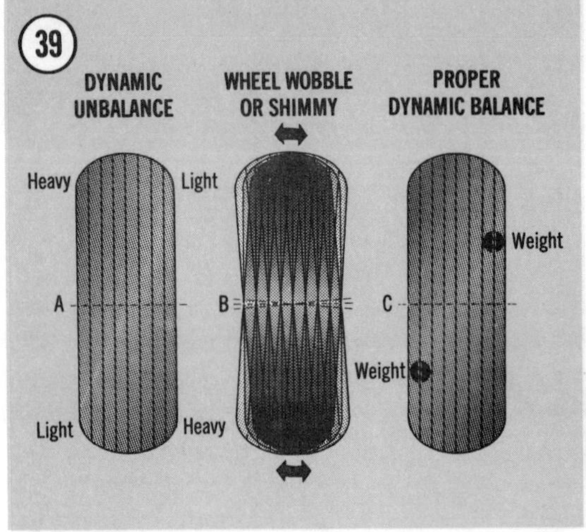

Figure 37 identifies wear patterns and indicates the most probable causes.

WHEEL BALANCING

All four wheels and tires must be in balance along two axes. To be in static balance **(Figure 38)**, weight must be evenly distributed around the axis of rotation. (A) shows a statically unbalanced wheel; (B) shows the result — wheel tramp or hopping; (C) shows proper static balance.

To be in dynamic balance **(Figure 39)**, the centerline of the weight must coincide with the centerline of the wheel. (A) shows a dynamically unbalanced wheel; (B) shows the result — wheel wobble or shimmy; (C) shows proper dynamic balance.

NOTE: If you own a 1982 model, first check the Supplement at the back of the book for any new service information.

3

CHAPTER THREE

LUBRICATION, MAINTENANCE AND TUNE-UP

This chapter describes all the necessary maintenance procedures required to keep your Vanagon running properly. A carefully followed regime of preventive maintenance will pay for itself in fewer and lower overall repair bills. Tune-up specifications are presented in **Table 1**; recommended oil grades, fluids and capacities are shown in **Table 2**. Maintenance schedules are given in **Table 3**. **Tables 1-3** are at the end of the chapter. Vehicle identification codes and locations are provided at the end of the chapter.

The checks and maintenance schedules in this chapter are based on direct experience estimates which are much more conservative than those recommended by Volkswagen. However, if your Vanagon has been recently purchased you may wish to follow the maintenance schedules listed by Volkswagen in the service booklet provided with each vehicle.

JACKING, HOISTING AND TOWING

Many service procedures, checks or roadside emergencies require that the vehicle be raised on a hoist, supported by jackstands or towed.

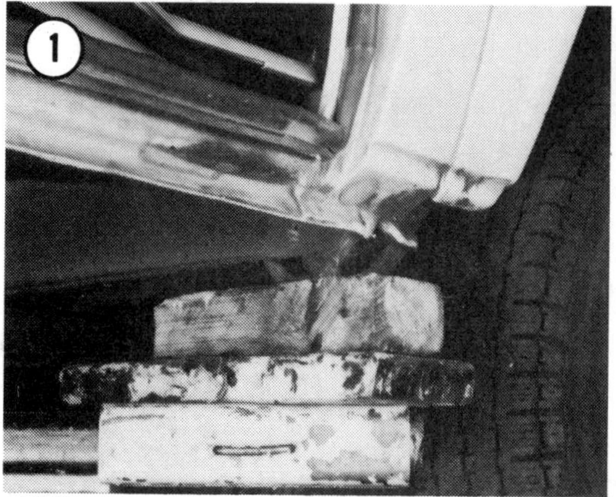

This section illustrates the safe methods of raising or towing the Vanagon without injuring yourself or damaging the vehicle.

Vehicle Raising

To lift the vehicle, place the floor jack, hoist pads or jackstands only under the front crossmember beams (**Figure 1**) or the rear crossmember beams (**Figure 2**).

Never try to raise or place jackstands under a vehicle on ground that is not level.

WARNING
Do not use the provided factory crank-jack when working under the vehicle. The crank-jack will not prevent the vehicle from rolling. If you must raise the vehicle with the crank-jack, ***always*** *use jackstands.*

Towing

When towing vehicles with manual transmissions, make sure that the transmission is in NEUTRAL.

Never tow a vehicle with an automatic transmission more than 30 miles without removing the drive axles or you will severely damage the transmission. See *Drive Axles* in Chapter Eight.

ROUTINE CHECKS

The following elementary inspections should be made at each fuel stop.

1. Check the engine oil level. To get a correct measurement the vehicle must be on level ground; turn the engine off and let it stand for a few minutes to allow the oil to run back into the crankcase. The oil dipstick is located behind the rear license plate; see **Figure 3**. Pull

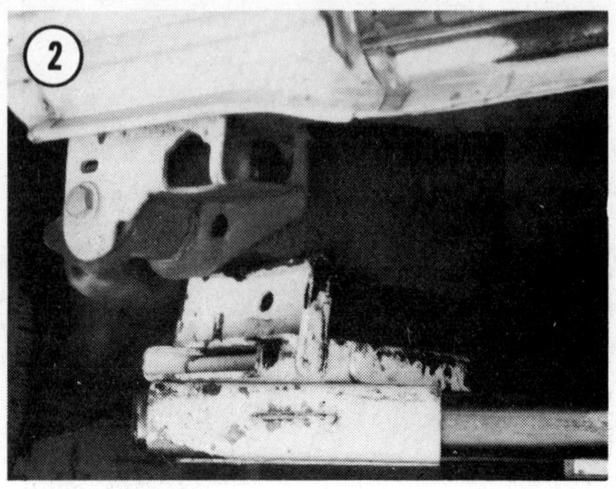

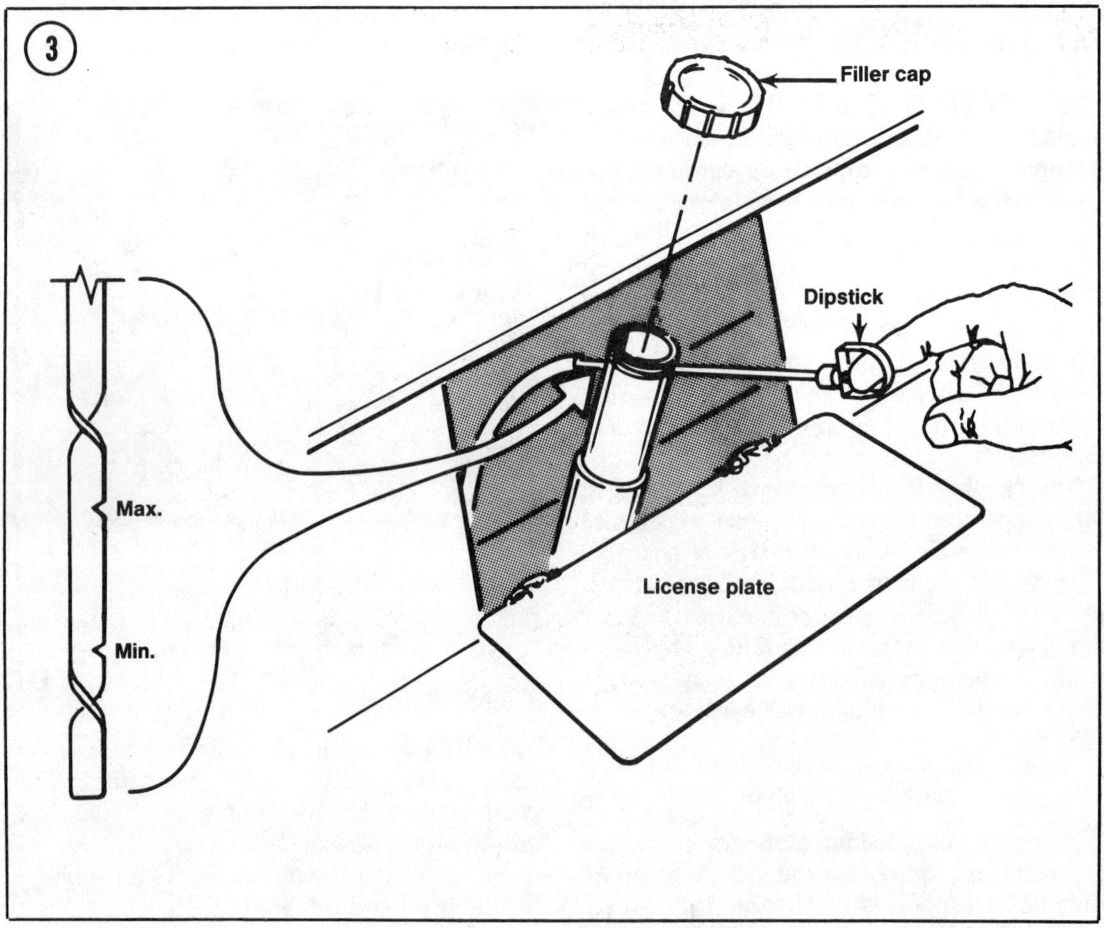

3

Filler cap

Dipstick

Max.

Min.

License plate

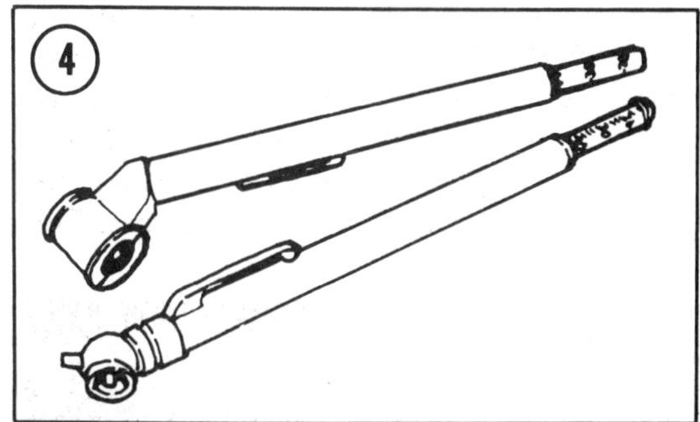

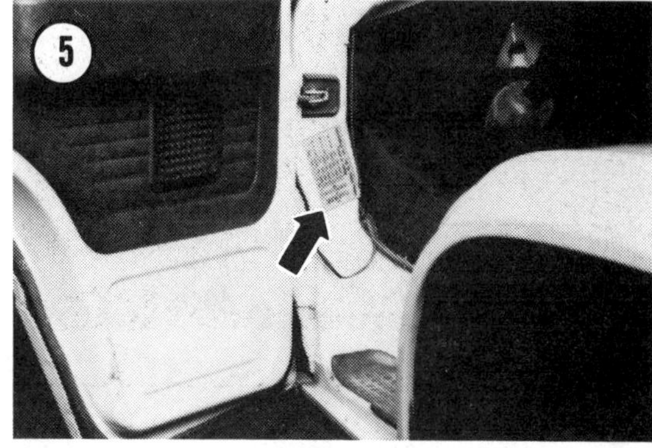

out the dipstick and wipe it clean with a rag. Reinsert it and push it in all the way. Pull the stick out again and note the oil mark. If the oil level is anywhere below the MAX mark on the dipstick, add oil until it reaches the MAX mark. See **Table 2** for recommended oil grades and capacities.

2. Check the tire pressures by using a pocket gauge like the ones shown in **Figure 4**. This should be done when the tires are cold, which usually means when the vehicle has not been driven for at least 3 hours or has been driven less than one mile. A decal listing cold tire pressures is located on the left door jam. See **Figure 5**. These specifications are for original-equipment tire sizes. Also, the maximum safe tire pressure is printed on each tire sidewall.

3. Check the hydraulic fluid level in the brake/clutch master cylinder reservoir. The reservoir is located on the driver's side on top of the instrument panel beneath a cover. See **Figure 6**. The fluid level should always be kept

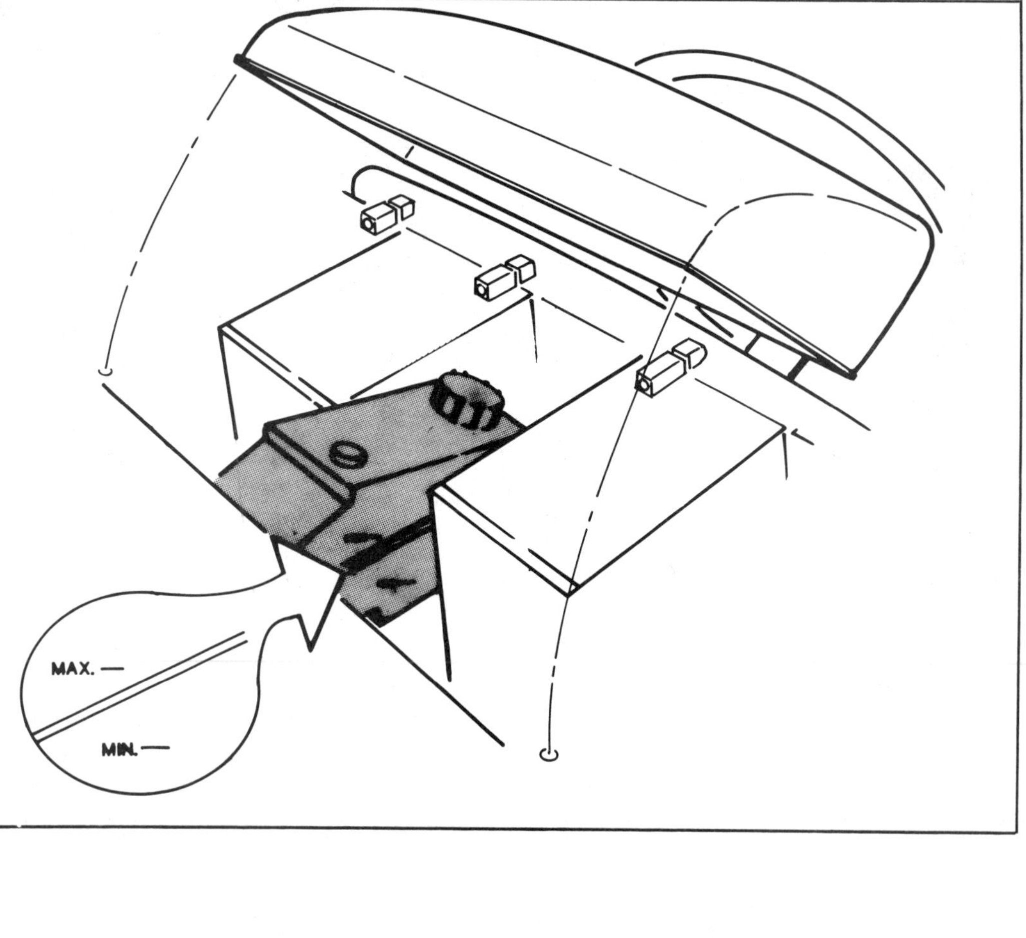

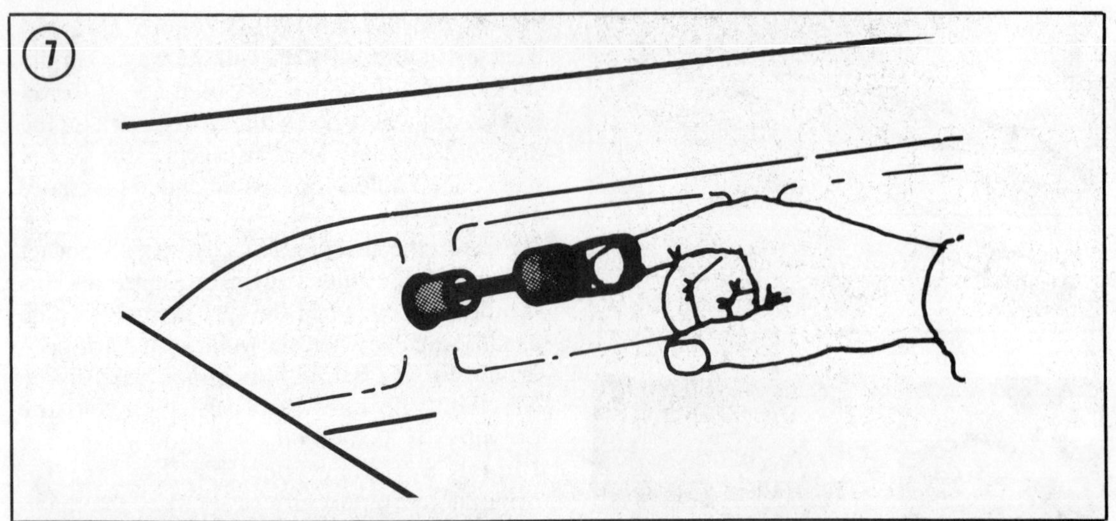

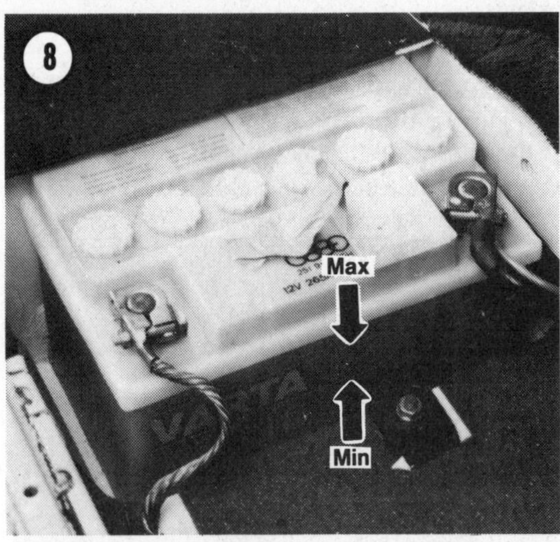

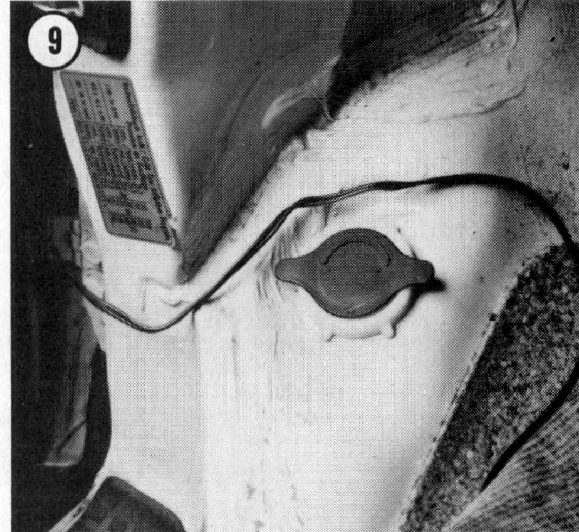

up near the MAX mark. See **Table 2** for oil grades, fluids and capacities.

4. On vehicles with automatic transmissions, check the automatic transmission fluid (ATF) level. The level should be checked when the ATF is warm (engine idling a few minutes). Park on level ground, set the parking brake, put the transmission in NEUTRAL and let the vehicle idle. Open the engine compartment, pull out the ATF dipstick (**Figure 7**) and wipe it off with a clean rag.

CAUTION

Always use a completely clean lint-free rag on the ATF dipstick. The slightest speck of dirt or lint can ruin an automatic transmission.

Reinsert the dipstick and withdraw it again; the ATF level is correct if the reading is between the 2 marks. If too low, immediately add ATF through the dipstick tube with a hose and funnel. See **Table 2** for recommended oil grades, fluids and capacities.

5. On non-maintenance free batteries, check the battery electrolyte level. The battery is located underneath the front passenger seat. To reach it, push the seat all the way forward (on vehicles with swivel seats, rotate the seat 180° to the left). The electrolyte level in each cell should be above the MIN mark on the side of the battery. See **Figure 8**. Fill only with distilled water.

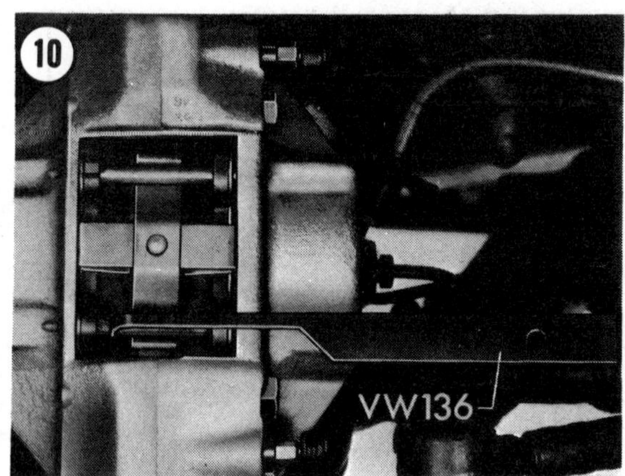

6. Check the level of the windshield washer container. The filler cap is located under the floor mat on the driver's side. See **Figure 9**. It's always good practice to keep the container full. If desired, use a special windshield cleaning solution (follow the manufacturer's instructions for use).

CAUTION
Do not use cooling system antifreeze as the runoff will damage paint.

7. Inspect the headlights, turn signals, side markers and brake lights for proper operation. If a bulb has burned out, replace it. See Chapter Seven.

PERIODIC CHECKS

These checks are performed less frequently than gas stop checks. Recommended time intervals are summarized in **Table 3**.

Fuel Lines and Tank

Rubber fuel lines often rot and crack due to constant exposure to engine heat, oil and road dirt. It is not uncommon for fuel lines to crack and spew gasoline throughout the engine compartment thus causing a serious fire.

The fuel lines should be meticulously checked inch by inch throughout the whole vehicle. Test each and every connection and pipe. Check the rubber filler hose connections to the gas tank and the lines to the expansion tanks. If cracks or defects in the piping are found, replace that entire piece immediately. See Chapter Six.

On vehicles with the Westfalia camper conversion, check the connections to the propane tank and to the stove and refrigerator for tightness with a wrench. If leaks are detected, immediately close the propane shutoff valves. See Chapter Eleven.

WARNING
Do not use an open flame (matches or gas lanterns) as a light source when checking the fuel system or camper propane system. If leaks are present, the fuel will explode, resulting in serious injury or death as well as the destruction of your vehicle. Use a flashlight.

Brakes

Check the thickness of the front disc pads and the rear drum shoes. Disc brake pads should be replaced if the lining thickness is less than 0.078 in. (2.0 mm). **Figure 10** shows how to measure front brake pad thickness with a special VW tool. Rear brake shoes should be replaced if the lining thickness is less than 0.098 in. (2.5 mm). See **Figure 11**. Never replace shoes or pads on one wheel only; do both front or both rear wheels at the same time.

Inspect the brake master cylinder, brake lines and connections, front calipers and rear slave cylinders for leaks. Defective components will be coated with a film of light oil. See Chapter Nine.

Clutch (Manual Transmission Models)

Check the clutch master cylinder, clutch lines and connections and rear slave cylinder for leaks. Defective components will be coated with a film of light oil. See Chapter Eight.

Suspension and Steering

Check the entire suspension and steering systems. Examine the rubber dust seals on the ball-joints and the tie rod ends. Check tie rods for tightness and damage. Check all the other suspension bolts for tightness. Inspect the tires for irregular wear which may indicate damaged or worn suspension parts. Examine the shock absorbers for oil streaks indicating leaks; replace if necessary. Jack up the front wheels and move them by hand. The steering wheel should move at the same time as the wheels; there should be no free play. Check the wheel bearing adjustment; repack with grease and readjust if necessary. See Chapter Ten.

Exhaust and Emission Control Systems

Raise the rear of the vehicle and check the tightness of all the exhaust pipe connections and exhaust manifolds. Check the mechanical EGR valve; readjust if necessary. See Chapter Six.

Vacuum Hoses

Inspect the fuel injection and the vacuum advance and retard hoses; look for cracks and loose connections. Replace any hose found defective. See Chapter Six.

Alternator Drive Belt

Since drive belt tension and conditon affect battery charging, it is important to check belt tension frequently. When tension is correct, the belt should deflect about 3/8 to 5/8 in. (10 to 15 mm) under moderate thumb pressure. Replace the belt if cracked or excessively worn.

To adjust belt tension, pull down the rear license plate and loosen the altenator bracket bolt (**Figure 12**). Push the left side of the alternator down until the proper tension is obtained; tighten the alternator bracket bolt. See Chapter Seven for drive belt replacement.

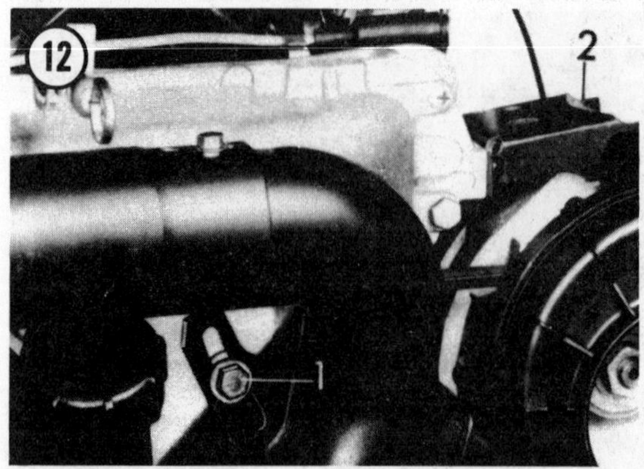

1. Pivot bolt 2. Bracket bolt

CV Joints

Check the CV (constant velocity) joint dust boots. If torn, the CV joint must be removed, cleaned and inspected for wear and a new dust boot (and possibly a CV joint) must be installed. Make sure that the CV joint bolts are torqued to 33 ft.-lb. (45 N•m). See Chapter Eight.

Tires and Wheels

Inspection

Check the condition of all the tires (including the spare). Check local traffic regulations concerning minimum tire tread depths. Original equipment tires have built-in tread wear indicators (**Figure 13**). Wear indicators appear as 1/2 in. (12.5 mm) bands when the tire tread depth becomes 1/16 in. (1.6 mm); the tire should be replaced at this point. Check the wheel lug nuts for tightness.

Tire rotation

For even wear, tires should be rotated as shown in **Figure 14**. If you notice unusual or uneven wear, the suspension may need alignment or the wheels may need balancing. Bring all alignment and balancing problems to a dealer or qualified tire shop.

Wiper Blades

Check operation of wipers. Also check the condition and alignment of wiper blades. See Chapter Seven. Check operation of washers and fill water reservoir.

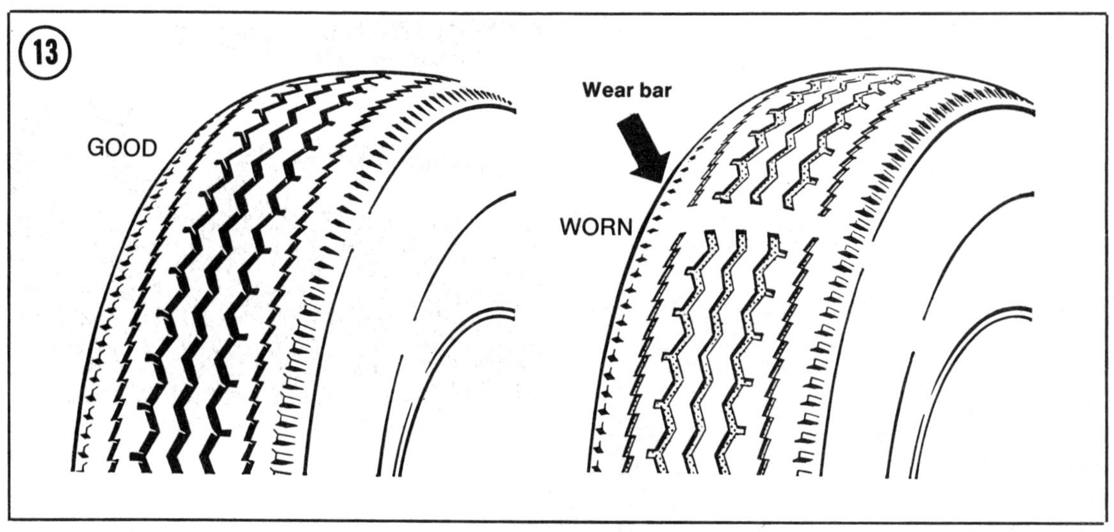

13
GOOD
Wear bar
WORN

14
Front
4-wheel rotation
Front
5-wheel rotation
BIAS
BELTED
TIRES
RADIAL
BELTED
TIRES
Front
5-wheel rotation
Front
4-wheel rotation

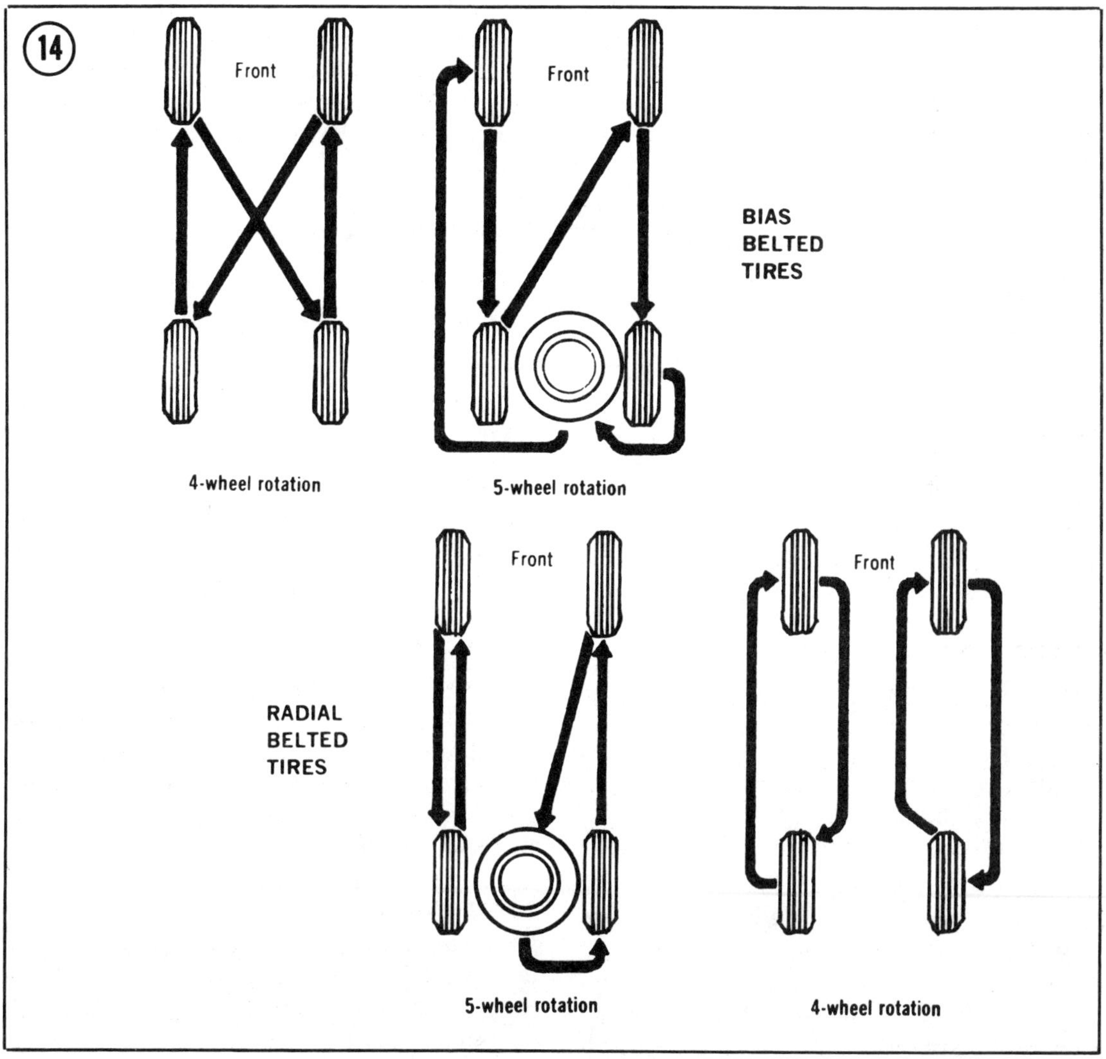

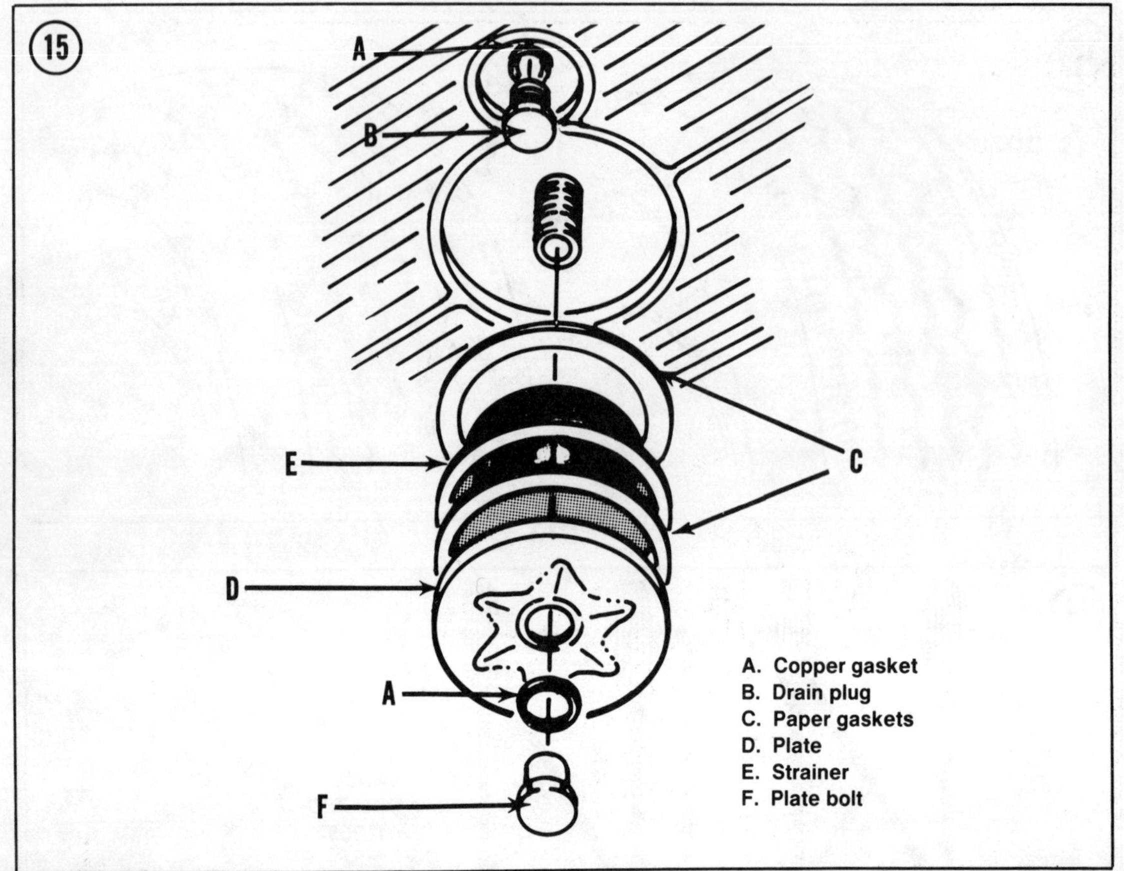

PERIODIC MAINTENANCE

Engine Oil and Filter Change

Engine oil should be changed every 3,000 miles (4,800 km), especially if the vehicle is driven in hot and dusty areas. Use only oils rated "For API service SE or SF." Non-detergent oils must never be used with air-cooled engines. See **Table 2** for recommended oil grades, fluids and capacities.

Change the oil filter every other oil change (every oil change if the vehicle is driven in hot and dusty areas).

1. When changing engine oil the vehicle must be on level ground. Start the engine and allow it to warm to operating temperature. Turn off the engine and let the vehicle stand at least 15 minutes; this lets oil flow to the bottom of the engine.
2. Place a container under the engine, remove the drain plug (**Figure 15**) and let the oil drain completely (10 to 15 minutes). Check the condition of the drain plug's copper sealing washer; replace if damaged. Reinstall the drain plug.
3. Remove the oil strainer. See **Figure 15**. Clean it with solvent (diesel fuel works nicely). Always use new gaskets when reinstalling the strainer.
4. If the oil filter is being changed, position the drain pan beneath it. Loosen the filter by turning it counterclockwise by hand or with a filter wrench. Remove and discard the old filter. Let the filter mounting drain for at least 5 minutes. Clean the filter mounting on the crankcase. Coat the rubber gasket on the new filter with a liberal amount of clean engine oil and screw the filter in until it contacts the seal on the crankcase. Tighten by hand 1/2 turn further; do not use a filter wrench to tighten.
5. Remove the oil filler cap in back of the rear license plate (**Figure 3**) and fill the crankcase with the recommended oil. See **Table 2** for recommended oil grades, fluids and capacities.

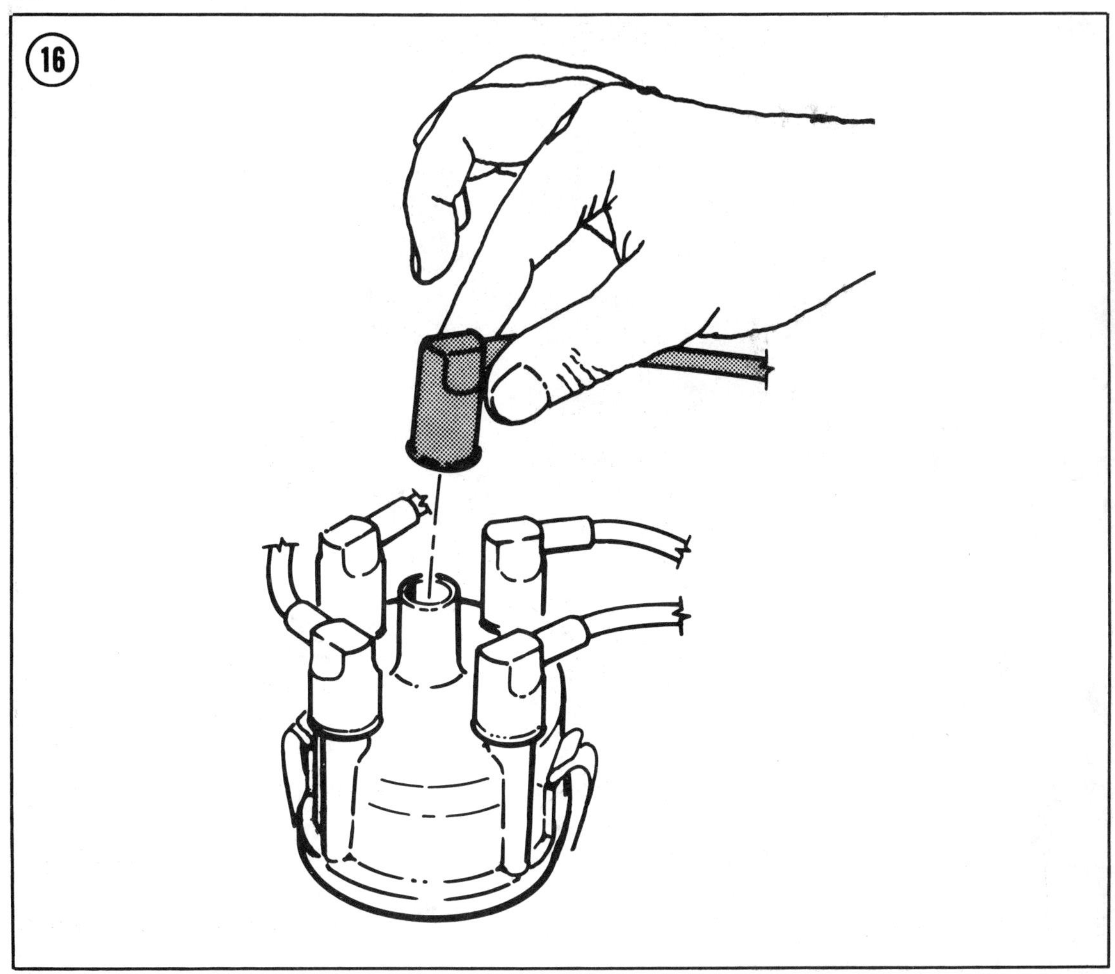

6. Open the engine compartment, pull the center wire (coil wire) out of the distributor cap (**Figure 16**) and ground the wire to the engine. Crank the engine over for about 30 seconds or until the oil pressure warning light goes out (this pumps oil up into the engine). Reconnect the coil wire to the distributor, start the engine and run it at idle for a couple of minutes. Turn off engine, check the oil level on the dipstick and top off if necessary. See **Figure 3**.

Air Cleaner

Remove and clean the air filter element every 3,000 miles (4,800 km). In very dusty areas the filter element must be cleaned more frequently. To remove the filter element, release the 5 snap clips and lift off the top of the air filter housing (**Figure 17**).

Remove the filter element and thoroughly clean the inside of the air cleaner housing with a lightly oiled lint-free cloth. Tap the filter lightly against your hand to shake out the dirt. Under no circumstances should the filter element be cleaned or soaked with gasoline, solvents or oil.

Replace the filter element every 6,000 miles (9,650 km) or more frequently if the vehicle is driven in dusty areas.

Fuel Filter

Replace the fuel filter every 6 months. To remove, clamp off the fuel lines feeding in and leading out of the filter (**Figure 18**). Loosen the hose clamps and cut the tie wraps which hold the filter and lines to the body. Pull out the old filter; install the new one with the arrow pointing to the fuel pump. Install new tie wraps

17

Filter element

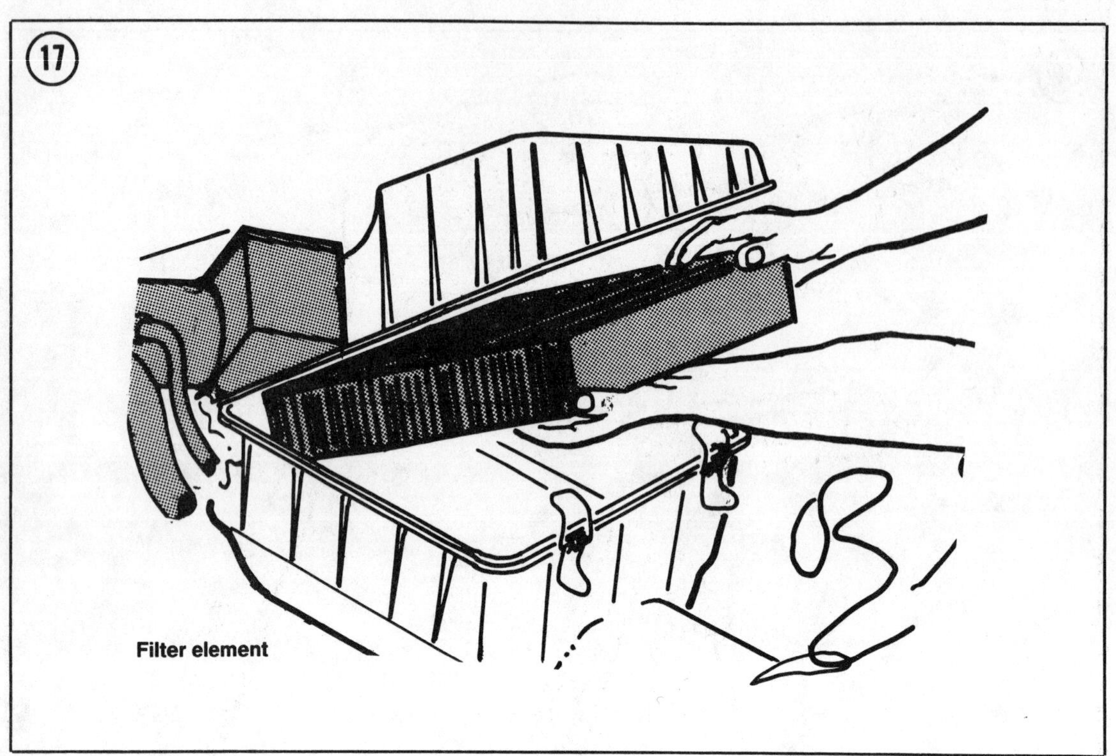

18

To engine
To fuel pump

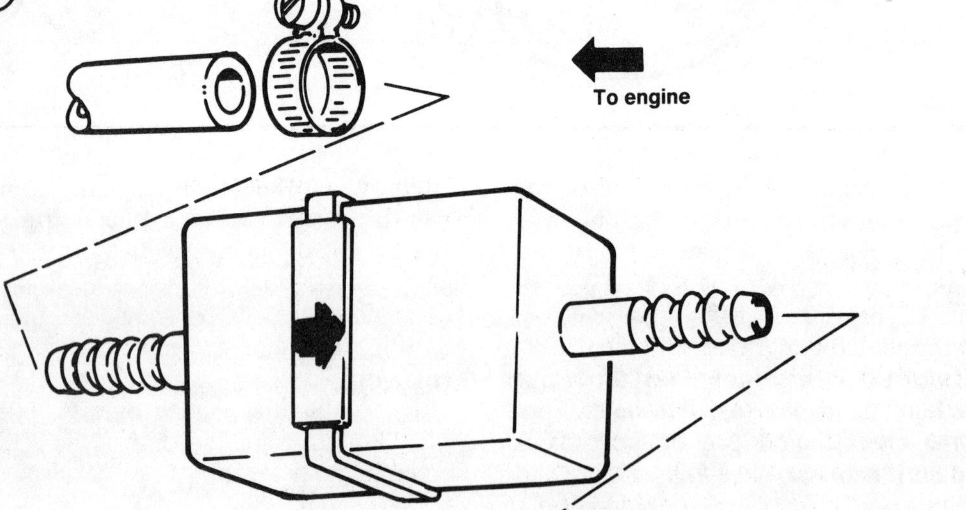

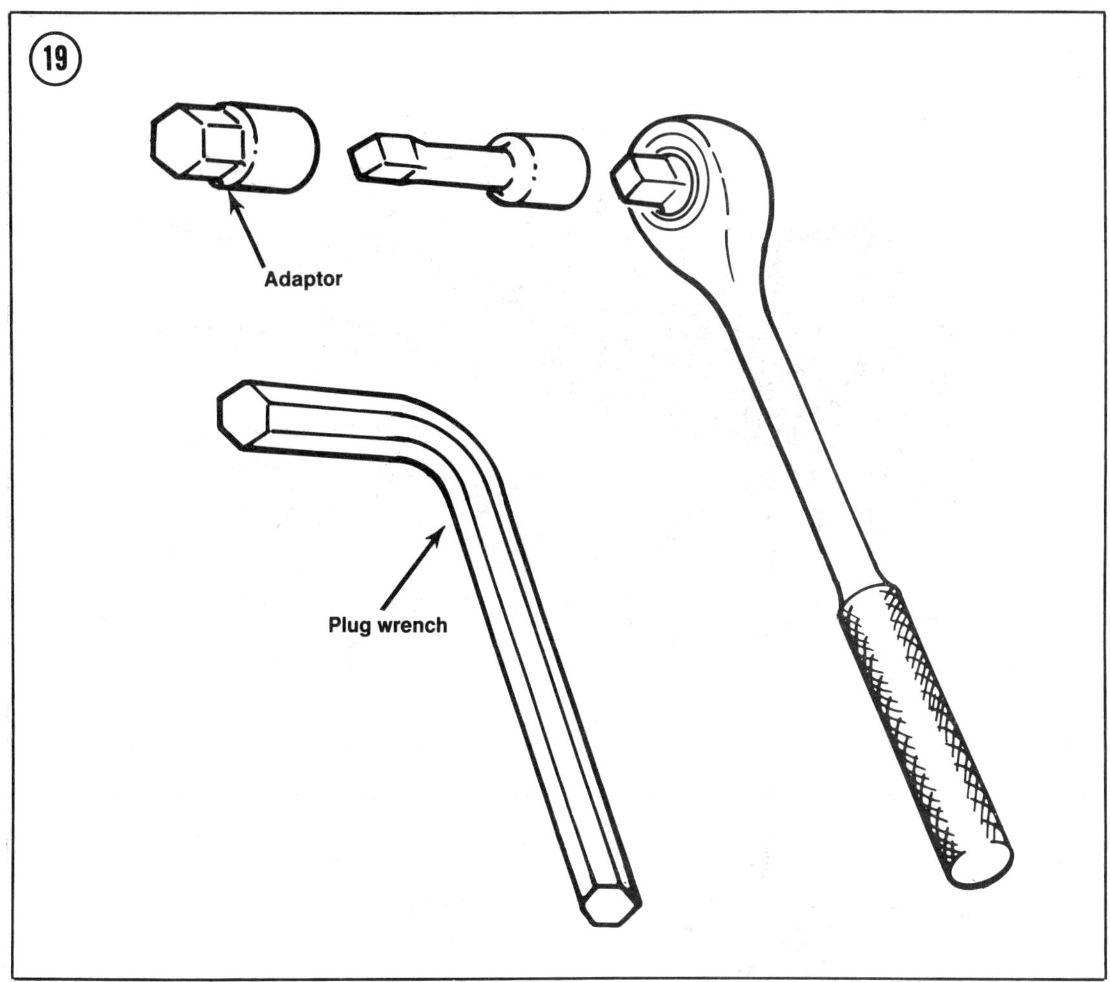

and secure the filter and lines to the body frame.

Manual Transmission and Final Drive

The manual transmission and final drive (differential) share the same fluid. Check the transmission oil level every 6,000 miles (9,650 km) or 6 months. Park the vehicle on level ground and set the parking brake. Remove the filler plug (a special tool is required as shown in **Figure 19**) on the right front section of the transmission just above the shifter mechanism. The gear oil should be even with the bottom of the plug hole; if not, add oil until it starts to spill from the filler hole. Reinstall the plug and wipe spilled oil off transmission. See **Table 2** for recommended oils, grades and capacities.

Automatic Transmission and Final Drive

Final drive and automatic transmission do not share the same oil. Change the automatic transmission fluid (ATF) every 22,500 miles (36,200 km) or 1 1/2 years. Also clean the ATF sump and strainer at this time.

Check the oil level of the final drive (differential gear) every 6,000 miles (9,650 km) or every 6 months.

Changing ATF

CAUTION

Do not remove ATF sump if you must work outdoors. Cleanliness is very important when working with an auto-

matic transmission. Blowing dust particles can settle on internal transmission parts and cause serious damage. Let your local repair shop change the fluid if you do not have access to a clean garage.

1. Park the vehicle on level ground and set the parking brake. Remove the filler tube from the ATF sump (**Figure 20**) and drain the fluid into a suitable container.

CAUTION
Do not start the engine or move the vehicle with the ATF drained.

2. Remove sump and gasket, ATF strainer cover and strainer (**Figure 21**). Clean the parts thoroughly with solvent and wipe dry with a clean lint-free cloth.
3. Reinstall the ATF strainer and strainer cover. Reinstall the sump (using a new rubber gasket). Evenly torque sump bolts to 14 ft.-lb. (20 N•m) and reinstall the filler tube.
4. Refill transmission with ATF through dipstick tube using a funnel and hose. See **Table 2** for recommended oils, grades and capacities.
5. Start the engine; move the gear selector through all positions, ending in NEUTRAL.
6. Check the ATF level with the dipstick and top up to the lower mark if necessary.
7. Let the engine idle for a few minutes to warm the ATF; check the level again. ATF must be between the 2 marks on the dipstick. Add ATF if necessary; do not overfill above the top mark. Excess ATF will cause a transmission malfunction; it will have to be drained away.

Changing final drive fluid

1. Park the vehicle on level ground and set the parking brake. Remove the final drive oil filler

20

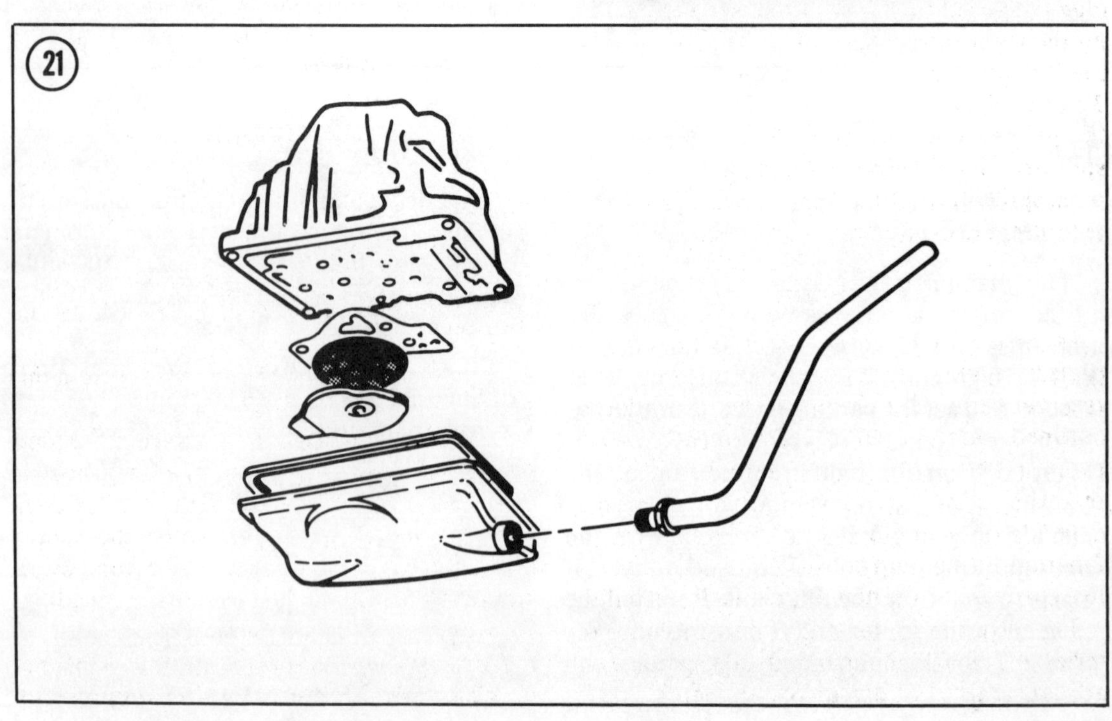
21

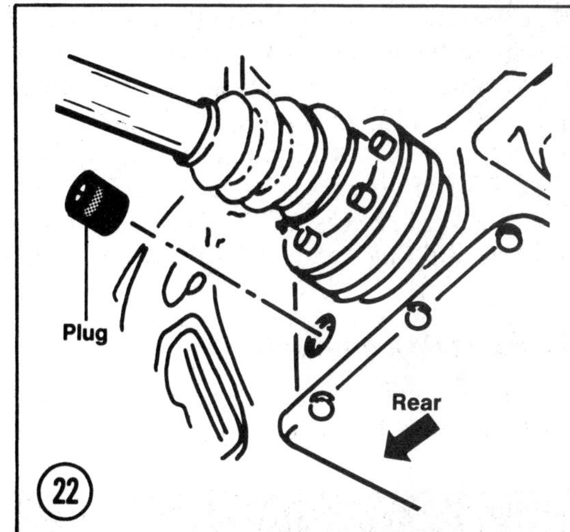

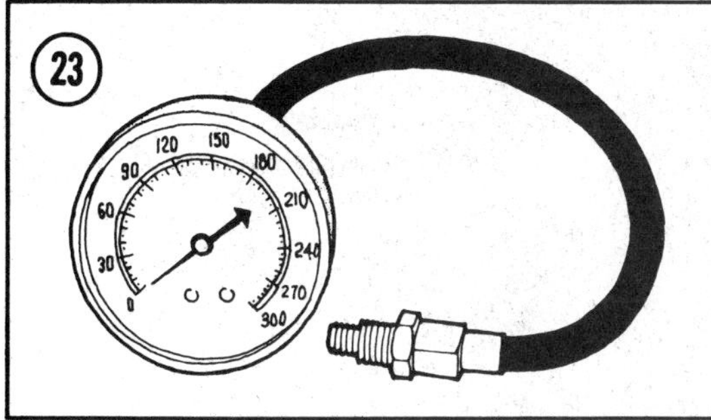

plug (a special tool is required; see **Figure 19**) on the right side in back of and slightly below the constant velocity joint (**Figure 22**).

2. The oil should be even with the bottom of the plug hole; if not, add oil until it starts to spill from the filler hole. Reinstall the plug and wipe spilled oil off final drive. See **Table 2** for recommended oils, grades and capacities.

TUNE-UP

In order to maintain your Vanagon in perfect running condition, the engine must receive periodic tune-ups. The procedures outlined here should be performed at least every 6,000 miles (9,650 km) or every 6 months. Since proper engine operation depends on a number of interrelated system functions, a tune-up consisting of only one or two corrections will not produce lasting results.

The procedures in this chapter require a series of visual and mechanical checks and adjustments, followed by an instrument checkout. The instruments required are described in detail within Chapter One. **Table 3** summarizes tune-up specifications. Tune-up consists of the following jobs, done in the order listed:

a. Engine compression test
b. Spark plug replacement
c. Spark plug wire inspection (replacement if required)
d. Distributor cap and rotor inspection (replacement if required)
e. Breaker point replacement/adjustment and condenser replacement (California excluded)
f. Dwell angle check (California excluded)
g. Ignition timing adjustment
h. Idle speed and mixture adjustment

CAUTION

On California models with breakerless ignition systems do not connect any condenser/suppressor or any kind of test light to terminal 1 on the ignition coil. Do not connect any kind of test equipment requiring a 12-volt supply to terminal 15 on the ignition coil. Do not crank the engine over with the center wire (terminal 4 wire) of the distributor disconnected without grounding this wire to the engine with a jumper wire. Do not disconnect the battery when the engine is running. If you do any of the above, the breakerless ignition system will be damaged.

COMPRESSION TEST

An engine with low or uneven cylinder compression cannot be properly tuned. In view of this, the engine should be given a compression test before proceeding with the tune-up.

1. Put the transmission in NEUTRAL, set the parking brake and block the wheels.
2. Remove the spark plugs as described in this chapter.
3. Screw a compression gauge like the one shown in **Figure 23** into each spark plug hole in turn. Have an assistant turn the engine over with the starter while you watch the gauge; crank the engine over at least 4 compression strokes to obtain the highest possible reading. Record the reading for each cylinder.

Each cylinder should produce 85-135 psi (6.0-9.5 bar). The minimum reading for any

3

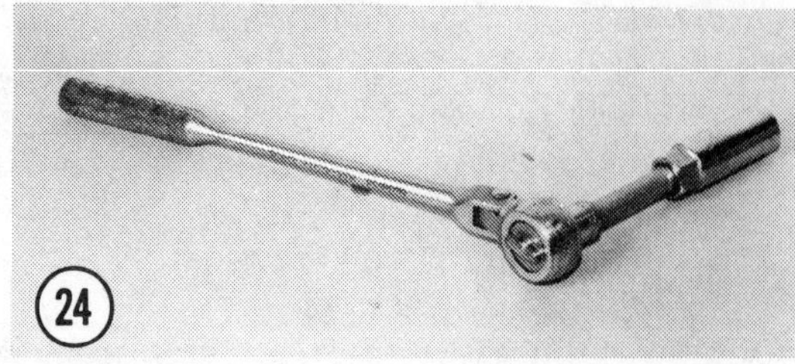

cylinder is 71 psi (5.0 bar). The maximum acceptable pressure difference between cylinders is 42 psi (3.0 bar).

If low or uneven compression readings were recorded for one or more cylinders, pour about a tablespoon of clean motor oil through the spark plug hole of each low-reading cylinder. Crank the engine through several strokes and recheck compression. If compression improves, the problem is most likely worn piston rings (new pistons and cylinders are needed). If no improvement is noted, in all probability the cylinder head valves are burned, sticking or not properly seating (cylinder heads need rebuilding). If 2 cylinders on the same side read low and the oil does not improve compression, the cylinder head may be loose (cylinder heads need re-torquing). Chapter Four gives procedures on how to repair all of these problems.

CAUTION

Take immediate steps to correct any compression defects found. Leaving anything unrepaired will quickly lead to severe engine damage, invariably costing you many more dollars to fix.

SPARK PLUG REMOVAL

1. Disconnect the spark plug wires by grasping the boot portion of the wire and pulling up.

CAUTION

Spark plug wires should never be removed by pulling on the wires; damage will result and the wires will have to be replaced.

2. Remove each spark plug with a wrench like the one shown in **Figure 24**.
3. Inspect each spark plug; compare its appearance with Figure 17 in Chapter Two. Electrode appearance is a good indicator of performance in each cylinder and permits early recognition of trouble.

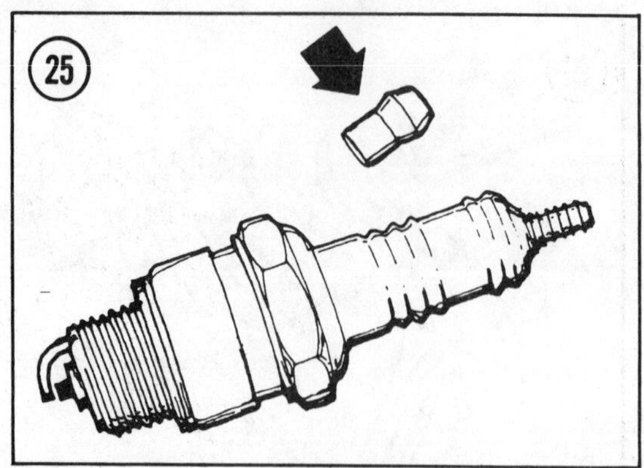

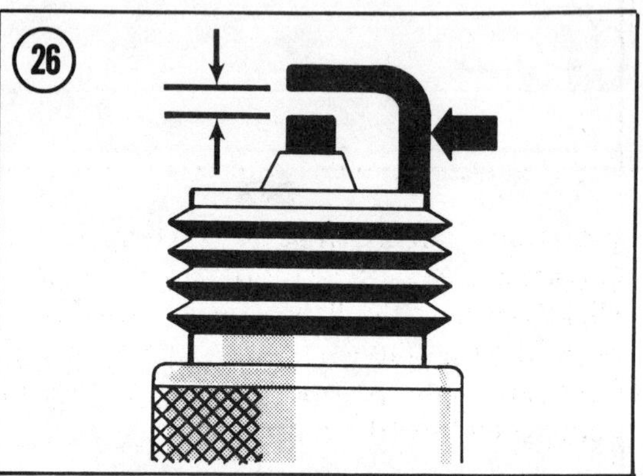

SPARK PLUG REPLACEMENT

Spark plugs should be replaced whenever the engine is tuned. If misfiring occurs between tune-up intervals, spark plugs in good condition can often be cleaned, regapped and reinstalled with acceptable results. If all new plugs are being installed, skip Steps 1-3 in the following procedure. See **Table 1** for spark plug types.

1. Inspect plugs and replace those with badly worn electrodes and/or glazed, blistered or broken porcelain insulators; compare the plugs with Figure 17 in Chapter Two.
2. Clean serviceable plugs with an abrasive cleaner (wire brush or sandblast). File the center electrode flat.
3. Verify that all plugs to be reinstalled are the same and of the proper heat range; see **Table 1**.
4. Remove each plug from the box; do not screw on the end pieces that are loose in the package (**Figure 25**).
5. Check the plug gap (**Table 1** and **Figure 26**) by inserting the correct gauge wire between the

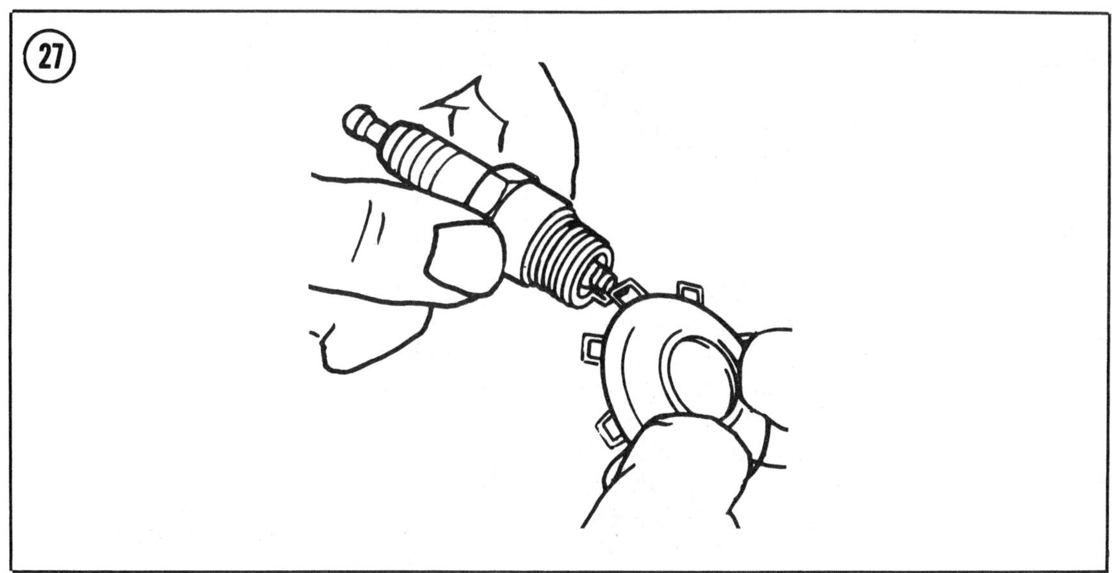

center and side electrode of each spark plug (**Figure 27**). If the gap is correct, you will feel a slight drag as you pull the wire through. If there is no drag or the gauge won't pass through, bend the side electrode with the slot on the gapping tool to set the proper gap.

CAUTION
Always adjust gap by bending the negative or side (never center) electrode. Most spark plug feeler gauges have a slot which can be used for bending the electrode. Never adjust the gap by tapping the electrode on a hard surface. This may cause damage to the plug insulator.

6. Apply aluminum anti-seize compound to the plug threads. Screw the plugs into the holes and torque them to 22 ft.-lb. (30 N•m). Do not overtighten. Always use a torque wrench; the VW cylinder heads are made of aluminum and are easily damaged.

NOTE
If the cylinder head plug threads are stripped, cracked or excessively worn see ***Cylinder Heads*** *in Chapter Four. This section gives instructions on how to repair spark plug hole threads without removing cylinder heads.*

7. Reconnect the spark plug wires.

SPARK PLUG WIRE INSPECTION

Check the spark plug wires if they have been in service for a year or longer. If they are oil soaked, cracked, stiff or brittle, replace them. Inspect the spark plug wire connectors for cracks or burn tracks; replace if necessary. Check the rubber air sealing boots on the plug connectors; they should be soft and pliable and make tight contact against the metal of the cooling air shroud. If not, unscrew the connector from the ignition wire and replace the boot with a new one. **Figure 28** shows ignition wire routing.

NOTE
If replacing the ignition wires, save the old plug connector and the longest wire for an emergency. Keep them in the vehicle at all times.

Ignition wires, plug connectors and sealing boots can be purchased separately or in whole kits from auto parts suppliers or VW dealers. When purchasing a whole wire kit, make sure the kit is made specifically for the Vanagon and that it is already assembled.

DISTRIBUTOR

California models utilize a breakerless ignition system; 49-state and Canadian models use a breaker point system.

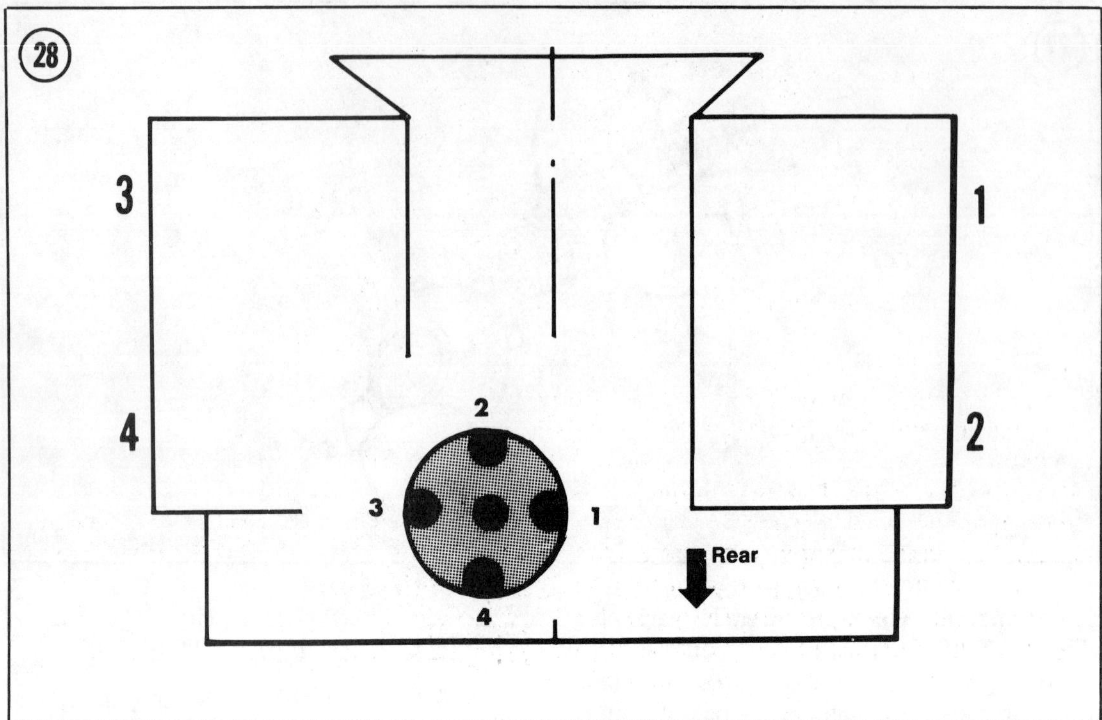

Distributor Cap and Rotor Inspection

1. Gently pull out all the ignition wires from the top of the distributor cap. Pry back the distributor cap clips with a screwdriver and remove the cap and rotor (**Figure 29**).
2. Wipe away all grease and dirt and check cap and rotor for cracks, wear or damage. See **Figure 30**. Minor burning on the rotor can be cleaned off by using a fine grit emery cloth. Replace parts as necessary.
3. Install the distributor cap and rotor. Push the ignition wires into the top of the distributor cap. See **Figure 28** for ignition wire routing.

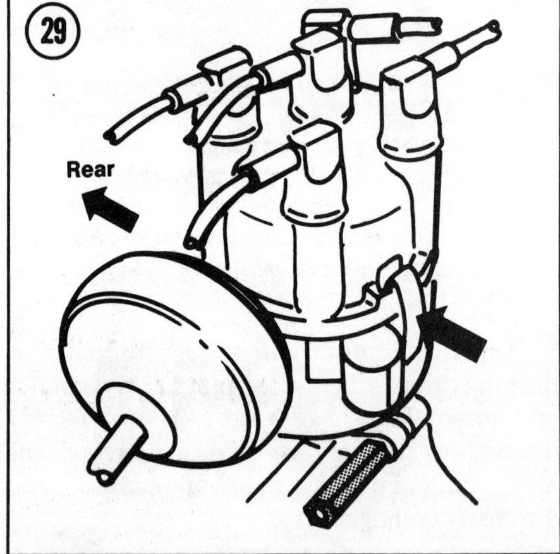

Breaker Point Replacement and Adjustment

1. Remove the distributor cap, rotor and dust cover.
2. Remove the small screw which holds the breaker points in place. See **Figure 31**. Remove old points and install new points.
3. Remove the 3 bolts which hold the plastic screen over the cooling fan and insert a socket wrench with extension onto the center cooling fan nut. See **Figure 32**. Turn the engine over clockwise (with wrench) until the plastic heel of the breaker points rests on the high point of one of the distributor cam lobes (**Figure 31**).
4. Loosen the small breaker point screw, insert a 0.016 in. (0.4 mm) feeler gauge between the breaker points and set the point gap. See **Figure 33**. Tighten the small screw. Apply a small amount of distributor cam lubricant to the cam lobes.

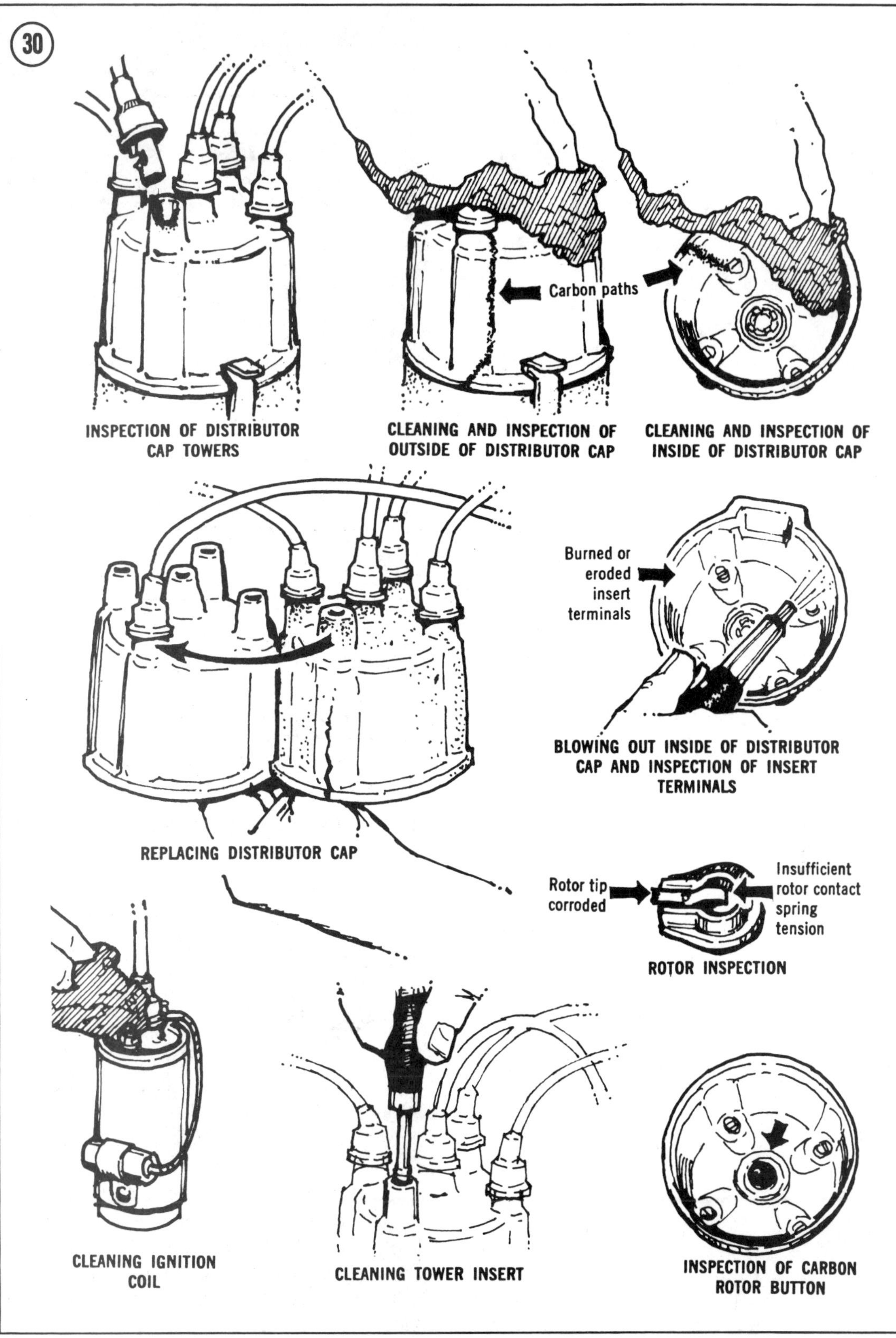

INSPECTION OF DISTRIBUTOR CAP TOWERS

CLEANING AND INSPECTION OF OUTSIDE OF DISTRIBUTOR CAP

CLEANING AND INSPECTION OF INSIDE OF DISTRIBUTOR CAP

REPLACING DISTRIBUTOR CAP

BLOWING OUT INSIDE OF DISTRIBUTOR CAP AND INSPECTION OF INSERT TERMINALS

ROTOR INSPECTION

CLEANING IGNITION COIL

CLEANING TOWER INSERT

INSPECTION OF CARBON ROTOR BUTTON

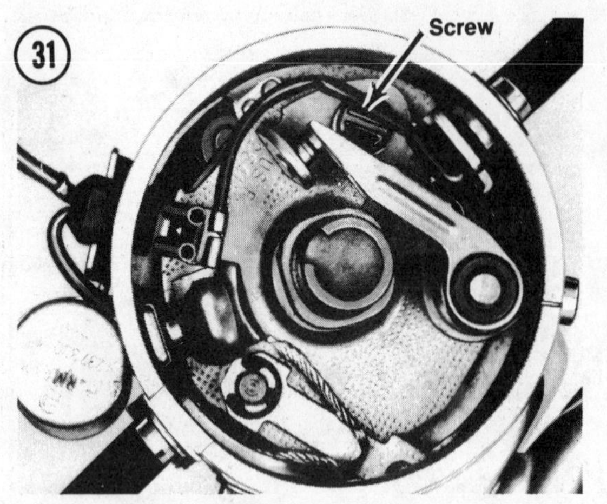

32

License plate

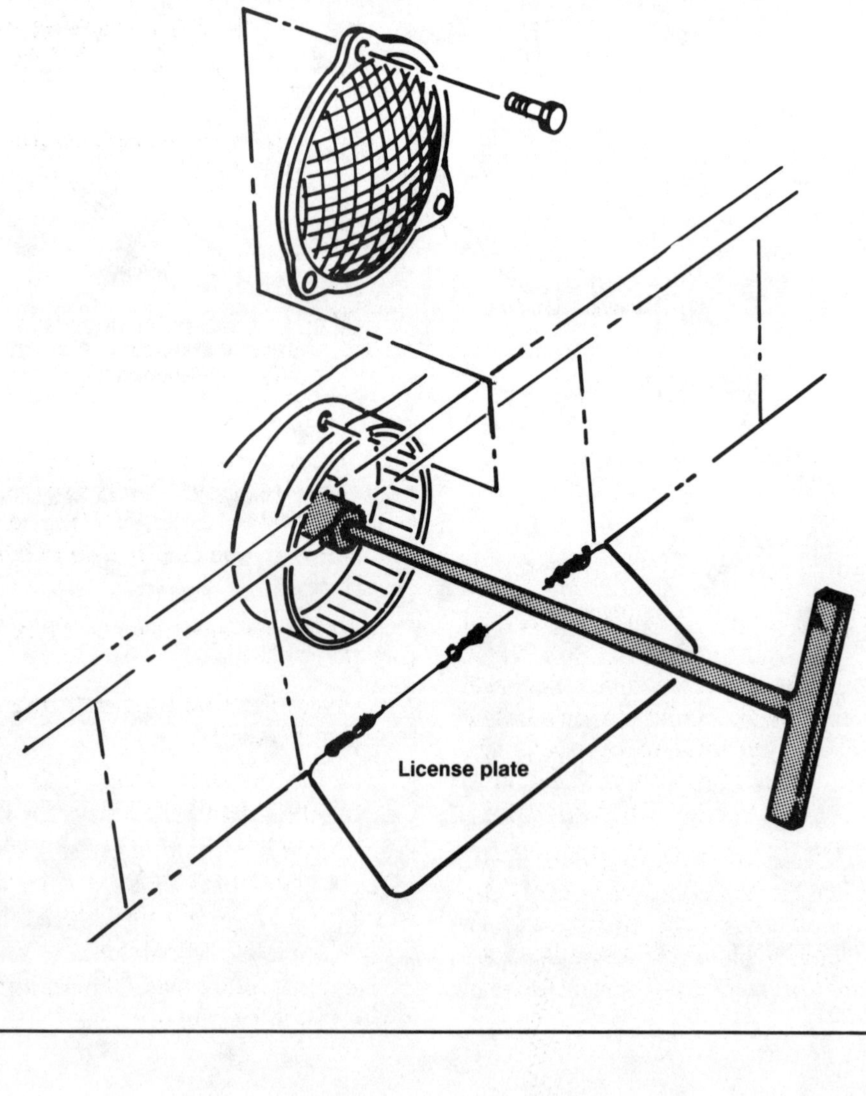

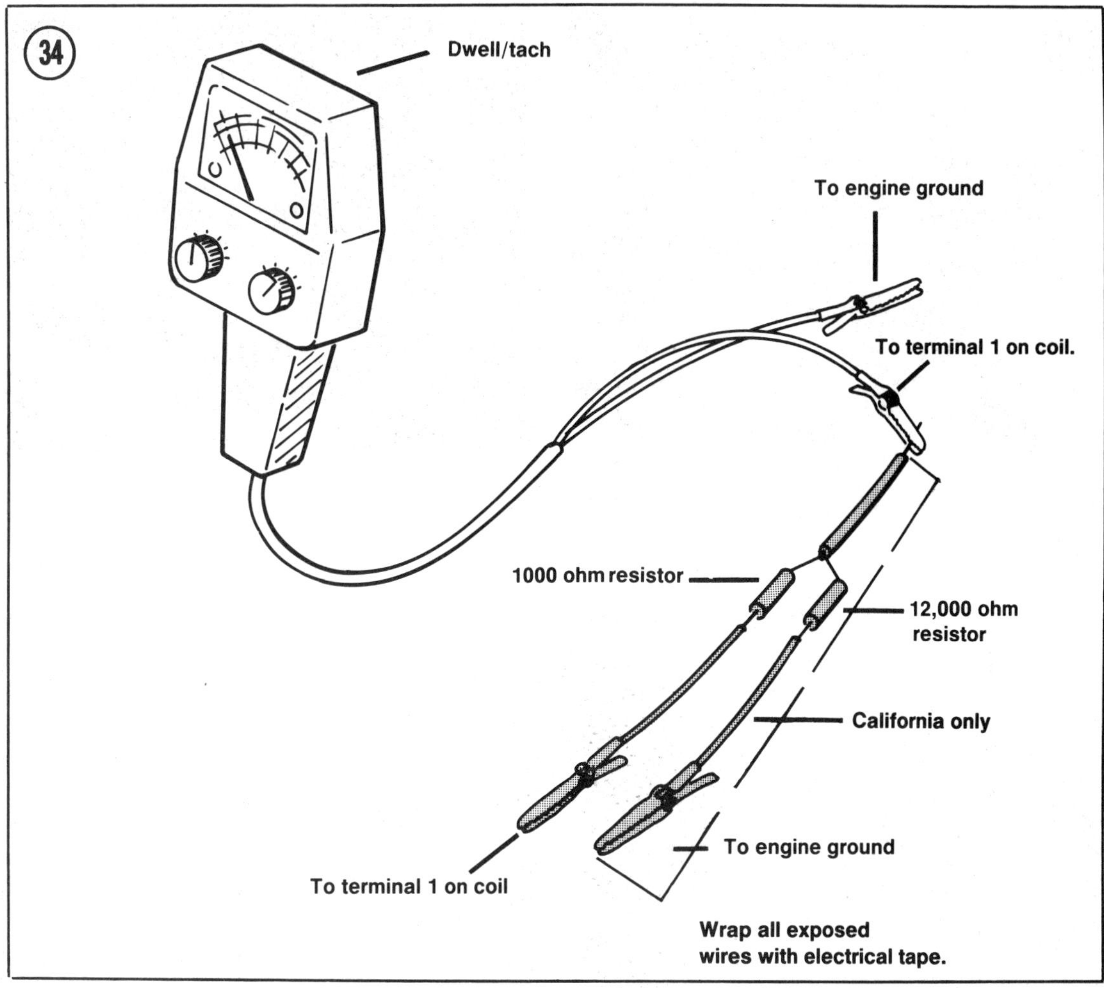

5. Reinstall the dust cover, rotor, distributor cap and plastic screen.

Dwell Angle Adjustment (Breaker Point System)

Dwell angle is the distance (in degrees) of distributor cam rotation during which the breaker points remain closed. Since this angle is determined by breaker point gap, dwell angle is an accurate determination of point gap. Dwell angle is also a good way to check point wear without removing the distributor cap.

The preferred method for setting dwell angle is to first set the breaker point gap with a feeler gauge and then check the setting with a dwell/tach meter. Many dwell meters intended for tuning and testing incorporate a tachometer as well.

It is very important that breaker points be set to the proper gap. Points with an excessive gap result in a weak spark at high engine speeds. Points set too closely tend to burn and pit rapidly.

1. Set the parking brake and block the drive wheels.

2. Connect the dwell meter to the engine as shown in **Figure 34**.

3. Pull the vacuum advance line off the distributor and plug the line. Start the engine.

4. Make sure the meter is switched to DWELL. Note the reading; dwell angle should be between 44-50° (for new points) with a wear limit of 42-58° (for old points).

5. Readjust point gap, if necessary, as described in this chapter.

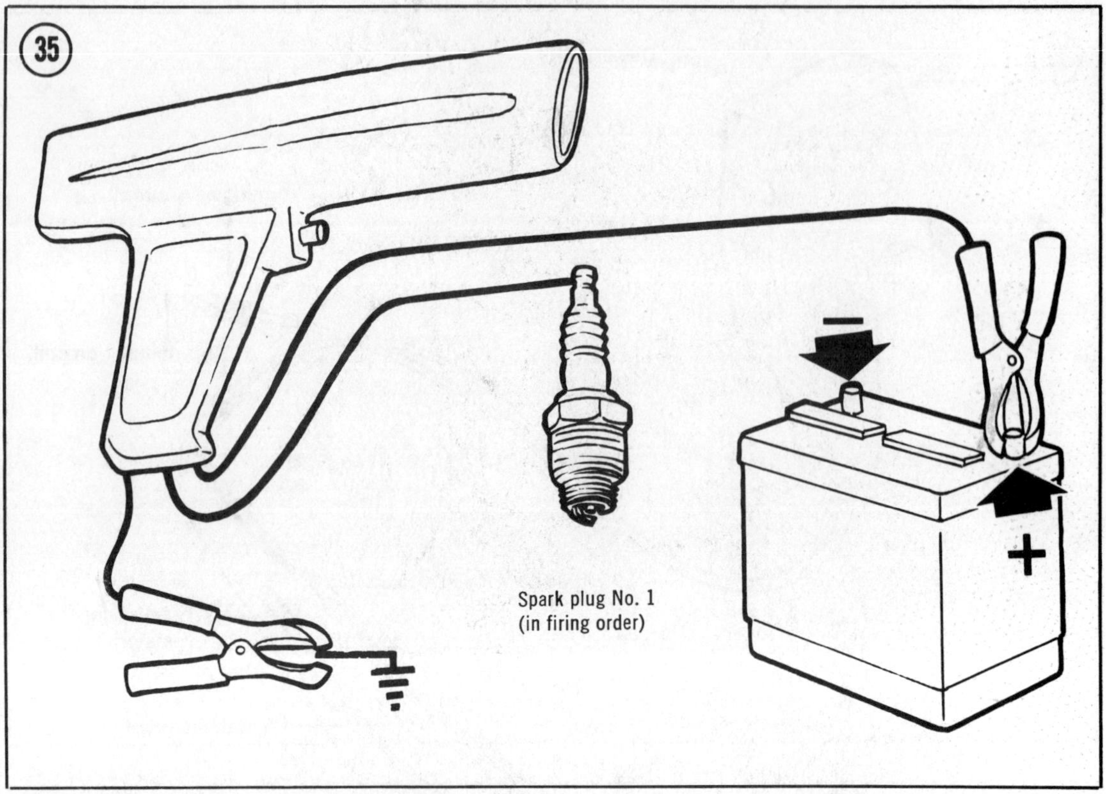

35

Spark plug No. 1
(in firing order)

IGNITION TIMING ADJUSTMENT

Ignition timing should be checked and adjusted (if required) only after breaker point replacement and dwell angle adjustment have been completed.

1. Connect a tachometer/dwell meter to the engine as shown in **Figure 34**. The special resistor set-up shown in **Figure 34** must be used on California models with breakerless ignition.
2. Connect the timing light to the engine as shown in **Figure 35**.
3. Set the parking brake and block the drive wheels. Start the engine and allow it to warm to operating temperature. Engine oil must be at least 86° F (30° C).

4A. On 49-state and Canadian models perform the following:

a. Check engine idle speed with the tach/dwell meter. Compare with specifications in **Table 1**. Adjust if necessary; see procedure in this chapter.
b. Pull the vacuum line off the distributor and plug the line; check the dwell angle with the dwell meter and readjust if necessary. See procedure in this chapter.
c. Shine the timing light onto the timing scale; the red dot on the scale should align with the notch in the pulley (7.5° BTDC) as shown in **Figure 36**. If not, loosen the distributor clamp bolt (**Figure 37**). Slowly turn the distributor body until the red dot and the notch align. Tighten the clamp bolt. Unplug and reconnect the distributor vacuum line and remove test equipment.

4B. On California models perform the following:

a. Disconnect the 2 plugs from the idle stabilizer and connect them together (**Figure 38**).

36

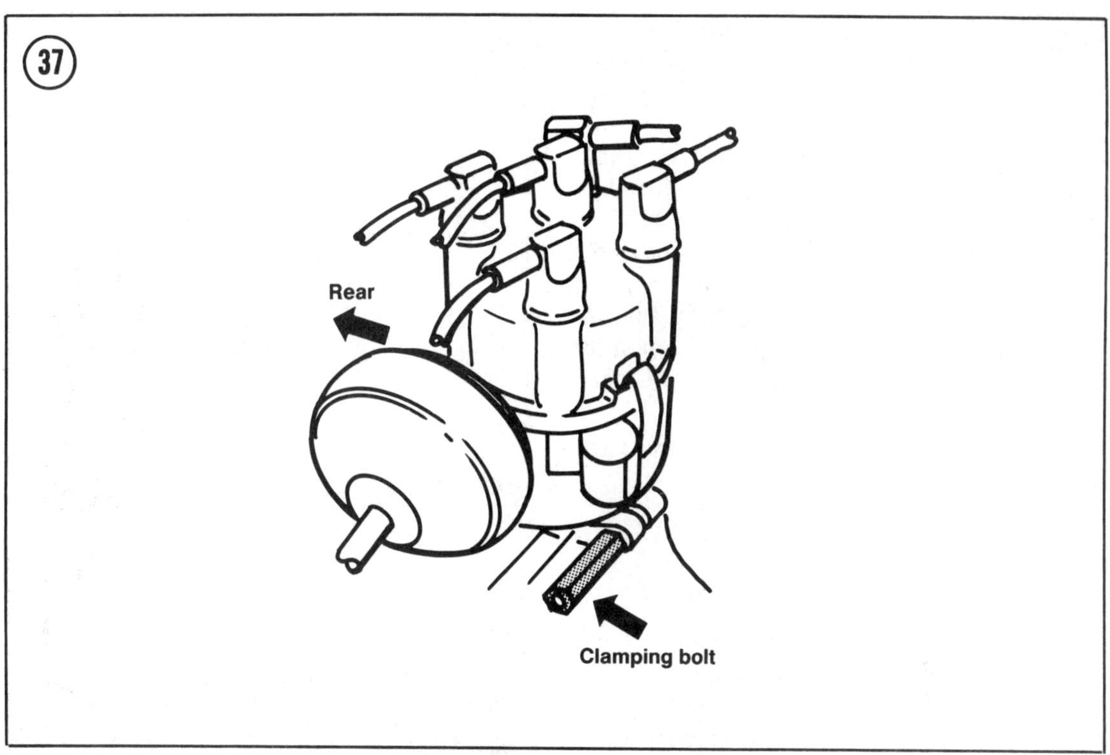

38

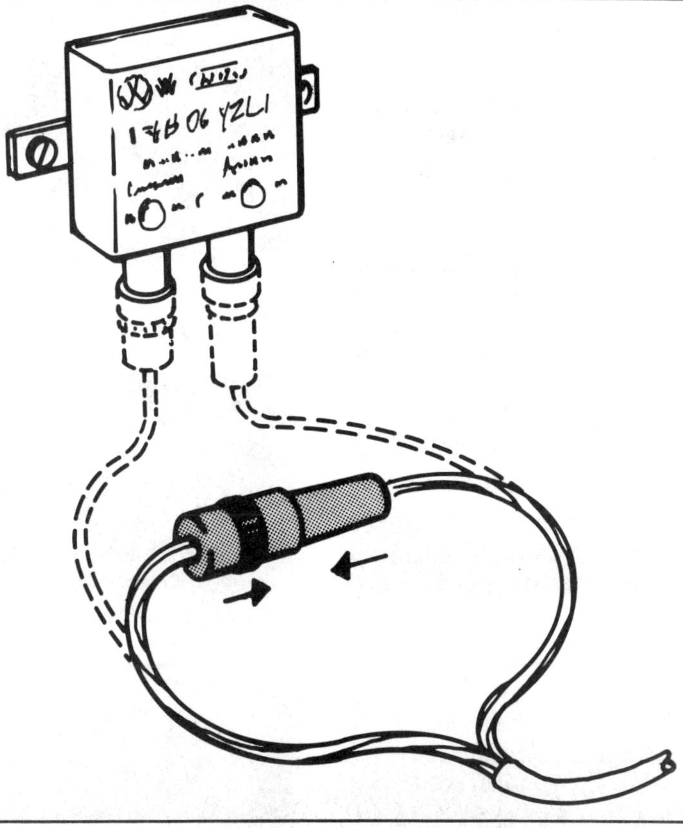

b. Check engine idle speed with the tach/dwell meter. Compare with specifications in **Table 1**. Adjust if necessary; see procedure in this chapter.
c. Shine the timing light onto the timing scale; the red dot on the scale should align with the notch in the pulley (5° ATDC) as shown in **Figure 39**. If not, loosen the distributor clamp bolt **(Figure 37)** and slowly turn the distributor body until the red dot and the notch align. Tighten the clamp bolt and reconnect the idle stabilizer plugs.

5. Disconnect the timing light and the tach/dwell meter from the engine.

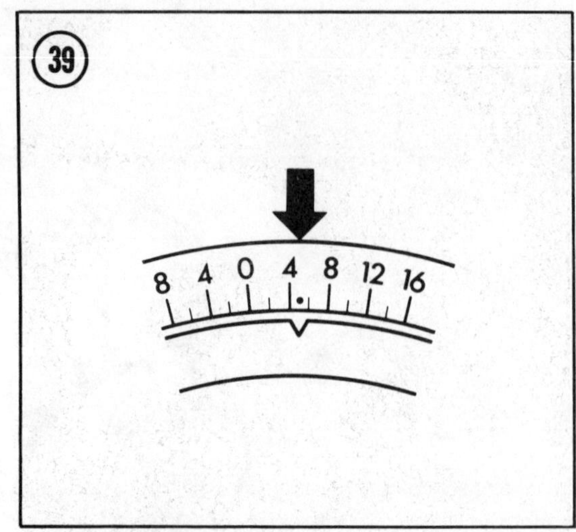

IDLE SPEED AND MIXTURE ADJUSTMENT

Idle speed and mixture adjustment should be done at the same time. A CO meter is required for idle mixture adjustment. Meters can be obtained from many equipment rental yards.

Idle speed can be set without adjusting the mixture, but the engine emissions will probably rise to an illegal level.

1. Set the parking brake and block the drive wheels. Start the engine and allow it to warm to operating temperature. Engine oil must be at least 140° F (60° C).

2. Turn off all electrical equipment. Disconnect the charcoal canister hose from the air cleaner housing and plug the hose **(Figure 40)**.

NOTE
Dwell angle and engine timing must be set to specifications before adjusting idle speed. See procedures in this chapter.

3. Connect the tach/dwell meter to the engine. A special resistor set-up as shown in **Figure 34** must be used for California models with breakerless ignition.

NOTE
If the vehicle has been parked outside at temperatures below 50° F (10° C) it must be brought inside a garage; the intake air sensor must warm up to at least 68° F (20° C).

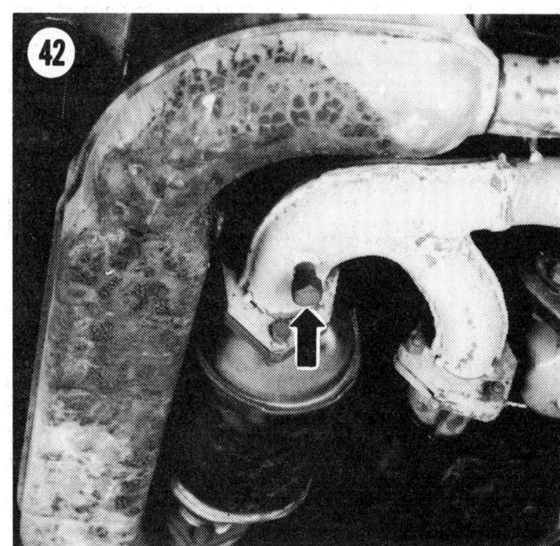

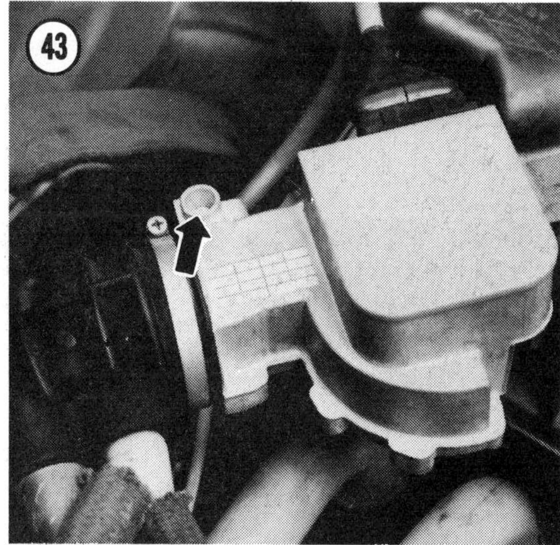

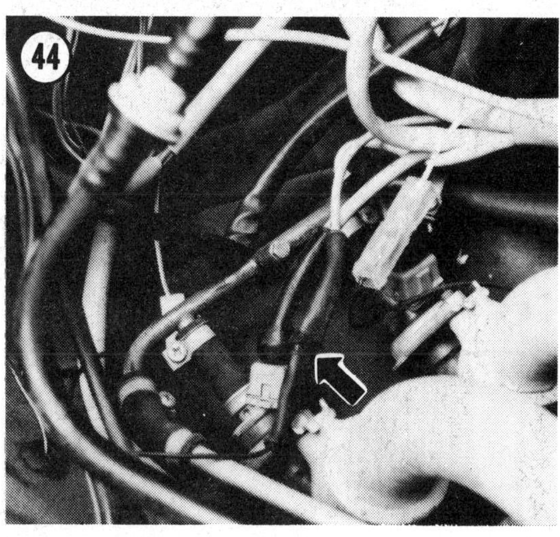

4A. On 49-state and Canadian models perform the following:

a. Check and, if necessary, adjust the engine idle speed to specifications (**Table 1**) by turning the idle speed screw (**Figure 41**).
b. Insert the CO probe ahead of the catalytic converter at the probe receptacle (**Figure 42**).
c. Check and, if necessary, adjust idle mixture to a CO level of 1.0 +/-0.5% by removing the metal cap and turning the adjusting screw (**Figure 43**). Reinstall the metal cap.
d. Disconnect the CO meter and probe; unplug and reconnect the charcoal canister hose to the air cleaner assembly.

4B. On California models perform the following:

a. Check the idle speed with the tach/dwell meter (idle stabilizer must be connected); it should be between 850-950 rpm.
b. Disconnect the 2 plugs from the idle stabilizer and connect them together (**Figure 38**).
c. Check the idle speed with the tachometer; adjust if necessary to 850-950 rpm by turning the idle speed adjusting screw (**Figure 41**).
d. Reconnect the idle stabilizer.
e. Slowly increase the engine speed to 1,000 rpm and release the throttle. Idle speed must return to 850-950 rpm.
f. Connect the CO meter.
g. Disconnect the oxygen sensor plug (**Figure 44**).
h. Insert the CO probe ahead of the catalytic converter at the probe receptacle (**Figure 42**).
i. Check and, if necessary, adjust idle mixture to a CO level of 0.7+/-0.4% by removing the metal cap and turning the adjusting screw (**Figure 43**). Reinstall the metal cap.
j. Reconnect the oxygen sensor.
k. Disconnect the CO meter and probe; unplug and reconnect the charcoal canister hose to the air cleaner assembly.

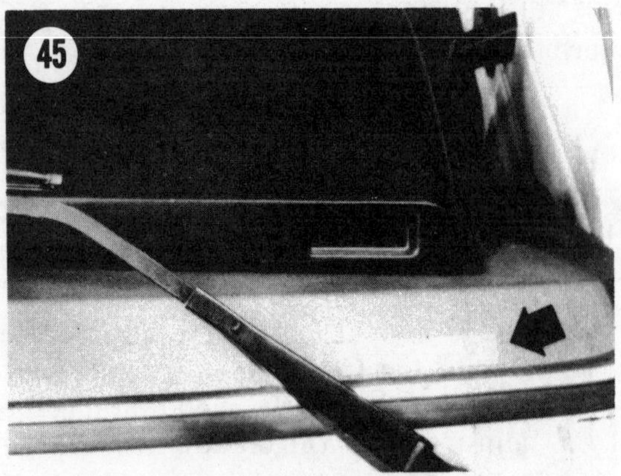

45

46

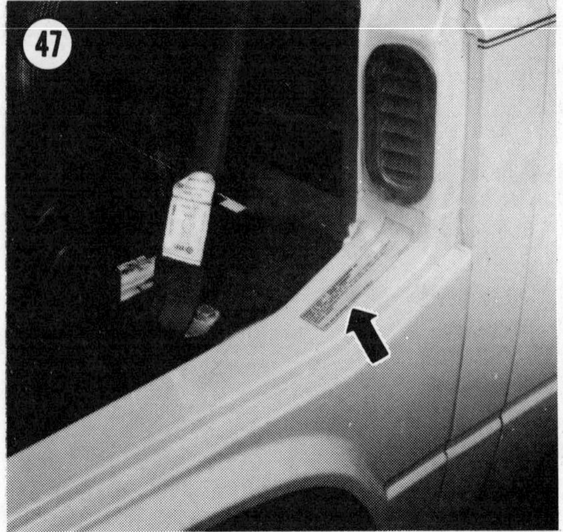

47

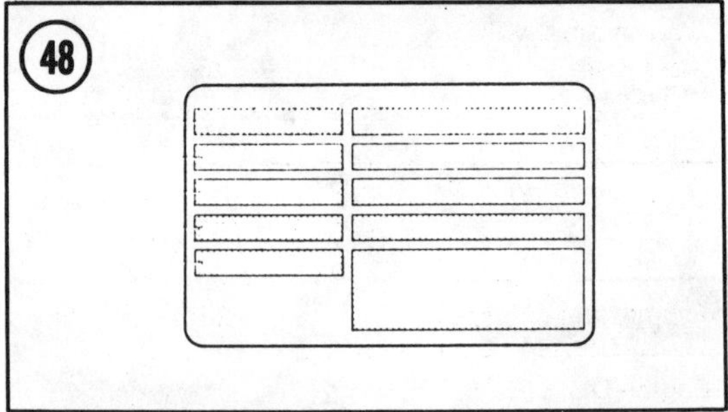

48

VEHICLE IDENTIFICATION CODES

All replacement parts should be ordered by the year the vehicle was made and by serial number. VW has a habit of making minor changes in the middle of a production run.

Several identification plates are on the Vanagon. The vehicle identification number (VIN) is located on the driver's side of the dashboard near the windshield (**Figure 45**). The engine number is stamped on the engine crankcase in front of the main cooling fan housing (**Figure 46**); this number should be recorded and kept in a secure place in the event the engine is stolen. The vehicle safety compliance sticker is located on the driver's side door jam (**Figure 47**). Located under the dashboard on the driver's side is the vehicle identification label (**Figure 48**); this label contains engine and transmission codes.

3

TABLE 1 TUNE-UP SPECIFICATIONS

SPARK PLUGS			
Plug Type			
Bosch		W145M2 or W8CO	
Beru		145/14/3L	
Champion		N288	
Plug Gap		0.023-0.028 in. (0.6-0.7 mm)	
Plug Torque		22 ft.-lb. (30 N•m)	
IGNITION SYSTEM			
Firing Order		1-4-3-2	
Distributor	**California**		**49 States and Canada**
Dwell	Electronic Ignition		44-50°
Point Gap	Electronic Ignition		0.016 in. (0.4 mm)
Ignition Timing			
49 States and Canada		7.5° BTDC	
California		5° ATDC	
Idle Speed	**California**		**49-States and Canada**
Manual Trans.	850-950 rpm		800-950 rpm
Automatic Trans.	850-950 rpm		850-1000 rpm
Vacuum Advance/Retard			
Hose/Hoses	ON		OFF
Valve Clearance	Adjustment not required		(Hydraulic Lifters)

TABLE 2 RECOMMENDED LUBRICANTS AND CAPACITIES

Temperature Range	Recommended Type	Capacity
Engine Oil		
Below -13° F	SAE 5E *	3.7 U.S. qt. (3.5L[1])
Between -13° F & 13° F	SAE 10W *	3.2 U.S. qt. (3.0L[2])
Between 5° F & 40° F	SAE 20-20W *	
Between 40° F & 68° F	SAE 30W *	
Above 68° F	SAE 40W *	
Manual Transaxle		
Below -13° F	ATF (DEXRON)	3.7 U.S. qt. (3.5 L)
Between -13° F & 0°F	Gear oil SAE 80W	
Above 0° F	Gear oil SAE 90W	
Automatic Transaxle		
All temperatures	ATF (DEXRON)	Dry fill: 6.4 U.S. qt. (6.0 L) Refill: 3.2 U.S. qt. (3.0 L)
Automatic Transaxle Final Drive		
Below -13° F	ATF (DEXRON)	1.25 U.S. qt. (1.36 L)
Between -13° F & 0°F	Gear oil SAE 80W	
Above 0° F	Gear oil SAE 90W	
Hydraulic Brake/Clutch Fluid		
All temperatures	DOT 3 or DOT 5	Keep Filled

* Use oils rated for API service SE, or SF only.
1. With filter change.
2. Without filter change.

TABLE 3 SCHEDULED CHECKS AND MAINTENANCE

Every 7,500 miles or 6 months
Engine oil and filter change
Every 15,000 miles or 1 year
Engine tune-up Fuel lines and tank Brakes Clutch Hydraulic fluid level Suspension Exhaust and emission control systems Vacuum hoses Alternator drive belt Tire and wheels Wiper blades Automatic transmission fluid level Automatic transmission final drive oil level Manual transmission oil level
Every 30,000 miles or 2 years
Change brake fluid Change ATF

NOTE: If you own a 1982 model, first check the Supplement at the back of the book for any new service information.

CHAPTER FOUR

4

ENGINE

This chapter details engine repair procedures for the Vanagon engine. Some repair situations require that the engine be removed from the vehicle; if in doubt, refer to the procedure in question before starting work.

The Vanagon is powered by a flat design 120 cu. in. (1,970 cc) air-cooled 4-cylinder engine which operates on a 4-stroke cycle. The cylinders are horizontally opposed and slightly offset in 2 pairs. Each cylinder has its own finned barrel for cooling. Cylinder pairs share a common finned aluminum cylinder head with 2 valves per cylinder.

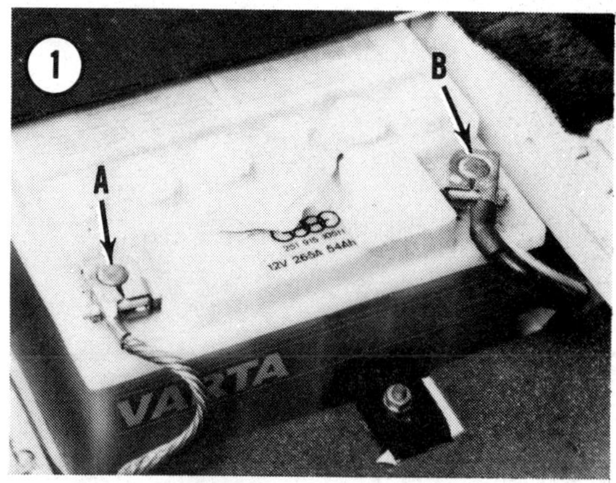

A. Negative B. Positive

The cylinders mount into an aluminum/magnesium alloy crankcase which is manufactured in 2 precision machined, matched (non-interchangeable) halves. The crankshaft turns inside 4 main bearings and the camshaft inside 3 bearings.

Volkswagen often makes design changes in the middle of a production run. For this reason, *always* order parts by year, chassis number and engine number; see Chapter Three for vehicle codes.

Table 1 presents engine tightening torques and **Table 2** lists engine specifications. All tables are at the end of this chapter.

ENGINE REMOVAL

1. Drain the engine oil.
2. Disconnect the positive and negative leads from the battery (**Figure 1**).

WARNING
Never attempt to remove the engine without first removing the positive and negative leads from the battery. If you try to remove the engine with the battery connected a serious electrical fire will most likely be the result.

3. To remove the air cleaner assembly, air flow sensor and the air intake duct as one unit:

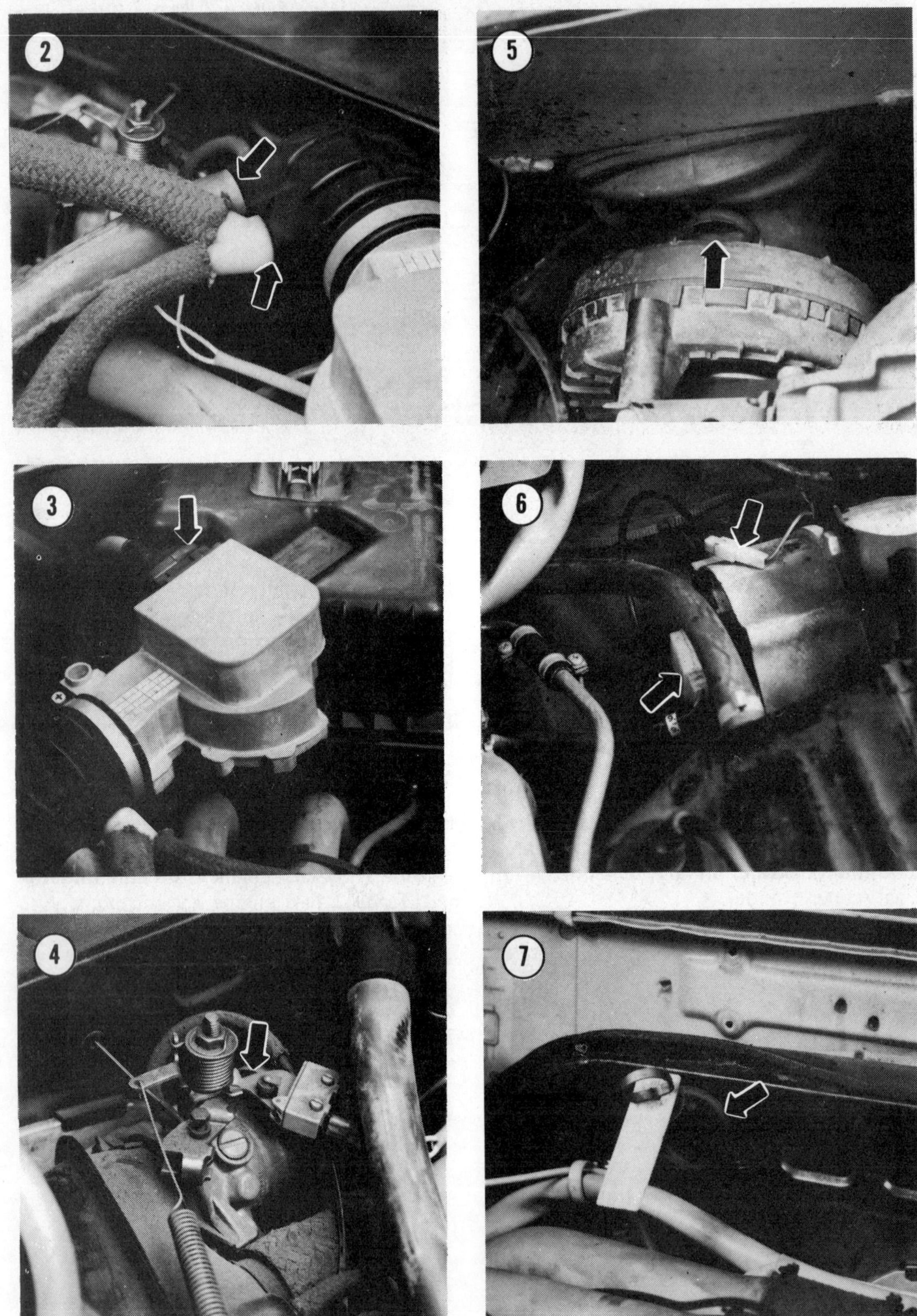
2
5
3
6
4
7

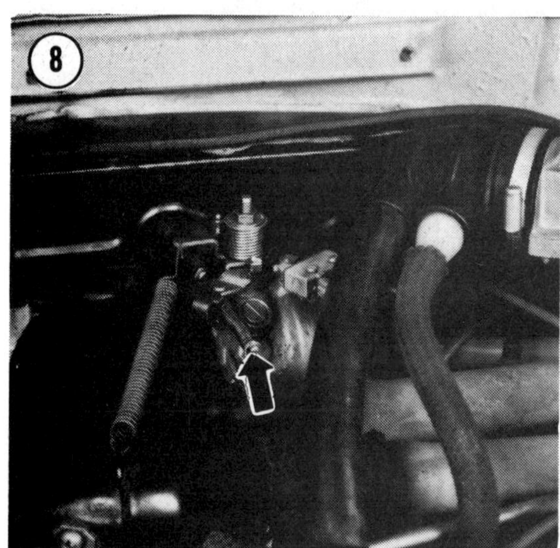

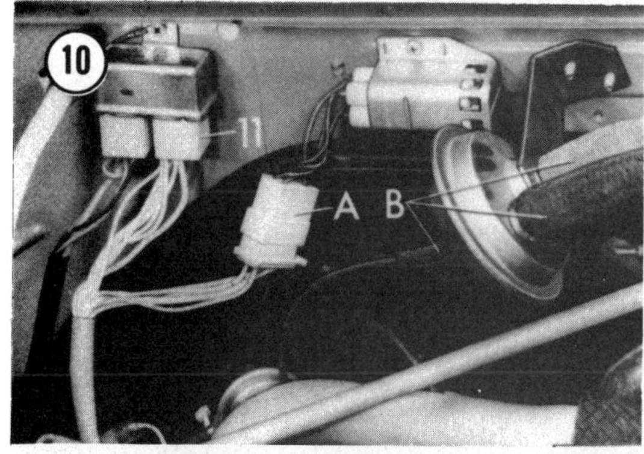

A. Resistor connector
B. Deceleration valve hoses

11. Double relay

   a. Remove the hoses which connect to the intake air hose (**Figure 2**).
   b. Disconnect the electrical plug from the air intake sensor (**Figure 3**).
   c. Loosen the hose clamp holding the air intake hose to the throttle valve (**Figure 4**).
   d. Remove the air cleaner assembly, air intake sensor and the intake air hose as one unit.

4. Carefully pull out the rubber heater booster boot (**Figure 5**).
5. Disconnect the alternator wires (**Figure 6**).
6. Disconnect the multi-pin connector from the fuel injection control unit.
7. Pull out the engine oil dipstick.
8. Pull out the automatic transmission dipstick, if so equipped. Remove the ATF filler tube grommet (**Figure 7**).
9. Disconnect the throttle valve linkage. On automatic transmission vehicles, see **Figure 8**. For manual transmissions, see **Figure 9**.
10. On 49-state and Canadian models, disconnect the double relay and resistor plugs and deceleration valve hoses (**Figure 10**).
11. On California models perform the following:
   a. Disconnect the double relay and the electrical connector for the series resistance block above (**Figure 11**).
   b. Disconnect the Hall control unit and idle stabilizer plugs (**Figure 12**).
   c. Disconnect the wire from the oxygen sensor (**Figure 13**).

12
BOSCH

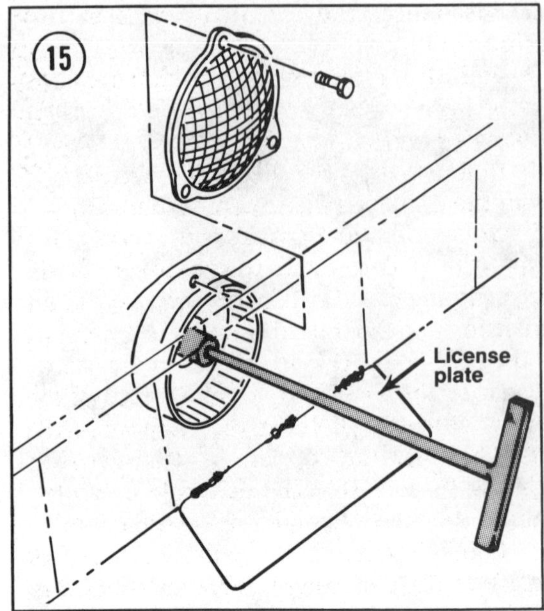
15
License plate

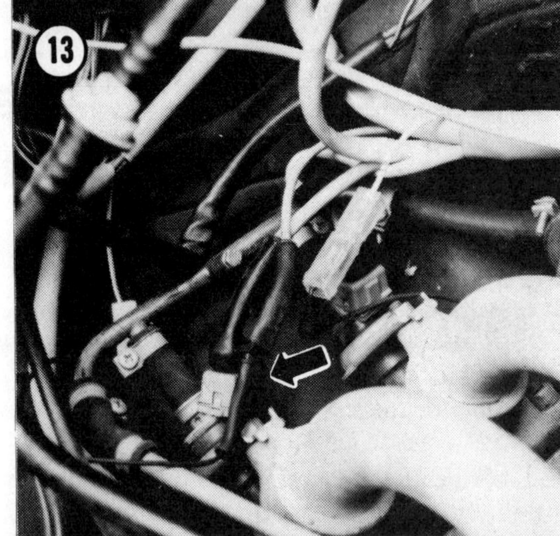
13

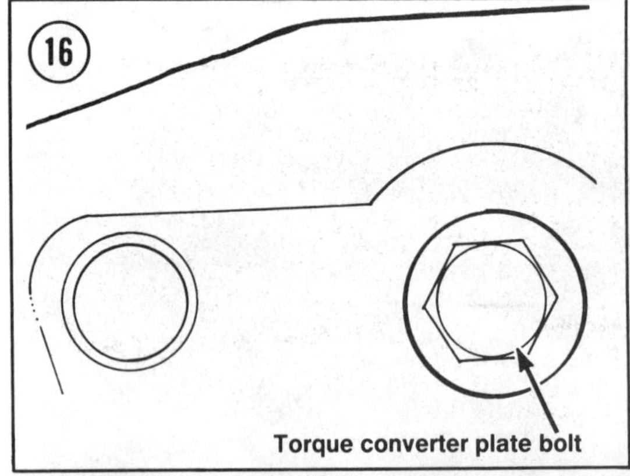
16
Torque converter plate bolt

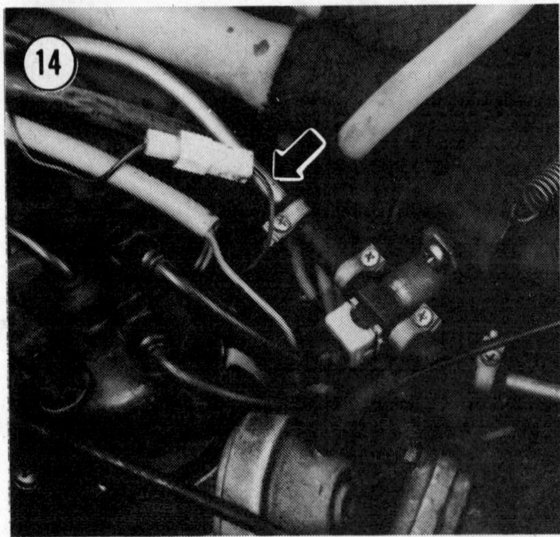
14

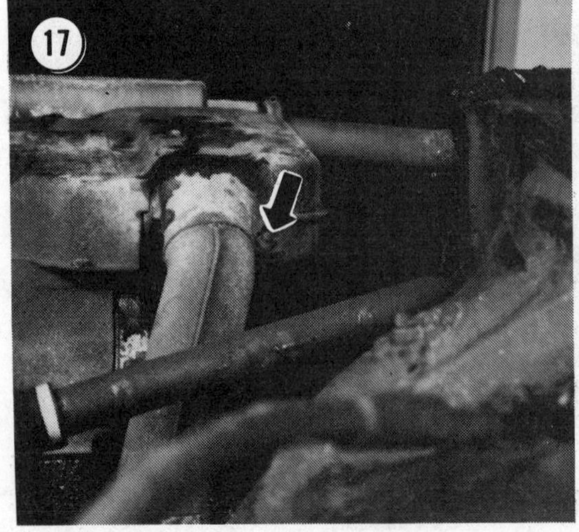
17

12. Disconnect the electrical wires at the ignition coil.
13. Pull off the oil pressure switch wire connector just in front of the distributor on the cooling air shroud.
14. Remove the brake booster vacuum line from the intake air distributor (**Figure 14**).
15. On automatic transmission models, remove the plastic mesh screen covering the large cooling fan. Put a socket wrench with an extension and flexible drive onto the center nut of the cooling fan (**Figure 15**). Turn the engine over with the wrench and remove each of the torque converter bolts as they appear in the large hole in the top of the transmission housing (**Figure 16**). The bolt hole is located behind the intake manifold for cylinder No. 3.
16. Loosen the clamps and pull the tubes off of the heater flap housings where they connect to the heat exchangers (**Figure 17**). There is one tube on either side of the engine.

17. Disconnect the electrical wires on the starter (**Figure 18**).
18. Clamp off and disconnect the fuel line which leads out of the fuel pressure regulator on the transmission side of the front cover plate.
19. Clamp off and disconnect the fuel line which leads into the engine on the transmission side of the front cover plate.
20. On manual transmission models, loosen the transmission carrier bolt (**Figure 19**).
21. On automatic transmission models, perform the following:
   a. Detach the throttle valve pushrod (**Figure 20**).
   b. Slip the pushrod out of the front cover plate into the engine compartment.
   c. Loosen the transmission carrier bolt (**Figure 19**).
22. Raise the rear of the vehicle at least 12 inches higher and support it with jackstands (see jacking instructions in Chapter Three).
23. Fashion a transmission sling as shown in **Figure 21** or position blocks under the transmission. The sling or the blocks must be directly under and slightly to the front of the drive shafts. Leave approximately 3 1/4 inches (80 mm) between transmission and the sling or blocks. If blocking, use a small square piece of hard wood for the top block.
24. Slide a floor jack under the engine and raise it until it contacts the center bottom of the crankcase. Raise it far enough to put slight pressure on the engine.

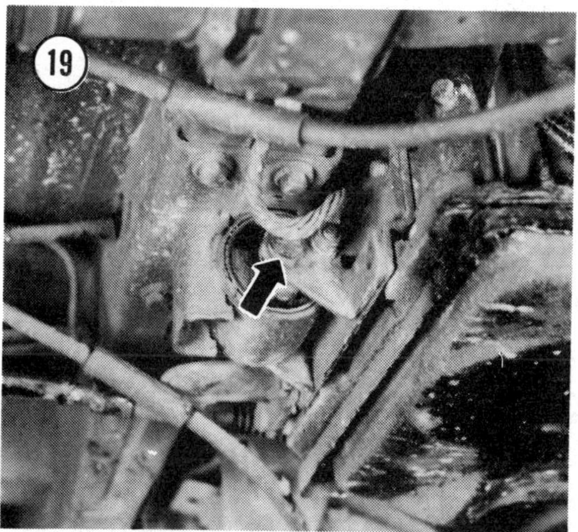

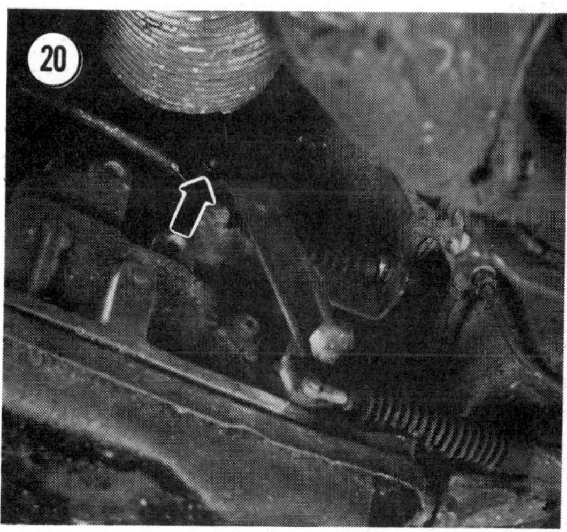

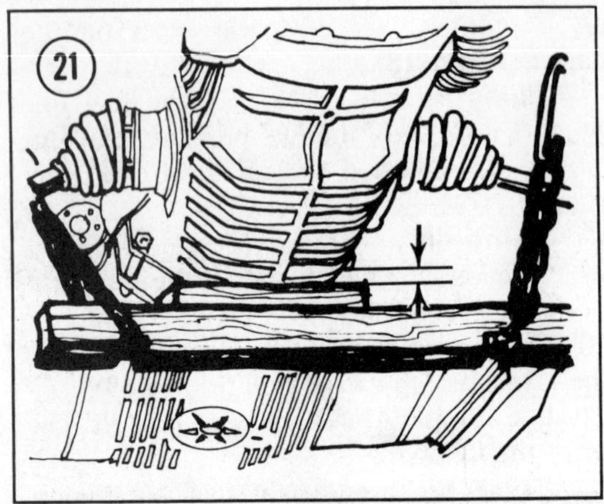

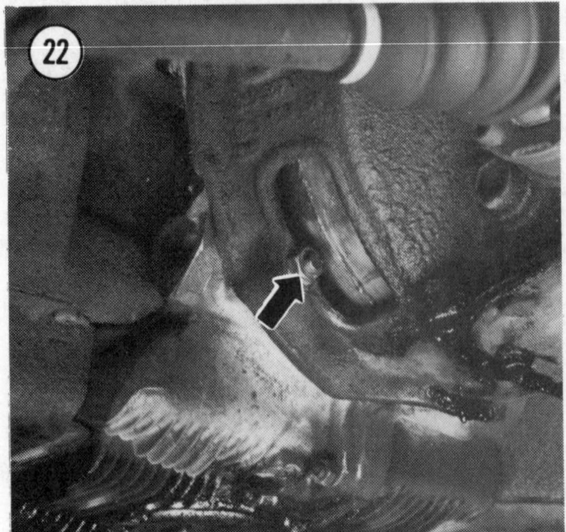

NOTE
A small square of plywood should go between the jack and the bottom of the engine to prevent damage.

25. Disconnect the 2 top large engine-to-transmission mounting bolts.
26. Remove the bottom engine-to-transmission mounting nuts. **Figure 22** shows an automatic transmission nut which is in the same area as the manual transmission nut; remember, there are 2 nuts on the bottom.
27. Remove the engine carrier bolts (**Figure 23**). Lower the engine until the transmission rests upon the sling or blocks. Grasp the rear of the engine and pull it out and clear of the transmission with a gentle side-to-side rocking motion. At this point you may want to have an assistant balance the engine on the jack from above.

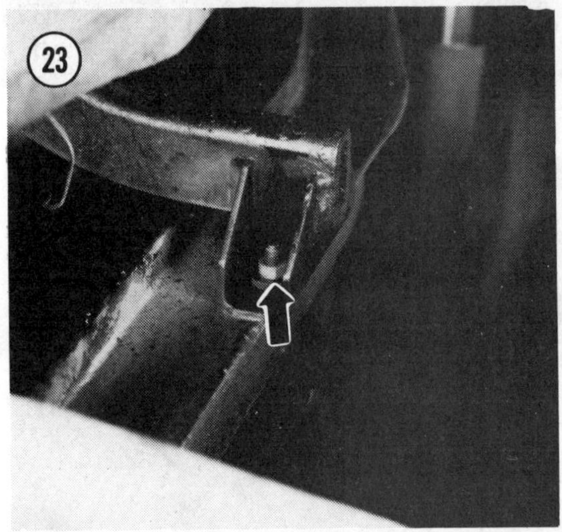

CAUTION
*The transmission must be in a holding sling (not on blocks) as shown in **Figure 21** if the vehicle is to be moved after removing the engine. Do not let the transmission dangle freely; this will damage the shift linkage and it will have to be replaced.*

28. Lower the engine and pull it from under the vehicle.

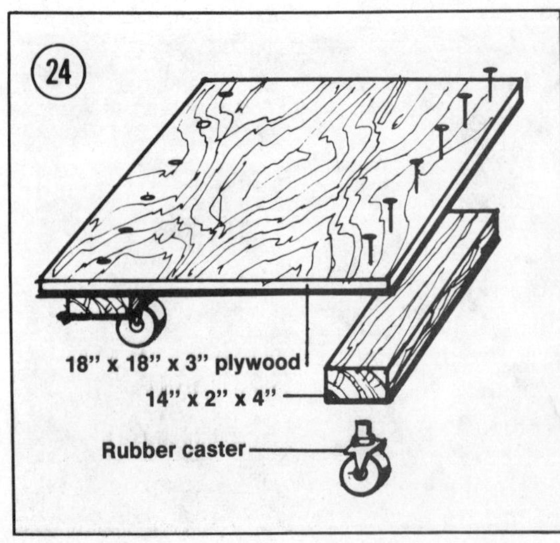

NOTE
*To permit easy mobility of the engine, construct a roller dolly as shown in **Figure 24**. Have an assistant help you lift*

the engine onto the dolly. This dolly makes engine disassembly simple because you can just sit in one place, turn the engine and remove the parts.

ENGINE INSTALLATION

See **Table 1** for torque specifications.

1. Perform the following before installing the engine:
   a. Inspect the clutch throw-out bearing, clutch disc and pressure plate for cracks and wear; replace if necessary. Also make sure the clutch disc is properly centered (Chapter Eight).
   b. Lightly coat the splines of the transmission drive shaft and the contact points of the clutch throw-out bearing and release lever with molybdenum disulfide grease.
   c. Lubricate the starter bushing with heavy-duty bearing grease.
   d. Clean the transmission housing flange and the engine flange thoroughly.
2. Put manual transmissions in gear to steady the transmission input drive shaft.
3. Lift the engine into place with a hydraulic floor jack.
4. Push the engine into the transmission housing until it is flush all the way around. If the engine will not slide into the transmission housing freely, rotate the crankshaft slightly so the splines in the transmission input drive shaft and the clutch disc hub will align.

NOTE

Before installing mounting bolts make sure that electrical wiring or cables are not trapped between the engine and the transmission mounting surfaces. It is very disheartening to fully assemble the engine and then find an electrical wire trapped between the engine and transmission.

5. Install the top engine-to-transmission mounting bolts and the bottom mounting bolt nuts; torque to specifications (**Table 1**).
6. Raise the engine and transmission with the floor jack and install the engine carrier bolts; torque to specifications (**Table 1**).
7. Remove the transmission sling or blocks.
8. Torque the transmission carrier bolts to specification.
9. On manual transmissions, attach the throttle cable to the throttle valve and adjust; see Chapter Six.
10. On automatic transmissions, install the throttle valve pushrod on the transmission selector lever and throttle valve and adjust; see Chapter Six.
11. Perform Steps 1-19 in *Engine Removal* in reverse order, then remove the jackstands and lower the vehicle.

ENGINE DISASSEMBLY/ASSEMBLY

4

The following sequences are designed so that the engine need not be disassembled any further than necessary to perform a particular service.

Each sequence includes numbers of detailed procedures required to complete the service. Unless otherwise noted, procedures for major assemblies in these sequences are included in this chapter.

Cylinder Head Service

1. Disconnect engine electrical connectors.
2. Remove fuel injection intake manifolds and injector rigs (Chapter Six).
3. Remove distributor (Chapter Seven).
4. Remove engine cooling shrouds (Chapter Five).
5. Remove exhaust system (Chapter Six).
6. Remove valve rocker assemblies.
7. Remove cylinder heads.
8. Remove and inspect valves, guides and seats.
9. Assembly is the reverse of these steps.

Pistons and Cylinders

1. Perform Steps 1-8 of *Cylinder Head Service.*
2. Remove cylinders.
3. Remove pistons from connecting rods.
4. Assembly is the reverse of these steps.

Engine Overhaul

1. Perform Steps 1-8 of *Cylinder Head Service.*
2. Perform Steps 1-3 of *Pistons and Cylinders.*
3 Remove fuel injection air intake distributor (Chapter Six).
4. Remove cooling fan housing and shrouds (Chapter Five).

5. Remove engine carrier bar.
6. Remove oil cooler, filter and filter adaptor.
7. Remove oil pump and cover.
8. Remove clutch pressure plate and disc (Chapter Eight).
9. Remove flywheel or torque converter plate.
10. Separate crankcase halves.
11. Remove camshaft and bearings.
12. Remove crankshaft and bearings.
13. Remove connecting rods from crankshaft.
14. Assembly is the reverse of these steps.

OIL COOLER

The oil cooler cannot be replaced without first removing the cooling fan housing; see Chapter Five. If the oil cooler has been leaking, first check the oil pressure relief valve for damage or sticking, which could cause high oil pressure. Check the oil cooler fins for bulging or cracking. Coolers which are cracked or have bulging fins (caused by excessive pressure) should be replaced.

Removal

1. Remove the cooling fan housing and the left rear heating air duct. See Chapter Five.
2. Remove the 3 nuts which hold the cooler to the crankcase mounting and slide it off the long studs.
3. Remove the rubber seals from the crankcase mounting.

Cleaning and Inspection

1. Pour solvent into the cooler and cover up the holes with your fingers. Shake the cooler, like you would rinse out a jar. Do this at least a dozen times until all the loose particles are washed free. Rinse 3 more times with clean solvent.
2. Check that no thin cooling fins are touching and that no parts are loose. Bent or smashed fins can be straightened out with needlenose pliers.

Installation

1. Clean the rubber seal mounting holes with a clean rag.
2. Install new rubber seals into the mounting.

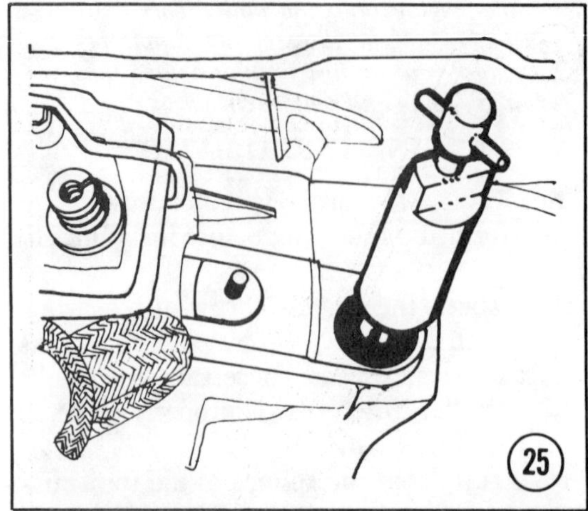
25

26

3. Install the oil cooler and nuts. Tighten all nuts evenly until the cooler touches the crankcase mounting, then tighten just a bit more.

DISTRIBUTOR DRIVE SHAFT

Removal

The distributor drive shaft may be removed with the engine installed. A special shaft extractor is required (**Figure 25**) which can be purchased at VW part stores. The drive shaft does not have to be removed if the engine is to be completely disassembled; it can be removed when the crankcase halves are separated.

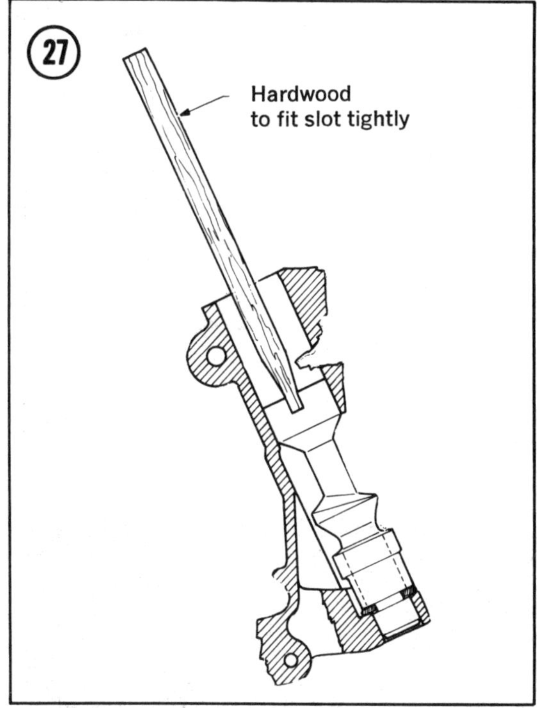

1. Remove the distributor cap.
2. Turn the engine over with a socket wrench on the center nut of the cooling fan (**Figure 15**) until the distributor rotor contact aligns with the notch on the distributor housing upper rim (where the No. 1 spark plug wire goes) and the timing notch on the main cooling fan pulley aligns with the TDC mark on the engine timing scale (**Figure 26**).
3. Remove the distributor (Chapter Seven).

NOTE
Do not turn the engine over after removing the distributor or timing will be lost. If you do, see ***Finding Top Dead Center*** *in this chapter.*

4. Fish for the little spring on top of the distributor drive shaft with a magnet tool. Do not lose it!
5. Insert a VW distributor shaft extracting tool (**Figure 25**) into the shaft hole and tighten the clamp. Rotate the tool counterclockwise and pull up simultaneously. Another method which sometimes works is shown in **Figure 27**.
6. Reach down through the distributor drive shaft hole and carefully lift out the thrust washer with a magnet tool or a hooked wire.

CAUTION
Do not drop the washer into the crankcase if you do not intend to disassemble the crankcase. On rare occasions it is possible to fish it out if dropped; usually it means completely disassembling the engine.

Inspection

Check the distributor drive gear for wear. If the gear is worn you should also look down into the shaft hole with a flashlight and visually inspect the brass crankshaft gear for damage. A cracked or worn crankshaft gear must be replaced; this means completely disassembling the engine.

4

Installation

This procedure should be performed after the engine is completely assembled (except distributor) or at least when the cylinder heads and rocker arms are installed.

1. Make sure that No. 1 piston is at TDC of its compression stroke. If not, see *Finding Top Dead Center* in this chapter.
2. Insert a small wire rod (coat hanger wire) down to the bottom of the distributor shaft hole.
3. Coat the thrust washer with a liberal amount of heavy grease. Slide the thrust washer onto the wire rod and let it drop down into place. Do not remove the wire until the washer is centered; the wire keeps the washer from dropping into the crankcase. Cut another length of wire; use it to center the thrust washer over the distributor shaft base support hole. Remove the wires; the grease will hold the washer in place.
4. Oil the distributor shaft and insert it with the slot at a 12° angle to the crankcase seam and the small half-crescent slot pointing toward the oil cooler (**Figure 28**). Push the shaft down with a large flat-blade screwdriver until you are certain it is seated against the thrust washer.
5. Crank the engine over by hand 1/3 turn; watch the distributor drive shaft. If the shaft turns, it is seated properly. If not, don't force it or you'll damage the drive gear on the crankshaft. Pull out the shaft and reinsert it.
6. Once the shaft is seated properly, insert a wire guide into the hole on the top of the

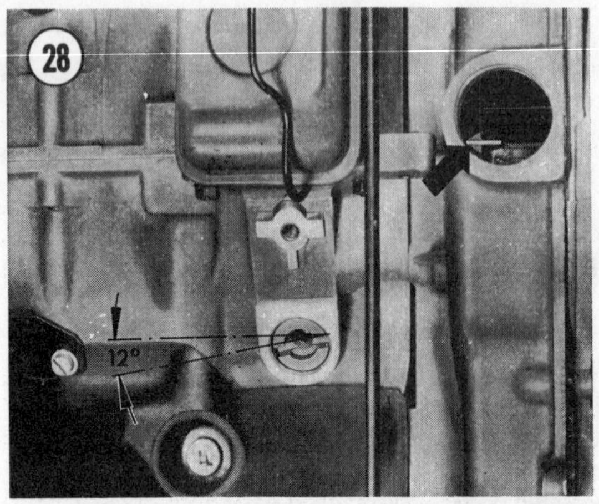

distributor drive shaft. Slide the spring over the wire into the drive shaft. See **Figure 29**. Remove the wire. The small spring holds the drive shaft down when the distributor is installed and prevents it from drifting up out of the crankshaft drive gear during operation.

Finding Top Dead Center

Perform the following to find top dead center (TDC) for the No. 1 piston:

1. Remove No. 1 cylinder spark plug and No. 1 and No. 2 cylinder head valve cover. Look into the No. 1 spark plug hole with a flashlight and turn engine over slowly with a socket wrench on the center nut of the cooling fan (**Figure 15**). Watch both piston and valve rocker arm movement.
2. When piston moves down and intake valve (inner valve) is open, piston is on *intake stroke.*
3. When piston moves all the way up from bottom position and both valves are closed, piston is at top of *compression stroke.*
4. Next, piston moves down with both valves closed; this is the *power stroke.*
5. Piston then moves up with exhaust valve (outer valve) open; this is the *exhaust stroke.*

FLYWHEEL/TORQUE CONVERTER DRIVE PLATE

NOTE

When removing the flywheel or torque converter drive plate, the front engine oil seal must be removed and replaced with a new one. Also, the crankshaft end play must be correctly reset. Failure to do either will result in front oil seal leaks and greatly reduced engine life.

Removal

1. On manual transmissions perform the following:
   a. Remove the clutch pressure plate and the clutch disc (Chapter Eight).
   b. Hold the flywheel in a special flywheel retainer as shown in **Figure 30**. If special retainer is not available, use the set-up shown in **Figure 31**. Remove the 5 bolts holding the flywheel to the crankshaft and the 5-hole washer plate.
   c. Pull the flywheel off; don't lose the metal dowel pin on the end of the crankshaft.
2. On automatic transmissions perform the following:
   a. Fashion a special tool as shown in **Figure 32** and screw it into the torque converter drive plate holes.

(31)

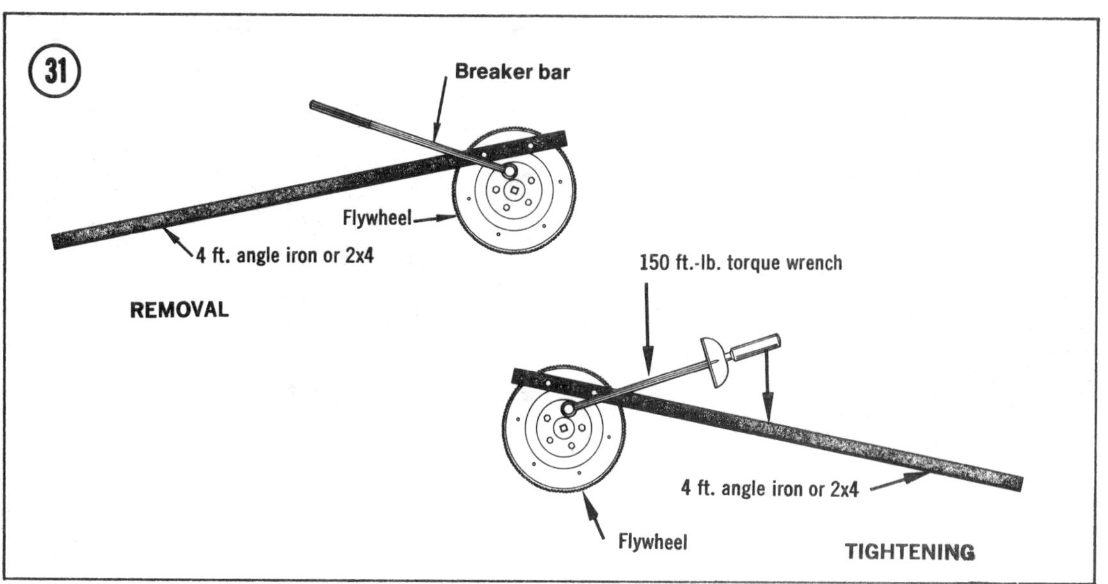

(32)

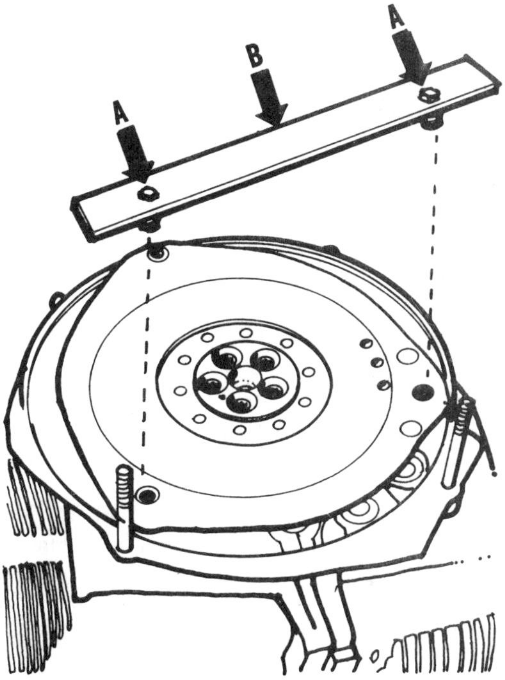

A. Torque converter bolts   B. Drilled bar stock

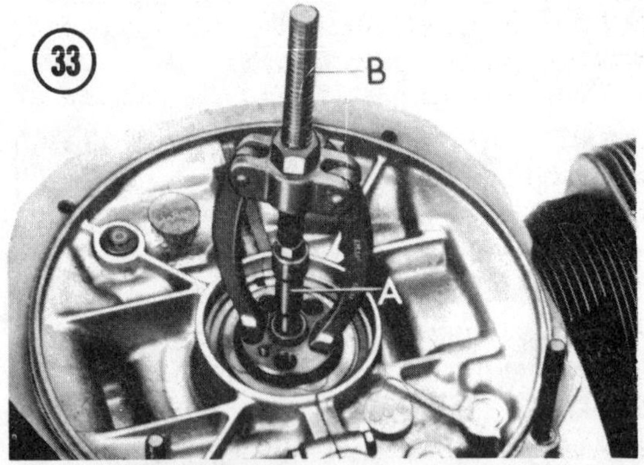

A. Puller adaptor B. Puller

b. Remove the 5 splined bolts (this requires a special splined socket) holding the torque converter drive plate to the crankshaft.
c. Pull the torque converter drive plate off; don't lose the metal dowel pin on the end of the crankshaft.

3. Remove the front oil seal; see procedure in this chapter.

4. Remove the end play shims (thin steel rings) located in back of the oil seal. Hang them in a safe place where they won't get damaged or rusty.

Inspection

1. Check the flywheel gear teeth for wear or damage. If teeth are only slightly damaged, up to 0.08 in. (2.03 mm) may be machined off the clutch side. Rechamfer the edges of the teeth after machining.

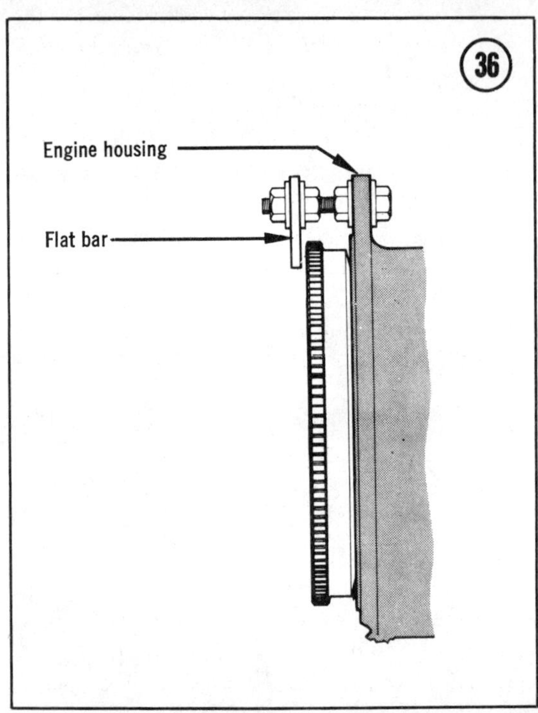

2. Examine the clutch disc surface; if it's excessively rough or gouged and grooved, have the flywheel resurfaced.

3. On manual transmissions, examine the pilot needle bearing and felt washer for the transmission input drive shaft located in the center of the crankshaft. *These are very important components!* The needle bearing rollers should all be present and not sloppy or loose. The felt washer must not be excessively worn. If necessary, install a new bearing and felt washer using the special tools shown in **Figure 33** and **Figure 34**.

4. Check the flywheel runout (warpage). Maximum allowable variation is 0.012 in. If greater, the flywheel must be machined true or replaced. To check runout, bolt the flywheel (using the 5-hole washer plate) onto the crankshaft, tighten the bolts and perform Step 5A or 5B.

5A. *Dial indicator method*:

   a. Attach a dial indicator as shown in **Figure 35**.
   b. Push the flywheel toward the crankshaft as far as possible. Adjust the dial indicator so that it just touches the flywheel. Set the indicator to zero.
   c. While pushing the flywheel in, rotate it, noting the variation (if any) on the dial indicator.

5B. *Bar stock method*:

   a. Attach a piece of bar stock through the transmission bolt hole with a piece of threaded stock as shown in **Figure 36**.
   b. Push the flywheel toward the crankshaft as far as possible. Set the bar (use a feeler gauge) 0.012 in. from the face of the flywheel and tighten the nuts.
   c. Mark the rim of the flywheel in 6 equal segments.
   d. While pushing the flywheel in, rotate it and measure the distance between the bar stock and the flywheel at each marked point.

6. Check the torque converter drive plate for hairline cracks; look closely at the area around the 3 converter bolt holes. Lay the plate on a flat surface (such as plate glass) and check for warpage. If cracks or warpage are found, replace the plate.

7. Check the front oil seal bearing surface. This is the concave area which surrounds the crankshaft bolt holes; it faces toward the crankshaft and makes contact with the front oil seal. Wipe the surface clean and check for grooves worn by the front oil seal. If a groove can be felt by touch (a discolored line is okay), replace the flywheel or torque converter drive plate. A groove will allow engine oil leakage.

Installation

1. Check the crankshaft end play and install a new front oil seal; see procedures in this chapter.

2. Push the dowel pin (preferably a new one) into the end of the crankshaft.

3. Clean the surfaces where the flywheel or converter drive plate meet the end of the crankshaft.

4. Pry the old rubber O-ring out of the flywheel or converter drive plate, clean out the slot and install a new O-ring.

5. Apply a dab of heavy grease to the pilot needle bearing and felt washer in the end of the crankshaft.

6. Align the dowel pin hole in the flywheel or converter drive plate and the dowel pin on the end of the crankshaft. Push the flywheel or converter drive plate onto the crankshaft.

7. On manual transmissions, use a new 5-hole washer plate and screw in the flywheel bolts hand-tight. Use a special flywheel retainer as shown in **Figure 30**. If a retainer is not available use the set-up shown in **Figure 31**. Torque the flywheel bolts to specifications; see **Table 1**.

8. On automatic transmissions, install the bolts in the torque converter drive plate (using the special splined socket). Torque to specifications; see **Table 1**.

CRANKSHAFT END PLAY

Crankshaft end play must be checked and adjusted any time the engine is completely disassembled or whenever the flywheel or torque converter drive plate is removed. End play should also be checked whenever the engine is removed for any reason. End play should be checked with the clutch pressure plate and disc installed. If found to be incorrect, the pressure plate and disc must be removed to reset the end play.

End play is determined by the total thickness of the 3 shims (thin steel rings) which slide in between the flywheel or torque converter drive plate and the No. 1 crankshaft main bearing. Shims come in 5 thicknesses (**Table 3**); they may be purchased at foreign auto parts stores or VW dealers.

New shims will have the thickness printed on the side; old worn shims will have to be checked for thickness with a micrometer.

End play must be within 0.003-0.005 in. (0.07-0.13 mm), with a wear limit of 0.006 in. (0.15 mm).

Two methods may be used to check end play. By far the easiest method is the dial indicator method. If a dial indicator is not available, the bar stock method can be used.

Dial Indicator Method

To check end play without removing the flywheel or torque converter drive plate and with clutch assembled, perform Steps 1, 6 and 7. If end play is incorrect perform the entire procedure below.

1. Remove the rear oil seal. See procedure in this chapter.
2. On manual transmissions, remove the clutch pressure plate and disc. See Chapter Eight.
3. Remove the flywheel or torque converter drive plate. See procedure in this chapter.
4. Remove the front oil seal. See procedure in this chapter.
5. Reinstall the flywheel or torque converter drive plate with only 2 shims and without the rubber O-ring. Tighten the flywheel or torque converter drive plate bolts.
6. Attach the dial indicator as shown in **Figure 35**. Push the flywheel or torque converter drive plate as far as possible toward the crankshaft. Adjust the dial indicator until it just touches the flywheel or torque converter drive plate; set the indicator to zero.
7. Gently pry the flywheel or torque converter drive plate out with a screwdriver. Read the end play on the dial indicator and record the figure on paper. Repeat this several times to ensure accuracy.
8. Calculate the thickness of the third shim to be inserted by subtracting the desired end play from the reading on the dial indicator.
9. Remove the flywheel or torque converter drive plate, install the third shim as calculated and reinstall the flywheel or torque converter drive plate.
10. Recheck the end play. If correct, remove the flywheel or torque converter drive plate again and install the front oil seal (see procedure in this chapter). If end play is incorrect, repeat Steps 5-9.
11. Install a new rear oil seal.
12. See *Flywheel/Torque Converter Drive Plate* in this chapter for proper installation procedure.

Bar Stock Method

To check end play without removing flywheel or torque converter drive plate and with clutch assembled, perform Step 1 and Steps 6-10. If end play is incorrect perform entire procedure below.

1. Remove the rear oil seal. See procedure in this chapter.
2. Remove the front oil seal. See procedure in this chapter.
3. On manual transmissions, remove the clutch pressure plate and disc. See Chapter Eight.
4. Remove the flywheel or torque converter drive plate. See procedure in this chapter.
5. Install the flywheel or torque converter drive plate with only 2 shims and without the rubber O-ring. Tighten the bolts.
6. Attach a 7 in. (18 cm) length of 3/8 in. (9.5 mm) threaded stock through the crankcase bolt hole; secure with 2 nuts. See **Figure 36**.
7. Attach a piece of flat bar stock to the threaded stock with 2 nuts; leave the nuts loose. With a large screwdriver, carefully pry between the crankcase and the flywheel to move the crankshaft all the way forward. Have someone hold the screwdriver in this position.
8. Adjust the flat bar on the threaded rod until it just touches the surface of the flywheel. Tighten the nuts in this position.
9. Remove the screwdriver and push the flywheel back as far as possible.
10. Measure the gap between the flat bar stock and the flywheel. This is the endplay. Repeat this several times to ensure accuracy.
11. Calculate the thickness of the third shim to be inserted by subtracting the desired end play from the measured gap.
12. Remove the flywheel or torque converter drive plate and install the third shim as calculated.
13. Reinstall the flywheel or torque converter drive plate.
14. Recheck the end play. If it is correct, remove the flywheel or torque converter drive plate and install the front oil seal (see procedure in this chapter). If end play is incorrect, repeat Steps 5-14.
15. See *Flywheel/Torque Converter Drive Plate* in this chapter for proper installation procedure.

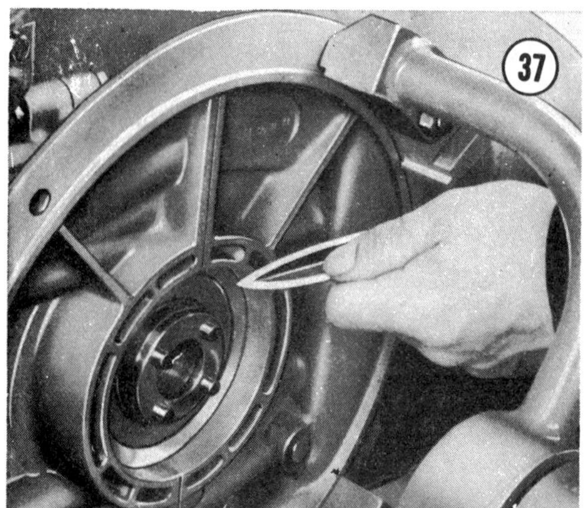

FRONT OIL SEAL

The front oil seal normally leaks a small amount of oil which lubricates the seal lip and prevents it from burning. This leaking causes a thin smear of oil to coat the transmission case. This smear does not indicate a defective seal.

Leakage from a defective seal will coat the transmission case heavily, with oil leaking from the front of the engine to the ground. Oil will most likely invade the clutch assembly and cause it to slip.

Replace the seal if:

a. Leaking appears excessive
b. Flywheel or torque converter drive plate is removed
c. Oil seal is removed for any reason (never reuse a seal)

Removal

1. Remove the clutch pressure plate and disc (manual transmissions only); see Chapter Eight.

2. Remove the flywheel or torque converter drive plate. See procedure in this chapter.
3. Carefully pry out the old seal with a large flat-blade screwdriver. Don't nick the crankcase surface. Discard the old seal.
4. Leave all end play shims (thin steel rings) on the crankshaft end.

Installation

1. Check and, if necessary, adjust crankshaft end play before installing new oil seal. See procedure in this chapter.
2. Clean the recess between the crankcase and the crankshaft. If necessary, remove any metal burrs from the crankcase so that the oil seal seats properly (**Figure 37**). Carefully clean all metal flakes out of the recess.
3. Make sure that the proper end play shims are in place. Install the oil seal with the closed side facing out. Use the special tool shown in **Figure 38** or put the seal in place and gently tap it with a hammer and a small flat block of wood, working slowly and evenly around the seal until it is flush with the outer edge of the crankcase recess.

REAR OIL SEAL

Removal

1. If engine is assembled, remove the cooling fan. See Chapter Five for procedure.
2. Remove the fan hub with a special puller plate as shown in **Figure 39**. The puller plate can be improvised by inserting three 1/8 in. (3.25 mm) thick strips of metal between the

case and the fan hub. Insert the hub bolts to hold the strips in place. Tighten the bolts evenly (don't let the strips slip out) and the hub will be pushed off the crankshaft.
3. Carefully pry out the old seal with a heavy flat-blade screwdriver. Don't nick the crankcase. Discard the old seal.

Installation

1. Clean the recess between the crankcase and crankshaft. If necessary, remove any metal burrs from the crankcase so that the oil seal seats properly (**Figure 37**). Carefully clean all metal flakes from the recess.
2. Install the oil seal with the closed side facing out. Use the special tool shown in **Figure 40** or put the seal in place and gently tap it with a hammer and a small flat block of wood, working slowly and evenly around the seal until it is flush with the outer edge of the crankcase recess. The special tool can be improvised with a large nut and bolt which fit the threaded hole in the crankshaft end and a large washer that will slip over the bolt.
3. Install the Woodruff key in the crankshaft and gently tap the fan hub on with a hammer.

TDC SENSOR

The TDC sensor is located in the right crankcase half. See **Figure 41**. The flywheel must be removed to replace the sensor.

Replacement

1. Cut off wire at the sensor.
2. Drive old sensor out of the crankcase to the front (toward the flywheel).

3. Drive a new sensor in as far as it will go with an old piston pin and a rubber mallet. Do not damage inner ring of sensor.

NOTE
Use a special oversize sensor as a replacement; this is available at foreign auto parts suppliers or from VW dealers.

VALVE ROCKER ASSEMBLY

Removal

1. Clean away the road dirt around and on the valve covers.
2. Pry the valve cover spring down with a large screwdriver and remove the valve cover.
3. Remove the 4 nuts which hold the rockers to the cylinder head (**Figure 42**); keep the nuts separate from other hardware.
4. Pull off the rocker arms and shafts.

5. Remove all 4 pushrods and store them so they may be reinstalled in exactly the same position (**Figure 43**).

Rocker Shaft Disassembly/Assembly

Refer to **Figure 44** for the following procedure.

1. Mark the rocker arms so they may reinstalled in the same position.
2. Slide all the parts off the shaft.
3. Clean all parts in solvent. Examine the bearing surfaces of the shaft and rocker arms. Small irregularities may be removed with crocus cloth. Check the rocker arm seat and ball sockets for wear.
4. Coat all parts with assembly lubricant and reassemble.

Installation and Adjustment

1. Roll each pushrod on a flat surface to check for bends. Replace as required.
2. Install pushrods in cylinder head in original positions.

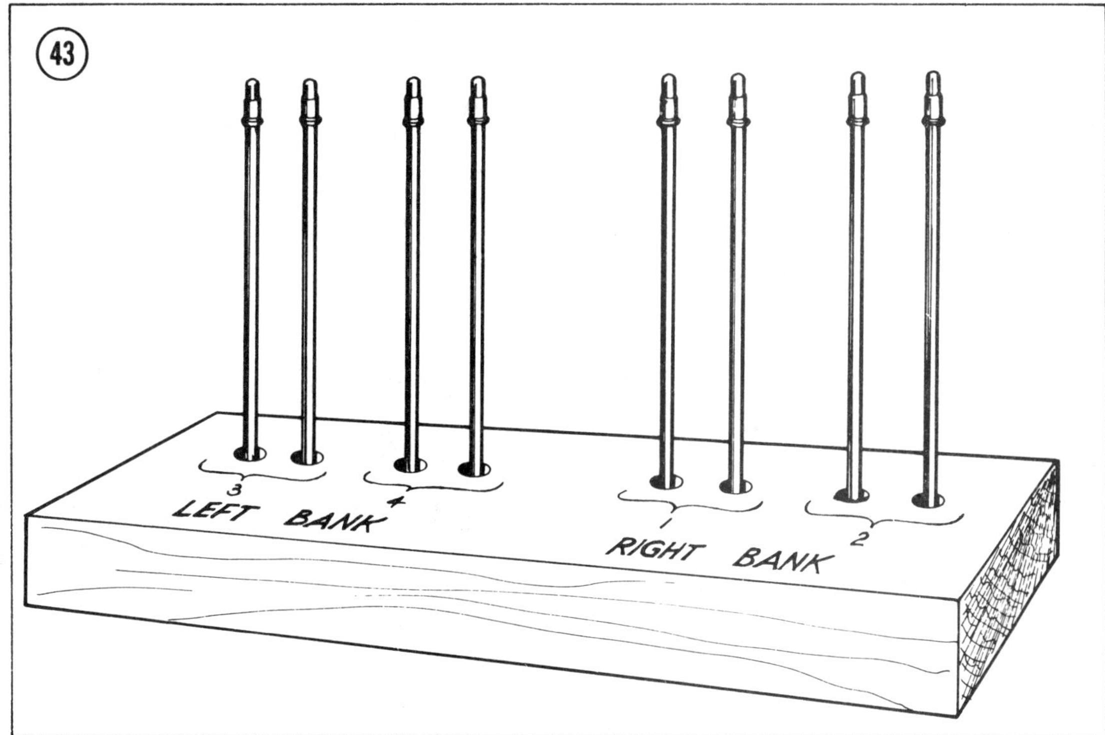

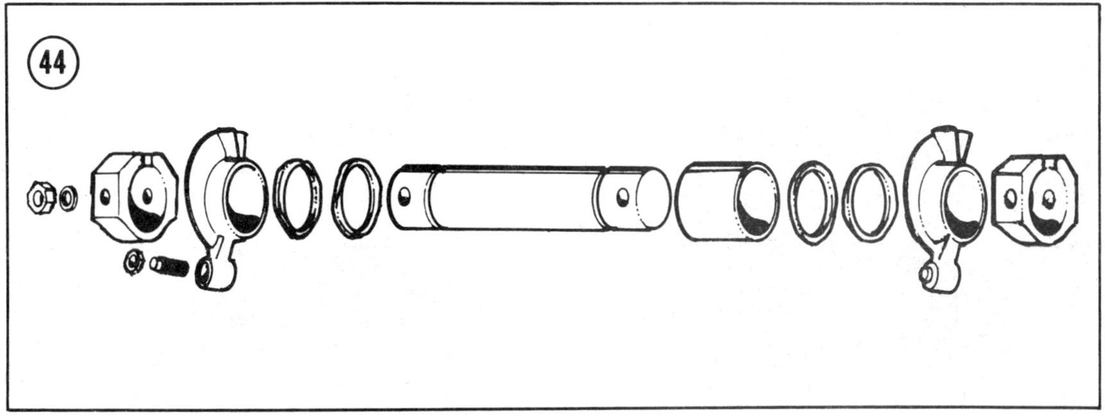

3. If engine is still in vehicle and oil has not been drained, check hydraulic valve lifters. See procedure in this chapter.
4. Install rocker shaft assemblies. Note the chamfered edge points *out* and the slots point *down*. See **Figure 42**.
5. Make sure the pushrod ball ends are centered in the rocker arm sockets.
6. Torque the rocker arm retaining nuts to specifications. See **Table 1**.
7. Check rocker arm adjusting screws; make sure they make slightly off-center contact with the valve stems as shown in **Figure 45**.
8. To adjust intake and exhaust valves perform the following:
   a. Turn crankshaft until No. 1 cylinder is at top dead center of compression stroke.
   b. Loosen the rocker arm adjusting locknuts on cylinder No. 1.
   c. Turn the adjusting screws in until they just make contact with the valve stem, then turn adjusting screws in 2 more turns.
   d. Hold the screws in this position and tighten the locknuts.
   e. Turn crankshaft 180° counterclockwise and adjust valves for cylinder No. 2.
   f. Repeat Steps a through e for cylinders No. 3 and No. 4.

CYLINDER HEADS

The cylinder heads may be removed with the engine installed. Although this makes component removal more difficult, it can save you the tedious job of engine removal.

Removal

1. Remove the valve rocker assemblies as described in this chapter.

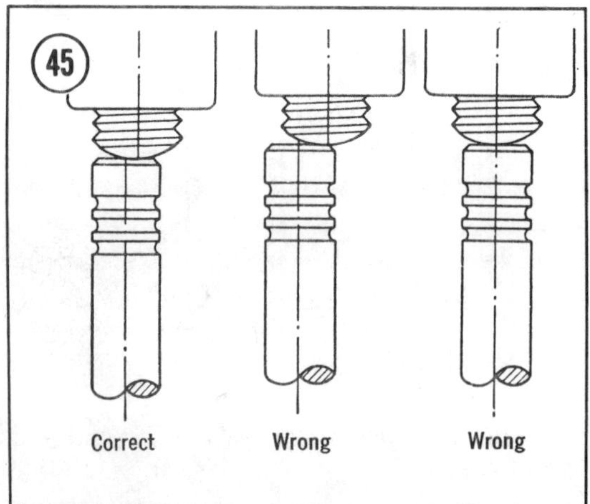

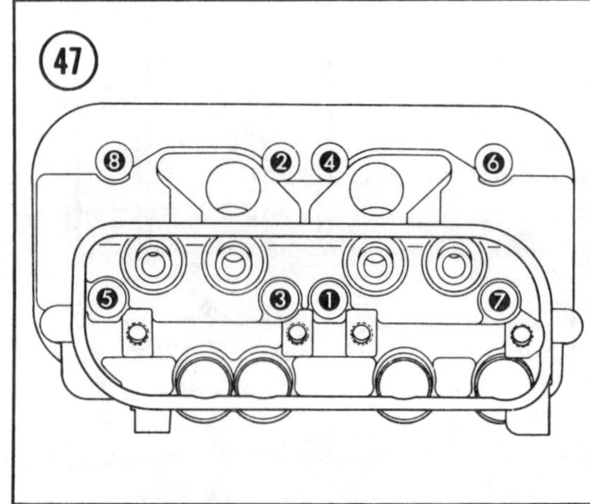

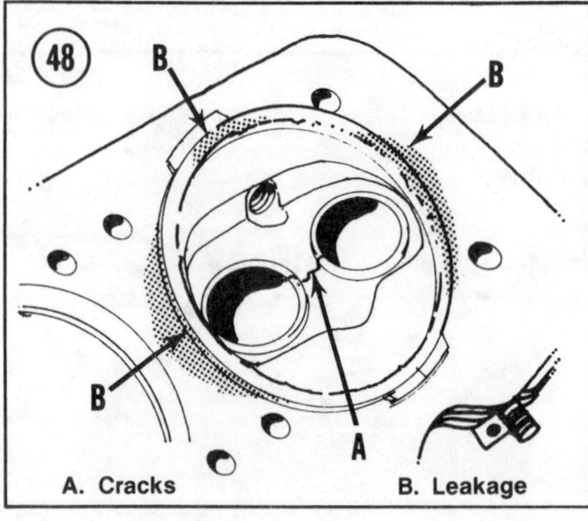

A. Cracks B. Leakage

2. Remove the pushrod tube retaining springs (**Figure 46**).
3. Loosen all 8 cylinder head nuts gradually and evenly in the sequence shown in **Figure 47**. Remove the nuts and washers. Keep this hardware separate. It is special (very expensive) and only available from VW dealers.
4. Pull the cylinder head off. If it stuck, carefully pry the head and the cylinders apart. In particularly tough cases, tap on the bottom edge of the head with a hammer and block of wood. Never hammer or pry on the fragile cooling fins.
5. Remove the copper sealing rings; they may be stuck inside the cylinder head or on cylinder shoulders.
6. If performing a valve job, it is unnecessary to remove the cylinders. Tie them in place with a soft wire and cover them with a plastic bag for protection.

Cleaning and Inspection

1. Without removing valves, carefully scrape all carbon from the cylinder head combustion chambers and valves with a soft scraper or wire brush. Take care not to gouge the soft aluminum or to scrape the copper sealing ring areas.
2. After carbon is removed from combustion chambers, both sets of valves and intake/exhaust ports, clean the entire cylinder head with solvent.
3. Have an assistant hold the cylinders in place and rotate the crankshaft until each piston in turn is at top dead center. Carefully scrape the carbon off the tops of the pistons. Take extreme care not to scrape the cylinder liners. Do not scrape the carbon ridges off the cylinder tops.
4. Check all studs for tightness. If a stud can't be tightened, have a machinist drill the hole out and install a thread coil (Heli-coil) insert.
5. Check between the valves for cracks (**Figure 48**). If cracks are found, the cylinder head must be replaced.

CAUTION
Cracks between valves cannot be successfully welded; the valve seats will fail and the valve will break off and be sucked right through the top of the piston. This totally destroys an engine.

6. Check the spark plug hole threads. If thread segments are cracked or stripped see *Repairing Spark Plug Threads* in this chapter.
7. Check the sealing ring surfaces for leakage. The head must be brought to a machinist and flycut if either of the following is found:
   a. If the sealing rings were partially burned away (the sealing surface on the head is likely to have been burned away).
   b. If the head is loose and there is much blackening due to leaking exhaust gases (see the areas marked "b" in **Figure 48**).

CAUTION
If one cylinder head must be flycut, the other should be cut to match, otherwise, 2 cylinders will run off balance (more compression than the others). The engine will not last very long like this.

8. Check the pushrod tubes for cracks, bends or dents. Replace if necessary.

Installation

1. Install new rubber sealing rings on the pushrod tubes. The white one goes toward the cylinder head; the black goes toward the crankcase.
2. Insert new copper sealing rings into the combustion chambers of the cylinder head.
3. Place the cylinder head on the crankcase studs and push it in all the way until it rests on the cylinders.
4. Install the special cylinder head nuts and washers. Torque them to specifications (**Table 1**).
5. Slip the pushrod tubes through the pushrod tube holes in the cylinder head and into the crankcase (**Figure 49**). Remember, the end of the pushrod tube with the black seal goes into the crankcase.
6. Install the pushrod tube retaining clips (**Figure 46**).
7. Install the rocker arm assembly. See procedure in this chapter.

Repairing Spark Plug Threads

If the spark plug threads are stripped or the segments are broken, have a machinist tap the hole out and put in a thread coil (Heli-coil) insert. If you want to do the job yourself, VW

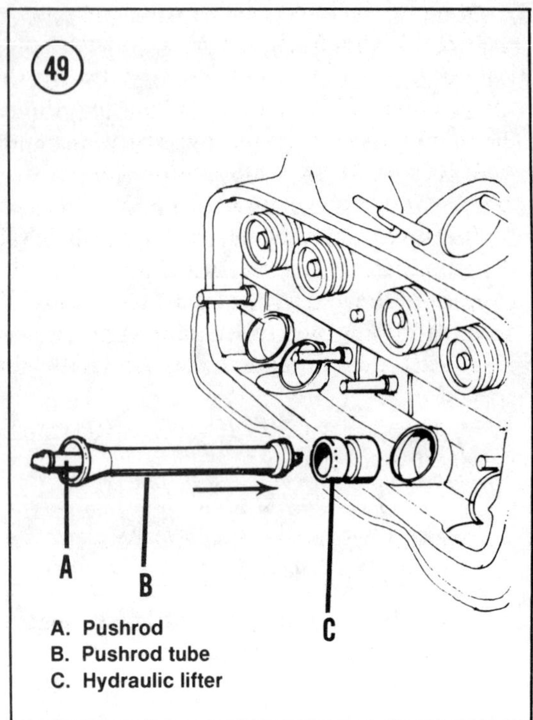

A. Pushrod
B. Pushrod tube
C. Hydraulic lifter

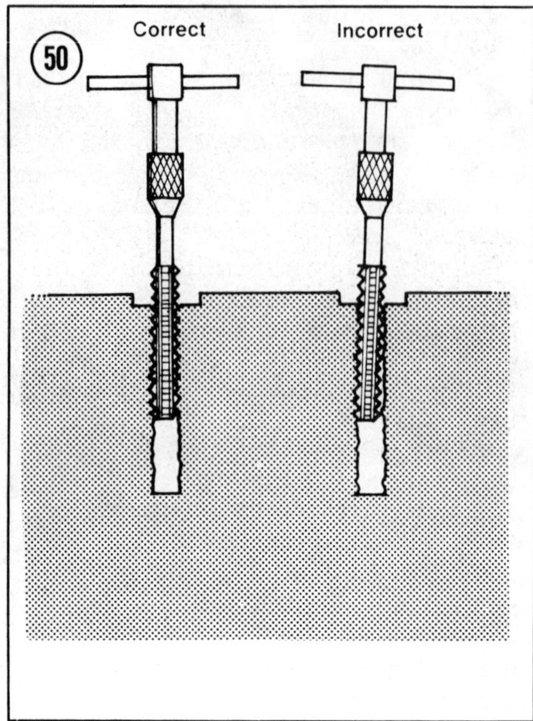

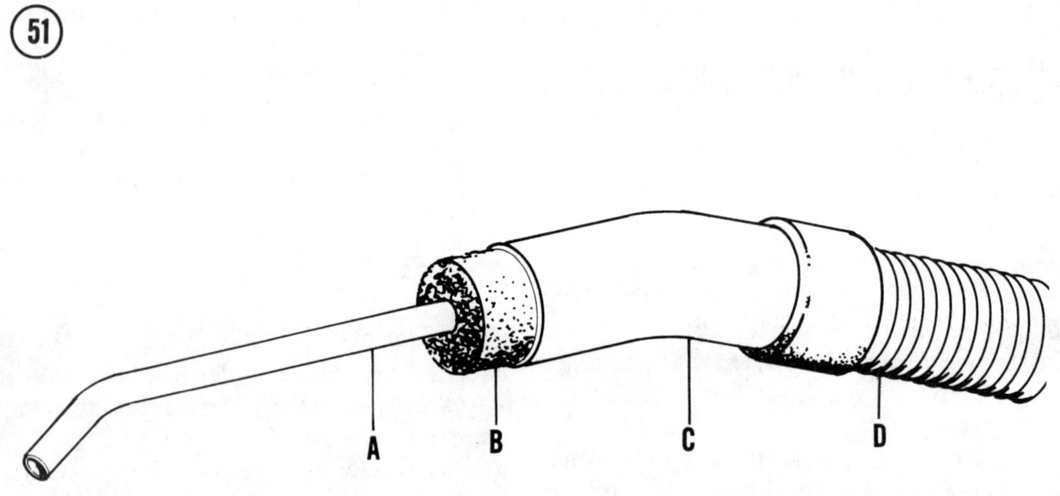

51

A
B
C
D

A. Aluminum pipe
B. Cork plug
C. Plastic pipe
D. Vacuum hose

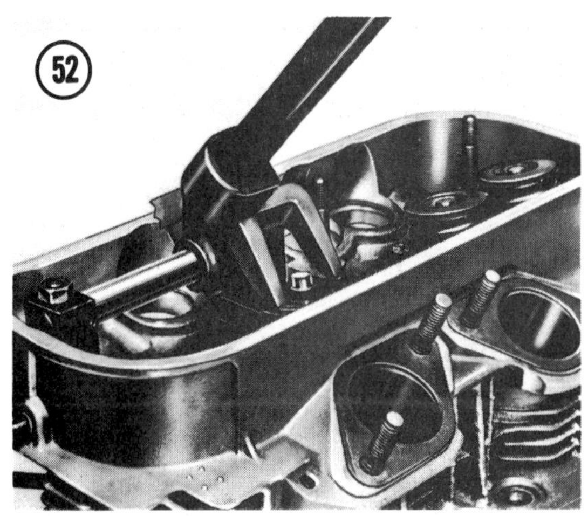

Thread-coil taps and inserts are available at foreign auto parts suppliers.

Cylinder heads need not be removed to install thread-coil inserts, although removal is recommended. The following procedure is designed to save you an engine teardown when and where it is not feasible.

1. Remove the spark plug wire and the spark plug from the cylinder head.
2. Shine a light down into the spark plug hole; turn the engine over until the piston moves all the way to top dead center. Crank the piston back down a little, but not so far that it goes out of sight.
3. Lightly coat the Thread-coil tap with oil.
4. Insert the tap into the spark plug hole. Align the tap with the centerline of the hole (**Figure 50**).
5. Start the tap in the hole; turn it one full turn clockwise. Then *stop* and turn it 1/3 turn counterclockwise to break up the chips.

CAUTION
Turning the tap 1/3 turn back after each cut is very important. If you don't, the tap will break off in the hole.

6. Continue through the hole after the starting cut by turning the tap 1/2 turn clockwise and stopping and turning it 1/3 turn counterclockwise to break up the chips. Occasionally apply a drop of oil to the tap (not too much or it will be difficult to remove the chips later). Remove tap from hole when completely through.
7. Make a vacuum cleaner hose adaptor as shown in **Figure 51**. Insert it into the spark plug hole and work it around to vacuum up the metal chips. This method will get out almost all of the chips. Having the piston near top dead center keeps them confined to an area accessible to the vacuum adaptor.
8. Remove the coil wire (center wire) from the distributor and ground the wire. Crank the engine over with the starter for about 30 seconds to blow out any remaining chips.
9. Install the Thread-coil insert with the special tool.
10. Connect the coil wire. Install the spark plug and spark plug wire.

VALVES AND VALVE SEATS

If a single defect is found with any of the valves, valve seats or valve guides for a specific cylinder, the other components for that cylinder must also be replaced or reconditioned.

NOTE
The valve guides must be replaced before the valve seats are reconditioned. Only new guides can accurately guide the valve seat cutter.

Reworking the valve train requires special tools and grinding equipment. These are available at many tool stores, but the cost can be more than removing the heads yourself and having them rebuilt.

Valve Removal/Installation

1. Remove the cylinder head.
2. Compress the valve springs with a spring compression tool. See **Figure 52**.
3. Remove the valve spring caps, springs, oil deflector rings and valves. Mark them so they can be replaced in their original position.
4. See *Cleaning and Inspection*. New or reground valves must be lapped before installing valve springs; see procedure in this chapter.
5. Coat the valve stems with engine assembly lubricant and insert them into cylinder head.
6. Install the valve springs.
7. Install the valve spring caps. Compress springs and install valve keepers.

(53)

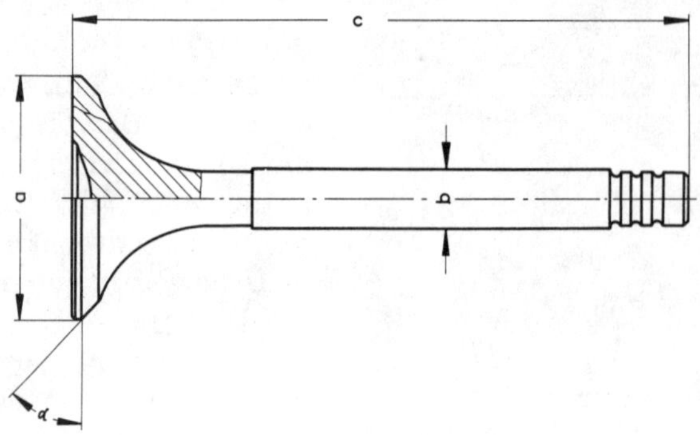

Intake valve	Exhaust valve
a 1.547 in. (39.3 mm) diameter	a 1.299 in. (33.0 mm) diameter
b 0.313 in. (7.95 mm) diameter	b 0.351 in. (8.92 mm) diameter
c 4.540 in. (115.4 mm) length	c 4.540 in. (115.4 mm) length
a 29°30'	*a* 45°

Cleaning and Inspection

1. Clean valves with a wire brush and solvent.
2. Discard burned, warped or cracked valves.

WARNING
Cylinder head valves are sodium filled. Sodium can be dangerous if exposed to water. Do not grind discarded valves to make punches or drifts.

3. Measure valve stems for wear. Compare with specifications in **Figure 53**; replace if necessary.
4. Scrape all carbon from valve guides, being careful not to mark the inside of the guides or the valve seats.
5. Insert the good or new valves in their corresponding seats. Hold them slightly off their seat with your finger on the valve stem. Rock the valve sideways. If it rocks more than 0.047 in. (1.2 mm), the valve guide is worn and it should be replaced. See **Figure 54**.

6. Measure the valve spring heights (**Figure 55**). All should be of equal length with no bends or other distortion. Replace any defective springs.
7. Inspect valve seats; if they are worn or burned (burning appears as little pit holes) they must be reconditioned. See *Valve Seat*

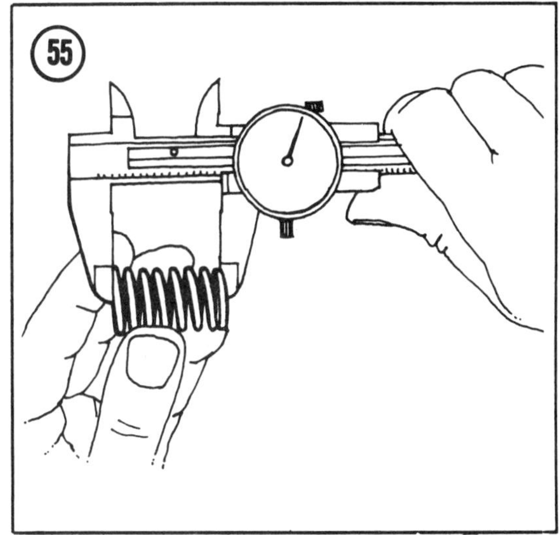

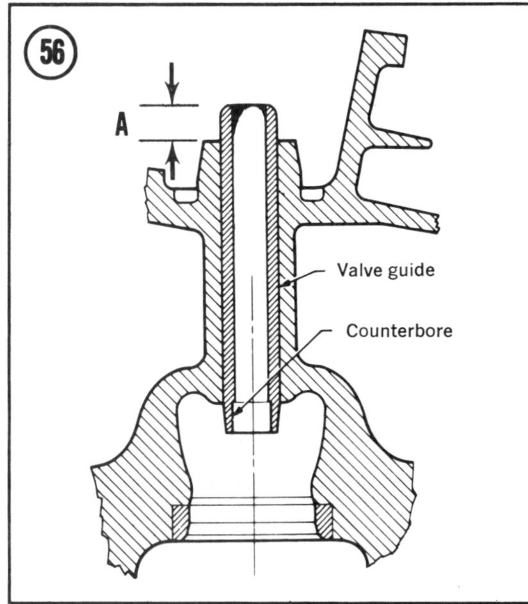

Reconditioning in this section. Seats and valves in near perfect condition can be restored by lapping with carborundum paste. However, lapping is always inferior to precision grinding or cutting.

Valve Guide Replacement

When the valve guides are worn so that there is excessive stem-to-guide clearance (valve rocking), the valve guides must be replaced. Replace all valve guides even if only one is worn.

1. Measure the exact distance that valve guides extend above the cylinder head. See dimension "A" in **Figure 56**.
2. Drill out the old guide from the rocker arm side with a shouldered 11 mm drill to a depth of 1 1/2 in. (38 mm). This will leave a shoulder for the punch **(Figure 57** and **Figure 58)**. Be sure that the head is firmly clamped in the drill press at the proper angle.
3. Place the punch into the drilled guide. The punch should be just a few thousandths of an inch (hundredths of a millimeter) smaller than the 11 mm shouldered drill. Hold the punch firmly and drive the guide out of the cylinder head **(Figure 57)**.
4. Accurately measure the valve guide bore. Note this figure for obtaining new oversize guides.

NOTE
Driving out the old guide increases the bore size. Oversize valve guides should be used. Replacement valve guides should be 0.001-0.002 in. (0.03-0.06 mm) larger than the measured bore size. Oversize guides are available from foreign parts suppliers or from VW dealers.

5. Coat the valve guide with clean engine oil and press it into the cylinder head from the rocker arm side **(Figure 59)**. The top of the valve guide should protrude the exact amount measured in Step 1.

NOTE
Chill the valve guides in a freezer (so they will shrink) for at least 40 minutes before pressing them in. Heat up the cylinder head (so it will expand) by placing it in the hot sun or in a 150° oven for at least 20 minutes. This will make guide installation easier.

6. The valve should be able to drop freely in the guide without binding or dragging. If not, ream the guide until the valve drops smoothly without excessive rocking play.

Valve Seat Reconditioning

This job is best left to a VW dealer or machine shop. They have the special equipment and knowledge required for this exacting job.

4

57

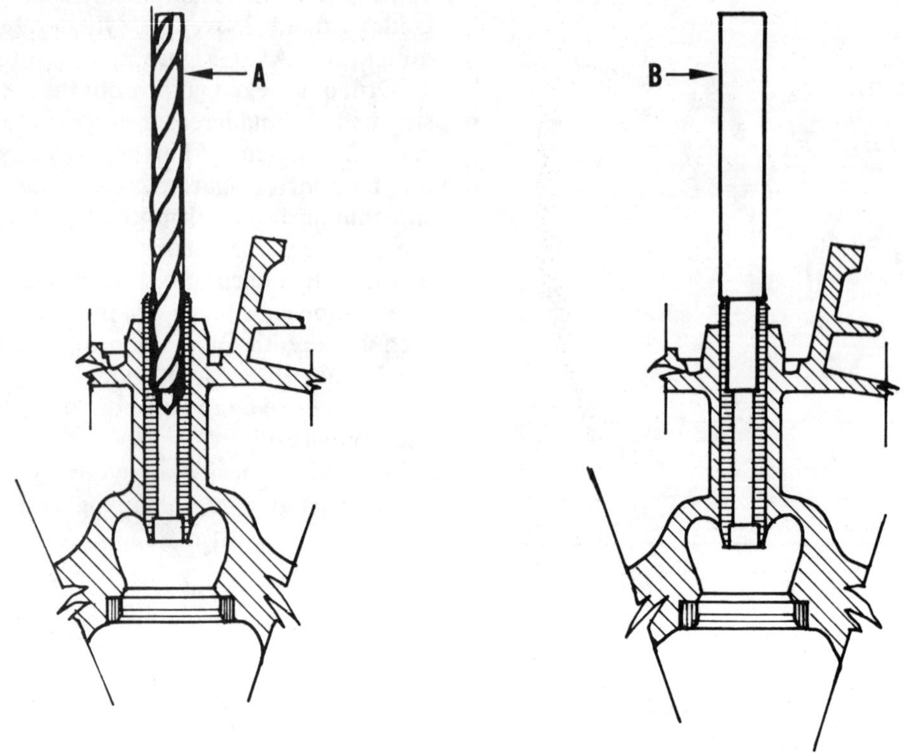

A

B

A. Shouldered drill
B. Punch

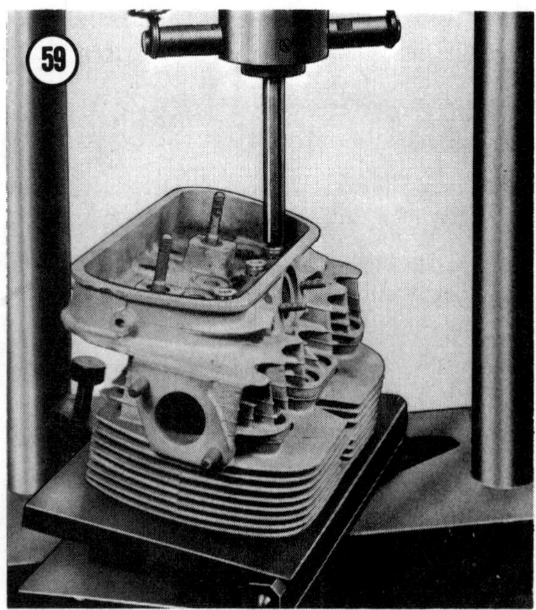

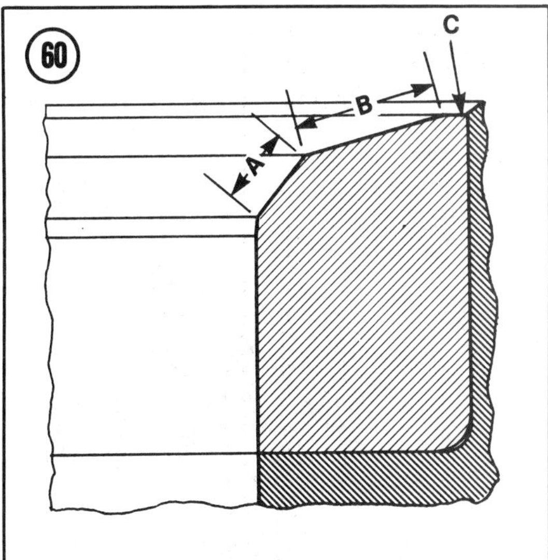

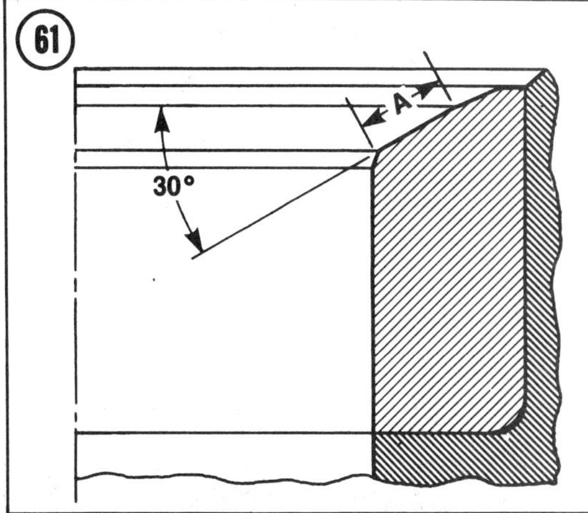

The following procedure is provided in the event you are not near a dealer and the local machine shop is not familiar with the Vanagon.

See **Figure 60** for the following explanation. Damaged or burned seats can be reconditioned if the width of dimension "a" is maintained at 0.070-0.086 in. (1.8-2.2 mm) for intake valves and 0.078-0.098 in. (2.0-2.5 mm) for exhaust valves. Also, dimension "b" must not exceed the outer diameter of valve seat insert at "c." Once limits have been exceeded, the cylinder head must be replaced.

1. *Intake valves*: Use the 30° cutter to cut the 30° face (**Figure 61**).
2. *Exhaust valves*: Use a 45° cutter to cut the 45° face (**Figure 62**).
3. Slightly chamfer the bottom of the 30 or 45° seat with a 75° cutter (**Figure 63**).
4. *Intake valves*: Narrow the width of 30° face (dimension "a") to 0.070-0.086 in. (1.8-2.2 mm) by cutting the top of the face with a 15° cutter (**Figure 64**).
5. *Exhaust valves*: Narrow the width of the 45° face (dimension "a") to 0.078-0.098 in. (2.0-2.5 mm) by cutting the top of the face with a 15° cutter (**Figure 64**).
6. Lap the valve into the valve seat. See procedure in this chapter.

Valve Lapping

Valve lapping is a method of fine honing the valve seats and valve faces. It can be used to

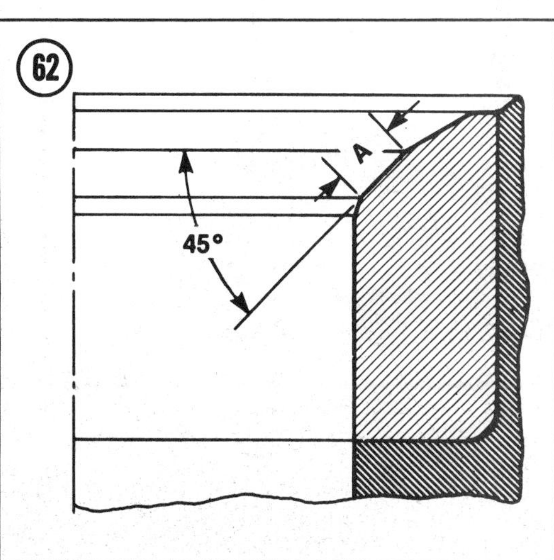

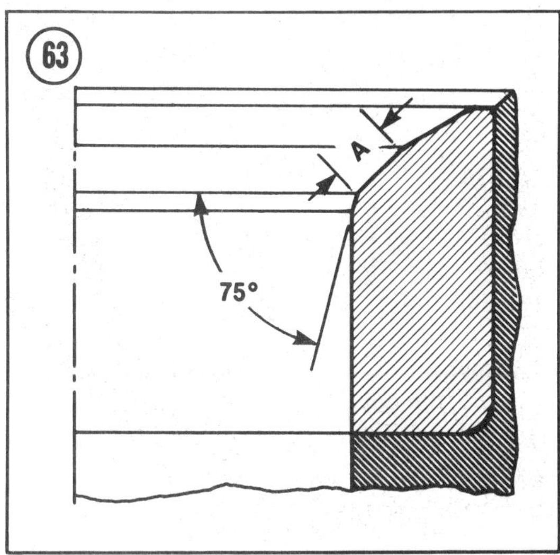

4

remove minor imperfections from valve seats and valve faces. Newly refaced valves and reconditioned valve seats should be lapped before final assembly. This procedure requires a suction cup lapping tool like the one shown in **Figure 65**.

1. Dab a small amount of extremely fine grit lapping compound onto the valve seat.
2. Insert the valve into the guide. Place a lapping tool on the valve (**Figure 66**). Spin the tool between the palms of your hands only 1/2 of a turn either way several times.
3. Lift the valve and turn it 3/4 of a turn.
4. Repeat Steps 2 and 3, 6 times per valve.
5. Wipe the lapping compound off of all the valves.
6. Coat the valve seats with blue layout ink. Let the ink dry.
7. Insert the valves into the guides.
8. Rotate the valve about 1/4 turn with light pressure against valve seat.
9. Lift the valve out. If the valve seats properly, the blue layout ink will transfer evenly onto the valve.

CYLINDERS AND PISTONS

VW cylinders and pistons may be rebuilt individually by honing the cylinder bores and installing new rings on the pistons or they may be purchased in brand new sets (bore kits) which are matched and weighed. Honing cylinders and installing new piston rings is a lot of work and it usually doesn't last long because cylinder liners wear in a taper.

Honing does not correct tapered wear. Tapered wear causes the rings to constrict and expand every time the piston goes from the bottom of the bore to the top. After a short while (several thousand miles), the piston rings will most likely break up. This situation is made worse by the fact that VW engines operate at high temperatures and high rpm.

Usually, when an individual piston and cylinder wear out the others are not far behind. Pistons and cylinders are not normally sold individually but rather in complete sets of 4 (including piston pins) called "bore kits." The cost to rebuild all 4 cylinders and pistons is only slightly less than the purchase price of a new bore kit. Direct experience has shown that

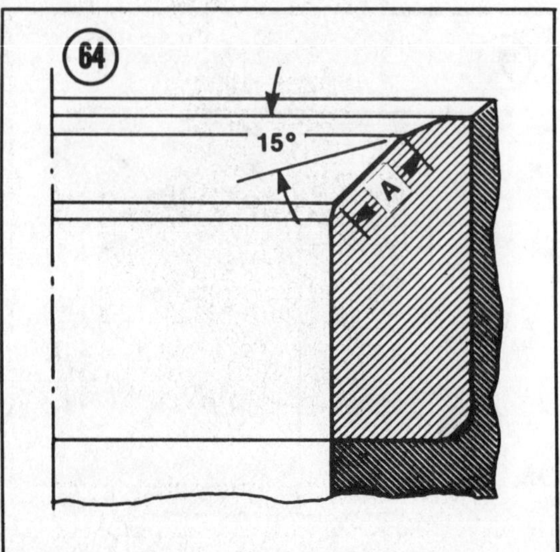

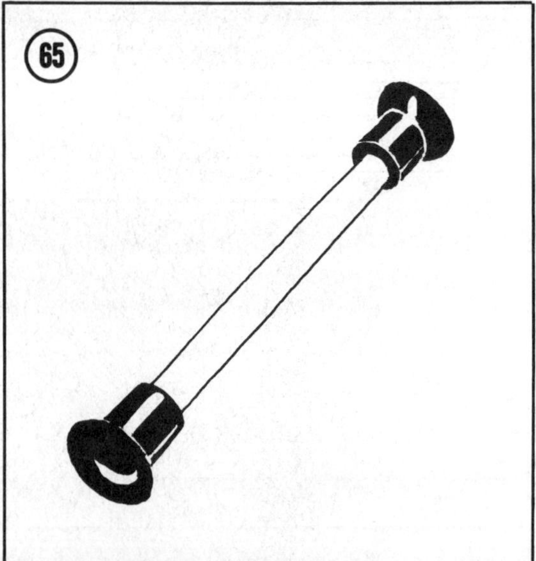

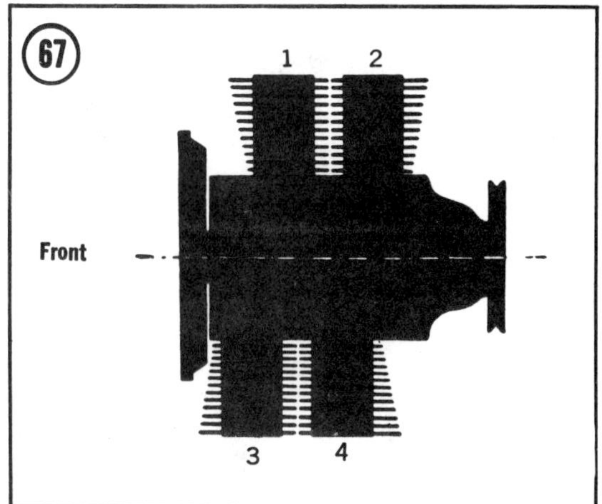

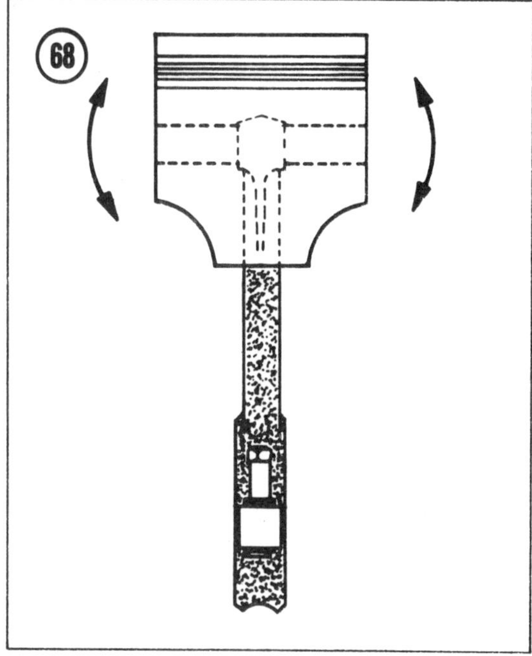

complete bore kit replacement is the preferable method, so only complete bore kit replacement and removal/installation procedures will be described in this chapter.

Removal

1. Remove the valve rocker assembly, pushrods and cylinder head using the procedures given in this chapter.
2. Mark the cylinder numbers on each cylinder and piston. Carefully pull the cylinder liner out of the crankcase and off of the piston. **Figure 67** shows correct cylinder numbers.

4

NOTE
Stubborn liners may be gently tapped from side to side with a rubber mallet. Be careful not to break off the cooling fins. Do not pry between the base of the liner and the crankcase with a screwdriver or metal bar; this will ruin the crankcase.

3. Rotate the crankshaft until the desired piston is at top dead center.

CAUTION
When rotating the crankshaft, make sure the skirts of the exposed pistons do not catch upon the crankcase. This will crack the piston.

4. Before removing the piston pin, hold the connecting rod tightly and rock the piston as shown in **Figure 68**. Any rocking movement (do not confuse with sliding motion) indicates wear in the piston pin, piston pin bore or connecting rod bushing. It is possibly a combination of all 3. Mark the piston, piston pin and rod for further examination.
5. Turn the engine up on the front end (flywheel side). Jam a few rags around the engine to catch leaking oil.
6. Use snap ring pliers to remove the piston pin snap rings (**Figure 69**).
7. Heat the piston with a small butane torch to 176° F (80° C). The piston pin will probably drop right out, but it may need to be tapped out with a wooden dowel and hammer. Hold the piston so that no sideways force is applied to the connecting rod.

Inspection and Cleaning

These procedures are given to help in determining whether a new bore kit is necessary. If you have doubts concerning the condition of any parts take them to a machine shop specializing in foreign autos for inspection.

1. Check the cylinder liners for excessive tapered wear. See **Figure 70**. Take several micrometer readings at least 0.4-0.6 in. (10-15 mm) from the top of the liner. The maximum permissible out-of-round is 0.0004 in. (0.01 mm). Another method (far less exacting) is to feel for a ridge at the top of the liner (not the carbon ridge). An exaggerated example of this is illustrated in **Figure 71**. If a ridge can be felt, it's time for new liners and pistons. Check the liners for scoring (gouges which travel the length of the liner). Scoring can be the cause of excessive exhaust smoke.
2. Examine the pistons. Check each ring groove for burrs, dented edges and side wear. A good way to tell if the rings are bad is to look at the piston below the rings; if there is excessive blackening (blow-by), the rings and cylinder liners are probably worn.
3. To check the piston pin bore of the piston, push the pin through the piston. If it moves through easily, the bore is worn or pounded out of round. The pin should move through with moderately heavy thumb pressure.
4. Check the connecting rod ends. Push the piston pin through the rod bore; it should move through the rod with an interference fit (light thumb pressure). If the piston pin can be rocked within the rod bushing, the bushing is worn excessively and must be replaced. If the rod bushing is excessively blackened or has slid out of the bore, the rod should also be replaced. See *Connecting Rods* in this chapter before installing cylinders and pistons.

Installation

If the crankcase studs are removed, install them before proceeding.

1. Place new gaskets on the crankcase ends of the cylinder liners.
2. Rotate the crankshaft until connecting rod No. 1 is at top dead center.

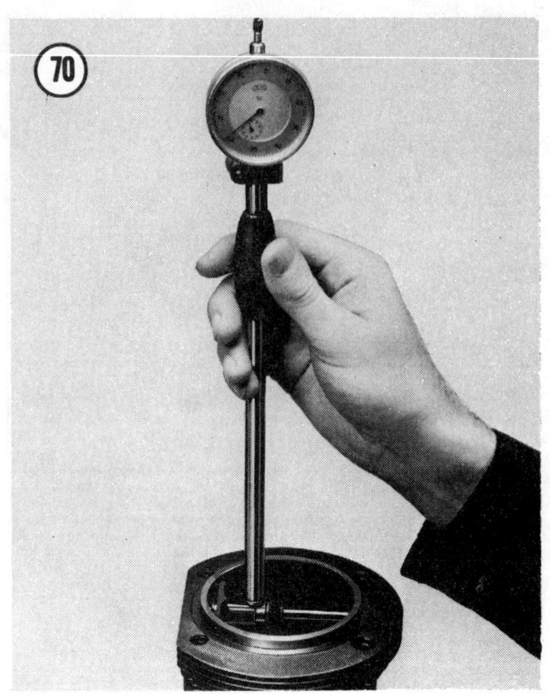

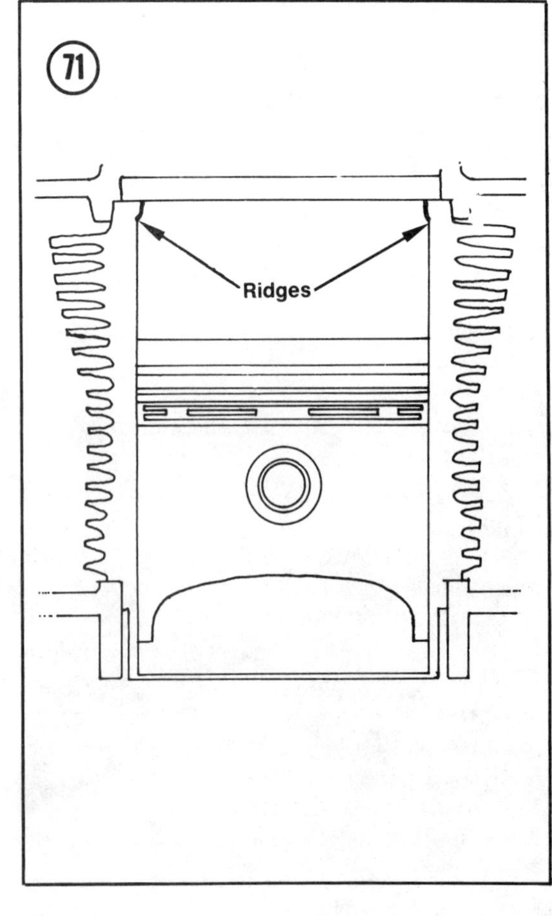

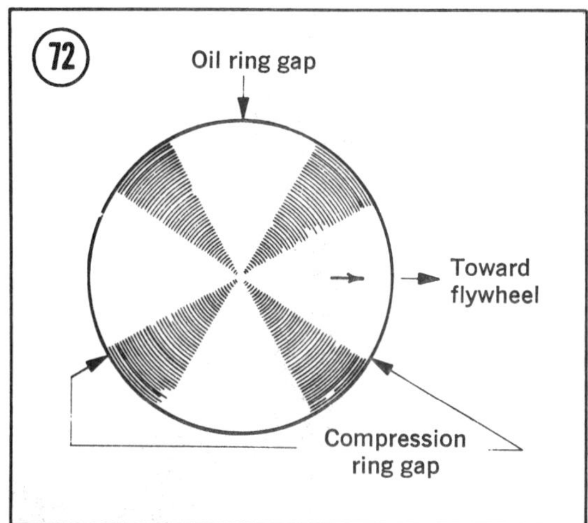

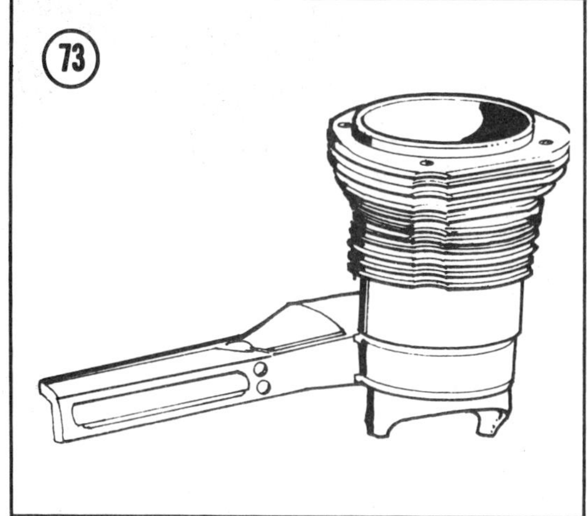

3. If installing new bore kit, push the pistons out of the liners.
4. Lay out the liners and pistons according to the connecting rod with which they will be installed.
5. Space the ring gaps 120° apart as shown in **Figure 72**. Make sure the oil ring gap is pointing straight up and that the arrow on the piston crown points toward the flywheel.
6. Compress the piston rings with a ring compression tool like the one shown in **Figure 73**. If a compression tool is not available use a large hose clamp wide enough to cover the piston rings. Gently slip the piston into the liner, making sure the arrow is pointing at a right angle to the flat cut on the cooling fins. When liner is installed on the engine studs the arrow must point toward the flywheel. On cylinders No. 1 and No. 3, arrow points away from flat cut. On cylinders No. 2 and No. 4, arrow points toward flat cut.
7. Push the pistons to the bottom of the liners until the piston pin bore holes are totally exposed. Do not push the piston out any farther or the piston rings will pop out and have to be reinserted using the method described in Step 6.
8. Slip the liner over the engine studs and onto connecting rod No. 1 or No. 3 so that the arrow points toward the flywheel.

NOTE
Install liners on only one side of the engine at a time.

9. Gently tap in the piston pin using a wooden dowel slightly smaller than the outer diameter of the pin itself. When the pin touches the connecting rod, align the piston so the end of the pin will slip through the connecting rod bushing without binding. Tap the pin through the connecting rod into the other side of the piston.
10. Insert the snap rings (**Figure 69**). Push the cylinder liner into the crankcase.
11. Determine which way the piston will face when installed on No. 2 or No. 4 connecting rod (arrow on piston must point to flywheel). Install the snap ring into the piston pin bore hole that will face cylinder No. 1 or No. 3. The snap ring will be almost impossible to insert once the other liner is installed. Install the piston pin from the side of the piston which faces the rear of the engine. Install the remaining snap ring. Push the cylinder liner into the crankcase.
12. Install cylinders on the other side of engine using the same procedures given in Steps 8-11.

OIL PUMP

The oil pump (**Figure 74**) is a gear type pump driven by a shaft from a slot in the end of the camshaft. Oil pumps can be replaced with the engine installed, however, the cooling fan housing must be totally removed, the engine must be supported with a floor jack and the rear engine carrier must be removed to gain access. If you suspect oil pump problems, first check oil pressure with the engine installed using the procedure below.

4

(74) OIL PUMP

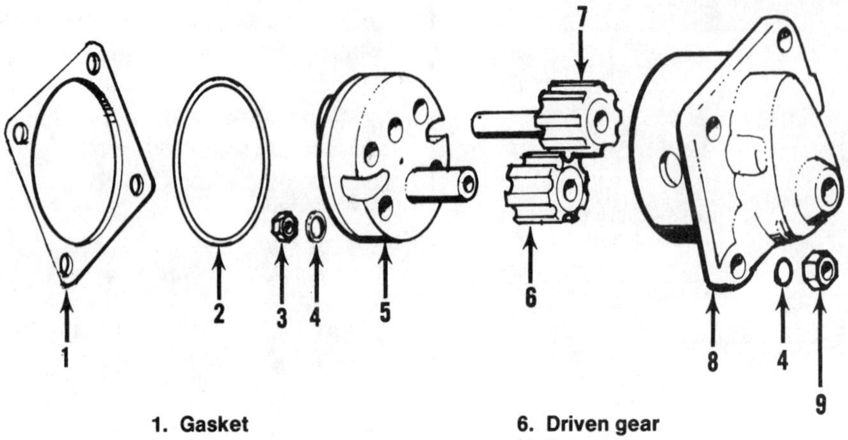

1. Gasket
2. O-ring
3. Cover nut
4. Spring washer
5. Cover
6. Driven gear
7. Drive gear
8. Housing
9. Housing nut

(75)

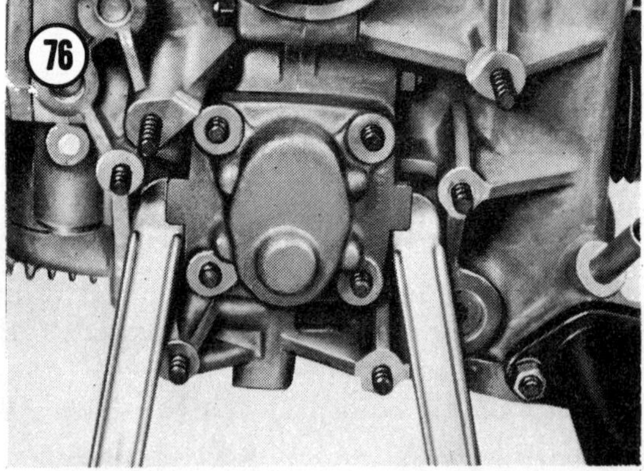

(76)

Checking Oil Pressure

1. Remove the oil pressure warning switch (**Figure 75**).
2. Screw an oil pressure gauge into the crankcase in place of the pressure warning switch.

CAUTION
The oil pressure gauge must have metric pipe threads or the crankcase will be damaged and the warning switch will not screw back in.

3. Set the parking brake and start the engine; slowly increase the engine speed to 2,000 rpm. Note the pressure reading. The pressure should be between 38-45 psi with a minimum allowable pressure of 29 psi.
4. Let the engine warm to operating temperature. Slowly increase the engine speed to 2,000 rpm. The pressure should stay within specifications. If pressure drops off sharply when engine is warm, either an engine oil passage in

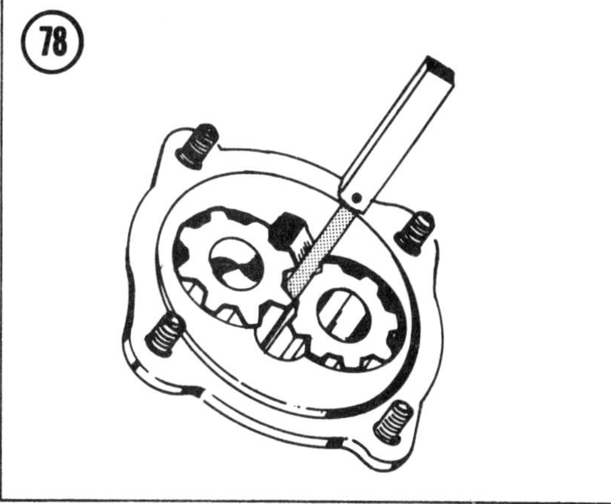

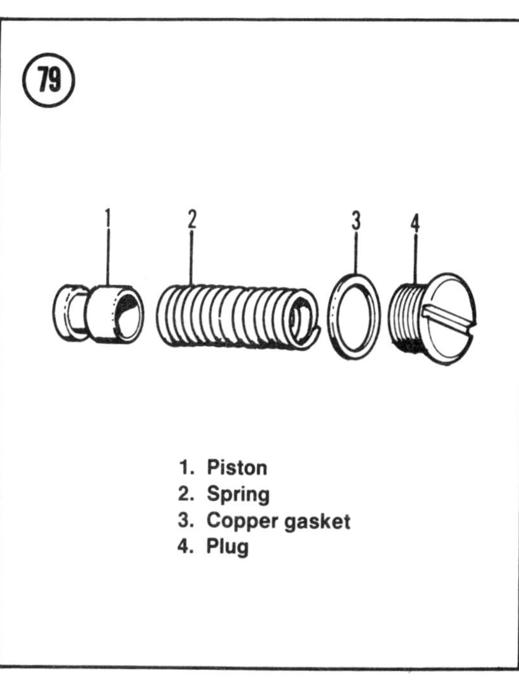

1. Piston
2. Spring
3. Copper gasket
4. Plug

the crankcase is cracked, main bearings are severely worn or a main bearing journal is cracked.

Removal

1. Remove the pump housing nuts.
2. Pry the oil pump housing off the crankcase (**Figure 76**).
3. Remove the pump cover nuts and pull the cover off with a special tool (**Figure 77**).
4. Remove the pump gears.

Inspection

1. Clean all parts thoroughly in solvent.
2. Check oil pump housing and cover for scoring. Check gear shafts and gears for scoring. If scoring is found, replace the pump.
3. Check gear backlash; insert a feeler gauge between the gear teeth as shown in **Figure 78**. The gap between the pump gears should not exceed 0.008 in. (0.02 mm); if it does, replace the pump.

Installation

1. Coat gears and shafts with assembly lubricant and insert gears in oil pump housing.
2. Install a new rubber seal on the cover. Oil the seal and install the cover in the housing. Put a drop of Loctite on the housing threads and install the housing nuts.
3. Make sure that the pump gears turn freely and install the oil pump in the crankcase with a new gasket. The pump shaft must fit in the slot in the camshaft.
4. Turn the crankshaft a couple of times to center the pump and tighten the pump housing nuts to 18 ft.-lb. (25 N•m).

OIL PRESSURE RELIEF VALVES

There are 2 oil pressure relief valves, one located on the bottom rear of the engine near the oil pump and the second between cylinder No. 1 pushrod tubes.

Removal

Refer to **Figure 79** for the following procedure.

1. Unscrew the plug and remove the copper gasket.

4

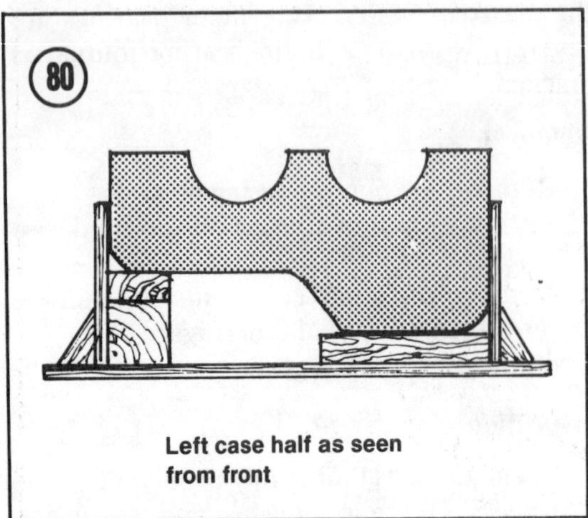
Left case half as seen from front

2. Remove the spring and piston. If the piston is stuck, reach up into the bore with a magnet tool and pull it out.

Inspection

1. Check the crankcase bore and piston for signs of scoring and seizure. Dress up the bore and piston with crocus cloth. Replace the piston if necessary.
2. Check the unloaded length of the spring; it should measure approximately 1.54 in. (39 cm). If not, replace the spring.

Installation

Install the piston, spring, copper gasket and plug in the order shown in **Figure 79**.

OIL STRAINER

The oil strainer may be removed with the engine installed; see *Engine Oil and Filter Change* in Chapter Three.

CRANKCASE

Disassembly

1. Double-nut the cylinder head studs and remove them from the crankcase. This is not absolutely necessary, but it makes it easier to dissassemble and assemble the engine without a VW engine stand.
2. Pull out the hydraulic lifters with a magnet tool. Remove the oil strainer from the bottom of the engine.

NOTE
Store the hydraulic lifters with the body down to prevent oil leakage. If they are to be reused, store them in order so they may be returned to their original positions.

3. Tip the crankcase up on its left side so that the large case nuts are exposed. Support the engine in a VW engine stand or an engine jig like the one shown in **Figure 80**. Cylinder head studs must be removed if case is to lay in wooden jig.
4. Remove all the small (13 mm) nuts around the crankcase seam, then remove the 6 large (17 mm) case nuts.
5. Carefully check around the case for any remaining nuts.
6. Separate the case halves by lifting up on the right case half and tapping against the left case half with a rubber hammer or a block of wood.

CAUTION
Never try to pry the crankcase halves apart with a screwdriver or pry bar. This will damage the sealing surfaces and cause oil leaks.

7. Remove the camshaft end seal **(Figure 81)** and lift the camshaft out.
8. Lift the crankshaft out.
9. Remove the oil pressure relief valves. See procedure in this chapter.
10. Carefully pry out the main bearing and cam bearing inserts. Remove the main bearing dowel pins **(Figure 82)**.

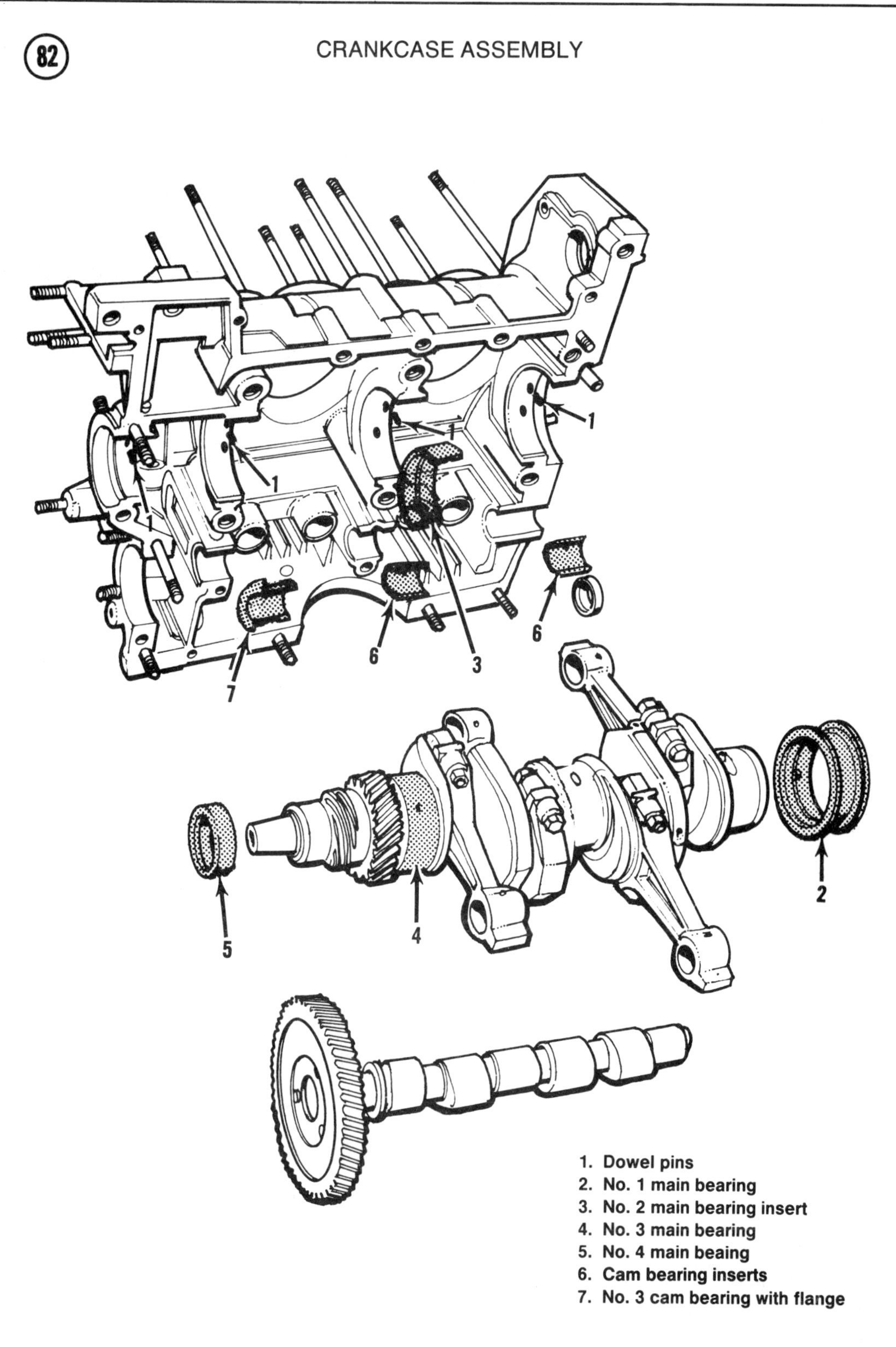
82
CRANKCASE ASSEMBLY
1
1
1
1
7
6
3
6
2
4
5
1. Dowel pins
2. No. 1 main bearing
3. No. 2 main bearing insert
4. No. 3 main bearing
5. No. 4 main beaing
6. Cam bearing inserts
7. No. 3 cam bearing with flange

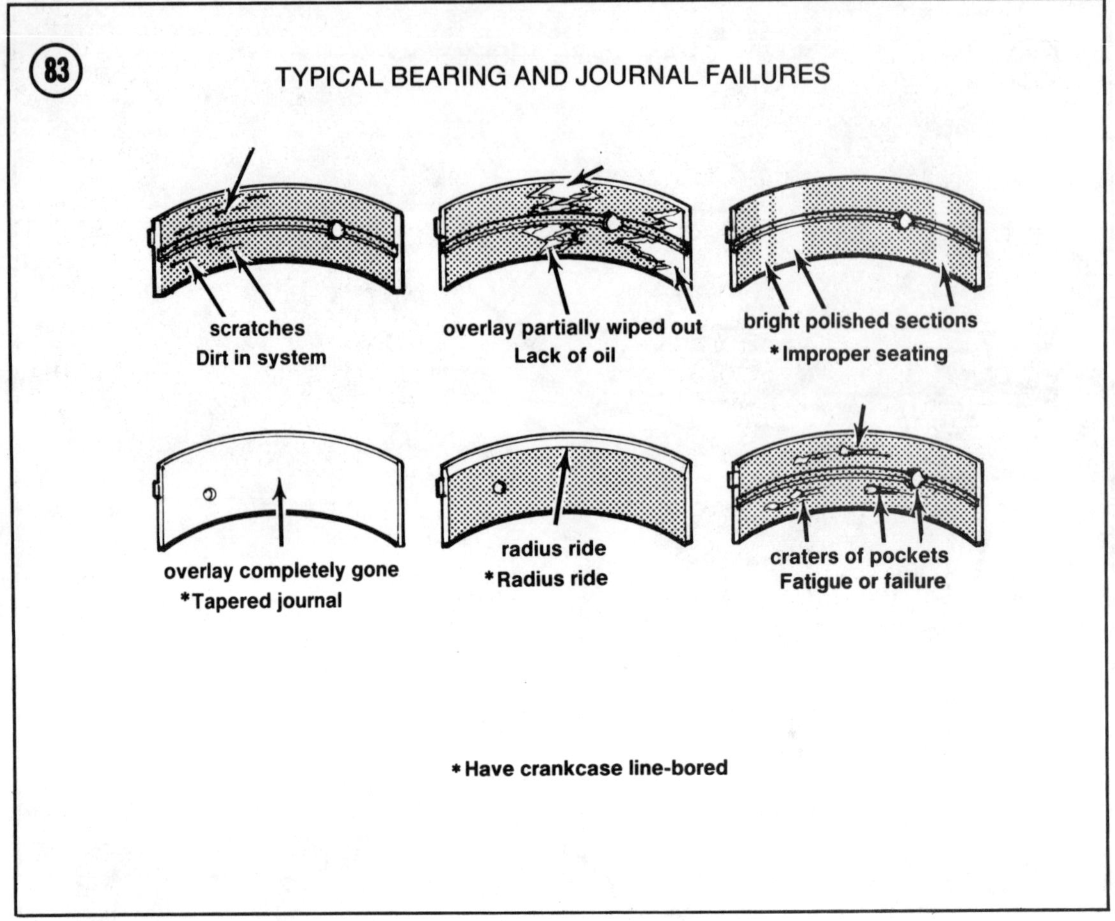

Inspection

1. Clean and flush both halves of the crankcase with solvent. Blow out oil passages with compressed air. Remove all traces of sealing compound on the mating surfaces.
2. Check both crankcase halves (inside and out) for cracks. Cracks will appear as a hairline and may run several inches in any direction. Do not confuse a crack with a mold line. Press heavily against the suspected crack with your thumbs; if a thin line of oil is squeezed out, it is definitely a crack. If in doubt, bring the crankcase to an automotive machine shop for inspection. Cracked crankcases cannot be repaired by welding; they must be replaced.
3. Check all studs in the crankcase for looseness. If any cannot be tightened, have a machinist install thread-coil (Heli-coil) inserts.
4. Check the main bearing bore (crankshaft bore) for scuffing or out-of-roundness. Scuffing will appear as a scrubbed area where the main bearing slid back and forth. The dowel pin hole under a slipping bearing will be out-of-round and the dowel pin will fit loosely.
5. Put the case halves together without the camshaft or crankshaft and torque the 6 large case nuts to specifications (**Table 1**). Check the crankcase bore for out-of-round (main bearing pounding) with inside calipers.
6. Check No. 1 bearing main journal thrust cut for nicks and burrs. If the thrust cut is damaged it must be remachined.
7. If you plan to rebuild the crankcase, it would be best to take it to a machine shop and have the case line-bored and the No. 1 main bearing journal thrust cut. New bearings must fit tightly into the journals for proper crankshaft operation. **Figure 83** shows typical bearing defects.

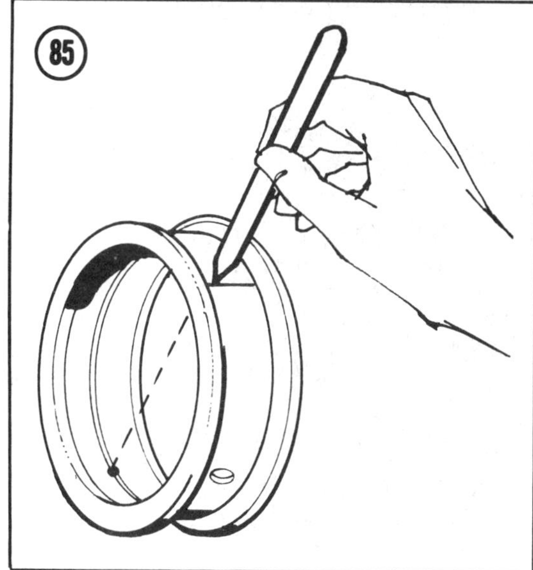

Assembly

NOTE
When reassembling the crankcase it is a good idea to use new crankshaft main bearings and new camshaft bearings. New main bearings must be used if a new or reground crankshaft is being installed or if the crankcase has been line-bored.

Prior to installing bearings, wipe all journal and bearing surfaces clean. Refer to **Figure 82** for the following procedure.

1. Install new dowel pins into the left case half main bearing journals (**Figure 84**). Install the No. 2 main bearing dowel pin into the right case half.
2. Install the crankshaft bearing inserts for No. 2 main bearing into both case halves. Make sure they are on the dowel pins and pushed all the way down in the journal.
3. Coat the inside of No. 1 and No. 4 main bearings and crankshaft journals with assembly lubricant.
4. Slide No. 1 main bearing (with thrust flanges) onto the flywheel end of the crankshaft. The offset dowel pin hole in the bearing must go toward the flywheel.
5. Slide No. 4 bearing onto the timing gear (rear) end of the crankshaft. The groove inside the bearing must go toward the rear oil seal.
6. Mark No. 1, No. 3 and No. 4 main bearings with a felt-tip marker directly opposite the dowel pin hole (**Figure 85**). This will greatly speed crankshaft installation.
7. Lift the crankshaft assembly by connecting rods No. 1 and No. 2 (**Figure 86**). Hold the crankshaft over the main bearing journals and have an assistant align the marks on the bearings so they point straight up from the case half. Carefully lower the crankshaft into the main bearing journals. The main bearings must be on (not held up on) the dowel pins. Connecting rods No. 3 and No. 4 must protrude through the cylinder liner holes. As the bearings seat in the journal there may be a

slight click. If the bearing hangs up on the dowel pin, gently lift up on the crankshaft, rotate the bearing slightly and drop it into place. After the bearings are seated make sure that none will rotate.

8. Carefully rotate the crankshaft until the centerpunched marks on the timing gear face toward the camshaft journals.

9. Install the camshaft bearing inserts into the left and right case half camshaft journals. The tabs in the bearings must engage the recess of the journals. Install No. 3 cam bearing (with the flange) in the No. 3 cam bearing journal on left case half. Coat the bearings with assembly lubricant.

10. Install the camshaft so that the "0" mark fits between the crankshaft gear teeth marked with lines (**Figure 87**). This alignment is critical because it establishes correct valve timing.

NOTE

For the following procedures have all the right tools and parts laid out and ready to install. Time in this phase is critical; the case halves must be put together with a minimum of delay.

11. Spread a coat of non-hardening sealing compound on the crankcase mating surfaces in the shaded areas shown in **Figure 88**. Keep the

87

88

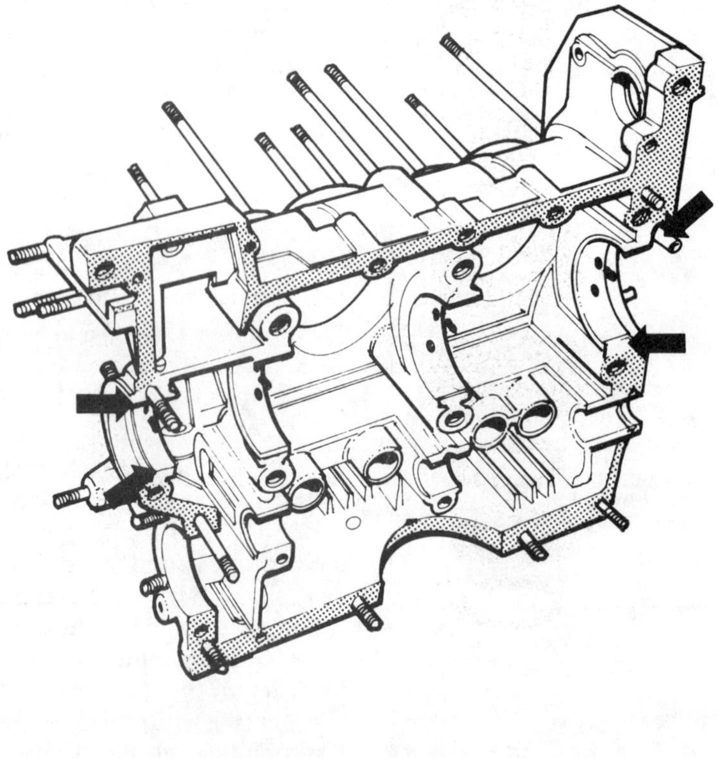

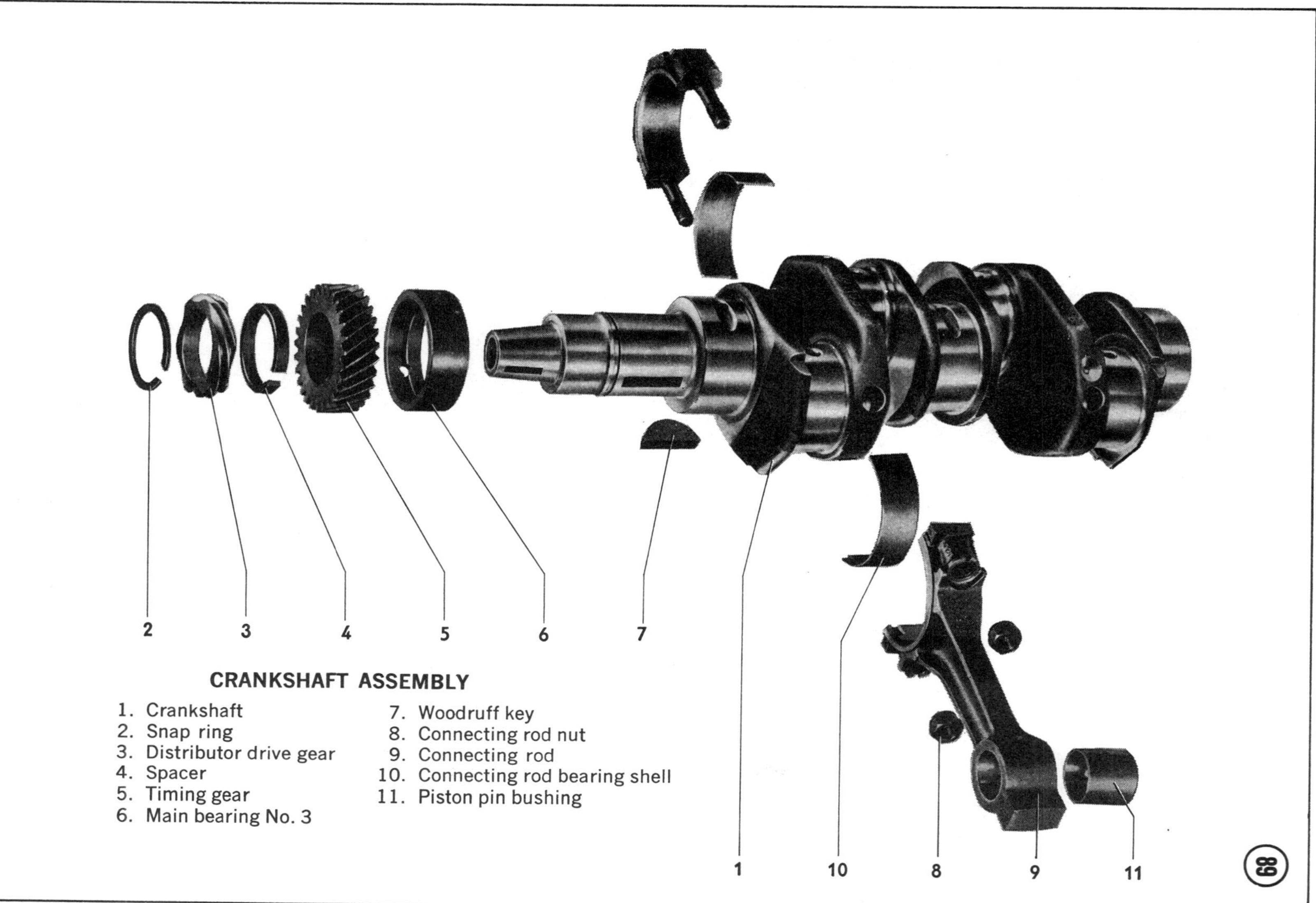

CRANKSHAFT ASSEMBLY

1. Crankshaft
2. Snap ring
3. Distributor drive gear
4. Spacer
5. Timing gear
6. Main bearing No. 3
7. Woodruff key
8. Connecting rod nut
9. Connecting rod
10. Connecting rod bearing shell
11. Piston pin bushing

sealing compound away from No. 1 and No. 4 main bearings (see areas marked with arrows in **Figure 88**). Let the first coat set for a few minutes, then spread another thin coat and let it set.

NOTE
A good sealing compound to use is Gasgacinch. This compound does not harden; if applied correctly and evenly the case halves will not leak oil.

12. Coat the camshaft end seal with a liberal amount of sealer and insert it in the left case half with the closed side facing out (**Figure 81**). Do not allow the sealer to come close to No. 1 cam bearing; if it does, wipe it out.
13. Hold up connecting rods No. 1 and No. 2. Slide the right case half down onto the left case half studs.
14. Put a couple drops of thread locking compound (Loctite) on all the small case stud threads. Install all the small case nuts and washers hand-tight.

NOTE
The tightening sequence described in the next steps is very important. Throughout the process, turn the crankshaft occasionally. If there is any binding, ***stop****. Take the case apart and find the trouble. Usually, it is a main bearing off its dowel pin. If the case must be taken apart, wipe away all the sealer and apply a new coat.*

15. Coat the large case studs, nuts and washers for the main bearing studs with sealer. Install the washers, then the nuts with their sealing rings facing out. Start with the center 2 nuts and work out; torque to specifications in **Table 1**.
16. Torque all the small case nuts to specifications (**Table 1**).
17. Wipe up all the excess case sealant squeezed into the front and rear oil seal areas.

CRANKSHAFT

Removal

1. When the right half of the crankcase has been removed, the crankshaft may be easily lifted out.

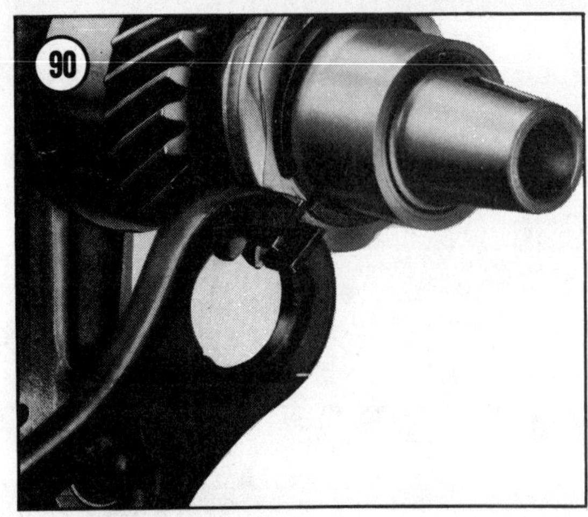

2. Remove the bearing inserts from the crankcase halves. If they are to be reused mark them with pencil (on the backside) so they may be reinstalled in the same position. Store in a safe place.

NOTE
When reinstalling the crankshaft it is a good idea to use new main bearings. New main bearings must be used if a new or reground crankshaft is being installed or if the crankcase has been line-bored.

Gear and Bearing Disassembly

Refer to **Figure 89** for the following procedure.

1. Slide No. 1 and No. 4 main bearings off the front and rear of the crankshaft. Mark the back of the inserts and store them in a safe place.

2. Use expanding pliers to remove the gear retaining snap ring (**Figure 90**).

3. Heat the timing and distributor gears (only) with a butane torch so they will expand. With a large gear puller, pull on the innermost gear (timing gear) to remove both gears as shown in **Figure 91**. Put Woodruff keys in a safe place so they won't get lost. If a gear puller is not available, bring the crankshaft to a VW repair shop or dealer for gear removal.

4. Slide No. 3 main bearing off the crankshaft. Mark it and store it safely.

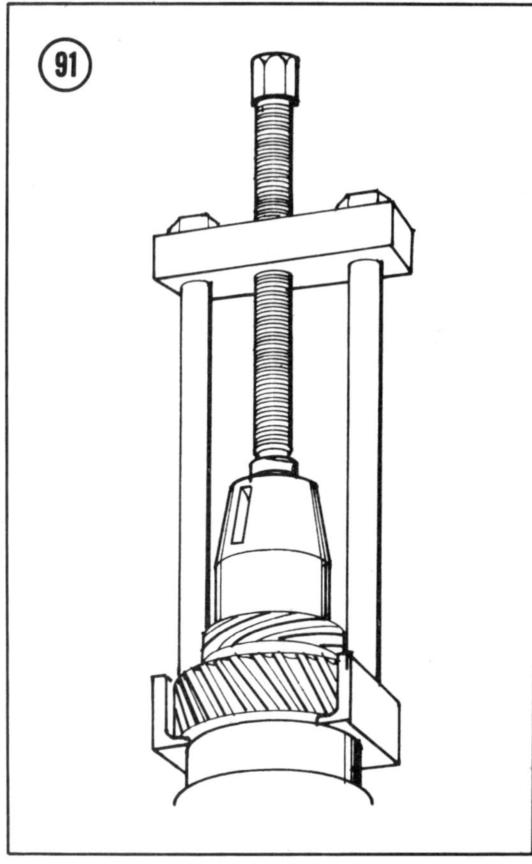

Inspection

1. Check connecting rod end play, then remove all connecting rods. Both procedures are described in *Connecting Rod Removal* in this chapter.
2. Clean the crankshaft thoroughly with solvent. Clean the oil passages with pipe cleaners or rifle brushes. Flush thoroughly with clean solvent and blow dry with compressed air.
3. Carefully check each bearing for scratches, ridges scoring, nicks, etc. Very minute nicks and scratches may be removed with an extremely fine hone stone. All bearing surfaces should have a dull gloss finish without any discoloration (blue or straw brown heat marks).
4. Even if the surface finish appears undamaged, take your crankshaft to a local automotive machine shop. They can check for out-of-roundness, taper, and wear on the journals. They will also check the crankshaft alignment and inspect for cracks (Magnaflux).
5. Fit the large Woodruff key inside the slot of the large timing gear. The key must fit very snugly and not wobble around. Fit the small key into the distributor gear slot; again the key must not fit loosely. If necessary, replace key. If a new Woodruff key fits the crankshaft slot loosely, replace the crankshaft. This same procedure applies to the cooling fan hub Woodruff key and crankshaft slot.

Gear and Bearing Assembly

Refer to **Figure 89** for the following procedure.

1. Wipe No. 3 crankshaft bearing journal clean. Coat journal and No. 3 bearing with assembly lubricant. Note that dowel pin hole in No. 3 bearing is offset. Slide No. 3 bearing onto the crankshaft so the dowel pin hole is toward the flywheel end of the crankshaft.
2. Temporarily bolt the flywheel to the end of the crankshaft. Stand the crankshaft up on the flywheel.
3. Insert the large Woodruff key in the crankshaft slot. Wrap No. 4 main bearing journal with a couple layers of tape. This will protect the bearing surface when the timing gear is driven on.
4. Heat the timing gear with a butane torch. Fit the gear over the crankshaft with the centerpunched marks facing up (away from flywheel). Align the slot in the timing gear with the Woodruff key.
5. Slip a length of 2 in. (5.1 cm) diameter pipe over the crankshaft and drive the gear into position.
6. Slide the spacer ring in place and align its slot with the Woodruff key.
7. Heat the brass distributor gear in the same manner as the timing gear. Fit the gear over the crankshaft and align the slot in the gear with the Woodruff key. Drive the gear down with the pipe until it is against the spacer ring.
8. Install the gear retaining snap ring with expanding pliers (**Figure 90**).
9. Remove the flywheel and peel the protective tape off No. 4 main bearing journal.
10. Leave No. 1 and No. 4 main bearings off until ready to install the crankshaft. See *Crankcase Assembly*.

4

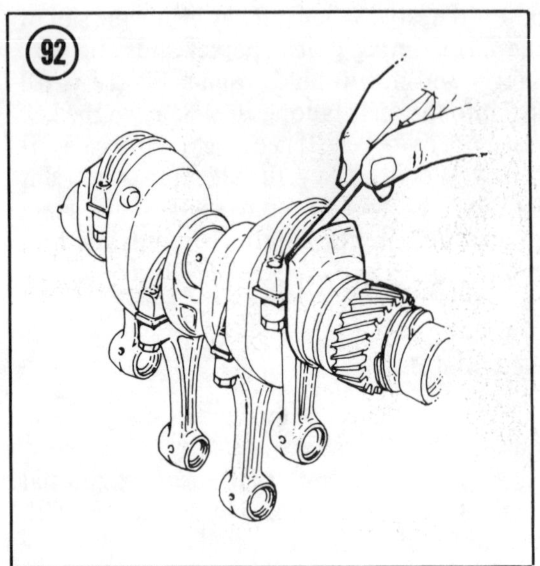

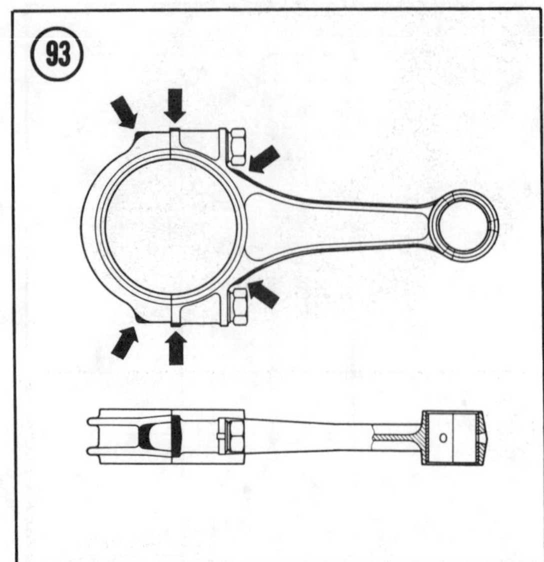

Installation

Installation is simply a matter of setting the crankshaft in place after the crankcase is prepared for assembly. See *Crankcase Assembly*.

CONNECTING RODS

Rods which are found to be defective should be replaced. Cross check with the crankshaft size for correct rod bearing insert size.

Removal

1. Remove the crankshaft from the crankcase.
2. File tiny identification marks on each rod to indicate its position for reassembly. Refer to **Figure 67** for correct cylinder locations.
3. Insert a feeler gauge between the side of the rod and the crank throw (**Figure 92**). If this gap is greater than 0.027 in. (0.7 mm), mark the rod for replacement.
4. Clamp the crankshaft down or have someone hold it. Remove *only* the connecting rod nuts. Give the rod a sharp tug; it should come free from the crankshaft.
5. Remove the bearing inserts from the rods and caps. Mark the back of the inserts with rod numbers for later inspection and reassembly. Do not mix up the bearings.
6. Install the caps on the rods to keep them together.

Inspection

1. Discard any rods which show excessive end play. See Step 3 in *Removal* procedure.
2. Check each rod for obvious damage such as cracks and burns.
3. Check the piston pin bushings for wear, burning or scoring. Push the pin through the rod bore; it should move through the rod with an interference fit (light thumb pressure). If the pin can be rocked within the rod, the rod bushing is worn excessively and must be replaced. If the rod bushing is excessively blackened or the edge is protruding out of the bore, the rod should also be replaced or reconditioned.
4. Take the rod to a machine shop and have it checked for twisting and bending.
5. Weigh each rod on a very accurate scale; they should be within 6 grams of each other. If not, find the lightest rod and lighten the others to match it. As much as 8 grams total may be removed by carefully filing away metal in the areas indicated in **Figure 93**.
6. Examine the bearing inserts for wear, scoring or burning. They may be reused if in good condition (**Figure 83**), but as long as the engine is apart you should consider installing new rod bearings. If the bearing is to be discarded, make a note of the bearing size stamped on the back of the insert; a previous owner may have used undersize bearings.

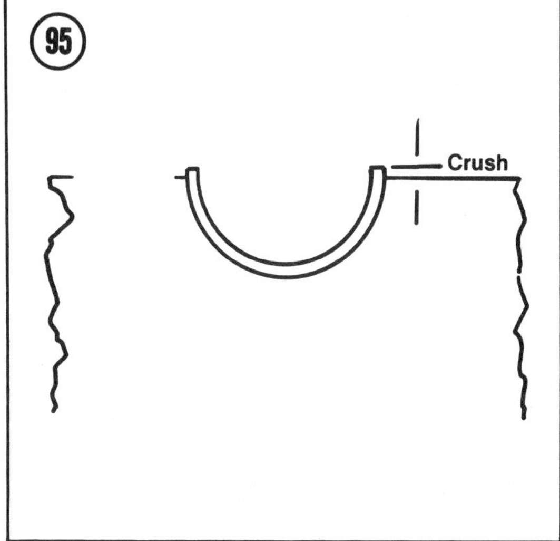

Installation

NOTE
If a new or reground crankshaft is to be used, do not reuse the old connecting rod bearings no matter what condition they are in. It is also a good idea to use all new or reconditioned connecting rods with the new or reground crank.

1. Remove the rod cap from the rod and discard the old nuts; you must use new nuts.
2. Carefully match the stamped numbers on the side of each rod to its matching rod cap (**Figure 94**). The numbers must be on the same side when the rod cap is installed.
3. Install the bearing inserts in the rods and caps. Press the bearings in with your thumbs on the ends of the bearing. Do not press down in the middle of the bearing. Be sure the tang on the bearing fits into the notch on the rod and cap.

NOTE
*The bearing insert ends will extend slightly above the cap or rod (**Figure 95**). Do not file any part of the rod, cap or bearing for a different fit.*

4. Cut a piece of Plastigage the width of the rod bearing. Assemble the No. 3 rod and cap on the crank throw for cylinder No. 3 (the one closest to the flywheel) with the Plastigage inserted between the bearing insert in the rod cap and the crank throw. Make sure that the forge mark of the rod faces up as shown in **Figure 96**. Tighten the nuts to 25 ft.-lb. (33.9 N•m).
5. Remove the bearing cap and measure the width of the Plastigage following the manufacturer's instructions. This is the bearing clearance; it should be 0.0008-0.028 in. (0.02-0.07 mm) with a wear limit of 0.006 in. (0.15 mm). If it is not right, check that you have installed the proper size bearings.
6. Wipe out the strip of Plastigage, coat the bearing and crank throw with assembly lubricant and reinstall the rod to the correct crank throw. Tighten the nuts to specifications in **Table 1**. As the rod nut is being torqued, the rod may bind up on the crank throw; this can be relieved by lightly tapping upon the rod with a hammer.
7. Repeat Steps 4-6 for each rod. Be sure that you assemble each rod with the forge mark

facing up and on the crank throw originally used for that rod. Reconditioned rods may be installed upon any crank throw. Make sure that the rod and cap numbers are aligned.

8. Peen each rod nut into the slot on the rod to lock it in place (**Figure 97**).

CAMSHAFT

Removal

1. When the right half of the crankcase has been removed, lift the camshaft out.
2. Remove the camshaft bearing inserts from the crankcase halves. Mark the back of each insert as it is removed so that it may be reinstalled in the same position.

Inspection

1. Check cam lobes for wear (**Figure 98**). Cam lobes should not be scored and the edges should be square. Slight damage may be removed with a silicon carbide oilstone. Use a 100-200 grit to start with, then polish with a 280-320 grit. Heavy damage means that a new camshaft must be installed.
2. Check camshaft runout at the center bearing as shown in **Figure 99**. Bearing runout must not exceed 0.0015 in. (0.04 mm).
3. Examine the timing gear rivets and check for gear looseness.
4. Check the bearing inserts for wear, scoring or burns (**Figure 83**). Replace if necessary.
5. Check hydraulic valve lifters as described in this chapter.
6. Slightly chamfer the edges of all the bearing bores to prevent bearing pressure seizure.
7. Check the timing gear teeth for wear and proper tooth contact with the small timing gear on the crankshaft.

Installation

Installation is simply a matter of setting the camshaft in place after the crankcase is prepared for assembly. See *Crankcase Assembly.*

NOTE

If a new camshaft is being installed new cam bearings must also be used. If excessive cam lobe wear or scoring was the reason for the new cam, also install new hydraulic lifters. The old lifters are most

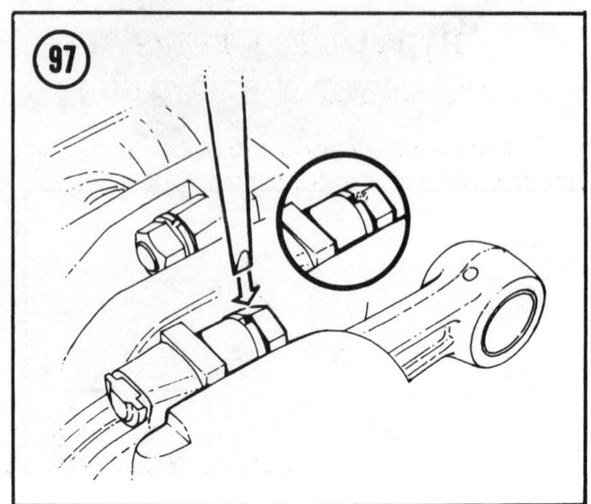

likely unevenly worn and scored and they will quickly tear up a new cam. If the old cam is to be reused it is a good idea to also install new cam bearings. If the crankcase was cam-bored, oversized cam bearings must be used.

HYDRAULIC LIFTERS

Removal/Installation

1. Remove the pushrod tubes. See procedure under *Cylinder Heads* in this chapter.
2. Take the lifters out of the crankcase with a magnetic tool. Lay them out so they may be returned to their original positions in the crankcase.
3. To install lifters, simply insert them into the crankcase and reinstall the pushrod tubes.

NOTE
If a new camshaft is being installed new hydraulic lifters must also be used. The old lifters are most likely unevenly worn and scored and they will quickly tear up a new cam.

4

TABLE 1 ENGINE TIGHTENING TORQUES

Connecting rods nuts	25 ft.-lb.	(35 N•m)
Crankcase halves small nuts	14 ft.-lb.	(20 N•m)
Crankcase halves sealing nuts	22 ft.-lb.	(30 N•m)
Cylinder head nuts		Torque in three stages:
	1. 10 ft.-lb.	(13.6 N•m)
	2. 16 ft.-lb.	(21 N•m)
	3. 22 ft.-lb.	(30 N•m)
Rocker arms to cylinder head	11 ft.-lb.	(15 N•m)
Cooling fan to hub	14 ft.-lb.	(20 N•m)
Hub to crankshaft	22 ft.-lb.	(30 N•m)
Spark plugs	22 ft.-lb.	(30 N•m)
Engine to transmission	22 ft.-lb.	(30 N•m)
Engine carrier to body	18 ft.-lb.	(25 N•m)
Engine support to crankcase	14 ft.-lb.	(20 N•m)
Oil pump to crankcase	18 ft.-lb.	(25 N•m)
Oil cooler adapter to crankcase	18 ft.-lb.	(25 N•m)
Flywheel to crankshaft	80 ft.-lb.	(110 N•m)
Torque converter plate to crankshaft	65 ft.-lb.	(90 N•m)
Clutch to flywheel	18 ft.-lb.	(25 N•m)
Torque converter to drive plate	18 ft.-lb.	(25 N•m)

Table 2 ENGINE SPECIFICATIONS

GENERAL	
No. of cylinders	4
Bore, in. (mm)	3.7 (94)
Stroke	2.80 (71)
Displacement	120.2 (1970)
Compression ratio	7.3:1
Firing order	1-4-3-2
Output (SAE) bhp @ rpm	67 @ 4,200
Torque (SAE) foot-pounds @ rpm	101 @ 3,000
Weight (dry) lb. (kg)	282 (128)
CYLINDERS	
Bore, in. (mm)	3.70 (94)
Cylinder/piston clearance, in. (mm)	0.0016-0.0023 (0.04-0.06)
Out-of-round, in. (mm)	0.0004 (0.01)
Oversize available, mm	0.5, 1.0
PISTONS	
Material	light alloy
Permissible weight deviation in same engine, grams	4
PISTON RINGS	
Number per piston	3
Compression	2
Oil control	1
Ring end gap, in. (mm)	
Top compression	0.014-0.021 (0.35-0.55)
Bottom compression	0.014-0.021 (0.35-0.55)
Oil control	0.010-0.016 (0.25-0.40)
Ring side clearance, in. (mm)	
Top compression	0.0023-0.0035 (0.06-0.09)
Bottom compression	0.0016-0.0027 (0.04-0.07)
Oil control	0.0008-0.0019 (0.02-0.05)
PISTON PINS	
Diameter, in. (mm)	0.9445-0.9448 (23.996-24.000)
Clearance in rod, in. (mm)	0.0004-0.0012 (0.01-0.03)
CRANKSHAFT	
Number of main bearings	4
Main bearing journal diameter, in. (mm)	
Bearings 1-3	2.3609-2.3617 (59.97-59.99)
Bearing 4	1.5739-1.5748 (39.98-40.00)
Connecting rod journal diameter, in. (mm)	2.1644-2.1653 (54.98-55.00)
Main bearing clearances	
Bearings 1 and 3	0.002-0.004 (0.05-0.10)
Bearing 2	0.0012-0.0035 (0.03-0.09)
Bearing 4	0.002-0.004 (0.05-0.10)
End play, in. (mm)	0.0027-0.005 (0.07-0.13)
Permissible out-of-round	
Main bearing journal, in. (mm)	0.0012 (0.03)
Connecting rod journal, in. (mm)	0.0012 (0.03)

(continued)

Table 2 ENGINE SPECIFICATIONS (continued)

CONNECTING RODS	
Weight deviation in same engine, grams	6
Side clearance, in. (mm)	0.004-0.016 (0.1-0.4)
Connecting rod bearing clearance, in. (mm)	0.0008-0.0027 (0.02-0.07)
Piston pin bushing diameter, in. (mm)	0.9454-0.9457 (24.015-24.024)
CAMSHAFT	
Number of bearings	3
Bearing diameter, in. (mm)	0.9837-0.9842 (24.99-25.00)
Bearing clearance, in. (mm)	0.0008-0.0020 (0.02-0.05)
End play, in. (mm)	0.0016-0.0051 (0.04-0.13)
TIMING GEARS	
Backlash, in. (mm)	0.000-0.002 (0.00-0.05)
VALVES — INTAKE	
Head diameter, in. (mm)	1.4764 (37.5)
Stem diameter, in. (mm)	0.3125-0.3129 (7.94-7.95)
Valve guide inside diameter, in. (mm)	0.3150-0.3157 (8.00-8.02)
Valve face angle	29° 30′
Valve seat angle	30°
Valve seat width, in. (mm)	0.07-0.08 (1.8-2.2)
VALVES — EXHAUST	
Head diameter, in. (mm)	1.286-1.299 (32.7-33.0)
Stem diameter, in. (mm)	0.3507-0.3511 (8.91-8.92)
Valve guide inside diameter, in. (mm)	0.3534-0.3538 (8.98-8.99)
Valve face angle	45°
Valve seat angle	45°
Valve seat width, in. (mm)	0.078-0.098 (2.0-2.5)
VALVE SPRINGS	
Length, in. (mm)	1.14 (29)
@ load, lb. (kg)	168-186 (76.5-84.5)
OIL SYSTEM	
Oil pressure (SAE 10W-30 @ 158°F and 2,500 rpm)	28 psi (2.0 kg/cm²) min.
Oil pressure relief valve spring	
Length, in. (mm)	1.54 (39.0)
@ load, lb. (kg)	15-19 psi (6.8-8.8)

Table 3 END PLAY SHIM THICKNESS

0.0095 in. (0.24 mm)	0.0134 in. (0.34 mm)
0.0118 in. (0.38 mm)	0.0142 in. (0.36 mm)
0.0126 in. (0.32 mm)	0.0150 in. (0.38 mm)

NOTE: If you own a 1982 model, first check the Supplement at the back of the book for any new service information.

CHAPTER FIVE

COOLING, VENTILATION AND HEATING

The cooling, heating and ventilation systems on the Vanagon are closely related. Cool air from a large fan mounted on the rear end of the crankshaft cools the engine (**Figure 1**). Cooling air is directed to the cylinder heads and cylinders by metal cover shrouds (**Figure 2**).

Cooling air temperature and warm-up rate are thermostatically controlled. The thermostat is positioned on the engine where it can sense the temperature of the cooling air as it leaves the cooling shrouds. This is an accurate method of determining engine temperature. When the engine is started from cold, the thermostat is constricted, holding 2 air control plates partially closed and limiting the volume of cooling air blown to the engine from the large cooling fan. The engine warms up quickly without full cooling air flow. Once the engine is warm, the thermostat expands, allowing the air control plates to fully open permitting the maximum volume of cool air to be admitted.

The heating and ventilation system for the Vanagon is shown in **Figure 3**. A squirrel cage (heater blower) fan is bolted to the alternator and driven by the alternator belt. This fan blows air to the heat exchangers. The hot air from the heat exchangers is allowed to flow through the system by 2 flaps controlled by cables from the vehicle dashboard. Hot air leaving the engine area is routed under the vehicle via a duct to the front warm air distributor where it enters the interior.

Some models have (as optional equipment) a heater booster which is explained in this chapter.

The ventilation system is a forced air type. Air is taken in from the front of the vehicle through the plastic grille, behind which is located the ventilation chamber. Cool air is routed through the chamber into the vehicle by air hoses and ducts. See **Figure 3**.

COOLING SYSTEM

Fan Housing Removal/Installation

The rear fan housing may be removed with the engine installed, but component removal will be slightly more difficult. If the fan housing is to be removed with the engine installed, a portion of the exhaust system must be disassembled and removed so that the fan housing will come out. Refer to **Figure 1** for the following procedure.

1. If the engine is installed perform the following (see *Exhaust System Removal/Installation*, Chapter Six):
   a. On California models, remove the muffler and crossover pipe first. Support

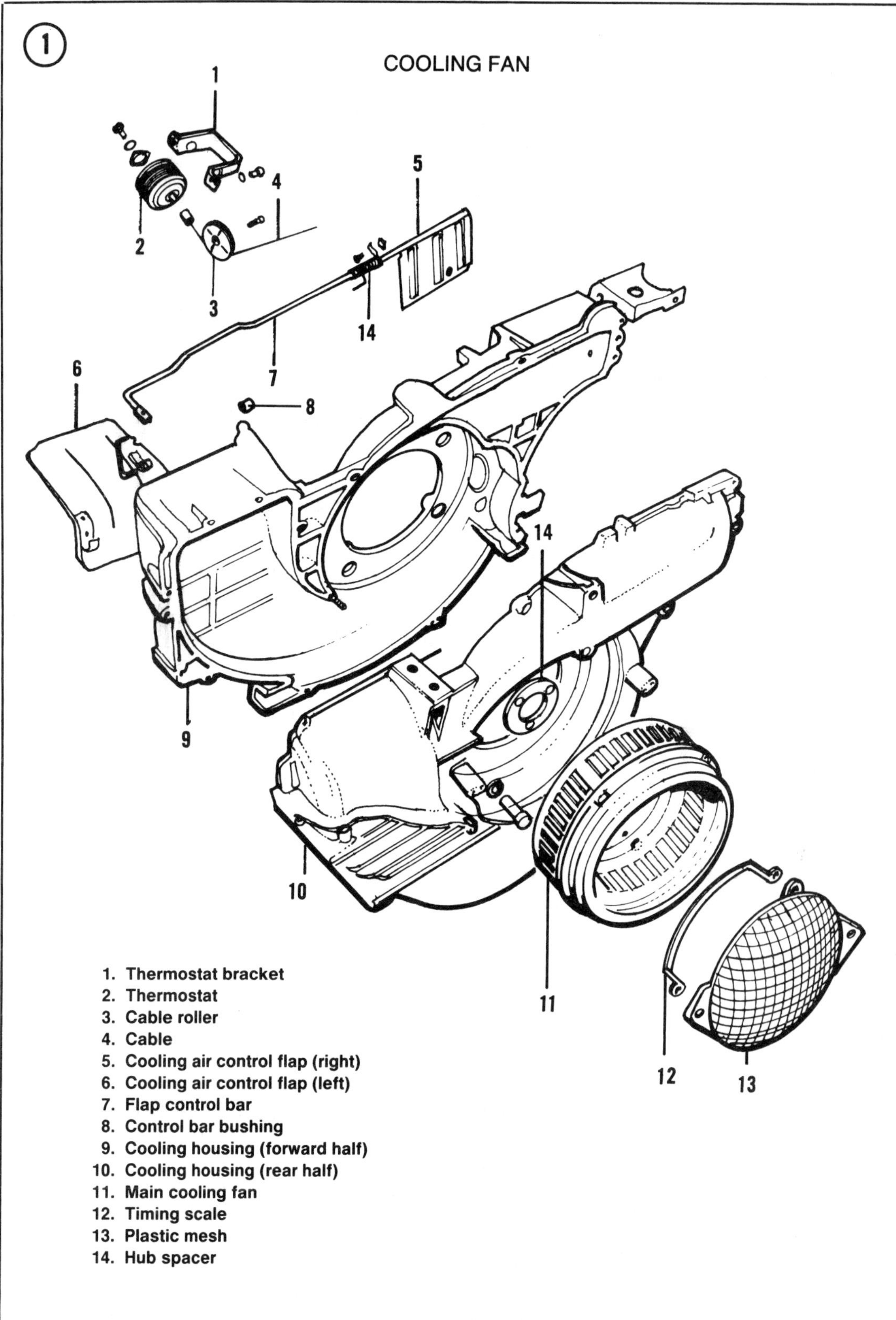

1. Thermostat bracket
2. Thermostat
3. Cable roller
4. Cable
5. Cooling air control flap (right)
6. Cooling air control flap (left)
7. Flap control bar
8. Control bar bushing
9. Cooling housing (forward half)
10. Cooling housing (rear half)
11. Main cooling fan
12. Timing scale
13. Plastic mesh
14. Hub spacer

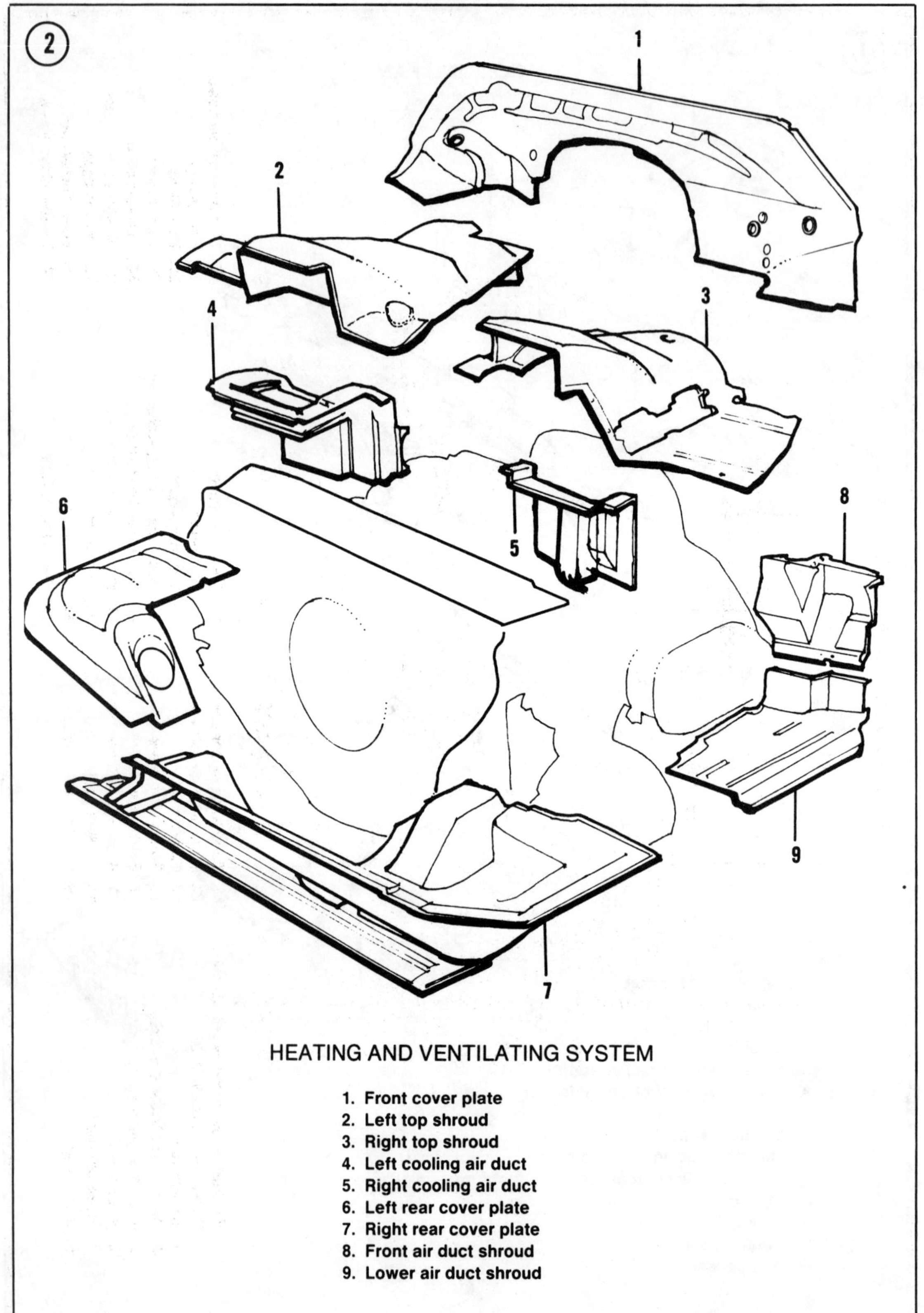

HEATING AND VENTILATING SYSTEM

1. Front cover plate
2. Left top shroud
3. Right top shroud
4. Left cooling air duct
5. Right cooling air duct
6. Left rear cover plate
7. Right rear cover plate
8. Front air duct shroud
9. Lower air duct shroud

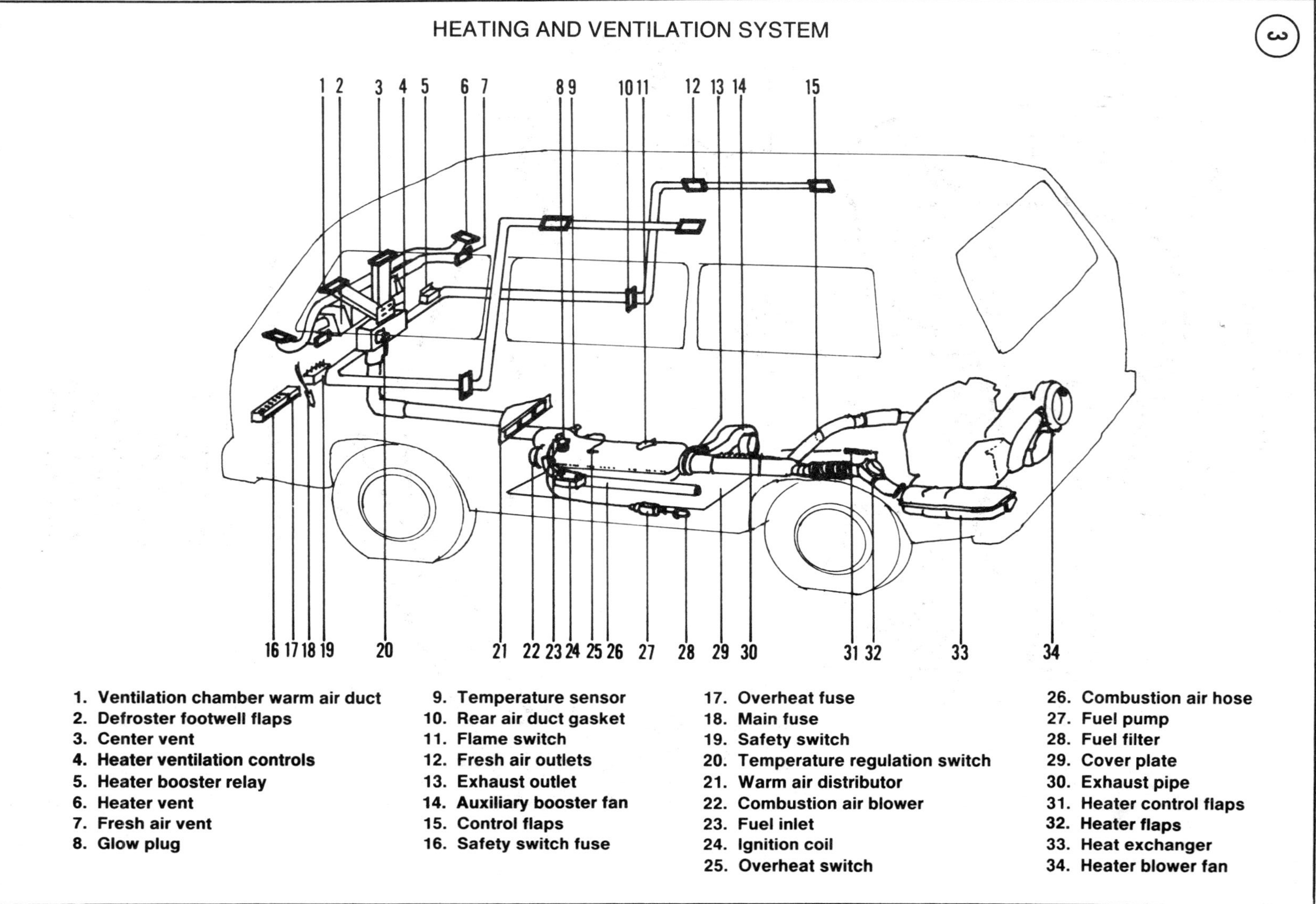
3
HEATING AND VENTILATION SYSTEM
1 2
3
4
5
6 7
8 9
10 11
12 13 14
15
16 17 18 19
20
21
22 23 24 25 26
27
28
29
30
31 32
33
34
1. Ventilation chamber warm air duct
2. Defroster footwell flaps
3. Center vent
4. Heater ventilation controls
5. Heater booster relay
6. Heater vent
7. Fresh air vent
8. Glow plug
9. Temperature sensor
10. Rear air duct gasket
11. Flame switch
12. Fresh air outlets
13. Exhaust outlet
14. Auxiliary booster fan
15. Control flaps
16. Safety switch fuse
17. Overheat fuse
18. Main fuse
19. Safety switch
20. Temperature regulation switch
21. Warm air distributor
22. Combustion air blower
23. Fuel inlet
24. Ignition coil
25. Overheat switch
26. Combustion air hose
27. Fuel pump
28. Fuel filter
29. Cover plate
30. Exhaust pipe
31. Heater control flaps
32. Heater flaps
33. Heat exchanger
34. Heater blower fan

5

the left exchanger with blocks; if allowed to hang down the heat exchanger will be damage.

b. On 49-state and Canadian models, remove the muffler, catalytic converter, EGR pipe and crossover pipe first.

c. Remove the rubber heater blower boot (**Figure 4**).

2. Remove the plastic warm air duct and elbow pipe which lead from the heater blower (**Figure 5**).

3. Remove the 3 bolts which secure heater blower housing to the alternator. Remove the heater blower housing.

4. Remove the plastic screen mesh (also timing scale) which covers the large cooling fan (**Figure 5**).

WARNING
Before removing the alternator, always disconnect the battery. This will prevent accidental electrical fires, injury and possible loss of the vehicle.

5. Remove the alternator. See *Alternator Removal/Installation* in Chapter Seven.

6. Remove the 3 bolts which hold the cooling fan to the center hub on the rear of the crankshaft. Pull the fan out of the housing.

7. Remove the small bolts that hold the cooling fan housing halves together. When all the small bolts are removed, separate the fan housing halves. It may be necessary to gently pry them apart with a screwdriver.

8. Disconnect the thermostat cable (**Figure 6**).

9. Remove the bolts which hold the front half of the cooling fan housing to the crankcase (**Figure** 7). Remove the housing half from the engine.

10. Remove the fan hub with a special puller plate as shown in **Figure 8**. The puller plate can be improvised by inserting three 1/8 in. (3.25 mm) thick strips of metal between the case and the fan hub. Insert the hub bolts to hold the strips in place. Tighten the bolts evenly (don't allow the metal strips to slip out) and the hub will be pushed off the crankshaft. Make sure that the Woodruff key in the crankshaft end is aligned properly before reinstalling the fan hub.

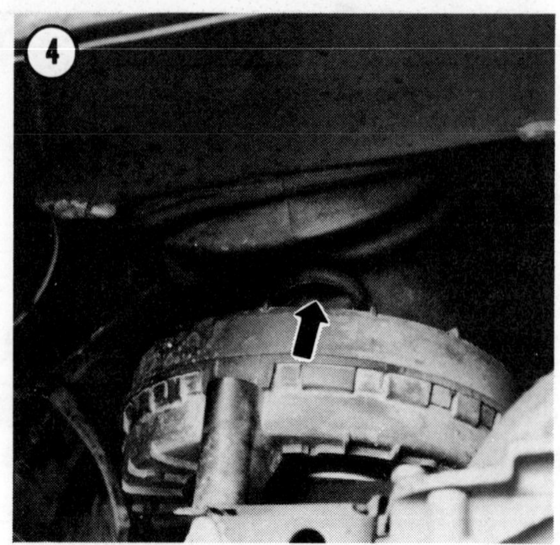

NOTE
*Before reinstalling the fan hub, install a new rear oil seal. See **Rear Oil Seal** in Chapter Four.*

11. Installation is the reverse of removal. See *Cleaning and Inspection* before installation. After installation adjust the thermostat cable; see procedure in this chapter.

Cooling Shrouds Removal/Installation

The metal cooling shrouds should be removed with the engine out of the vehicle.

WARNING
Before working on electrical lines, always disconnect the battery. This will prevent accidental electrical fires and injury.

Refer to **Figure 2** for the following procedure.

1. Remove the engine (Chapter Four).
2. Remove the air cleaner assembly and all the fuel injection components from the top of the engine (Chapter Six).
3. Disconnect the EGR pipe at the muffler and at the EGR valve (Chapter Six).
4. Remove the distributor (Chapter Seven).
5. Remove any other engine accessory which may hinder removal of the cooling shrouds.

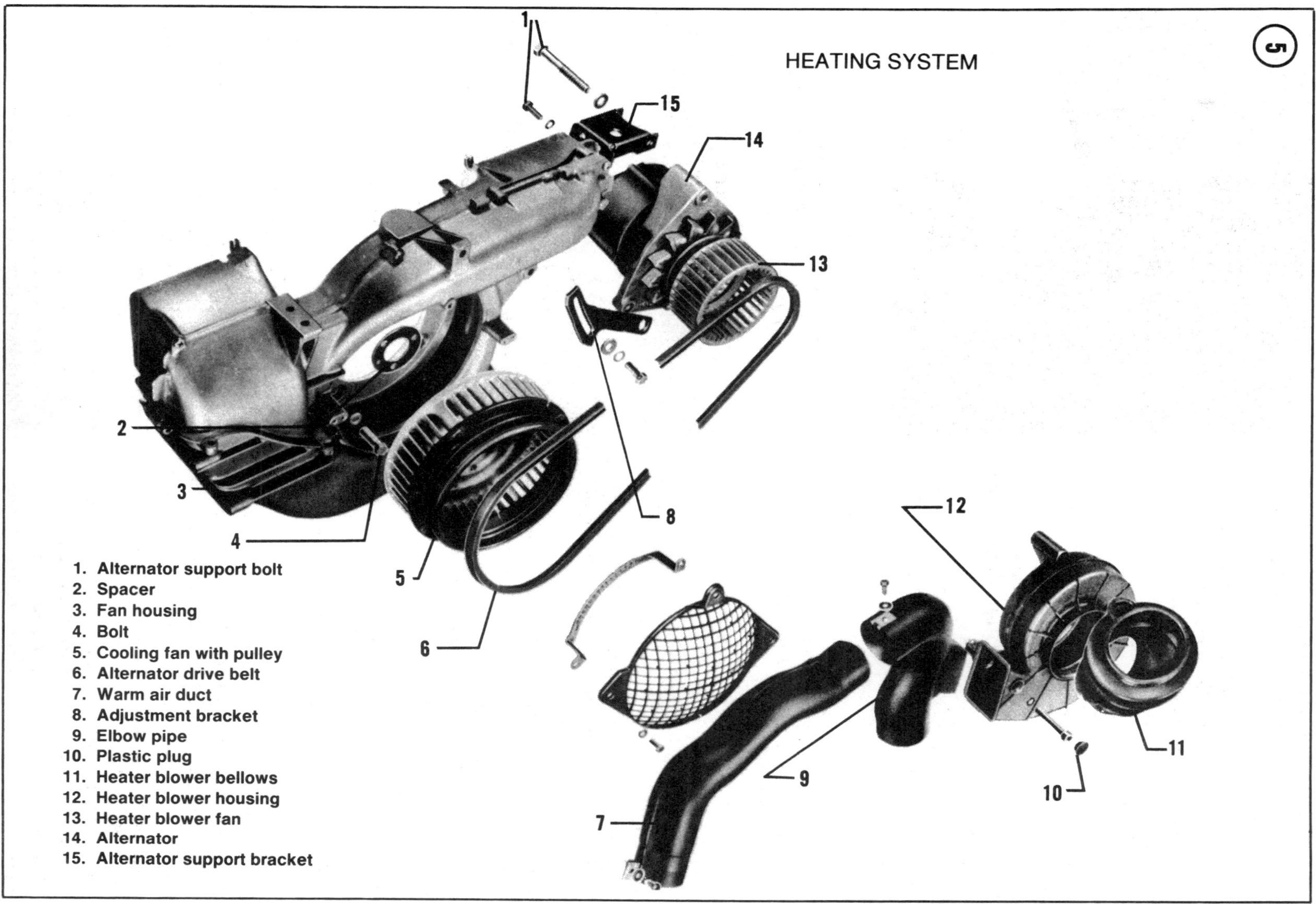

HEATING SYSTEM

1. Alternator support bolt
2. Spacer
3. Fan housing
4. Bolt
5. Cooling fan with pulley
6. Alternator drive belt
7. Warm air duct
8. Adjustment bracket
9. Elbow pipe
10. Plastic plug
11. Heater blower bellows
12. Heater blower housing
13. Heater blower fan
14. Alternator
15. Alternator support bracket

6. Remove the plastic warm air duct and elbow pipe which lead from the heater blower (**Figure 5**). Remove the right and left rear cover plates.
7. Remove the front cover plate.
8. Remove the right and left top shrouds.
9. Remove the right and left, front and lower air duct shrouds.
10. Remove the left and right cooling air ducts.
11. Installation is the reverse of removal. See *Cleaning and Inspection* before installing shrouds. After installation, adjust the thermostat cable; see procedure in this chapter.

NOTE

To prevent rattling and air leaks, use new screws when installing the cooling shrouds.

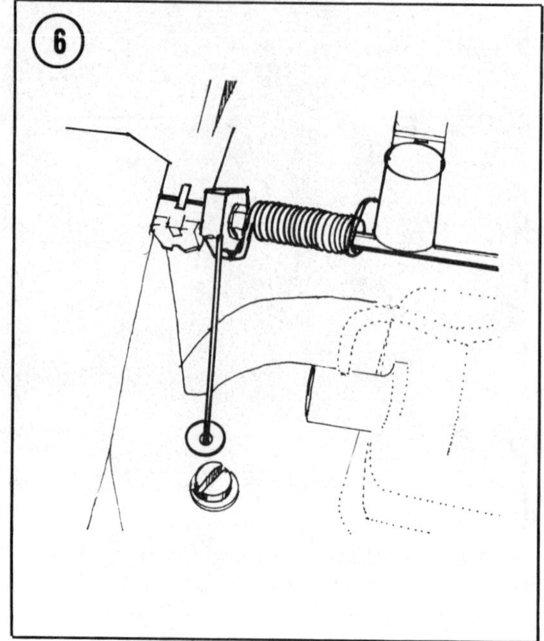

Fan and Shrouds Cleaning and Inspection

1. The interior of the cooling fan housing should be kept absolutely clean. Over the course of many miles, dirt and oil may cake up inside. The best way to clean out the housing is to take the disassembled halves to a coin-operated car wash and blast the dirt out with high-pressure soap and water.
2. Clean out the interior of the heater fan housing, the warm air duct and elbow pipes. Care should be exercised when handling plastic parts. They should be cleaned by hand using soapy water and a scrub brush. Avoid the use of solvents and harsh cleansers.
3. Check the fan housing halves for cracks. Cracks should be welded.
4. Inspect the air cooling flaps for freedom of movement. If necessary, oil the connecting bar between the flaps and the bushings in which it turns. Replace any part in which wear or visible damage is found.
5. Check the small bolts that hold the fan housing halves together. If they are stripped, use longer bolts which will protrude through the other side of the housing. Secure the protruding bolt with a nut and a lockwasher.
6. Check the large cooling fan for cracks where it bolts to the hub in the crankshaft. Inspect the crankshaft hub for stripped threads or cracks.

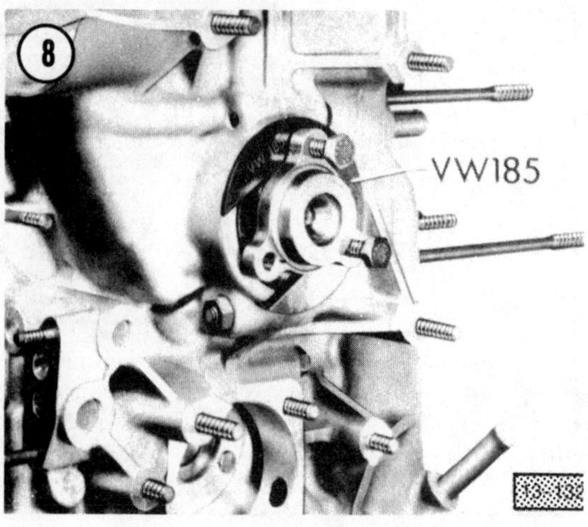

9

10

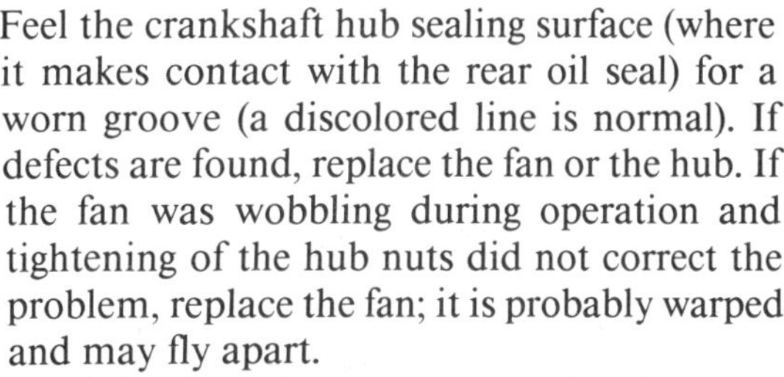

Feel the crankshaft hub sealing surface (where it makes contact with the rear oil seal) for a worn groove (a discolored line is normal). If defects are found, replace the fan or the hub. If the fan was wobbling during operation and tightening of the hub nuts did not correct the problem, replace the fan; it is probably warped and may fly apart.

7. If the shrouds are rusty, sand and repaint them. Use a rust-preventive black paint.

Air Control Thermostat Removal/Installation

The thermostat is held in a bracket which is bolted to the crankcase directly under cylinders No. 1 and No. 2.

1. Remove the right lower air duct shroud to gain access to the thermostat (**Figure 2**).
2. Loosen the small bolt (holding the thermostat) in front of the bracket (**Figure 9**).
3. Hold the hex head on the thermostat cable with a wrench and unscrew the thermostat by hand until it comes out (**Figure 10**).
4. Installation is the reverse of removal. After installation adjust the cable; see procedure in this chapter.

Thermostat Cleaning and Testing

The thermostat should be free of grease; if not, clean it with solvent. Immerse the thermostat in a pan of hot water (185-194° F/85-90° C) for at least 5 minutes. The thermostat should expand to a length of at least 1 13/16 in. (46 mm); if not, replace it. See dimension "a" in **Figure 11**.

Check the cable roller (**Figure 12**). It should roll freely without binding; if not, lubricate or replace it.

Thermostat Adjustment

CAUTION

The thermostat cable can only be adjusted when the engine is stone cold (the thermostat contracted) or the adjustment will be wrong and the engine will overheat.

1. Make sure that the return spring ends are hooked to the cable bracket and the retaining boss (**Figure 13**).

NOTE

Broken springs must be replaced. To replace the spring, the fan housing must be completely disassembled and the control plates removed. See ***Fan Housing Removal/Installation*** *in this chapter.*

2. Loosen the cable bracket screw (**Figure 6**).
3. Rotate the bracket to the closed position (indicated by the large arrow) to close the control plates (**Figure 14**). Take up any cable slack by pulling up on the cable with pliers in

the direction indicated by the small arrow.

4. Tighten the cable bracket screw (**Figure 6**).

HEATING AND VENTILATION

Heater Cable Replacement

The heater cables work in 2 sets: the inner control flap cables and the outer control flap cables. The inner 2 cables attach to heater control levers on the dashboard and run under the body to a point over the transaxle where they connect to the outer cables. The outer 2 cables run from this point and connect to the heater control flaps.

Inner cable replacement

1. Remove the instrument panel to gain access to the heater system controls (Chapter Seven).
2. Push the heater knob in the direction shown in **Figure 15** and loosen the retaining bracket which holds the cables. Unhook the cables from the control unit.
3. Loosen the cable connectors on the heater control flaps (**Figure 16**).
4. Disconnect the inner cables from the outer cables near the heater control flaps (**Figure 17**).
5. Trace the inner cables through the under body. Pull the cables out of the holding fittings and replace with new cables.
6. Push the control knob to the left as shown in **Figure 15**. Connect the cables to the control unit and tighten the retaining bracket.
7. Connect the inner cables to the outer cables (**Figure 17**).

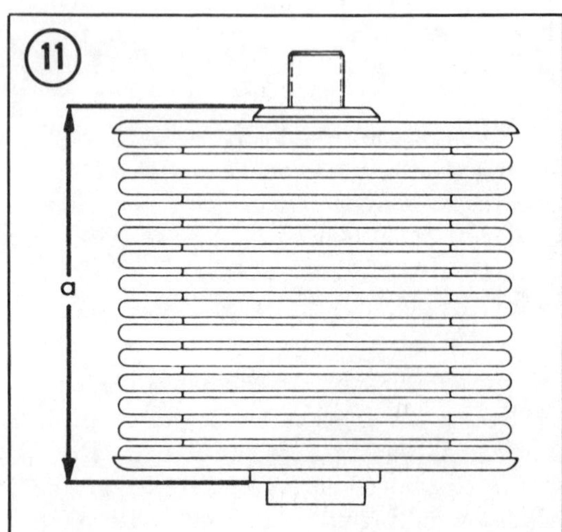

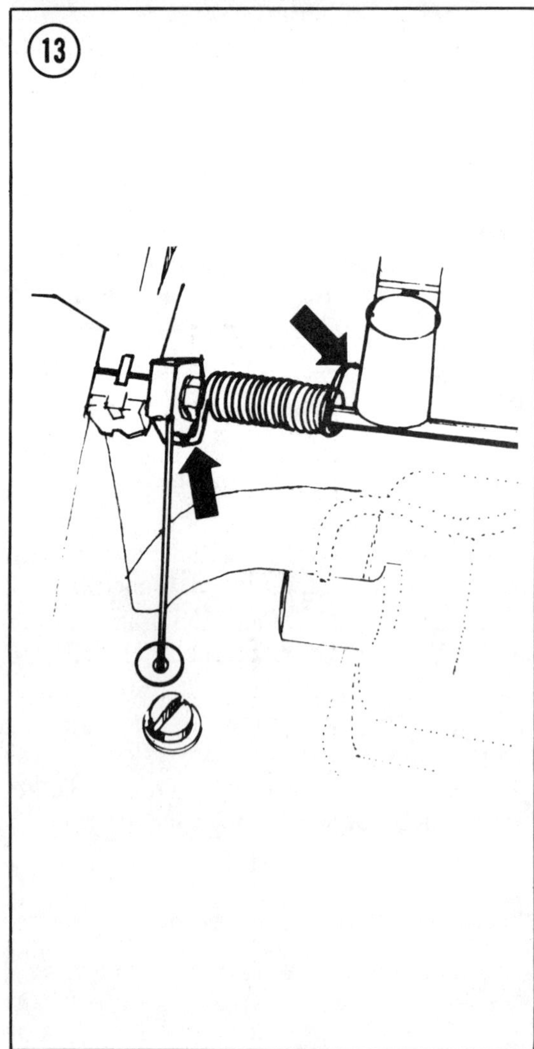

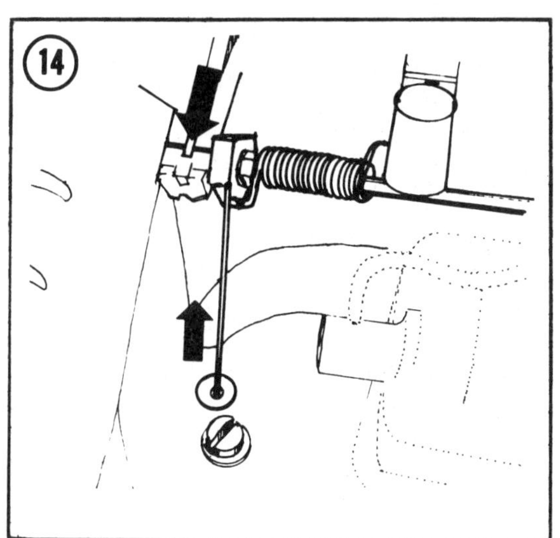
14

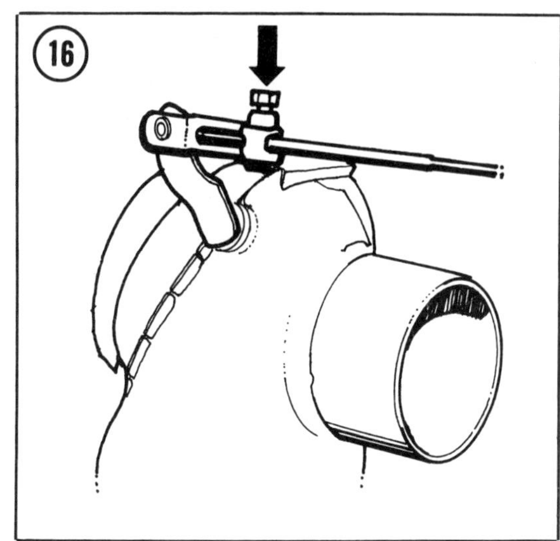
16

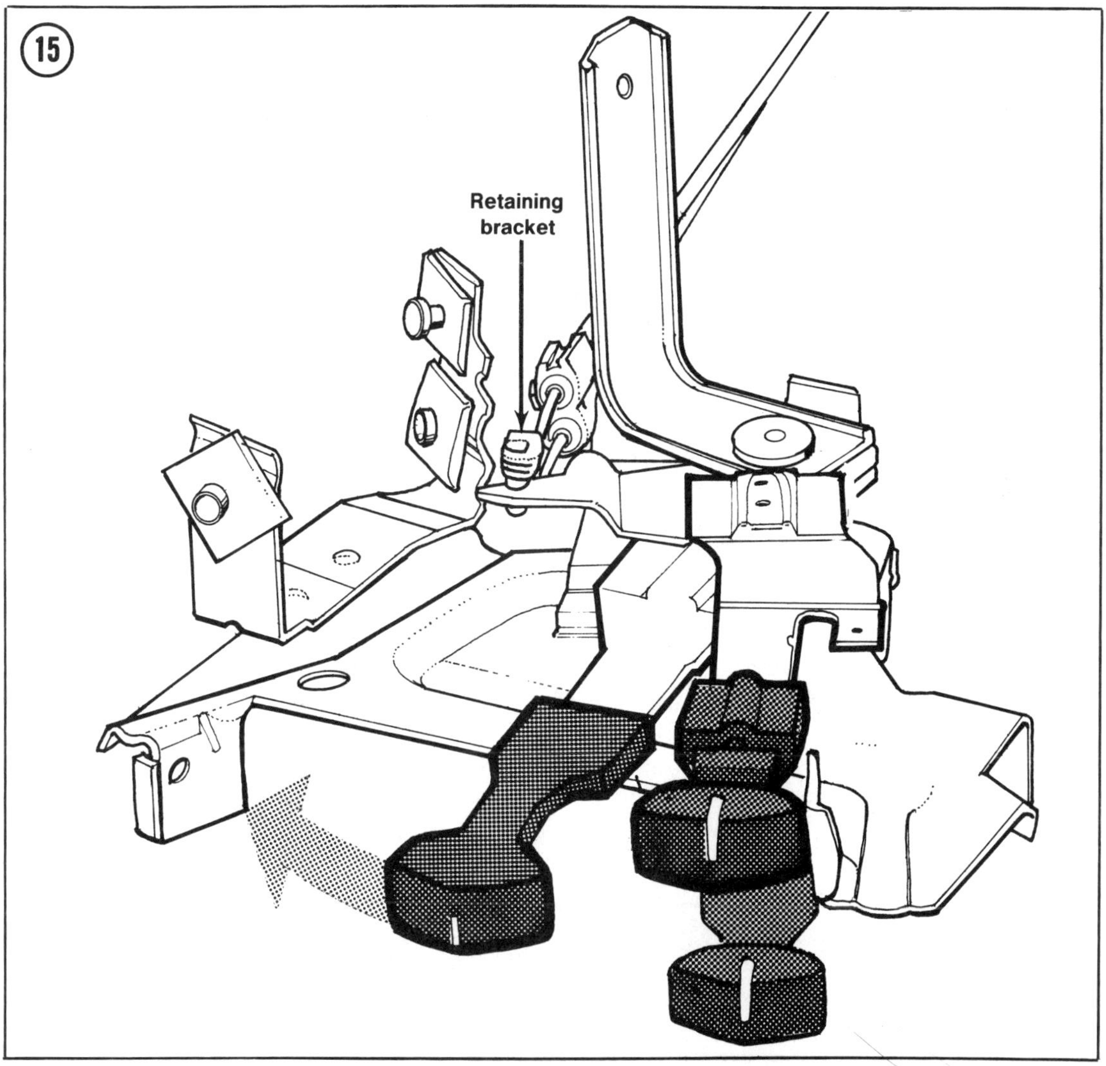

15
Retaining bracket

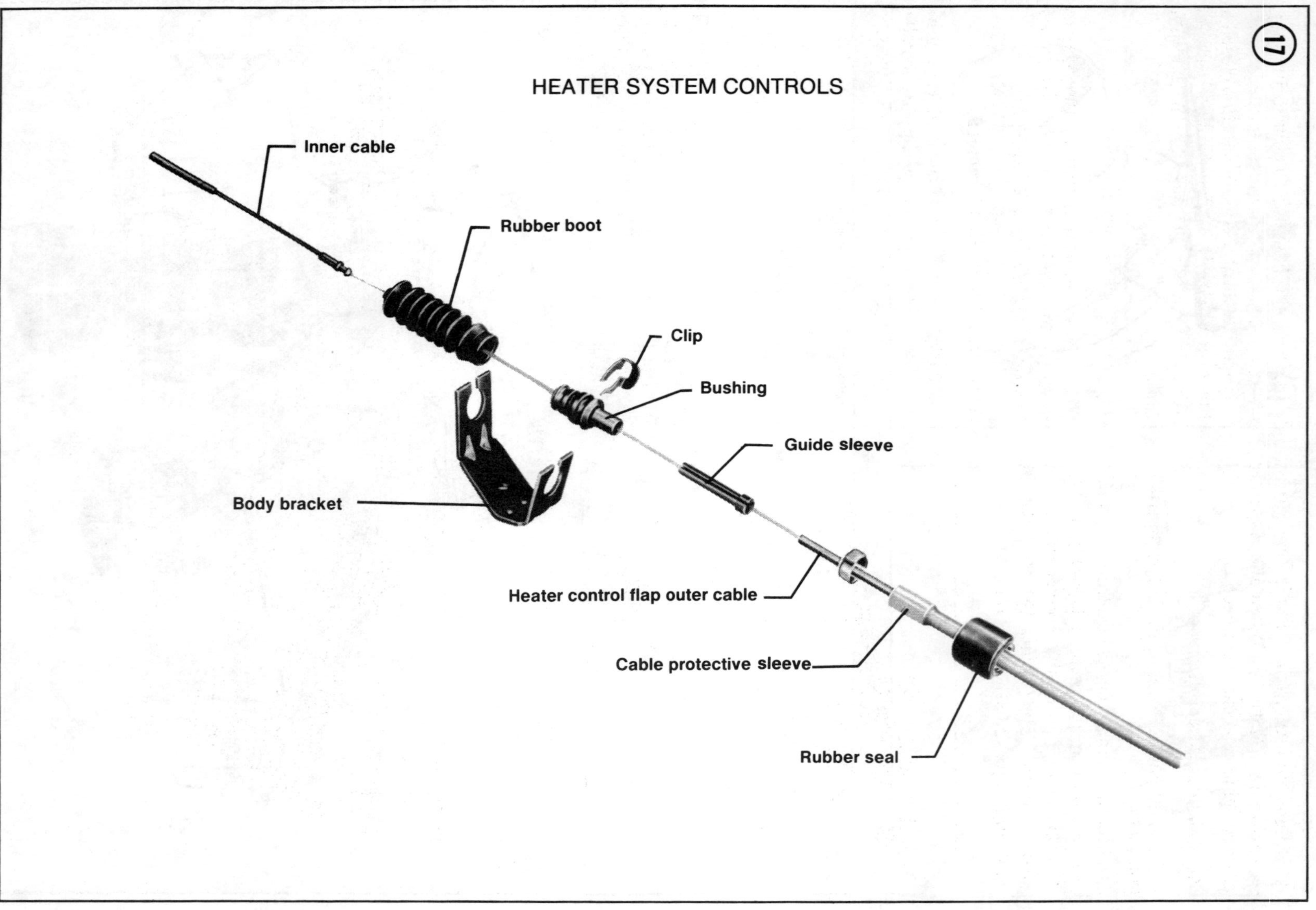
17
HEATER SYSTEM CONTROLS
Inner cable
Rubber boot
Clip
Bushing
Guide sleeve
Body bracket
Heater control flap outer cable
Cable protective sleeve
Rubber seal

8. Rotate the heater control unit flaps closed as shown in **Figure 18**. When the flaps are closed, tighten the cable connector.

Outer cable replacement

1. Push the control knob to the left as shown in **Figure 15**.
2. Disconnect the inner cables from the outer cables near the heater control flaps (**Figure 17**).
3. Loosen the outer cable connection on the heater control flaps (**Figure 16**). Remove the cable and replace with a new one.

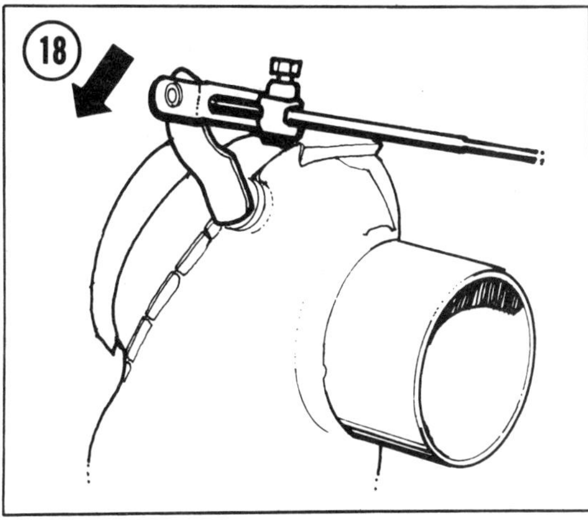

4. Connect the new outer cable to the inner cable.
5. Rotate the heater control unit flap closed as shown in **Figure 18**. When the flap is closed, insert the cable end and tighten the cable connector.

Heat Exchanger Replacement

Removal and installation of the heat exchangers are described in *Exhaust System Removal/Installation* in Chapter Six.

Heater and Ventilation Chambers

Figure 19 shows the heater and ventilation chambers as they look when they are installed in the dashboard and in an exploded view.

Removal/Installation

Refer to **Figure 19** for the following procedure.

1. Remove the instrument panel (Chapter Seven).
2. Disconnect the cables from the heat/ventilation control levers. Pull the heater control knobs off the levers then pry the trim plate off the dashboard. Remove the control lever assembly.

5

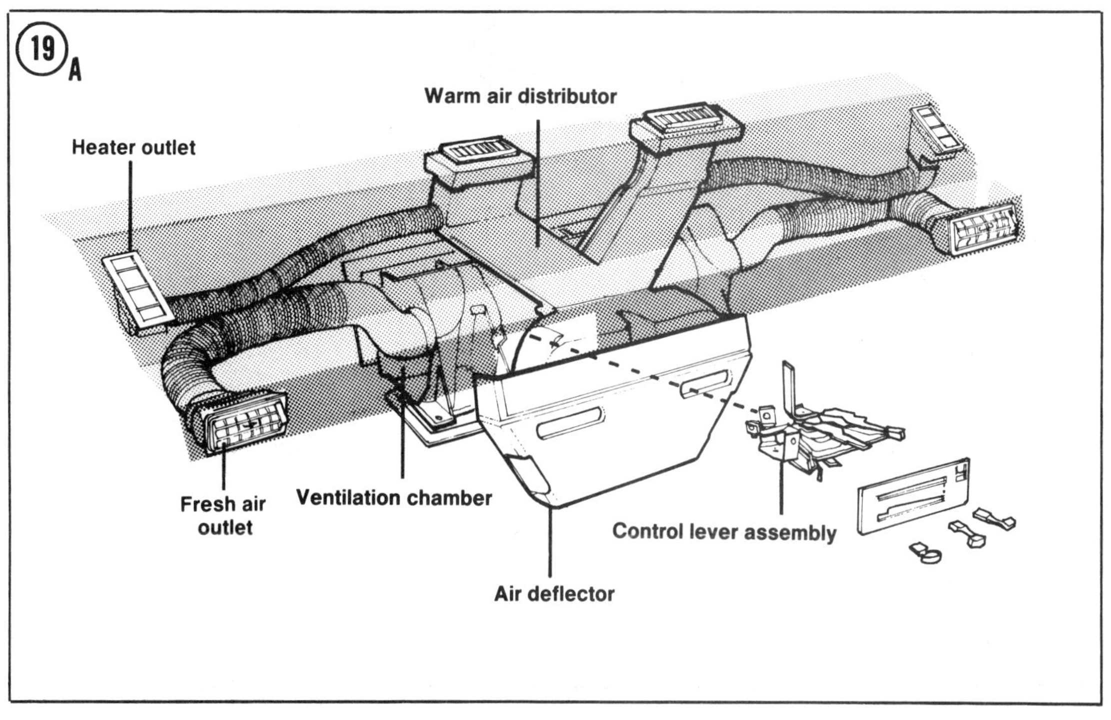

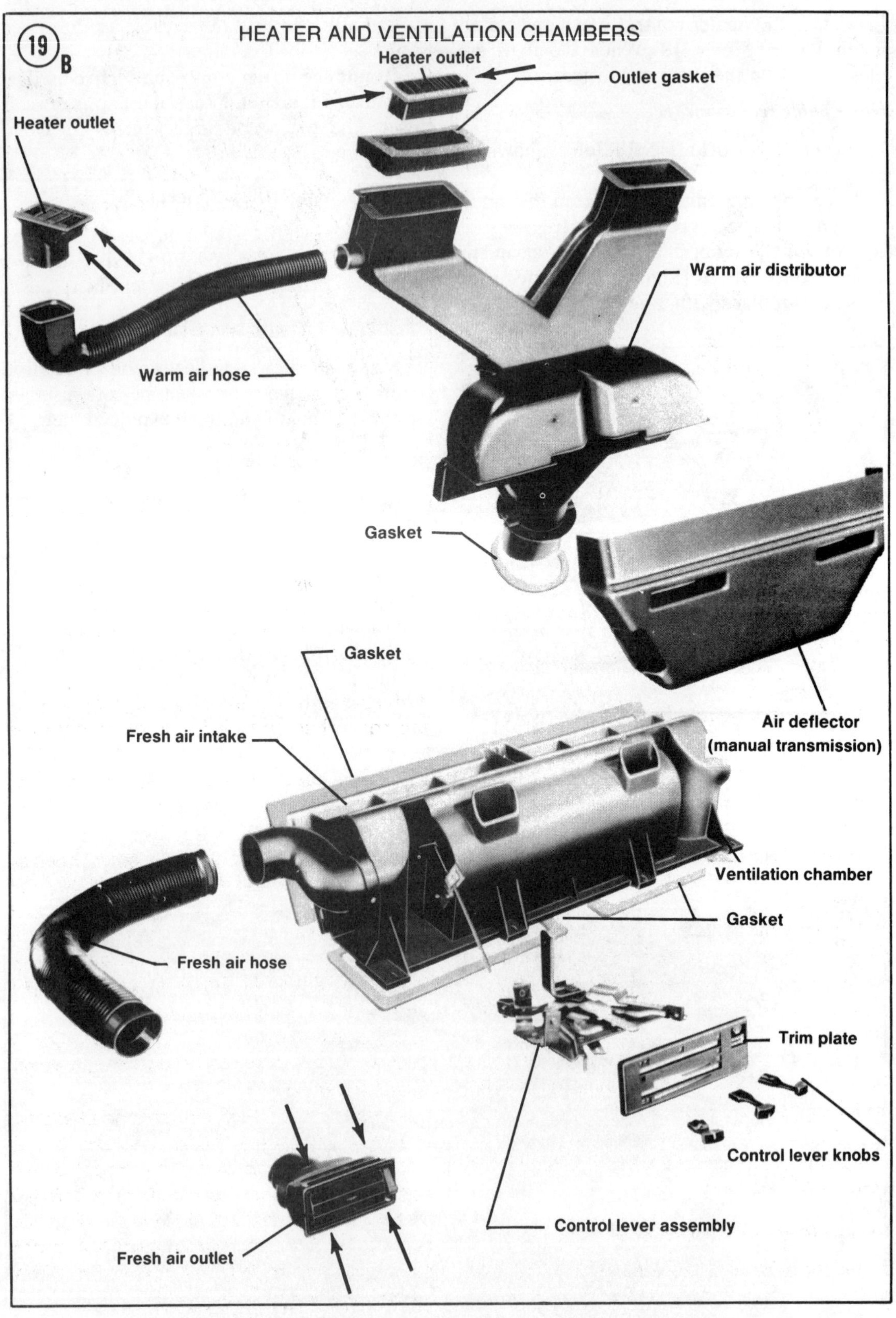
19 B
HEATER AND VENTILATION CHAMBERS
Heater outlet
Outlet gasket
Heater outlet
Warm air distributor
Warm air hose
Gasket
Gasket
Air deflector
(manual transmission)
Fresh air intake
Ventilation chamber
Gasket
Fresh air hose
Trim plate
Control lever knobs
Control lever assembly
Fresh air outlet

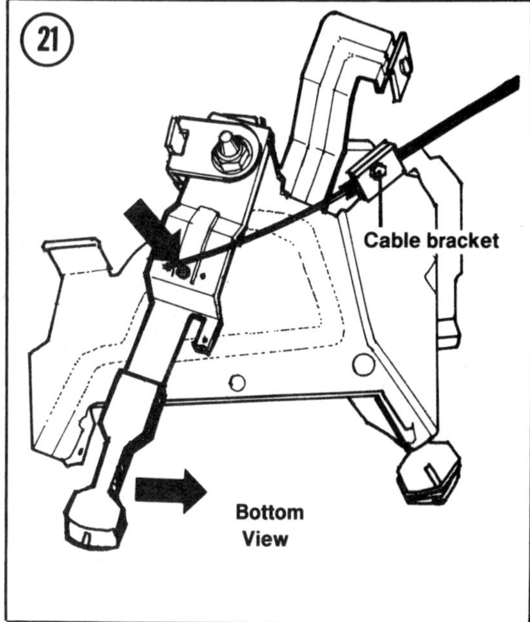

3. Remove the air deflector by pulling it straight out toward the shift lever. Automatic transmission shift lever must be in DRIVE for deflector removal.
4. Pull the warm air hoses off of the warm air distributor.
5. Remove the heater outlets by reaching behind the dashboard and pressing in the 2 lugs which clip the units in.

6. Remove the spare tire to gain access to the bottom of the warm air distributor. Loosen the clamp and pull the large heating air hose off the connection on the bottom of the warm air distributor.
7. Unscrew the fasteners which hold the warm air distributor in place and remove it from the body.
8. Pull the fresh air hoses off of the air distributor.
9. Remove the fresh air outlets by reaching behind the dashboard and pressing in the 4 lugs which clip the units in.
10. Remove the screws which hold the ventilation chamber to the body. Remove the ventilation chamber.

Installation/Cable Adjustment

1. Perform Steps 3-10 in *Removal* in reverse order.

NOTE
When installing the ventilation and heating chambers, use a silicone sealer along with new sealing gaskets. This will prevent future water leakage.

2. Install the control lever assembly. Install the trim plate and push the knobs onto the levers.
3. Loosen the outer heater flap control cables at the heater flaps (**Figure 16**).
4. Loosely install the heater flap cables in the retaining bracket then push the control knob to the left as shown in **Figure 15**. Connect the heater flap cables to the control unit and tighten the bracket.
5. Rotate the heater flap closed as shown in **Figure 18**. When the flap is closed, tighten the outer cable connector (**Figure 16**).
6. Close the flap in the ventilation chamber by pulling the chamber lever against spring tension (**Figure 20**).
7. Hook the cable in the lower lever as shown in **Figure 21**. Loosely install the cable in the retaining bracket. Push the lever in the direction of the arrow then tighten the cable bracket.
8. Pull the rod (attached to the cable under the vehicle) for the passenger compartment warm air distributor in the direction of the arrow shown in **Figure 22**.

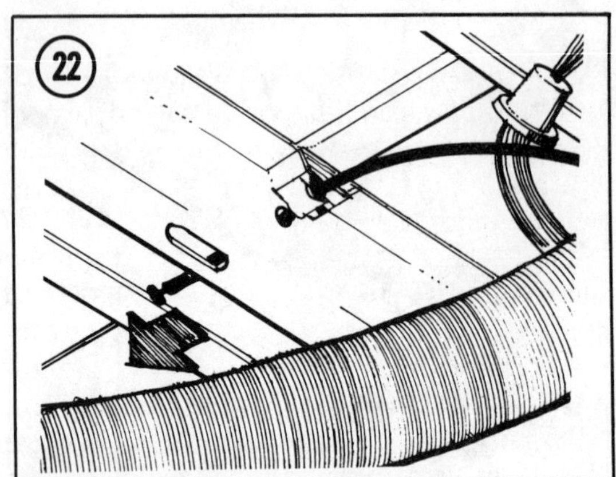

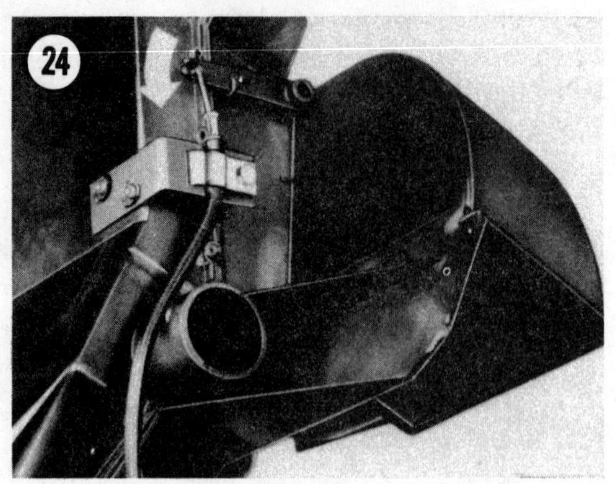

23

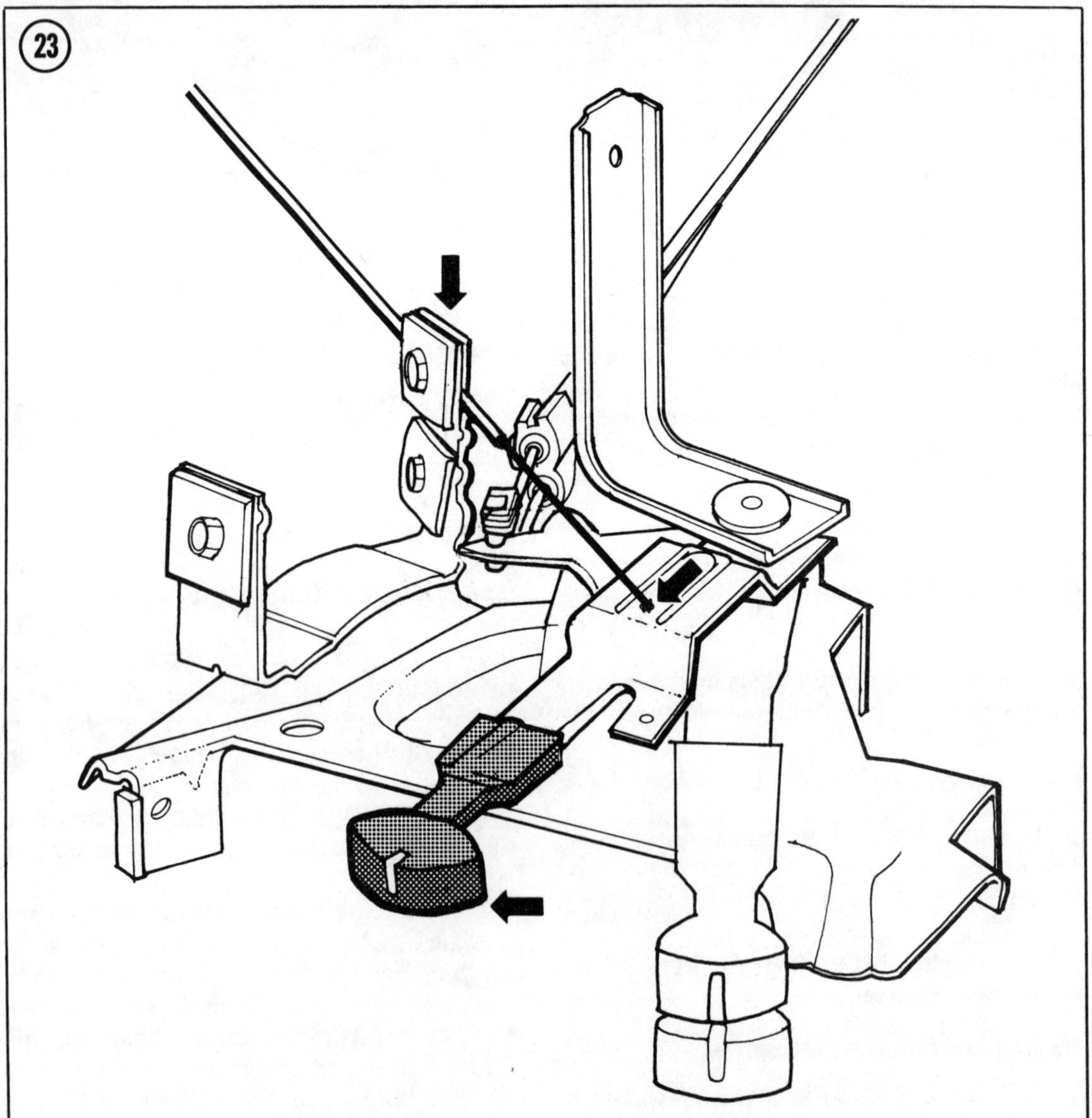

9. Push the upper control lever in the direction of the arrow shown in **Figure 23**. Hook the cable for the passenger compartment warm air distributor to the upper control lever. Install and tighten the cable in the lever bracket.

10. Push the driver's warm air distributor control lever in the direction of the arrow shown in **Figure 24**.

11. Loosely install the cable in the retaining bracket and hook the warm air distributor cable to the upper lever as shown in **Figure 25**. Tighten the cable bracket.

HEATER BOOSTER

The heater booster is an optional gasoline furnace (mounted under the vehicle) designed to assist the heat exchangers in extremely cold weather. **Figure 3** shows where the booster is located under the vehicle.

The heater booster burns fuel drawn from the vehicle's fuel tank at a rate of 2 U.S. pints per hour (1 liter per hour), increasing the temperature of the air from the heat exchangers to a desired level by thermostatic control.

Hot air from the heater booster is blown to the warm air distributor by a fan. The heat produced by the heater booster will vary ac-

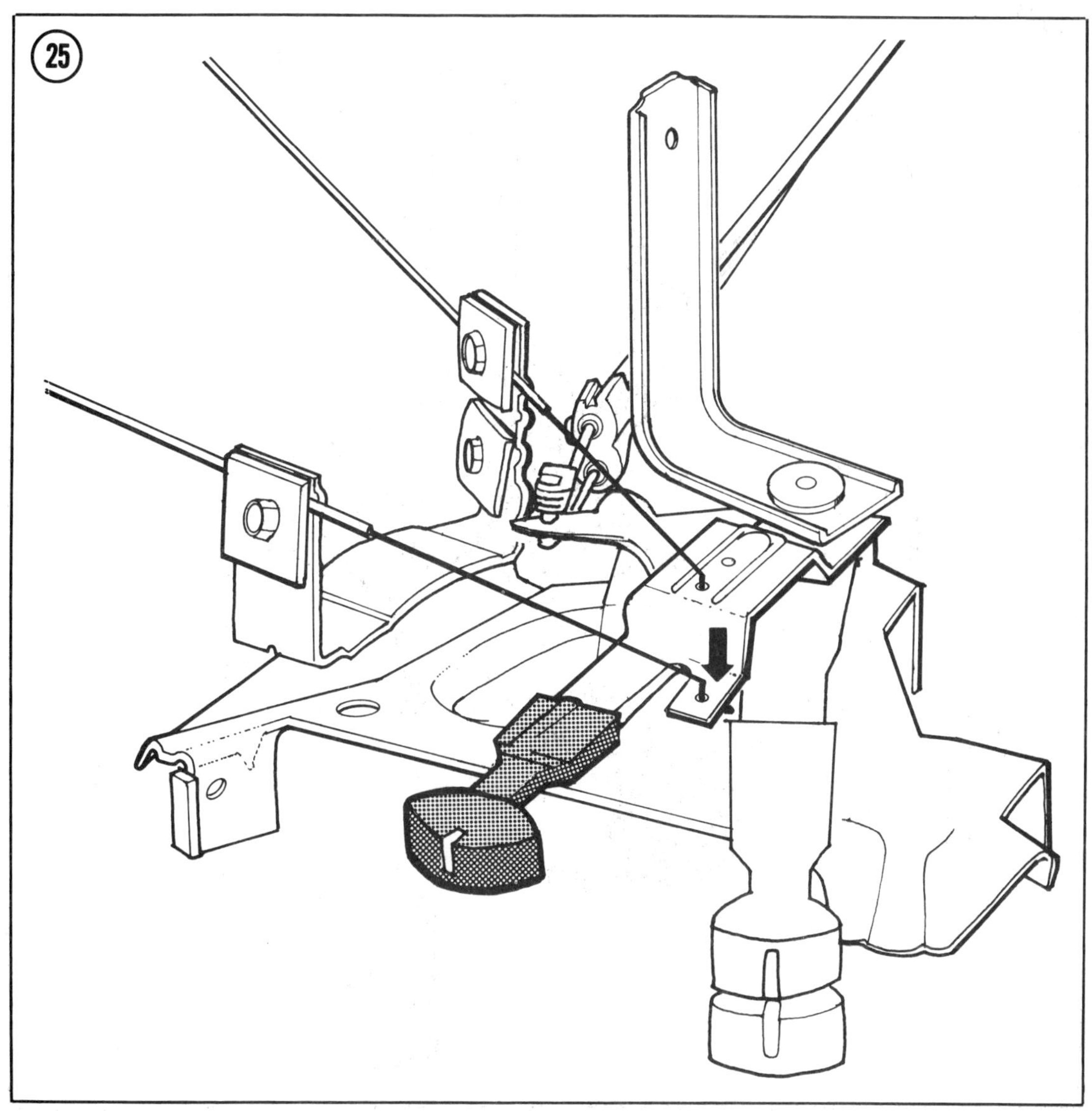

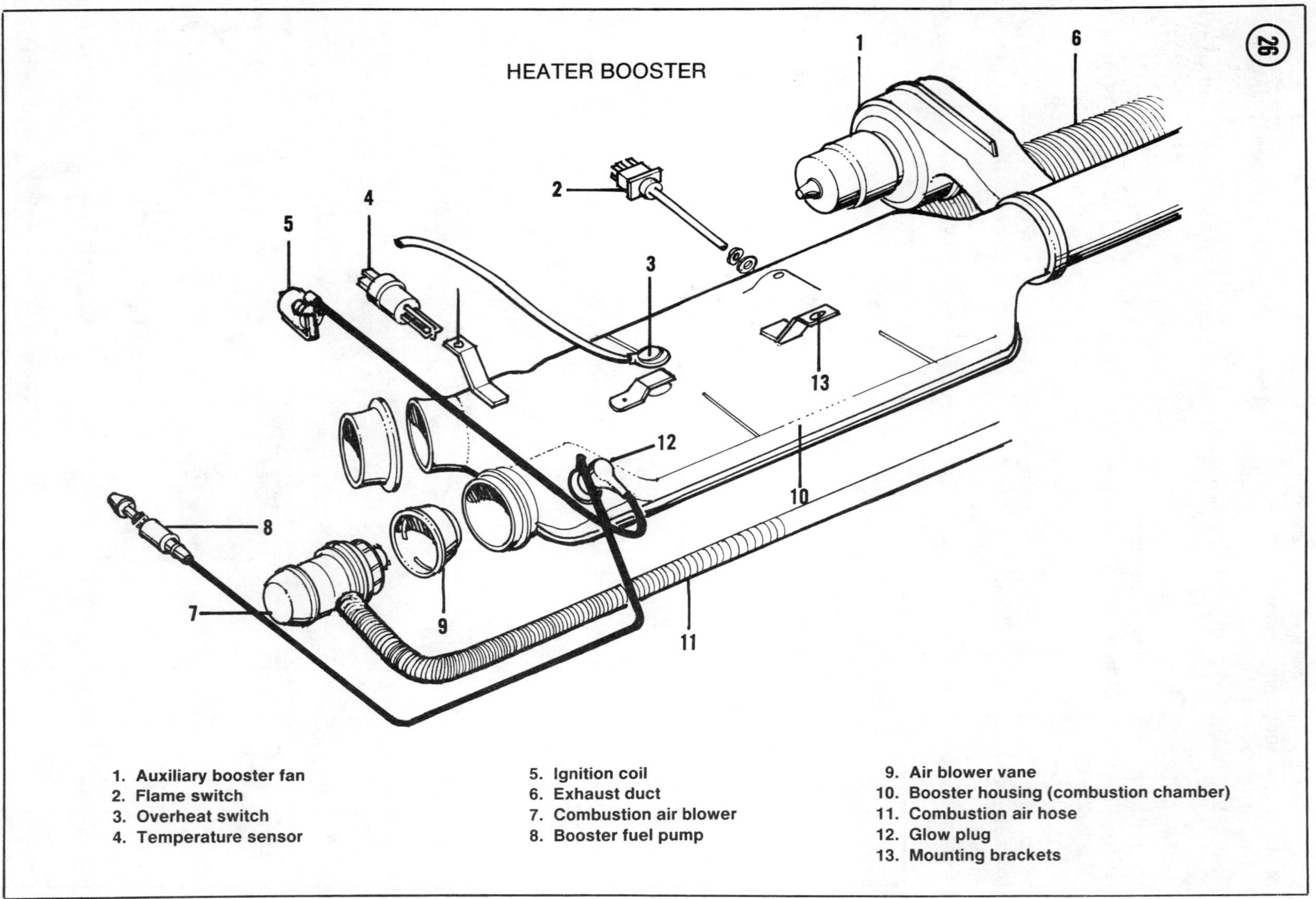
26
HEATER BOOSTER
1
2
3
4
5
6
7
8
9
10
11
12
13
1. Auxiliary booster fan
2. Flame switch
3. Overheat switch
4. Temperature sensor
5. Ignition coil
6. Exhaust duct
7. Combustion air blower
8. Booster fuel pump
9. Air blower vane
10. Booster housing (combustion chamber)
11. Combustion air hose
12. Glow plug
13. Mounting brackets

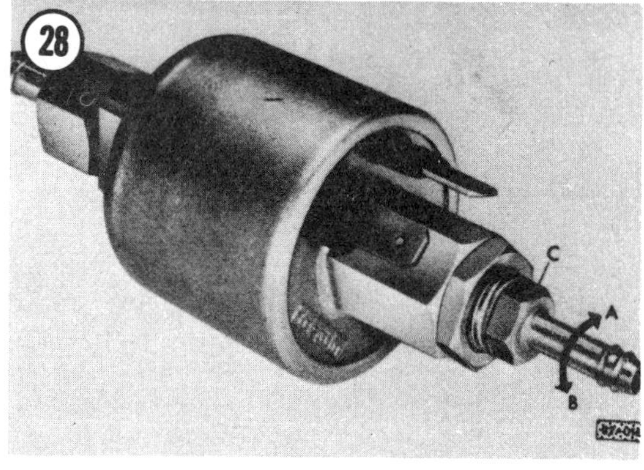

cording to the temperature of the warm air from the heat exchangers. The booster will automatically shut down when the engine supplies sufficient heat by itself. If the engine is not running or will not run (emergencies), the heater booster alone can heat the vehicle.

Operation

Refer to **Figure 3** and **Figure 26** for the following explanation. When the heater booster is switched on from the temperature regulating switch in the driver's compartment, the following are activated:

a. Heater booster relay

b. Booster fuel pump

c. Combustion air blower

d. Glow plug and ignition coil

e. Auxiliary booster fan

f. Flame switch

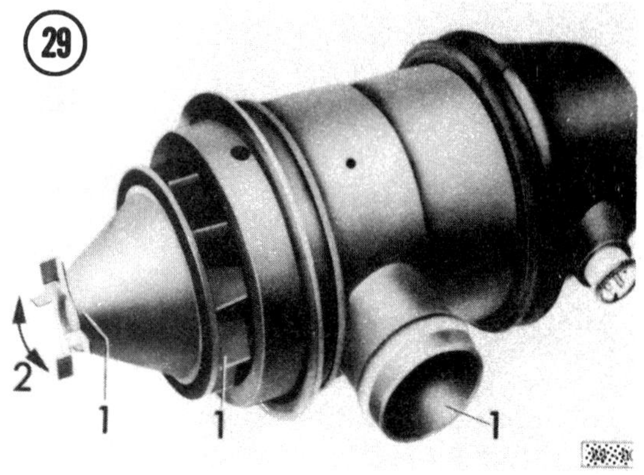

g. Overheat kill switch

h. Temperature sensor

Fuel is taken from the main fuel line at a tee connection (**Figure 27**, arrow A indicates fuel flow direction) then routed through an electric fuel pump (**Figure 28**) that supplies gasoline to the heater booster combustion chamber.

Air for combustion is provided by the combustion air blower (**Figure 29**). The air and gasoline mixture is ignited by a glow plug mounted in the combustion chamber body (**Figure 30**) powered by an ignition coil (**Figure 31**). Combustion heat is sensed by the flame switch (**Figure 32**) which controls the glow plug and ignition coil.

The auxiliary booster fan (**Figure 33**) supplies extra air for the combustion chamber heat exchanger. An overheat safety switch (**Figure 34**) shuts the entire system down if dangerous temperatures are reached in the combustion chamber.

Hot air leaving the combustion chamber heat exchanger is checked by the temperature sensor (**Figure 35**); this information is sent to the heater relay and cross checked with the driver's setting of the temperature regulating switch. If the air gets too hot, the heater booster will shut down; it will start once again when the air cools.

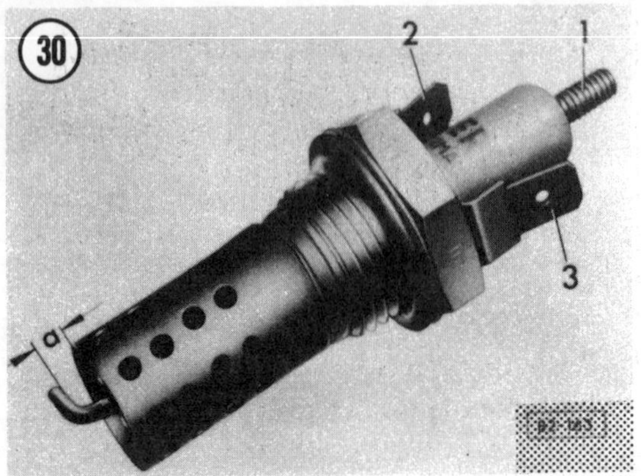

Removal/Installation

Refer to **Figure 26** for the following procedure.

1. Disconnect the battery.
2. Disconnect and plug the fuel line where it connects to the heater booster.
3. Remove all the electrical lines from the heater booster body. Mark and tag the components and lines with tape for correct reinstallation.
4. Disconnect the large hose pipes from each end of the booster.
5. Disconnect the exhaust pipe and the combustion air hose.
6. Remove the bolts which hold the booster to the underbody, then carefully lower it.
7. Installation is the reverse of removal.

Disassembly/Assembly

Refer to **Figure 26** for the following procedure.

1. Remove the combustion air blower and vane housing.
2. Gently pry up the little metal flap and remove the overheat switch.
3. Remove the glow plug.
4. Remove the flame switch.
5. Remove the temperature sensor.
6. Assembly is the reverse of disassembly. Make sure the drain hole in the air blower points straight down.

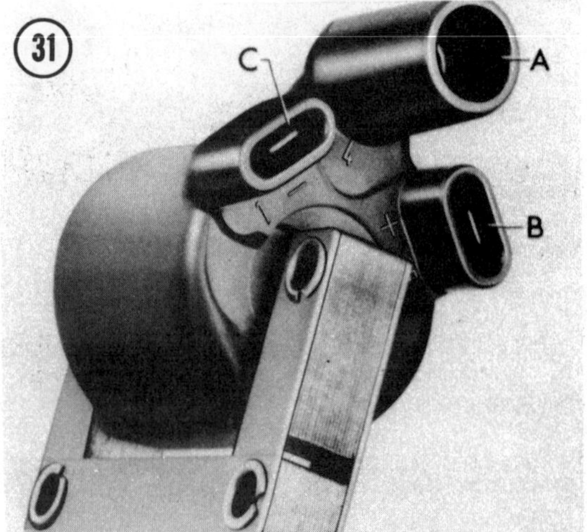

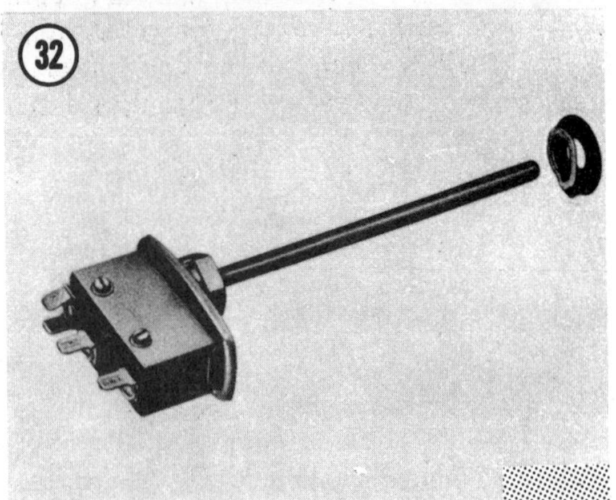

Inspection

1. Check the heater booster housing for distortion caused by excessive heat and for cracks, rust or burn-through. Replace the housing if damage is found.

2. Check the ceramic ring that the overheat switch sits in. If the ring is damaged in any way, replace it.

3. Examine the adaptor for the glow plug. If carbon fouled, clean with a stiff brush.

4. Check the combustion air blower vane housing for burns; replace if necessary. Turn the blower blades over by hand; check shaft for freedom of movement. If the shaft drags or grinding sounds can be heard when turning the blades, replace the blower. Reinstall the blower with the small drain hole facing straight down.

5. Look into the combustion chamber and check for carbon fouling; clean out if necessary.

6. Clean out the fresh air inlet if dirty.

7. Inspect the exhaust outlet; if tar-like deposits are found, replace the whole booster housing.

8. Check the glow plug. The electrode should not be burned away or carbon fouled. Clean with a wire brush if necessary.

NOTE: If you own a 1982 model, first check the Supplement at the back of the book for any new service information.

CHAPTER SIX

FUEL, EXHAUST, AND EMISSION CONTROL SYSTEMS

AFC FUEL INJECTION SYSTEM

The AFC (air flow controlled) electronic fuel injection system, manufactured by the Robert Bosch Company, is standard equipment on all Vanagons.

Fuel injection—unlike carburetion—does not rely upon a partial vacuum caused by inrushing air to draw fuel into the engine. Instead, fuel is injected at low pressure directly behind each intake valve in the cylinder heads. Fuel injection pulses are timed with the firing of the engine to make sure that fuel is fully vaporized when it is sucked into the cylinders.

The quantity of the fuel injected is determined by the electronic control unit (ECU) which factors in variables such as engine temperature, outside air temperature and engine load demands.

The major components which comprise the fuel injection system are the fuel supply system, air system and the electronic control system. These systems are described in the following paragraphs. Refer to **Figure 1** for location of AFC components.

Fuel Supply System

Figure 2 is a simplified drawing of the fuel system. The fuel supply system consists of the fuel tank, fuel lines, fuel pump, filter, injector rig, pressure regulator, 4 injectors and a cold start valve.

When the ignition key is turned on, the fuel pump is also activated. The pump draws fuel from the front-mounted fuel tank through a filter, then delivers it to the lines of the injector rig and finally to 4 electromagnetic fuel injectors.

Fuel pressure is maintained in the injector rig and injectors at 28 psi by the fuel pressure regulator. Excess fuel from the regulator is returned to the fuel tank.

Figure 3 shows a typical fuel injector. When the control unit sends an electrical pulse through the winding in the injector, the injector needle is pulled off its seat. This allows pressurized fuel to spray from the injector into the cylinder head. A return spring seats the needle at the end of the pulse.

If the engine and outside air are cold, extra fuel is needed to start the engine. The cold start

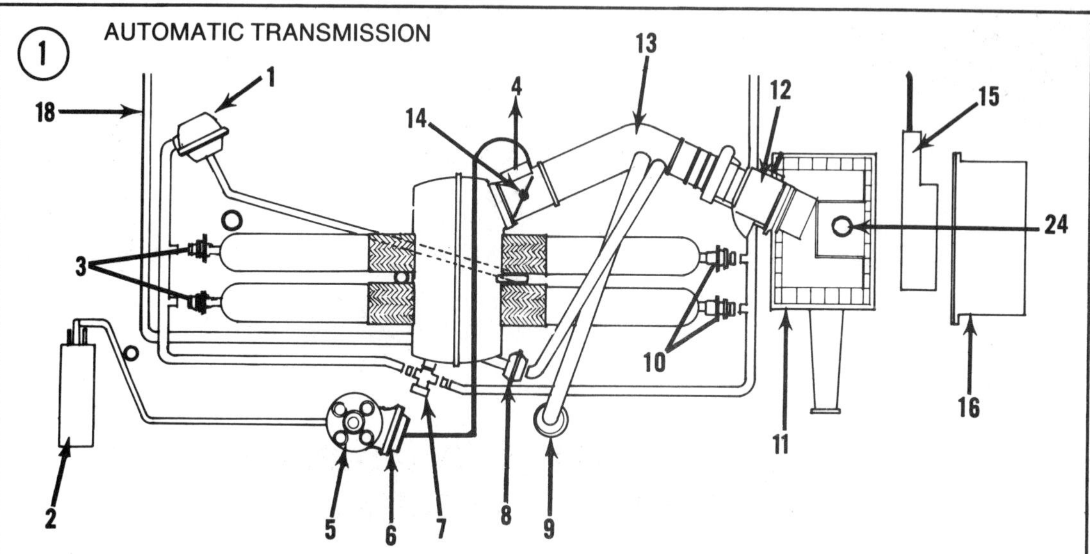

1. Fuel pressure regulator
2. Ignition coil
3. No. 3 and No.4 fuel injectors
4. Full throttle switch
5. Distributor
6. Vacuum advance unit reload unit
7. Cold start valve
8. Auxiliary air regulator
9. Crankcase vent cap
10. No. 1 and No. 2 fuel injectors
11. Air cleaner housing
12. Intake air sensor
13. Intake air hose
14. Throttle valve
15. Multi-pin connection
16. ECV electronic control unit
17. Decel valve (manual transmissions)
18. Brake vacuum scrud line
19. Vacuum retard line (California only)
20. Vacuum advance line
21. Oxygen sensor (California only)
22. Temperature sensor No. 2
23. Thermo time switch
24. Temperature sensor No. 1

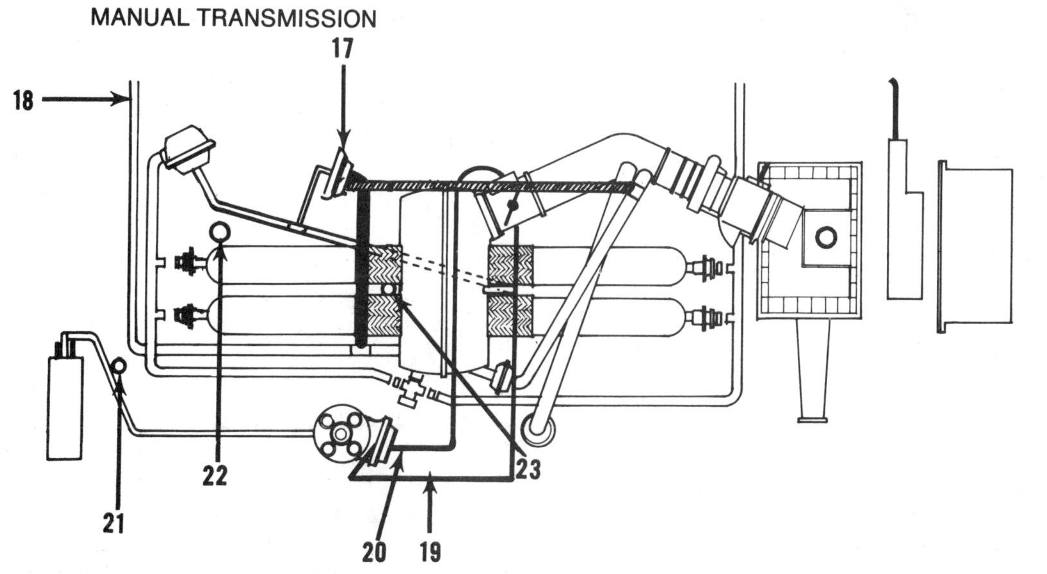

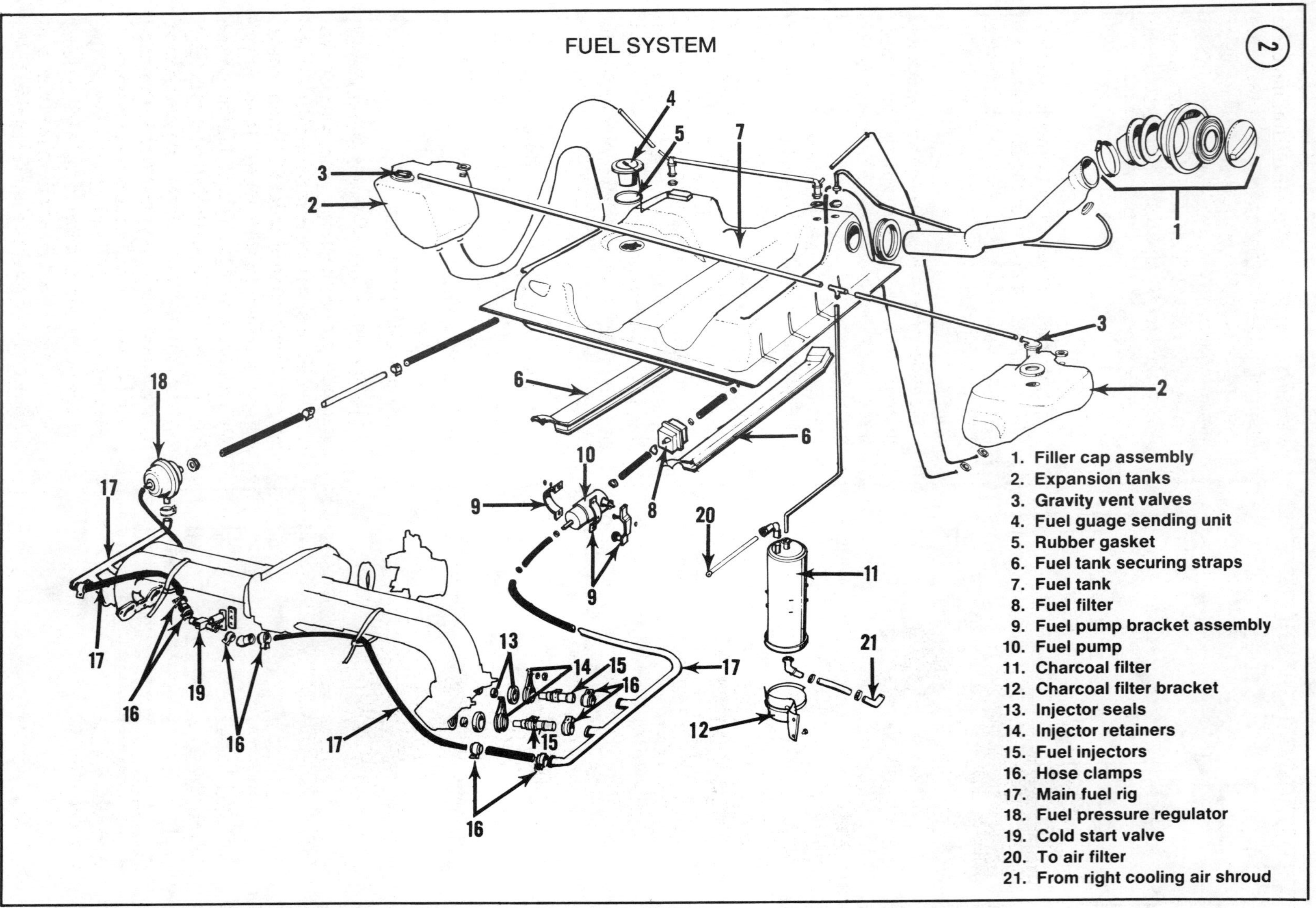
2
FUEL SYSTEM
1. Filler cap assembly
2. Expansion tanks
3. Gravity vent valves
4. Fuel guage sending unit
5. Rubber gasket
6. Fuel tank securing straps
7. Fuel tank
8. Fuel filter
9. Fuel pump bracket assembly
10. Fuel pump
11. Charcoal filter
12. Charcoal filter bracket
13. Injector seals
14. Injector retainers
15. Fuel injectors
16. Hose clamps
17. Main fuel rig
18. Fuel pressure regulator
19. Cold start valve
20. To air filter
21. From right cooling air shroud

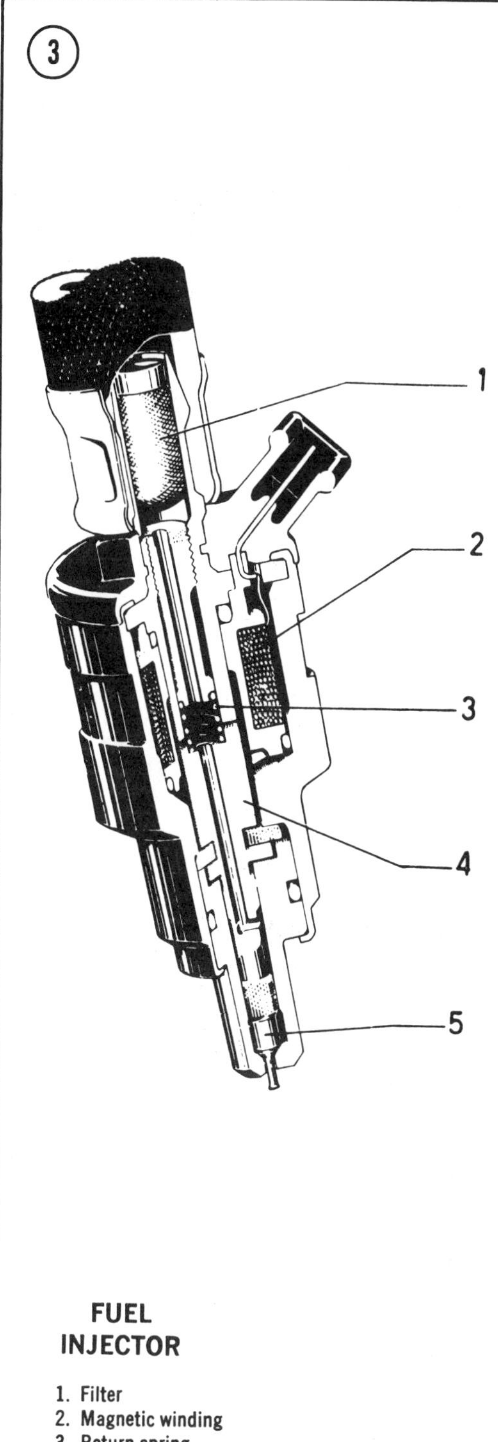

FUEL INJECTOR

1. Filter
2. Magnetic winding
3. Return spring
4. Magnetic armature
5. Sealing needle

valve (sometimes called the fifth injector) injects fuel directly into the intake air distributor only during the first few seconds of starter cranking. When this occurs the intake air distributor acts like a crude carburetor in which the fuel is vaporized, then drawn into the cylinders.

Air System

Figure 4 and **Figure 5** show the air system. The air system consists of the air cleaner, intake air distributor, throttle valve housing, intake manifolds and the auxiliary air regulator.

Outside air is drawn through an air cleaner, filtered, then passed through the air intake sensor into the throttle valve housing via the air intake hose.

The throttle valve regulates how much air is admitted to the engine. It is directly connected to the throttle pedal by a cable which runs through the vehicle body. When the engine is idling the throttle valve is completely closed. Idle air bypasses the throttle valve through a little hole in the throttle valve housing. The amount of air allowed to bypass (and therefore the engine idle speed) is regulated by the idle speed screw which threads into the bypass hole.

At idle, the air stator flap in the intake air sensor is also completely closed; idle air bypasses the stator chamber through a passage in the housing wall.

Electronic Control System

The electronic control system monitors and regulates engine functions. The components which comprise the system are the double relay, electronic control unit (ECU), air intake sensor, air temperature sensor (also called temperature sensor No. 1), temperature sensor No. 2, ignition distributor, thermo-time switch, full throttle switch, oxygen sensor (California models only) and series resistance block (49-state and Canadian models only).

The double relay controls the supply of voltage to the components of the AFC system. The unit is screwed to the body of the vehicle in front of and slightly above intake manifold No. 3 (**Figure 6**).

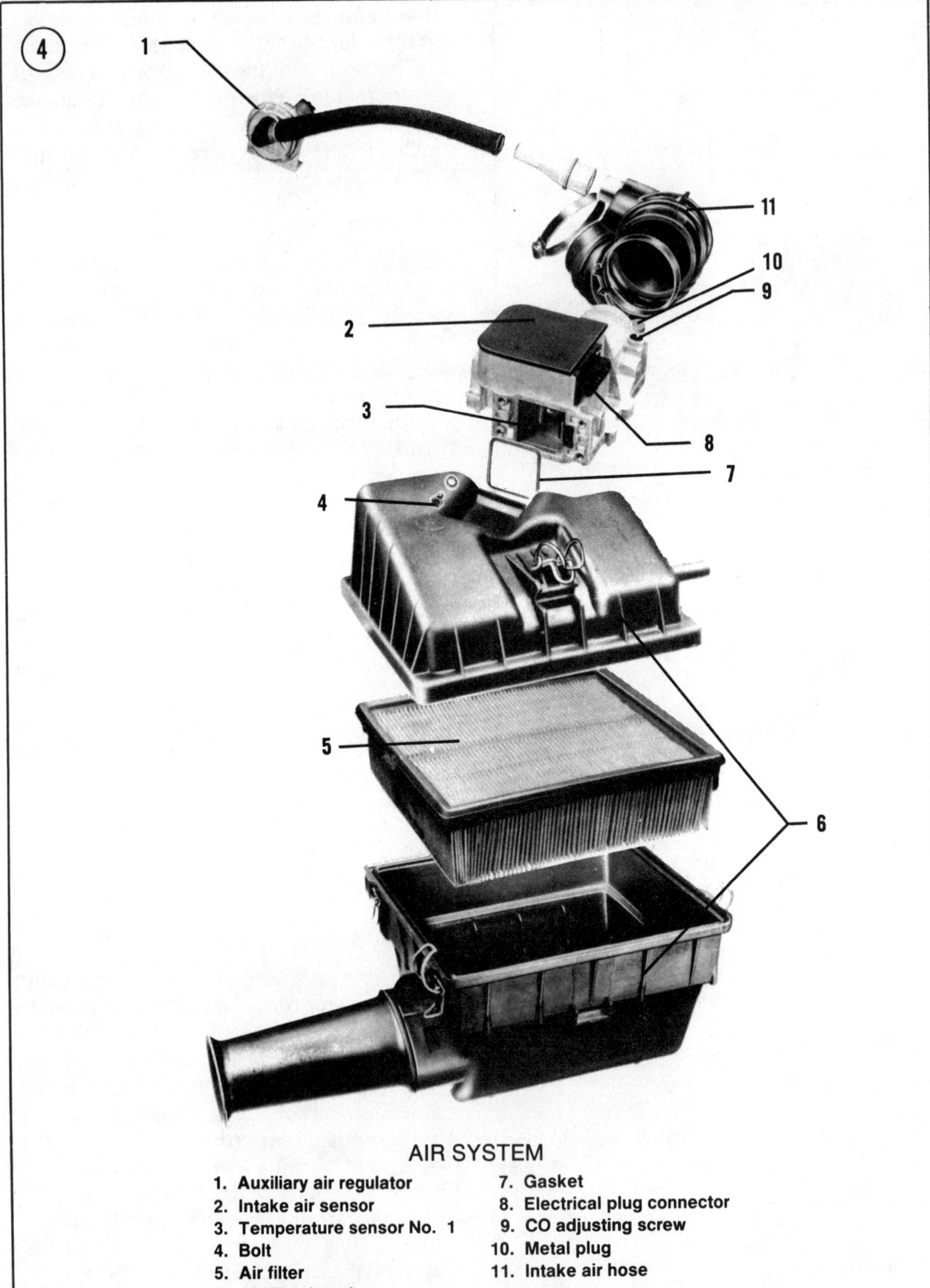

AIR SYSTEM

1. Auxiliary air regulator
2. Intake air sensor
3. Temperature sensor No. 1
4. Bolt
5. Air filter
6. Air filter housing
7. Gasket
8. Electrical plug connector
9. CO adjusting screw
10. Metal plug
11. Intake air hose

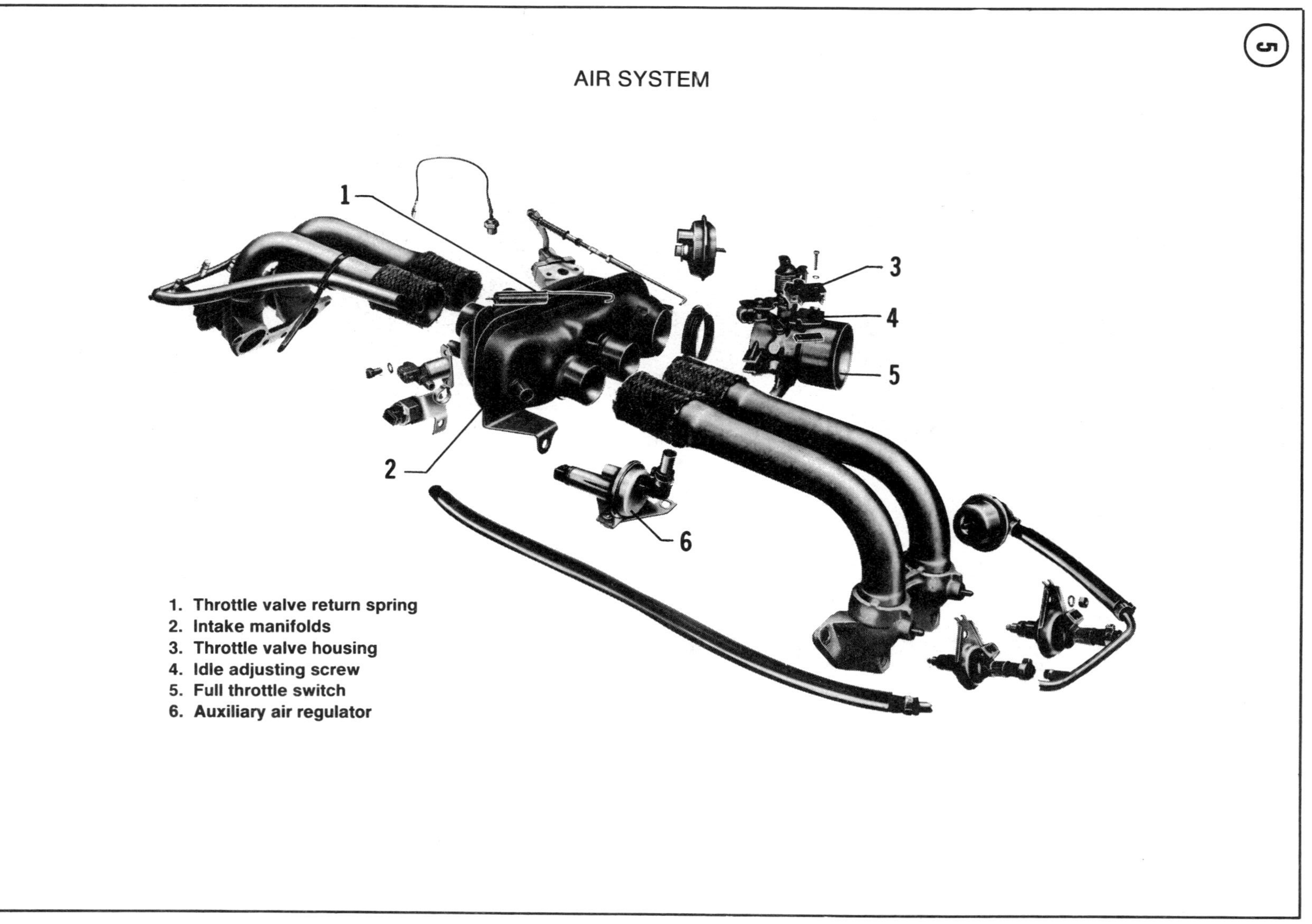

AIR SYSTEM

1. Throttle valve return spring
2. Intake manifolds
3. Throttle valve housing
4. Idle adjusting screw
5. Full throttle switch
6. Auxiliary air regulator

The ECU is the heart of the electronic control system (**Figure** 7). The unit is located in the engine compartment on the right-hand side, fastened to the body by a bracket. The ECU is a computer which monitors data from the engine sensors listed above. The ECU evaluates data such as engine speed, engine temperature, outside air temperature, intake air volume and load demands and then instantly orders engine control units in the fuel system to take proper action.

The air intake sensor is a 2-vane stator flap which operates a potentiometer and a fuel pump regulation switch (**Figure 8**). The air intake sensor tells the ECU how much air is being admitted into the engine. Inrushing air causes a slight depression (partial vacuum) in the stator chamber, pulling on the stator flap and causing it to open. A potentiometer connected to the stator measures how far the stator flap is open. The information is relayed to the ECU which uses the information to calculate fuel injection pulse durations.

The air temperature sensor (also called temperature sensor No. 1) is located within the air intake sensor housing (**Figure 9**). This sensor measures the temperature of the outside air drawn through the air cleaner. Temperature sensor No. 2 is located on the cylinder head in front of intake manifold No. 3. This sensor measures cylinder head temperature. The information from both sensors is used to calculate fuel mixture.

The ECU picks up ignition pulses from terminal No. 1 on the ignition distributor where the distributor condenser wire connects. These pulses are used to determine when to inject fuel.

The thermo-time switch is fastened to the crankcase beneath the intake air distributor directly under the outlet for intake manifold No. 4. The thermo-time switch is closed when cold, allowing the cold start valve to inject extra fuel into the air intake distributor for the first few seconds of starter cranking. After about 8 seconds the thermo-time switch opens, shutting off the cold start valve.

The full throttle switch is located on the throttle valve housing (**Figure 10**). The full throttle switch alerts the ECU when a heavy demand is placed upon the engine. When the throttle pedal is suddenly pushed down, the throttle valve lever opens and activates the switch. The ECU receives the signal, then directs the fuel injector to inject extra fuel, allowing the engine to generate more power.

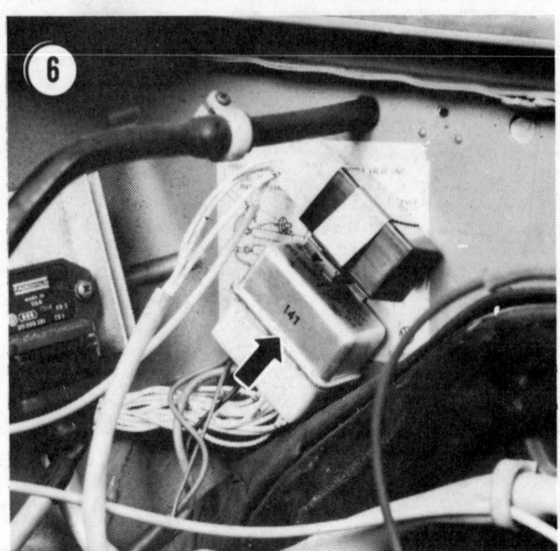

On California models, the oxygen sensor detects the amount of oxygen present in the exhaust gases and signals the ECU. This feedback system allows the ECU to constantly monitor the results of its signals to the fuel injectors.

TROUBLESHOOTING AND REPAIR

This section includes troubleshooting and repair procedures for the AFC system. Repair of the AFC system is not beyond the scope of mere mortals. Home service is possible if you have a few basic tools such as a combination ohmmeter/voltmeter/ammeter, a simple test light and a combination fuel pressure/vacuum gauge.

In order to test the AFC system you should be thoroughly familiar with the location and function of each component. If you are not, see **Figure 1** and refer to *AFC Systems* in this chapter.

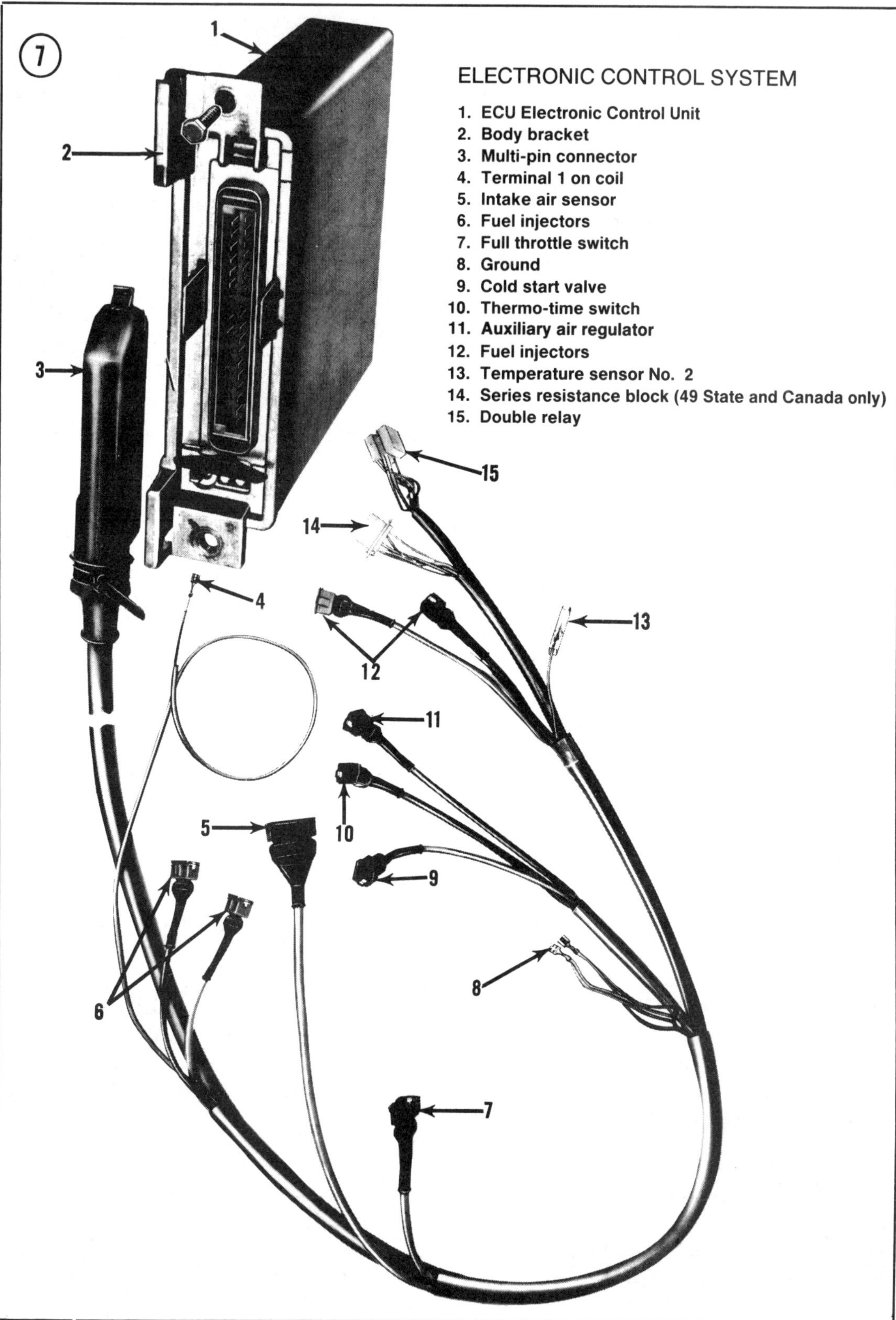
7
ELECTRONIC CONTROL SYSTEM
1. ECU Electronic Control Unit
2. Body bracket
3. Multi-pin connector
4. Terminal 1 on coil
5. Intake air sensor
6. Fuel injectors
7. Full throttle switch
8. Ground
9. Cold start valve
10. Thermo-time switch
11. Auxiliary air regulator
12. Fuel injectors
13. Temperature sensor No. 2
14. Series resistance block (49 State and Canada only)
15. Double relay
1
2
3
4
5
6
7
8
9
10
11
12
13
14
15

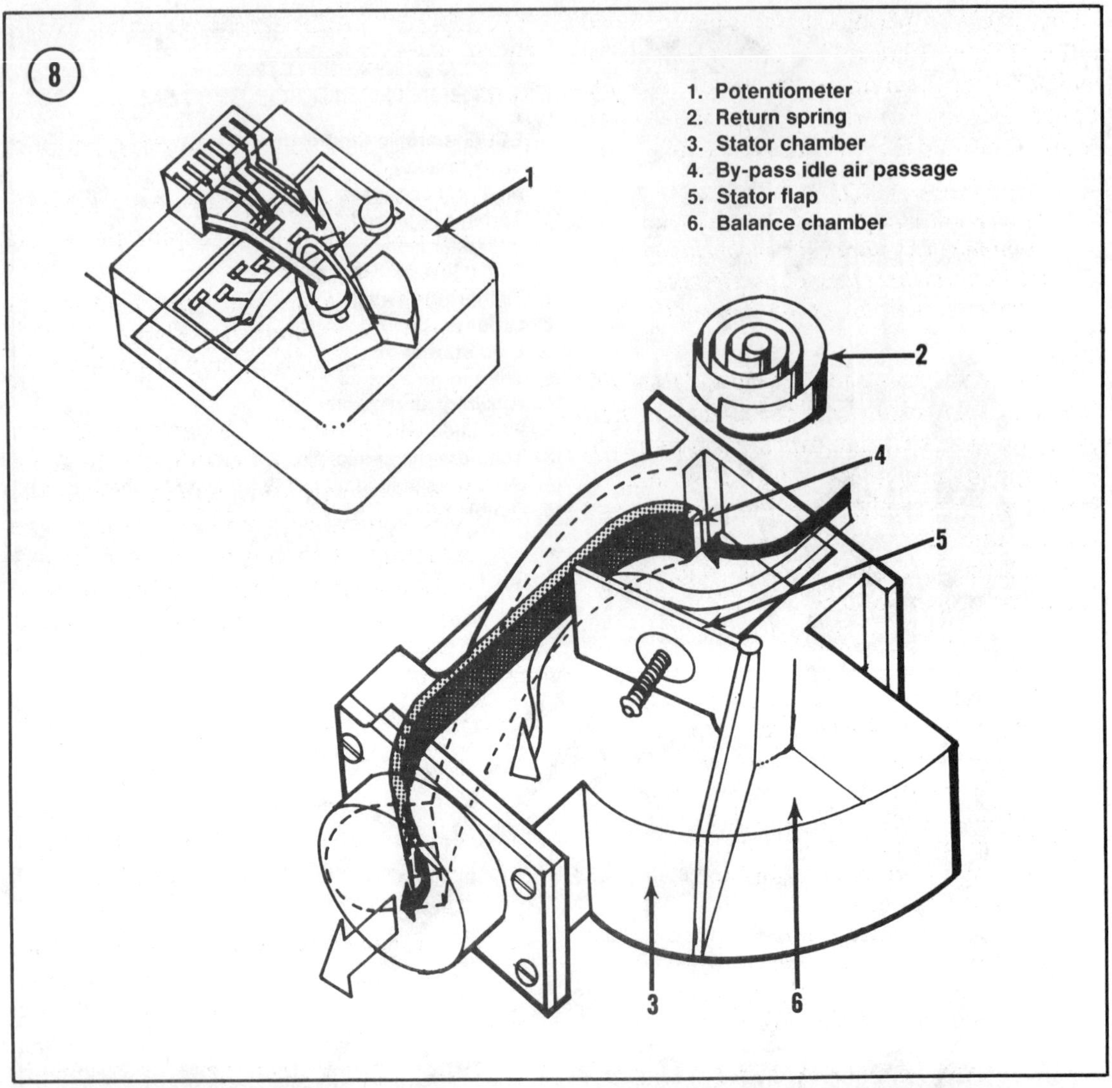
8
1. Potentiometer
2. Return spring
3. Stator chamber
4. By-pass idle air passage
5. Stator flap
6. Balance chamber
1
2
4
5
3
6

9

10

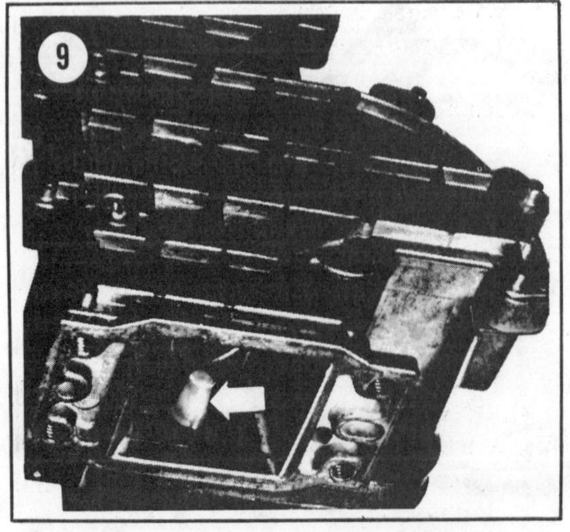

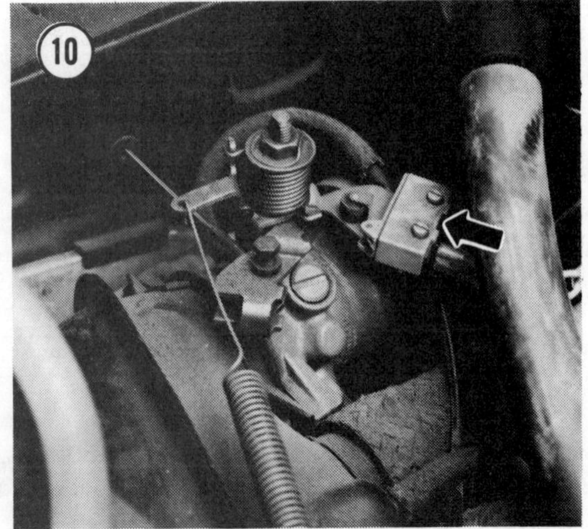

Fuel injection wiring diagrams are included in this chapter (**Figure 11A**) and in the general vehicle wiring diagrams at the end of the book. Refer often to the diagrams when troubleshooting; they will prove useful.

NOTE
Test procedures often refer to numbered terminals. The electrical components on the Vanagon have the electrical terminal numbers imprinted on the component body.

Whenever anything goes wrong and the AFC system is suspected, first check the ignition system wires, distributor cap, breaker points (if so equipped) and spark plugs. If nothing is wrong there, check the air system for leaks and cracked and loose hoses and connections. Check all the AFC electrical connectors in the engine for proper contact.

WARNING
Gasoline is highly flammable and explosive in enclosed areas. Do not smoke, run any kind of electrical power tools or have any open flames (such as gas home appliances) around when handling gasoline. When working with the AFC system you will sometimes be exposed to liquid gasoline and vapors. If you heed this warning you will be safe from possible serious injury. As extra protection to yourself and the vehicle, always have a fire extinguisher on hand when working with the AFC system.

AFC SYSTEM TEST

The entire AFC system may be checked electrically at the ECU plug connector. Disconnect the plug from the ECU and use an ohmmeter or a voltmeter according to **Figure 11B**.

If a component does not check out at the plug connector, check out the component using the individual procedures given in this chapter. If the component checks out fine, the Fuel Injection wiring harness is most likely faulty and should be replaced.

DOUBLE RELAY

If the engine refuses to start and nothing seems to be wrong with either the ignition system or the air system, it may be that the AFC system is not receiving power at all. Check the double relay.

Testing

1. To test current supply to the relay, perform the following:
   a. Unscrew the double relay from the vehicle body, but do not unplug the wiring connectors.
   b. Touch one lead from a test light to terminal 85 (ground). See **Figure 12**. This lead should be kept here throughout the entire sequence.
   c. Touch the other lead to terminal 88y and then to 88z. The tester should light up on both terminals. If the tester lights on 88y only, something is wrong with the double relay and it should be replaced. If 88y does not light, power is failing to reach the relay from terminal 30 on the starter. Check the electrical connections on the starter.
   d. Turn the ignition key to the RUN position. Touch the tester lead to terminal 86c. The tester should light; if not, power is not reaching the relay from ignition coil. Check the electrical connection at the ignition coil and associated wiring.
   e. Touch the tester lead to terminal 86a. Have an assistant turn the engine over with starter. The test light should light up. If not, power is not reaching the relay from terminal 50 on the starter solenoid. Check the connection at the solenoid and associated wiring.
2. To test relay function perform the following:
   a. Remove the double relay from the vehicle body; do not unplug the wiring connectors.
   b. Touch one lead from the test light to terminal 85 (ground). See **Figure 12**. This lead should be kept here throughout the next step.
   c. Touch the other lead to terminal 88d, which powers the fuel pump. Have an assistant crank the engine with the starter. If the tester does not light, the pump relay is failing to close; replace the double relay.

6

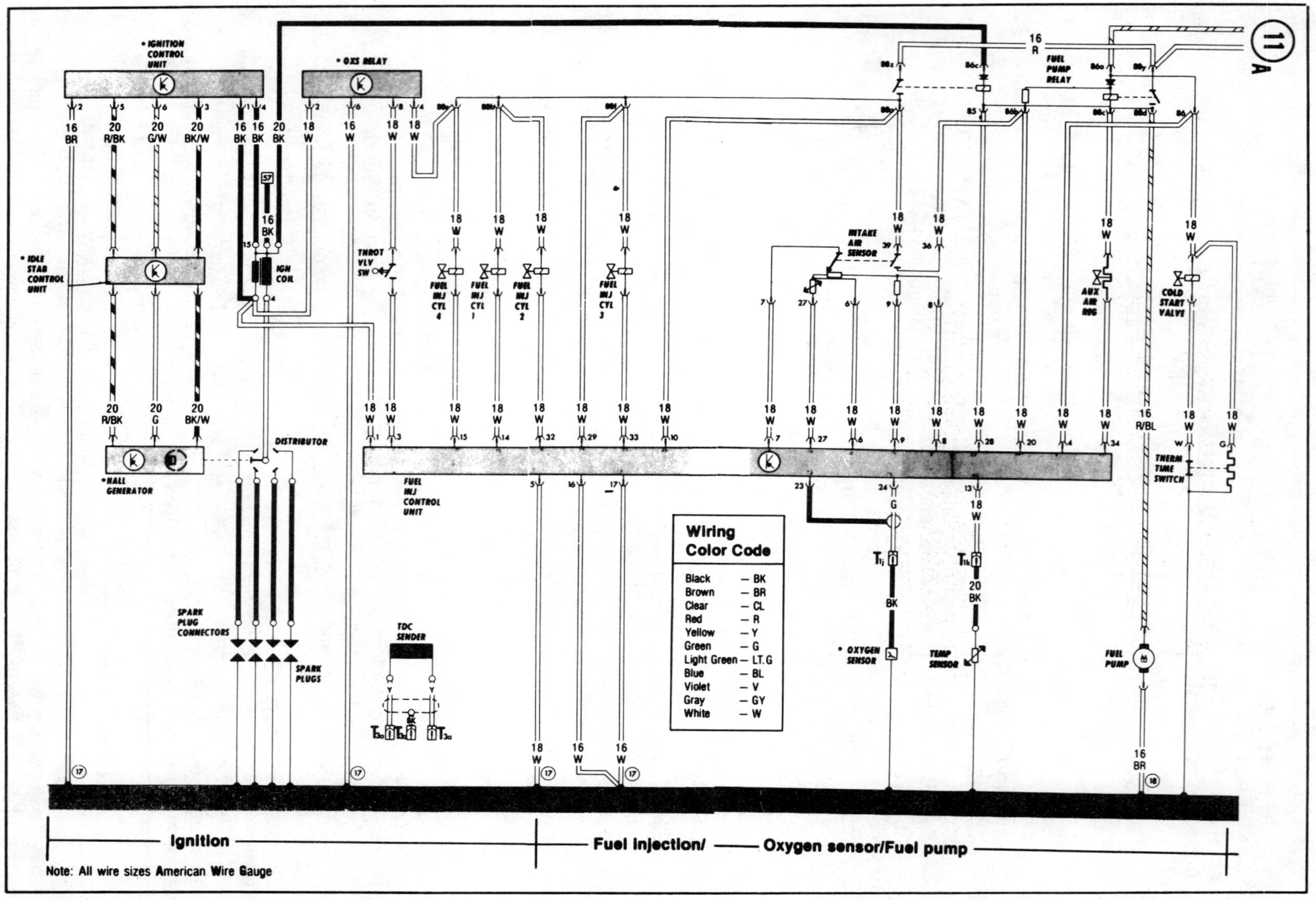
11A
IGNITION CONTROL UNIT
OXS RELAY
FUEL PUMP RELAY
IDLE STAB CONTROL UNIT
IGN COIL
THROT VLV SW
FUEL INJ CYL 4
FUEL INJ CYL 1
FUEL INJ CYL 2
FUEL INJ CYL 3
INTAKE AIR SENSOR
AUX AIR REG
COLD START VALVE
THERM TIME SWITCH
HALL GENERATOR
DISTRIBUTOR
FUEL INJ CONTROL UNIT
SPARK PLUG CONNECTORS
SPARK PLUGS
TDC SENDER
OXYGEN SENSOR
TEMP SENSOR
FUEL PUMP
Wiring Color Code
Black — BK
Brown — BR
Clear — CL
Red — R
Yellow — Y
Green — G
Light Green — LT.G
Blue — BL
Violet — V
Gray — GY
White — W
Ignition
Fuel Injection/
Oxygen sensor/Fuel pump
Note: All wire sizes American Wire Gauge

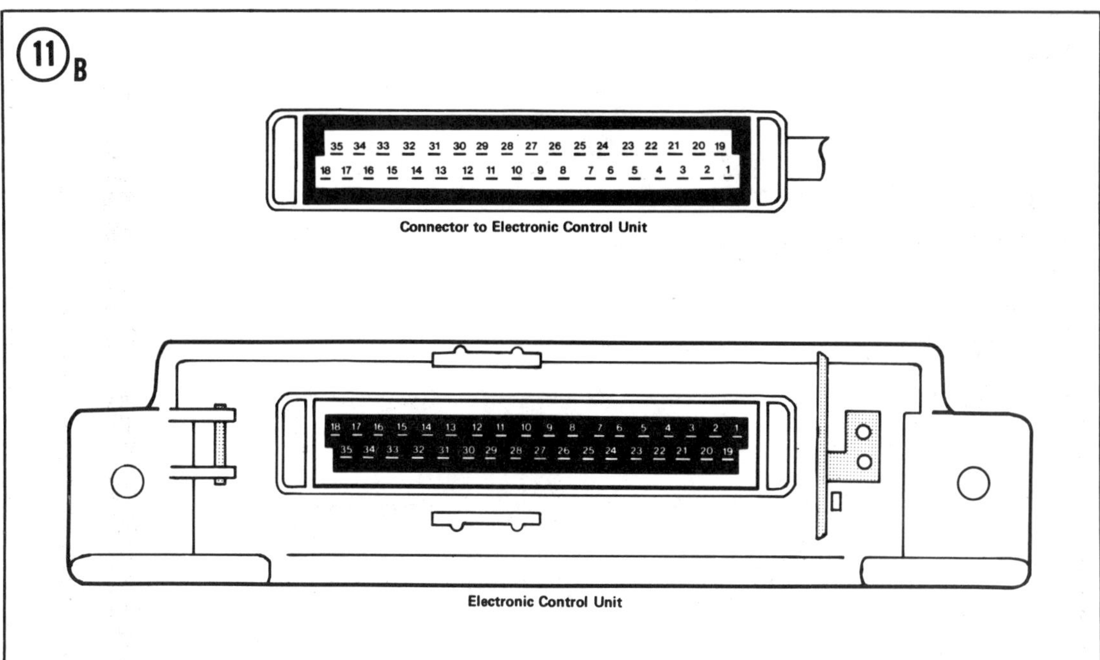

Ohmmeter to terminal:	Specifications	Checks
#1 and ground	Disconnect white injection wire at coil—infinite ohms; hook wire to ground—0 ohms	Wire to #1 terminal on coil
#3 and #18	Press accelerator pedal down fully—0 ohms	Full throttle enrichment circuit through throttle switch
#5 and ground	0 ohms	Ground circuit
#6 and #9	200-400 ohms	Air sensor circuit
#6 and #8	130-260 ohms	Air sensor circuit
#8 and #9	70-140 ohms	Air sensor circuit
#6 and #7	40-300 ohms	Air sensor circuit
#7 and #8	100-500 ohms	Air sensor circuit
#6 and #27	Max 2,800 ohms at 68° F	Air sensor circuit
#13 and ground	2,100-2,900 ohms at 68° F 270-390 at 176° F	Temperature sensor No. 2
#14 and #10	Approximately 7 ohms	Injector wire and resistor
#15 and #10	Approximately 7 ohms	Injector wire and resistor
#32 and #10	Approximately 7 ohms	Injector wire and resistor
#33 and #10	Approximately 7 ohms	Injector wire and resistor
#16 and ground	0 ohms	Ground circuit
#17 and ground	0 ohms	Ground circuit
#34 at control unit and #37 on the double relay	Approximately 30 ohms	Auxiliary air regulator and wires

Voltmeter to terminal	Specifications	Checks
#4 and ground	12 volts during cranking, 0 volts at all other times	Signal from starter
#10 and ground	12 volts with key on, 0 volts with key off	Voltage supply to computer
#20 and ground	12 volts with key on and intake a in sensor flap open	Pump circuit

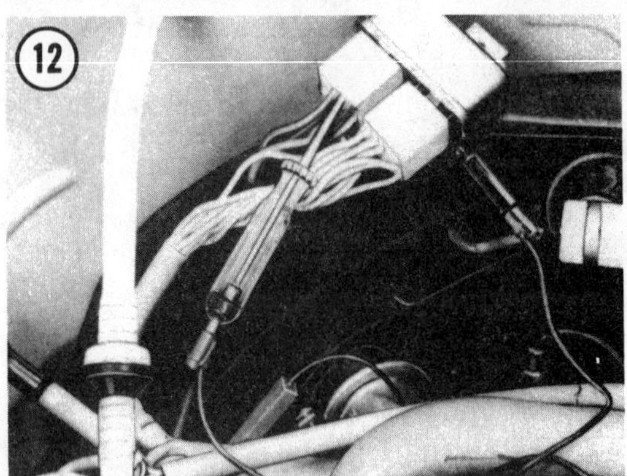

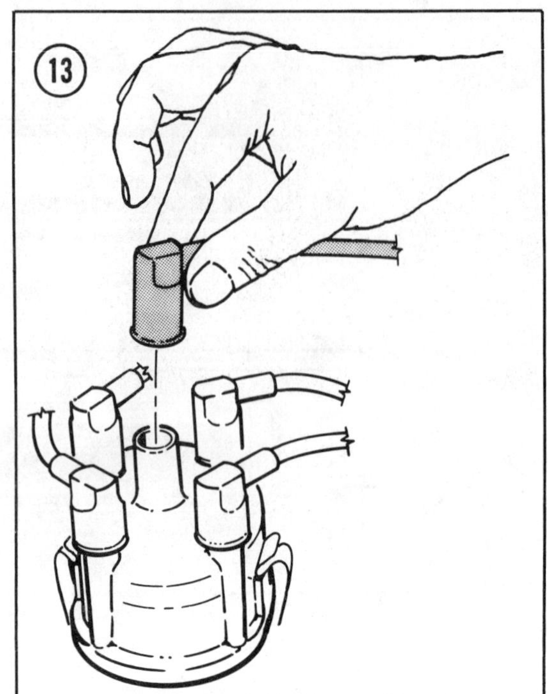

Replacement

Refer to **Figure 6** for the following procedure.

1. Disconnect the battery cables.
2. Unscrew the relay from the vehicle body and pull out the multi-pin electrical connectors.
3. Plug in the electrical connectors on the new relay and mount it on the body.
4. Reconnect the battery cables.

FUEL INJECTORS AND SERIES RESISTANCE BLOCK

Testing

1. To isolate a bad injector perform the following:

NOTE
This step assumes that the engine will run, but that it runs erratically or misfires.

a. Make sure that all the injector retainers are tightened. The injector may be loose and leaking air.

b. Disconnect and ground one spark plug wire at a time while the engine is running. When the spark plug wire for a cylinder with a faulty injector is removed, the engine misfiring will *not* increase. Removing the wire from a cylinder with a good injector will increase roughness and misfiring. Reconnect each wire before removing the next one.

WARNING
Hold the spark plug wire with an insulated tool to avoid painful shocks.

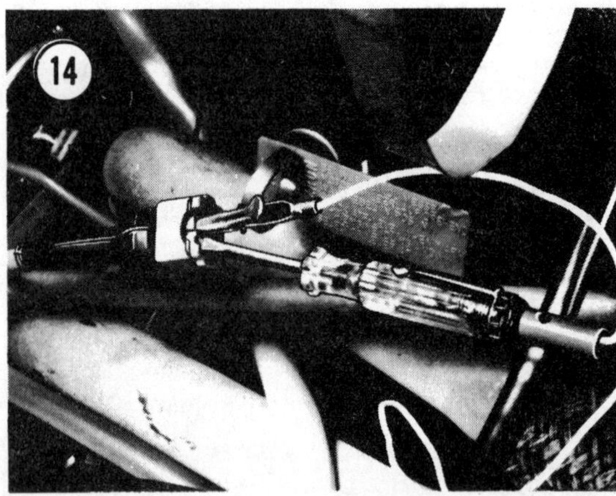

Do not leave the wire disconnected any longer than absolutely necessary or you may damage the ignition system or the exhaust system.

2. To check the voltage supply to the injector perform the following:

a. Disconnect the center wire (coil wire) from the distributor (**Figure 13**) and ground the wire.

b. Disconnect the injector plug from the injector.

c. Connect a test light to the injector plug lead as shown in **Figure 14**.

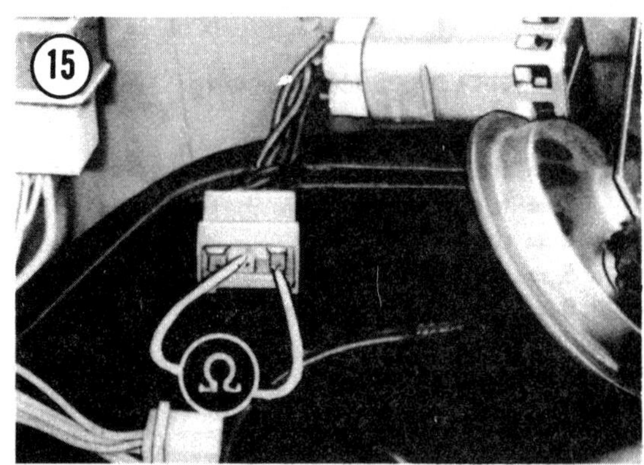

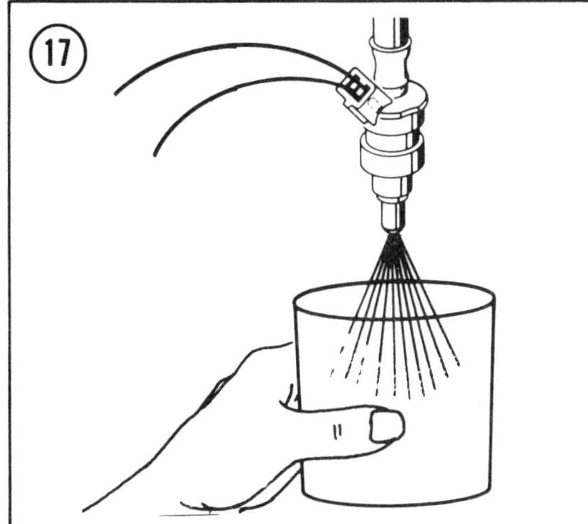

d. Have an assistant crank the engine with the starter while you watch the light. When the engine is turning the light should flicker. If not, the wiring harness is defective or the ECU is not operating properly (also see Step 3 for 49-state and Canadian models). If the tester lights, the fuel injection is probably faulty. Check it for proper operation using the procedure in Step 4.)

e. Reconnect the coil wire to the distributor.

3. 49-state and Canadian models only: If the test light did not light in Step 2D, check the series resistance block. Perform the following:

a. Pull the connector from series block.

b. Touch one ohmmeter lead to the center terminal and the other lead to the 2 outside terminals (**Figure 15**). The meter should read 5.5-6.5 ohms for each. If not, replace the series block by unscrewing it from the body and installing a new one.

NOTE
The series resistance block on California models is built into the ECU and cannot be checked.

4. To check the injector for leaks and proper fuel injection perform the following:

a. Disconnect the center wire (coil wire) from the distributor (**Figure 13**) and ground the wire.

b. Unbolt the retainer and pull the injector out of the cylinder head (**Figure 16**). Do not disconnect it from the main fuel rig. Also leave the electrical connector attached.

c. Check the injector seals. If they are hard and brittle, replace them; they will leak air.

d. Turn the ignition key to the second position and let the fuel pressure build up. The end of the injector may moisten with fuel but it should not leak more than 2 drops per minute. If it does, replace the injector.

e. Wipe the dirt off the end of the injector. Fashion a paper cylinder as shown in **Figure 17**. Hold the injector in the cylinder and have an assistant crank the engine with the starter.

f. The injector should spray an even pattern within the cylinder; if not, replace the injector. If the injector does not spray at all, check the fuel pressure as described under *Pressure Regulator* in this chapter. If the fuel pressure checks out okay and everything in the preceding steps of this test checked out okay, replace injector.

g. Touch the tester leads from an ohmmeter to the injection terminals. The meter should read 2-3 ohms. If not, the injection windings are probably shorted and it should be replaced.

h. Reconnect the coil wire to the distributor.

Injector Removal/Installation

Refer to **Figure 2** and **Figure 16** for the following procedure.

1. Remove the electrical connectors from the fuel injectors.

2. Loosen the hose clamps that secure the injector to the main fuel rig. Carefully pull the injector off the rig.

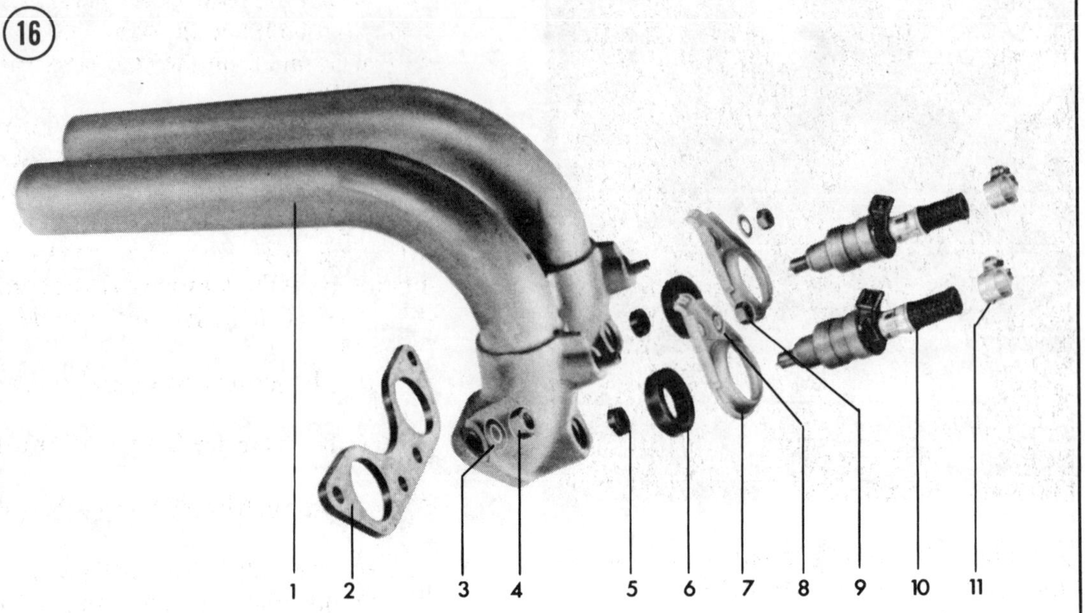

16
1
2
3
4
5
6
7
8
9
10
11

FUEL INJECTORS

1. Intake pipe
2. Seal
3. Lockwasher
4. Nut
5. Inner seal
6. Outer seal
7. Retainer
8. Lockwasher
9. Nut
10. Injector
11. Hose clamp

18

19

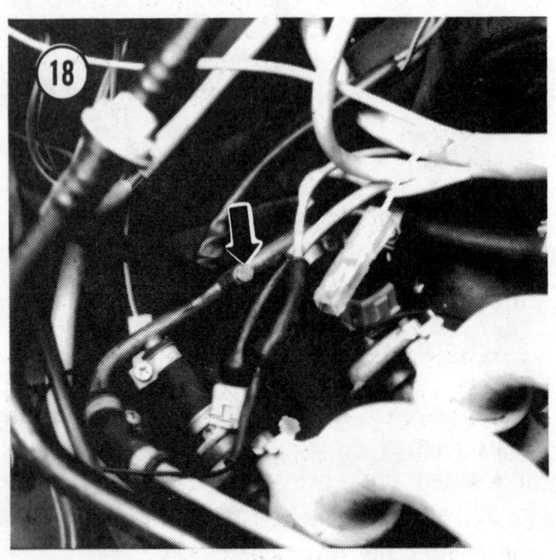

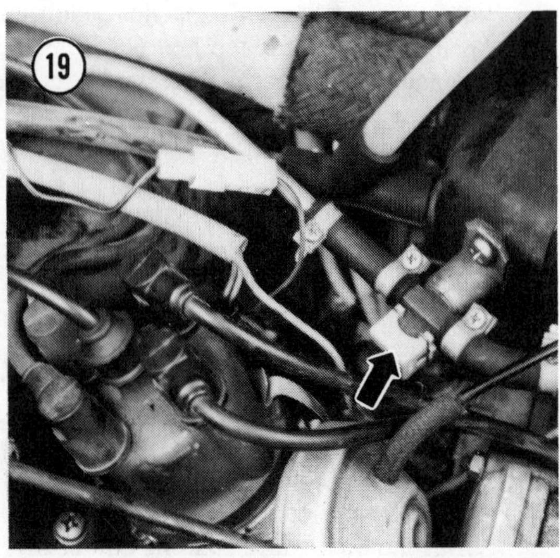

3. Unbolt the injector retainer and pull the injector out of the cylinder head.
4. Remove the inner seal from the end of the injector and the outer seal from the retainer.

NOTE
*When installing fuel injectors, **always** use new inner and outer seals.*

5. Installation is the reverse of removal.

COLD START VALVE

Testing

1. To check for proper operation perform the following:
   a. Connect a fuel pressure gauge to the tap between injectors No. 3 and No. 4 on the main fuel rig (**Figure 18**).
   b. Pull the center wire (coil wire) from the distributor cap and ground the wire (**Figure 13**).
   c. Crank the engine with the starter for a few seconds to build up fuel pressure, then turn the ignition off.
   d. Remove the electrical connector from the cold start valve (**Figure 19**).
   e. Fashion 2 jumper wires. Mark them "A" and "B."
   f. Connect one end of wire "A" to terminal 15 (+ terminal) on the ignition coil and the other end to either terminal on the cold start valve. Connect one end of wire "B" to any exposed metal part on the engine (ground) and the other end to the unused terminal on the cold start valve (**Figure 20**).
   g. Turn the ignition key to the second position and watch the pressure gauge. The pressure should drop slowly, showing that the cold start valve is injecting fuel into the intake air distributor. If the pressure does not drop, the valve is defective and should be replaced.
   h. Remove the jumper wires and pressure gauge.
2. To check the valve for leaks perform the following:
   a. Remove the electrical connector from the valve.
   b. Remove the valve from the intake air distributor without disconnecting it from the main fuel rig.
   c. Pull the center wire (coil wire) off the distributor cap and ground the wire (**Figure 13**).
   d. Crank the engine with the starter; this will build up fuel pressure.
   e. Check the end of the valve; it should not leak. If it does, replace it.

Removal/Installation

1. Disconnect the battery.
2. Remove the electrical connector from the valve.
3. Loosen the hose clamps and pull the main fuel rig hoses off the valve. Plug the fuel lines.
4. Remove the screws which hold the valve to the intake air distributor. Remove the valve and the gasket.
5. Installation is the reverse of removal.

THERMO-TIME SWITCH

Testing

To test the thermo-time switch for proper operation perform the following:

1. The engine and the thermo-time switch must be cold with the outside air temperature below 68° F (20° C). If necessary cool the switch with ice.
2. Pull the center wire off the distributor cap and ground the wire (**Figure 13**).

6

3. Remove the electrical connector from the cold start valve (**Figure 19**).
4. Touch the leads of a test light to the cold start valve electrical connector (**Figure 21**).
5. Have an assistant crank the engine with the starter for at least 25 seconds. Watch the test light; it should be brilliantly lit at first then become dimmer and go out in 8-11 seconds. If the tester did not go out when the starter was engaged the thermo-time switch is faulty (circuit will not open) and should be replaced.
6. If the tester did not light at all, check that power is reaching the thermo-time switch and the cold start valve. Touch one of the tester leads to a bare metal spot (ground) on the engine and the other to a terminal on the cold start valve electrical connector. Crank the engine with the starter; if the tester still does not light, touch the tester lead to the other terminal on the connector and crank the engine again. If the tester lights see Step 8.
7. If the tester still refuses to light the problem is most likely within the wiring to the double relay, the relay itself or the wiring between the relay terminal 86a and terminal 50 on the starter solenoid.
8. If power is reaching one of the terminals on the cold start valve connector as shown in Step 6, but the tester did not light in Step 5, the thermo-time switch is defective and should be replaced.

Removal/Installation

1. Remove the intake air distributor as described in this chapter.
2. Remove the electrical connector and remove the switch from the bracket.
3. Installation is the reverse of removal.

PRESSURE REGULATOR

Testing

To test the regulator for proper operation perform the following:

1. Start the engine and allow it to warm to operating temperature.
2. Turn the engine off. Connect a fuel pressure gauge to the tap between injectors No. 3 and No. 4 on the main fuel rig (**Figure 18**).

3. Disconnect and plug the small vacuum hose on the pressure regulator which leads to the intake air distributor (**Figure 22**).

4. Start the engine and let it idle; the pressure should be approximately 36 psi. Between 33-37 psi (2.35-2.65 kg/cm^2) is acceptable. If the pressure is much too high or too low see Step 6. If the pressure is correct, go to Step 5.

5. Unplug and reconnect the vacuum hose to the pressure regulator. The pressure must drop to approximately 29 psi. Between 26-30 psi (1.85-2.15 kg/cm^2) is acceptable. Again, if the pressure is too high or too low see Step 6. If the

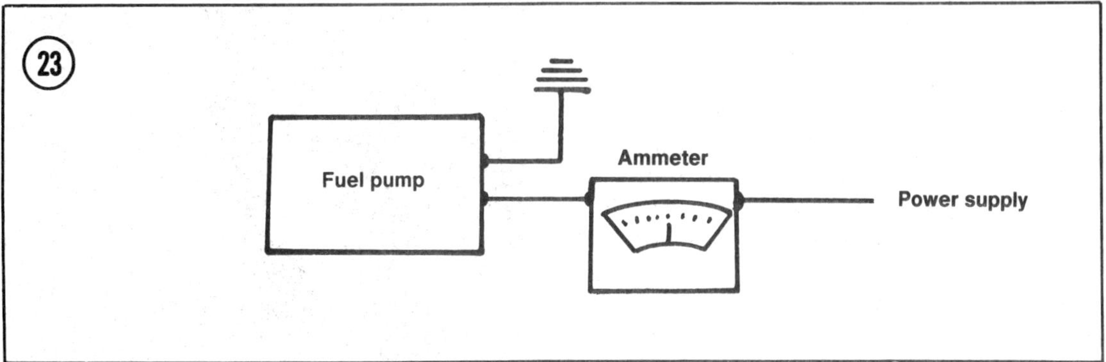

pressure checked out correctly in Step 4 and in this step, the regulator is functioning properly.

6. If the pressure is too low, first check the fuel filter for blockage and then check the fuel pump delivery rate. See *Fuel Pump* in this chapter for procedure. If the pressure is too high, check the return line to the fuel tank. If the fuel pump and return line are okay, replace the pressure regulator.

Removal/Installation

1. Disconnect the battery.
2. Disconnect the vacuum hose from the pressure regulator.
3. Loosen the fuel line hose clamps at the regulator. Pull the lines off and quickly plug them. One line can be removed inside the engine compartment; the other is accessible from the transmission side of the front cover plate.
4. Loosen the ring nut that holds the pressure regulator to the front cover plate. The ring nut is only accessible under the vehicle on the transmission side of the cover plate where the fuel line was disconnected.
5. Installation is the reverse of removal.

FUEL PUMP

Testing

1. To test pump for proper operation perform the following:
   a. With the ignition *off*, disconnect the return fuel line from the pressure regulator, which is under the vehicle on the transmission side of the front cover plate.
   b. Attach one end of a piece of fuel line about 3 ft. (1 meter) long to the return line fitting on the pressure regulator and insert the other end in a 1 quart (1 liter) graduated measuring container.
   c. Open the air cleaner housing and remove the filter element. Start the fuel pump by pushing and holding open the stator flap inside the intake air sensor with a length of dowel. Another method is to connect a jumper wire between terminals 36 and 39 on the intake air sensor electrical connector.
   d. Let the fuel pump run for approximately 30 seconds, then close the stator flap or disconnect the jumper wire.
   e. Measure the amount of fuel pumped into the container. It should be approximately 1/2 quart (500 cc). If the amount is less, check the fuel filter or the fuel pump ground connections; if these components check out okay see Step 2.
2. To check the fuel pump for proper electrical operation perform the following:
   a. With the ignition *off*, connect an ammeter in a series circuit to the fuel pump and the current supply as shown in **Figure 23.**
   b. Open the air cleaner housing and remove the filter element. Start the fuel pump by pushing and holding open the stator flap inside the intake air sensor with a length of dowel. Another method is to connect a jumper wire between terminals 36 and 39 on the intake air sensor electrical connector.
   c. The ammeter reading should be 6.5-8.5 amps. If the reading is lower, the pump may have a poor ground connection; if it is higher, the pump motor may be dragging. In this case, replace the pump.

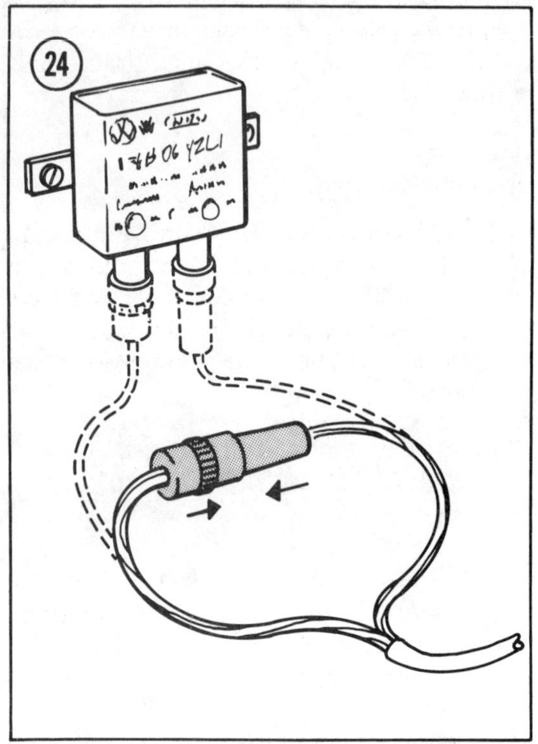

Removal/Installation

Refer to **Figure 2** for the following procedure.

1. Disconnect the electrical lines on the fuel pump.
2. Clamp off the fuel lines leading to and from the pump.
3. Remove the hose clamps on the fuel lines.

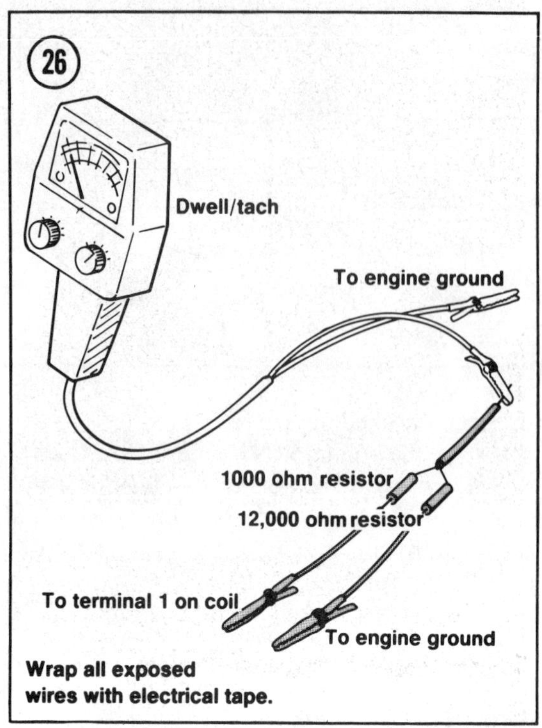

4. Remove the clamp which holds the pump to the shock bracket.
5. Installation is the reverse of these steps.

FULL THROTTLE SWITCH

Testing

To check for proper operation perform the following:

1. Start the engine and allow it to warm to operating temperature. Let the engine idle throughout the test.
2. Make sure that the idle speed and the ignition timing are set properly (Chapter Three).
3. On California models, disconnect the idle stabilizer plugs and connect them together as shown in **Figure 24**.
4. Connect a jumper wire to terminals 4 and 8 on the speed limit switch electrical connector shown in **Figure 25**.
5. Connect a tachometer to the engine as shown in **Figure 26**.
6. Operate the switch by hand (**Figure 27**). The engine idle should increase by 100 rpm. If not, replace the switch.
7. Turn the engine off. Touch the leads from the ohmmeter to the switch terminals (**Figure**

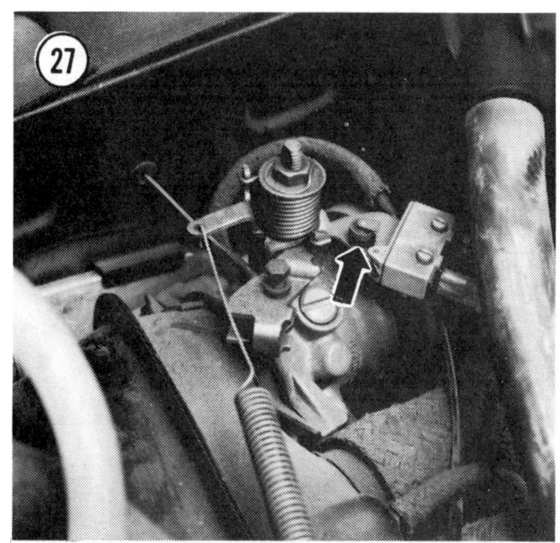

28). With the throttle valve closed the ohmmeter must read infinite resistance (no continuity). Open the throttle valve slowly; just before reaching full stop the meter must read 0 ohms (continuity). If not, the switch must be adjusted and rechecked. If the adjustment does not produce results, replace the switch.

Adjustment

1. Have an assistant fully depress the throttle pedal and hold it in that position.
2. Touch the leads of the ohmmeter to the switch terminals (**Figure 28**). Loosen the Allen head bracket screw and move the switch until the ohmmeter changes from no continuity to 0 ohms; the roller should be in the curved center of the lever. Tighten the Allen head bracket screw.

Removal/Installation

Disconnect the electrical wires and remove the Allen head bracket screw; remove the bracket and switch. Installation is the reverse of removal. When replacing or reinstalling the switch it must always be adjusted for proper operation.

SPEED LIMIT SWITCH (CALIFORNIA MODELS ONLY)

Testing

To test the speed limit switch for proper operation perform the following:

1. Start the engine and allow it to warm to operating temperature. Turn the engine off.
2. Touch the positive lead of a voltmeter to terminal 8 and the negative lead to terminal 6 on the switch (**Figure 25**). Do not disconnect the electrical connector.
3. Connect a tachometer to the engine.
4. Start the engine and increase speed to 3,000 rpm. The voltmeter should register battery current; if not, replace the switch.

FUEL SYSTEM AIR INTAKE SENSOR

Testing

To check the air intake sensor for proper operation perform the following:

1. Open the air cleaner housing and remove the air filter. Prop the air cleaner housing open with a block of wood.

2. Pull the multi-pin electrical connector off the sensor housing (**Figure 29**).

3. Using a length of dowel, reach into the air cleaner and push the sensor stator flap open to check for freedom of movement. If the flap sticks, it will most likely work properly once it is pushed open. If the stator flap is hard to move the sensor should be disassembled,

cleaned (if possible) and lubricated. See procedure in this section. If the flap cannot be made to move freely, the sensor must be replaced.

4. Check the fuel pump contacts by touching the ohmmeter leads to terminals 36 and 39 on the sensor (**Figure 30**). Push the stator flap fully open; the ohmmeter should read zero ohms. Release the flap; the ohmmeter should read infinity (no continuity).

5. Touch the ohmmeter leads to the following pairs of terminals, with the stator flap closed and the sensor at room temperature (**Figure 30**):

   a. Terminals 6 and 9: meter reading 200-400 ohms
   b. Terminals 6 and 8: meter reading 130-260 ohms
   c. Terminals 8 and 9: meter reading 70-140 ohms
   d. Terminals 6 and 7: meter reading 40-300 ohms
   e. Terminals 7 and 8: meter reading 100-500 ohms
   f. Terminals 6 and 27 (if applicable): meter reading should be 2300-2700 ohms with a maximum of 2,800 ohms at 68° F (20° C)

6. To check for a burned resistance strip, make sure that the stator flap is in the closed position. Connect the ohmmeter to terminals 7 and 8 and open the stator flap slowly. The resistance should not be lower than 40 ohms or higher than 500 ohms. Repeat this test on terminals 6 and 7; the reading should be the same.

Removal/Installation

1. Disconnect the fuel evaporation hose which leads into the air cleaner.
2. Remove the hoses from the intake air hose.
3. Loosen the large hose clamp which holds the intake air hose to the throttle valve.
4. Pull the multi-pin connector off the intake air sensor (**Figure 29**).
5. Remove the air cleaner housing, intake air sensor and intake air hose as one unit.
6. Remove the small bolts which hold the top half of the air cleaner housing to the intake air sensor.

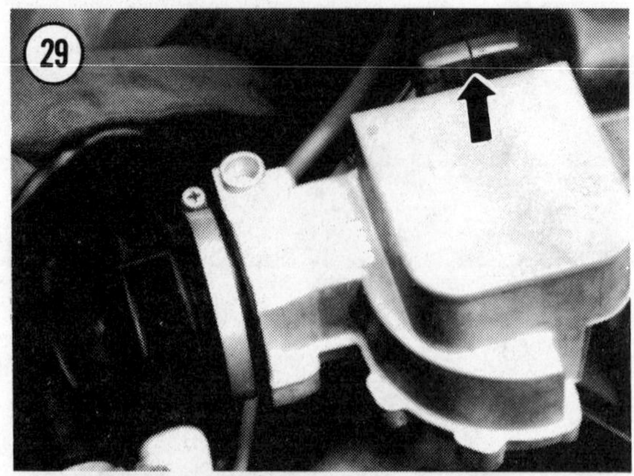

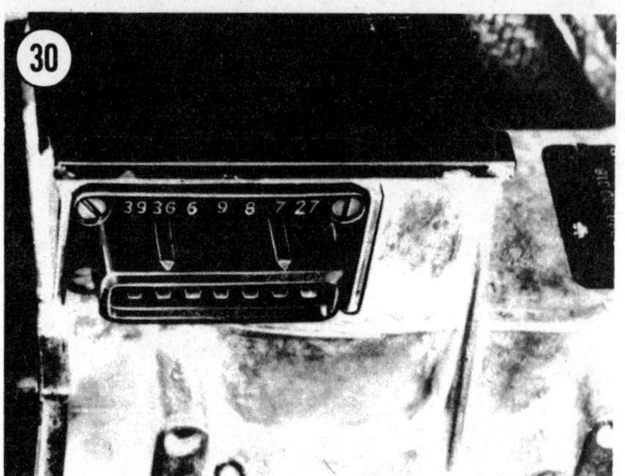

7. Separate the intake air sensor from the top half of the air cleaner.
8. Installation is the reverse of removal.

Disassembly/Assembly

Carefully take out the screws and pry off the bottom plate from the main sensor housing. Assembly is the reverse of disassembly. Always use sealer when installing the bottom plate; otherwise, the unit will leak air and not work properly.

TEMPERATURE SENSORS

Temperature sensor No. 1 is located within the intake air sensor (**Figure 9**) and can be tested as a unit with the procedure given in the intake air sensor section. However, a separate procedure is given in Step 1 of this section.

Temperature sensor No. 1 is also called the air temperature sensor. If temperature sensor No. 1 is found to be faulty, the whole intake air sensor must be replaced.

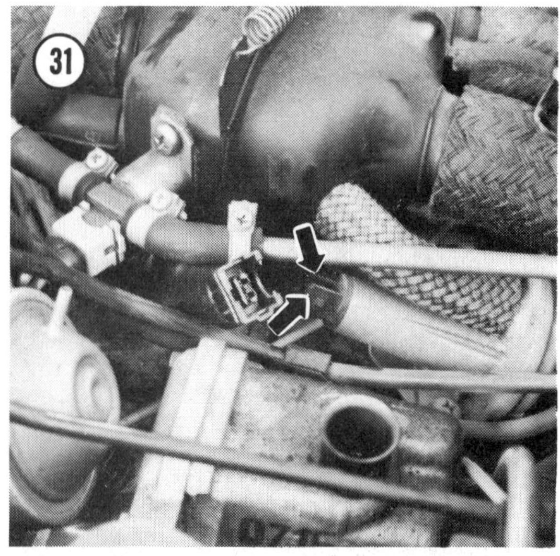

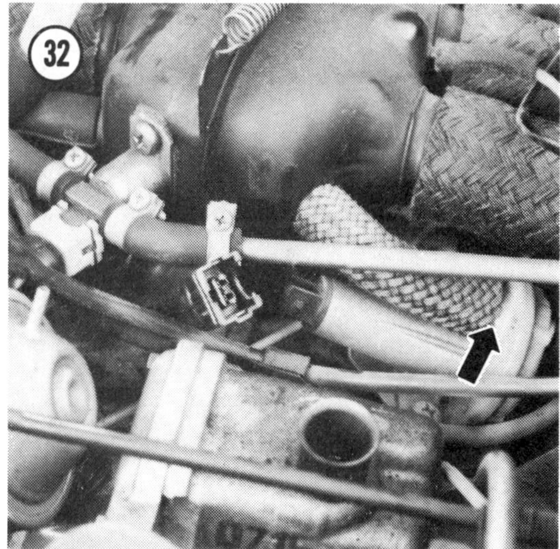

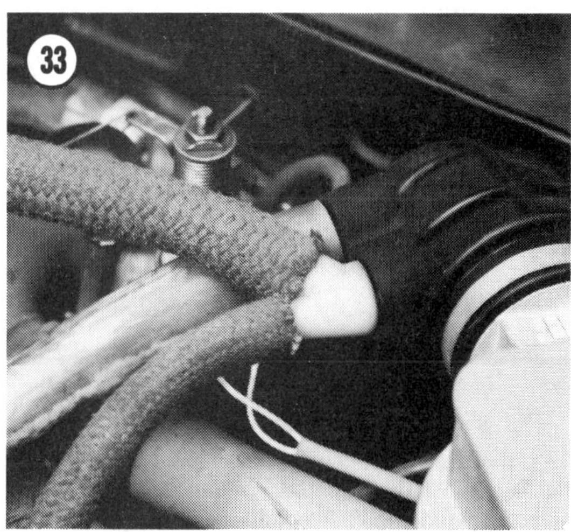

Temperature sensor No. 2 is installed in the cylinder head in front of intake manifold No. 3.

Testing

1. To check temperature sensor No. 1 perform the following:
   a. Pull the multi-pin electrical connector off the intake air sensor (**Figure 29**).
   b. Touch the leads from the ohmmeter to terminals 6 and 27 on the air intake sensor (**Figure 30**). The meter should read 2,300-2,700 ohms; if not, the sensor should be replaced.
2. To check temperature sensor No. 2 perform the following:
   a. Pull the wire off the sensor.
   b. Touch one lead of the ohmmeter to the terminal on the sensor and ground the other to a bare metal spot on the engine. The meter should read 7,000-11,600 ohms at 14° F (10° C); 2,100-3,100 ohms at 68° F (20° C); and 270-390 ohms at 176° F of engine oil temperature.
   c. If readings are too high, touch the ground lead to the steel casing of the sensor. If this gives a correct reading the problem is corrosion between the cylinder head and the sensor. Clean the threads to correct the problem. If the readings are still out of specification the sensor is defective and must be replaced.

6

AUXILIARY AIR REGULATOR

Testing

To check the air regulator perform the following:

1. Pull the electrical connector off the auxiliary air regulator. Touch both leads from the ohmmeter to the terminals on the air regulator (**Figure 31**). The ohmmeter should read approximately 30 ohms. If not, replace the regulator.
2. With a cold engine, pull off the hose which leads into the intake air distributor (**Figure 32**). Disconnect the other hose on the air regulator where it connects to the intake air hose (**Figure 33**) and blow into the regulator through the open end of this hose. Air must pass through

the regulator freely when it is cold; if not, the regulator should be replaced.

3. Reconnect the electrical connector to the auxiliary air regulator. Turn the ignition key to the second position; this will supply current to the air regulator and warm up the heating element. Keep the ignition on for 5 minutes, then blow through the regulator again. The air regulator should now be closed and air should not be able to pass through. If it's not closed, the regulator is defective and should be replaced.

Removal/Installation

1. Disconnect the electrical plug from the air regulator.
2. Remove the screws which hold the regulator to the mounting bracket.
3. Lift up the regulator and disconnect both of the air hoses.
4. Installation is the reverse of removal.

DECEL VALVE (MANUAL TRANSMISSION ONLY)

A vehicle with a faulty decel valve will idle too fast or irregularly.

Testing

1. To check the decel valve perform the following:
   a. Start the engine and let it warm up to operating temperature.
   b. While the engine is running, find the hose which runs from the decel valve to the tee connection on the intake air hose and pinch the hose closed (**Figure 34**). If the idle speed drops the decel valve is defective and should be replaced.
2. To be sure of a faulty decel valve perform the following:
   a. Turn off the engine and disconnect the hose at the tee connection on the intake air hose (**Figure 35**). Plug the tee connection.
   b. Start the engine. Work the throttle valve with your hand and rev the engine up to around 3,000 rpm for a few seconds. At the same time, keep your thumb on the open end of the disconnected hose.

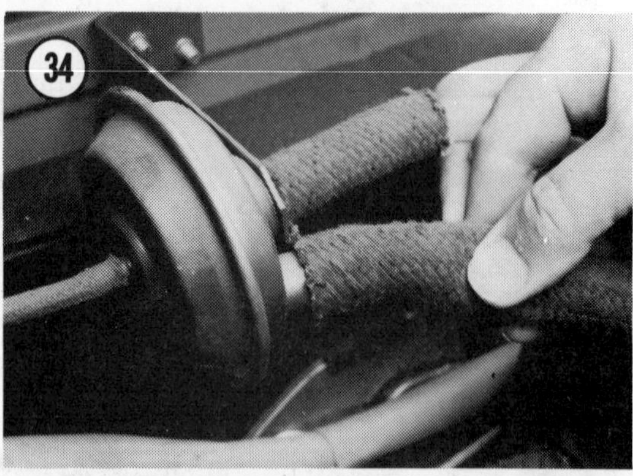

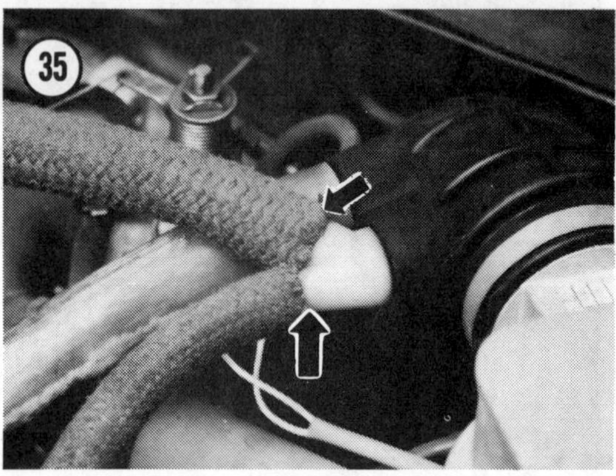

   c. Let the throttle valve snap closed; you should be able to feel a suction on the open end of the hose. If not, the decel valve is defective and must be replaced.

Removal/Installation

1. Disconnect the air hoses from the valve.
2. Remove the screws which hold it to the body and remove the valve.
3. Installation is the reverse of removal.

OXYGEN SENSOR (CALIFORNIA MODELS ONLY)

Testing

NOTE
A carbon monoxide (CO) meter is required to check the oxygen sensor. If a CO meter is not available this procedure should be left to a VW dealer or qualified specialist.

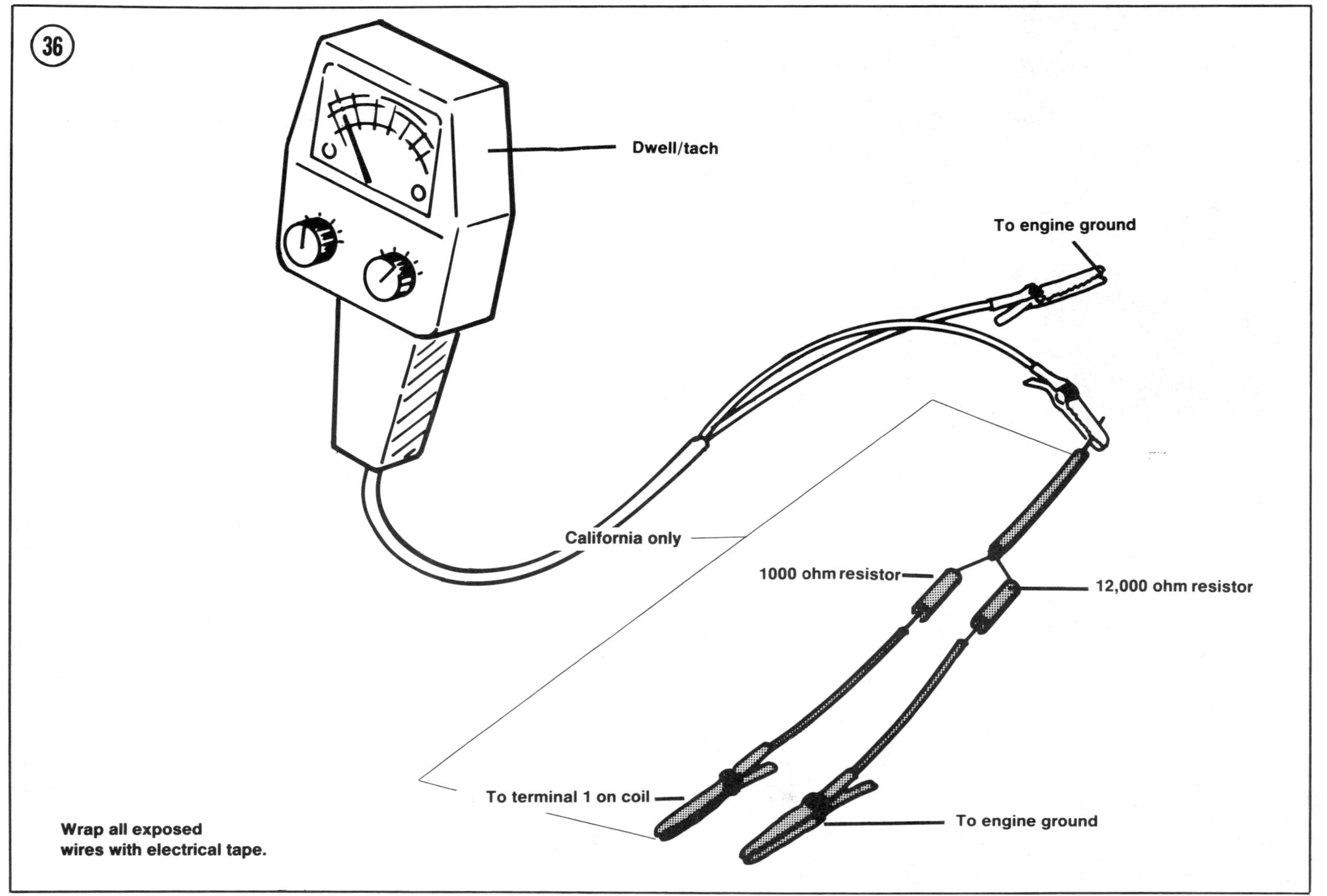
36
Dwell/tach
To engine ground
California only
1000 ohm resistor
12,000 ohm resistor
To terminal 1 on coil
To engine ground
Wrap all exposed
wires with electrical tape.

6

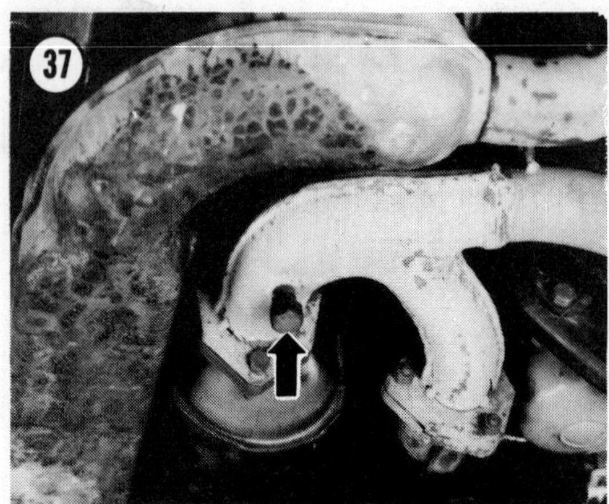

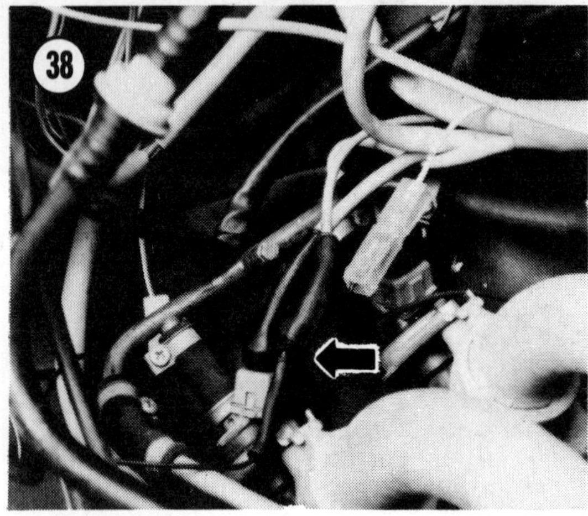

To check the oxygen sensor perform the following:

1. Connect a tachometer to the engine. When using a tach/dwell meter with California models a special condenser set-up as shown in **Figure 36** must be used.
2. Connect the CO meter to the test port in front of the catalytic converter (**Figure 37**).
3. Start the engine and allow it to warm to operating temperature. Oil temperature must be at least 140° F (60° C) and intake air sensor temperature must be at a room temperature of 68° F (20° C) before testing.
4. Check and, if necessary, adjust the idle speed (Chapter Three).
5. Disconnect the wire from the oxygen sensor (**Figure 38**). Check the CO level with the meter; it should be 0.7 + /-0.4%.
6. Let the engine idle. Remove and plug the vacuum hose on the fuel pressure regulator

(**Figure 22**). The CO level should increase to approximately 2.5%.

7. Reconnect the oxygen sensor wire. The CO level must be 0 to 0.7 + /-0.4% if the oxygen sensor is functioning properly. If not, the oxygen sensor is faulty, the wire between the sensor and the ECU is faulty (see Step 8) or there is a leak in the exhaust system between the catalytic converter and the cylinder head.
8. If you suspect a defective wire pull the multi-pin connector off the ECU. Touch the ohmmeter leads to terminal 24 (**Figure 11B**) on the multi-pin connector and the terminal on oxygen sensor. If the meter reads 0 ohms, the wire is fine. If the meter reads infinity, there is a defect in the wire.

Removal/Installation

The oxygen sensor is removed by loosening the unit with a wrench and removing it from the exhaust pipe. Installation is the reverse of removal. Coat the sensor threads with electrically conductive antiseize compound (don't get the compound in the sensor slots). Torque the sensor to 40-55 N•m.

AIR CLEANER

Filter Element Replacement

Refer to Chapter Three for procedure.

Removal/Installation

Refer to **Figure 4** for the following procedure.

1. Disconnect the fuel evaporation hose which leads into the air cleaner (**Figure 39**).
2. Open the housing halves and remove the filter element.

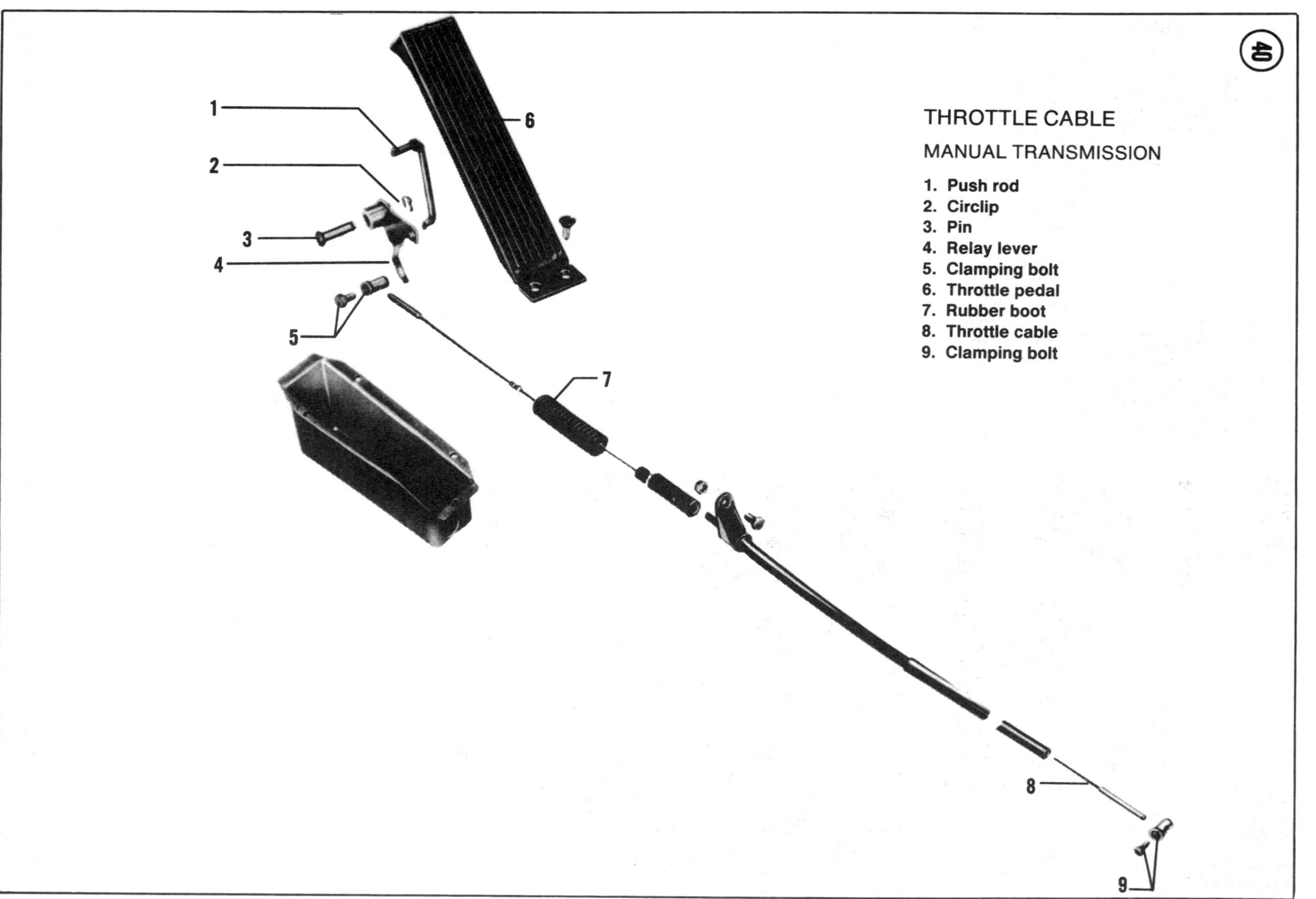
40
THROTTLE CABLE
MANUAL TRANSMISSION
1. Push rod
2. Circlip
3. Pin
4. Relay lever
5. Clamping bolt
6. Throttle pedal
7. Rubber boot
8. Throttle cable
9. Clamping bolt
1
2
3
4
5
6
7
8
9

3. Loosen the large hose clamp which holds the intake air hose to the intake air sensor.
4. Pull the multi-pin connector off the intake air sensor (**Figure 29**).
5. Remove the intake air sensor and the top half of the air cleaner housing as one unit. Remove the small bolts inside the top half of the housing; separate the intake air sensor and the top half of the housing.
6. Pull the lower half of the air cleaner housing from the engine.
7. Installation is the reverse of removal.

THROTTLE CABLE (MANUAL TRANSMISSION)

NOTE

Any time the throttle cable is removed, disconnected or replaced, the linkage must be readjusted. If it is not readjusted, the fuel injection system will not function properly.

The throttle cable connects the throttle pedal, through the underbody frame and front cover plate, to the throttle valve on the intake air distributor.

Replacement

Refer to **Figure 40** for the following procedure.
1. Loosen the clamping bolt on the throttle lever and disconnect the cable (**Figure 41**).
2. Remove the spare tire to gain access to the throttle pedal mechanism under the vehicle. Remove the cover plate (**Figure 42**).
3. Loosen the front clamping bolt (**Figure 43**) and pull the cable out of the cable guide tube.
4. Slip the rubber boot on the new cable end, insert it into the guide tube and coat it with axle grease as you push it in. Push the cable all the way through until the steel end appears in the engine compartment.
5. Connect the forward end of the cable to the clamping bolt and reinstall the cover plate. Install the spare tire. After installation, adjust the cable; see procedure in this chapter.

Adjustment

1. Have an assistant hold the throttle pedal all the way to the floor.

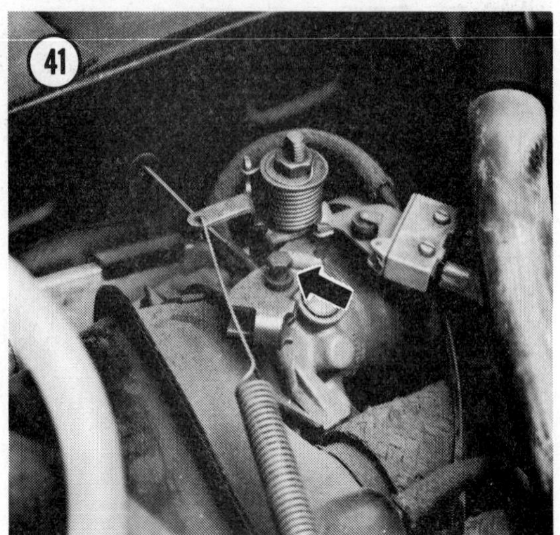

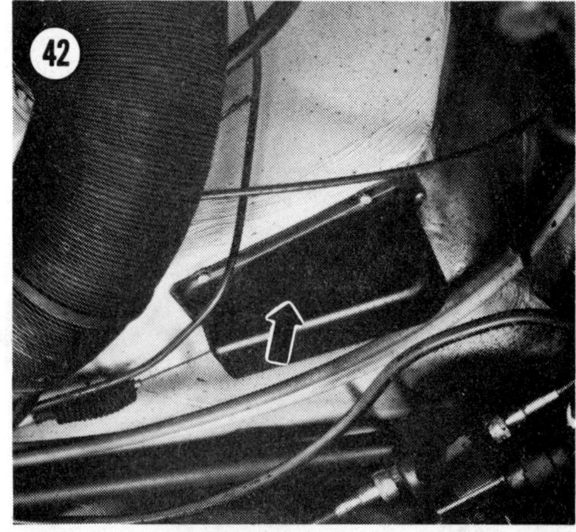

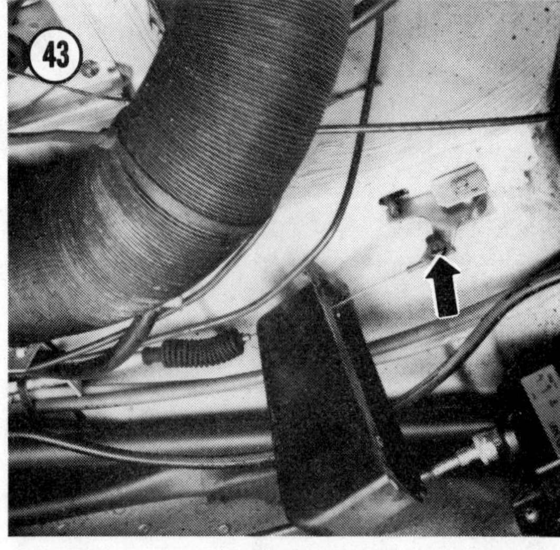

2. Insert the steel end of the cable into the clamping bolt on the throttle valve lever (**Figure 41**).
3. Open the throttle valve by hand until a gap of 0.040-0.060 in. (1.0-1.5 mm) is obtained between the throttle valve lever and the stop on the housing. See dimension A in **Figure 44**. When the proper gap is obtained tighten the clamping bolt.

THROTTLE CABLE (AUTOMATIC TRANSMISSION)

NOTE
Any time the throttle cable or throttle valve pushrod is removed, disconnected or replaced, the linkage must be readjusted. If it is not readjusted, the fuel injection system will not function properly and the automatic transmission will not shift properly.

The throttle cable connects the throttle pedal, through the underbody frame, to the shifter lever on the transmission. The shifter lever is connected to the throttle valve lever by the throttle valve pushrod. See **Figure 45**.

Replacement

Refer to **Figure 45** for the following procedure.
1. Remove the spare tire to gain access to the throttle pedal mechanism.
2. Remove the cover plate (**Figure 42**).
3. Loosen the clamping bolt (**Figure 43**) and pull the steel end of the cable out of the pedal lever. Pull the rubber boot off the cable end.
4. From under the vehicle, pop the cable connector off the shifter lever (**Figure 46**). Pull the boot off the cable end and pull the cable through the guide tube.
5. Insert the new cable into the guide tube from the transmission end, coating it with axle grease as it is being pushed in, until the steel end appears from the guide tube in the front of the vehicle.
6. Install the rubber boot on the transmission end of the cable and snap the connector onto the shifter lever.
7. Install and/or adjust the throttle valve pushrod before installing the cable's steel end in the front clamping bolt and installing the cover plate. After the pushrod is adjusted, adjust the throttle cable. See procedure in this chapter.

6

Cable Adjustment

Refer to **Figure 45** for the following procedure.
1. Remove the spare tire to gain access to the pedal mechanism.
2. Remove the cover plate (**Figure 42**).
3. If the cable was disconnected, install the rubber boot onto the pedal end of the cable. Install the cable's steel end in the front clamping bolt and tighten the nut (**Figure 43**).
4. Have an assistant hold the throttle pedal all the way to the floor.
5. Measure the free play between the transmission lever and its internal stop. See dimension A in **Figure 47**. There should be approximately 1/32-3/32 in. of free play. If not, loosen the front clamping bolt and adjust by letting out or pulling in more cable. Tighten the clamping bolt.
6. Reinstall the cover plate and install the spare tire.

Throttle Valve Pushrod Removal/Installation

Refer to **Figure 45** for the following procedure.
1. To remove the pushrod, gently pry the circlip off the throttle valve end of the adjusting

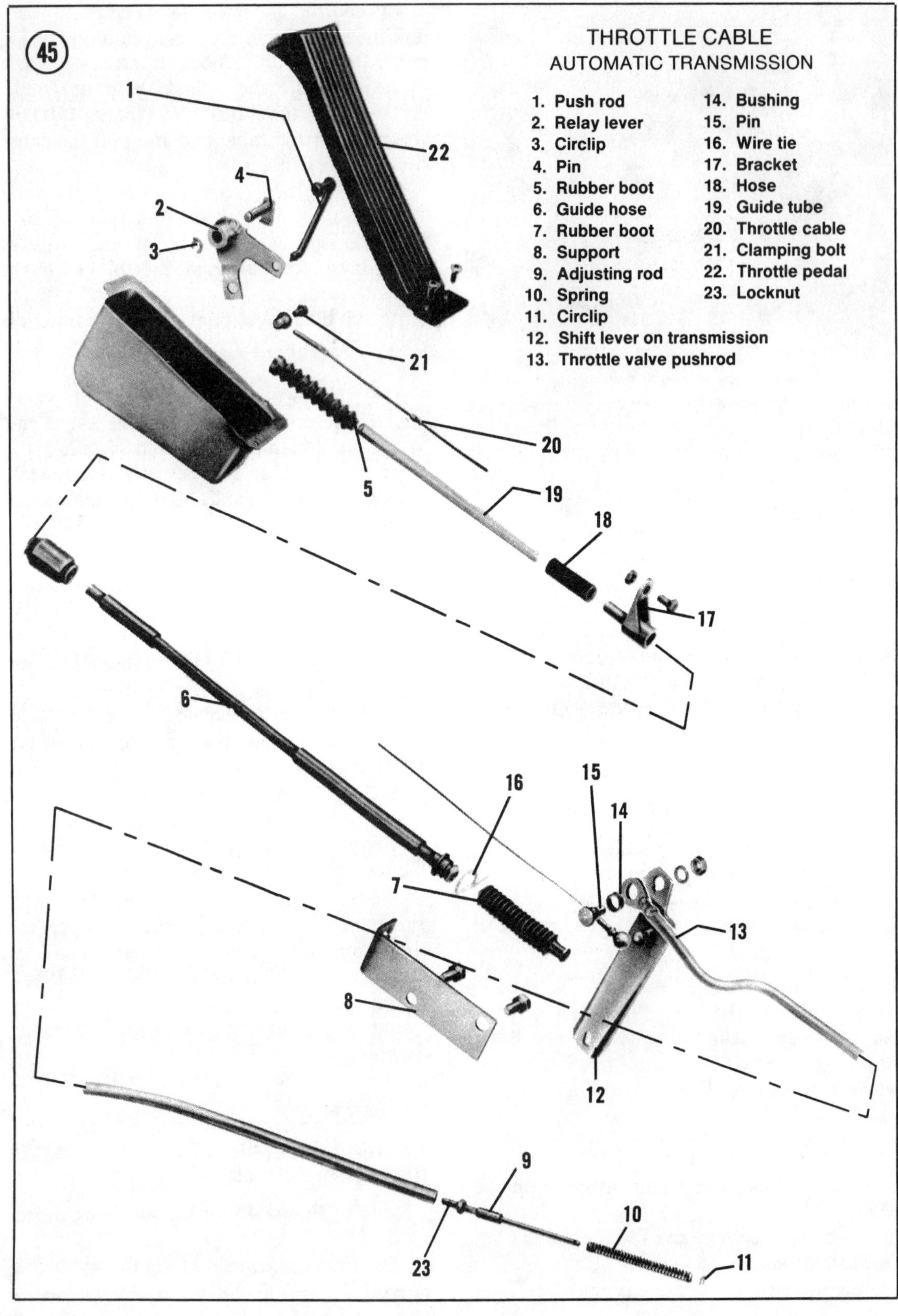
45
THROTTLE CABLE
AUTOMATIC TRANSMISSION
1. Push rod
2. Relay lever
3. Circlip
4. Pin
5. Rubber boot
6. Guide hose
7. Rubber boot
8. Support
9. Adjusting rod
10. Spring
11. Circlip
12. Shift lever on transmission
13. Throttle valve pushrod
14. Bushing
15. Pin
16. Wire tie
17. Bracket
18. Hose
19. Guide tube
20. Throttle cable
21. Clamping bolt
22. Throttle pedal
23. Locknut

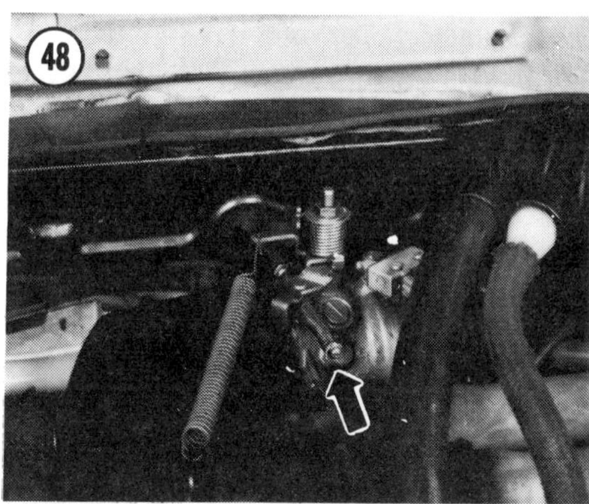

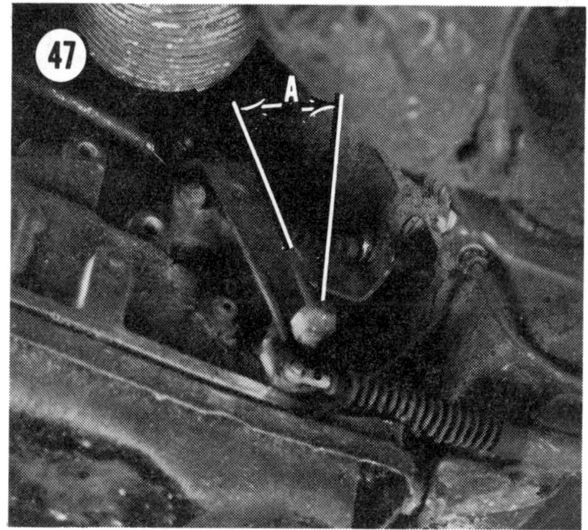

rod (**Figure 48**). Be careful not to lose the clip or let the spring fall down into the engine.
2. Unbolt the pushrod from the shifter lever (**Figure 49**).
3. Installation is the reverse of removal. The spring and circlip should not be installed until the rod is adjusted. See procedure in this chapter.

Pushrod Adjustment

Refer to **Figure 45** and **Figure 50** for the following procedure.

1. Pop the cable connector off the shifter lever if it's not off already (**Figure 46**).
2. Loosen the locknut. Remove the circlip and spring from the end of the throttle valve pushrod if they are not off already (**Figure 48**).
3. Start the engine and let it warm to operating temperature.
4. Check and, if necessary, adjust the idle speed (Chapter Three).
5. Shut the engine off.
6. Pull the throttle valve pushrod in the direction of arrow B in **Figure 50** until it stops.
7. While holding the throttle valve pushrod, turn the adjusting rod on the end of the pushrod with a screwdriver until the larger diameter shoulder just touches the swivel pivot on the throttle lever.
8. Install the spring and circlip.
9. Start the engine and recheck the idle speed. Adjust if necessary by turning the adjusting rod with a screwdriver. Only minor adjustment should be necessary.
10. Tighten the locknut.
11. Snap the cable connector onto the shifter lever.

12. Install the rubber boot on the throttle cable end. Insert the steel end in the front clamping bolt, but do not tighten the nut. The throttle cable must be adjusted before installing the cover plate; see procedure in this chapter.

INTAKE MANIFOLDS

Removal/Installation

1. Remove the air cleaner assembly, intake air sensor and intake air hose. See procedures in this chapter.
2. Fashion a special tool as shown in **Figure 51**.
3. Use the special tool to slide the 4 hoses off the intake air distributor and onto the intake manifolds **(Figure 52)**.
4. Remove the fuel injectors from the heads as described in this chapter; they do not have to be disconnected from the main fuel rig.
5. Remove the 4 nuts and washers securing the manifold to the cylinder heads and carefully lift the manifold out taking care not to drop anything into the cylinder heads. Plug the intake port with rags.
6. Installation is the reverse of removal. Be sure to install a new gasket with the manifold.

INTAKE AIR DISTRIBUTOR

Removal/Installation

1. Remove the air cleaner assembly, intake air sensor and intake air hose as one unit. See procedures in this chapter.
2. Remove the intake manifolds. See procedure in this chapter.
3. Disconnect the throttle linkage from the throttle valve.
4. Disconnect the EGR crossover pipe from the EGR valve.

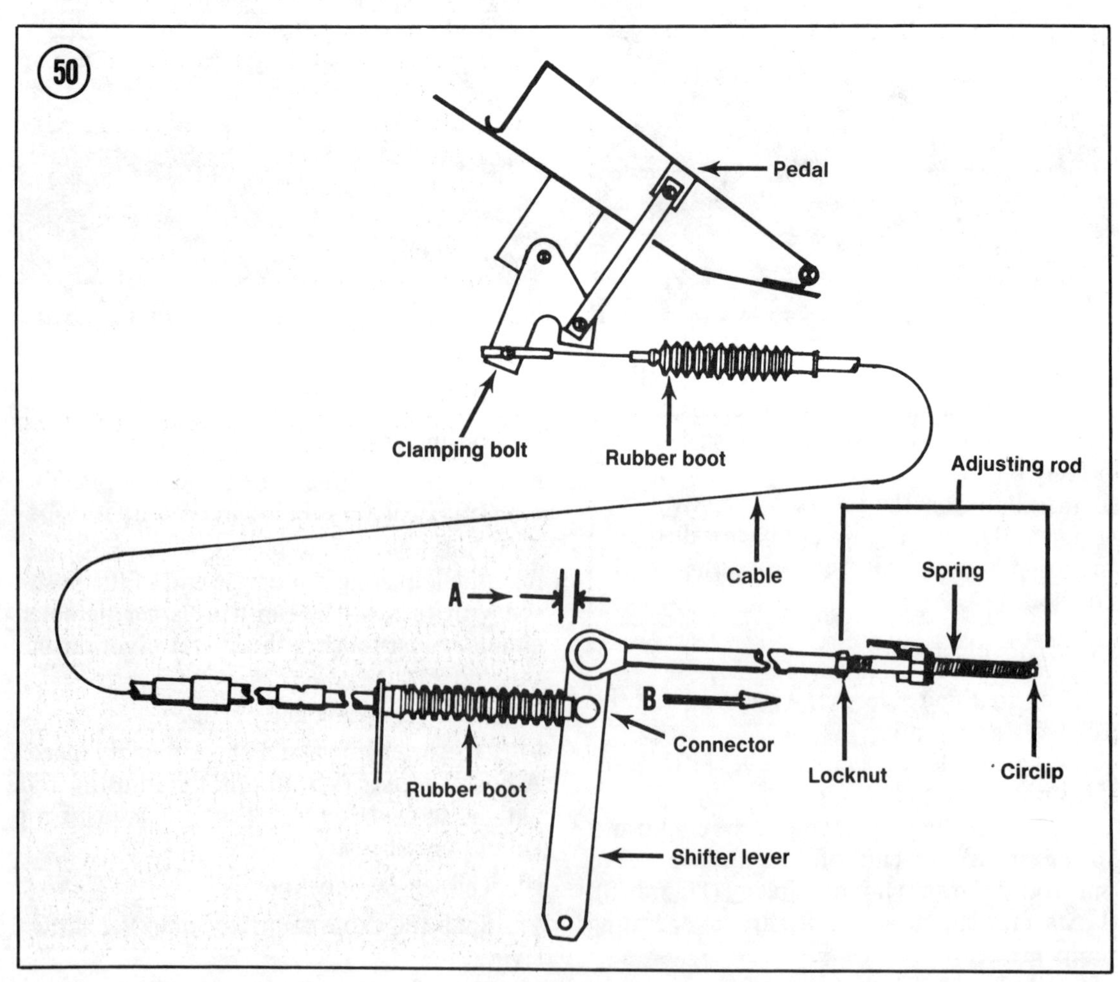

5. Remove the vacuum hoses which attach to the intake air distributor. Mark them for correct installation.
6. Disconnect the electrical wires and the main fuel rig lines to the cold start valve. Plug the fuel lines.
7. Loosen the bolts securing the air distributor to the crankcase. Remove the air distributor.
8. Installation is the reverse of removal.

EXHAUST SYSTEM

Exhaust gases are routed through heat exchangers, a catalytic converter and a muffler. The system for 49-state models is shown in **Figure 53**. Refer to the emission control systems section of this chapter for information on the EGR system. Canadian models have a system similar to that shown in **Figure 53** but without EGR. The California model exhaust system is shown in **Figure 54**.

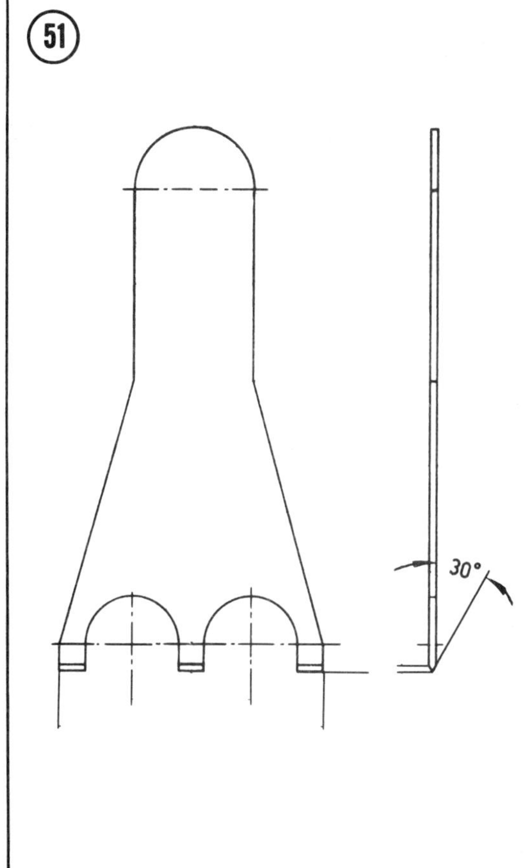

Removal/Installation

The exhaust system can easily be removed with the engine installed. Refer to **Figure 53** and **Figure 54** for the following procedure.

1. Remove the clamps which hold the muffler to the crossover pipes. Disconnect the muffler clamp and pull the muffler off the exhaust pipe.

2A. On California models, perform the following:
   a. Remove the left lower air duct from the left heat exchanger. Disconnect the left heat exchanger from the front of the catalytic converter and lower it carefully; do not allow it to drop.
   b. Unbolt and remove the catalytic converter.
   c. Remove the crossover pipe.
   d. Remove the lower air shrouds.
   e. Remove the right lower air duct from the right heat exchanger.
   f. Remove the left lower air duct from the left heat exchanger.
   g. Unbolt the left exhaust manifold and the right heat exchanger/exhaust manifold from the cylinder heads.
   h. Remove the exhaust seals from the cylinder heads.
   i. Installation is the reverse of removal.

2B. On 49-state and Canadian models, perform the following:
   a. Remove the catalytic converter.
   b. Unbolt the EGR exhaust pipe, then remove the crossover pipe.

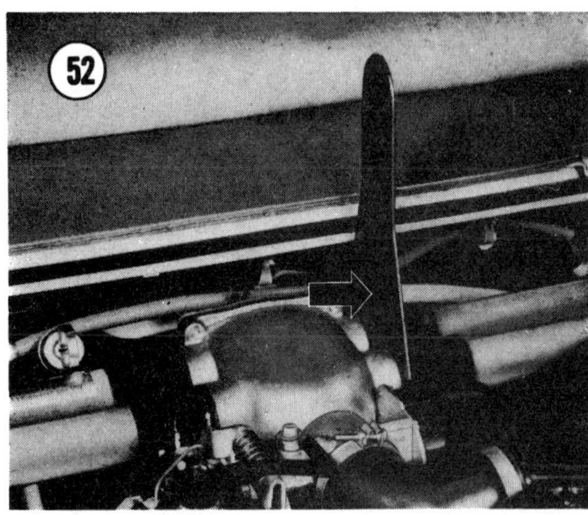

6

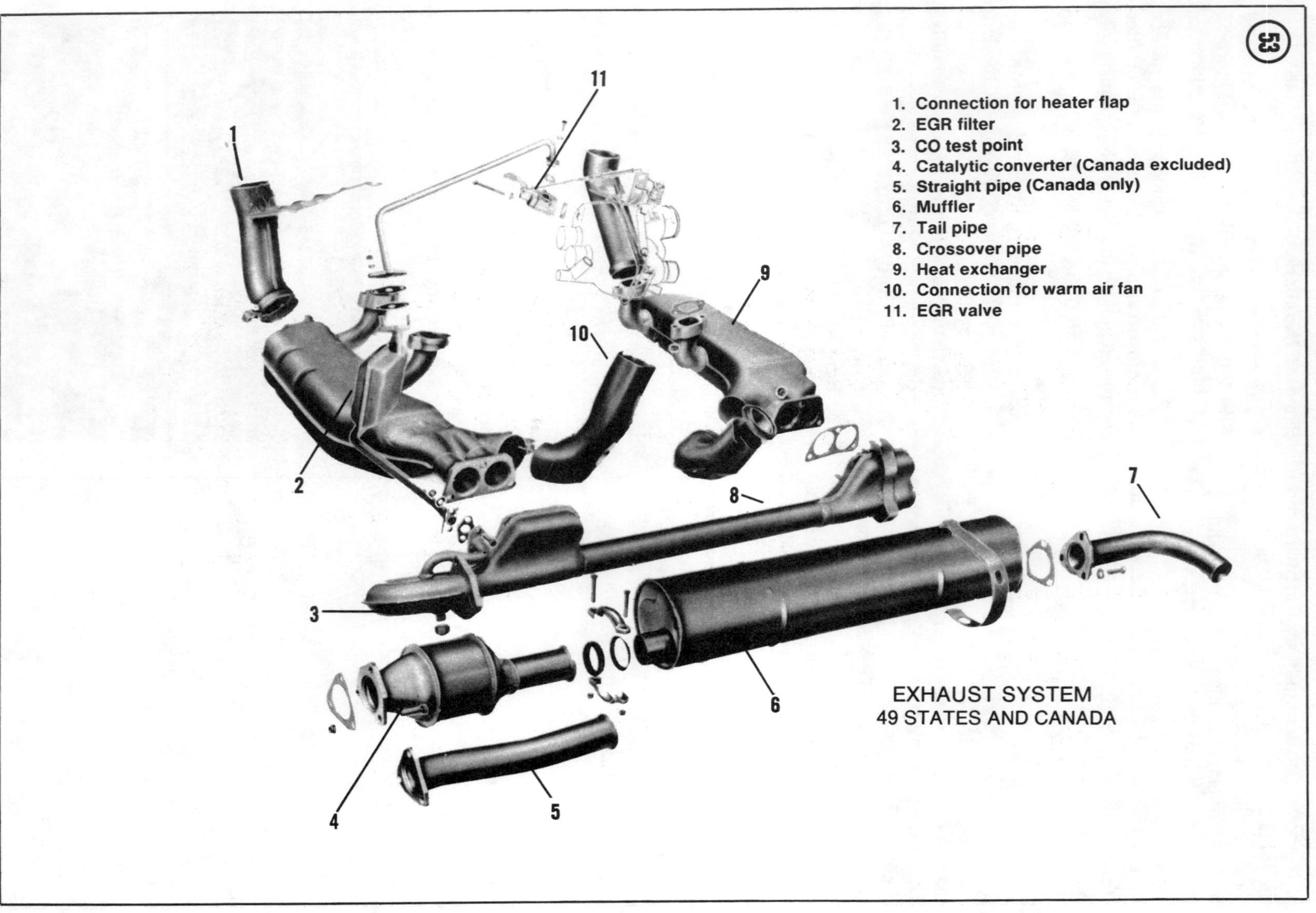
53
1. Connection for heater flap
2. EGR filter
3. CO test point
4. Catalytic converter (Canada excluded)
5. Straight pipe (Canada only)
6. Muffler
7. Tail pipe
8. Crossover pipe
9. Heat exchanger
10. Connection for warm air fan
11. EGR valve
11
1
9
10
2
8
7
3
6
4
5
EXHAUST SYSTEM
49 STATES AND CANADA

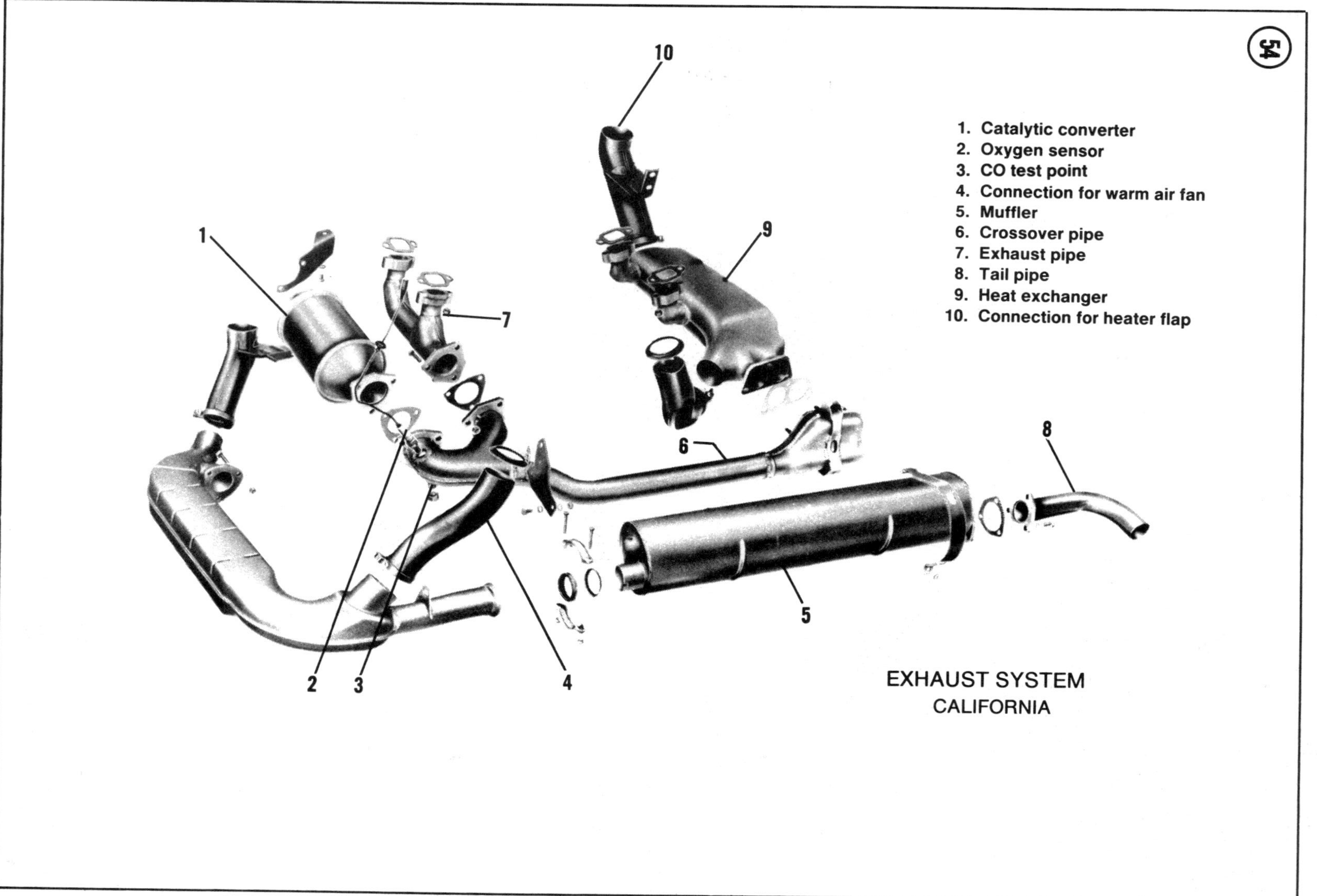

EXHAUST SYSTEM
CALIFORNIA

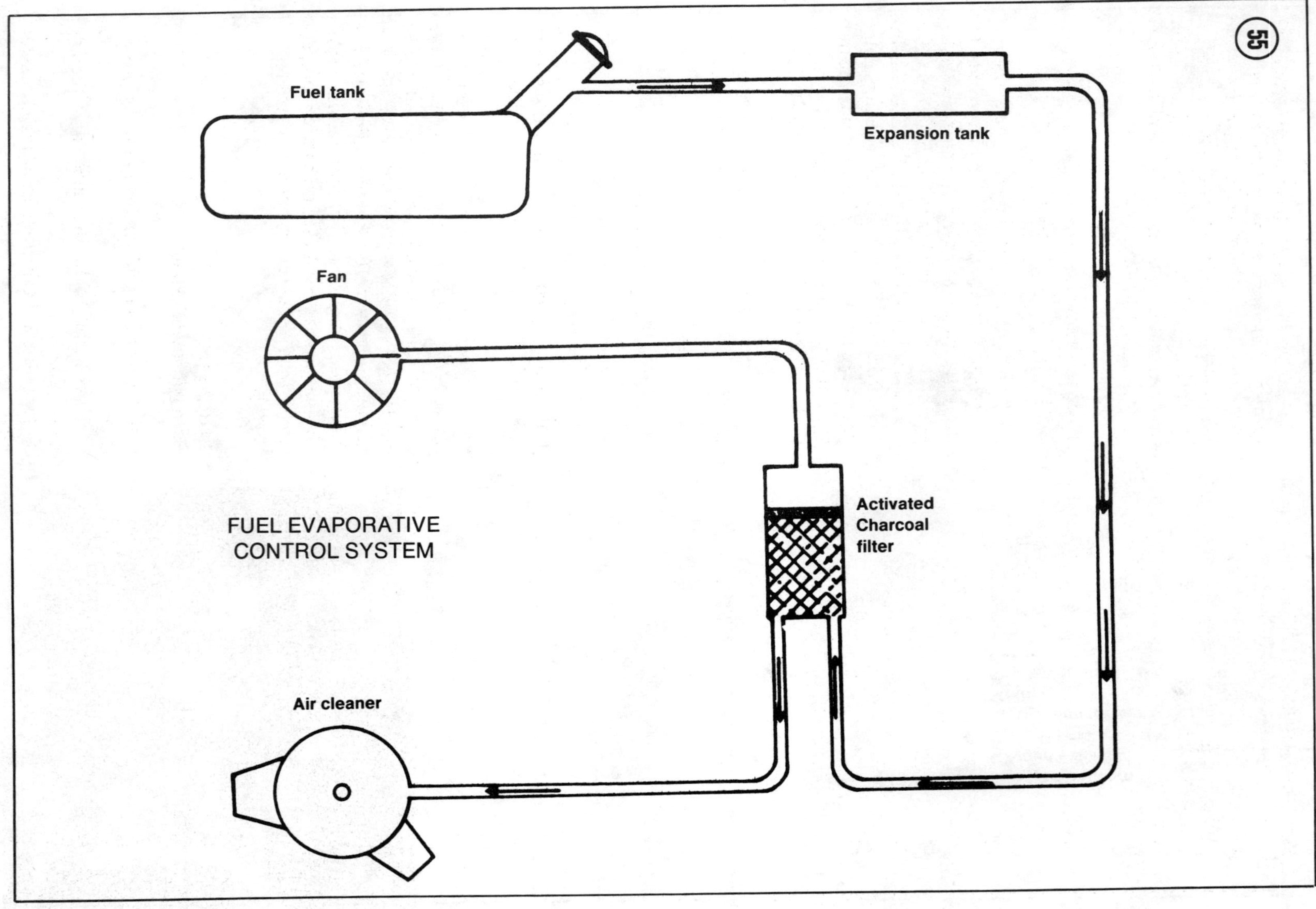
55
Fuel tank
Expansion tank
Fan
Activated
Charcoal
filter
FUEL EVAPORATIVE
CONTROL SYSTEM
Air cleaner

c. Remove the right and left lower air ducts.
d. Remove the lower air shrouds.
e. Unbolt the left and right heat exchangers/exhaust manifolds from the cylinder heads.
f. Remove the exhaust seals.
g. Installation is the reverse of removal.

WARNING
Always use new exhaust seals and gaskets when installing the exhaust system or dangerous fumes may leak into the vehicle when the engine is running.

Inspection

Check all components for cracks, burn-through or rust. Minor defects may be welded, however, this is not recommended for heavy damage. Heavily damaged components should be replaced; repair should not be attempted.

EMISSION CONTROL SYSTEM

Fuel Evaporative Control System

All Vanagons are equipped with a fuel evaporative system to prevent release of fuel vapor into the atmosphere. This system is shown along with the fuel system in **Figure 2** and in **Figure 55**. Fuel vapor from the fuel tank passes through the expansion tanks to the charcoal canister. When the engine is running, cool air from the fan housing forces the fuel vapor into the air cleaner where it takes part in the normal combustion process.

There is no preventive maintenance required other than checking tightness and condition of the lines connecting the parts of the system. The expansion tank is an integal part of the fuel tank. The charcoal canister is under the vehicle, on the right-hand side, bolted slightly to the rear of the fuel tank.

Positive Crankcase Ventilation (PCV) System

When the engine is running a small amount of combustion gas from the cylinder leaks by the piston rings and enters the crankcase. If this gas were to leak freely into the atmosphere it would greatly increase vehicle emissions. Instead this gas is routed from the top of the crankcase through a breather cap and hose into the intake air hose where the gas takes part in the normal combustion process (**Figure 56**).

6

This system needs no preventive maintenance other than occasionally checking that the hose is not cracked and that the connections are tight.

Exhaust Gas Recirculation (EGR) System

Vanagons sold in the United States (except California) are equipped with an EGR system (**Figure 57**). The EGR system is designed to cut emission of oxides of nitrogen (NOx). A portion of the exhaust gases passes through the EGR filter to the EGR valve located at the throttle valve housing. During partial engine loads, the vacuum within the intake air distributor opens the EGR valve, admitting exhaust gases into the air distributor. Addition of this gas lowers combustion chamber temperature thus reducing formation of oxides of nitrogen.

EGR Valve Removal/Installation

Refer to **Figure 57** for the following procedure.

1. Unbolt the EGR filter pipe from the exhaust pipe.
2. Unbolt the EGR filter from the crossover pipe.

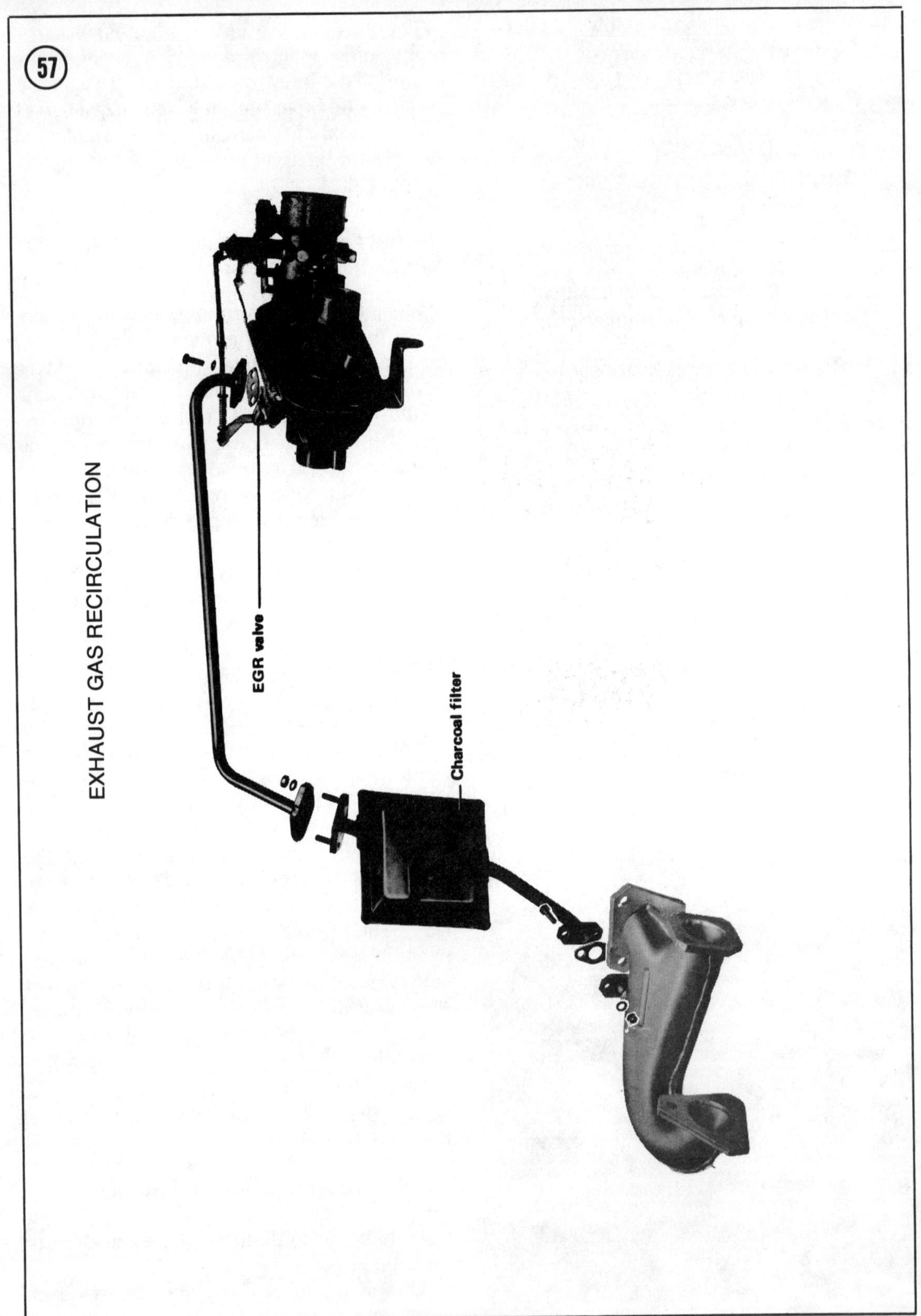
57
EXHAUST GAS RECIRCULATION
EGR valve
Charcoal filter

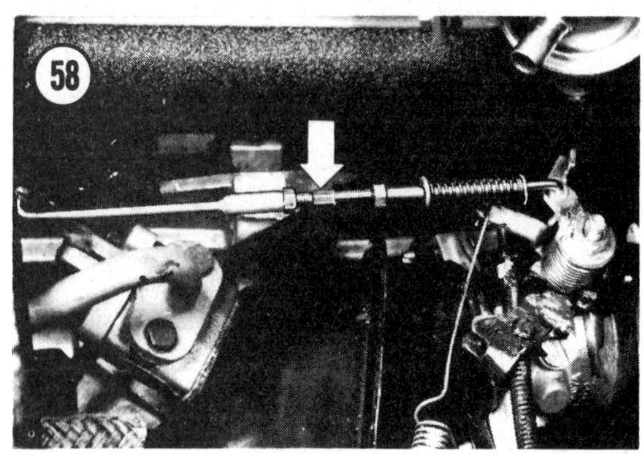

3. Unbolt the crossover pipe from the EGR valve.
4. Installation is the reverse of removal. After installation, adjustment of the linkage between the throttle valve and the EGR valve is recommended.

WARNING
Always use new gaskets when installing the EGR system or there will be a danger of exhaust leakage. The system will not operate properly if there is a leak.

Adjustment

1. Start the engine and allow it to warm to operating temperature.
2. Check and, if necessary, adjust idle speed (Chapter Three).
3. Turn the hex nut on the linkage rod (**Figure 58**). Shorten the linkage until the idle speed suddenly drops (caused by the valve opening).
4. Turn the hex nut the opposite direction (lengthen the rod) 1 1/16 turns for manual transmissions or 5/6 turn for automatic transmissions. The idle speed should return to normal; if not, turn the nut just a little more.

CHAPTER SEVEN

ELECTRICAL SYSTEMS

This chapter includes service procedures for the battery, starter, charging system, lighting system, fuses, instruments and windshield wipers. Wiring diagrams are included at the end of the book. **Table 1** and **Table 2** are at the end of the chapter.

BATTERY

The battery is located under the front passenger seat. The stock battery which comes with the Vanagon requires regular maintenance and checking.

Care and Inspection

1. Slide the passenger seat all the way forward. Camper vehicles must rotate the swivel seat all the way to the left to gain access.
2. Remove the battery hold-down clamps.
3. Disconnect the battery cables and remove the battery (**Figure 1**).
4. Clean the top of the battery with baking soda and water solution. Scrub with a stiff bristle brush. Wipe the battery clean with cloth moistened in ammonia or baking soda solution.

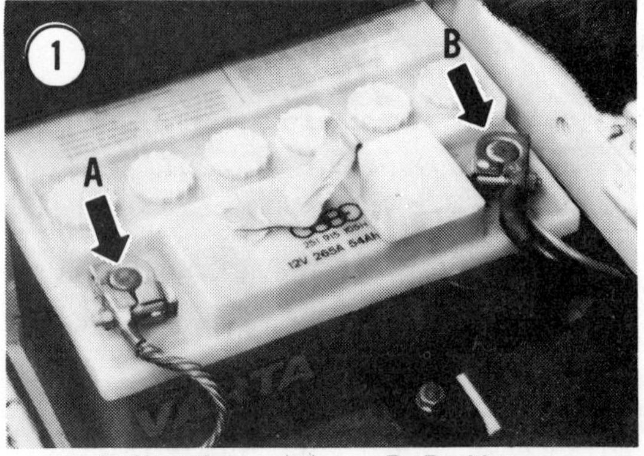

A. Negative **B. Positive**

CAUTION
Keep the baking soda solution out of the battery cells or the electrolyte will be seriously weakened.

5. Clean the battery terminals with a stiff wire brush or one of the many tools made for this purpose.
6. Examine the entire battery for cracks.
7. Install the battery and reconnect battery cables, positive to positive and negative to negative.

8. Coat the battery connections with a light mineral grease or petroleum jelly after tightening.

9. Check the electrolyte level; top up with distilled water if necessary.

Testing

Hydrometer testing is the best way to check the condition of the battery. Use a hydrometer with numbered graduations from 1.100 to 1.300 rather than the type with colored bands (**Figure 2**).

To use the hydrometer, squeeze the rubber ball, insert the tip in the cell and release the ball (**Figure 3**). Draw enough electrolyte to float the weighted float inside the hydrometer. Note the number in line with the surface of the electrolyte; this is the specific gravity for this cell. Squeeze the electrolyte back into the cell from which it came. The specific gravity of the electrolyte in each battery cell is an excellent indication of that cell's condition. See **Table 1**.

If the cells test in the poor range, the battery will require recharging. If one or more cells test out dead or very low, the cell may be shorted and the battery will have to be replaced.

CAUTION
Disconnect both battery cables before connecting charging equipment.

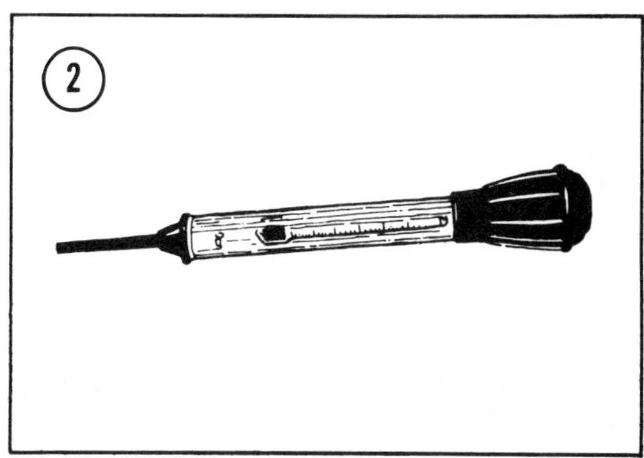

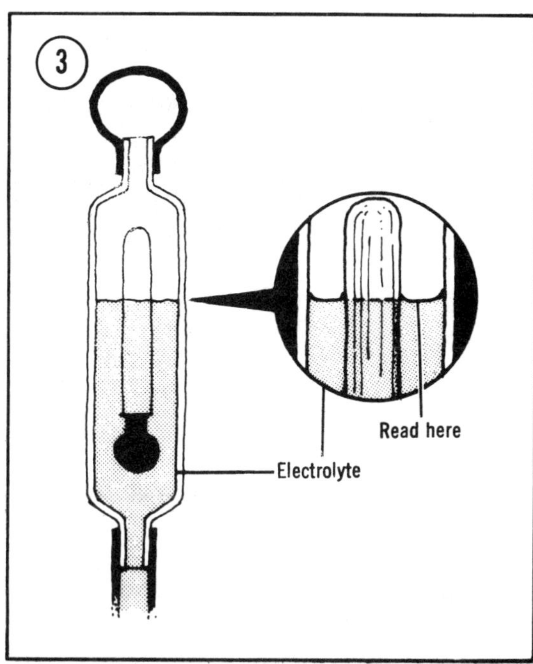

ALTERNATOR

All Vanagons have an alternator-based 12-volt electrical system. The alternator generates alternating current (AC) which is converted into direct current by silicone diodes within the alternator housing. The alternator is mounted on the right side of the cooling fan housing and is driven by a fan belt which is turned by the main cooling fan (**Figure 4**).

7

Belt Replacement

Refer to **Figure 4** for the following procedure.

1. Disconnect the battery (**Figure 1**).
2. Remove the rubber heater blower bellows (**Figure 5**).
3. Remove the elbow air duct.
4. Remove the heater blower housing.
5. Remove the plastic screen mesh which guards the main cooling fan.
6. Loosen the alternator adjusting bolt (**Figure 6**).
7. Rotate the alternator counterclockwise to take tension off the belt. Remove the old fan belt and slip the new one on.
8. Installation is the reverse of removal. Adjust the alternator belt tension; see procedure in this chapter.

Belt Adjustment

Since drive belt tension and condition affect battery charging, proper tension is important. When tension is correct, the belt should deflect

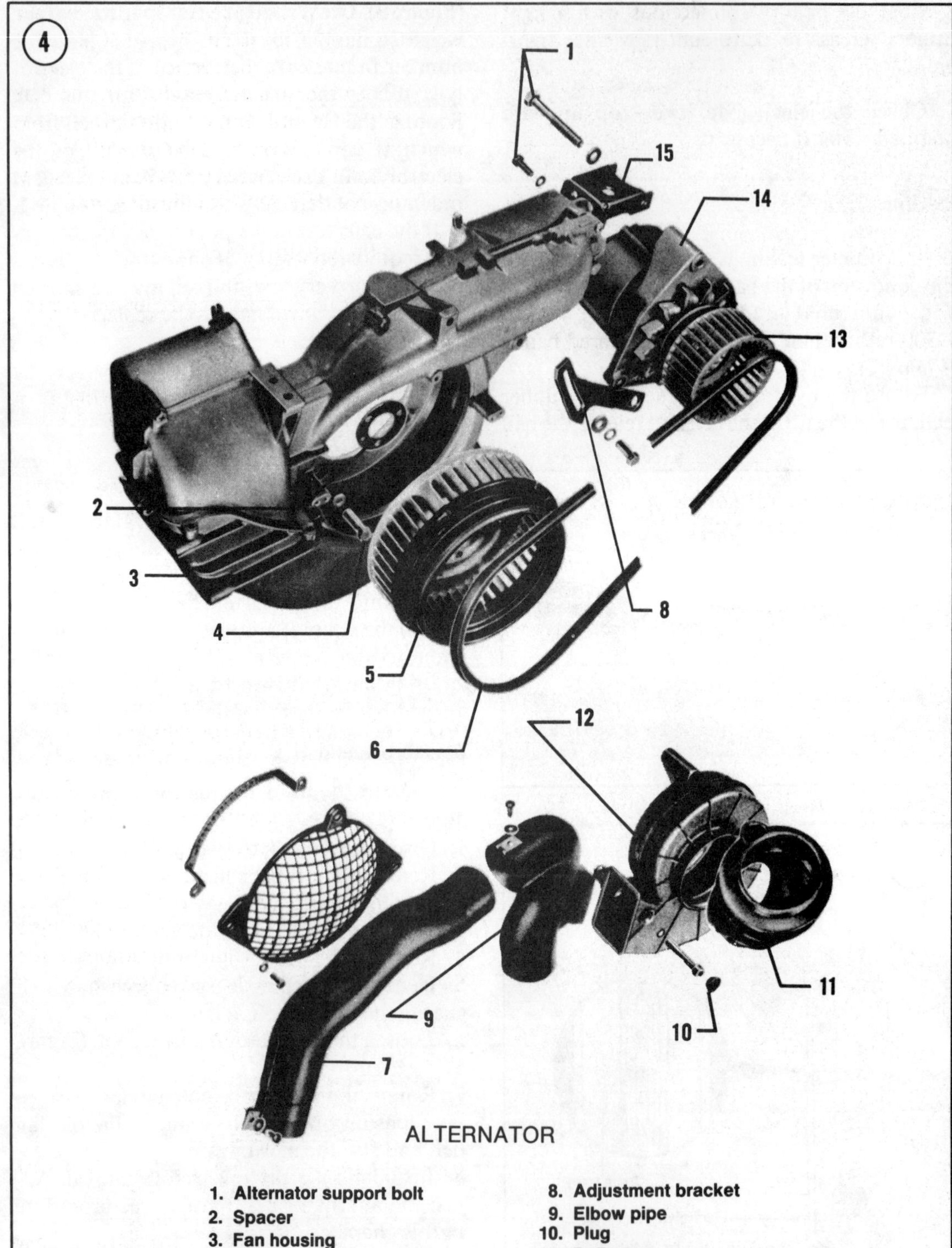

ALTERNATOR

1. Alternator support bolt
2. Spacer
3. Fan housing
4. Bolt
5. Cooling fan with pulley
6. V-belt
7. Warm air duct
8. Adjustment bracket
9. Elbow pipe
10. Plug
11. Bellows
12. Heater blower housing
13. Heater blower fan
14. Alternator
15. Alternator support

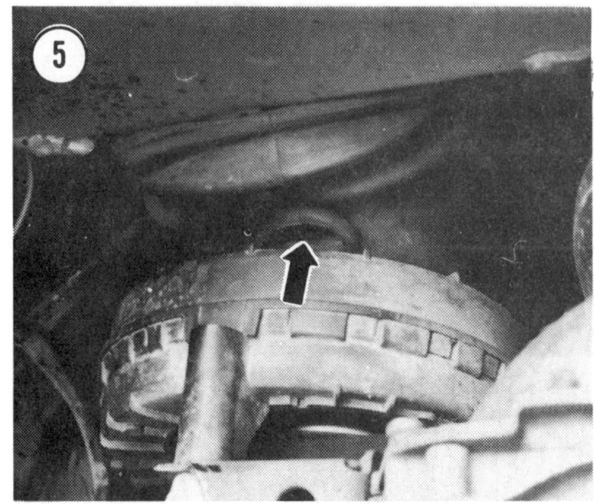

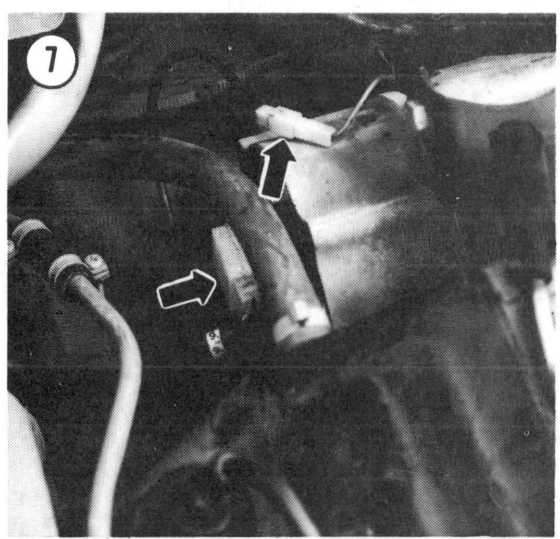

about 3/8 to 5/8 in. (10 to 15 mm) under moderate thumb pressure. Replace the belt if cracked or excessively worn.

To adjust belt tension, pull down the rear license plate and loosen the alternator adjusting bolt (**Figure 6**). Push the left side of the alternator down until the proper tension is obtained, then tighten the adjusting bolt.

Removal/Installation

Refer to **Figure 4** for the following procedure.

1. Disconnect the battery cables (**Figure 1**).
2. Remove the rubber heater blower bellows (**Figure 5**).
3. Remove the elbow air duct.
4. Remove the heater blower housing.
5. Remove the plastic screen mesh which guards the main cooling fan.
6. Remove the adjusting bolt (**Figure 6**). Remove the bolt which holds the bracket to the alternator.
7. Remove the alternator belt.
8. Unplug the electrical connectors from the back of the alternator (**Figure 7**).
9. Remove the alternator support bolt and carefully lift the alternator out of the engine compartment.
10. Remove the heater blower fan. Make up a special tool with a length of pipe with a 2 inch (5 cm) inner diameter and an old fan belt. Slip one end of the fan belt over the heater blower fan pulley and slip the other end into the pipe; use this tool to keep the fan from turning while the fan belt is being removed (**Figure 8**).

7

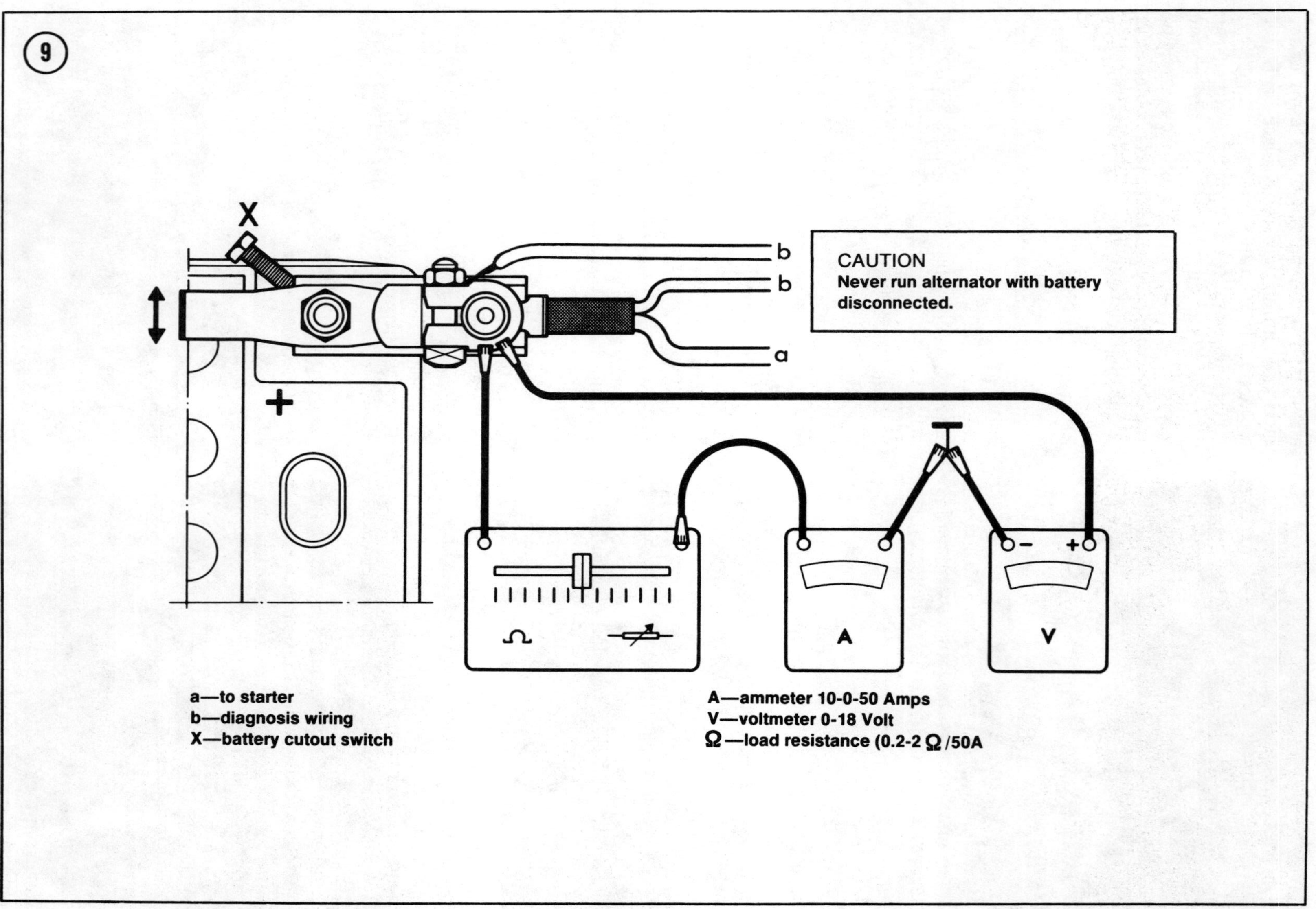
9
X
b
b
a
CAUTION
Never run alternator with battery disconnected.
+
A
V
–
+
a—to starter
b—diagnosis wiring
X—battery cutout switch
A—ammeter 10-0-50 Amps
V—voltmeter 0-18 Volt
Ω—load resistance (0.2-2 Ω/50A

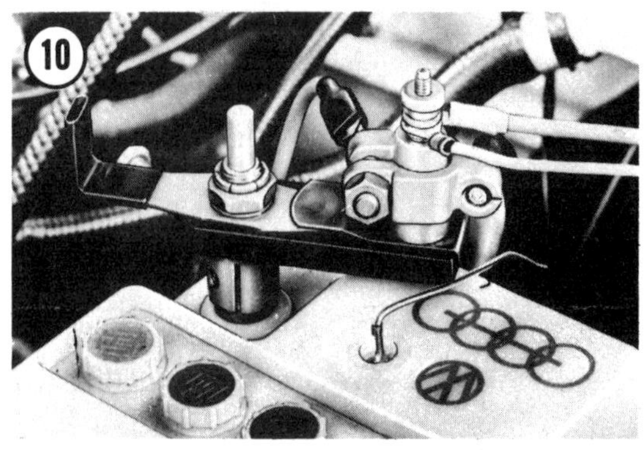

11. Installation is the reverse of removal. After installation, adjust the alternator belt tension. See procedure in this chapter.

Testing the Alternator

This test requires a special battery cut-out switch, a variable resistance device, an ammeter and a voltmeter hooked up to the battery as shown in **Figure 9**. If the alternator is found to be faulty, it should be replaced with a new or rebuilt unit.

1. Disconnect the negative and positive leads from the battery.
2. Connect the cut-out switch to the battery positive terminal. Connect the positive lead strap to the cut-out switch. Make sure the switch is closed (**Figure 10**).
3. Connect the variable resistance device, the ammeter and the voltmeter in series with the cut-out switch as shown in **Figure 9**.
4. Connect the battery negative lead. Start the engine and run it at 3,000 rpm.
5. Adjust the variable resistance device until the ammeter reads 25 amps.
6. Open the cut-out switch (**Figure 11**). Adjust the resistance device until the ammeter reads 40 amps. The voltmeter should read 13.5-14.5 volts. If the reading is low replace the suppressor condenser and the voltage regulator. Repeat the test. If the voltage is still low, replace the alternator.

STARTER

There are 2 types of starters used on the Vanagon; they are both manufactured by the Robert Bosch Company. Automatic transmissions employ a starter having 4 brushes; this is because of the heavy loads encountered when turning over the automatic transmission (**Figure 12**). Manual transmission starters have only 2 brushes (**Figure 13**). Both starters operate the same way and are very similar in appearance.

The starter is located under the vehicle, on the right-hand side, near the top of the transmission where it meets the engine crankcase.

7

Removal/Installation

1. Disconnect the battery (**Figure 1**).
2. Cut the plastic tie-wrap which holds a wiring harness to the body of the starter solenoid.
3. Mark the 2 smaller electrical wires which connect to terminals 30 and 16 with tape and a pen so they won't be mixed up when reinstalling the starter. Remove the electrical wires from the rear of the solenoid (**Figure 14**).
4. Remove the 17 mm nut which holds the starter to the transmission housing.
5. Remove the top right engine-to-transmission bolt.
6. Carefully lower the starter body.
7. Installation is the reverse of removal.

Solenoid Replacement

Refer to **Figure 12** and **Figure 13** for the following procedure.

1. Disconnect the large braided connecting wire between the starter and solenoid (**Figure 15**).
2. Remove the 2 screws securing the solenoid to the mounting bracket (**Figure 16**).

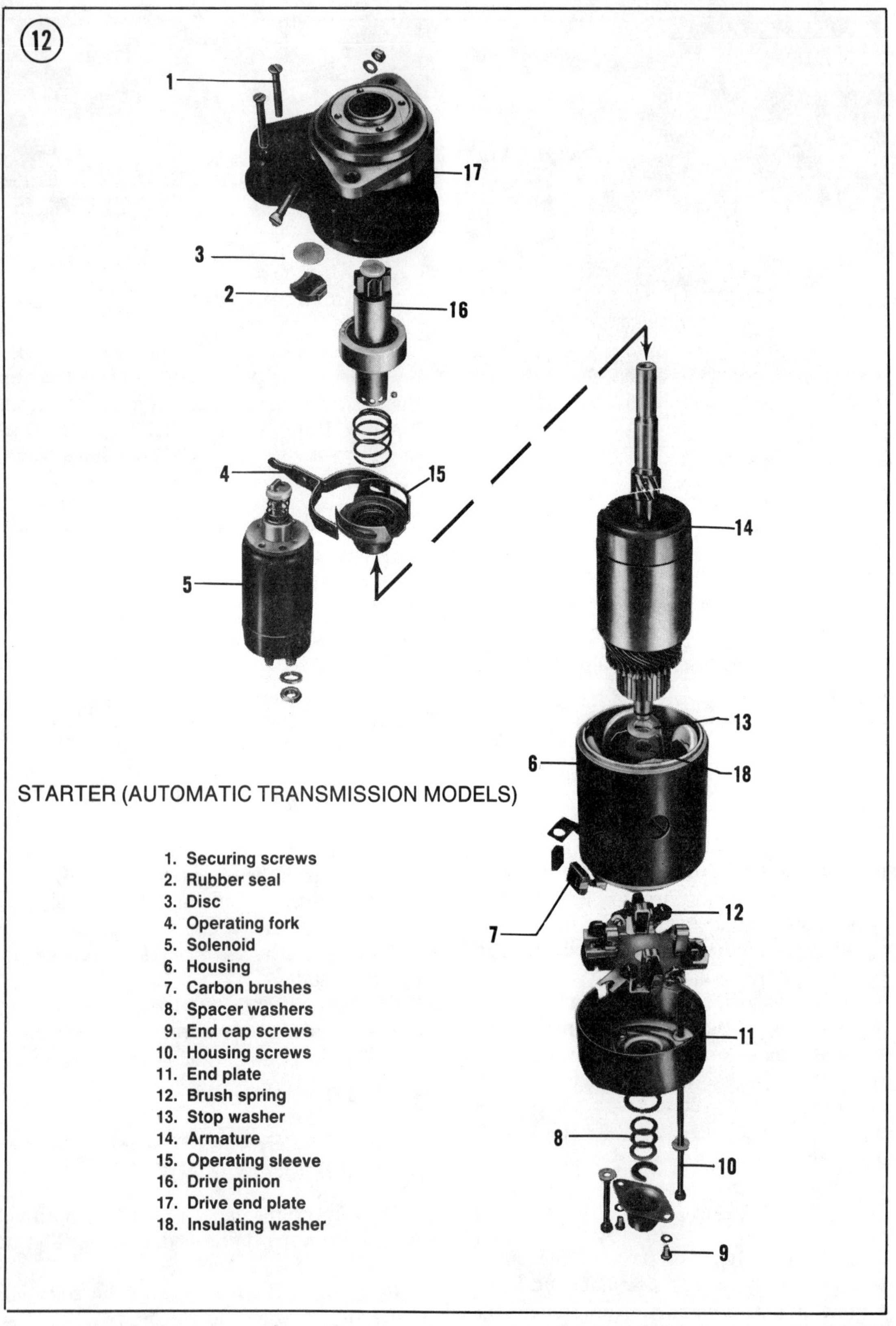
12
1
17
3
2
16
4
15
5
14
13
6
18
12
7
11
8
10
9
STARTER (AUTOMATIC TRANSMISSION MODELS)
1. Securing screws
2. Rubber seal
3. Disc
4. Operating fork
5. Solenoid
6. Housing
7. Carbon brushes
8. Spacer washers
9. End cap screws
10. Housing screws
11. End plate
12. Brush spring
13. Stop washer
14. Armature
15. Operating sleeve
16. Drive pinion
17. Drive end plate
18. Insulating washer

(13)

STARTER (MANUAL TRANSMISSION MODELS)

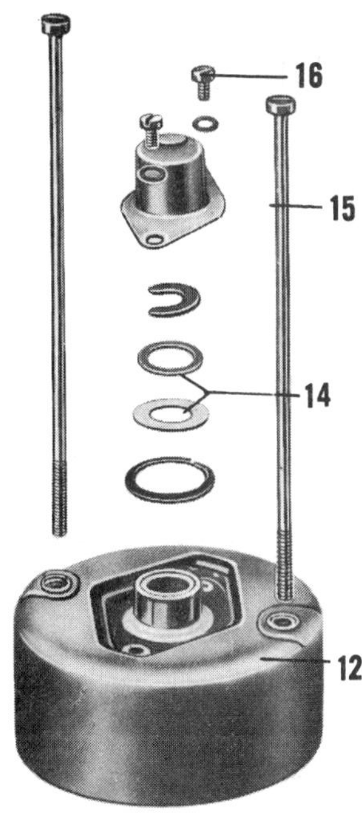

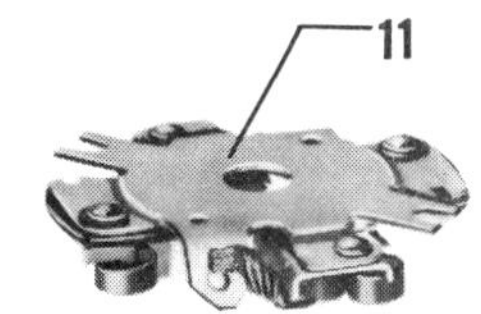

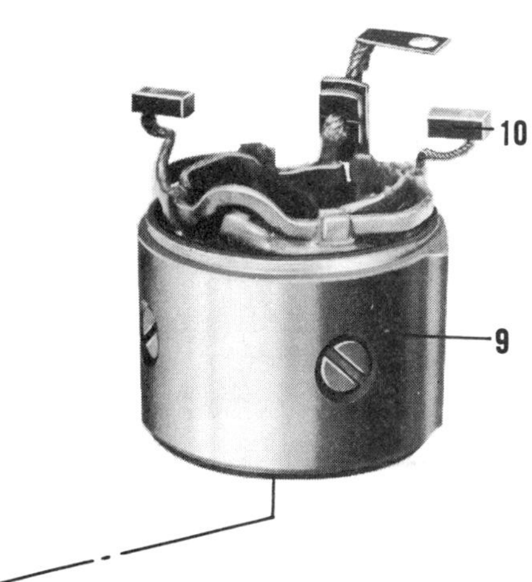

1. Armature
2. Operating fork
3. Disc
4. Rubber seal
5. Mounting bracket
6. Drive pinion
7. Stop ring
8. Circlip
9. Housing
10. Carbon brushes
11. Brush holder
12. End plate
13. Pivot bolt
14. Spacer washers
15. Housing screws
16. End cap screws
17. Solenoid

14

17

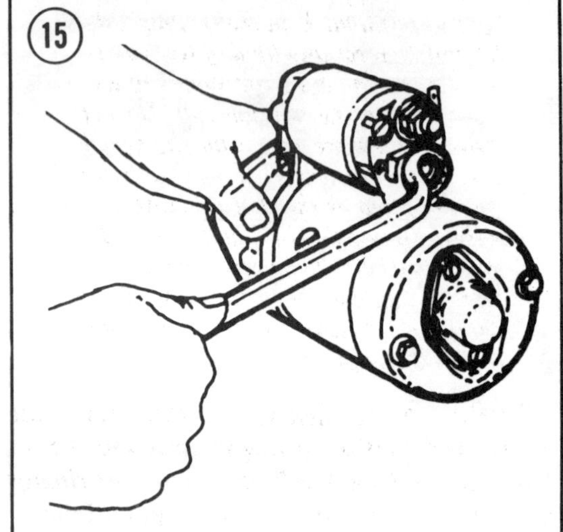
15

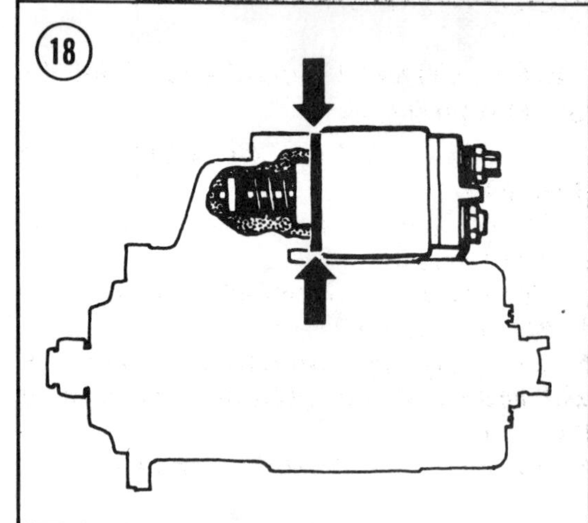
18

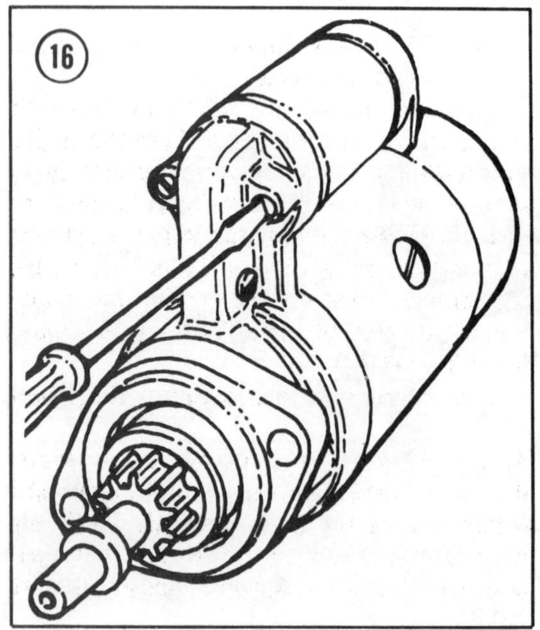
16

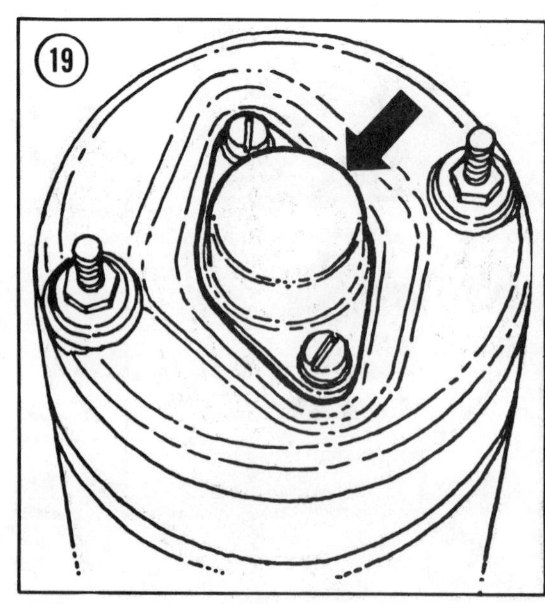
19

3. Lift the solenoid pull rod free of the operating lever and remove the solenoid (**Figure 17**).
4. Place a strip of plastic sealer on the outer edge of the new solenoid's face (**Figure 18**).
5. Rotate the drive gear pinion all the way out; this will bring the operating lever back so the solenoid can be hooked onto it.
6. Hook the solenoid pull rod lever onto the operating lever.
7. Install the 2 mounting screws and reconnect the large braided wire from the starter to the solenoid.

Brush Replacement

Refer to **Figure 12** and **Figure 13** for the following procedure.

1. Remove the end cap screws and end cap (**Figure 19**).
2. Pry out the locking ring and remove the shims (**Figure 20**).
3. Remove the 2 long housing screws.
4. Remove the end cover.
5. Gently pry the brush retainer springs back with needlenose pliers. Lift the brushes out of the holders.
6. Assembly is the reverse of these steps.

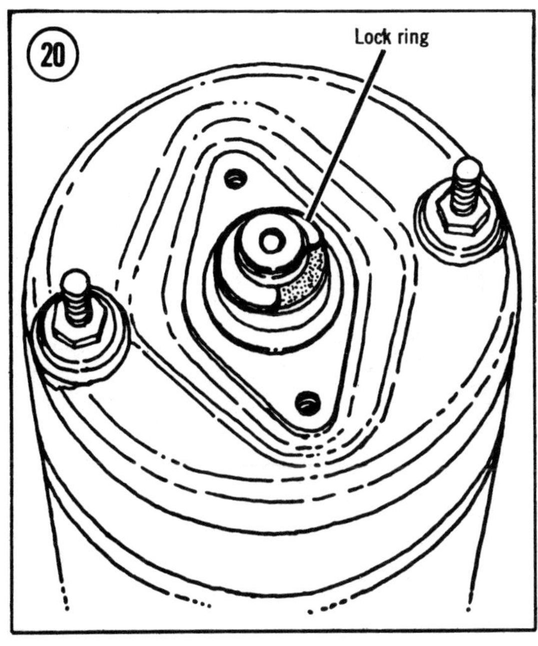

IGNITION SYSTEM

Distributor

There are 2 types of distributor used in the Vanagon. California models use a breakerless ignition system with a vacuum advance and retard unit (**Figure 21**).

All other 49-state and Canadian models use a breaker point distributor with a vacuum advance unit only (**Figure 22**).

CAUTION

On California models with breakerless ignition systems do not connect any condenser/suppressor or any kind of test light to terminal 1 on the ignition coil. Do not connect any kind of test equipment requiring a 12-volt supply to terminal 15 on the ignition coil. Do not crank the engine over with the center wire (terminal 4 wire) of the distributor disconnected without grounding this wire to the engine with a jumper wire. Do not disconnect the battery when the engine is running. If you do any of the above, the breakerless ignition system will be damaged.

Breaker point, distributor cap and rotor service and ignition timing are presented under *Tune-up* in Chapter Three. For *Distributor Drive Shaft Removal*, refer to Chapter Four.

Distributor Removal

1. Remove the distributor cap but leave the ignition wires connected.
2. Remove the plastic screen mesh which guards the main cooling fan. Turn the engine over with a socket wrench on the center nut of the cooling fan (as shown in **Figure 23**) until the distributor rotor points to the No. 1 cylinder mark on the rim of the distributor housing and the timing mark on the cooling fan pulley aligns with the "0" mark (TDC) on the timing scale (**Figure 24**).
3. Remove the distributor clamp nut (**Figure 22**).
4. On 49-state and Canadian models, disconnect the condenser wire from terminal 1 (- terminal) on the ignition coil. On California models, remove the Hall control unit connector from the distributor housing (**Figure 25**).

DISTRIBUTOR (BREAKERLESS IGNITION)

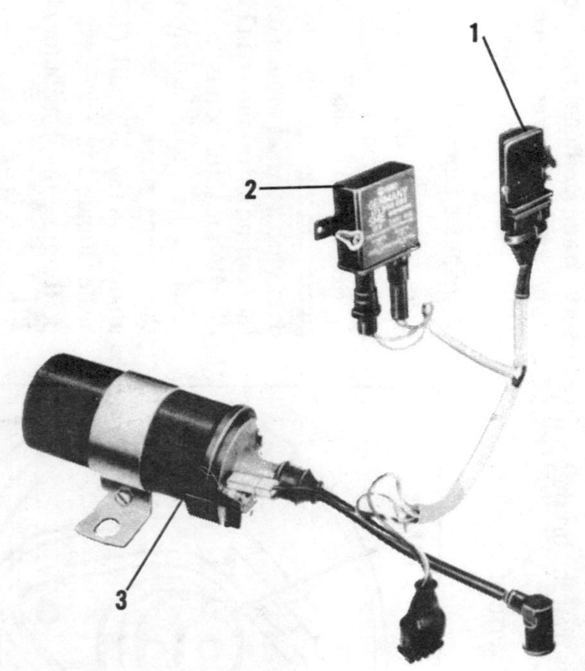

WARNING

Do not touch or remove ignition coil wire when running or cranking engine. Only disconnect wires of ignition system or connect/disconnect test instruments when ignition is turned **OFF**

CAUTION

Do not connect any test instruments on terminal 15 (+) of ignition coil, this could damage electronic parts. Use fuse No. 10 for connection.

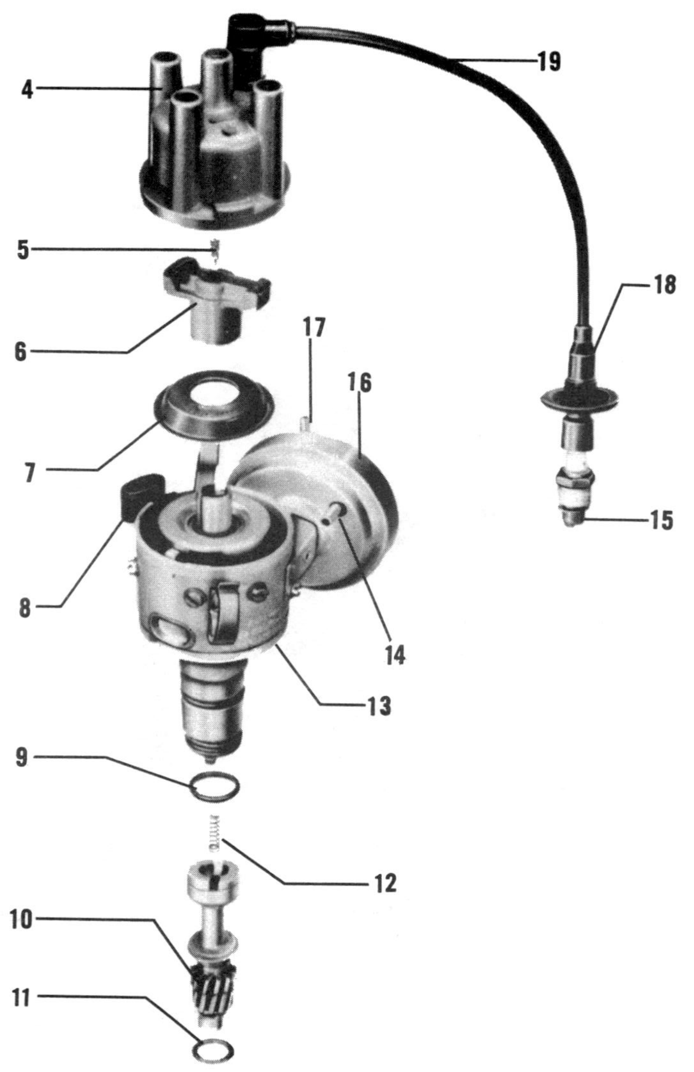

1. Hall control unit
2. Idle stabilizer
3. Ignition coil
4. Distributor cap
5. Carbon brush and spring
6. Rotor
7. Dust cover
8. Plug for Hall generator
9. Seal
10. Distributor drive
11. Thrust washer
12. Spring
13. Distributor
14. Retard connection
15. Spark plug
16. Vacuum unit
17. Advance connection
18. Spark plug connector
19. Ignition wire

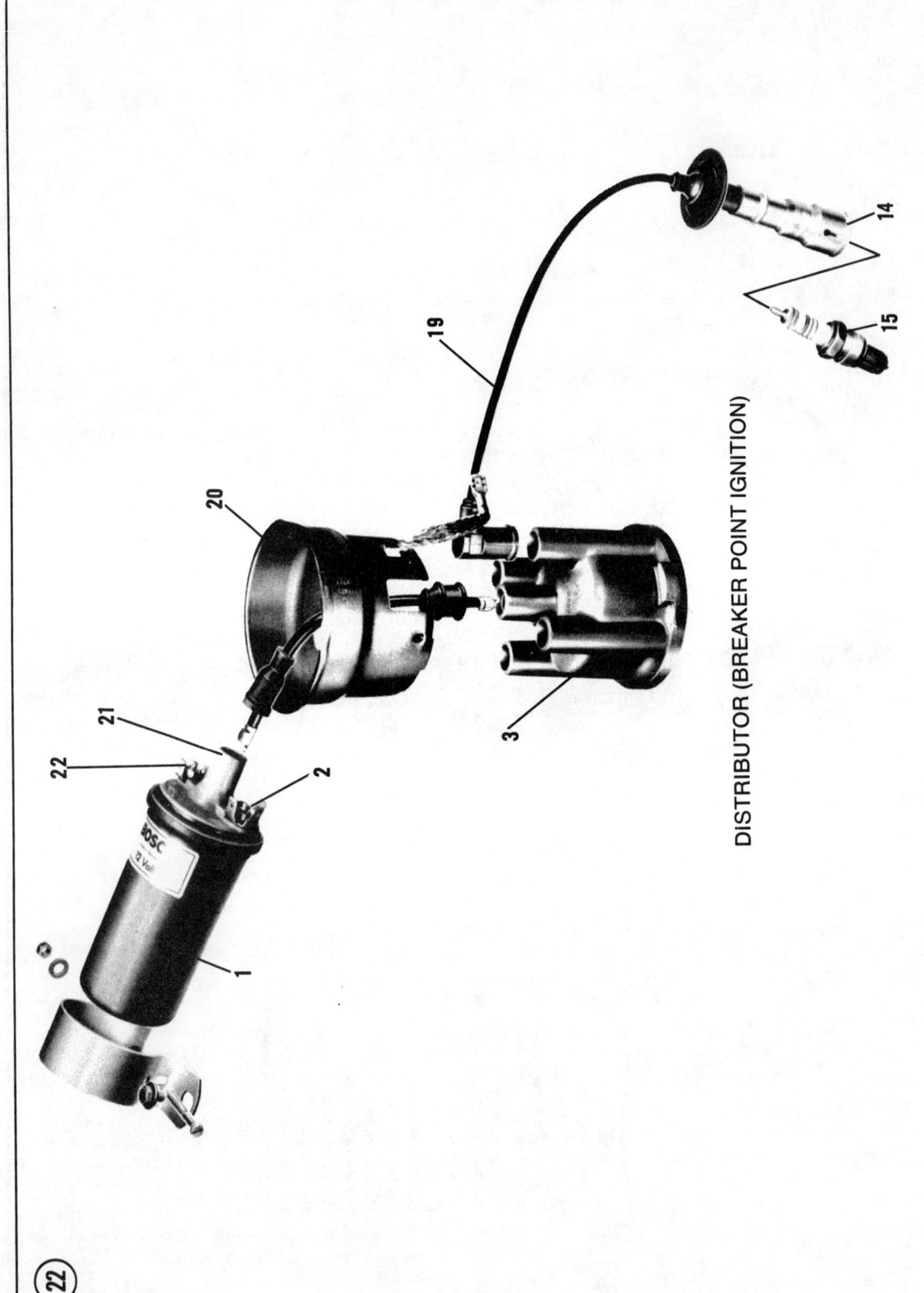

(22) DISTRIBUTOR (BREAKER POINT IGNITION)

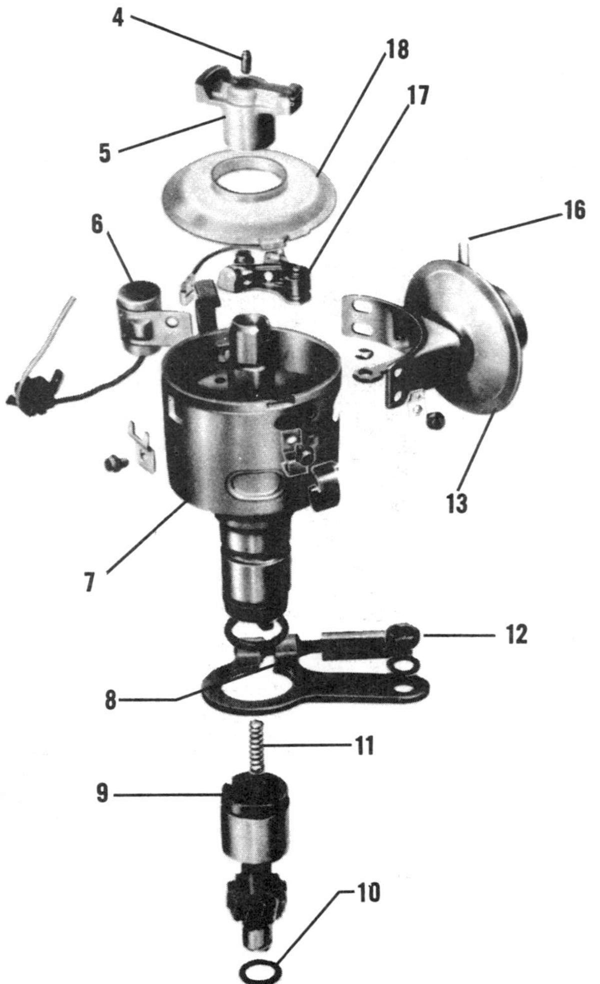

1. Ignition coil
2. Terminal 15 (+)
3. Distributor cap
4. Carbon brush and spring
5. Rotor
6. Condenser
7. Distributor
8. Clamping bolt
9. Distributor drive
10. Thrust washer
11. Spring
12. Distributor clamp nut
13. Vacuum advance unit
14. Spark plug connector
15. Spark plug
16. Vacuum hose connection
17. Breaker points
18. Dust cover
19. Ignition wires
20. Static shield
21. Terminal 4
22. Terminal 1 (-)

7

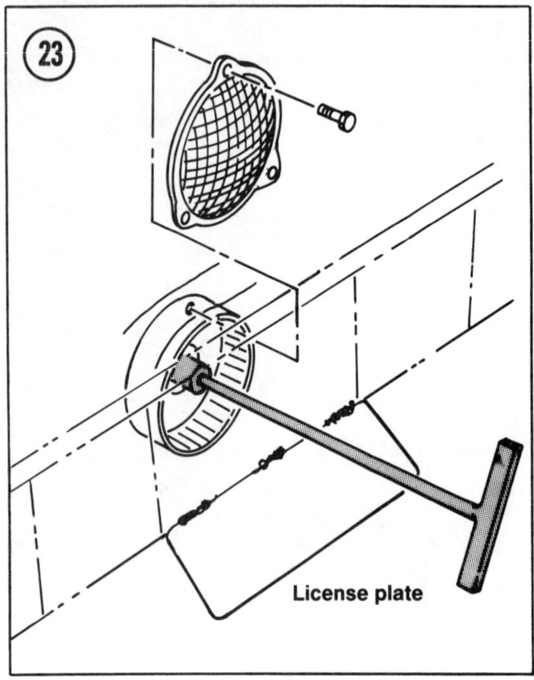

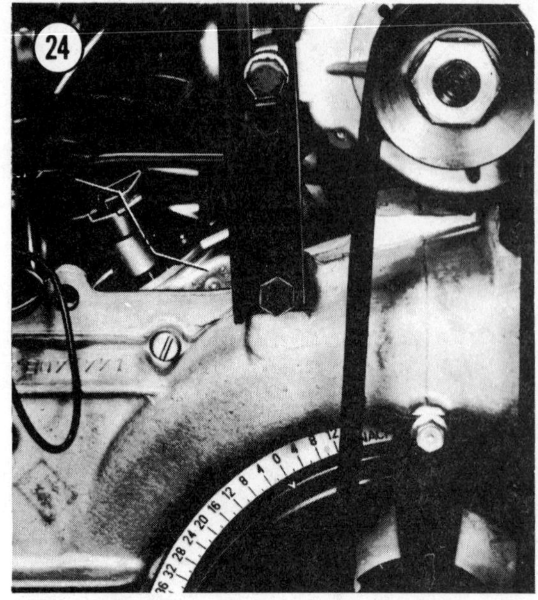

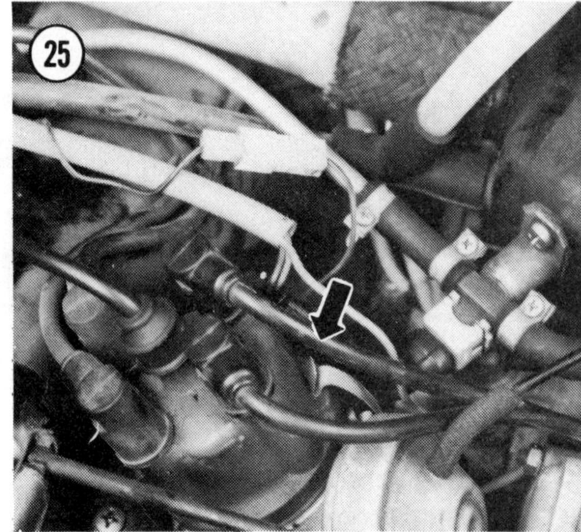

5. Pull straight up on the distributor; it should slide out of the crankcase.
6. Use a magnet tool to remove the small spring which goes between the distributor and the drive shaft.

Distributor Installation

1. Make sure that No. 1 piston is still at TDC of its compression stroke. If the engine has been turned over see *Finding Top Dead Center* in Chapter Four.
2. Cut a straight length of coat hanger wire; insert it into the distributor drive shaft hole, into the small hole in the top of the drive shaft. Slide the spring down the coat hanger onto the drive shaft. **Figure 26** shows the method.

NOTE

When installing the distributor, always use a new rubber sealing ring on the distributor shaft to prevent engine oil leakage.

3. Insert the distributor into the shaft hole as far down as it will go. Make sure that the bolt hole in the distributor clamp goes over the bolt protruding from the crankcase.
4. Gently but firmly push down on the distributor housing; at the same time turn the distributor shaft with the rotor. As the shaft

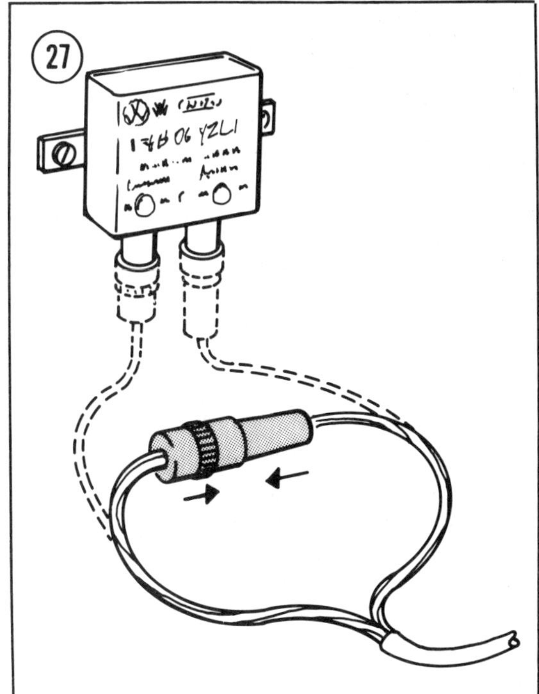

turns it will automatically seat in the distributor drive shaft. It will only go in one way; the rotor should point to the No. 1 cylinder mark on the distributor housing rim. Make sure it is seated properly. Turn the rotor back and forth; it should only go a few fractions of an inch in either direction. If not, remove the distributor and check that the spring is seated properly in the distributor drive shaft, then repeat Steps 3 and 4.

5. Install the clamp nut. Reset the ignition timing; see *Ignition Timing Adjustment* in Chapter Three.

Testing Hall Control Unit and Idle Stabilizer (California Models Only)

The Hall control unit and idle stabilizer are only used on California models with the breakerless ignition system.

1. Disconnect the plugs from the idle stabilizer and connect them together (**Figure 27**).
2. Pull out the center wire from the distributor (coil wire) and ground it to the engine with a jumper wire. Also disconnect the Hall control unit connector at the distributor.
3. Connect a voltmeter positive lead to the ignition coil terminal 15 and the voltmeter negative lead to the coil terminal 1.
4. Have an assistant turn the ignition key to the second position.
5. The voltmeter should read 5-6 volts for approximately 1 second then drop to 0. If the voltage reads anything above 0 for more than 1 second turn off the ignition immediately. If the voltage checked out okay proceed to Step 6.
6. Touch the center green wire of the Hall unit electrical connector on the distributor (**Figure 25**) to ground with a jumper wire. The voltage should briefly increase to approximately 5-6 volts; if not, replace the Hall unit. If the voltage checked out okay proceed to Step 7.
7. Connect the voltmeter positive lead to the red and black wire and the voltmeter negative lead to the brown and white wire of the Hall unit electrical connector on the distributor. Have an assistant turn the ignition on. The voltmeter should read approximately 10 volts; if not, replace the Hall unit.
8. To test the Hall generator perform the following:
   a. Connect a test light between terminal 15 and terminal 1 on the ignition coil.
   b. Crank the engine with the starter; the test light must flicker. If not, replace the Hall unit.

9. To test the idle stabilizer perform the following:
   a. Connect the center wire (coil wire) to the distributor cap.
   b. Set the parking brake and block the drive wheels.
   c. Connect a timing light to the engine as shown in **Figure 28**.
   d. Start the engine and allow it to warm to operating temperature.
   e. Shine the timing light onto the timing scale. *On manual transmissions,* have an assistant put the transmission in 4th gear, slowly let out the clutch and let it slip but do not fully engage it (only just enough to create a load). *On automatic transmissions,* apply the brakes, put the transmission selector in DRIVE and accelerate the engine to create a load.
   f. The timing must advance with the increased engine load; if not, replace the idle stabilizer.

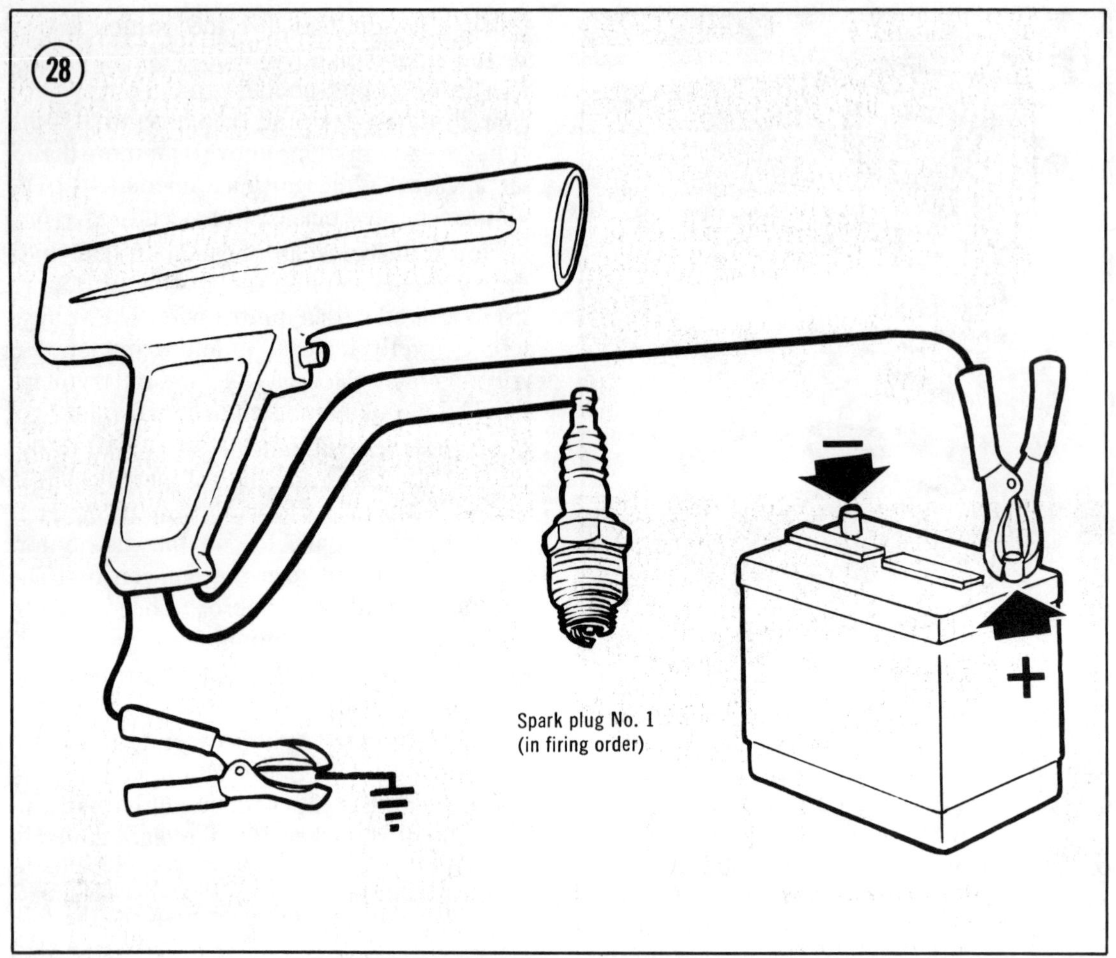

Ignition Coil Testing

Two types of ignition coil are used on the Vanagon. One type is used with the breakerless distributor (California models); the other is used with the breaker point distributor (49-states and Canada). The different types must never be interchanged.

1. Remove all the wires from the coil.
2. Touch the leads from an ohmmeter to terminals 1 and 15. Measure the resistance between the terminals; it should be 2.6-3.1 ohms for 49-state and Canadian models and 0.550-0.750 ohms for California models. If not, replace the coil.
3. Measure the resistance between terminals 1 and 4 with the ohmmeter. It should be 6,000-12,000 ohms for 49-state and Canadian models and 2,500-3,500 ohms for California models. If not, replace the coil.

FUSE AND RELAY PANEL

The fuse panel is located within the vehicle, under the left side of the dash panel (**Figure 29**). The function of each fuse is clearly marked on the fuse cover. See **Table 2** for fuse location and function.

Whenever a fuse blows, determine the reason for the failure before replacing the fuse. Usually the trouble is a short circuit in the wiring. This may be caused by worn-through insulation or a wire which works its way off the terminal connector and shorts to ground. Always carry several spare fuses in the glove compartment.

CAUTION

Never substitute metal foil or wire for a blown fuse. An overload will most likely result in an electrical fire and the complete loss of the vehicle.

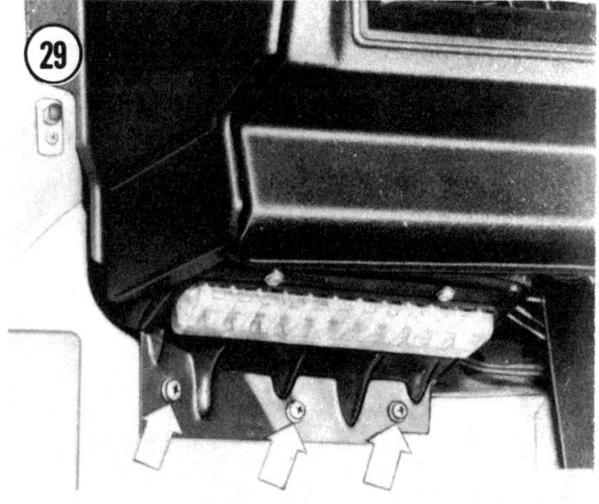

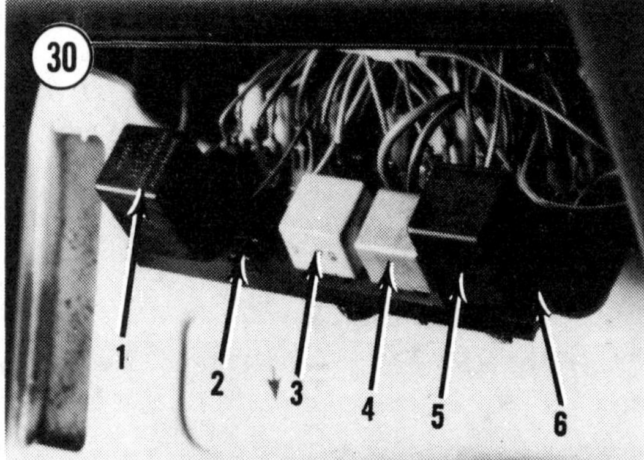

1. Hazard flasher relay
2. Not used
3. Load reduction relay
4. Ignition key warning buzzer/relay
5. Intermittant windshield wiper/washer relay (optional)
6. 8A overheat fuse for heater booster

The relay panel is located on the reverse side of the fuse panel. To gain access remove the screws shown in **Figure 29**. Pull the panel down to reveal the relay panel. **Figure 30** shows relay location and function. The relays are removed by unplugging them from the panel.

LIGHTING SYSTEM

Headlight Replacement

1. Remove the front grille by turning the retaining screws 90° (**Figure 31**).

2. Remove the 3 screws which secure the retaining ring to the adjusting ring (**Figure 32**).

3. Pull the sealed beam headlight out.

4. Disconnect the plug from the rear of the sealed beam unit (**Figure 33**).

5. Installation is the reverse of these steps.

6. Adjust the headlights according to local regulations. Headlights are adjusted by turning the adjusting screws shown in **Figure 34**.

Rear Light Replacement

The lights which make up this assembly include the turn signal light, taillight bulb, back-up light and brake light.

7

33

36

34

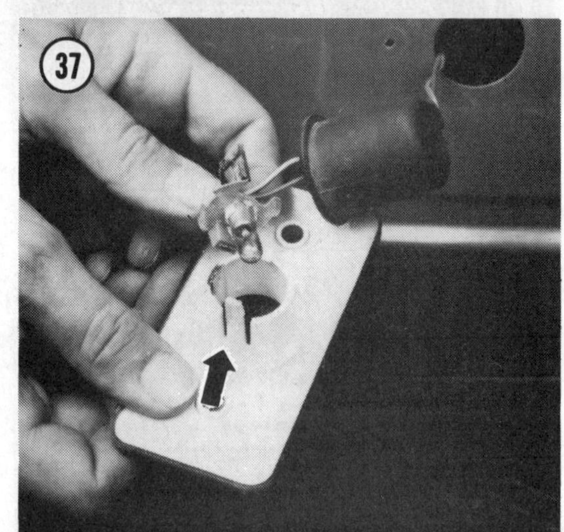
37

35

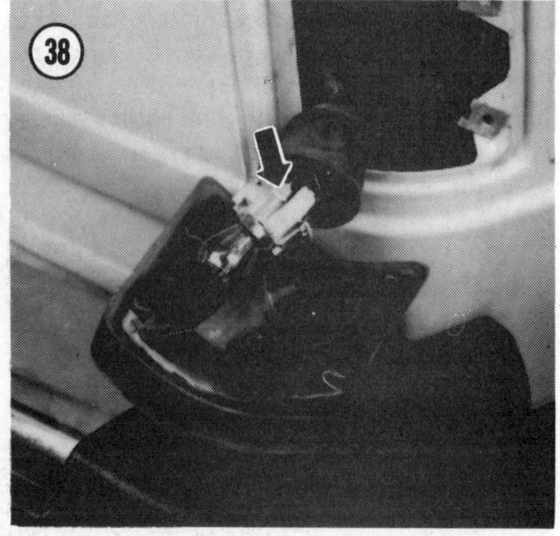
38

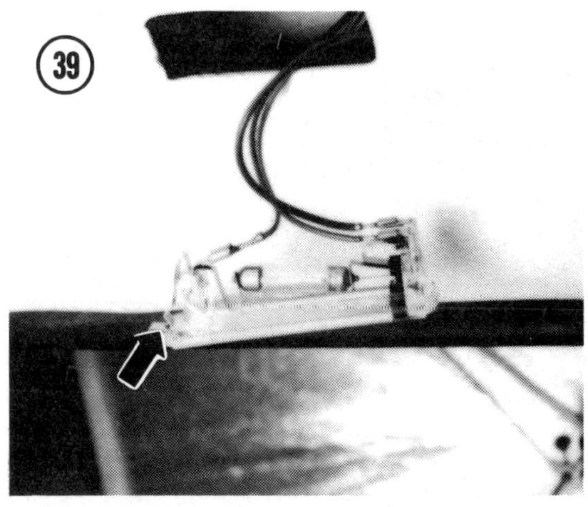

1. Remove the rear lens screws. Pull out the lens with the bulb housing and lay it on the bumper as shown in **Figure 35**.

NOTE
The taillight electrical connector and boot may be pulled from the rear of the bulb housing at this time.

2. Pry the 2 side springs on the bulb housing (arrows, **Figure 35**) apart and separate the housing from the lens (**Figure 36**).
3. Bulbs are removed by pushing in and turning; the bulb will then pull free from bulb housing. New bulbs are installed in the same manner.
4. Install the lens assembly in the reverse order.

Side Marker Light Replacement

1. Remove the lens screws and pull out the lens.
2. Pull back the rubber boot.
3. Pry the plastic spring clip backward and remove the bulb holder. See arrow in **Figure 37**.
4. The bulb is removed by pushing in and turning; the bulb will then pull free from bulb housing. The new bulb is installed in the same manner.
5. Install the lens assembly in the reverse order.

Front Marker Light Replacement

There is one bulb in the running light and turn signal light assembly.

1. Remove the lens screws and pull out the lens. Lay it on the bumper.
2. Pull back the rubber boot.
3. Pry the plastic spring clip backward and remove the bulb holder. See arrow in **Figure 38**.
4. The bulb is removed by pushing in and turning; the bulb will then pull free from bulb housing. The new bulb is installed in same manner.
5. Install the lens assembly in the reverse order.

Interior Light Replacement

1. Pry the clip up with a screwdriver and pull the lens out of the body. See arrow in **Figure 39**.
2. Pull out the bulb from between the 2 spring contacts and install the new bulb.
3. Press lens back into body recess.

ELECTRICAL SWITCHES

The switches which are on the instrument panel are the headlight switch, rear window defogger switch and the emergency flasher switch. Electrical switches are removed from the rear of the panel by compressing the plastic springs on the rear of each switch and pulling to the front of the vehicle.

Four switches are located on the steering column; they are the horn switch, turn signal switch, windshield wiper switch and ignition switch. Access to the turn signal and wiper switches requires that the steering wheel be removed. Access to the ignition switch requires that the column lock housing be pulled off. However, the ignition lock may be removed without removing the lock housing.

Switch Removal/Installation

Refer to **Figure 40** for the following procedure.

1. Gently pry out the horn cover. Disconnect the electrical wires.
2. Remove the large steering wheel nut.
3. Pull off the steering wheel.
4. Take out the column cover screws and remove the column covers.

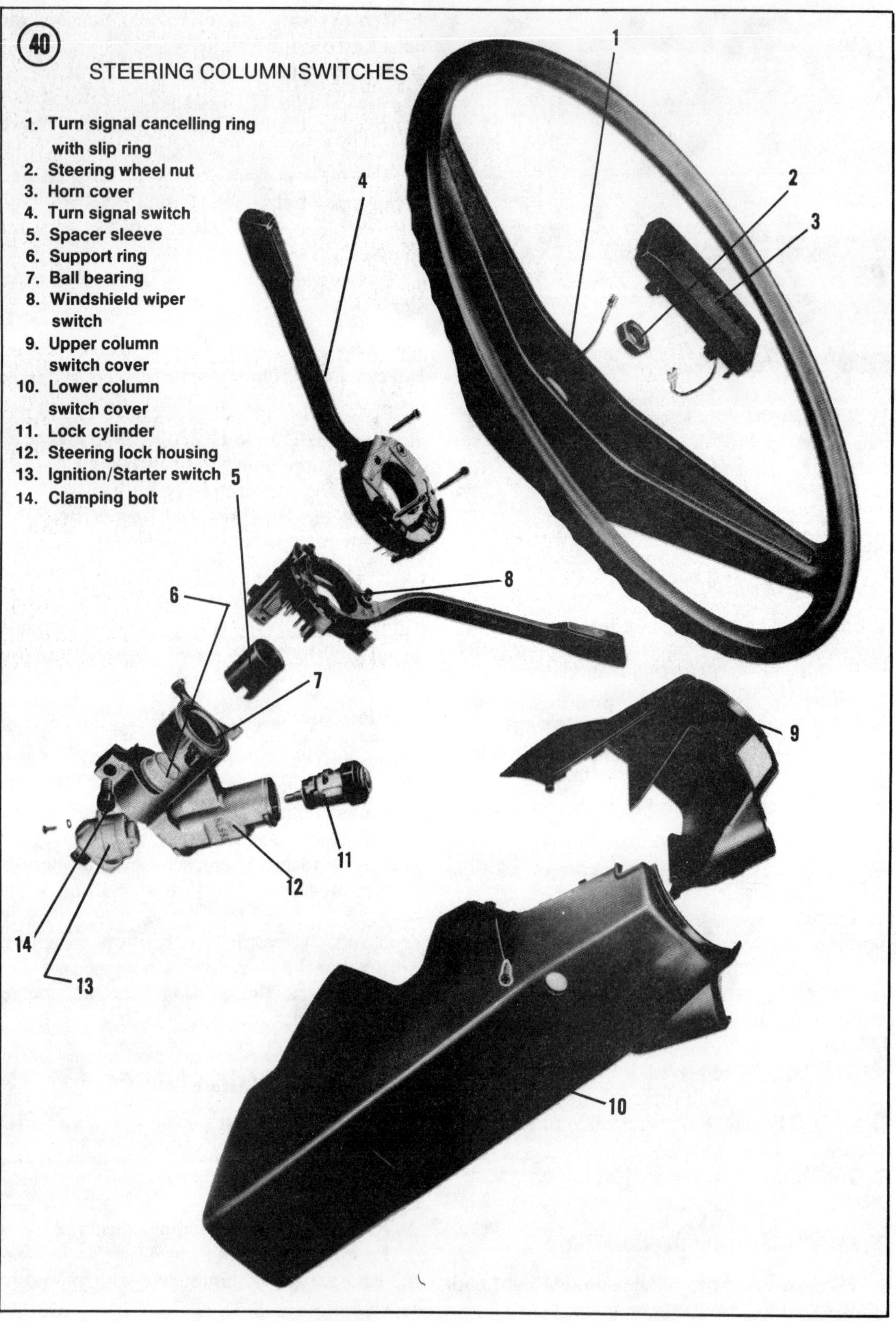
40
STEERING COLUMN SWITCHES
1. Turn signal cancelling ring with slip ring
2. Steering wheel nut
3. Horn cover
4. Turn signal switch
5. Spacer sleeve
6. Support ring
7. Ball bearing
8. Windshield wiper switch
9. Upper column switch cover
10. Lower column switch cover
11. Lock cylinder
12. Steering lock housing
13. Ignition/Starter switch
14. Clamping bolt
1
2
3
4
5
6
7
8
9
10
11
12
13
14

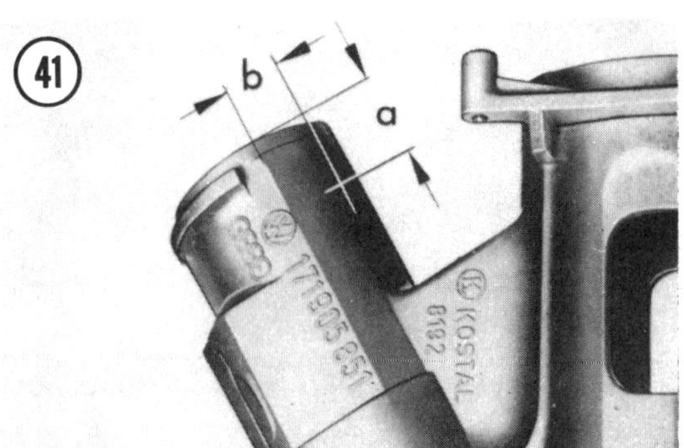

A. 1/2 in. (12 mm) B. 3/8 in. (10 mm)

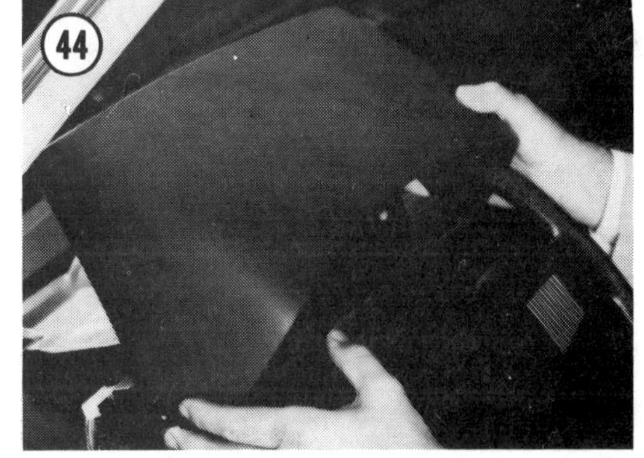

5. To remove the turn signal switch, remove and mark the electrical wiring for correct installation. Remove the 3 securing screws and pull the switch off the column.

6. To remove the windshield wiper switch, remove and mark the electrical wiring for correct installation, then pull the switch off the column. The same screws which hold the turn signal switch also hold the wiper switch.

7. To remove only the ignition lock without removing the column lock perform the following:

a. Carefully drill a 1/8 in. (3 mm) hole into the column housing in the exact spot shown in **Figure 41**. This is to gain access to an internal release pin.

b. Press in the pin with a punch and withdraw the lock from the cylinder.

8. To remove the steering column lock and ignition switch, perform the following:

a. Remove the clamping bolt on the steering lock housing.

b. Remove and mark the electrical wiring for correct installation.

c. Remove the lock housing and spacer sleeve with a puller as shown in **Figure 42**.

d. Take out the ignition switch by removing the clamping screw; the switch will slide out of the lock housing.

9. Installation is the reverse of removal. The lock housing is installed by driving the unit back into place with a hammer and length of pipe that will fit over the column shaft. The spacer sleeve is installed in the same manner; the top edge of the sleeve must be at least 2 in. (51 mm) from the top of the column. See dimension "a" in **Figure 43**.

INSTRUMENT PANEL

The instrument panel is a modular type, with all the instruments fitted into a molded

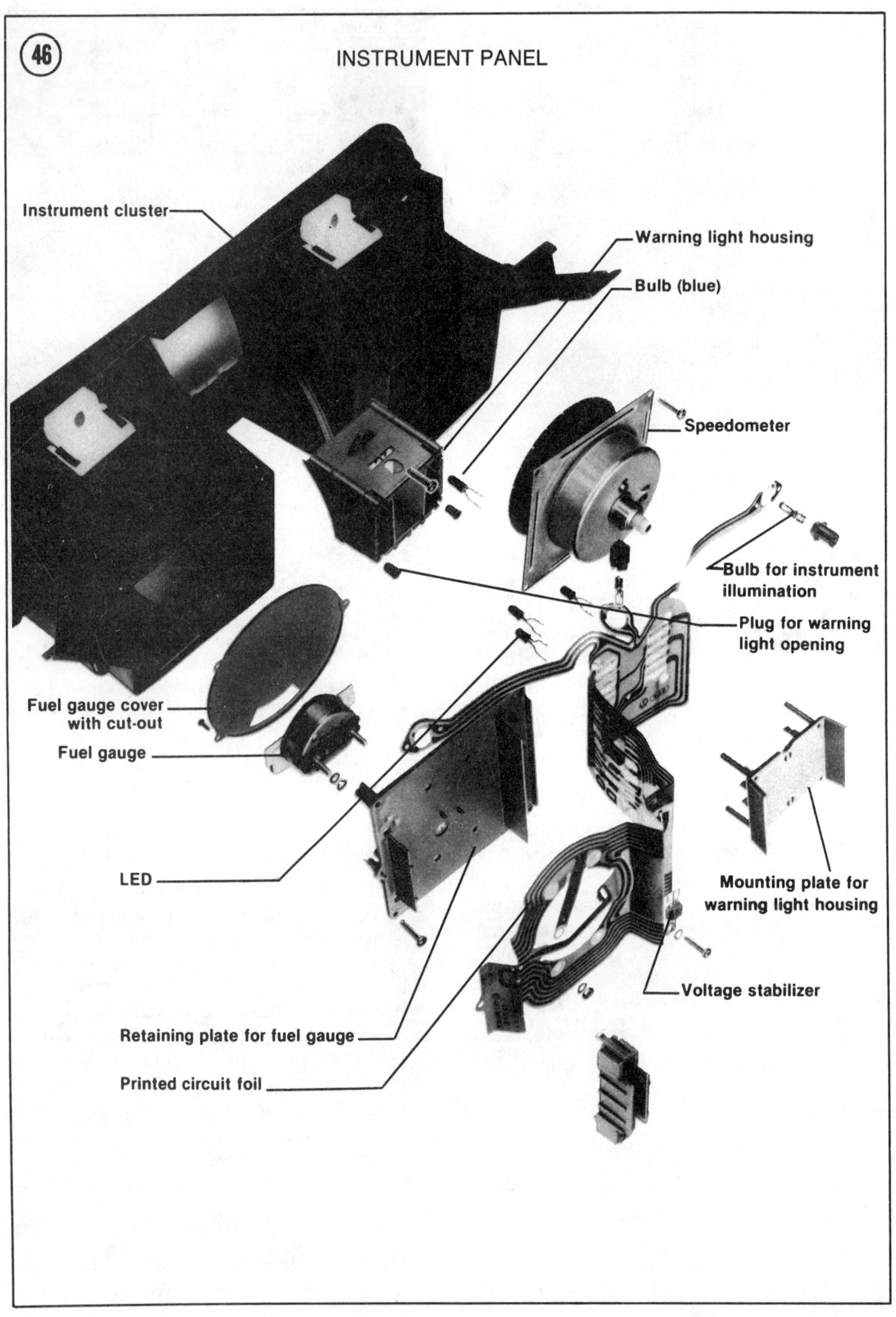
46
INSTRUMENT PANEL
Instrument cluster
Warning light housing
Bulb (blue)
Speedometer
Bulb for instrument illumination
Plug for warning light opening
Fuel gauge cover with cut-out
Fuel gauge
LED
Mounting plate for warning light housing
Voltage stabilizer
Retaining plate for fuel gauge
Printed circuit foil

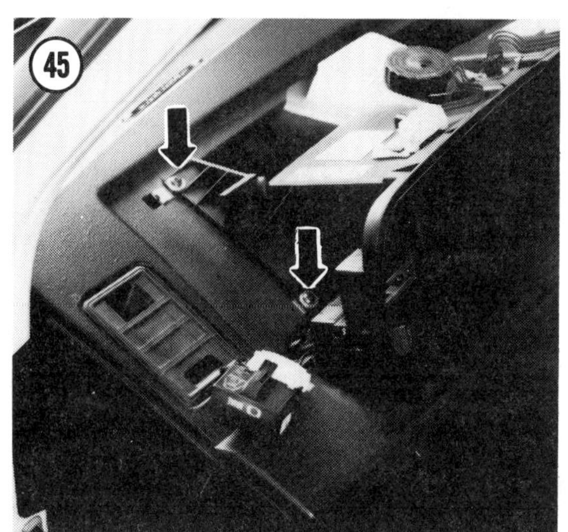

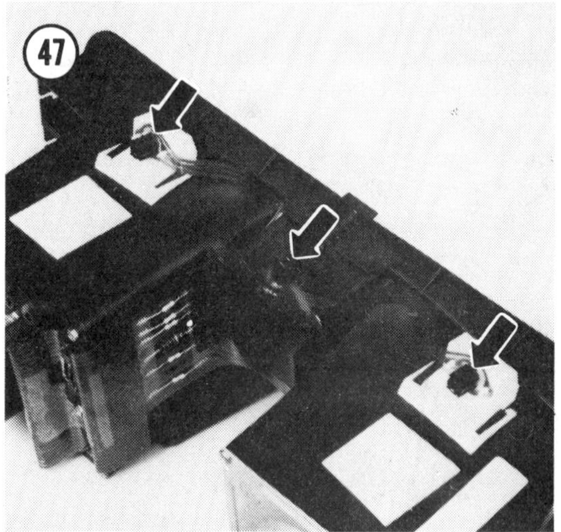

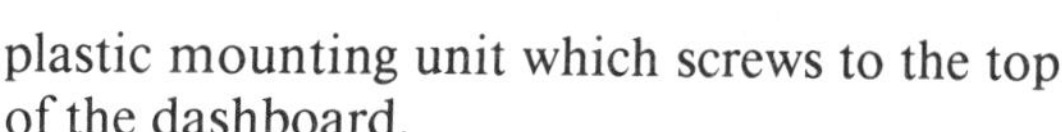

plastic mounting unit which screws to the top of the dashboard.

Three small bulbs light the speedometer, the warning light housing and the fuel gauge. Illumination for the individual warning lights is provided by LED's (light emitting diodes).

Removal/Installation

1. Remove the instrument cover as shown in **Figure 44**.
2. Carefully pull the multi-connector off the back of the instrument panel.
3. Unscrew the speedometer cable from the back of the speedometer.
4. Remove the headlight, brake warning light, rear window defogger and emergency flasher switches from the rear of the instrument panel without disconnecting the electrical connectors.
5. Remove the 4 screws which hold the panel to the dash and lift it out (**Figure 45**).
6. Installation is the reverse of removal.

Disassembly/Assembly

Refer to **Figure 46** for the following procedure.

1. Remove the instrument panel.
2. Carefully pry off the warning light housing.
3. Remove the multi-connector frame.
4. Remove the screw and nuts which hold the ribbon connector to the instrument housing.
5. Carefully remove the ribbon connector.
6. Remove the fuel gauge/clock retaining plate.
7. Remove the warning light housing.
8. Remove the speedometer.
9. Assembly is the reverse of disassembly.

Replacing Instrument Bulbs

Replacement of the speedometer and warning light housing bulbs does not require disassembly of the instrument panel.

Remove the instrument cover (**Figure 44**). Turn the bulb holder in the top of the speedometer, warning light housing or clock housing (**Figure 47**); the holder with the bulb will pop out. Remove the bulb from the holder and replace with a new one.

Testing and Replacing LED's

This procedure requires the use of a homemade tester like the one shown in **Figure 48**.

For U.S. models refer to **Figure 49** and for Canadian models refer to **Figure 50** for LED identification.

1. Disassemble the instrument panel.
2. Touch the leads of the tester to the negative and positive connections of each LED. The LED should light; if not, replace it. For U.S. models see **Figure 51** and for Canadian models see **Figure 52** for terminal locations.
3. Pull out the bad LED and plug in a new one; make sure to get the LED leads into the correct connections (**Figure 53**). The negative terminal lead on the LED is slightly wider than the positive.
4. Assemble the instrument panel.

HORN

If the horn works, but not loudly or not at the correct pitch, make sure that it is not touching

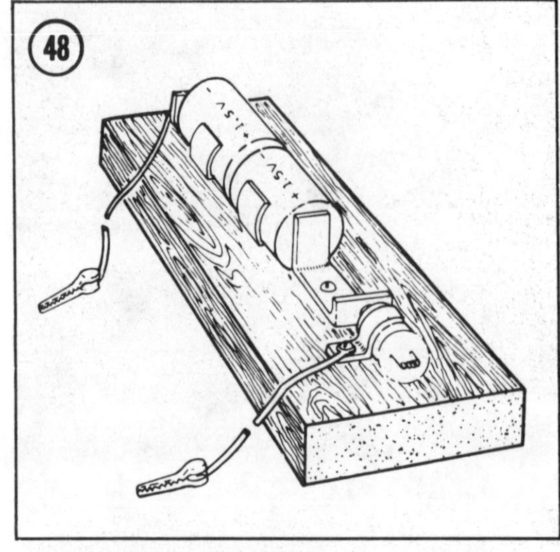

48

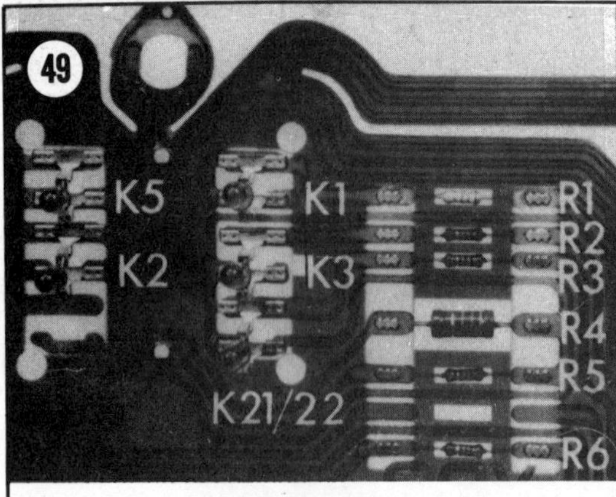

49

K1 LED (red) high beam

K2 LED (red) alternator

K3 LED (red) oil pressure

K5 LED (green) turn indicator

K21/22 LED (red) EGR or OXS

R1 Resistor for K1 (470)

R2 Resistor for K3 (470)

R3 Resistor for K21/22 (470)

R4 Resistor for voltage stabilizer (150)

R5 Resistor for K2 (470)

R6 Resistor for K5 (470)

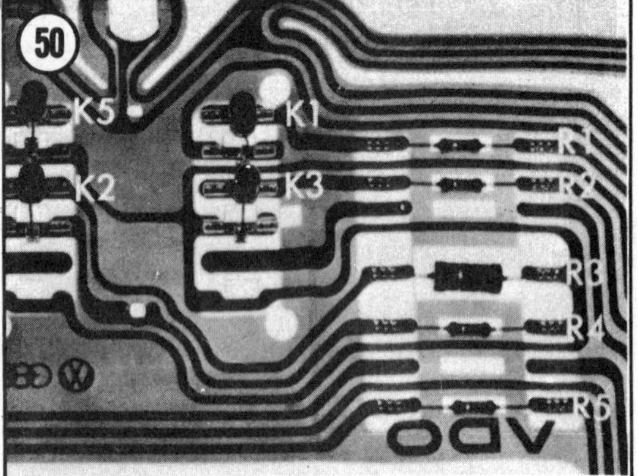

50

K1 bulb (blue) high beam

K2 LED (red) alternator

K3 LED (red) oil pressure

K5 LED (green) turn indicator

R1 Series resistor for K1 (270)

R2 Resistor for K3 (470)

R3 Resistor for alternator preexciter circuit (150)

R4 Series resistor K2 (470)

R5 Series resistor for K5 (470)

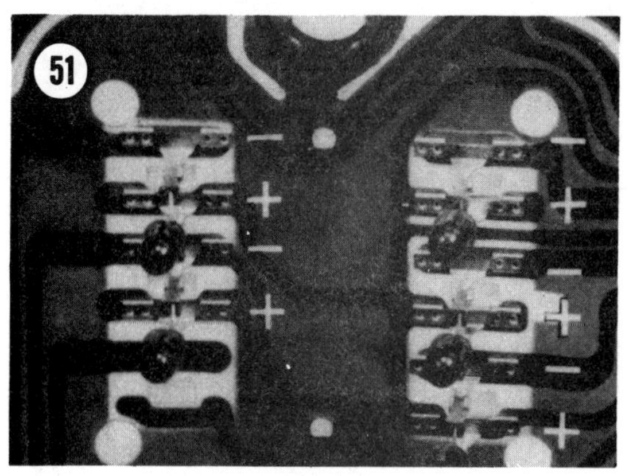

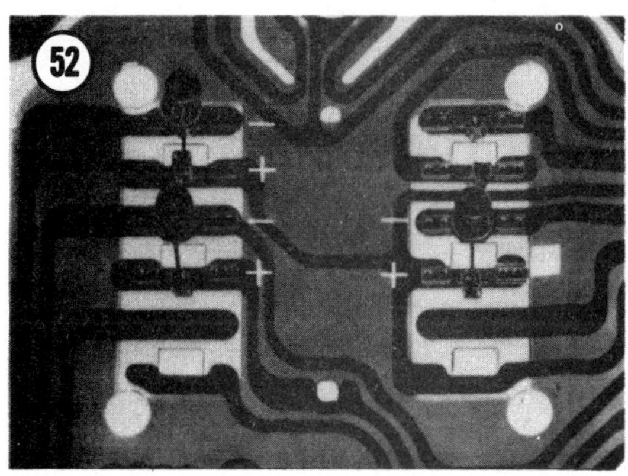

the body of the vehicle. On some VW horns the pitch and loudness can be adjusted by removing the rear seal on the horn and turning the adjusting screw. If the horn does not work at all, check the wiring to the horn and check the horn switch (**Figure 40**). Carefully pry up the switch cover and make sure the electrical wiring is still connected.

Horn Replacement

The horn is mounted under the front end on the right-hand side of the bumper (**Figure 54**).

1. Disconnect the battery negative cable.

2. Remove the nut securing the horn to the bracket.

3. Disconnect the wiring from the horn.

4. Installation is the reverse of removal.

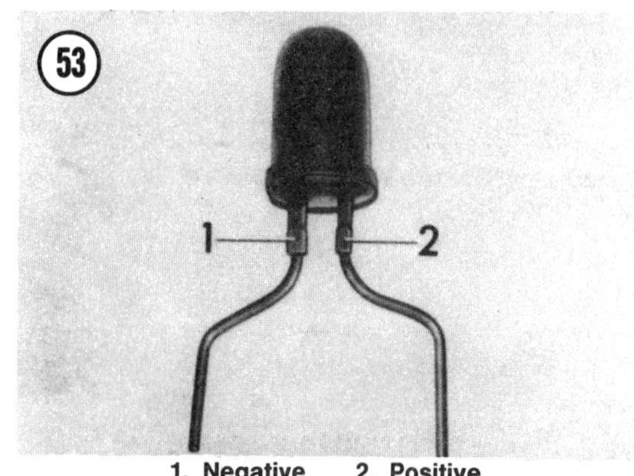

1. Negative 2. Positive

WINDSHIELD WIPER SYSTEM

Wiper Assembly Removal/Installation

The wiper motor is located in the dashboard panel on the right-hand side. Refer to **Figure 55** for the following procedures.

1. To remove the motor perform the following:
   a. Remove the glove compartment.
   b. Remove the protective dust caps on the right wiper arm and remove the wiper arm nuts (**Figure 56**). Pull the blade and arm off the wiper shaft.
   c. Working under the dash, unfasten the left relay rod from the right arm shaft.
   d. Remove the electrical wiring connector from the wiper motor.

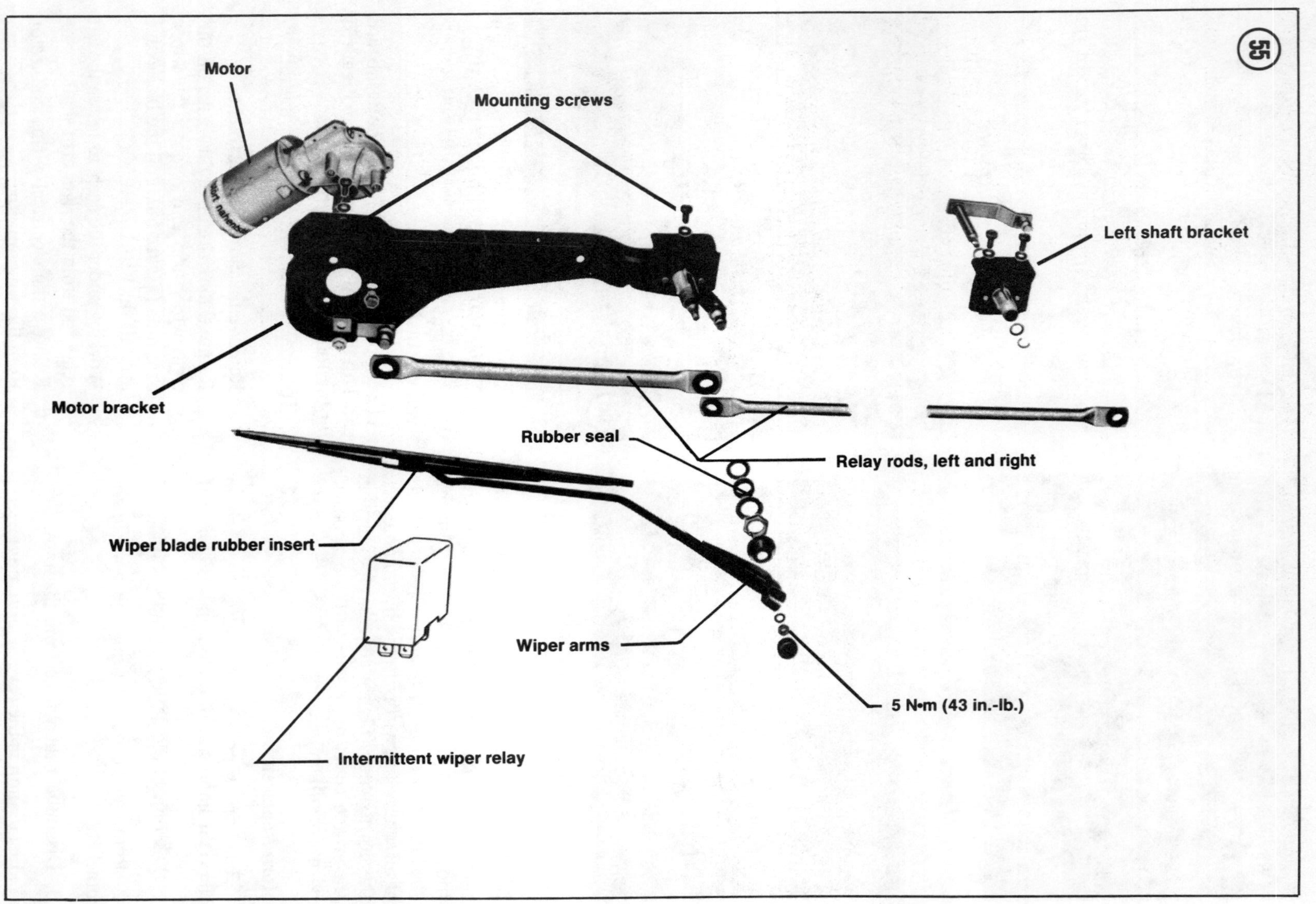
55
Motor
Mounting screws
Left shaft bracket
Motor bracket
Rubber seal
Relay rods, left and right
Wiper blade rubber insert
Wiper arms
5 N•m (43 in.-lb.)
Intermittent wiper relay

e. Remove the right wiper shaft retaining nut and rubber sealing washers.
f. Remove the mounting screws and pull the motor bracket from under the dash.

2. To remove the left wiper shaft bracket perform the following:

a. Remove the instrument panel to gain access to the left side wiper shaft bracket. See procedure in this chapter.
b. Remove the left wiper shaft retaining nut and rubber sealing washers.
c. Remove the protective dust caps on the left wiper arm and remove the wiper arm nuts; pull the blade and arm off the wiper shaft (**Figure 56**).
d. Remove the left shaft bracket mounting screws.
e. Disconnect the left relay rod from the left wiper arm shaft. Slide the left relay rod out under the dash toward the passenger side.
f. Pull the wiper shaft bracket out of the dash.
g. Pull the wiper shaft bracket out of the dash.

3. Installation is the reverse of removal. Install the wiper motor bracket with the wiper motor in the park position as shown in **Figure 57**. After installation adjust the wiper blades so they are 2 3/4 in. (70 mm) from the bottom of the windshield. See dimension A in **Figure 58**.

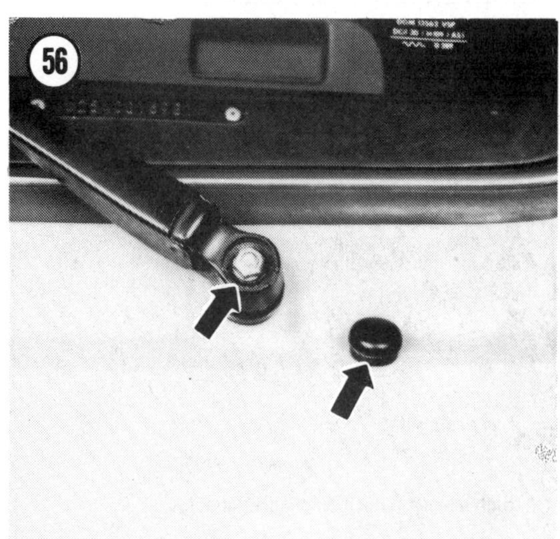

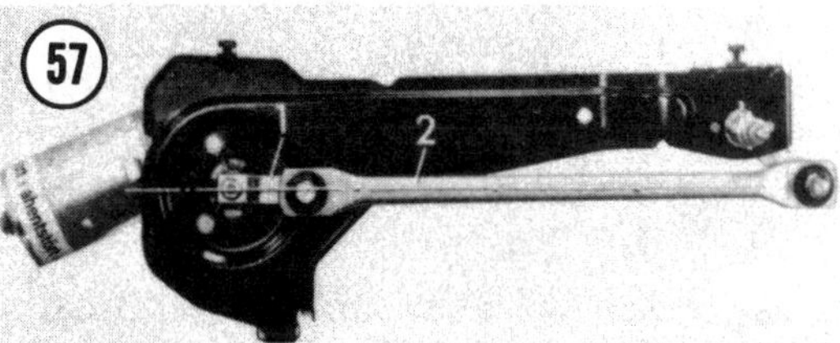

Table 1 BATTERY CONDITION

Specific Gravity	Percent Charged
1.110-1.130	Discharged
1.140-1.160	Almost discharged
1.170-1.190	One-quarter charged
1.200-1.220	One-half charged
1.230-1.250	Three-quarters charged
1.260-1.280	Fully charged

Table 2 FUSE LOCATION AND FUNCTION

1. 8 ampere	Parking light left, side marker left
2. 8 ampere	Parking light right, license plate light, side marker left
3. 8 ampere	Low beam left
4. 8 ampere	Low beam right
5. 8 ampere	High beam left, including indicator lights
6. 8 ampere	High beam right
7. 8 ampere	Accessories
8. 8 ampere	Interior lights, cigarette lighter, stop lights
9. 16 ampere	Emergency hazard flasher system
10. 16 ampere	Windshield wiper/washer pump, rear window defogger
11. 8 ampere	Turn signals
12. 8 ampere	Horn, back-up lights

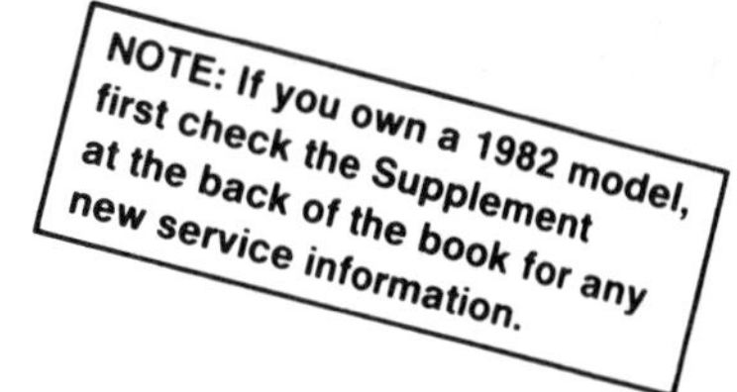
NOTE: If you own a 1982 model, first check the Supplement at the back of the book for any new service information.

CHAPTER EIGHT

CLUTCH, TRANSAXLE AND DRIVE AXLES

This chapter covers service procedures for the clutch, automatic and manual transaxles and drive axles. Torque specifications are presented in **Table 1** at the end of this chapter.

CLUTCH

The VW clutch consists of a single dry clutch disc and a diaphragm pressure plate mounted on the flywheel (**Figure 1**). The clutch is hydraulically operated. The clutch master cylinder is located under the dashboard and the clutch slave cylinder is on top of the transaxle. The clutch master cylinder shares a fluid reservoir with the brake master cylinder.

CLUTCH HYDRAULIC SYSTEM

This chapter contains removal and installation procedures for the clutch master and slave cylinders. If either unit leaks or fails to hold pressure, it should be replaced with a new or rebuilt unit.

Clutch Master Cylinder Removal/Installation

Refer to **Figure 2** for the following procedure.

1. Remove the instrument panel to gain acess to the clutch master cylinder (Chapter Seven).
2. Spread rags under the master cylinder to catch spilling fluid.
3. Pull out the hydraulic fluid reservoir line at the connection on the master cylinder and plug the line to keep the fluid from draining. Be careful not to pull on the fluid line; you might pull it out of the reservoir.
4. Unbolt the hydraulic line at the master cylinder; cap the end of the line.
5. Remove the cotter pin from the pedal clevis and remove the shaft.
6. Remove the bolts which hold the master cylinder to the body bracket. Pull the master cylinder out of the bracket.
7. Installation is the reverse of removal. After installation, the system must be bled and the clevis rod adjusted; see procedures in this chapter.

Clutch Slave Cylinder Removal/Installation

Refer to **Figure 2** for the following procedure.

1. Disconnect the hydraulic line from the slave cylinder and plug the line.
2. Remove the bolts which hold the slave cylinder to the transaxle bracket.

3. Pop the slave cylinder off of the clutch lever ball.
4. Remove the slave cylinder from the transaxle.
5. Installation is the reverse of removal. After installation, the system must be bled; see procedure in this chapter.

Clutch Bleeding

The clutch system requires bleeding whenever air enters the system. Air can enter the system when the clutch master cylinder or slave cylinder are serviced or when the hydraulic fluid reservoir runs dry. Air can also enter through a damaged line or hose or a severely worn master or slave cylinder. Find the damaged line and replace it before bleeding; badly worn master or slave cylinders will usually leak amounts of hydraulic fluid which are quite easy to spot. Refer to **Figure 2** for the following procedure.

1. Remove the instrument panel cover (**Figure 3**). Remove the cap from the reservoir.
2. Pack rags around the reservoir; spilled hydraulic fluid will drip into the electrical components under the dashboard and flow onto the carpet.
3. Check the fluid level and top off if necessary. Use a funnel when adding fluid to prevent accidental spillage.
4. Remove the rubber cap from the bleeder valve on the slave cylinder.

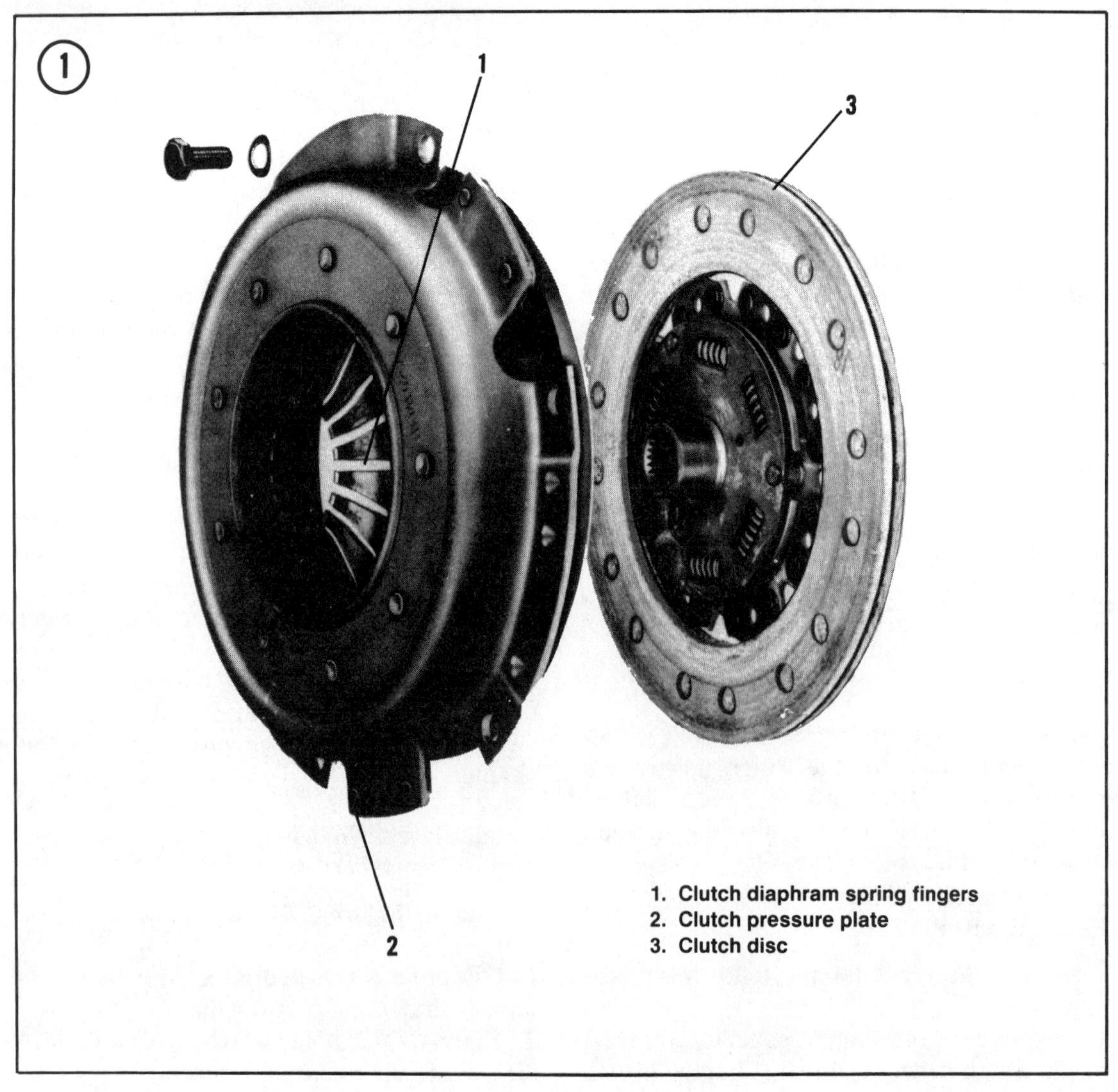

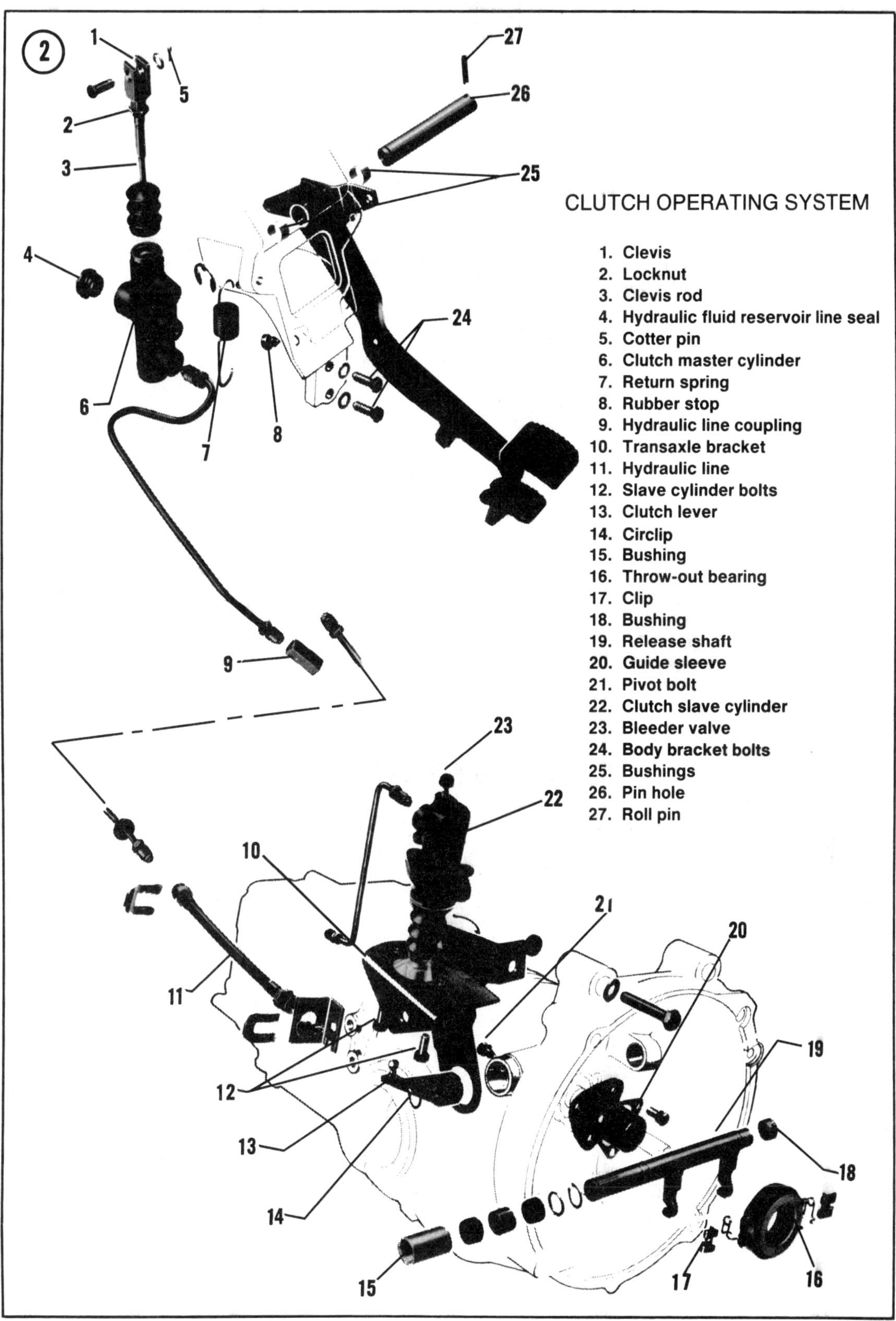
2
CLUTCH OPERATING SYSTEM
1. Clevis
2. Locknut
3. Clevis rod
4. Hydraulic fluid reservoir line seal
5. Cotter pin
6. Clutch master cylinder
7. Return spring
8. Rubber stop
9. Hydraulic line coupling
10. Transaxle bracket
11. Hydraulic line
12. Slave cylinder bolts
13. Clutch lever
14. Circlip
15. Bushing
16. Throw-out bearing
17. Clip
18. Bushing
19. Release shaft
20. Guide sleeve
21. Pivot bolt
22. Clutch slave cylinder
23. Bleeder valve
24. Body bracket bolts
25. Bushings
26. Pin hole
27. Roll pin

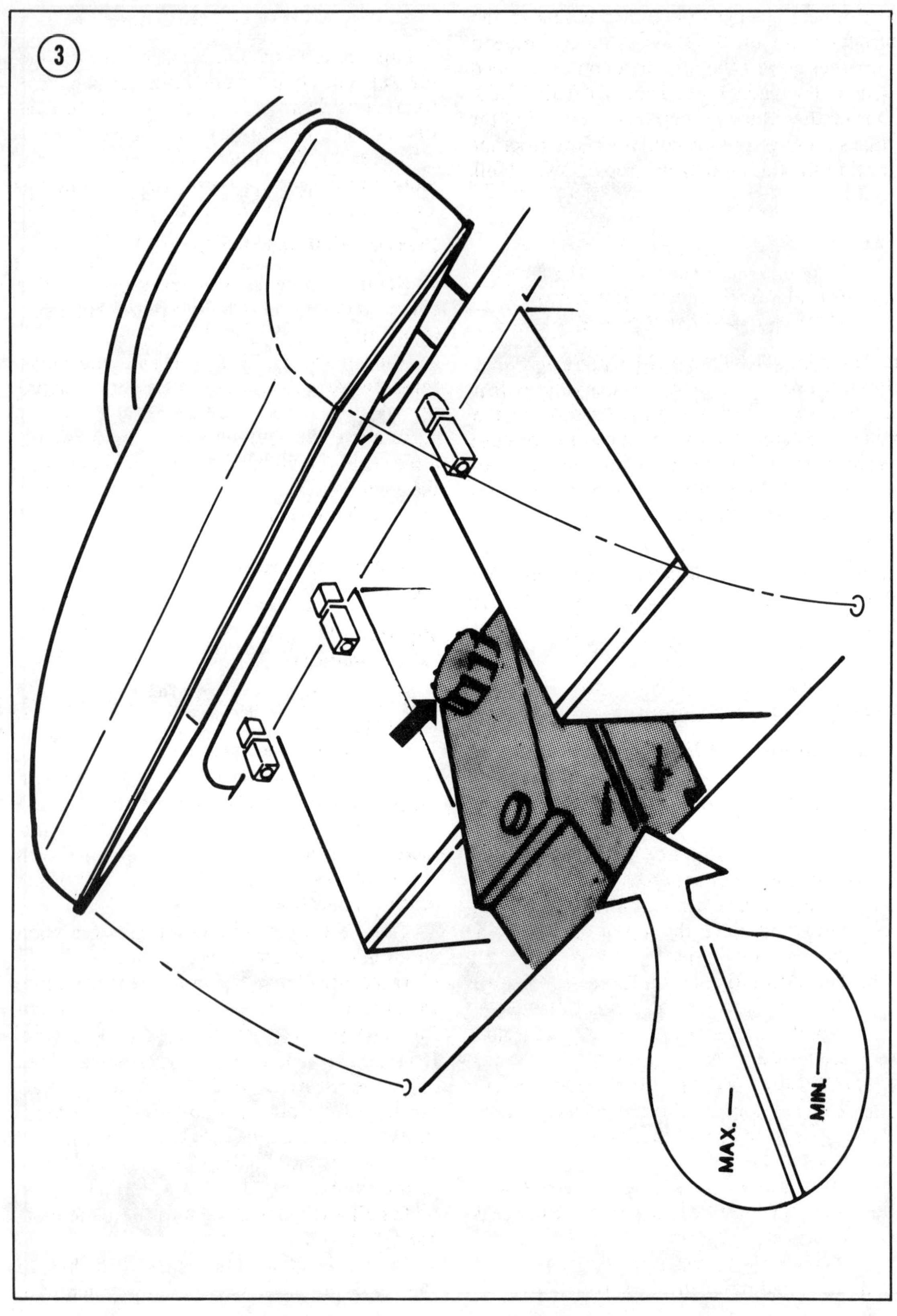
3
MAX.
MIN.

5. Connect a length of rubber tubing to the bleeder valve on the slave cylinder. Suspend the other end of the tube in a container filled with a few inches of clean hydraulic fluid. During the following steps keep the end of the tube submerged in the container; never let the level in the fluid reservoir drop below 1/2 full.

NOTE

If the hydraulic fluid reservoir is accidentally drained, both hydraulic systems (clutch and brakes) must be bled.

6. Have an assistant slowly depress and hold the clutch pedal. Open the bleeder valve with a wrench about 3/4 of a turn. As soon as the pedal is all the way down, close the bleeder valve. Repeat this step as many times as necessary, until fluid with no air bubbles issues from the tube in the container.

7. When the system is bled, discard the hydraulic fluid in a jar or bottle; never reuse this fluid. Top up the resevoir with clean hydraulic fluid.

Pedal Free Play Adjustment

Refer to **Figure 2** for the following procedure.

1. To check the pedal free play perform the following:
   a. Check the pedal free play by pushing down on the pedal with your hand until resistance is felt; that is, until you feel the clevis rod touch the top of the piston in the master cylinder.
   b. There should be around 3/16 in. (4.5 mm) free play between the clevis rod and the top of the master cylinder piston. If not, see Step 2.
2. To adjust the pedal perform the following:
   a. Remove the instrument panel to gain access to the pedal mechanism (Chapter Seven).
   b. Loosen the locknut on the clevis rod. Turn the rod until the proper clearance is obtained.
   c. Tighten the locknut.
   d. Reinstall the instrument panel.

CLUTCH MECHANISM

This section contains servicing procedures for the clutch pressure plate, clutch disc, throw-out bearing and throw-out bearing operation lever (**Figure 1** and **Figure 2**).

Access to the clutch mechanism may be gained in one of 2 ways—either by removing the engine or by removing just the transaxle.

Pressure Plate and Disc Removal

1. Remove the engine or the transaxle. For engine removal see Chapter Four. Transaxle removal is presented in this chapter.
2. Make marks on the flywheel and the clutch pressure plate for proper installation (**Figure 4**).
3. Remove the pressure plate bolts. Work around the pressure plate several times with the wrench and loosen them evenly. Do not remove them one at a time or the pressure plate will warp.
4. Remove the pressure plate and the clutch disc. Perform *Cleaning and Inspection.*

Pressure Plate and Disc Installation

Refer to **Figure 1** and **Figure 2** for the following procedure.

1. Wash your hands before proceeding.
2. Sand the friction surface of the flywheel and the pressure plate friction plate with a medium fine emery cloth. Sand lightly across the surfaces (not around) until they are covered with fine scratches. This breaks the glaze and aids in seating a new disc.
3. Clean the flywheel and the pressure plate with non-petroleum based solvent.
4. Insert the clutch disc in the flywheel. Place the pressure plate in position and line it up with the mark you made in the removal procedure. If installing a new or rebuilt pressure plate, align the clutch assembly with the balance marks 180° from each other. The balance marks, painted on the edge of the flywheel and the clutch assembly, show the heaviest portion of the component.
5. Install and tighten the pressure plate bolts *hand-tight* only.
6. Center the clutch disc hub with the hole in the center of the flywheel with a clutch pilot

tool (**Figure 4**), available in auto part stores, or a length of dowel. The clutch disc must be very close to center or the transmission shaft will not slide through.
7. Tighten the pressure plate bolts evenly and torque to specifications; see **Table 1**.
8. Install the engine or the transaxle.

Throw-out Bearing and Release Lever Removal/Installation

Refer to **Figure 2** for the following procedure.

1. Remove the engine or the transaxle. For engine removal see Chapter Four. Transaxle removal is presented in this chapter.
2. Remove the retaining clip, pry the retaining spring back and slip the bearing off the release lever. Perform *Cleaning and Inspection.*
3. To remove the throw-out bearing release lever perform the following.
   a. Remove the throw-out bearing.
   b. Remove the snap ring from the end of the release lever with a pair of snap ring pliers.
   c. Pull the clutch lever off the release lever. Some clutch levers may just slip off; others may need coaxing with a hammer and a drift or a puller. Do not hammer on the end of the release lever; you will ruin it.
   d. Remove the pivot bolt.
   e. Rotate the release lever up and slide it to the left side of the transmission housing. The rubber bushing housing and bushings will pop out where the clutch lever was removed; pull them off the release lever. The right-hand side of the release lever will pop out of the transmission housing; pull this end back and slide the lever to the left. The right side of the release lever will come free and out of the transaxle housing.
   f. Perform *Cleaning and Inspection.*
   g. Installation is the reverse of removal. When installing the center bushing, align the hole with the pivot bolt hole in the transaxle housing; slide the bushing in and install the pivot bolt immediately.

Cleaning and Inspection

Never replace a clutch part without giving thought to the reason for failure. To do so will only invite future trouble.

1. Clean the flywheel face and pressure plate assembly in a non-petroleum base cleaner.
2. Check the friction surface of the flywheel for cracks and grooves. Attach a dial indicator and check the runout; see *Flywheel/Torque Converter Drive Plate* in Chapter Four. If necessary have the flywheel machined.
3. Check the pressure straps between the friction plate and the cover for cracks and rivet tightness (**Figure 5**). If any defects are found, replace the plate.
4. Check the diaphragm spring fingers for wear; lightly scored fingers may be reused (**Figure 6**). Plates with heavily scored fingers must be replaced.
5. Check the friction plate for warpage with a straightedge and a feeler gauge as shown in

Figure 7. Plates which are warped more than 0.012 in. (0.3 mm) must be replaced.

CAUTION
Pressure plate rebuilding and repair requires special tools and skills. Do not attempt repairs unless you are properly trained and have the tools required for the job.

6. The assembled thickness of the disc should be no less than 0.36 in. (9.128 mm) (**Figure 8**). Replace if thinner.
7. Check the disc for cracks, oil, burns, loose/cracked springs or loose rivets. Replace if defects are found.
8. Check the throw-out bearing for wear. Turn the bearing with your hand; it should turn smoothly without rumbling or grinding. If not, replace it.

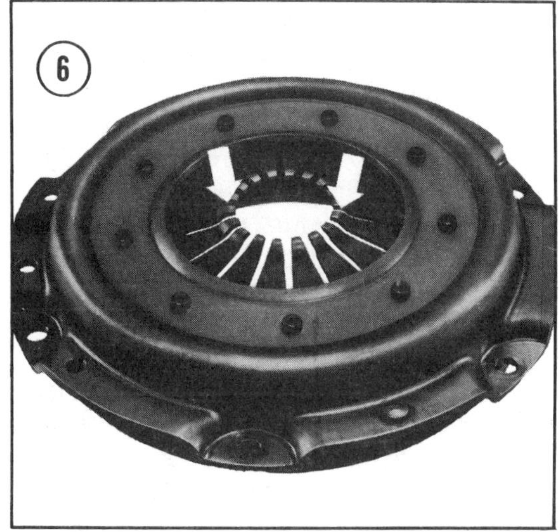

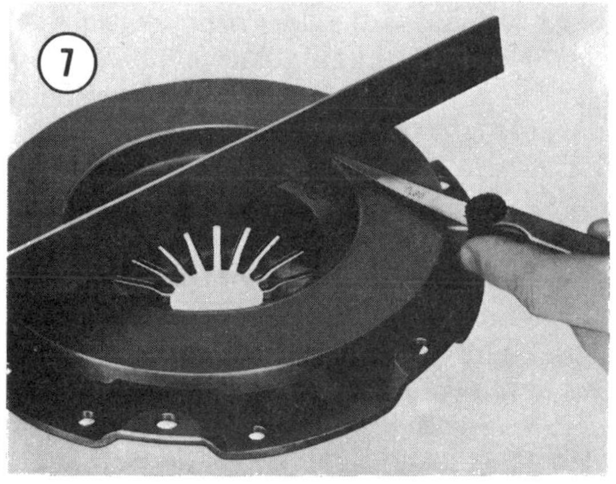

CAUTION
The throw-out bearing is prelubricated and sealed. Do not wash it in solvent or the bearing will be ruined; just wipe it with a clean cloth.

9. Check the release lever; if the forks are bent, excessively worn or cracked, replace the lever.

TRANSAXLE REMOVAL INSTALLATION

Repairs requiring disassembly of the transaxle are not possible without a large assortment of special VW tools. Lubrication and maintenance procedures for the manual and automatic transaxles are presented in Chapter Three.

Most adjustments such as selector fork positions and bearing preload must be done on special test jigs; these adjustments are impossible while the parts are installed in the case. The price of the test jigs and special tools far exceeds the cost of several brand new transaxles.

A considerable amount of money can be saved by removing the old transaxle and installing a new or rebuilt one yourself. This chapter details removal and installation procedures for the manual and automatic transaxles, plus service for the drive axles and CV (constant velocity) joints.

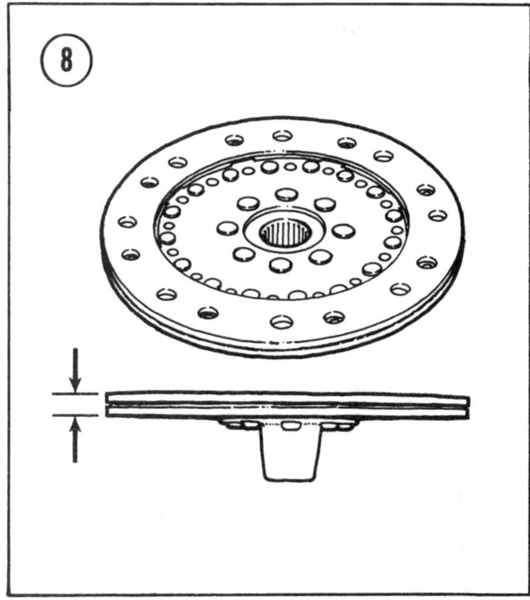

Manual or automatic transaxles may be removed from the vehicle independently of the engine. The following procedure can be used whether or not the engine is in the vehicle.

1. Raise the rear of the vehicle at least 1 ft. (30 cm) and support it with jackstands.
2. Disconnect the battery.

WARNING
When removing the transmission you will have to handle the electrical wiring on the starter. Failure to disconnect the battery may result in a fire, personal injury and loss of the vehicle.

3. Remove the Allen head bolts which hold the CV joints and axles to the transaxle. **Figure 9** shows a typical CV joint-to-transaxle arrangement. Hang the axles up under the vehicle with wire.
4. Disconnect the electrical wiring to the starter (**Figure 10**). The starter may be removed or left in place. See Chapter Seven for starter removal.
5. On manual transaxles, detach the transaxle shifter linkage. Refer to **Figure 11** and perform the following:
   a. Remove the nut which holds the guide pin.
   b. Remove the nut which secures the relay lever to the transaxle shifter shaft.
   c. Remove the hydraulic line from the clutch slave cylinder and cap the end of the line.
6. On automatic transaxles, refer to **Figure 12** and perform the following:
   a. Pop off the throttle cable from the shift lever on the transaxle.
   b. Disconnect the throttle valve pushrod at the throttle valve (**Figure 13**) and at the shift lever on the transaxle; slip it out of the vehicle underbody.
   c. Detach the selector lever cable from the selector lever by removing the circlip at the end of the cable (**Figure 14**).
   d. Disconnect the filler tube from the side of the transaxle and drain the fluid into a suitable container (**Figure 15**).
   e. Remove the ground strap and the selector cable bracket (**Figure 16**).
7. Hold up the transaxle with a floor jack and a special support like the one shown in **Figure 17**. If a special support is not available, improvise one and secure it to the top of the jack. If the engine was already removed and a transaxle support rig like the one shown in **Figure 18** was used, it must be removed.
8. To remove the transaxle with the engine in place perform the following. If the engine is already out of the vehicle go to Step 9.
   a. Use a jack to support the front of the engine (the part closest to the flywheel). Place a piece of wood between the jack and the bottom of the engine to prevent damage.
   b. Remove the 4 large (17 mm) nuts and bolts which hold the engine and the transaxle together. Two are on top and two are on the bottom of the transaxle.

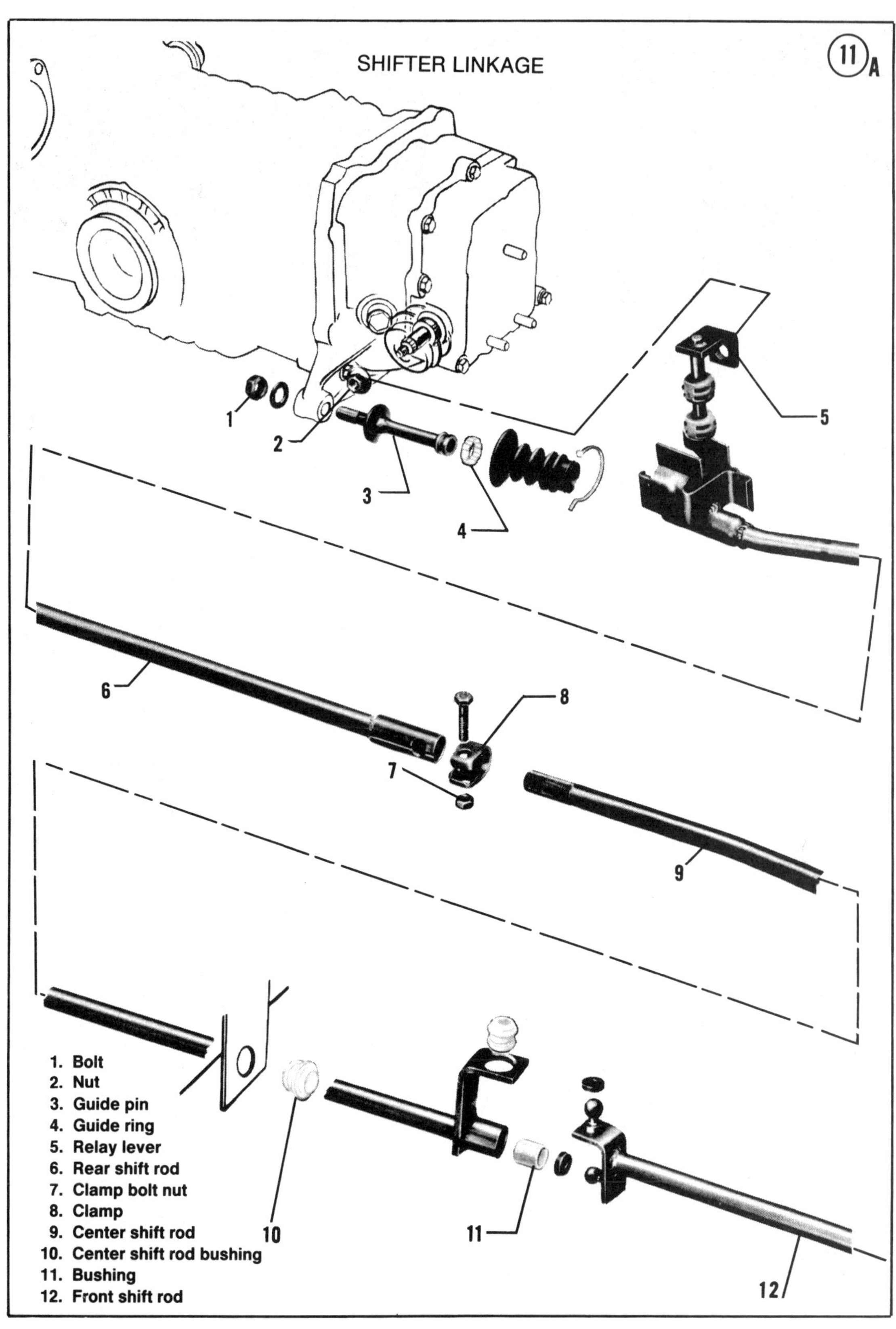
SHIFTER LINKAGE
11A
1
2
3
4
5
6
7
8
9
10
11
12
1. Bolt
2. Nut
3. Guide pin
4. Guide ring
5. Relay lever
6. Rear shift rod
7. Clamp bolt nut
8. Clamp
9. Center shift rod
10. Center shift rod bushing
11. Bushing
12. Front shift rod

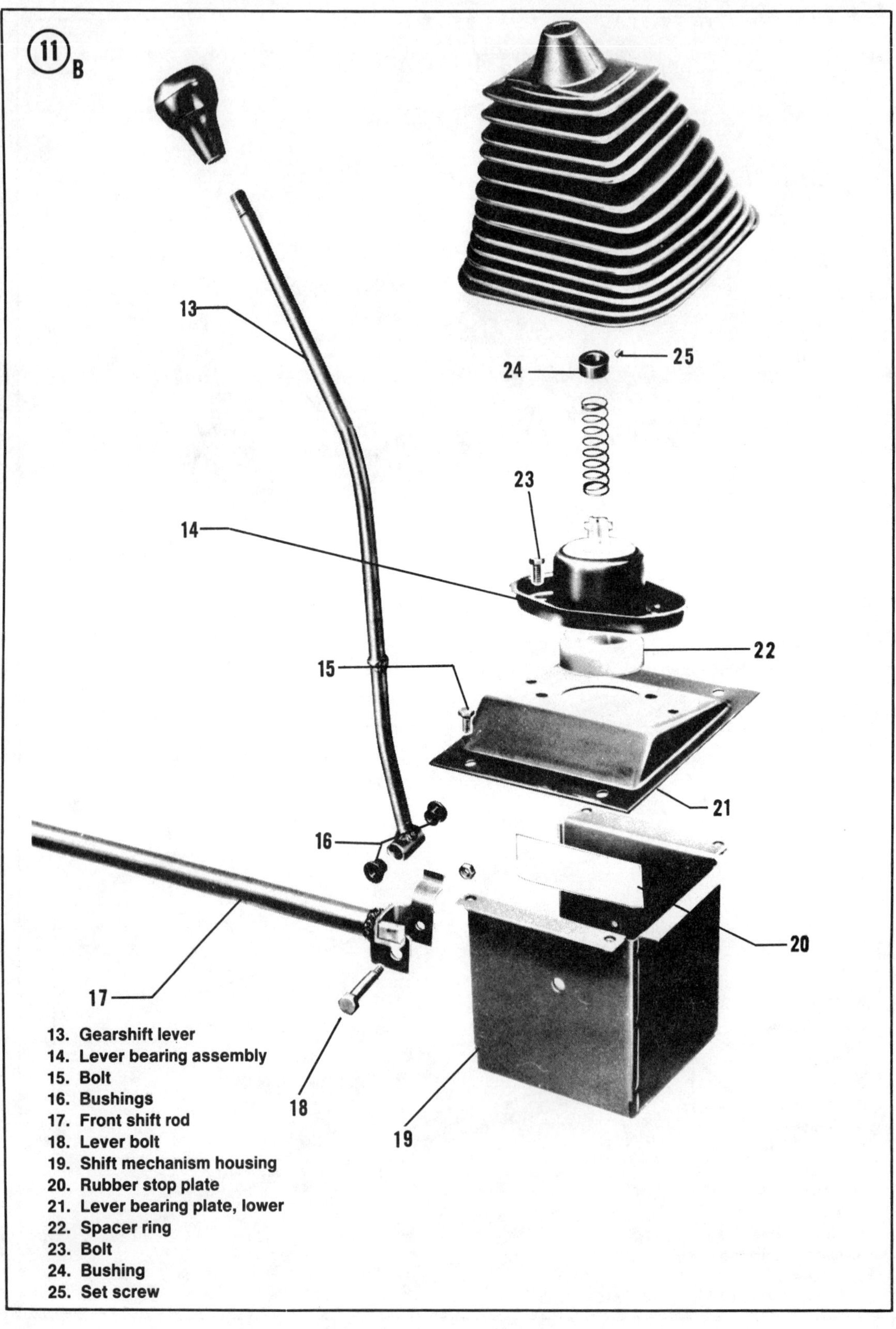

13. Gearshift lever
14. Lever bearing assembly
15. Bolt
16. Bushings
17. Front shift rod
18. Lever bolt
19. Shift mechanism housing
20. Rubber stop plate
21. Lever bearing plate, lower
22. Spacer ring
23. Bolt
24. Bushing
25. Set screw

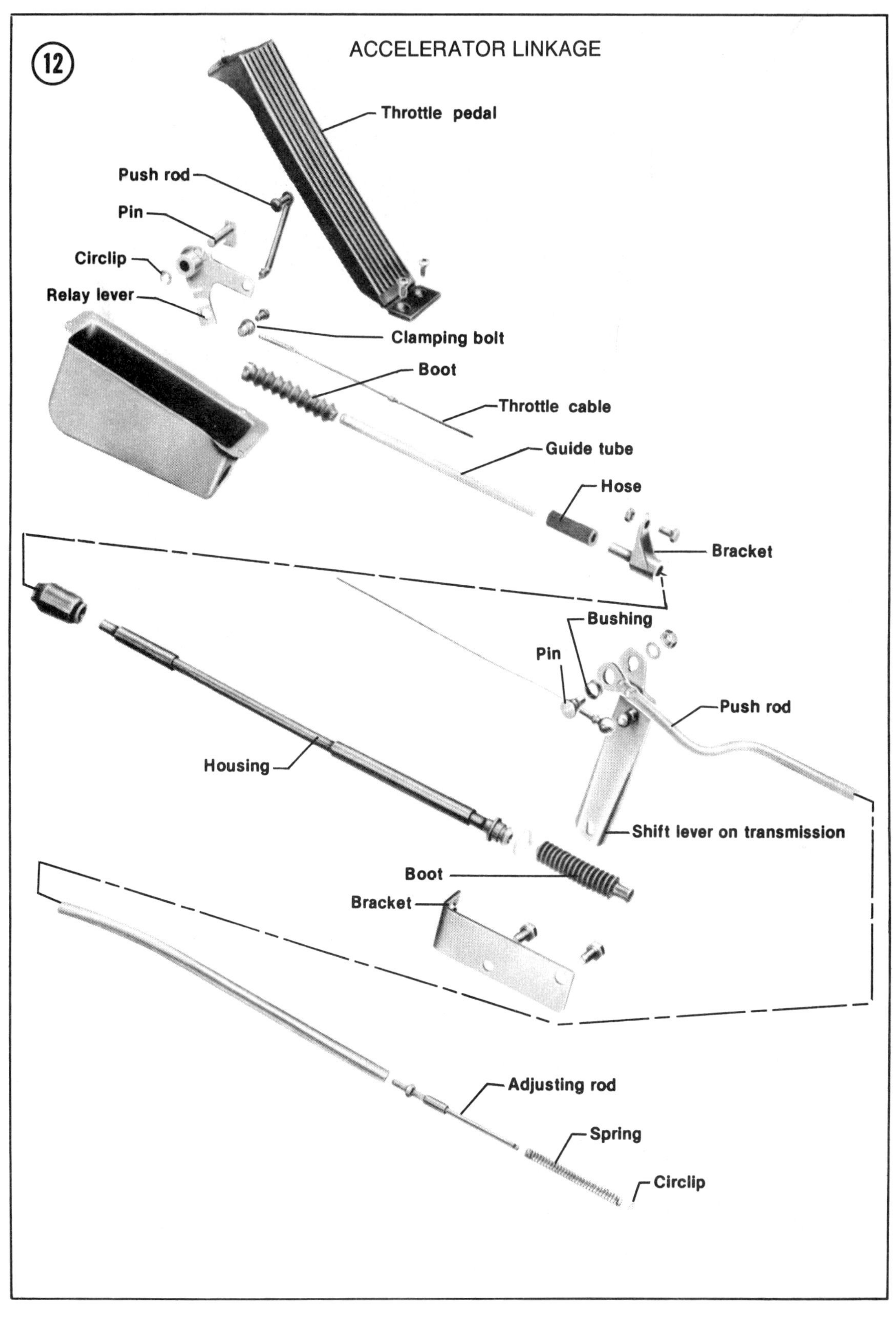
12
ACCELERATOR LINKAGE
Throttle pedal
Push rod
Pin
Circlip
Relay lever
Clamping bolt
Boot
Throttle cable
Guide tube
Hose
Bracket
Bushing
Pin
Push rod
Housing
Shift lever on transmission
Boot
Bracket
Adjusting rod
Spring
Circlip

13

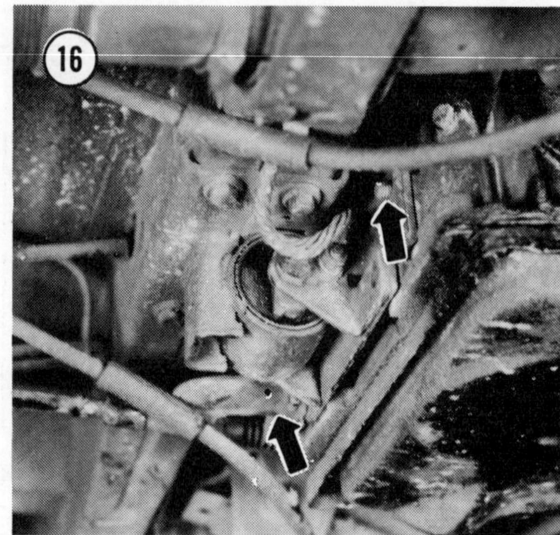
16

14

17

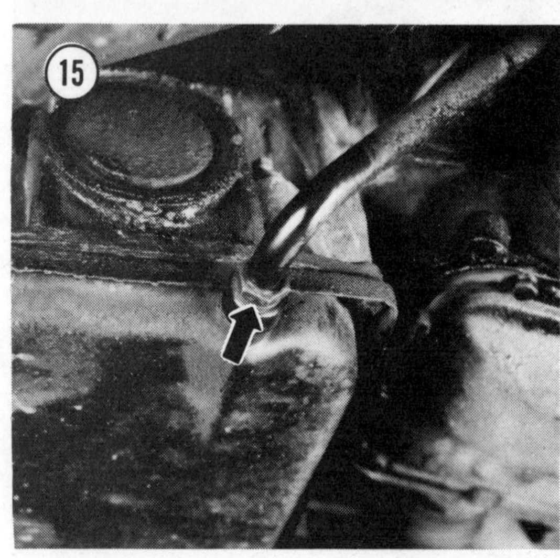
15

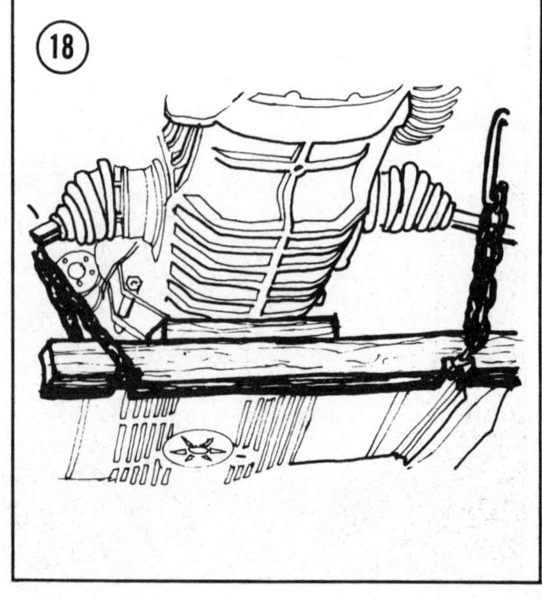
18

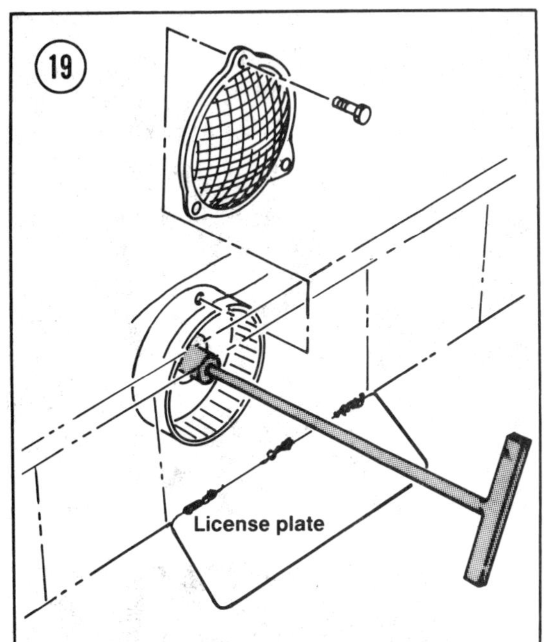

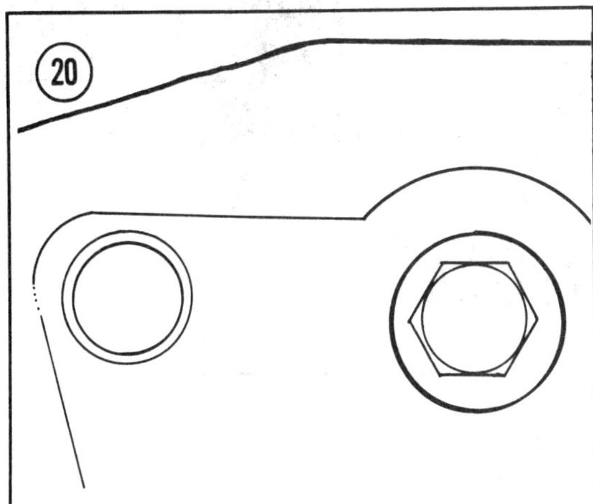

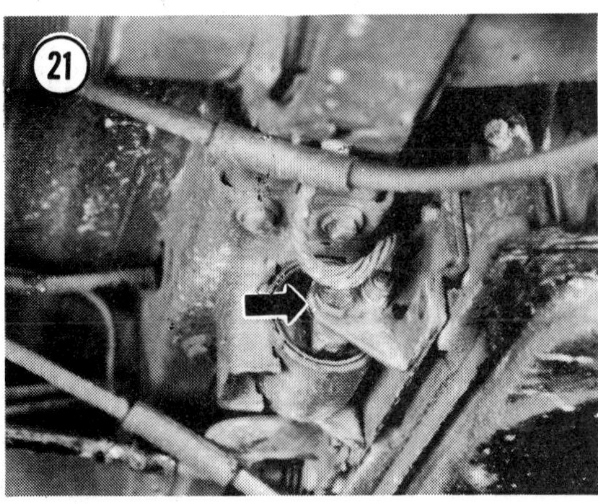

c. On automatic transaxles, remove the bolts which hold the torque converter to the torque converter drive plate. First, remove the plastic screen mesh which protects the main cooling fan. Turn the engine over with a socket and a T-handle wrench on the center nut of the cooling fan (**Figure 19**) until each torque converter bolt appears in the bolt hole on the top of the crankcase on the left-hand side (**Figure 20**).

9. Remove the transaxle carrier support bolts. **Figure 21** shows an automatic transaxle carrier; the manual transaxle carrier is similar.

10. If the engine is removed, lower the floor jack supporting the transaxle. If the engine is installed, it may be necessary to lower the jack supporting the engine a couple of inches (no more) to give the transaxle room to slip off the engine. Slide the transaxle forward and off the engine; lower the floor jack supporting it to the ground.

CAUTION

On manual transaxles, do not let the transmission hang down on the transaxle input shaft. This will bend the shaft and it will have to be replaced, which means totally disassembling the transaxle.

11. Installation is the reverse of removal. See **Table 1** for torque specifications. Note the following:

a. During manual transaxle installation, it may be necessary to turn the engine over by hand to align the splines of the transaxle drive shaft and the clutch disc hub so that the engine and transaxle may slide together.

b. After manual transaxle installation, adjust the shift linkage as described in this chapter. Bleed the clutch.

c. After automatic transaxle installation, adjust the shift selector linkage; see procedure in this chapter. Also adjust the throttle cable and throttle pushrod linkages (Chapter Six).

d. When the transaxle has been installed fill it with the recommended lubricant. **Ta-**

ble 2 presents recommended lubricants and capacities.

MANUAL TRANSAXLE REPAIR/ADJUSTMENT

The services described in the following procedures are the only repairs and adjustment possible for the amateur mechanic. All other jobs should be entrusted to a dealer or other qualified specialist.

Main Shaft Oil Seal Replacement

Refer to **Figure 22** for the following procedure.

1. Remove the engine (Chapter Four) or the transaxle (see procedure in this chapter).
2. Remove the throw-out bearing; see the procedure in this chapter.
3. Remove the throw-out bearing guide sleeve.
4. Use a hook type tool as shown in **Figure 23** to pry out the old seal. Be careful not to damage the seal recess in the housing. The seal may be pried out with the main shaft in place.
5. Wipe out the seal recess with a clean rag.
6. Push new seal onto the main shaft and up against transaxle housing.
7. Use a length of pipe that will fit over the transaxle rear main shaft and large enough in diameter to bear against the outer edge of the rear main seal. A smaller diameter pipe will damage the main seal. Drive the main seal into

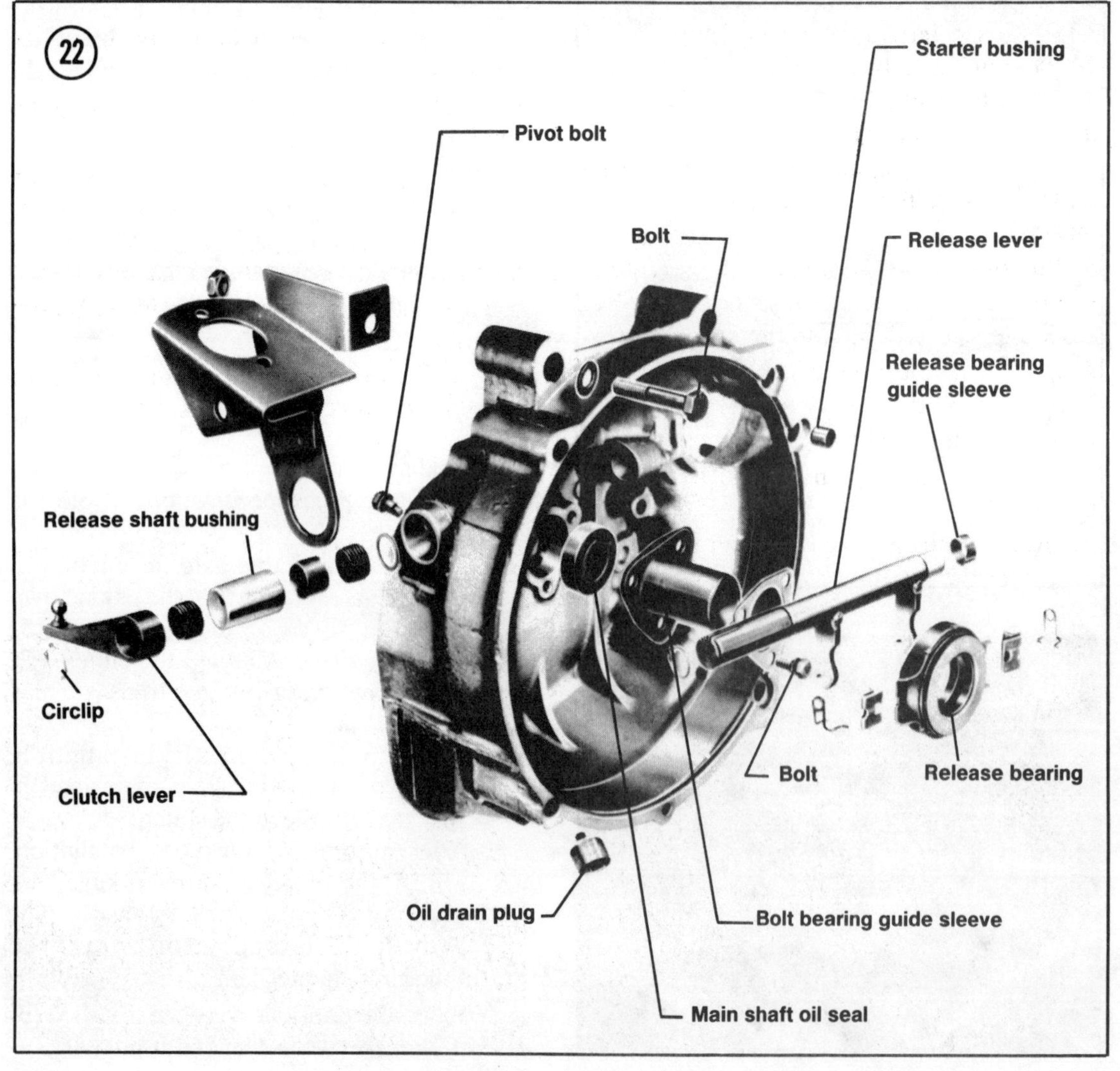

the recess with the pipe and a hammer until it is flush with the clutch housing. A special tool like the one shown in **Figure 24** can also be used.

Starter Drive Bushing Replacement

The starter bushing may be replaced without removing the engine and transaxle, but a special tool is required. Without the special tool, this procedure requires the removal of either the engine or the transaxle to gain access.

To replace the bushing with the engine and transaxle installed perform the following:

1. Disconnect the battery.
2. Remove the starter (Chapter Seven).
3. Use a special starter bushing puller which can be purchased from VW parts stores.
4. Insert the puller into starter bushing though the transaxle housing from the starter side.
5. Tighten the tool; this will expand the collet on the end of the tool and lock it into the bushing.
6. Pull out the old bushing.
7. Loosen the tool and release the old bushing. Lock the new bushing into the tool.
8. Insert the tool and the new bushing into the transaxle housing. Gently tap the new bushing into the transaxle housing with a hammer.
9. Put a few dabs of heavy grease into the bushing.
10. Remove the tool and reinstall the starter.

To remove the bushing with either the engine or transaxle removed perform the following:

1. If the starter is installed, remove it (Chapter Seven).
2. Drive the starter bushing out of the transaxle housing with a length of dowel and a hammer.
3. Drive the new bushing into the transaxle housing the same way. Make sure that it goes in straight.
4. Put a few dabs of heavy grease on the bushing.
5. Reinstall the starter.

Shift Lever Removal/Installation

Refer to **Figure 11** for the following procedure.

1. Unscrew and remove the shifter knob.
2. Pull up the rubber dust boot.
3. Remove the small bolts which hold the lever assembly to the lever plate.
4. Remove the spare tire to gain access to the shift mechanism housing. Remove the housing.
5. Remove the lever bolt and the bushings.
6. Pull out the lever and the lever bearing assembly.
7. Installation is the reverse of removal. Adjust the shift linkage after installation.

Shift Linkage Adjustment

Refer to **Figure 11** for the following procedure.

23

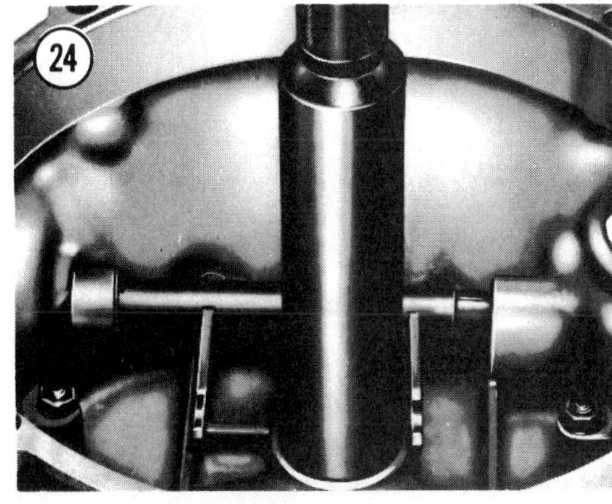

24

8

1. Loosen the clamp which secures the center and the rear shift rod.
2. To make sure the transaxle is in NEUTRAL, perform the following:
   a. If the engine is not installed, turn the transaxle drive shaft by hand. It should turn easily and the wheels should not turn. If the transaxle is in gear, reach under the vehicle and move the relay lever on the side of the transaxle until it is in the NEUTRAL position.
   b. If the engine is installed, push the vehicle forward slightly. If the transaxle is in gear, the engine will turn over and the vehicle will be hard to push. Reach under the vehicle and move the relay lever on the side of the transaxle until it is in the NEUTRAL position.
3. Remove the spare tire to gain access to the shifter mechanism.
4. Put the shifter in NEUTRAL.
5. Loosen the bolts holding the lever assembly to the lever plate.
6. There are 2 small holes drilled in the lever bearing assembly plate. Align these holes with the holes drilled in the lower bearing plate; tighten the bolts.
7. Move the stop finger of the front shift fork to the center of the rubber stop in the shift mechanism housing.
8. Adjust the shift rod end until a gap of 3/4 in. (19 mm) exists (dimension A, **Figure 25**).
9. Tighten the rod clamp.
10. Check that all gears engage smoothly; check the reverse gear lockout. If necessary, readjust.

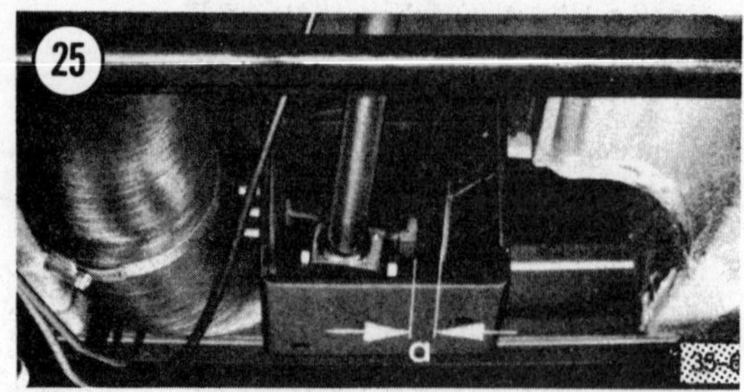

AUTOMATIC TRANSAXLE REPAIR/ADJUSTMENT

The procedures in the following paragraphs are the only jobs possible for the amateur mechanic. All other jobs should be entrusted to a dealer or other qualified specialist.

Torque Converter Removal/Installation

The torque converter is located between the engine and the automatic transaxle. It receives engine output and passes it to the transaxle. The torque converter and the automatic

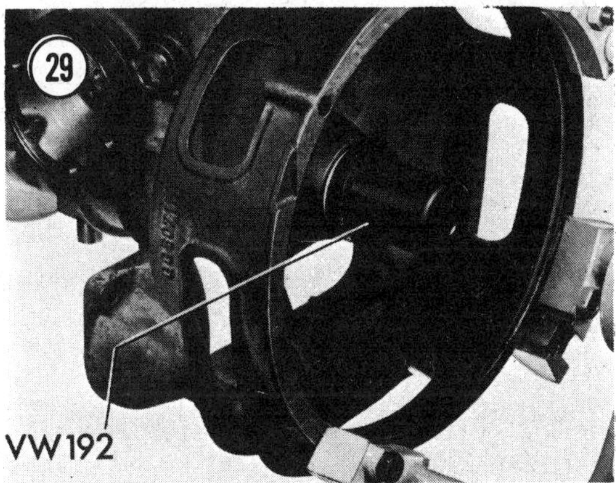

transaxle share the same automatic transmission fluid (ATF).

1. Remove the engine (Chapter Four) or remove the transaxle (this chapter).
2. Pull the torque converter off the input shaft of the transaxle.
3. Installation is the reverse of removal. If the torque converter must be replaced, use one that has the same letter code printed on the side (**Figure 26**).
4. After installation, fill the transaxle with automatic transmission fluid. See **Table 2**. Allow the engine to idle in NEUTRAL and continue adding fluid until the recommended amount has been added and the dipstick reading is correct. This ensures that the torque converter is completely filled.

Torque Converter Inspection

1. Check the converter hub for scoring. Make sure the cooling vanes are secure and tight (**Figure 27**). If damage is found, replace the converter.
2. Push the converter back onto the transaxle shaft. Rotate the converter to make sure the turbine within turns freely; if not, it must be replaced.

Torque Converter Seal Replacement

1. Remove the engine (Chapter Four) or remove the transaxle (this chapter).
2. Remove the torque converter.
3. Use a hook type tool to pry out the old seal shown in **Figure 28**. Be careful not to damage the seal recess in the housing.
4. Wipe out the seal recess with a clean rag.
5. Push new seal onto the main shaft and up against transaxle housing.
6. Use a length of pipe that fits over the transaxle rear main shaft and that is large enough in diameter to come to the outer edge of the rear main seal. A smaller diameter pipe will damage the main seal. Drive the main seal into the recess with the pipe and a hammer until it is flush with the housing. A special tool like the one shown in **Figure 29** can also be used.

Shift Lever Removal/Installation

Refer to **Figure 30** for the following procedure.

1. Remove the shift lever handle setscrew. Remove the handle from the lever.
2. Carefully pry up the shift lever guide plate.
3. Unscrew and remove the lever cover.
4. Remove the spare tire to gain access to the bottom of the lever mechanism.
5. Remove the shift rod bolt and bushings.
6. Unbolt the shift lever support from the vehicle body.
7. Installation is the reverse of removal. After installation adjust the cable as described in this chapter.

Shift Linkage Cable Replacement

Refer to **Figure 30** for the following procedure.

1. Unbolt the shift linkage cable bracket from the underbody.
2. Remove the circlip and pull the cable end off the transmission shift lever (**Figure 14**).

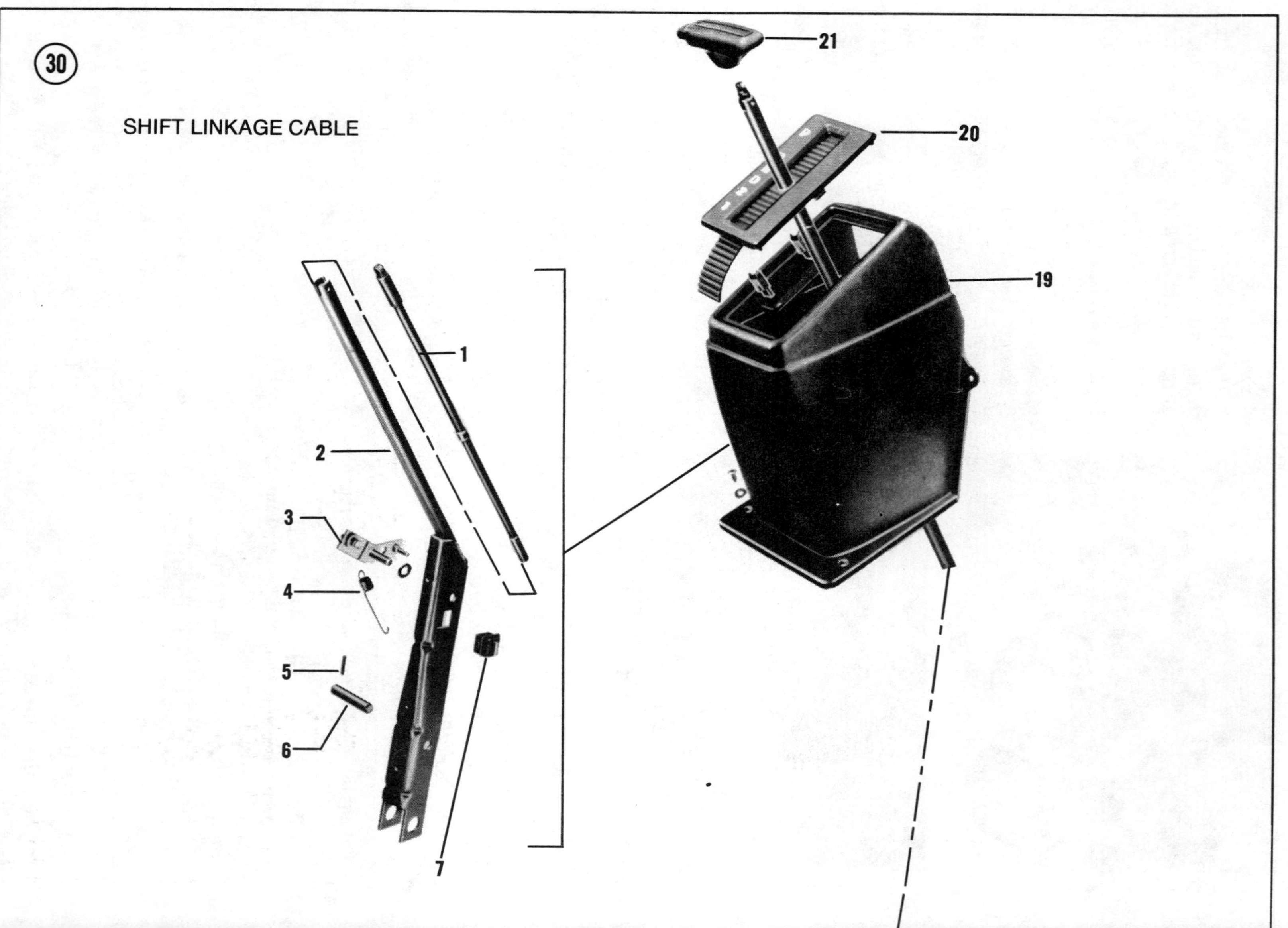
30
SHIFT LINKAGE CABLE
21
20
19
1
2
3
4
5
6
7

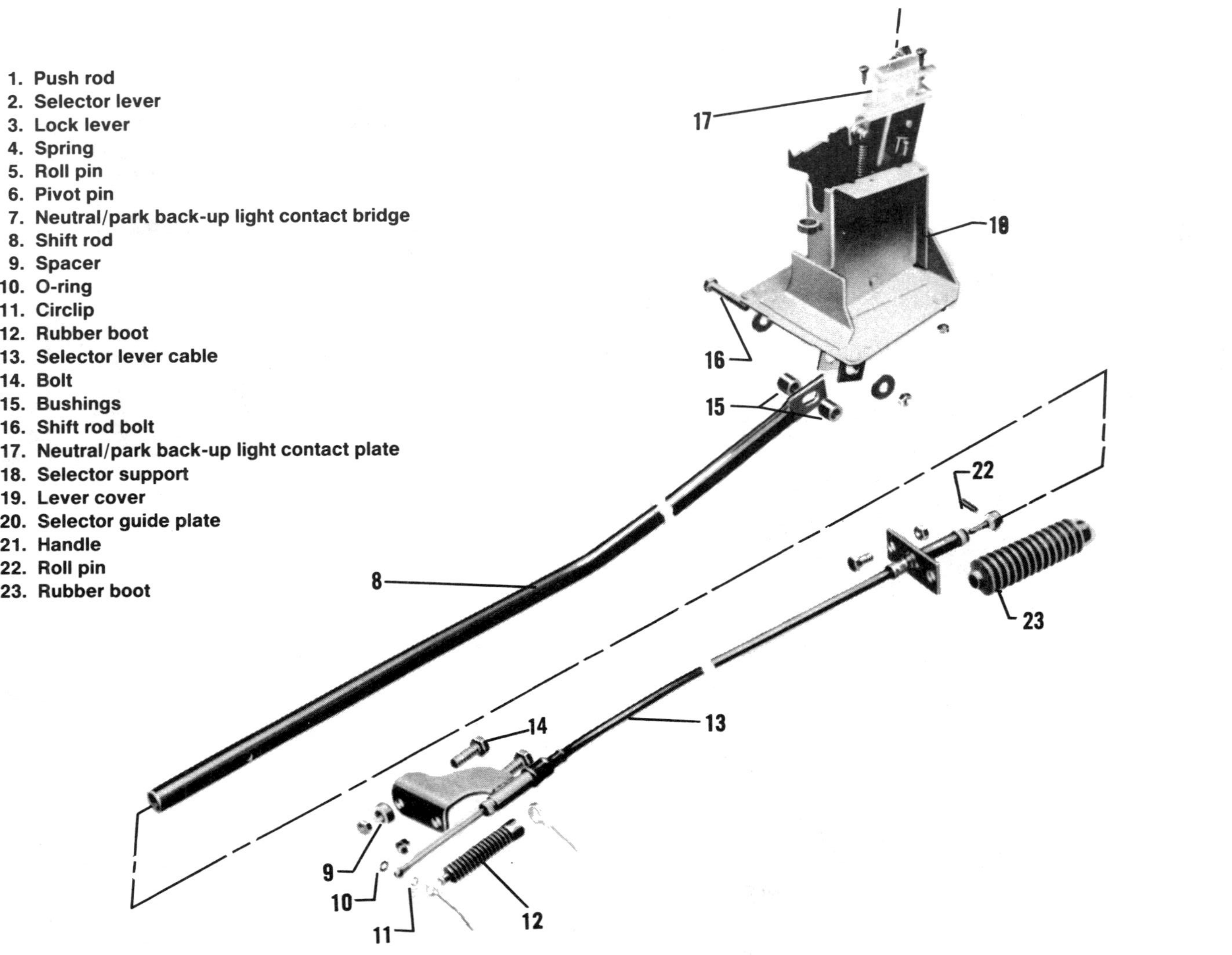
1. Push rod
2. Selector lever
3. Lock lever
4. Spring
5. Roll pin
6. Pivot pin
7. Neutral/park back-up light contact bridge
8. Shift rod
9. Spacer
10. O-ring
11. Circlip
12. Rubber boot
13. Selector lever cable
14. Bolt
15. Bushings
16. Shift rod bolt
17. Neutral/park back-up light contact plate
18. Selector support
19. Lever cover
20. Selector guide plate
21. Handle
22. Roll pin
23. Rubber boot
17
18
16
15
22
8
23
14
13
9
10
11
12

8

3. Remove the shift rod bolt and bushings; push the rod to the rear of the vehicle.
4. Push the roll pin out of the shift rod.
5. Pull the old cable out of the cable tube and insert the new one, coating it with grease as it's pushed in.
6. Perform Steps 1-4 in reverse order. After installation adjust the cable as described in this chapter.

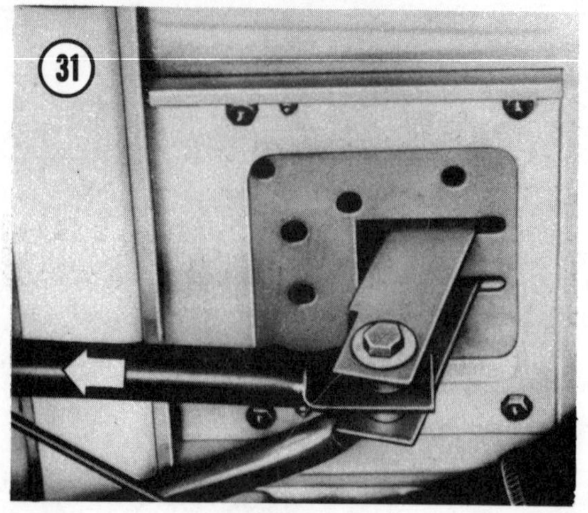

Shift Linkage Cable Adjustment

Refer to **Figure 30** for the following procedure.

1. Put the shift lever in PARK.
2. Remove the spare tire to gain access to the lower shifter mechanism.
3. Loosen the shift rod bolt. Push the rod to the rear of the vehicle (**Figure 31**).
4. Tighten shift rod bolt.
6. Reinstall the spare tire.

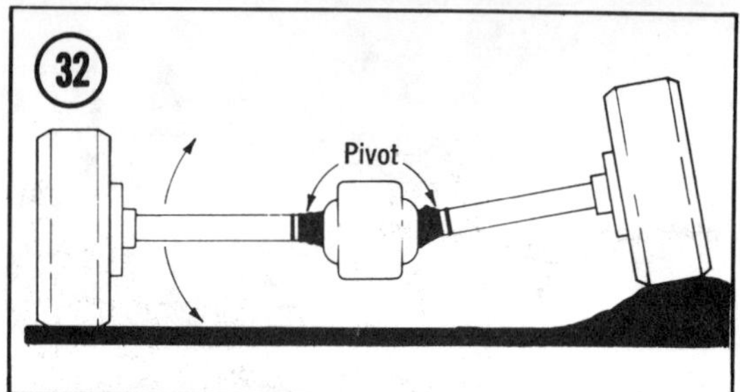

DRIVE AXLES

The drive axles on the Vanagon have a constant velocity (CV) joint at each end. Instead of traveling in an arc (**Figure 32**), wheels travel vertically (**Figure 33**). Negative camber increases during cornering under load.

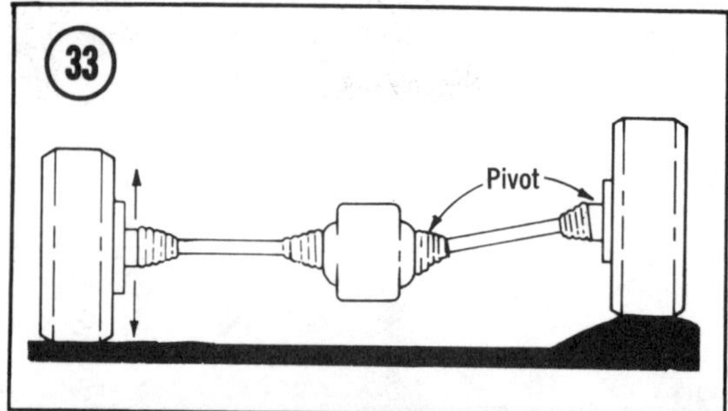

Removal/Installation

1. Block the drive wheels.
2. Remove the Allen head bolts which hold the CV joints and axle to the transaxle and the rear axle shaft (**Figure 9**). Pull the axle and CV joints off the vehicle.
3. Installation is the reverse of removal. During installation torque the Allen head bolts to specifications; see **Table 1**.

REAR AXLE BOOTS

Boot replacement is possible without removing the axle shafts, however, a split boot must be installed. If the boot has ripped open, dirt has most likely entered the CV joint and it should be completely disassembled and cleaned as described in this chapter.

1. Remove the retaining clamps on the boot.
2. Cut off the old boot with a sharp knife.
3. Clean the exposed area with a dry, clean rag.
4. Install the boot with the split toward the rear. Tighten the boot screws. Install and

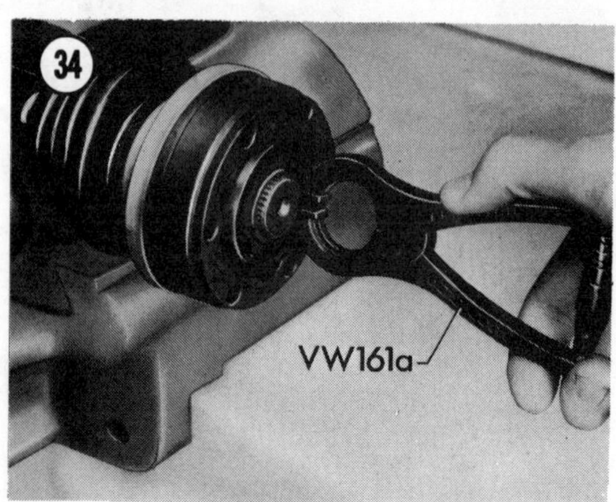

tighten the boot clamps. Do not overtighten screws or clamps.

CONSTANT VELOCITY JOINTS

Disassembly

1. Remove the circlip from the end of the axle (**Figure 34**).
2. Remove the clamps which hold the rubber dust boot to the CV joint and the axle (**Figure 35**). Slide the boot down the axle.
3. Use a drift to knock off the protective cap from the CV joint (**Figure 36**).
4. Press the drive shaft out of the CV joint as shown in **Figure 37**.

NOTE
If more than one CV joint is to be disassembled, do not mix up the parts. CV joints are sized and matched; parts may not be interchanged.

5. Rotate the ball hub and cage; press it out of the outer ring as shown in **Figure 38**.
6. Remove the ball bearings from the cage.
7. Align the groove in the ball hub with the cage edge; remove the hub from the cage (**Figure 39**).

Cleaning and Inspection

NOTE
If any part of the CV joint is found to be damaged, replace the entire unit.

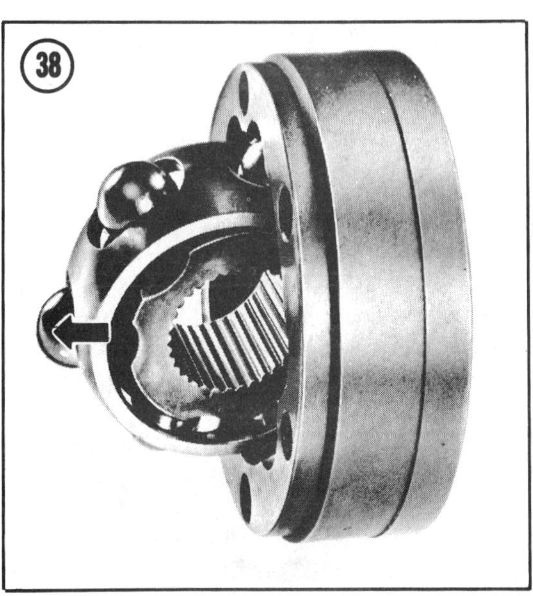

8

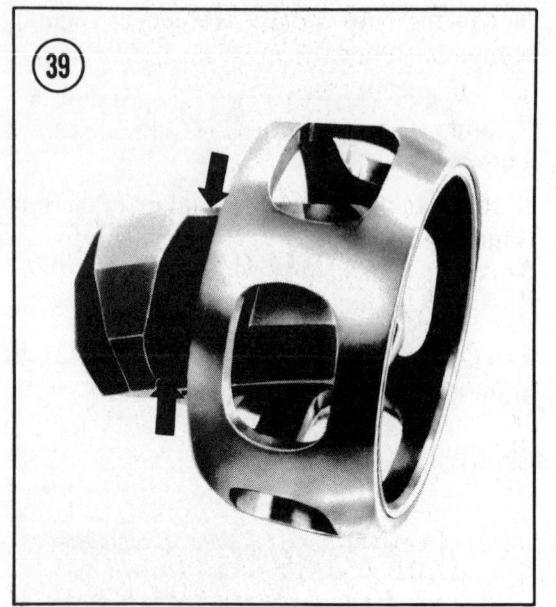
39

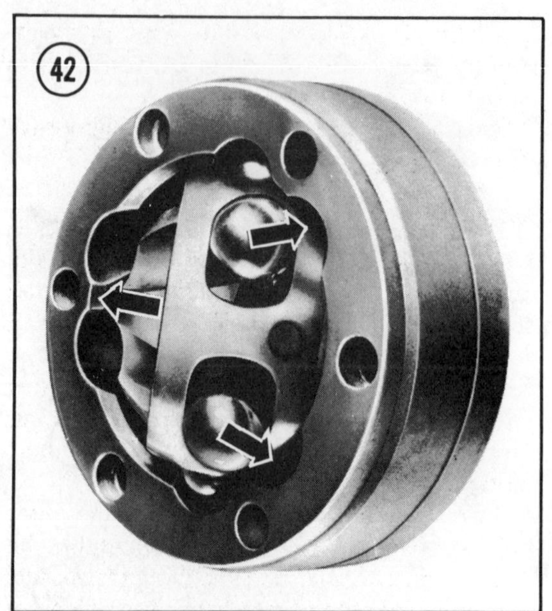
42

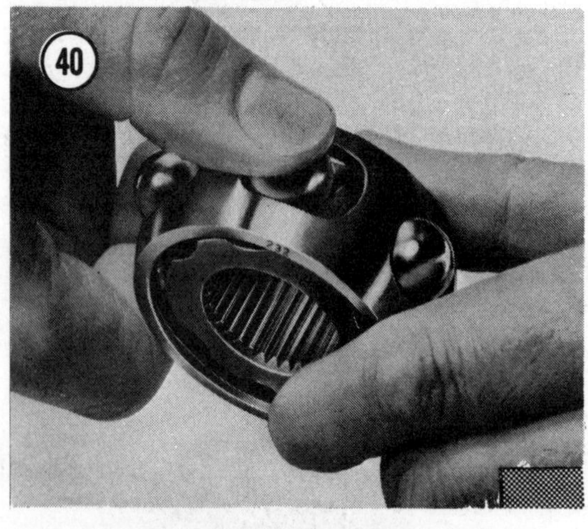
40

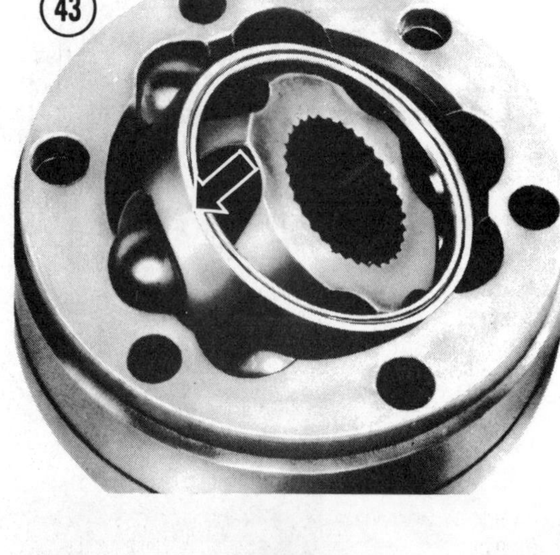
43

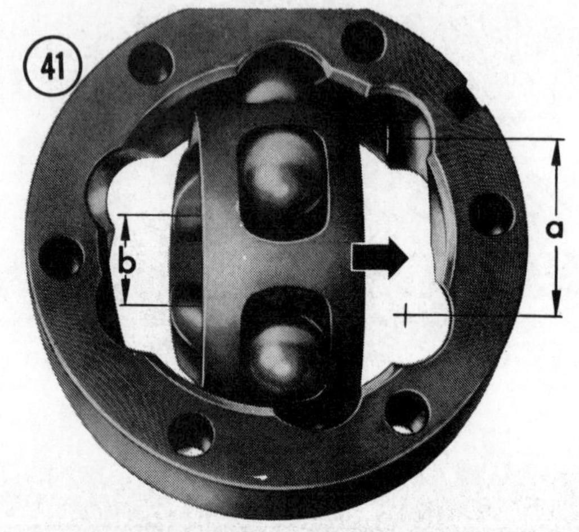
41
a
b

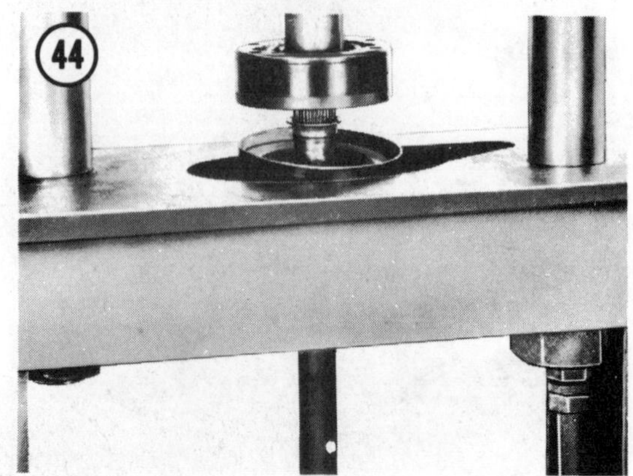
44

1. Clean all parts in solvent. Wipe them absolutely clean and lay them out on a clean surface for assembly.
2. Inspect all parts for scoring, pitting or heat discoloration.

Assembly

1. Align the groove in the ball hub with the cage edge; install the hub in the cage (**Figure 39**).
2. Press the balls into the cage (**Figure 40**).
3. Hold the outer ring so the large diameter end faces up. Look at the ball groove spacing. Note that dimension A is wider than dimension B (**Figure 41**).
4. Insert the ball hub and cage into the outer ring as shown in **Figure 42**. Make sure that the widely spaced balls line up with the widely spaced grooves and that the chamfered end of the hub faces toward the large diameter end of the outer ring when the hub is pivoted.
5. Pivot the ball hub until the balls fit into their grooves.
6. Press the cage in the area indicated by the arrow in **Figure 43** until the hub swings into position.
7. Check the operation of the hub by hand. It should be possible to move the hub in and out through its full range.
8. Slide the rubber boot and the protective cap onto the drive shaft.
9. Press the CV joint onto the drive shaft as shown in **Figure 44**.
10. Install the circlip onto the end of the drive shaft (**Figure 34**).
11. Pack about 2 ounces (60 grams) of lithium grease (with molybdenum disulfide additive) between the protective cap and the CV joint. Do not get any grease on the contact surfaces between the cap, joint and rubber boot. Pack another ounce (30 grams) of grease into the end of the joint which faces the axle shaft or the transaxle.
12. Tap the protective cap into place over the joint.
13. Slide the rubber boot over the metal cap. Tighten both clamps securing the boot.
14. Squeeze the rubber boot by hand to force any grease which has oozed out back into the joint.

8

TABLE 1 CLUTCH AND TRANSAXLE TIGHTENING TORQUES

Item	Ft.-lb.	N•m
Engine to transmission	22	30
Engine carrier to body	18	25
CV joint to transaxle	33	45
Transaxle mount to body	22	30
MANUAL TRANSAXLE		
Clutch master cylinder body bracket bolts	18	25
Clutch slave cylinder transaxle bracket bolts	18	25
Guide sleeve bolts	11	15
Transaxle to transaxle bracket bolt	33	45
Guide pin nut	33	45
Relay lever nut	14	20
Pivot bolt	11	15
Clutch pressure plate to flywheel	18	25
Flywheel to crankshaft	80	110
AUTOMATIC TRANSMISSION		
Torque converter plate to crankshaft	65	90
Torque converter to plate	22	30

Table 2 RECOMMENDED LUBRICANTS AND CAPACITIES

Temperature Range	Recommended Type	Capacity
Manual Transaxle		
Below -13° F Between -13° F & 0°F Above 0° F	ATF (DEXRON) Gear oil SAE 80W Gear oil SAE 90W	3.7 U.S. qt. (3.5 L)
Automatic Transaxle		
All temperatures	ATF (DEXRON)	Dry fill: 6.4 U.S. qt. (6.0 L) Refill: 3.2 U.S. qt. (3.0L)
Automatic Transaxle Final Drive		
Below -13° F Between -13° F & 0°F Above 0° F	ATF (DEXRON) Gear oil SAE 80W Gear oil SAE 90W	3.7 U.S. qt. (3.5 L)

CHAPTER NINE

BRAKES

The brake system has 2 independent hydraulic circuits. Each circuit controls either the front disc brakes or the rear drum brakes. **Table 1** brake specifications is located at the end of the chapter.

When the brake pedal is depressed, pressure in the front half of the master cylinder operates one front and the opposite rear brake; pressure from the rear half operates the two remaining brakes. If one circuit should fail, the other should work, permitting a safe stop with 2 wheels.

The master cylinder is operated through a vacuum servo. The vacuum servo uses the difference between engine vacuum and atmospheric pressure to reduce pedal pressure required from the driver.

Two warning pressure switches on the master cylinder indicate with a light on the dash panel if pressure in either circuit fails. If the warning light goes on during vehicle operation, check the entire system immediately.

The cable-operated handbrake acts upon the rear brake shoes. When the hand lever is drawn up, the rear brake shoes expand to provide parking brakes.

NOTE

Procedures in this chapter require the removal of brake lines and brake part bolts. A special VW brake tool for disconnecting brake lines is available in many foreign parts stores. This tool will greatly speed disassembly/assembly and bleeding.

MASTER CYLINDER

Removal/Installation

Refer to **Figure 1** and **Figure 2** for the following procedure.

1. Remove the instrument panel to gain access to the master cylinder (Chapter Seven).
2. Spread rags under and around the master cylinder to catch spilling fluid.
3. Drain the hydraulic fluid reservoir and pull it off the top of the master cylinder.
4. Unbolt the hydraulic lines at the master cylinder and cap the end of the lines.

NOTE

You can use the rubber dust caps off of the wheel cylinder bleeder valves to plug the lines.

5. Remove the vacuum hose from the vacuum servo.
6. Remove the clevis shaft.
7. Remove the nuts which hold the master cylinder and the vacuum servo to the pedal bracket. Pull the cylinder and servo out of the dash as one unit.
8. Remove the bolts which hold the pedal bracket to the body.

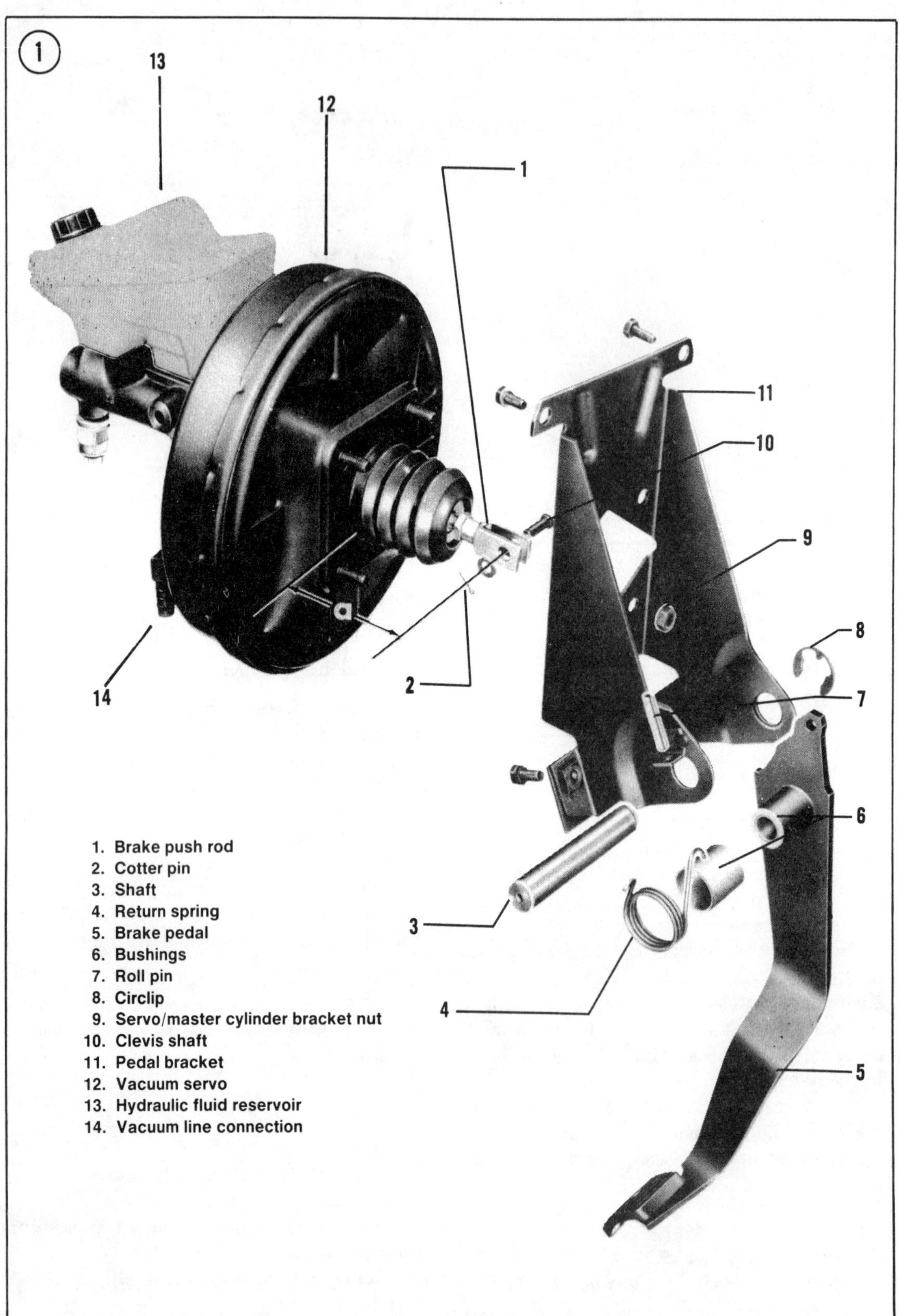
1
13
12
1
11
10
9
8
7
6
2
14
3
4
5
a
1. Brake push rod
2. Cotter pin
3. Shaft
4. Return spring
5. Brake pedal
6. Bushings
7. Roll pin
8. Circlip
9. Servo/master cylinder bracket nut
10. Clevis shaft
11. Pedal bracket
12. Vacuum servo
13. Hydraulic fluid reservoir
14. Vacuum line connection

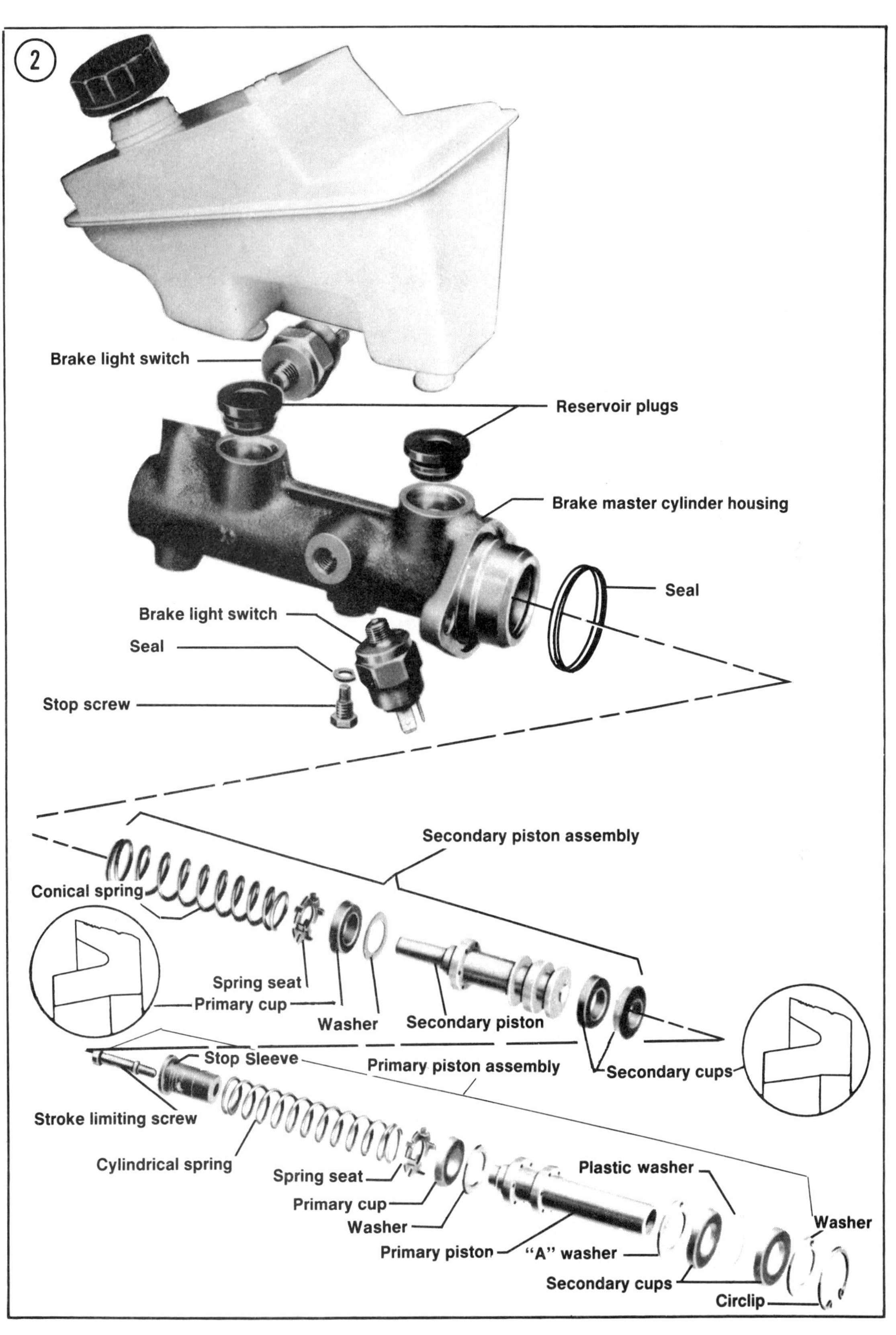
2
Brake light switch
Reservoir plugs
Brake master cylinder housing
Seal
Brake light switch
Seal
Stop screw
Secondary piston assembly
Conical spring
Spring seat
Primary cup
Washer
Secondary piston
Stop Sleeve
Primary piston assembly
Secondary cups
Stroke limiting screw
Cylindrical spring
Spring seat
Primary cup
Washer
Primary piston
Plastic washer
"A" washer
Secondary cups
Washer
Circlip

9. Remove the nuts which hold the master cylinder to the vacuum servo and separate them.
10. Installation is the reverse of removal. Before installing master cylinder and vacuum servo, adjust the pushrod to 4 3/8 in. (111.5 mm); see dimension A in **Figure 1**. After installation the system must be bled; see procedure in this chapter.

Disassembly

When disassembling the master cylinder lay out the parts as they are removed to avoid confusion when replacing old parts with new ones from the rebuild kit. Refer to **Figure 2** for the following procedure.

1. Remove the brake light switches from the master cylinder.
2. Pull out the rubber hydraulic fluid reservoir plugs.
3. Clamp the cylinder in a vise with soft jaws. Remove the snap ring with snap ring pliers (**Figure 3**). Do not let the primary piston pop out.
4. Carefully remove the primary piston and cylindrical spring from the cylinder.
5. Pull out the secondary piston. Tip the cylinder over and let the conical spring fall out.
6. See *Cleaning and Inspection* in this chapter.

Cleaning and Inspection

1. Carefully cut the rubber cups off the pistons with a single-edge razor blade.
2. Clean all parts in clean denatured alcohol or brake fluid.
3. Examine the pistons and the inside of the cylinder for rust, pitting or cracks. Pits will appear as small discolored cavities. If severe pitting is found, replace the entire unit. If very minor pitting or rust spots are present, try to remove them with brake fluid and a rag or with crocus cloth. If the damage cannot be removed, replace the parts.
4. If the cylinder and piston are free of defects, reassemble as described in this chapter.

WARNING

Cylinders with pitting must not be rebuilt. Hydraulic fluid leaks through the pits around the sealing cups or rings. This will degrade braking power and you may wind up in an accident.

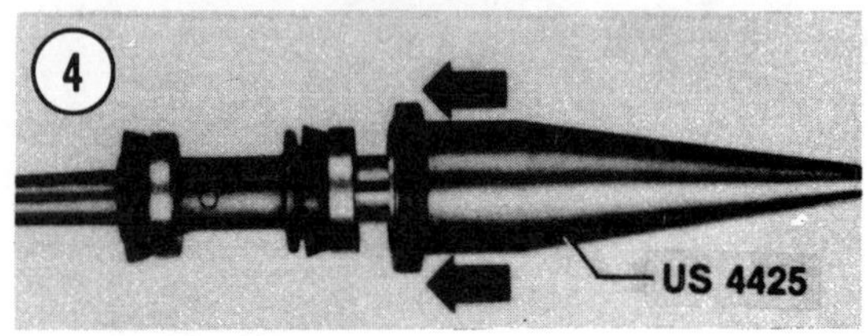

Assembly

Refer to **Figure 2** for the following procedure. Soak all new rubber parts in clean brake fluid for 15 minutes prior to assembly to make them pliable.

1. Push the washer, primary cup and spring seat onto the secondary piston. Make sure the sealing edges of the cup point to the front of the piston.
2. Install the secondary cups on the secondary piston. The sealing edges of the cups must point in opposite directions. Gently pry the cups over the cup retaining walls on the piston with a small blunt instrument or use a special tool as shown in **Figure 4**.
3. Drop the conical spring into the cylinder bore.
4. Lubricate the cups on the secondary piston with clean brake fluid.
5. Slip the washer, primary cup and spring seat onto the end of the primary piston.

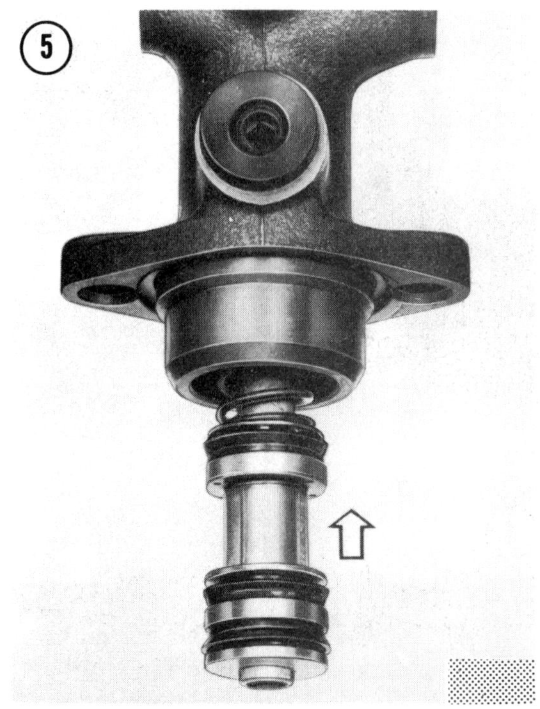

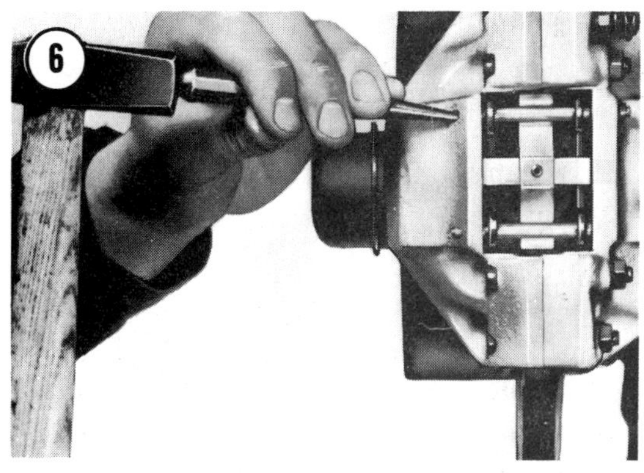

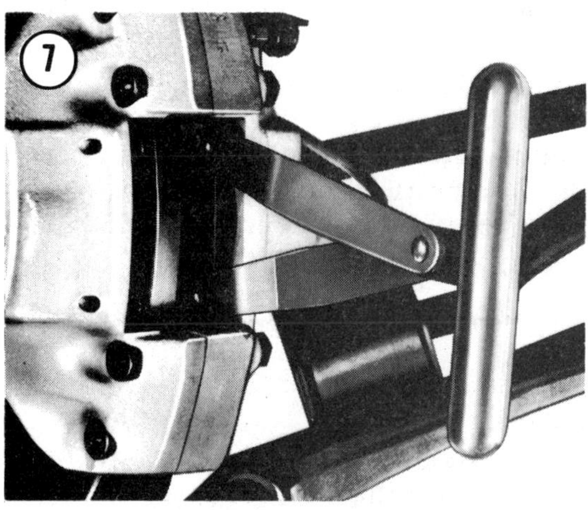

6. Install the stop sleeve and spring on the primary piston. Install the stroke limiting screw and turn it all the way in until it seats.
7. Slip the "A" washer, one secondary cup, spacer washer, another secondary cup and the "B" washer onto the end of the primary piston.
8. Clamp the cylinder in a soft-jaw vise with the bore vertical.
9. Slip the secondary piston into the cylinder bore as shown in **Figure 5**. Work the lips of the cups into the bore with a blunt instrument.
10. Slip the primary piston into the cylinder bore. Work the lip of the cups into the bore with a blunt instrument. Push the piston in as far as it will go and install the snap ring.

NOTE
You may want to have an assistant hold the primary piston while you install the snap ring.

FRONT DISC PAD REPLACEMENT

1. Loosen the front wheel lug nuts.
2. Jack up the front of the vehicle and position it on jackstands.
3. Remove the front wheels.
4. Knock out the pad pins with a hammer and a small drift (**Figure 6**). Remove the spreader spring.
5. Extract the old pads. Use a tool like the one shown in **Figure 7** or a U-shaped piece of wire with a hook at each end.

NOTE
If the brake pads are to be reinstalled, mark them so they can be reinstalled in the same position.

6. Carefully clean out the cavity which holds the pads. Inspect the rubber caps; if they are damaged, replace them. If dirt has penetrated the cylinder due to a damaged cap, rebuild the caliper as described in this chapter under *Front Brake Calipers.*
7. Before installing the new pads, push the pistons back into the cylinders. Use an expansion tool like the one shown in **Figure 8**. Another method is to pry with a large screwdriver between the caliper piston and the rotor.

9

CAUTION
The screwdriver blade must be resting near the rotor hub (not on the pad wear surface) or the rotor will be damaged.

Put a thin piece of wood over the piston, lever the piston back into the cylinder with the screwdriver and insert the disc pad. Repeat this with the other piston.

NOTE
The master cylinder may overflow when the pistons are pressed in. Draw some fluid out of the reservoir to prevent this (discard the fluid).

8. Make sure the brake pads slide smoothly within the caliper assembly.
9. Install the lower pad pin in the hole and tap it in with a hammer. Do not use a drift or you may drive it in too far.
10. Hook a *new* spreader spring under the lower pad pin. Hold the spring in place and install the upper pad pin.
11. Depress the brake pedal several times before driving the vehicle so the pads can align correctly to the brake rotor.

FRONT BRAKE CALIPERS

Two different types of brake calipers are used on the Vanagon: Teves (**Figure 9**) and Girling (**Figure 10**). Removal and installation procedures are the same for both types. If you are going to rebuild a caliper, be sure you get the correct replacement parts.

Removal/Installation

1. Loosen the front wheel lug nuts. Raise the front of the vehicle and position it on jackstands. Remove the front wheels.
2. Remove the disc pads. See *Front Disc Pad Replacement* in this chapter.
3. Disconnect the hydraulic line from the back of the caliper and plug the line.

NOTE
The hydraulic line does not have to be removed if the caliper is not to be disassembled. If the line is not disconnected, hang the caliper from the suspension with a length of wire to keep all strain off the line.

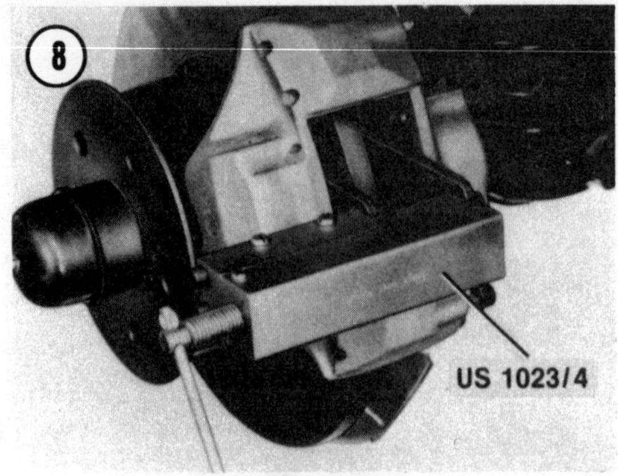

4. Two large shouldered bolts on the inboard side of the caliper hold it to the steering knuckle. Remove the bolts and pull the caliper off the disc rotor.

5. Installation is the reverse of removal. Torque the shouldered bolts to 115 ft.-lb. (160 N•m). After installation the system must be bled if the hydraulic line was disconnected; see procedure in this chapter.

Disassembly

If the caliper was leaking between the halves, it must be replaced. If the damage is less severe, the caliper can be disassembled, cleaned and reassembled as described in this chapter.

1. Clamp the caliper in a soft-jaw vise.

2. Carefully pry out the cap with a screwdriver (**Figure 11**).

3. Hold one of the pistons with a clamping tool (as shown in **Figure 12**) or with your hand. Hold the inboard (bleeder valve) side with the clamp first and blow out the outboard piston with compressed air. Insert a small diameter steel rod into the hydraulic line hole and push out the inboard piston. If this method does not work, rebuild one side of the caliper at a time.

4. Carefully pry out the piston seal (**Figure 13**).

5. See *Cleaning and Inspection* in this chapter.

Cleaning and Inspection

1. Carefully cut the rubber cups off the brake pistons with a single-edge razor blade.

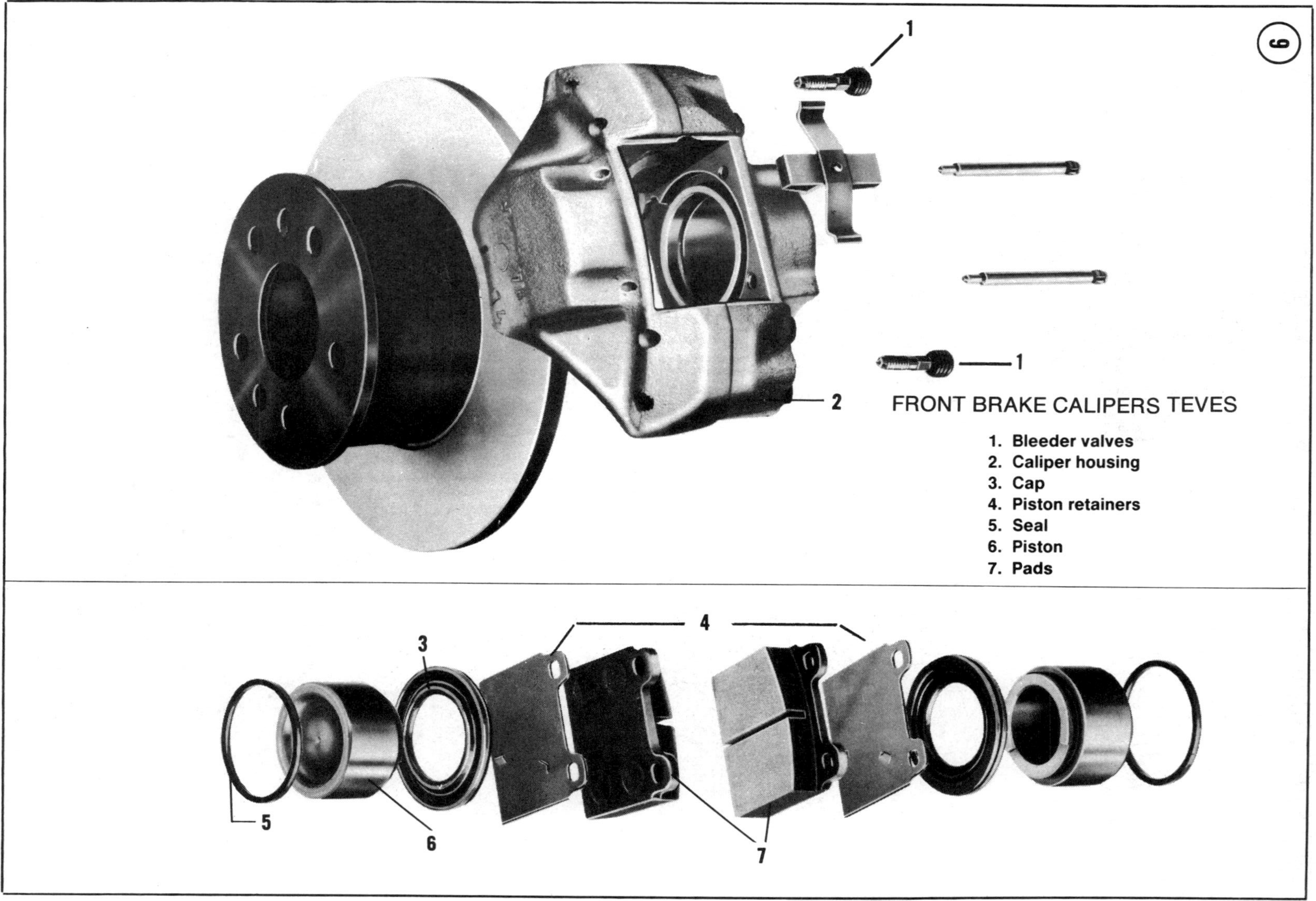
9
1
1
2
FRONT BRAKE CALIPERS TEVES
1. Bleeder valves
2. Caliper housing
3. Cap
4. Piston retainers
5. Seal
6. Piston
7. Pads
4
3
5
6
7

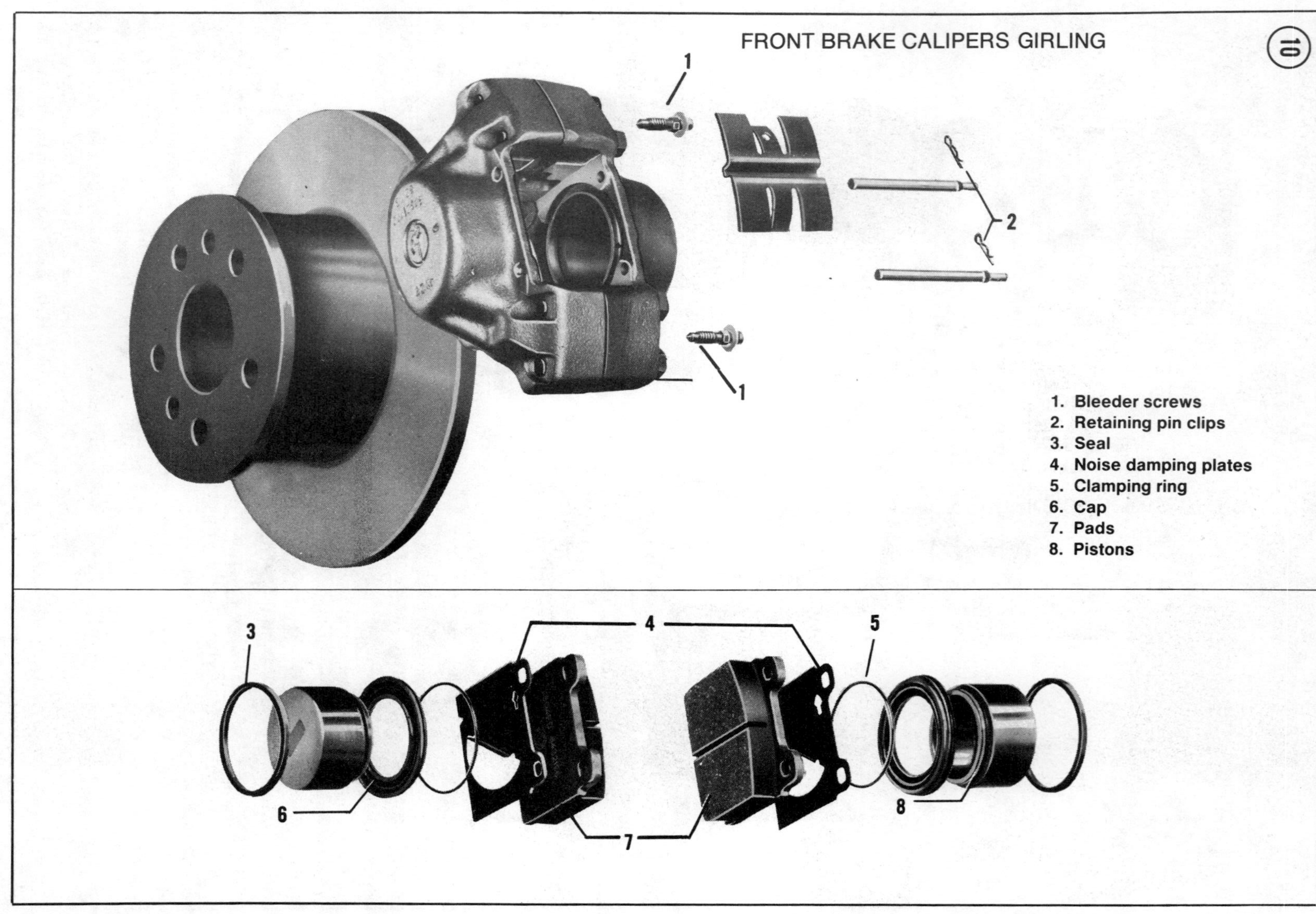
10
FRONT BRAKE CALIPERS GIRLING
1. Bleeder screws
2. Retaining pin clips
3. Seal
4. Noise damping plates
5. Clamping ring
6. Cap
7. Pads
8. Pistons
1
1
2
3
4
5
6
7
8

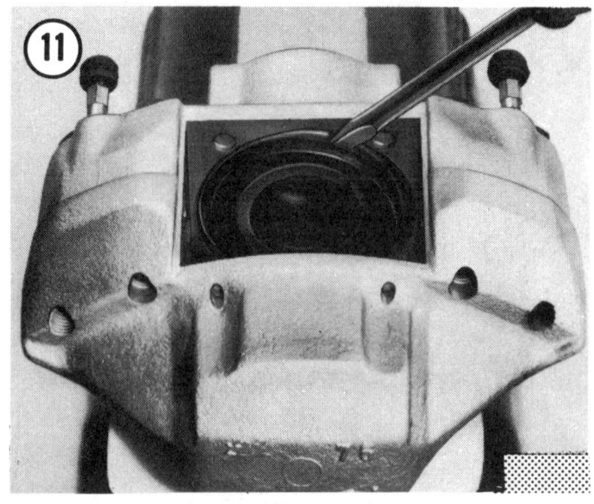

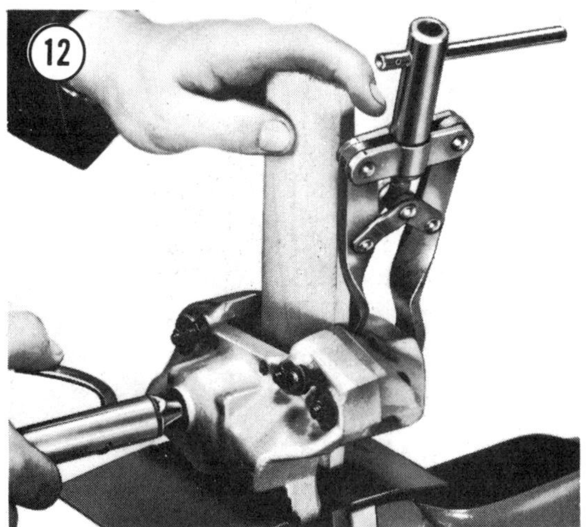

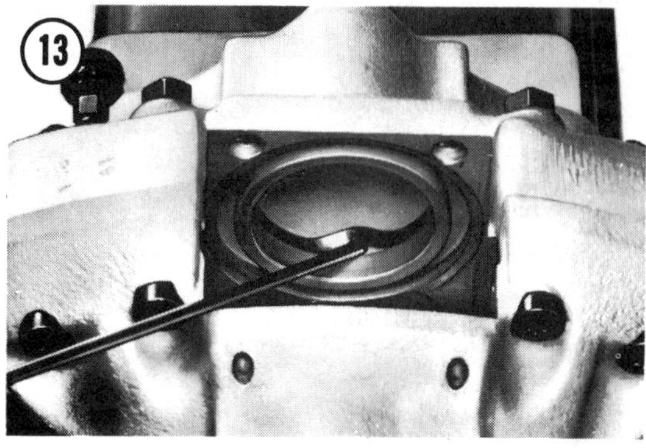

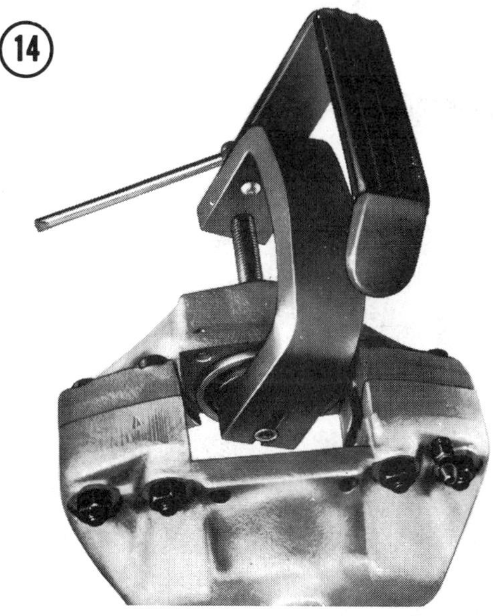

2. Clean all brake parts in clean denatured alcohol or brake fluid.

3. Examine the pistons and the inside of the cylinder for rust, pitting or cracks. Pits will appear as small discolored cavities. If severe pitting is found, replace the entire unit. If very minor pitting or rust spots are present, try to remove them with brake fluid and a rag or with crocus cloth. If the damage cannot be removed, replace the parts.

4. If the cylinder and piston are free of defects, reassemble as described in this chapter.

WARNING

Cylinders with pitting must not be rebuilt. Hydraulic fluid leaks through the pits around the sealing cups or rings. This will degrade braking power and you may wind up in an accident.

Assembly

Refer to **Figure 9** or **Figure 10** for the following procedure. Soak all new rubber parts in clean brake fluid for 15 minutes prior to assembly to make them pliable.

1. Install the piston seal in the cylinder.

2. Coat the entire piston with clean brake fluid.

3. Press the piston into the cylinder with a tool like the one shown in **Figure 14** or push it in by hand. Make sure the piston goes in straight.

4. Push down the inner lip of the cap (**Figure 15**). Use a special tool like the one shown in **Figure 16** to press it in. A piece of plastic pipe the same diameter as the cap and a clamp will also work. On Girling models, install the clamping ring with the cap.

9

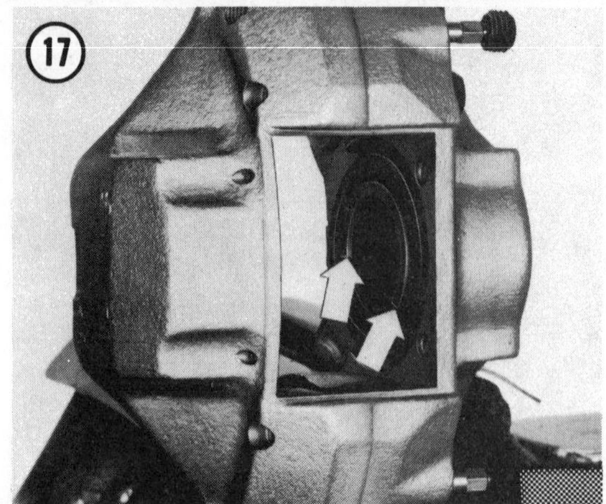

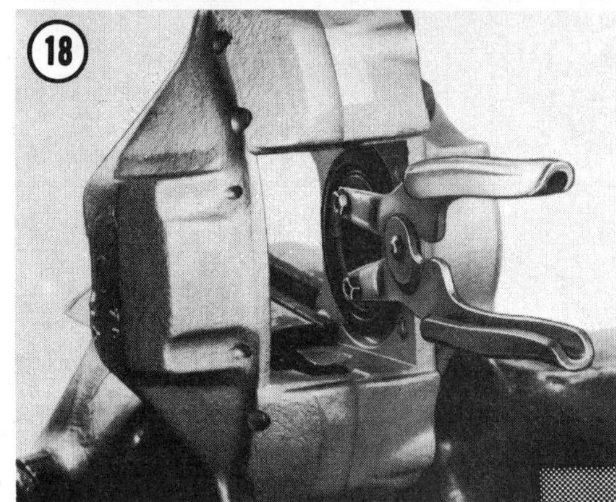

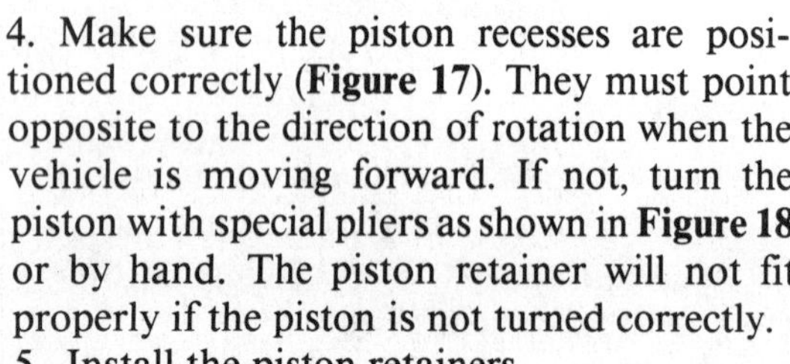

4. Make sure the piston recesses are positioned correctly (**Figure 17**). They must point opposite to the direction of rotation when the vehicle is moving forward. If not, turn the piston with special pliers as shown in **Figure 18** or by hand. The piston retainer will not fit properly if the piston is not turned correctly.
5. Install the piston retainers.

FRONT BRAKE ROTOR

Removal/Installation

Refer to **Figure 19** for the following procedure.

1. Loosen the front wheel lug nuts.
2. Raise the front of the vehicle and position it on jackstands.
3. Pry off the front grease cap with a tire iron, using the wheel nuts as a fulcrum, or use a special pry bar as shown in **Figure 20**.
4. Remove the front wheels.
5. Remove the calipers as described in this chapter. Leave the brake line attached; hang the caliper up with a piece of wire (**Figure 21**).
6. Insert a small chisel in the axle groove and pry up the peening nut collar.
7. Remove peening nut and thrust washer.
8. Pull the rotor off the axle.
9. Installation is the reverse of removal. Install new grease seals prior to installing rotors. After installation adjust the wheel bearings. See *Wheel Bearing Adjustment* in Chapter Ten.

Inspection

1. Check the rotors for scratches. Small marks on the disc are not important, but deep radial scratches (deep enough to snag a fingernail) reduce braking effectiveness and increase pad wear.

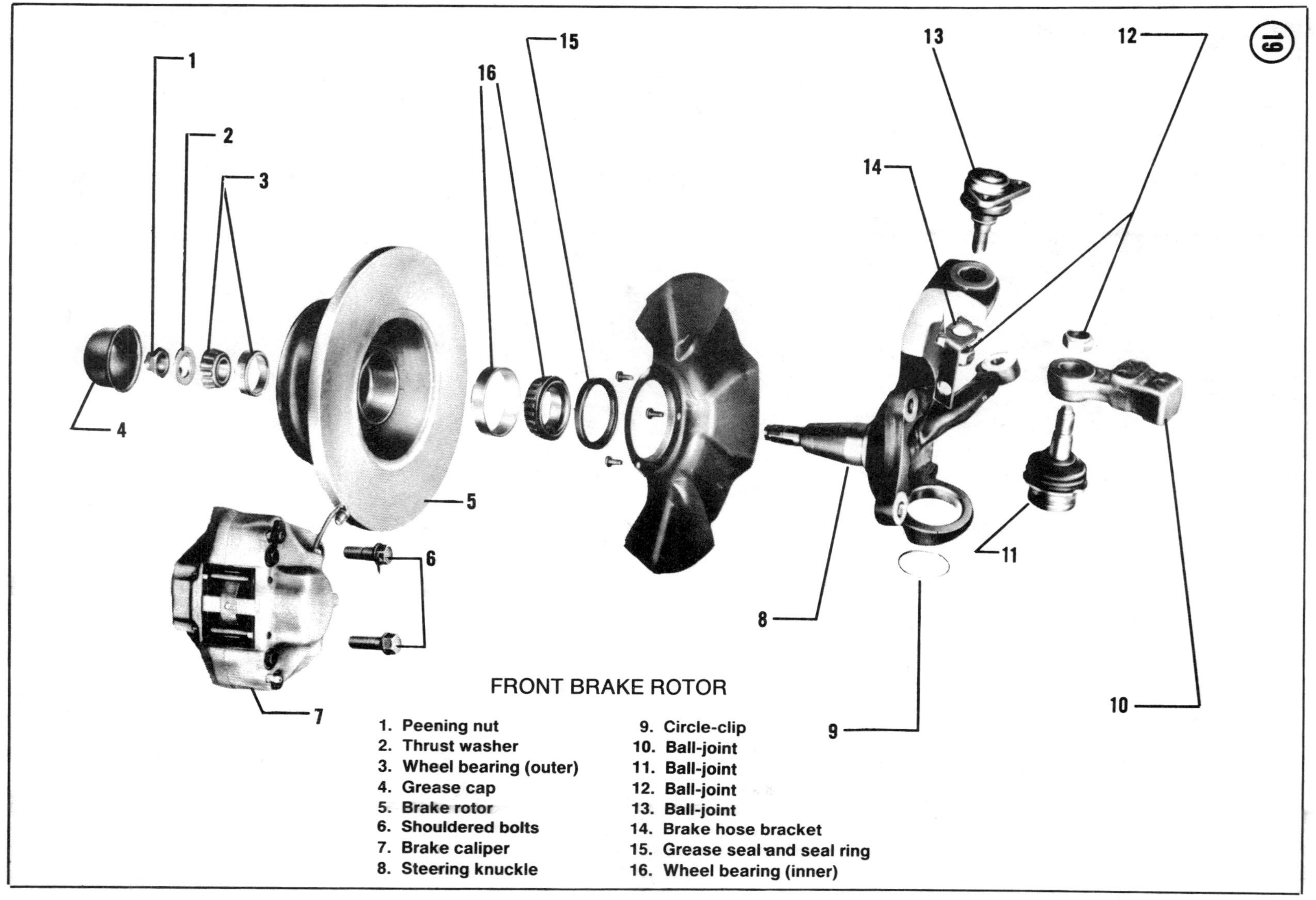

FRONT BRAKE ROTOR

1. Peening nut
2. Thrust washer
3. Wheel bearing (outer)
4. Grease cap
5. Brake rotor
6. Shouldered bolts
7. Brake caliper
8. Steering knuckle
9. Circle-clip
10. Ball-joint
11. Ball-joint
12. Ball-joint
13. Ball-joint
14. Brake hose bracket
15. Grease seal and seal ring
16. Wheel bearing (inner)

2. Check the rotor runout. Mount a dial indicator as shown in **Figure 22**. Turn the rotor; runout should not exceed 0.004 in. (0.1 mm).

NOTE
*The runout procedure assumes that the wheel bearings are adjusted properly. If in doubt, check them; see **Wheel Bearing Adjustment** in Chapter Ten.*

3. Check the thickness of the rotor with a micrometer. Take at least 12 measurements around the rotor about 1 in. from the outer edge. The thickness for new rotors is 0.512 in. (13 mm) with a service limit of 0.433 in. (11 mm). Measurements should not vary more than 0.0008 in. (0.02 mm). If the rotor is below or very close to the wear limit, it must be replaced.
4. If the rotor has excessively deep scratches, excessive runout, variation in thickness or is too thin, it must be replaced or machined. If machining the rotor would bring it below the minimum thickness of 0.453 in. (11.5 mm), it must be replaced.

NOTE
*If the rotor is machined, the wheel bearings must be removed and cleaned. See **Wheel Bearings/Disc Rotor Removal/Installation** in Chapter Ten.*

REAR BRAKE LINING REPLACEMENT

Brake linings must be replaced whenever they are found to be soaked with oil, grease or brake fluid. In addition, replace linings worn to less than 1/16 in. (0.5 cm); see Chapter Three for inspection procedures.

If brake drums have been turned, use oversize linings (see **Table 1** for brake specifications). Always replace linings on both rear wheels to ensure uniform braking.

Refer to **Figure 23** for the following procedure.

1. Remove the brake drum as described in this chapter.
2. Block the front wheels and release the parking brake.
3. Note where the return springs hook up. Grasp them with pliers and remove them.
4. Remove the adjuster spring.

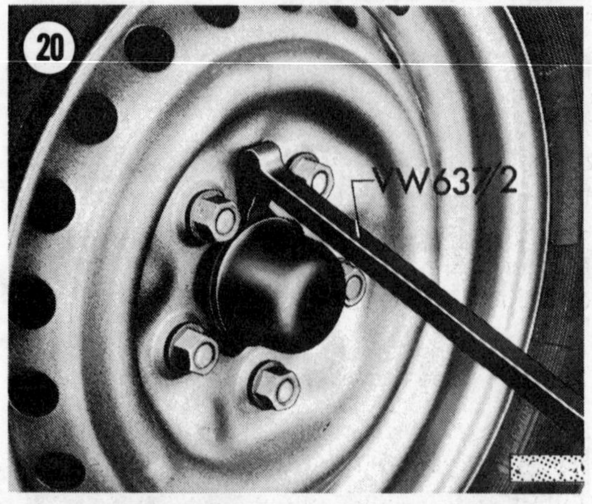

5. Remove the adjusting rod.
6. Unhook the parking brake cable from the rear shoe lever.
7. Remove the shoe retaining springs.
8. Remove the retainer and take the parking brake cable lever off the shoe (**Figure 24**).
9. Installation is the reverse of removal. Before installing brake drums, adjust brakes as described in this chapter.

REAR BRAKE DRUMS

The rear brake drums are split; the outer drum may be removed without removing the inner hub. For brake lining service it is best to remove both drum and hub as a unit for better component access. The drum and hub may be separated once they are removed from the axle.

Removal/Installation

Refer to **Figure 23** for the following procedure. To remove both drum and inner hub perform the following:

1. Put the transmission in gear and apply the parking brake.
2. Remove the cotter pin from the large nut on the axle.
3. Use a 1 in. drive socket and breaker bar to loosen the large axle nut. This size tool is recommended because smaller tools may fail under the extreme loads (the nut is torqued to 253 ft.-lb./350 N•m).
4. Loosen the rear wheel lug nuts.
5. Raise the rear of the vehicle and position it on jackstands.
6. Remove the rear wheel.
7. Remove the hub nut.
8. Release the parking brake.
9. Pull the drum and hub off the axle. They may slip easily off the axle or a puller like the one shown in **Figure 25** may have to be used.
10. See *Cleaning and Inspection.*
11. Installation is the reverse of removal. Do not apply final torque to the axle nut until the wheels are installed and the vehicle is off of the jackstands. Then torque the nut to 253 ft.-lb. (350 N•m).

To remove the brake drum *only* perform the following:

1. Loosen the rear wheel lug nuts.
2. Raise the rear of the vehicle and position it on jackstands. Release the parking brake.
3. Remove the rear wheel.
4. Pull the drum off the inner hub. You may have to tap on the rear edges of the drum with a hammer.
5. See *Cleaning and Inspection.*
6. Installation is the reverse of removal.

Cleaning and Inspection

See **Table 1** for brake specifications.

1. Clean all brake dust and dirt from the brake drum.

WARNING
Do not inhale brake lining particles; they are made with asbestos. Asbestos inhaled in even small quantities may cause lung damage. Wear a paper mask (available at drug stores) when working with brake linings. Wash your hands thoroughly after handling brake linings.

2. Remove grease and oil with cleaning solvent.
3. Measure the drums for out-of-roundness. See specifications in **Table 1**. If you do not have the equipment to do this, have the drums checked by a dealer or qualified specialist.
4. Inspect drums for scoring, cracking or heat discoloration (blue or straw color). If the drums are damaged, or you are in doubt, take them to a brake shop for inspection and machining. If the brake drums are machined, the old lining must be replaced with new oversize linings. The drums may only be machined oversized so much and then they must be replaced.

REAR WHEEL CYLINDER

Removal/Installation

Refer to **Figure 23** for the following procedure.

1. Remove the brake drum and linings as described in this chapter.
2. Remove the hydraulic line from the back of the cylinder and plug the line.
3. Remove the wheel cylinder bolt and pull the cylinder off the backing plate.

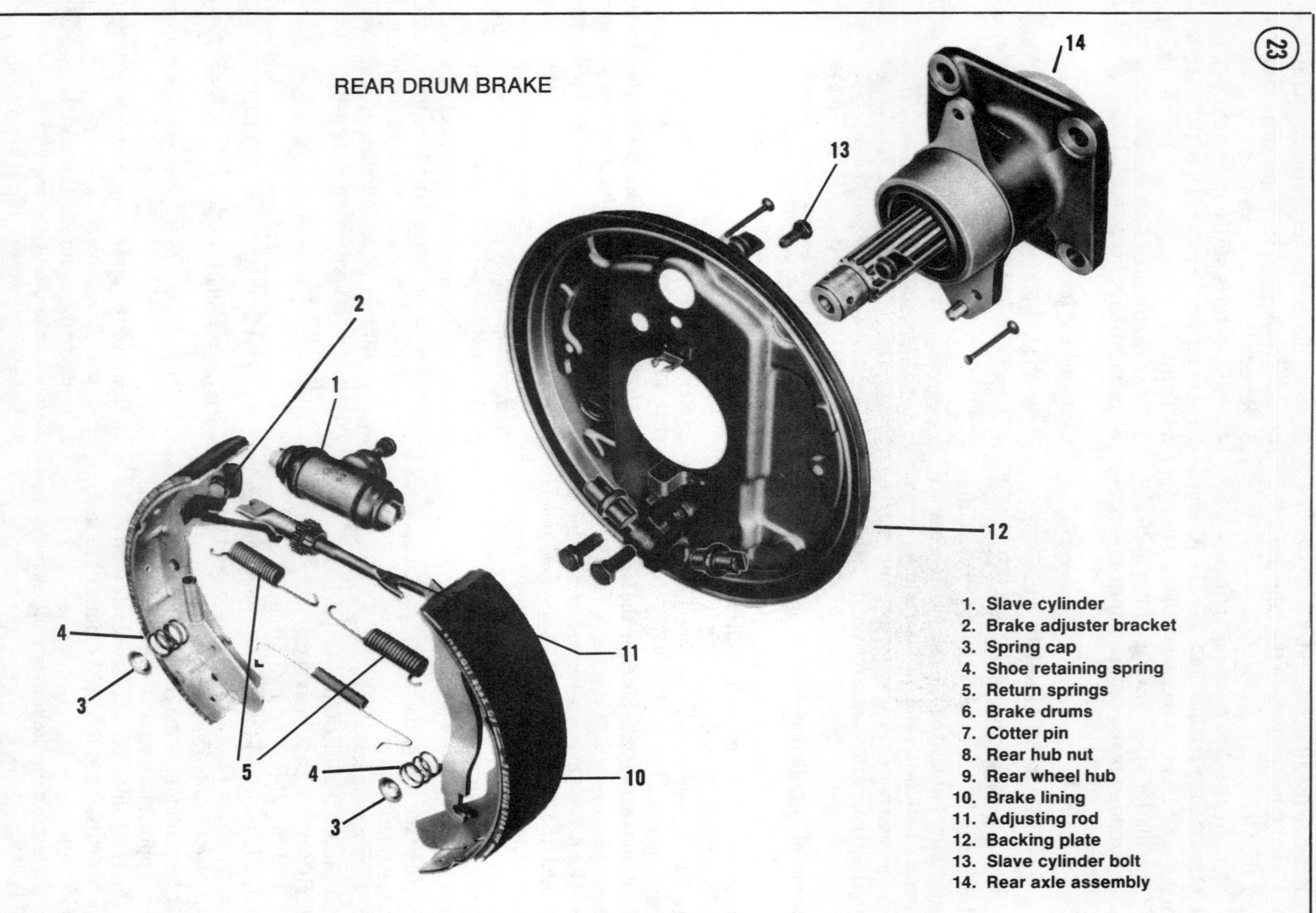
23
REAR DRUM BRAKE
1. Slave cylinder
2. Brake adjuster bracket
3. Spring cap
4. Shoe retaining spring
5. Return springs
6. Brake drums
7. Cotter pin
8. Rear hub nut
9. Rear wheel hub
10. Brake lining
11. Adjusting rod
12. Backing plate
13. Slave cylinder bolt
14. Rear axle assembly

9
6
7
8

4. Installation is the reverse of removal. When cylinder is installed, bleed the system and adjust the rear brakes as described in this chapter.

Disassembly

Refer to **Figure 26** for the following procedure.

1. Clamp the cylinder in a soft-jaw vise.
2. Pull the rubber dust boots off.
3. Pull the pistons out of the cylinder. Note how the pistons and the spring are installed.
4. Remove the bleeder valve.
5. See *Cleaning and Inspection* in this chapter.

Cleaning and Inspection

1. Carefully cut the rubber cups off the brake pistons with a single-edge razor blade.
2. Clean all brake parts in clean denatured alcohol or brake fluid.
3. Examine the pistons and the inside of the cylinders for rust, pitting or cracks. Pits will appear as small discolored cavities. If severe pitting is found, replace the entire unit. If very minor pitting or rust spots are present, try to remove them with brake fluid and a rag or with crocus cloth. If the damage cannot be removed, replace the parts.
4. If the cylinder and piston are free of defects, reassemble as described in this chapter.

WARNING

Cylinders with pitting must not be rebuilt. Hydraulic fluid leaks through the pits around the sealing cups or rings. This will degrade braking power and you may wind up in an accident.

Assembly

Refer to **Figure 26** for the following procedure. Soak all new rubber parts in clean brake fluid for 15 minutes prior to assembly to make them pliable.

1. Install the cups onto the pistons with the sealing edges pointing to the center of the cylinder.
2. Clamp the cylinder in a soft-jaw vise with the bore vertical.
3. Lubricate one of the cups on the piston with clean brake fluid. Push the piston into the cylinder and work the lips of the cup into the bore with a blunt instrument.
4. Put the spring in the center of the installed piston.
5. Install the other piston as described in Step 3.
6. Install the dust boots and the bleeder valve.

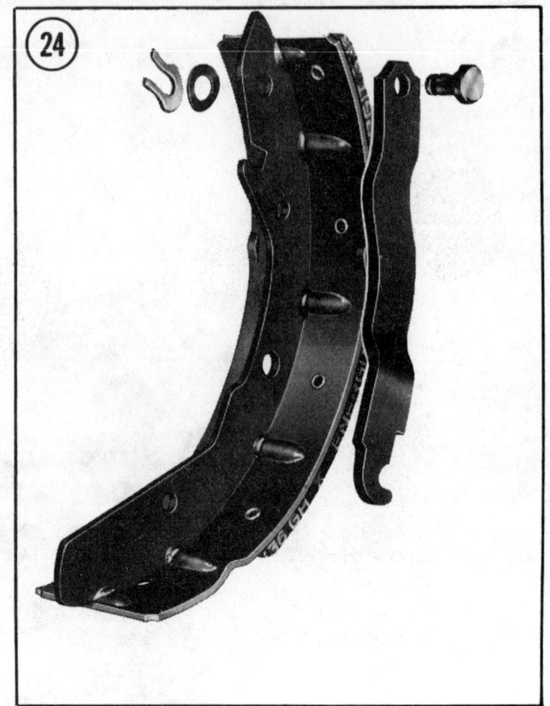

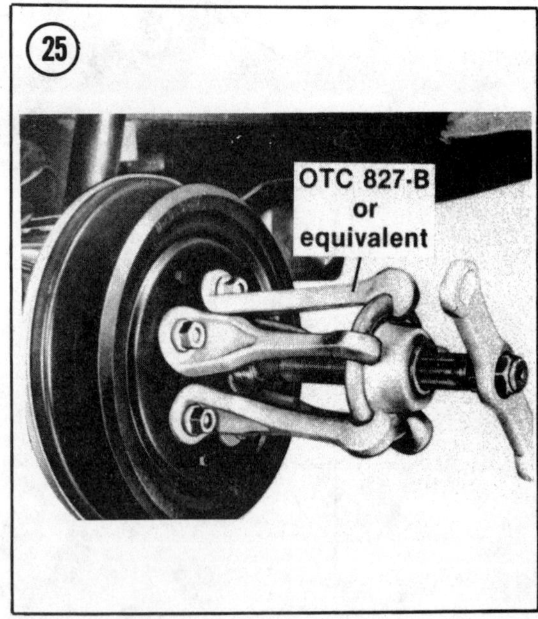

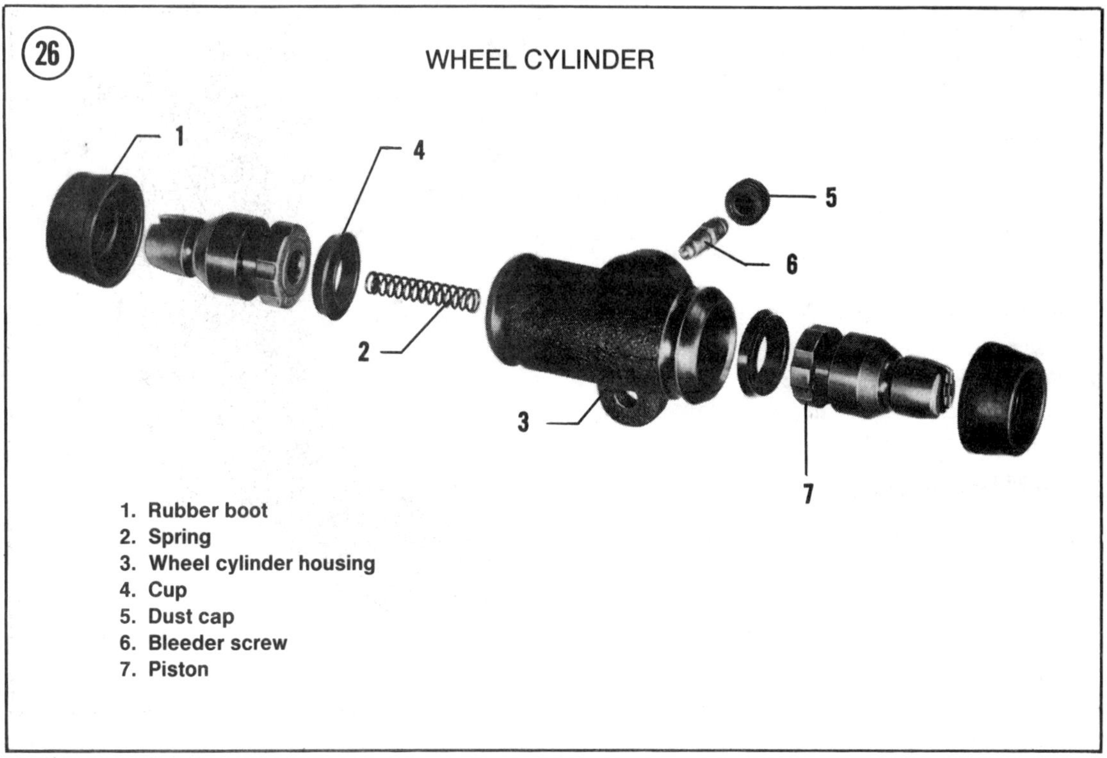

BRAKE ADJUSTMENT

Rear Drum Brakes

The following procedure applies only to rear drum brakes. Front discs do not require any adjustment.

Use the *Caliper Method* to adjust rear brakes after the linings have been replaced, before the hub and drum are installed. Use the *Hand Method* for periodic adjustment when linings have not been replaced.

Caliper method

1. Block the front wheels and release the parking brake.
2. Loosen the parking brake adjusting nut until the brake cables are very slack (**Figure 27**).
3. Measure and note the inner diameter of the brake drum.
4. Center the linings on the rear axle assembly; measure and note dimension A as shown in **Figure 28**.
5. Turn the adjuster until a clearance of 0.059 in. (1.5 mm) is obtained between the linings and the drum.
6. Install the brake drum.
7. Adjust the parking brake as described in this chapter.

Hand method

1. Install the brake drum.
2. Install the wheel. Keep the vehicle up on jackstands with the wheel off the ground.
3. Loosen the parking brake adjusting nut until the brake cables are very slack (**Figure 27**).

9

4. Insert a brake adjuster tool in the adjuster hole as shown in **Figure 29**. Turn the adjuster until the wheel is locked up tight. Turn the adjuster in the opposite direction until the wheel is just able to turn without the brakes rubbing.
5. Adjust the parking brake as described in this chapter.

Parking Brake Adjustment

The rear drum brakes must be adjusted before the parking brake can be adjusted. Refer to **Figure 30** for the following procedure.
1. Block the front wheels.
2. Raise the rear of the vehicle and position it on jackstands.
3. Release the parking brake.
4. Turn the adjusting nut (**Figure 27**) until there is a slight drag when the rear wheels are turned. Loosen the nut until the drag disappears.
5. Pull up the parking brake lever 2 notches. Turn each wheel by hand, make sure there is the same amount of drag at each rear wheel.
6. Pull the parking brake lever up an additional 2 notches; the rear wheels should be locked.

BRAKE PRESSURE REGULATOR

A brake pressure regulator in the rear brake circuit ensures optimum braking. The pressure regulator slowly allows more pressure to build up in the front hydraulic circuit than in the rear. This prevents premature rear wheel lock-up. The regulator should only be serviced by a brake shop or VW dealer.

Removal/Installation

1. Disconnect the hydraulic lines from the regulator. Plug the lines (**Figure 31**).
2. Unbolt the regulator from the underbody.
3. Installation is the reverse of removal. After installation, the brake system must be bled.

BRAKE BLEEDING

The brake system requires bleeding whenever air enters the system. Air can enter the system when the master cylinder, the wheel cylinders or the calipers are removed and

28

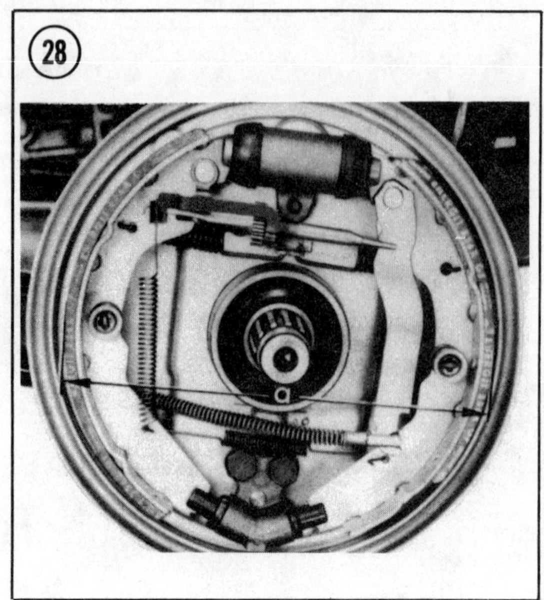

29

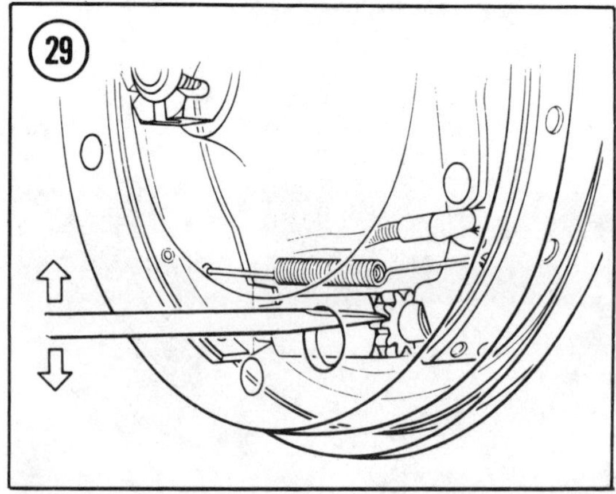

seviced or when the hydraulic fluid reservoir runs dry. Air can also enter through a damaged line or a severely worn master or wheel cylinder or front caliper. Find and replace the defective components before bleeding the system.
1. Remove the instrument panel cover (**Figure 32**). Remove the cap from the hydraulic fluid reservoir.
2. Pack rags around the reservoir to catch spilled hydraulic fluid.
3. Check the fluid level and top off if necessary. Use a funnel when adding fluid to prevent accidental spillage.
4. Remove the rubber caps from all bleeder valves.

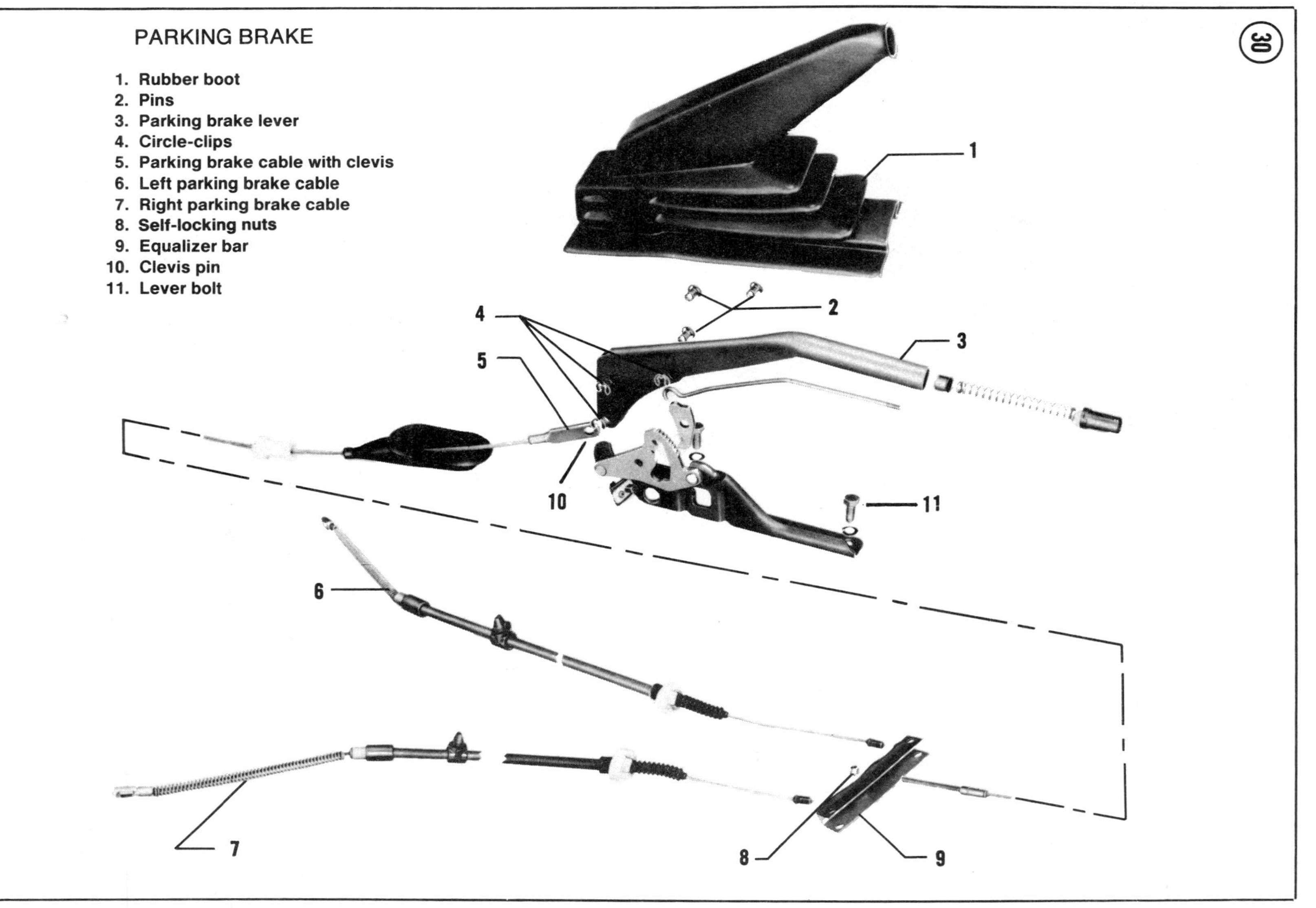
30
PARKING BRAKE
1. Rubber boot
2. Pins
3. Parking brake lever
4. Circle-clips
5. Parking brake cable with clevis
6. Left parking brake cable
7. Right parking brake cable
8. Self-locking nuts
9. Equalizer bar
10. Clevis pin
11. Lever bolt
1
2
3
4
5
10
11
6
7
8
9

5. Connect a length of rubber tubing to the bleeder valve on the right rear wheel. Suspend the other end of the tube in a container filled with a few inches of clean brake fluid (**Figure 33**). During the following steps keep the end of the tube submerged in the container. Never let the level in the master cylinder fluid reservoir drop below 1/2 full.

6. Have an assistant depress and hold the brake pedal. Open the bleeder valve with a wrench about 1/2 turn. As soon as the pedal is all the way down, close the bleeder valve. Repeat this step as many times as necessary, until the fluid leaving the tube has no air bubbles.

NOTE
If the hydraulic fluid reservoir is allowed to run dry, both the clutch and the brake systems must be bled.

7. Bleed the remaining valves as described in Step 6. Follow the sequence shown in **Figure 34**. Keep checking the fluid reservoir to be sure it doesn't run out of fluid. Each front caliper has 2 bleeder valves; they must be bled at the same time with 2 hoses.

8. When the system is bled, discard the used hydraulic fluid; never reuse this fluid. Top up the reservoir with clean brake fluid.

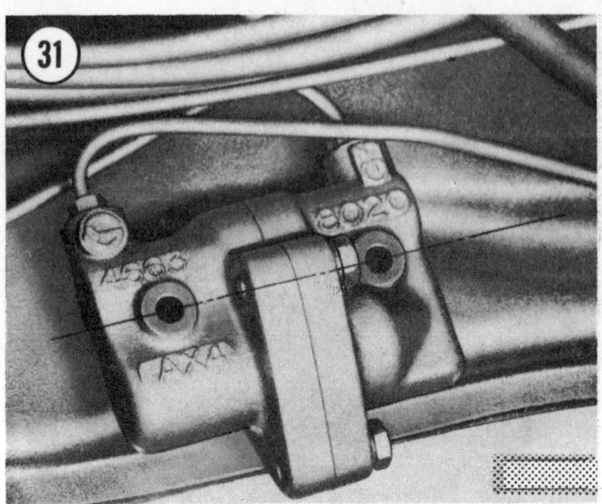

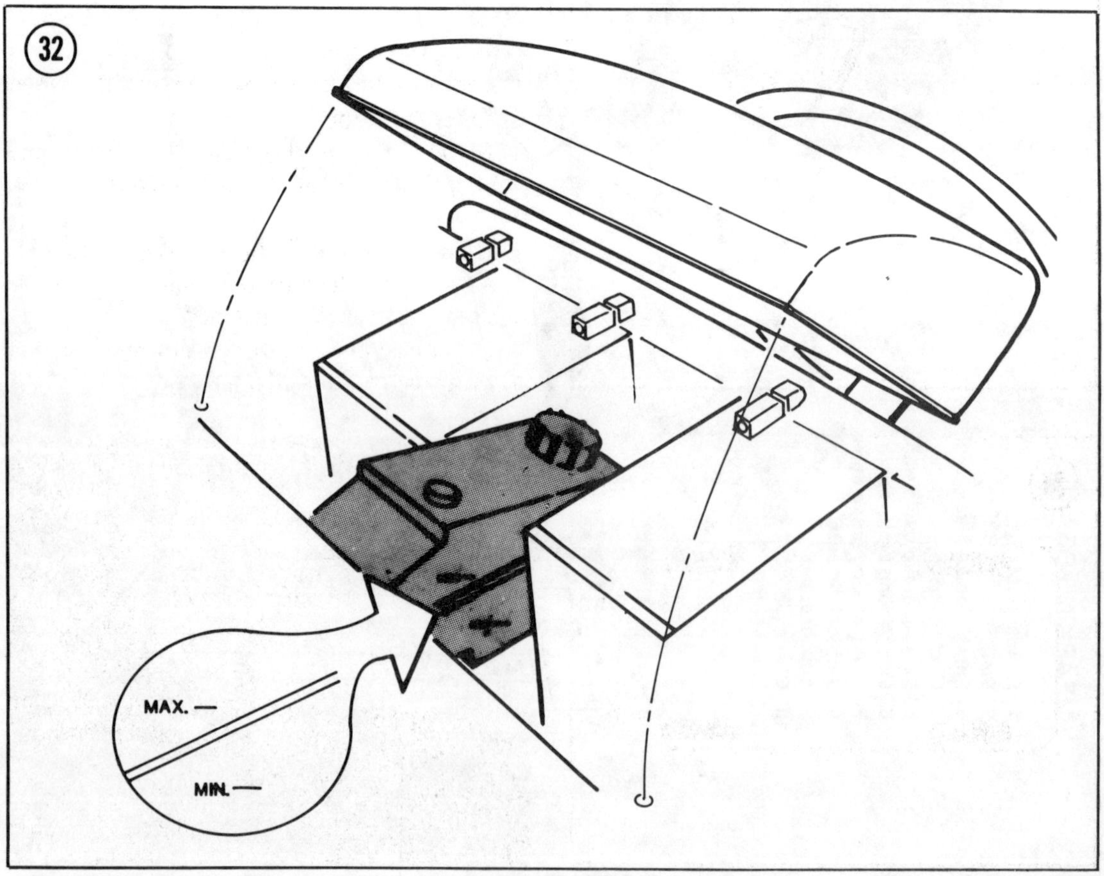

31

32

MAX.

MIN.

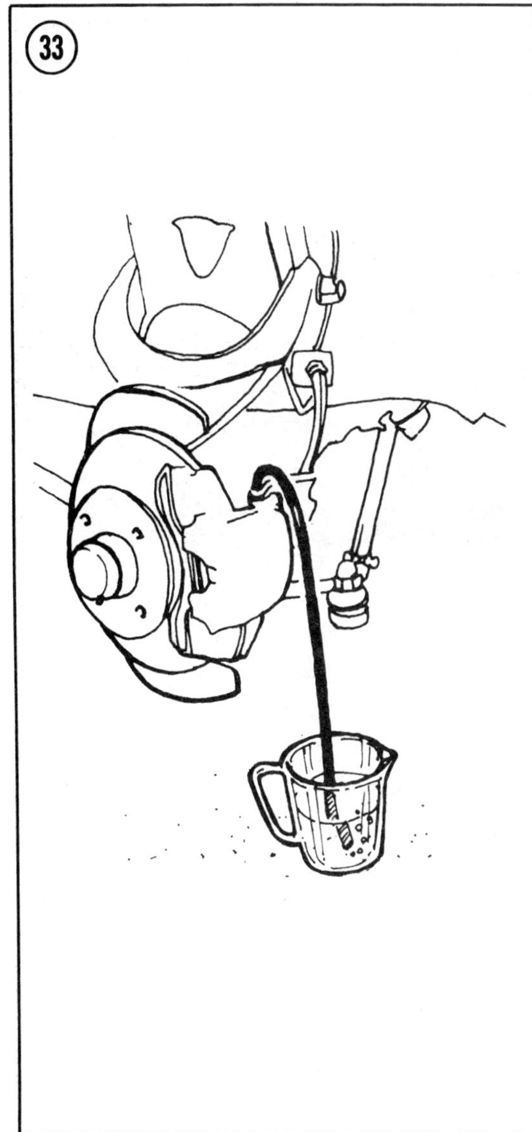

BRAKE LINES AND HOSES

Brake lines and hoses are made of special materials and to exact lengths. When replacement is necessary, obtain the new part from a VW dealer or specialist to ensure suitable strength and exact fit.

To replace a brake line:

1. Disconnnect the union nuts at both ends.
2. Unclip the line from the chassis and pull it out.
3. Install the new line in the chassis clips.
4. Moisten the ends of the line with brake fluid, then tighten the union nuts.
5. After installing new lines, the system must be bled as described in this chapter.

To replace a brake hose:

1. Remove the appropriate wheel.
2. Loosen the union nut and remove the hose clip from the bracket. **Figure 35** shows a typical hose arrangement.
3. Pull the hose from the bracket.
4. Disconnect the hose from the wheel cylinder or caliper.
5. Connect the new brake hose to the wheel cylinder or caliper.
6. Install the new hose in the bracket and tighten the union nut. Do not allow the hose to twist.
7. If a new front brake hose was installed, turn the wheel from lock to lock and check that the hose is not twisted or strained.
8. After installation, the system must be bled as described in this chapter.

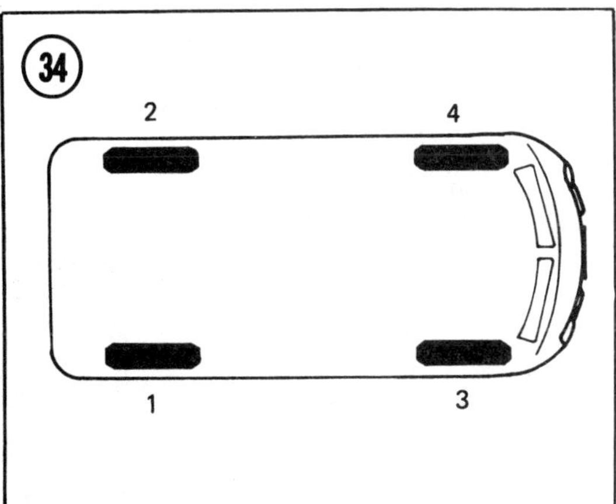

9

PARKING (HAND) BRAKE

Lever Removal/Installation

Refer to **Figure 30** for the following procedure.

1. Put the transmission in gear and block the rear wheels.
2. Pull the rubber boot off the parking brake lever.
3. Remove the lever bolts.
4. Detach the clevis pin from the cable clevis.
5. Installation is the reverse of removal. After installation adjust the parking brake as described in this chapter.

Cable Replacement

Refer to **Figure 30** for the following procedure.

1. Raise the rear of the vehicle and position it on jackstands.
2. Remove the rear brake drums as described in this chapter.
3. Unhook the cable from brake lever.
4. Unbolt the cable bracket from the rear of the backing plate and pull the cable out of the backing plate.
5. Pull the cable from the bottom of the vehicle.
6. Unhook the cable end from the equalizer bar.
7. Reverse these steps to install the new cable. Adjust the parking brake as described in this chapter.

Table 1 BRAKE SPECIFICATIONS

Brake disc	
Standard thickness	0.512 in. (13 mm)
Minimum thickness (wear limit)	0.433 in. (11 mm)
Minimum thickness (after machining)	0.453 in. (11.5 mm)
Maximum runout	0.004 in. (0.1 mm)
Brake drum	
Standard diameter	9.921 in. (252 mm)
Maximum diameter (wear limit)	9.980 in. (253.5 mm)
Maximum diameter (after machining)	9.960 in. (253 mm)

CHAPTER TEN

SUSPENSION AND STEERING

This chapter includes service, repair and adjustment procedures for the front suspension, steering, rear suspension and rear axles. Any time the suspension is disassembled and assembled the front or rear end should be aligned.

Wheel alignment is not possible for the home mechanic. Suspension repairs may be made within the confines of the home garage, after which the vehicle can be brought to a front-end shop for alignment.

Table 1 at the end of the chapter presents torque specifications.

WARNING
Never straighten or reuse bent suspension parts. A straightened or bent part is structurally weaker than an undamaged part and could fail, causing a serious accident.

WHEEL ALIGNMENT

Several angles affect the running and steering of the front wheels and rear wheels. These angles must be properly aligned to maintain directional stability, ease of steering and proper tire wear.

The angles involved are:

a. Caster
b. Camber
c. Toe-in
d. Steering axis
e. Toe-out on turns

Alignment is not possible for the home mechanic, as it requires the use of a front-end rack. This section is provided to instruct you in the theory and terminology of the suspension system.

Pre-alignment Check

Several factors influence the suspension angles or steering. Before the vehicle is brought in for alignment, perform the following checks; they may save you money.

1. Check tire pressure and wear.
2. Check the play in the front wheel bearings. Adjust if necessary.
3. Check play in ball-joints.
4. Check for cracks or breaks in the springs, control arms and rear trailing arms.
5. Remove any excessive load.
6. Check the condition of the shock absorbers.
7. Check steering gear.
8. Check play in ball-joints and tie rod parts.

A proper inspection of tire wear can point to several alignment problems. See *Tire Wear Analysis* in Chapter Two.

Caster

Caster is the inclination of the axis through the ball-joints from the vertical (**Figure 1**). Caster causes the wheels to return to a straight-ahead position after a turn. It also prevents the car from wandering due to wind, potholes or uneven road surfaces. Caster is set by lengthening or shortening the strut bar.

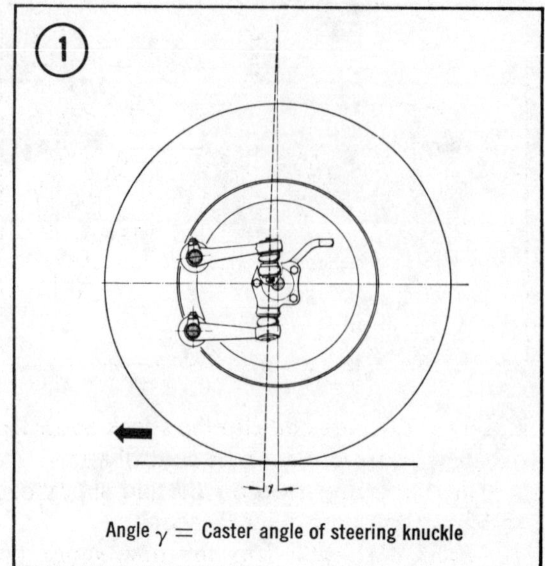

Angle γ = Caster angle of steering knuckle

Camber

Camber is the inclination of the wheel from vertical as shown in **Figure 2**. Positive camber occurs when the top of the tire is farther outward than the bottom.

Camber is adjusted by loosening the upper control arm shaft and rotating it until the proper setting is achieved. If the camber setting changes radically for any reason, check for bent suspension parts.

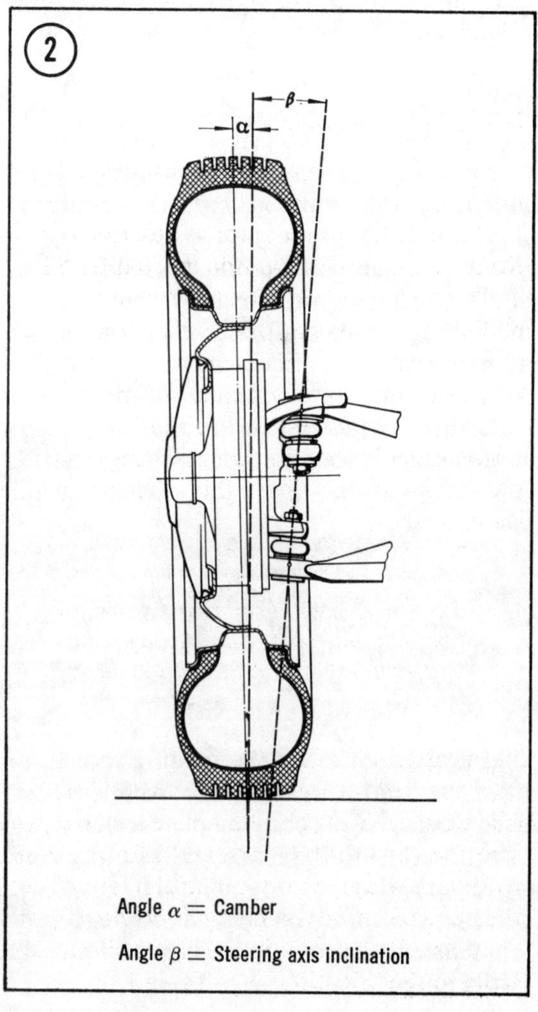

Angle α = Camber

Angle β = Steering axis inclination

Toe-in

Camber and rolling resistence tend to force the front wheels outward at their forward edge. To compensate for this tendency, the front edges are turned slightly inward when the car is at rest—this is toe-in (**Figure 3**).

Toe-out on Turns

The inside wheel in a turn is always at a greater angle than the outside wheel. In **Figure 4**, which shows a right turn, n1 is greater than n2, therefore, there is slight toe-out as a result of the turn. Toe-out is not adjustable.

FRONT SUSPENSION

Shock Absorber Replacement

Refer to **Figure 5** for the following procedure.

1. Set the parking brake.
2. Loosen the front wheel nuts.
3. Raise the front of the vehicle and position it on jackstands.
4. Remove the front wheel.
5. Place a small jack under the lower control arm. Raise the jack to compress the coil spring an inch.
6. Remove the upper shock nut.
7. Remove the lower shock bolt.

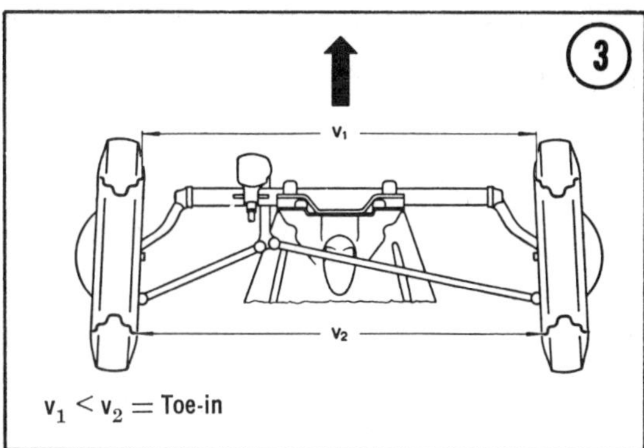

$v_1 < v_2$ = Toe-in

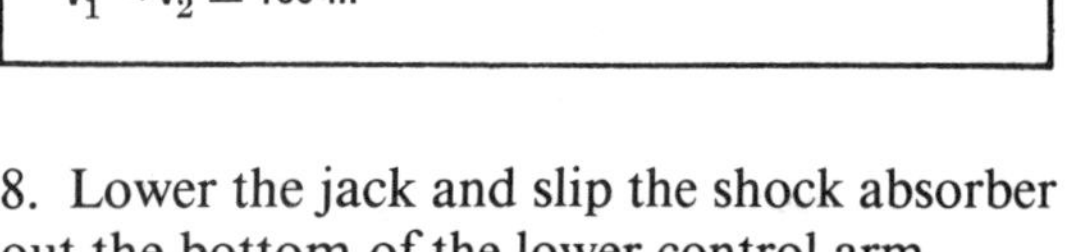

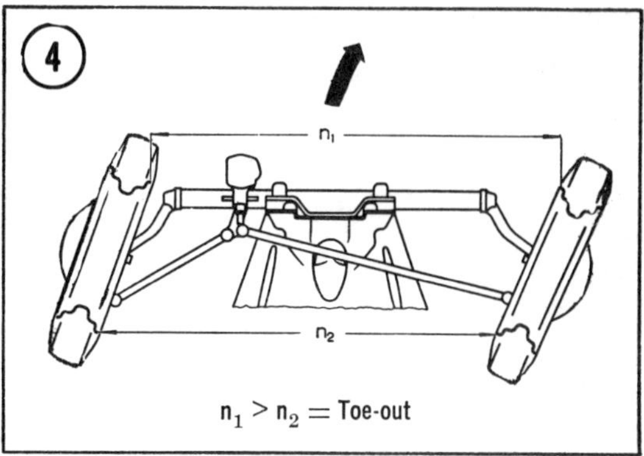

$n_1 > n_2$ = Toe-out

8. Lower the jack and slip the shock absorber out the bottom of the lower control arm.
9. Slip the bump stop off the old shock absorber; install it on the new shock.
10. Raise the jack; slip the new shock up through the lower control arm.
11. Install the upper shock nut and the lower shock bolt.

Wheel Bearing Removal/Installation

Refer to **Figure 6** for the following procedure.

1. Remove the brake rotor as described under *Rotor Removal/Installation* in Chapter Nine.
2. Pry the grease seal out of the rotor.
3. Pull the inner and outer roller bearings out of the rotor.
4. Knock the inner and outer bearings out of the rotor with a soft copper drift. For installation, inner and outer bearings must be pressed into rotor. Leave this job to a machine shop.

NOTE
Do not remove inner bearings for inspection only as they are damaged during removal and must always be replaced.

5. Installation is the reverse of removal. Install new grease seals prior to installing rotor. Use a round piece of metal plate which will fit into the rotor hub. Work seal into rotor hub with the plate and hammer until it is flush with the hub. See *Wheel Bearing Adjustment* in this chapter after installation. Torque all nuts and bolts to specifications, see **Table 1**.

NOTE
If the rotor has been turned, the wheel bearings should be removed and cleaned. Also, the old bearing grease must be removed from the rotor hub and new grease must be packed in before and after the bearings are reinserted.

Cleaning and Inspection

1. Clean all parts thoroughly in solvent before inspection.
2. Be sure all the old grease is removed from the rotor hub and bearings (inner and outer).
3. Check the inner and outer hub bearings for signs of wear, galling, scoring, chipping, rust or heat discoloration. Rotate the bearings and check for roughness and excessive noise. Replace any suspect bearings.

Wheel Bearing Adjustment

Refer to **Figure 6** for the following procedure.

1. Set the parking brake.
2. Raise the front of the vehicle and position it on jackstands.
3. If the wheels are not on, install them.
4. Pry off the front grease cap with a tire iron using the wheel nuts as a fulcrum or use a special pry bar like the one shown in **Figure 7**.
5. Insert a small chisel in the axle groove and pry up the peening nut collar (**Figure 8**).
6. Tighten the peening nut a little and turn the wheel several revolutions.
7. Loosen the peening nut until the thrust washer can be moved with a screwdriver. Do not pry or lever the thrust washer (**Figure 9**).

5

SHOCK ABSORBER

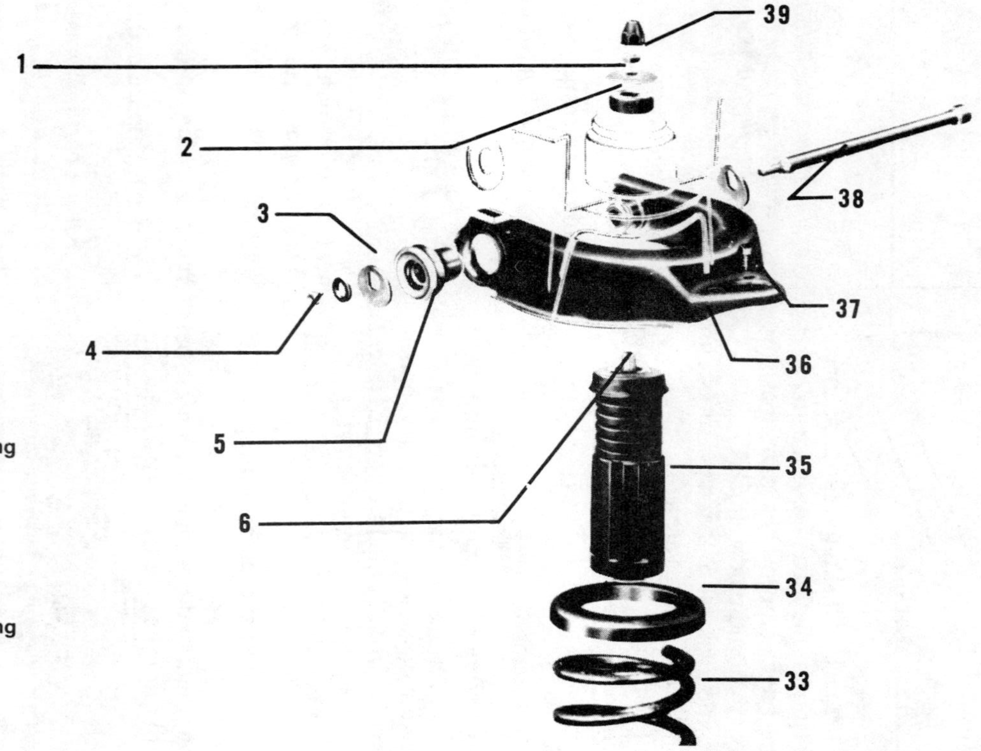

1. Washer
2. Bushing
3. Eccentric washer
4. Control arm shaft nut
5. Upper control arm bushing
6. Spacer sleeve
7. Stabilizer bar
8. Bushings
9. Stabilizer bar bracket
10. Stabilizer link
11. Lower control arm nut
12. Lower control arm bushing
13. Strut bar nut
14. Washers
15. Spacer sleeve
16. Bushings
17. Strut bar
18. Lower control arm bolt
19. Lower control arm
20. Washer

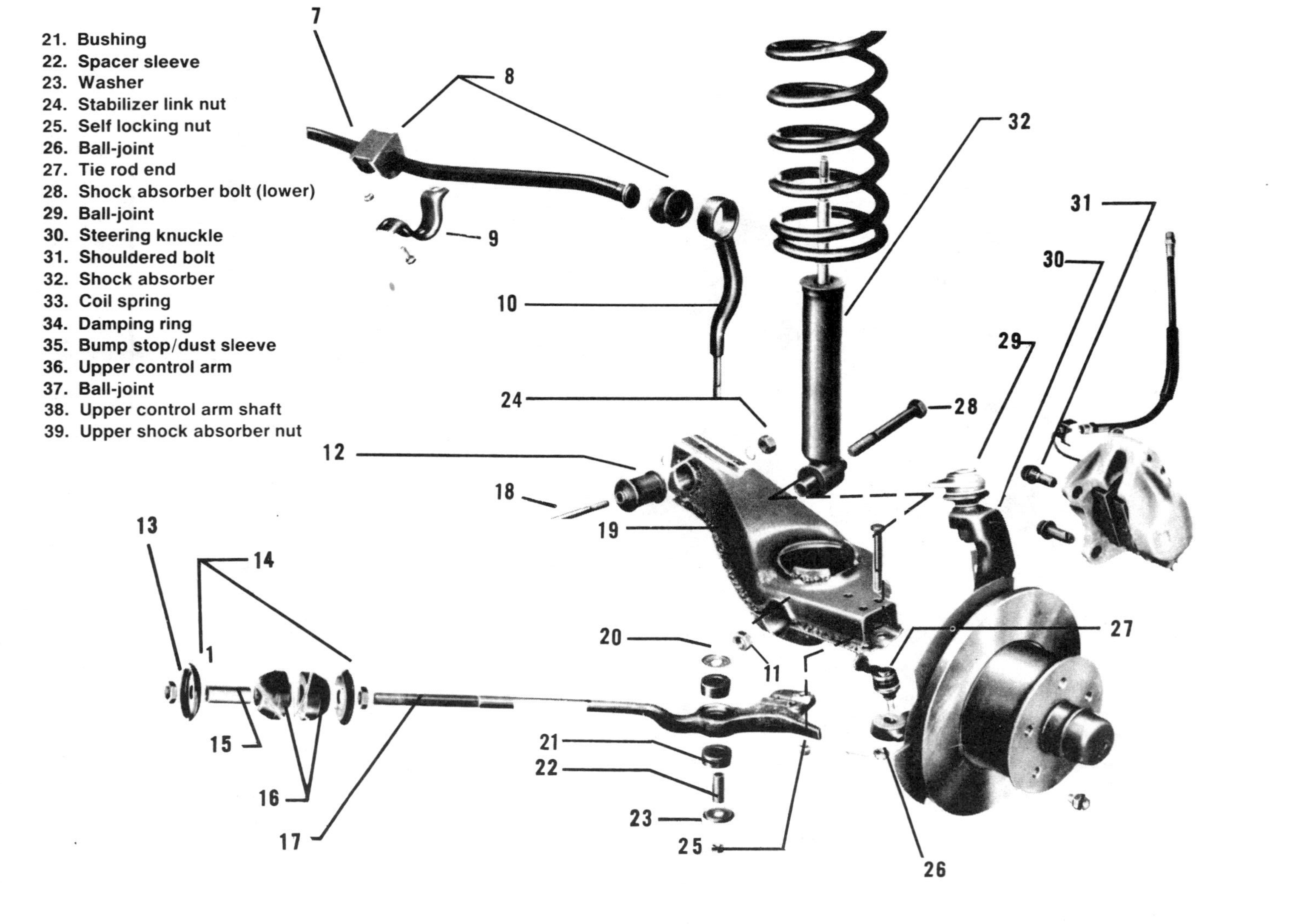
21. Bushing
22. Spacer sleeve
23. Washer
24. Stabilizer link nut
25. Self locking nut
26. Ball-joint
27. Tie rod end
28. Shock absorber bolt (lower)
29. Ball-joint
30. Steering knuckle
31. Shouldered bolt
32. Shock absorber
33. Coil spring
34. Damping ring
35. Bump stop/dust sleeve
36. Upper control arm
37. Ball-joint
38. Upper control arm shaft
39. Upper shock absorber nut
7
8
9
10
24
12
18
19
13
14
1
15
16
17
20
11
21
22
23
25
26
27
28
29
30
31
32

10

STEERING KNUCKLE

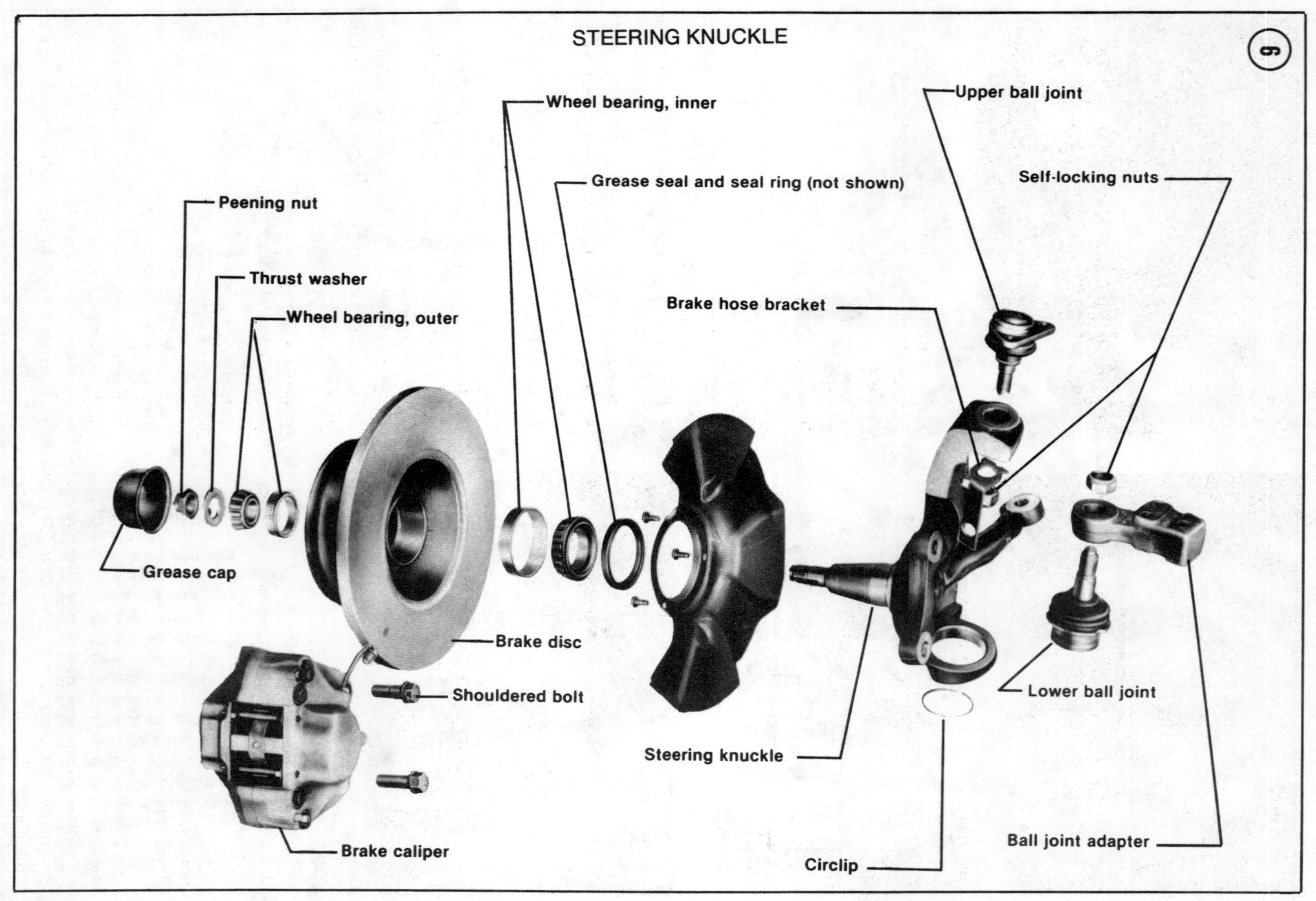

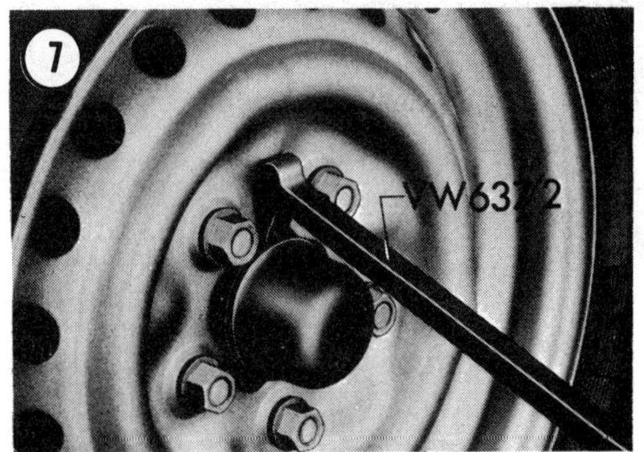

7

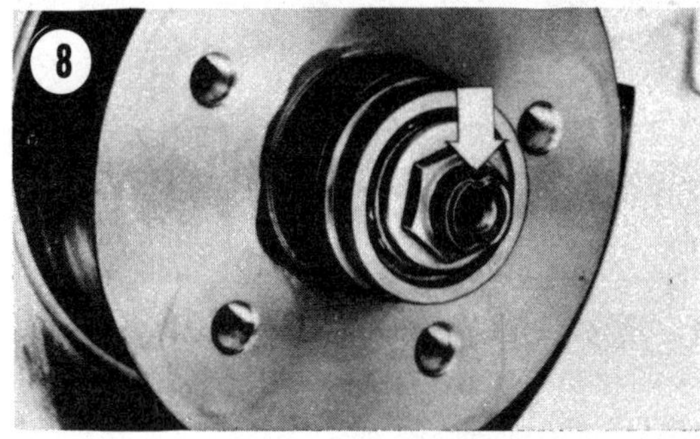

8

9

8. Re-peen the peening nut.
9. Install the grease cap.
10. Install the wheels and lower the vehicle.

Stabilizer Bar Removal/Installation

Refer to **Figure 5** for the following procedure.

1. Unbolt the stabilizer link from the strut bar.
2. Unbolt the stabilizer bar bracket from the underbody. Pull the link out of the strut bar.

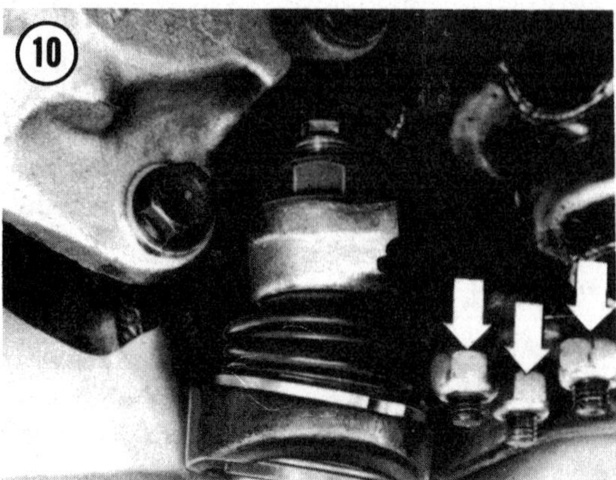

10

3. Installation is the reverse of removal. Torque all nuts and bolts to specifications; see **Table 1**.

Strut Bar Removal/Installation

Refer to **Figure 5** for the following procedure.

1. Set the parking brake.
2. Loosen the front wheel nuts.
3. Raise the front of the vehicle and position it on jackstands.
4. Remove the front wheel.
5. Remove the brake caliper and rotor (Chapter Nine).
6. Detach the stabilizer bar from the strut bar.
7. Remove the 3 nuts which hold the strut bar to the steering knuckle (**Figure 10**).
8. Remove the strut bar nut. Pull the strut bar out of the body. Keep track of the bushings, spacer sleeve and washers.
9. Installation is the reverse of removal. Torque all nuts and bolts to specifications; see **Table 1**.

Steering Knuckle Removal/Installation

Refer to **Figure 5** and **Figure 6** for the following procedure.

1. Set the parking brake.
2. Loosen the front wheel lug nuts.
3. Raise the front of the vehicle and position it on jackstands.
4. Remove the front wheel.
5. Remove the brake caliper and rotor (Chapter Nine).

6. Detach the strut bar from the bottom of the lower control arm; see procedure in this chapter.
7. Place a small jack under the lower control arm. Raise the jack just enough to keep the lower control arm from dropping when the steering knuckle is removed.
8. Press the tie rod end out of the steering knuckle arm using a press like the one shown in **Figure 11**. If a pressing tool is not available, loosen the locknut on the tie rod end. Unscrew the whole ball-joint and tie rod end by turning the steering knuckle.
9. Remove the nuts and bolts which hold the upper ball-joint to the upper control arm.
10. Lower the jack a little; the steering knuckle will drop and the ball-joint will come free of the upper control arm.
11. Installation is the reverse of removal. To install the tie rod, insert the threaded end into the knuckle arm. Pull it all the way in with the nut. Torque all nuts and bolts to specifications; see **Table 1**.

Ball-joint Replacement

Ball-joints are pressed into the steering knuckle; if they are worn, remove the steering knuckle as described in this chapter. Take the steering knuckle to a VW dealer to have the ball-joints replaced.

Control Arms Removal/Installation

Refer to **Figure 5** for the following procedure.
1. Set the parking brake.
2. Loosen the front wheel lug nuts.
3. Raise the front of the vehicle and position it on jackstands.
4. Remove the front wheel.
5. Remove the brake caliper and rotor (Chapter Nine).
6. Detach the strut bar from the lower control arm as described in this chapter.
7. Remove the shock absorber and steering knuckle as described in this chapter.
8. Lower the jack (used during steering knuckle removal) supporting the lower control arm and remove the coil spring. Mark the bottom and top for proper installation.

9. Remove the lower control arm bolt; pull the control arm off the body.
10. Remove the upper control arm shaft; pull the control arm off the body.
11. Installation is the reverse of removal. Torque all nuts and bolts to specifications; see **Table 1**.

STEERING

The steering system is shown in **Figure 12** and **Figure 13**. Steering gear components cannot be repaired or adjusted.

Steering Gear Removal/Installation

Refer to **Figure 13** for the following procedure.
1. Set the parking brake.
2. Turn the steering wheel from lock to lock. Count the number of turns the wheel makes and turn the wheel 1/2 the number of turns from lock; the wheel is now centered. Do not move the wheel.
3. Remove the bolts which retain the coupling disc between the connecting shaft and the 2-arm flange. Slip the coupling disc out.
4. Loosen the collar which connects the 2-arm flange and the input shaft for the steering gear. Slip the 2-arm shaft off the input shaft.
5. Pull the rubber dust boots outboard to reveal the tie rod ends where they connect to the steering gear.

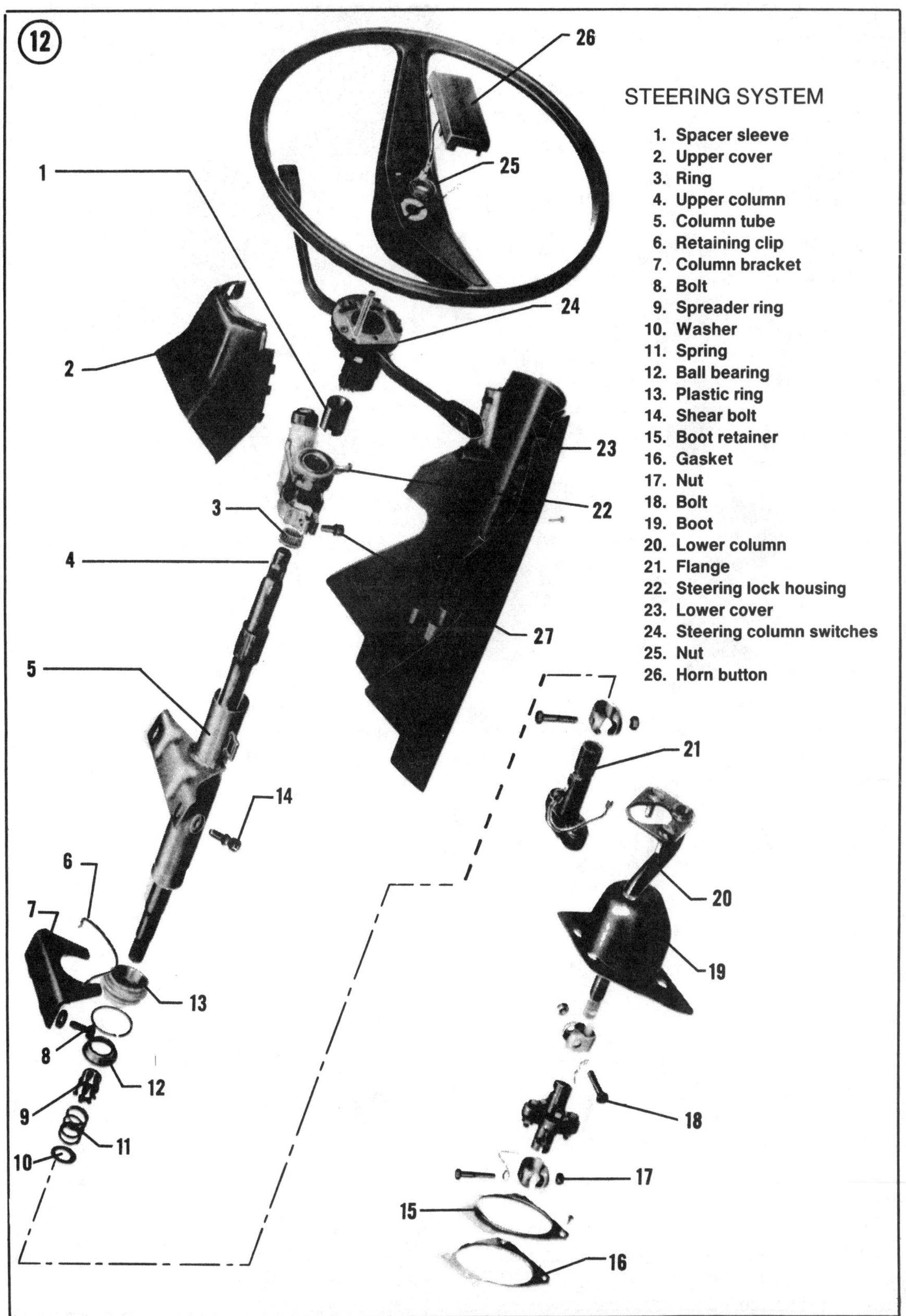

STEERING SYSTEM

1. Spacer sleeve
2. Upper cover
3. Ring
4. Upper column
5. Column tube
6. Retaining clip
7. Column bracket
8. Bolt
9. Spreader ring
10. Washer
11. Spring
12. Ball bearing
13. Plastic ring
14. Shear bolt
15. Boot retainer
16. Gasket
17. Nut
18. Bolt
19. Boot
20. Lower column
21. Flange
22. Steering lock housing
23. Lower cover
24. Steering column switches
25. Nut
26. Horn button

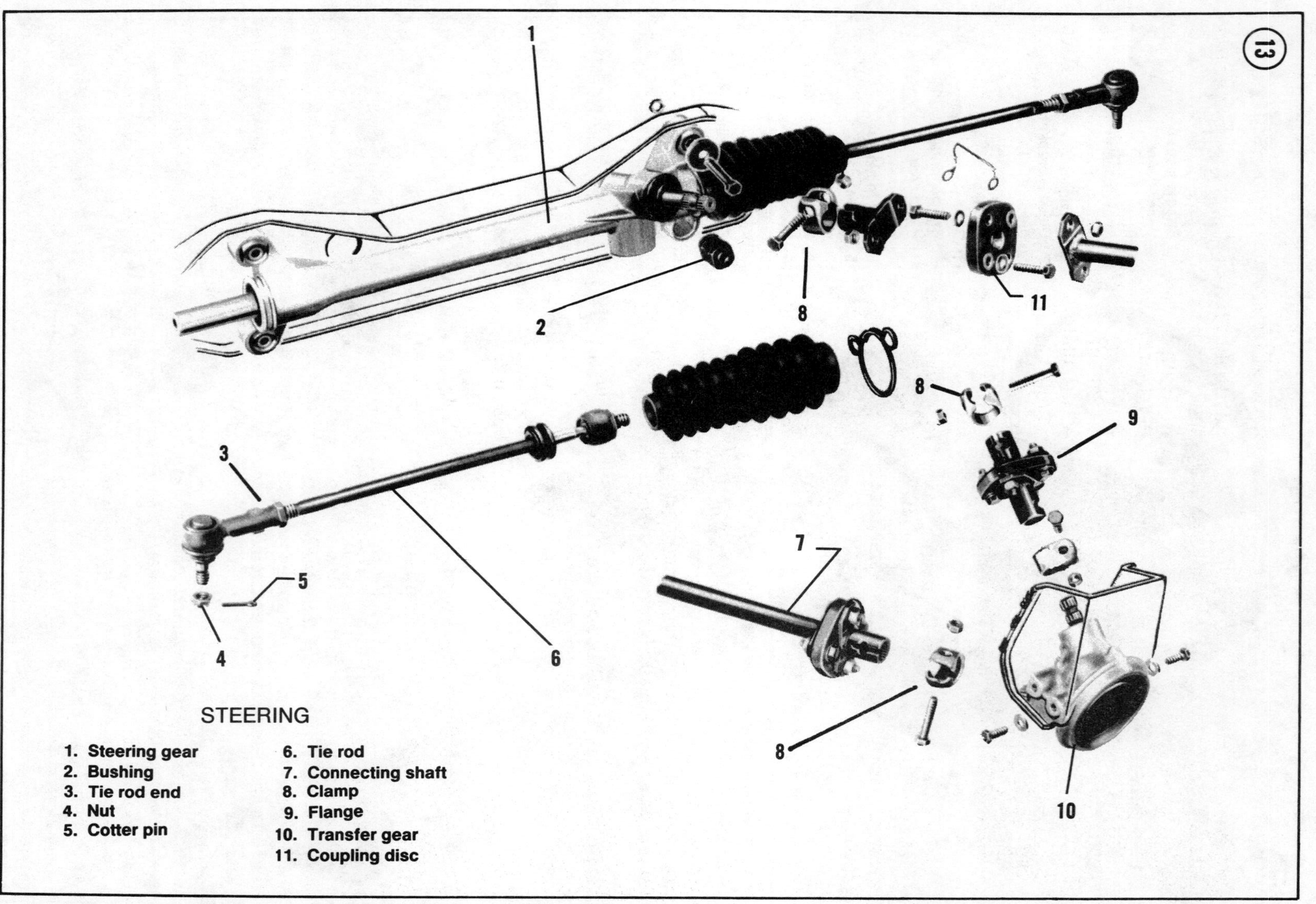
13
1
2
3
4
5
6
7
8
8
8
9
10
11
STEERING
1. Steering gear
2. Bushing
3. Tie rod end
4. Nut
5. Cotter pin
6. Tie rod
7. Connecting shaft
8. Clamp
9. Flange
10. Transfer gear
11. Coupling disc

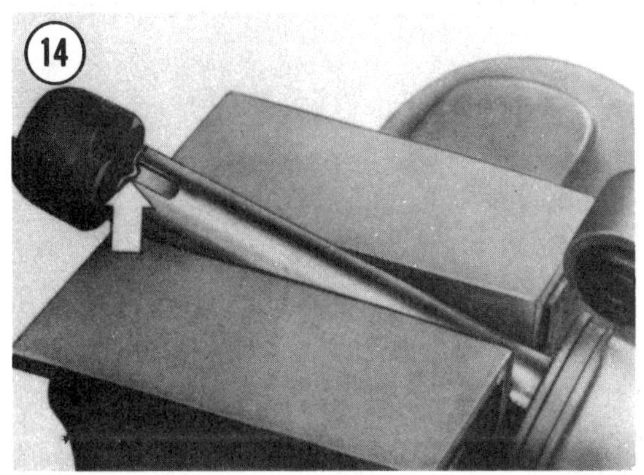

6. Unlock the tie rods from the steering gear by knocking the collar on the rod end out of the locking groove with a hammer and a small drift (**Figure 14**).
7. Use a wrench on the tie rod ends to unscrew them from the steering gear.
8. Remove the bolts which hold the steering gear to the body. Remove the steering gear.
9. Installation is the reverse of removal. Torque all nuts, bolts and components to specifications; see **Table 1**. After installing the steering gear the front wheels must be aligned.

If installing a new steering gear use the procedure in Step 2 to center the gear before installing. Turn the gear input shaft instead of the steering wheel.

Transfer Gear Removal/Installation

Refer to **Figure 13** for the following procedure.
1. Set the parking brake.
2. Turn the steering wheel from lock to lock. Count the number of turns the wheel makes and turn the wheel 1/2 the number of turns from lock; the wheel is now centered. Do not move the wheel.
3. Loosen the collars which connect the steering wheel shaft flange and connecting shaft to the transfer gear. Slip the collars up and off the transfer gear shafts.
4. Remove the bolts which hold the transfer gear to body.
5. Installation is the reverse of removal. Torque all nuts and bolts to specifications; see **Table 1**.

Steering Wheel Removal/Installation

Refer to **Figure 12** for the following procedure.
1. Gently pry out the horn cover. Disconnect the electrical wires.
2. Remove the large steering wheel nut.
3. Pull off the steering wheel.
4. Installation is the reverse of removal. Torque the steering wheel nut to 36 ft.-lb. (49 N•m).

Upper Steering Column Removal/Installation

Refer to **Figure 12** for the following procedure.
1. Remove the steering wheel as described in this chapter. Remove the turn, windshield wiper and ignition switches as described in Chapter Seven.
2. Drill out the head of the shear bolt.
3. Unbolt the column bracket from the body.
4. Loosen the collar which connects the flange to the upper and lower column.
5. Pull upward on the upper column and remove it.
6. Installation is the reverse of removal. When installing the upper column, use a new shear bolt and tighten it until the head breaks off. Torque all nuts and bolts to specifications; see **Table 1**.

10

Lower Column Removal/Installation

The upper column does not have to be removed to remove the lower column. Refer to **Figure 12** for the following procedure.
1. Loosen the collar which connects the flange to the upper and lower column.
2. Unbolt the flange from the lower column.
3. Loosen the collar between the steering wheel shaft flange and the lower column.
4. Unfasten the boot from the floor of the vehicle.
5. Remove the lower column assembly.
6. Installation is the reverse of removal. Torque all nuts and bolts to specifications; see **Table 1**.

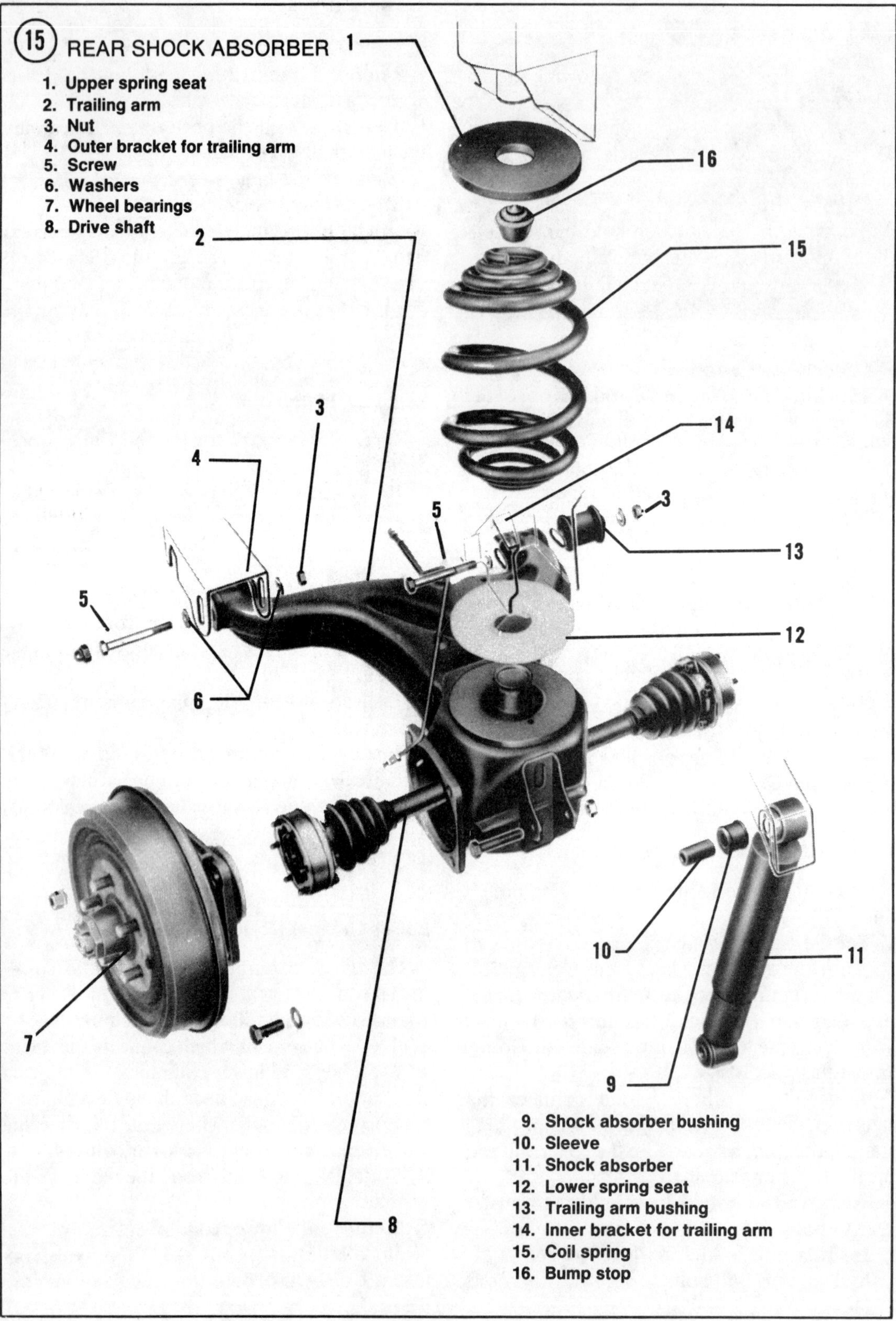
15
REAR SHOCK ABSORBER
1. Upper spring seat
2. Trailing arm
3. Nut
4. Outer bracket for trailing arm
5. Screw
6. Washers
7. Wheel bearings
8. Drive shaft
1
16
2
15
3
14
4
5
3
13
5
12
6
10
11
7
9
9. Shock absorber bushing
10. Sleeve
11. Shock absorber
12. Lower spring seat
13. Trailing arm bushing
14. Inner bracket for trailing arm
15. Coil spring
16. Bump stop
8

REAR SUSPENSION

Shock Absorber Replacement

Refer to **Figure 15** for the following procedure.

1. Loosen the rear wheel lug nuts.
2. Raise the rear of the vehicle; position it on jackstands.
3. Remove the rear wheel.
4. Remove the bolts which hold the shock to the trailing arm and the vehicle body.
5. Reverse these steps to install the new shock.

Rear Axle Assembly Removal/Installation

After removal of the rear axle assembly, disassembly and assembly should be left to a VW dealer or competent specialist. Special tools and skills are required to repair the rear axle.

Refer to **Figure 15** for the following procedure.

1. Loosen the rear wheel lug nuts.
2. Loosen the rear hub nuts. See *Brake Drum Removal/Installation* in Chapter Nine.
3. Raise the rear of the vehicle; position it on jackstands.
4. Remove the rear wheel.
5. Remove the drive axle and CV (constant velocity) joints (Chapter Eight).
6. Pull the brake drum and hub off the axle (Chapter Nine).
7. Unhook the parking brake cable from the lever on the brake shoe. Unbolt the cable bracket from the other side of the backing plate and pull the cable out.
8. Detach the brake hydraulic line from the slave cylinder on the inboard side of the backing plate and plug the line.
9. Remove thc bolts which hold the axle assembly to the trailing arm.
10. Pull the axle assembly out of the trailing arm.
11. Installation is the reverse of removal. Torque all nuts and bolts to specification; see **Table 1**. After installation the brake hydraulic system must be bled; also, the brake shoes and parking brake must be adjusted (Chapter Nine).

Trailing Arm Removal/Installation

Refer to **Figure 15** for the following procedure.

1. Remove the shock absorber and rear axle assembly; see procedures in this chapter.
2. Lower the trailing arm and remove the coil spring. Mark the top and the bottom for proper reinstallation.
3. Remove the trailing arm bolts. Pull trailing arm out of body.
4. Installation is the reverse of removal. Torque all nuts and bolts to specifications; see **Table 1**. After installation, the rear end must be aligned by a dealer or competent specialist.

Table is on the following page.

TABLE 1 TORQUE SPECIFICATIONS

STEERING	Ft.-lb.	N•m
Steering wheel nut	36	50
Collar nuts	14	20
Flange nuts	14	20
Transfer case to body	18	25
Tie rod locknut	58	80
Tie rod to steering gear	51	70
Steering gear to body	18	25
FRONT SUSPENSION	**Ft.-lb.**	**N•m**
Upper shock nut	22	30
Upper control arm to ball-joint	43	60
Brake caliper shouldered bolt	115	160
Tie rod ball-joint nut	22	30
Self-locking nuts-strut bar-steering knuckle: two stages	a. 47 b. 51	a. 65 b. 70
Stabilizer link nut	22	30
Strut bar nut	72	100
Lower shock bolt nut	108	150
Lower control arm nut	65	90
Upper control arm nut	54	75
Steering knuckle ball joint nuts	80	110
REAR SUSPENSION	**Ft.-lb.**	**N•m**
Shock absorber nuts	65	90
Axle assembly to trailing arm bolts	101	140
Trailing arm nuts	76	105
CV joint to transaxle	33	45

CHAPTER ELEVEN

BODY

This chapter details replacement or repair procedures for the key locks, seats, doors and door windows. Other body service requires special knowledge and/or tools and should be left to a body repair shop.

SEATS

Front Seat Removal/Installation

1. Lift the adjustment lever.

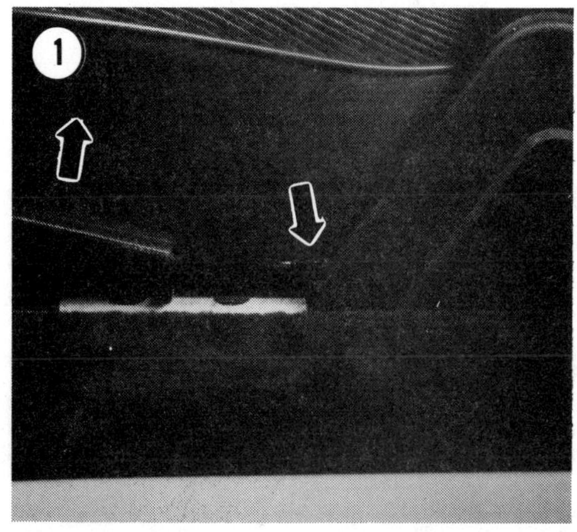

2. Slide the seat forward until it stops; lift the stop catch (**Figure 1**) and slide the seat forward again until it comes off the rails.
3. For installation, align the seat in front of the rails.
4. Slip the seat onto the rail with the adjustment lever held up. Push the seat all the way back and adjust to suit.

Center Bench Seat Removal/Installation

Remove the 4 bolts under the seat which hold it to the floor. Installation is the reverse of removal.

Rear Bench Seat Removal/Installation

Remove the bolts (beneath the seat covering) that hold the seat to each sidewall. Installation is the reverse of removal.

FRONT DOORS

Removal

Refer to **Figure 2** for the following procedure.

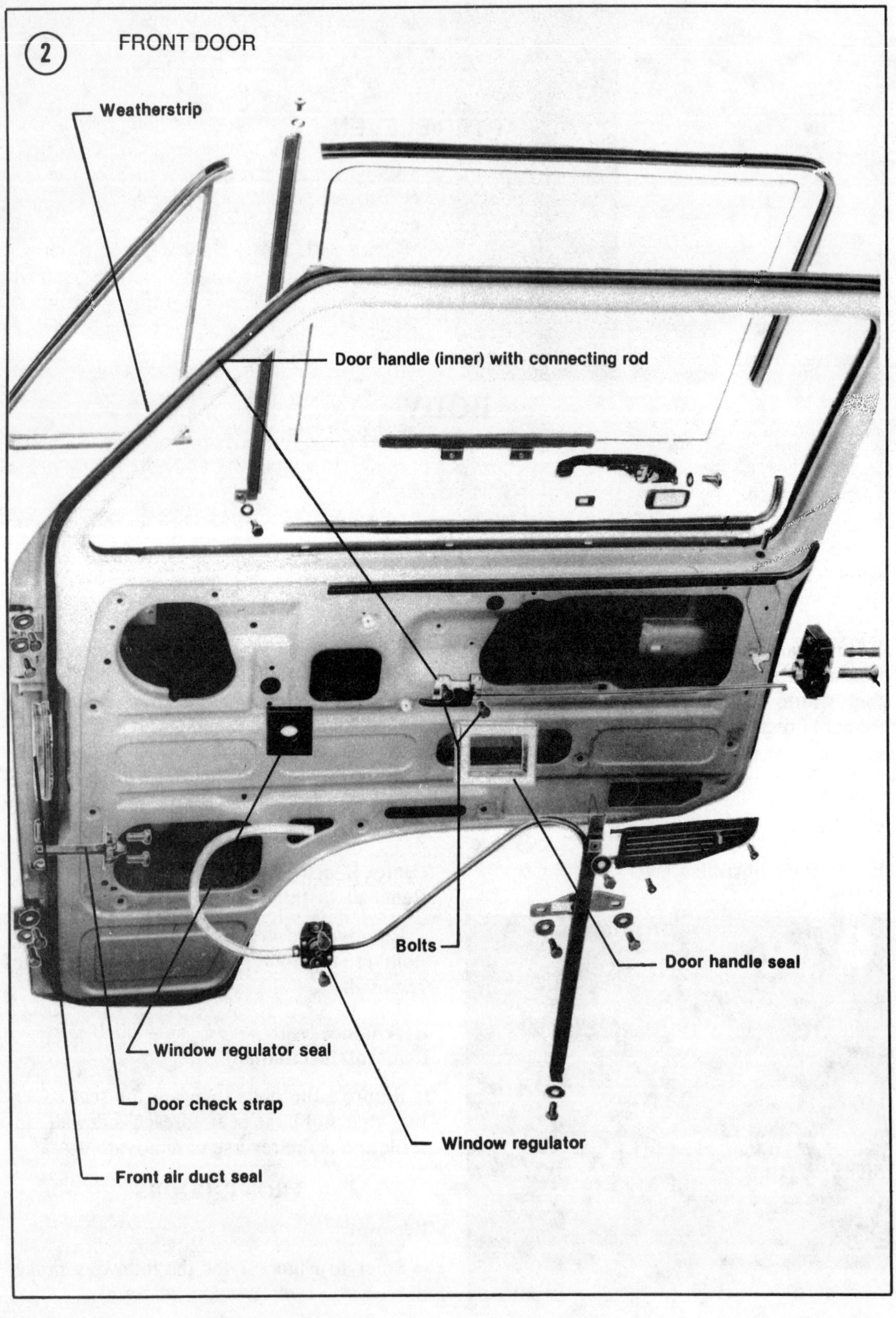
2
FRONT DOOR
Weatherstrip
Door handle (inner) with connecting rod
Bolts
Door handle seal
Window regulator seal
Door check strap
Window regulator
Front air duct seal

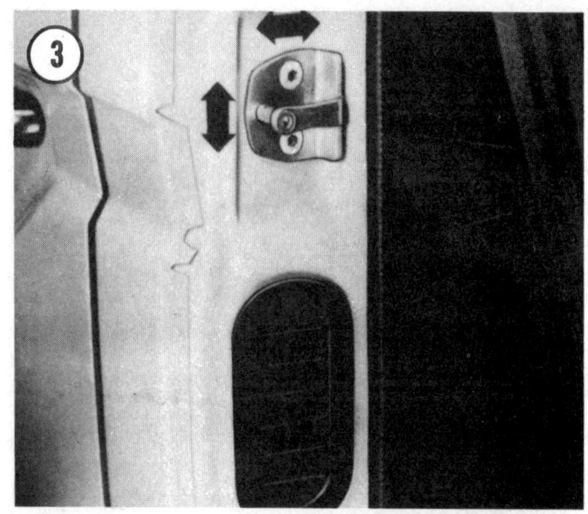

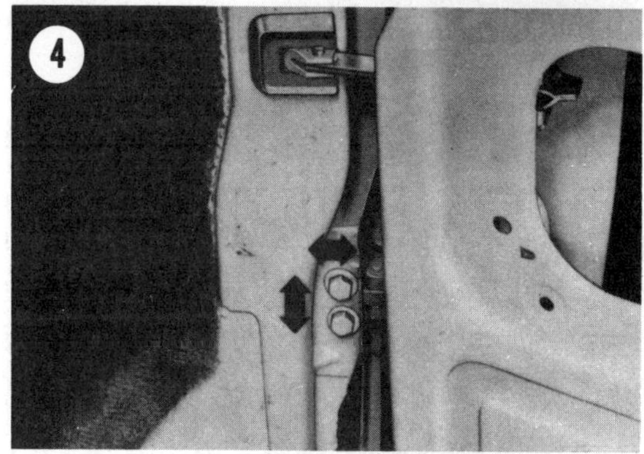

1. Open the door and remove the pin from the door check strap.
2. Remove the hinge bolts while an assistant supports the door.

Installation

1. Check the door weatherstripping. Replace if damaged.
2. Remove the door striker plate (**Figure 3**).
3. Loosely install the hinge bolts. Before tightening the hinge bolts, adjust the door until there is an even gap between the edge of the door and the body (**Figure 4**). Tighten the hinge bolts.
4. Install and adjust the striker plate.

Striker Plate Adjustment

1. If the door does not close properly, remove the striker plate and check the door alignment. If necessary, adjust the door. See *Front Door Installation*.
2. If the striker plate was removed, install it with the screws finger-tight.
3. Close the door until it is just about to come into contact with the striker plate.
4. Note the position of the plate in relation to the door lock. If it is misaligned, reposition it and tighten the screw.
5. Try to close the door. If it doesn't close, reposition the striker plate and try again (**Figure 3**). If it closes properly, the outer edge of the door near the handle will be flush with the quarter panel with it lifting slightly when closed.

Door Trim Panel Removal/Installation

Refer to **Figure 5** for the following procedure.

1. Remove the long Phillips head screws which secure the armrest and the door handle.
2. Carefully pry back the plastic cover on the window crank. Remove the screw under the cover and pull the crank off the door.
3. Carefully pry the plastic insert out of the door release latch plate (**Figure 6**).
4. Remove the screw which holds the release latch plate (**Figure 7**).
5. Work your fingers in between the trim panel and the door. Carefully pull the panel off the door. The panel is held in at this point by a dozen little hole clips which will pop out under moderate but steady pressure.
6. Installation is the reverse of removal.

WINDOWS

Window replacement should be limited to the door windows. Other windows require special skills and equipment for installation. Take these jobs to a local glass shop.

WARNING
When working with broken glass always wear suitable eye and hand protection to avoid injury. Completely clean up any shards before operating the vehicle.

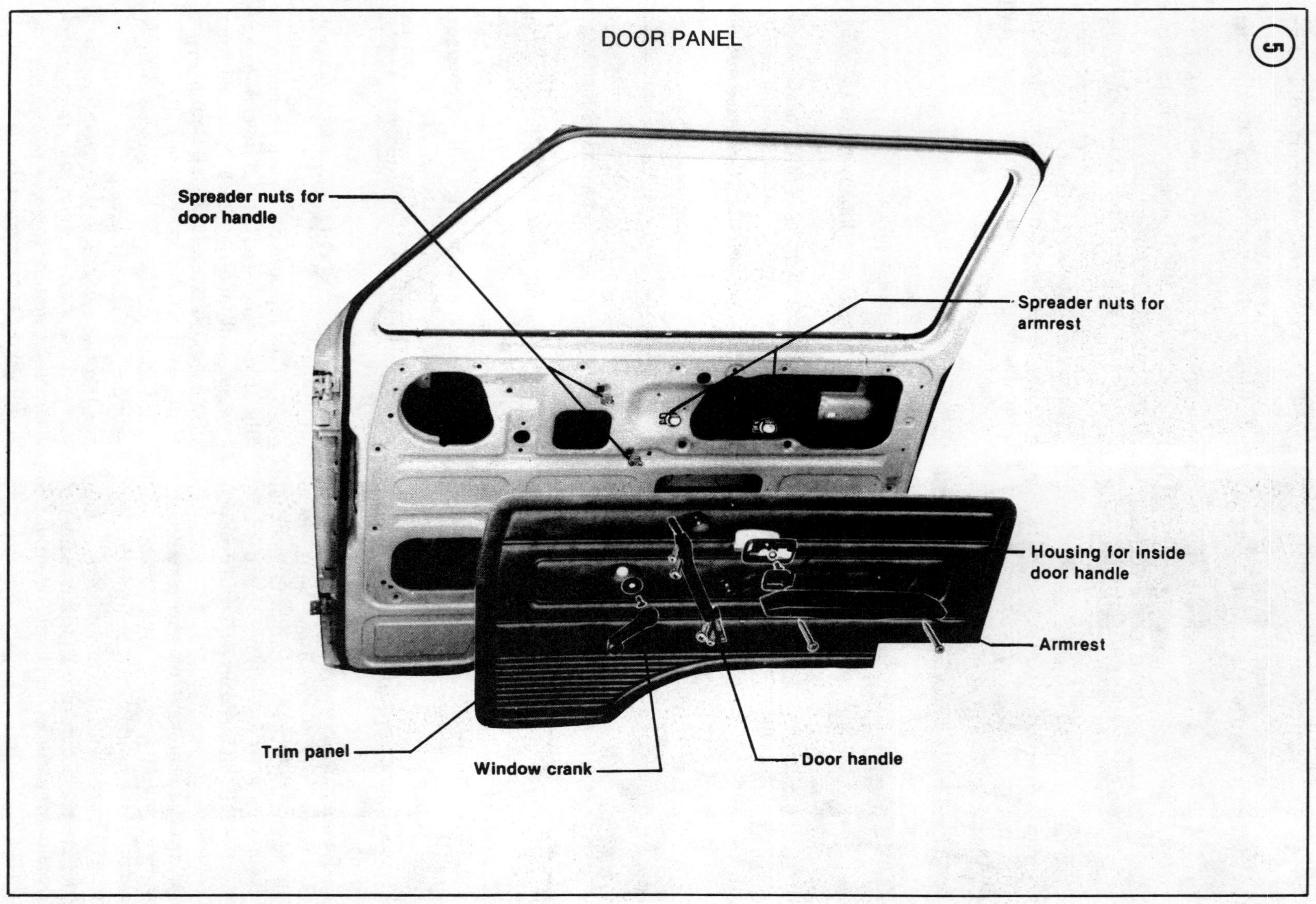
5
DOOR PANEL
Spreader nuts for door handle
Spreader nuts for armrest
Housing for inside door handle
Armrest
Trim panel
Window crank
Door handle

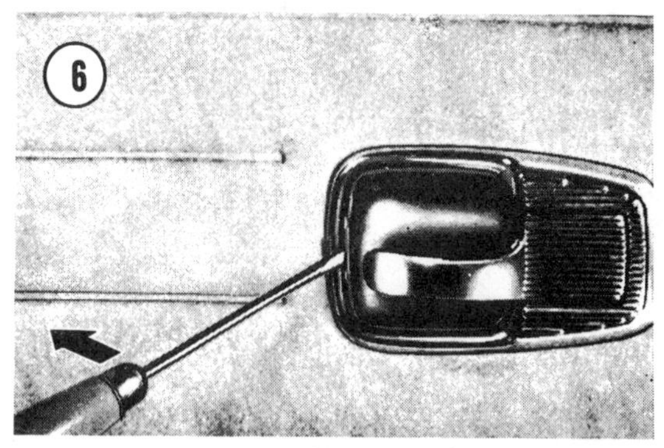

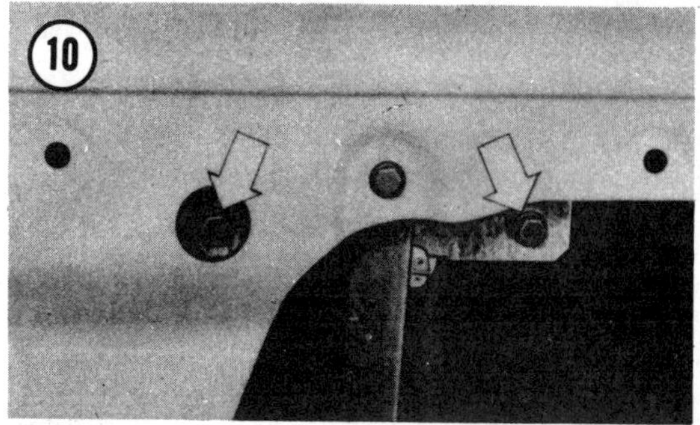

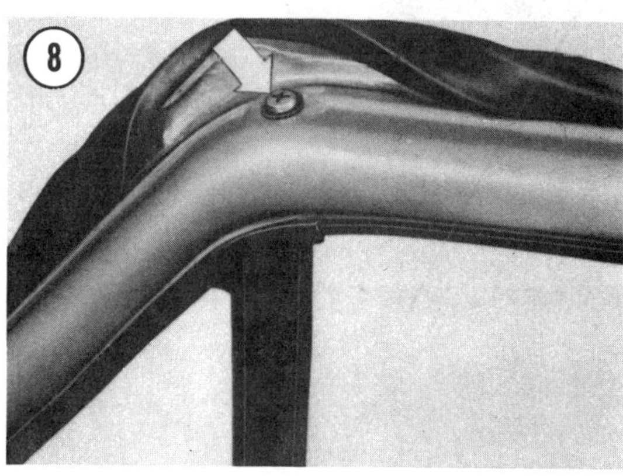

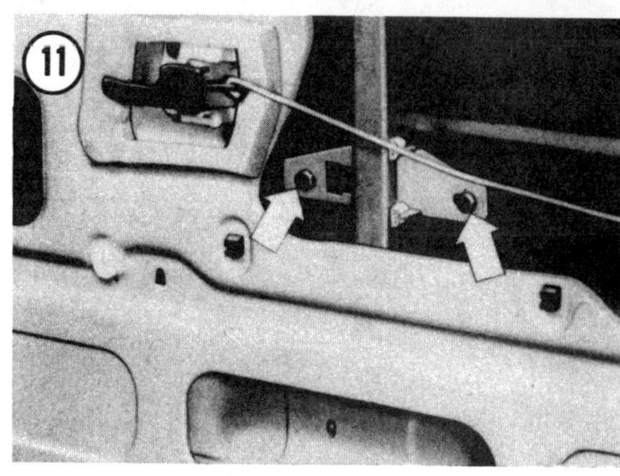

Door Window Replacement

Refer to **Figure 2** for the following procedure.

1. Remove the door trim panel. See procedure in this chapter.
2. Open the windwing. Peel up the weatherstripping and remove the screw which holds the top of the front guide channel to the door frame (**Figure 8**).
3. Remove the small bolt which holds the bottom of the channel to the door frame (**Figure 9**).
4. Crank down the old window until the regulator bolts appear in the door holes (**Figure 10**).
5. Remove the regulator bolts and lift the old window out of the door frame.
6. Slip the new window into the door frame.
7. Reinstall the window channel guide.
8. Install the window in the regulator channel with the bolts loose (**Figure 11**).
9. Crank the window all the way up and align the window with the front and upper guide channel. Tighten the regulator bolts.
10. Install the trim panel.

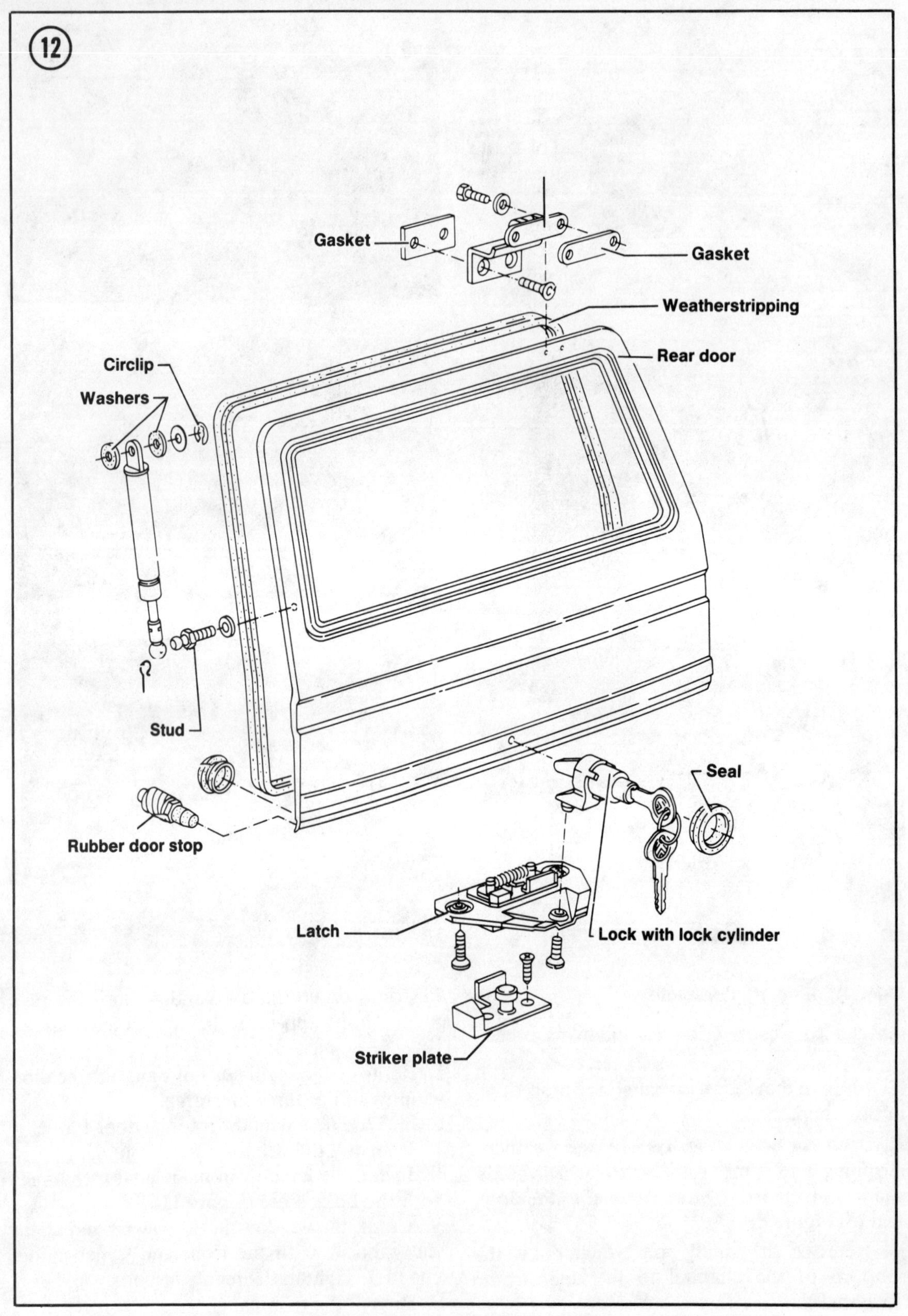
12
Gasket
Gasket
Weatherstripping
Rear door
Circlip
Washers
Stud
Seal
Rubber door stop
Latch
Lock with lock cylinder
Striker plate

REAR DOOR

Removal/Installation

Refer to **Figure 12** for the following procedure.

1. Remove the circlip from the end of the gas spring. Pull the ball-head connector off the stud.
2. Carefully disconnect the rear window defogger wire and pull it out of the door frame.
3. Have an assistant hold the door while you remove the hinge screws. Remove the rear door.

4. Install the door hinge screws hand-tight.
5. Move the rear door up and down until a gap of 1/2 in. (12 mm) exists between the body and the top of the door. See dimension "a" in **Figure 13**. Also adjust the door so there is an even gap at the sides.
6. Screw the rubber stop in or out until the rear door is flush with body panel when closed (**Figure 14**).
7. Install and reconnect the rear window defogger wire.
8. Push the ball-head connector onto the stud. Install the circlip.
9. Adjust the striker plate.

Striker Plate Adjustment

1. Open the rear door.
2. Loosen the striker plate screws just enough to allow the plate to move.
3. Close the rear door.
4. Open the rear door and tighten the striker plate screws.

KEY LOCKS

This section deals with only the front and rear door locks. For ignition switch lock refer to *Steering Column Switches* in Chapter Seven.

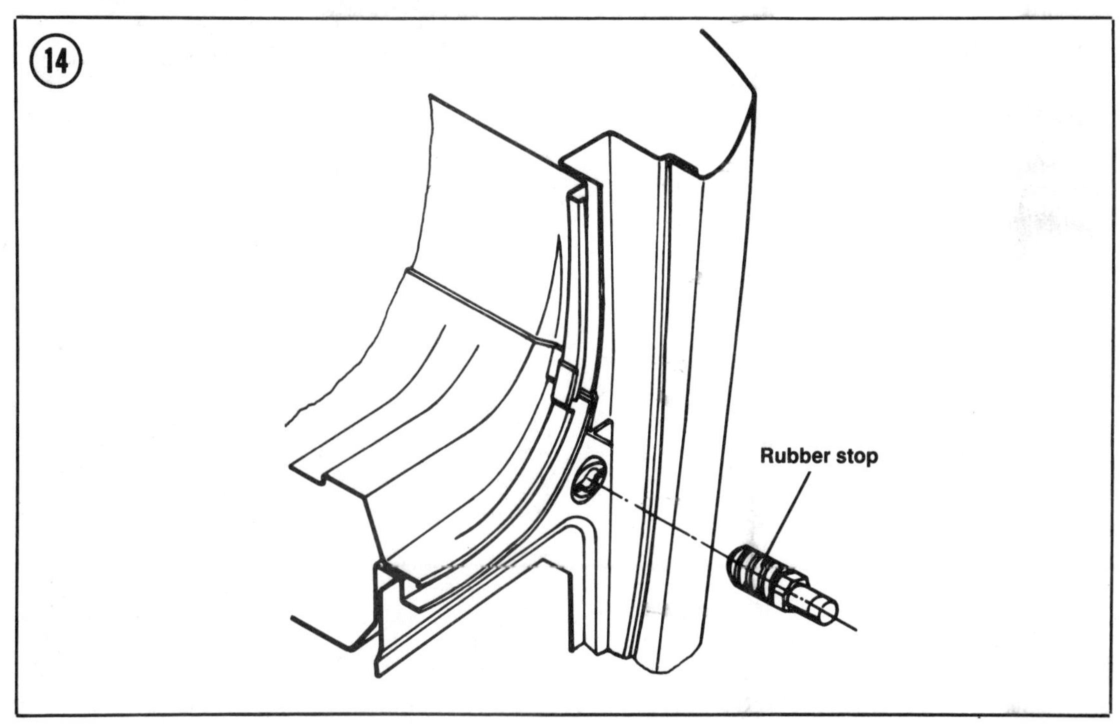

Front Door Lock Replacement

1. Open the door and peel back the weatherstripping from the area of the outer door handle.

2. Remove the handle securing screw (**Figure 15**). Push the handle forward and pull it out of the door frame.

3. Remove the screw which holds the tumbler in the door handle. Push the tumbler out and insert new tumbler.

4. Slip the handle in the door frame and install the securing screw.

5. Push the weatherstripping back into place.

Rear Door Lock Replacement

Refer to **Figure 12** for the following procedure.

1. Open the rear door.
2. Unscrew and remove the door latch.
3. Separate the lock cylinder from the latch.
4. Join the new lock to the latch and install in the door.
5. If necessary, adjust the striker plate.

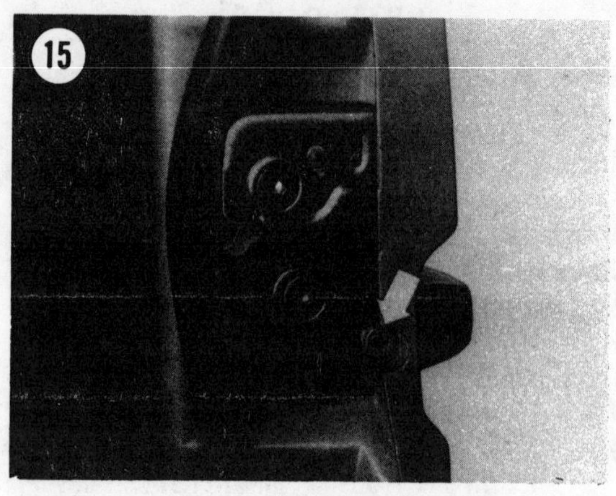

WESTFALIA CAMPER CONVERSION

Service to the camper refrigerator, water system and especially the stove and propane system should be left to qualified recreational vehicle repair shops or to the dealer. An electrical wiring diagram for the camper is included at the end of the book.

WARNING
Do not attempt to make stove or propane system repairs. Leave this to a qualified RV repair technician. Propane is highly explosive; mistakes made when servicing the stove or propane systems can produce disastrous results.

1982 SERVICE INFORMATION

This supplement contains service and maintenance information for the 1982 VW Vanagon. The information supplements the procedures in the main body (Chapters One through Eleven) of the book, referred to in this supplement as the "basic book." The chapter headings and titles in this supplement correspond to those in the basic book. If a chapter is not included in the supplement, there are no changes affecting 1982 models.

If your vehicle is covered by this supplement, carefully read the supplement and then read the appropriate chapters in the basic book before beginning any work.

CHAPTER THREE

LUBRICATION, MAINTENANCE AND TUNE-UP

PERIODIC MAINTENANCE (DIESEL)

Table 1 provides a maintenance schedule for 1982 models equipped with a diesel engine. Diesel maintenance procedures which differ from those used with the air-cooled engine are described in this supplement.

ROUTINE CHECKS (DIESEL)

The simple checks specified in Chapter Three of the main book should be performed at each fueling stop. Those specified in this supplement differ for the diesel engine.

1. *Check engine oil*—Oil should be checked with the engine warm and on level ground. Level should be between the 2 marks on the dipstick (A, **Figure 1**); never above or below. Top up if necessary with an oil designated API service SF/CC or SF/CD. Refer to **Table 2** for the correct viscosity range.
2. *Check coolant level*–Perform this check when the engine is cold. The coolant level should be between the minimum (cold) and maximum (hot) marks on the expansion tank (B, **Figure 1**).

Engine Oil and Filter

If the vehicle is given normal use, change the oil and filter every 7,500 miles or 6 months, whichever comes first. If the vehicle is used in dusty areas or for frequent short trips, stop-and-go driving or in extremely cold weather, change the oil and filter every 3,000 miles or 3 months.

Use an oil with an API designation of SF/CC or SF/CD. Multi-viscosity oils are preferred. To select the exact viscosity range, refer to **Table 2**.

To drain the oil and change the filter, you will need:

a. Drain pan (6 quarts or more capacity).
b. Oil can spout or can opener and funnel.
c. Filter wrench (VW part No. US 4774 and part No. US 4496).
d. 5 quarts of oil.
e. Adjustable wrench.
f. New oil filter.

There are several ways to discard the old oil safely. The easiest way is to pour it from the drain pan into a gallon bleach or milk container. The oil can then be taken to a service station for recycling.

NOTE

Check local regulations before disposing of oil in trash. Never let oil drain on the ground.

The drain pan can be cleaned with solvent or paint thinner, if available. If not, hot water and dishwashing liquid will work.

1. Warm the engine to operating temperature, then shut it off.
2. Place the drain pan under the crankcase drain plug (**Figure 2**). Remove the plug with the wrench and let the oil drain for at least 15 minutes. Check the condition of the drain

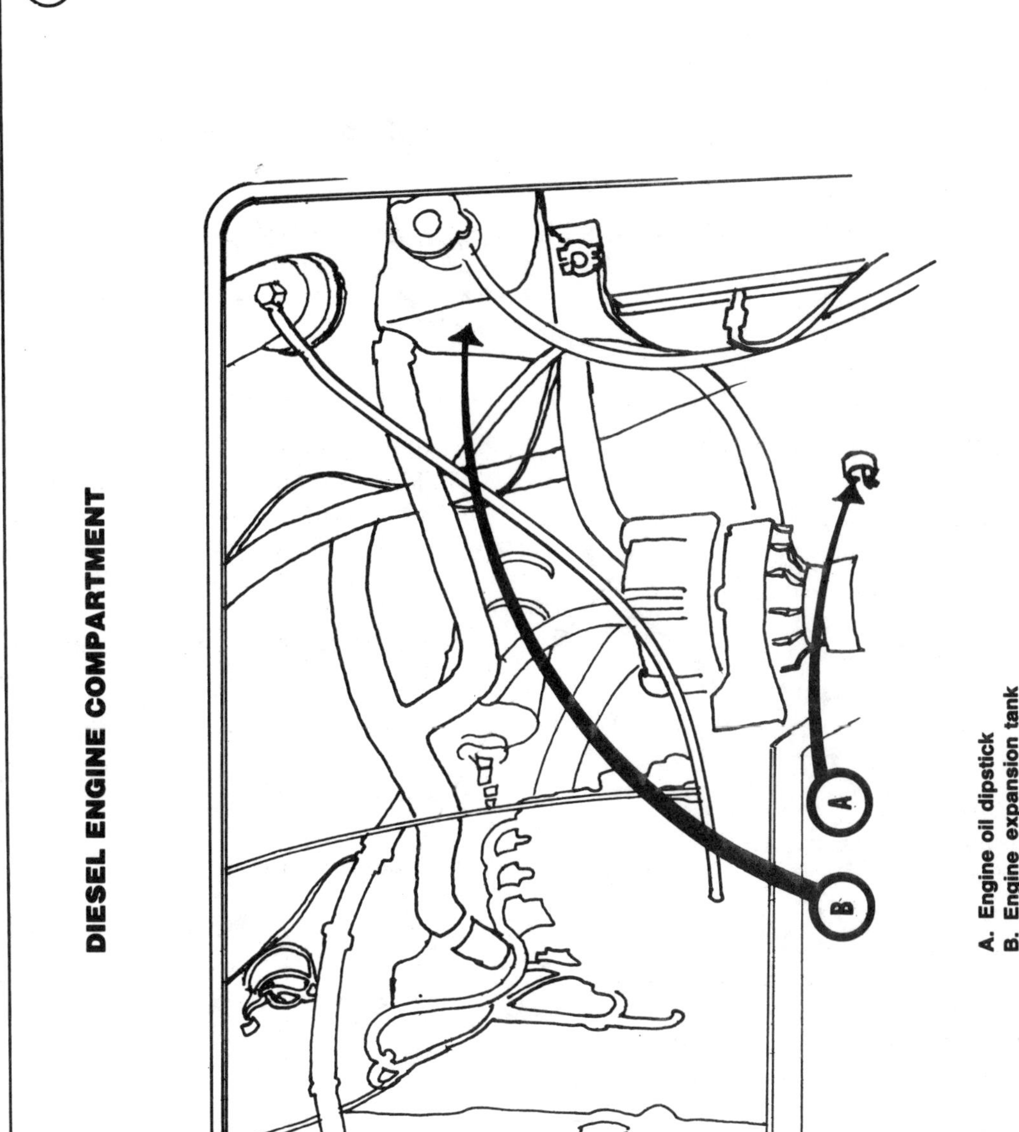
1
DIESEL ENGINE COMPARTMENT
A
B
A. Engine oil dipstick
B. Engine expansion tank

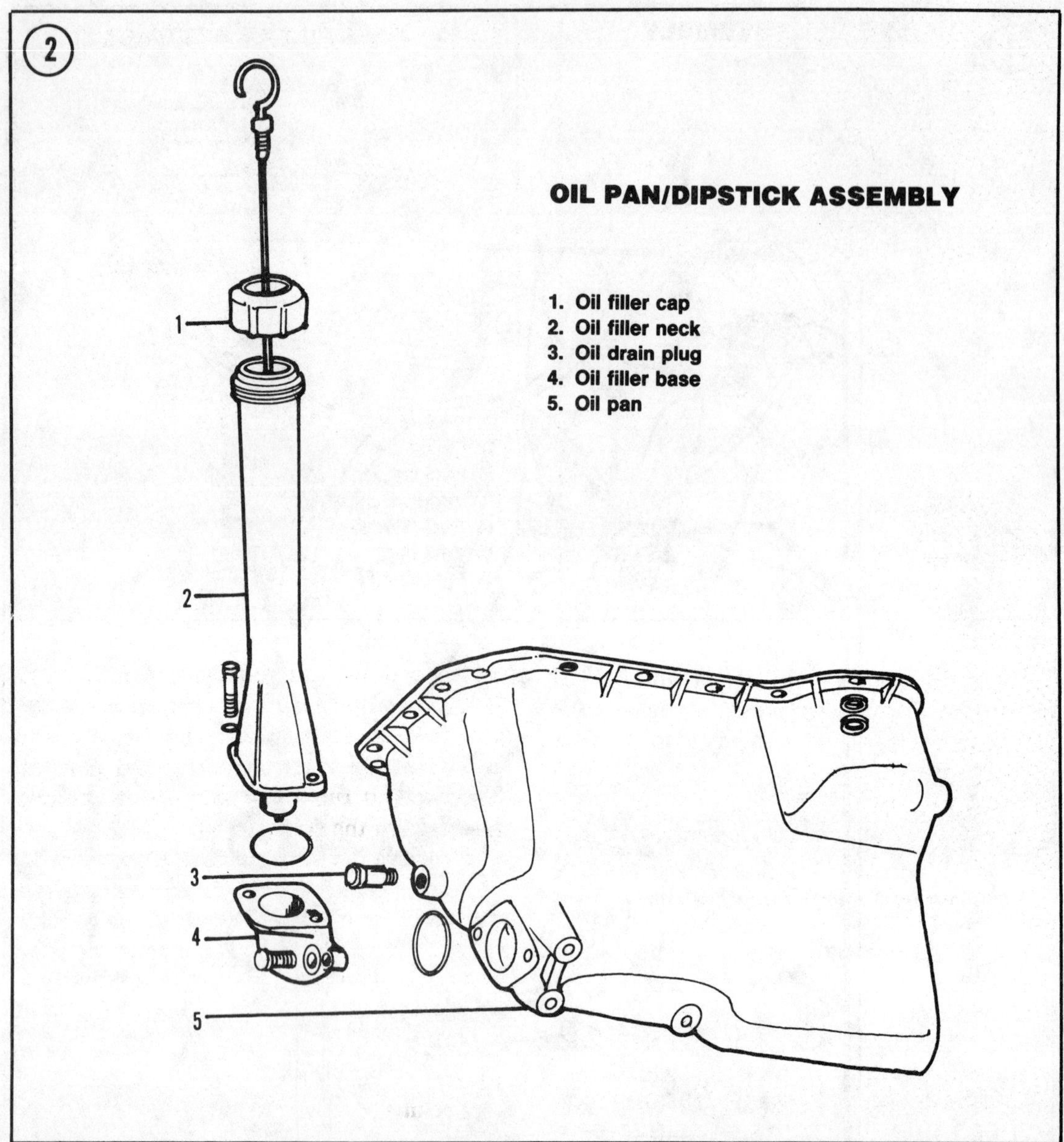

plug gasket and replace it if damaged. Reinstall the plug and gasket and tighten the plug to 14 ft.-lb. (20 N•m).

3. Move the drain pan beneath the oil filter. Loosen the filter with VW tool part No. US 4474 and remove the filter by unscrewing it counterclockwise.

4. Wipe the gasket surface on the oil cooler assembly (**Figure 3**) clean with a paper towel.

5. Coat the neoprene gasket on the new filter with clean engine oil. Install the filter with VW tool part No. US 4496.

NOTE
Use only a VW oil filter obtained from your dealer and follow the installation instructions (if any) printed on the filter container.

6. Remove the oil filler cap/dipstick assembly from the oil filler neck. See **Figure 2**.

7. Pour the oil into the oil filler neck. Wipe up any spills around the oil filler neck with a clean cloth or paper towel.

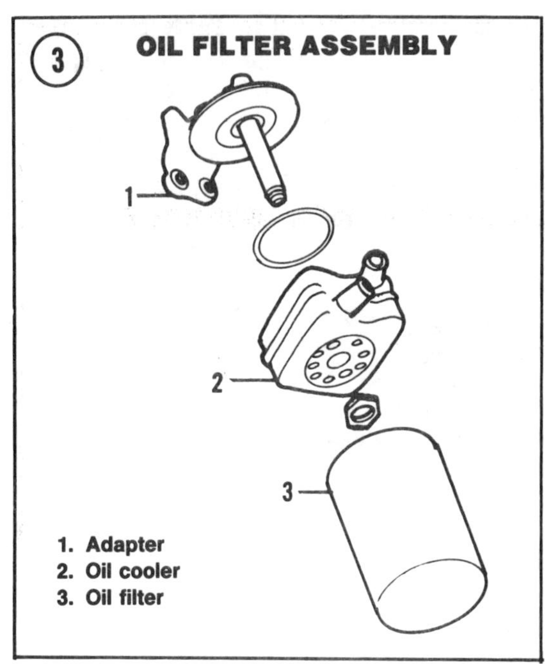

1. Adapter
2. Oil cooler
3. Oil filter

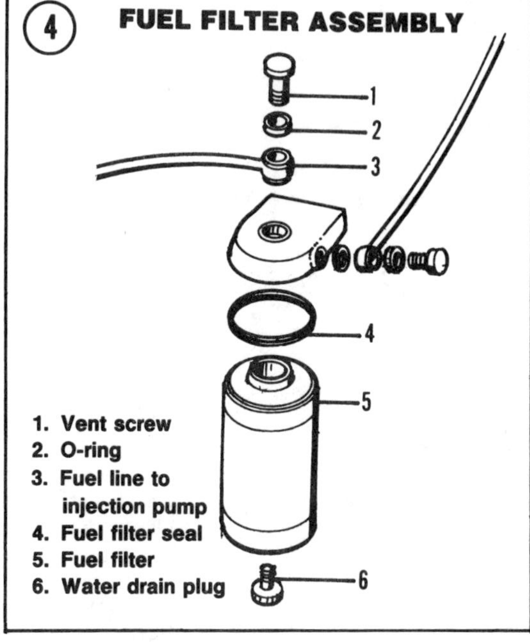

1. Vent screw
2. O-ring
3. Fuel line to injection pump
4. Fuel filter seal
5. Fuel filter
6. Water drain plug

8. Start the engine and let it idle. The instrument panel oil pressure light will remain on for a few seconds, then go out.

CAUTION
Do not rev the engine to make the oil pressure light go out. It takes time for the oil to reach all parts of the engine and revving it could damage dry parts.

9. While the engine is running, check the areas under and around the drain plug and filter for leaks.
10. Turn the engine off. Let the oil settle for several minutes, then recheck the level on the dipstick. Add oil, if necessary, to bring the level up to the "FULL" mark, but *do not overfill.*

Fuel Filter Service

Water should be drained from the fuel filter when the engine oil and oil filter are changed. Replace the fuel filter every 15,000 miles.

The filter is located under the vehicle near the fuel tank. Before attempting filter service, raise the vehicle with a jack and place it on jackstands.

Open the vent screw located on top of the filter. Loosen the water drain plug at the bottom of the filter housing. See **Figure 4**. Catch the water in a suitable container. Let the fuel flow until it runs clean, then tighten the drain plug and close the vent screw. Lower the vehicle to the ground and start the engine. Let it run a few minutes to remove any air from the system.

To replace the filter element, loosen it with VW tool part No. 4462 or equivalent and unscrew it by hand. Lubricate the new filter seal with clean diesel fuel and screw it onto the flange hand-tight. Do not tighten with a filter wrench.

Air Cleaner

At the intervals stated in **Table 1**, remove and clean or replace the air cleaner filter element. Release the 4 air cleaner cover clips and remove the cover. Remove the filter element and clean or discard according to service interval.

To clean a filter, tap it lightly against your hand to shake the entrapped dirt out. The filter element should not be cleaned or soaked with gasoline, solvents or oil under any circumstances.

Thoroughly clean the inside of the housing with a lightly oiled lint-free cloth. Install the filter element, position the cover and latch the 4 clips.

Cooling System Check and Service

WARNING
Personal injury is possible. Perform the cooling system service when the engine is cold. Disconnect the electrical connector at the fan motor before working on the cooling system.

At the intervals stated in **Table 1**, remove the expansion tank cap and visually inspect the level and condition of the coolant. If it looks dirty or rusty, flush the radiator and replace the coolant as described in the Chapter Five section of this supplement.

Inspect all radiator and heater hoses. Replace any hoses that are cracked, deteriorated or extremely soft/spongy. Make sure that all hoses are correctly installed and that all clamps are securely tightened.

Table 1 MAINTENANCE SCHEDULE (DIESEL ENGINE)

Every 7,500 miles	Change engine oil and filter
(6 months)	Service fuel filter
Every 10,000 miles	Check clutch adjustment
	Inspect front disc brakes
	Inspect rear drum brakes
	Check exhaust system
Every 15,000 miles	Have valve clearance adjusted
(12 months)	Have compression checked
	Have injection pump timing checked
	Have injector heat shields replaced
	Have oil pump drive gear checked
	Check condition/tension of drive belts
	Clean air cleaner filter element
	Replace fuel filter
	Check steering and suspension
	Check manual transaxle fluid level
	Check final drive fluid level
	Check wheel bearings
	Inspect/rotate tires
	Visually check engine compartment
	Check and service cooling system
Every 30,000 miles	Replace air cleaner filter element
(24 months)	Change automatic transmission fluid
Every 24 months	Drain, flush and refill cooling system
Every 45,000 miles	Have spur belt replaced

Table 2 OIL VISCOSITY RECOMMENDATIONS

Engine Oil Type	Temperature Range	Recommended Type
Single grade	Above 68° F	SAE 40W
	+32° to +78° F	SAE 30W
	+15° to +50° F	SAE 20W
	-5° to +25° F	SAE 10W
Multi-grade*	+15° to +80° F	SAE 20W-40, SAE 20W-50
	-5° to +50° F	SAE 10W-30, SAE 10W-40
	Consistently below -15° F	SAE 5W-20

* Recommended.

CHAPTER FOUR

ENGINE

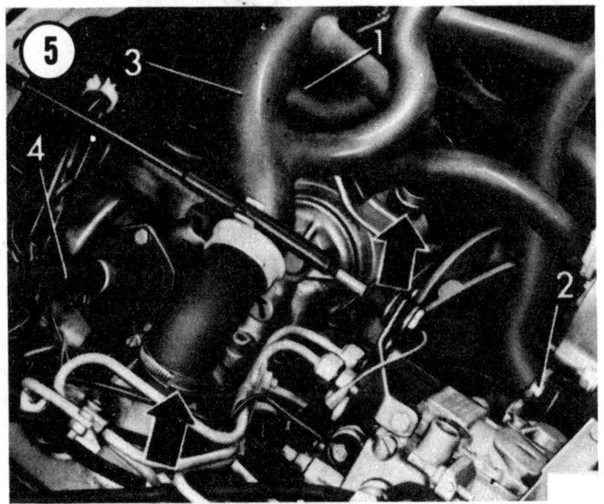

A 1.6L diesel engine is optional in 1982 Vanagons. This is a slightly modified version of the 1.6L diesel used in VW Rabbit, Scirocco and Jetta models. The engine is mounted transversely (sideways) and at an angle in the engine compartment.

An electrical ignition system, as used on a gasoline engine, is not necessary. The diesel engine relies instead on the heat generated by air compression within the combustion chamber for ignition.

Removal and installation procedures are provided in this chapter. Owner disassembly of the diesel engine is not recommended, especially if the vehicle is still under the manufacturer's warranty. Refer all mechanical work on the diesel engine to your VW dealer or a qualified specialist.

Removal

1. Set the parking brake and block the drive wheels.
2. Disconnect the negative battery cable.
3. Unsnap the 4 air cleaner housing clips and remove the air cleaner cover.
4. Remove the lower engine cover.
5. Remove the coolant expansion tank cap.
6. Place a clean container under the water pump. Disconnect the lower hose from the water pump at the connecting pipe (1, **Figure 5**). Let the coolant drain into the container. If coolant is clean, save for reuse.
7. Disconnect the center hose (2, **Figure 5**) from the water pump.
8. Disconnect the hose (3, **Figure 5**) from the cylinder head (lower arrow, **Figure 5**) and from the oil cooler (upper arrow, **Figure 5**). Move it to one side out of the way.
9. Remove vacuum hose (4, **Figure 5**) from the vacuum pump.
10. Refer to **Figure 6** and disconnect the wiring at the oil pressure switch (1), temperature sensors (2 and 3) and glow plugs (4).
11. Remove the coolant hose (5, **Figure 6**).

12. Refer to **Figure** 7 and remove the fuel supply (1) and return (2) lines at the injection pump.
13. Disconnect the throttle cable at the pump lever. Remove retaining clip (3, **Figure** 7) at bracket and move cable to one side out of the way.
14. Disconnect cold start cable at lockscrew (4, **Figure** 7). Remove retaining clip and move cable to one side out of the way.
15. Disconnect fuel shut-off solenoid wire (5, **Figure** 7).
16. Remove the fasteners holding the coolant reservoir. Remove the reservoir.
17. Remove the oil filler neck cap with dipstick (1, **Figure 8**).
18. Remove the nuts (2, **Figure 8**) from the rear engine mounts on each side. Leave the bolts in place.
19. Raise the vehicle with a jack and place it on jackstands.
20. Remove engine/transaxle mounting bolts (1, **Figure 9**).
21. Remove support member bolts (2, **Figure 9**). Remove support member.
22. Support the engine with engine crane and adaptor VW part No. 3058 as shown in **Figure 10**. Turn knob (arrow, **Figure 10**) as required to adjust adaptor to correct engine/transaxle angle.
23. Remove front engine mount nuts (arrow, **Figure 11**) on each side.
24. Remove all bolts from front and rear engine mounts. Lower engine/transaxle assembly until the fasteners holding the 2 units together can be reached.
25. Support transaxle with VW part No. 785/1B as shown in **Figure 12**.
26. Separate engine from transaxle and lower it from the vehicle.

Installation

Installation is the reverse of removal, plus the following:
1. Adjust the engine to transaxle angle before connecting the 2 assemblies.
2. Tighten engine to transaxle bolts to proper torque. M10 bolts should be torqued to 33 ft.-lb. (45 N•m) and M12 bolts to 58 ft.-lb. (80 N•m).

3. Tighten engine mount fasteners to 61 ft.-lb. (85 N•m) and support member fasteners to 33 ft.-lb. (45 N•m).
4. Make sure fuel supply and return pipe union screws are correctly installed. Fuel return pipe union screw is marked "OUT" on hex head. In addition, the return line is smaller in diameter than the supply line. Tighten union screws to 18 ft.-lb. (22 N•m).
5. Adjust the cold start cable as follows:
   a. Insert washer (1, **Figure 13**) on cable.
   b. Install cable in bracket with rubber bushing.
   c. Insert inner cable in pin (3, **Figure 13**).
   d. Install lock clip (2, **Figure 13**).
   e. Push cold start knob in fully and move lever in direction of arrow (**Figure 13**) until it stops.
   f. Pull inner cable tight. Fasten pin (3, **Figure 13**) with clamping screw.
6. Refill cooling system. See the Chapter Five section of this supplement.

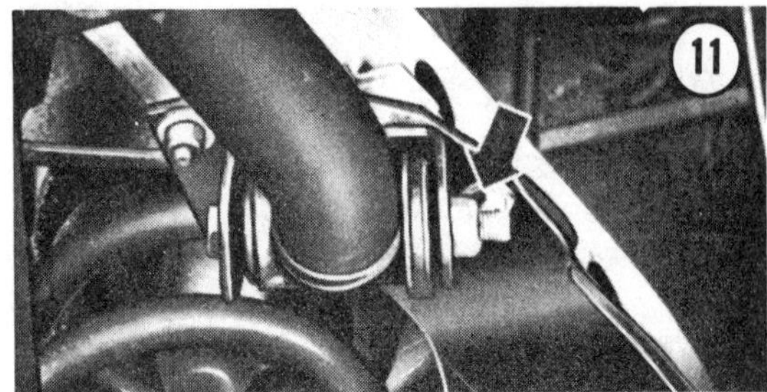

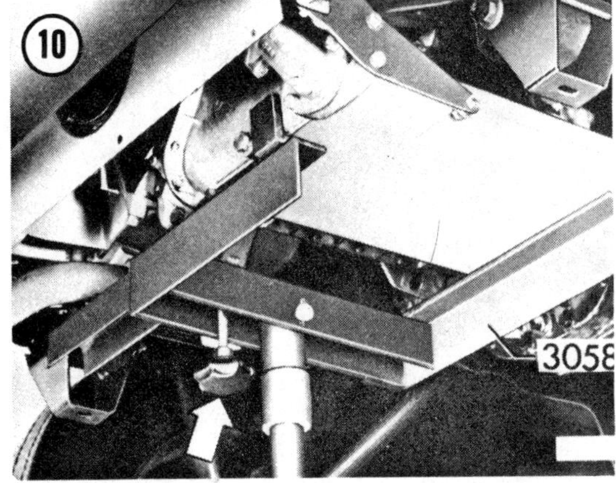

CHAPTER FIVE

COOLING, VENTILATION AND HEATING

WATER-COOLED ENGINE

The pressurized cooling system used on diesel powered Vanagon models consists of a radiator, water pump, electric cooling fan and motor, thermostat, coolant expansion tank, coolant reservoir, 2 thermoswitches and connecting hoses. See **Figure 14** and **Figure 15**. Cooling system components can be replaced with the engine in the vehicle.

The electric cooling fan is mounted in a shroud behind the radiator. Fan operation is controlled by 2 thermoswitches mounted in the radiator end tank (**Figure 15**).

The heater system is shown in **Figure 16**. An auxiliary gas heater similar to the heater

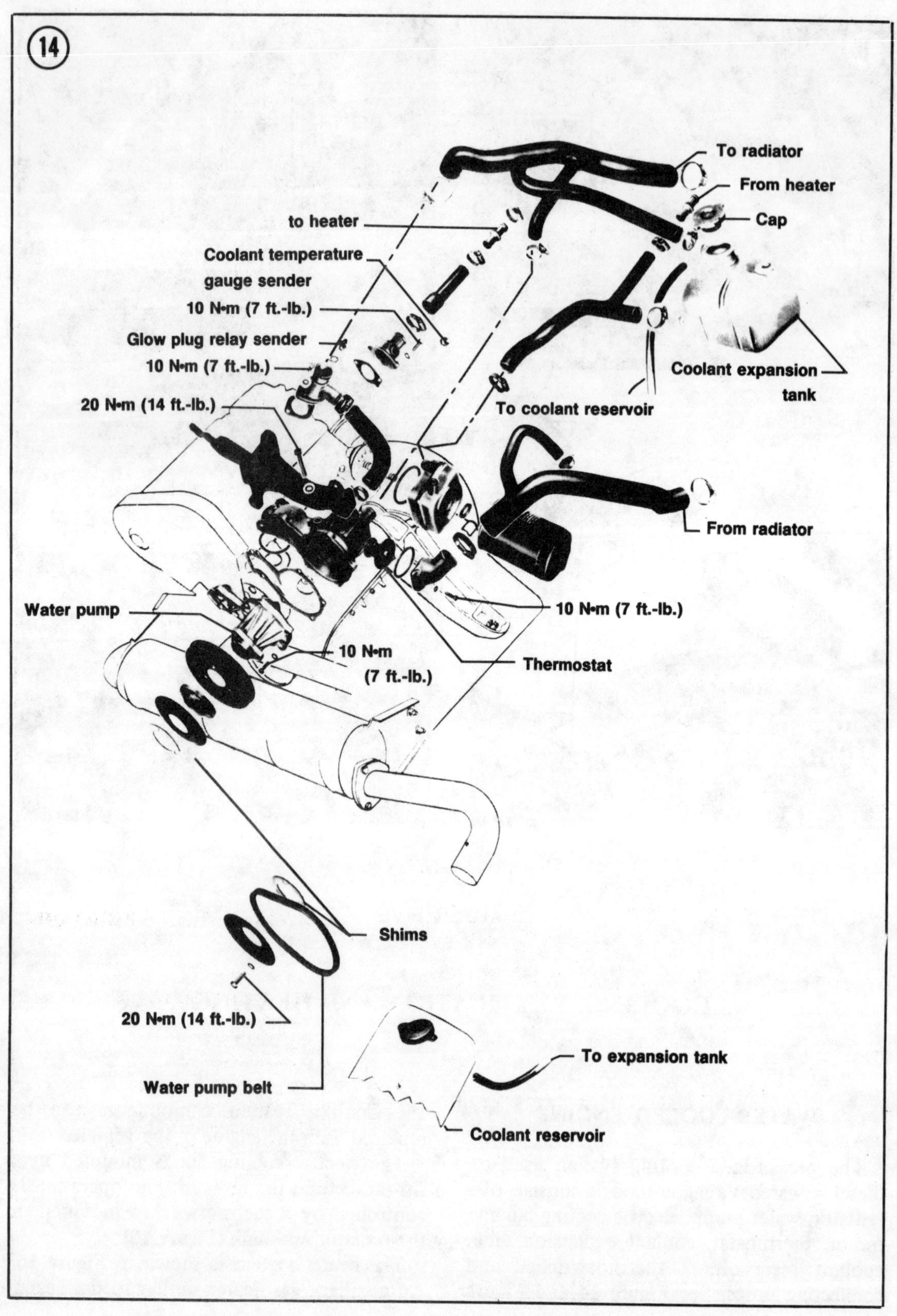
14
To radiator
From heater
Cap
to heater
Coolant temperature
gauge sender
10 N•m (7 ft.-lb.)
Glow plug relay sender
10 N•m (7 ft.-lb.)
20 N•m (14 ft.-lb.)
Coolant expansion
tank
To coolant reservoir
From radiator
Water pump
10 N•m (7 ft.-lb.)
10 N•m
(7 ft.-lb.)
Thermostat
Shims
20 N•m (14 ft.-lb.)
To expansion tank
Water pump belt
Coolant reservoir

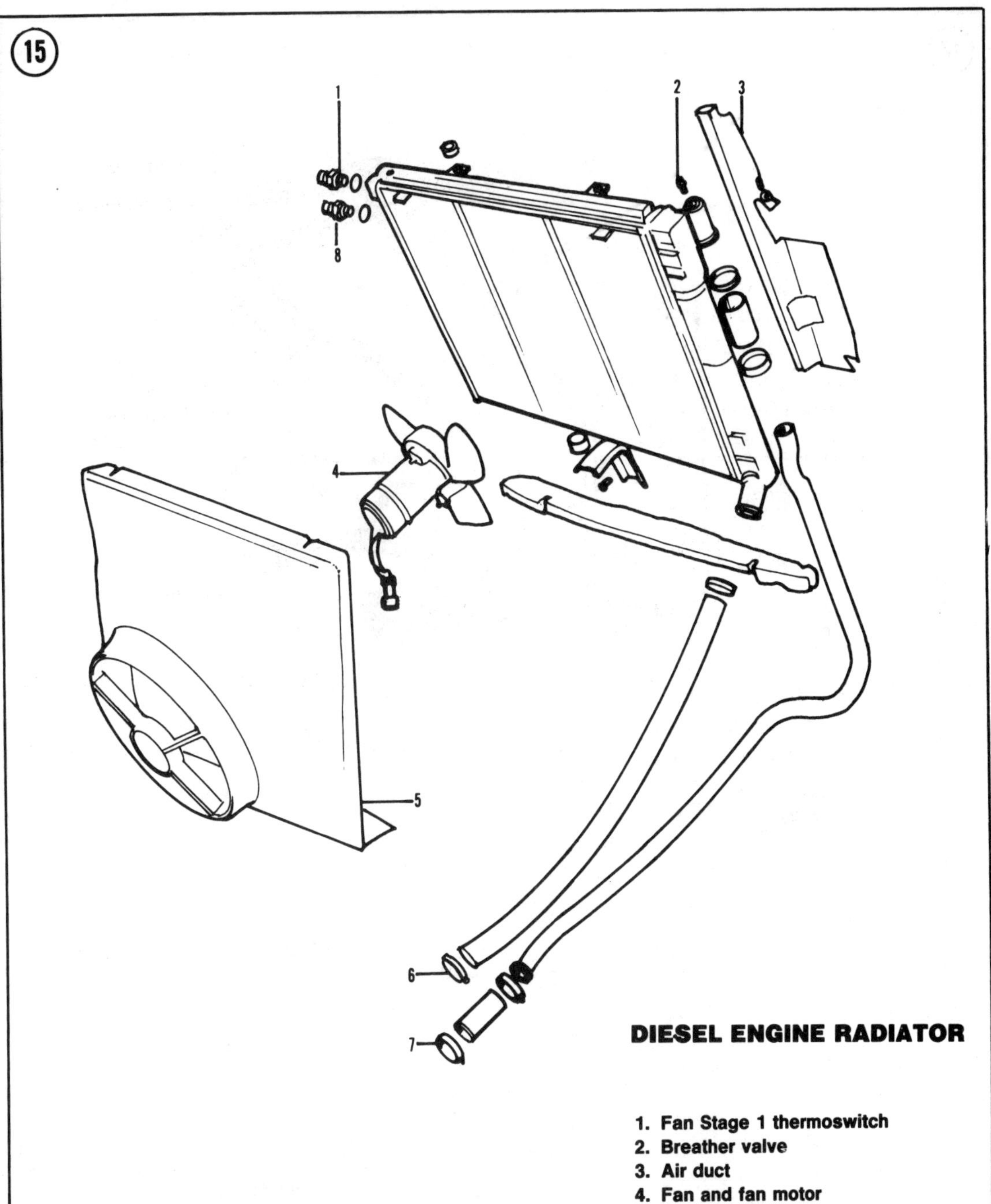

DIESEL ENGINE RADIATOR

1. Fan Stage 1 thermoswitch
2. Breather valve
3. Air duct
4. Fan and fan motor
5. Fan shroud
6. To cylinder head
7. To water pump
8. Fan Stage 2 thermoswitch

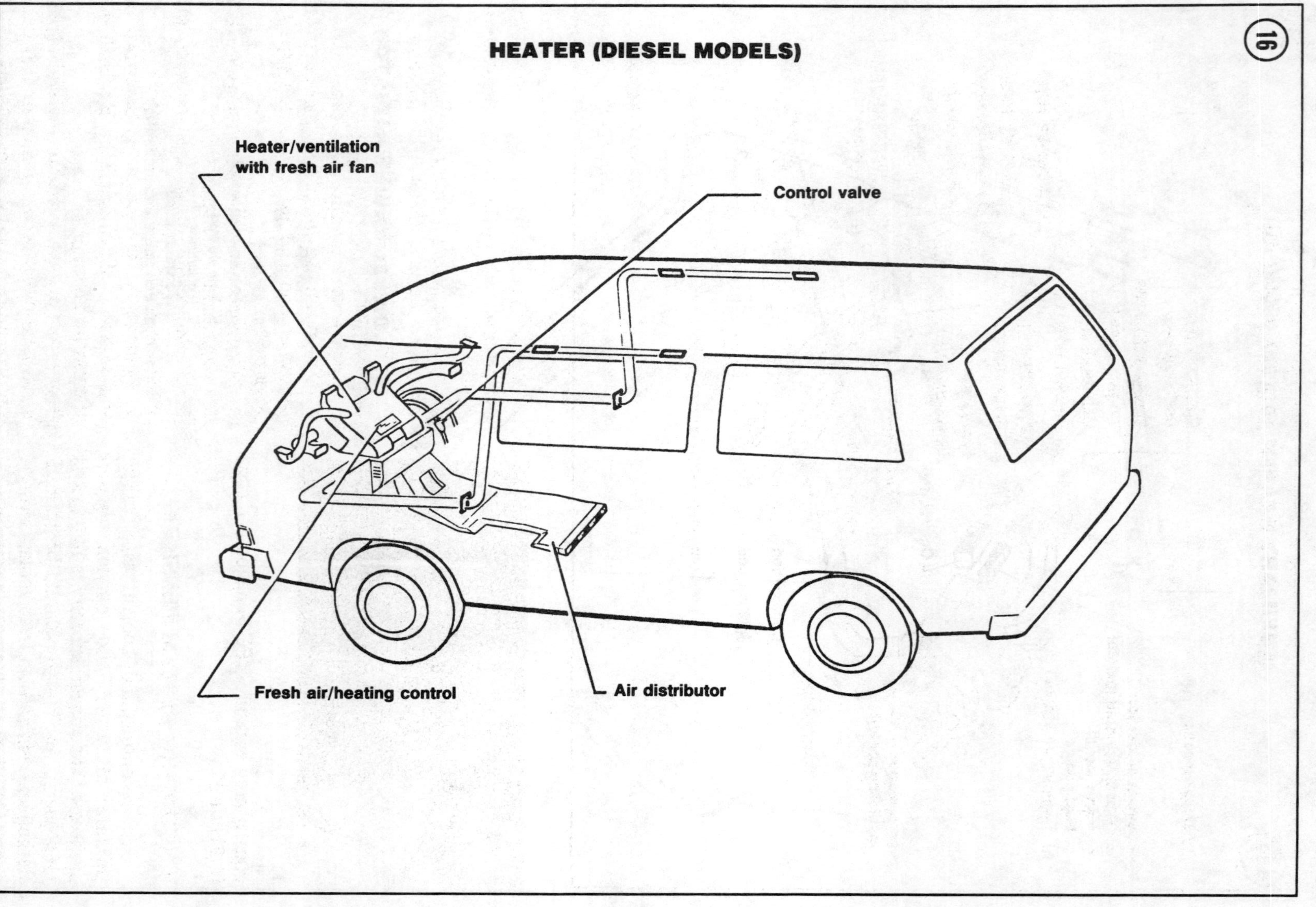
16
HEATER (DIESEL MODELS)
Heater/ventilation
with fresh air fan
Control valve
Fresh air/heating control
Air distributor

17

AUXILIARY HEATER (DIESEL MODELS)

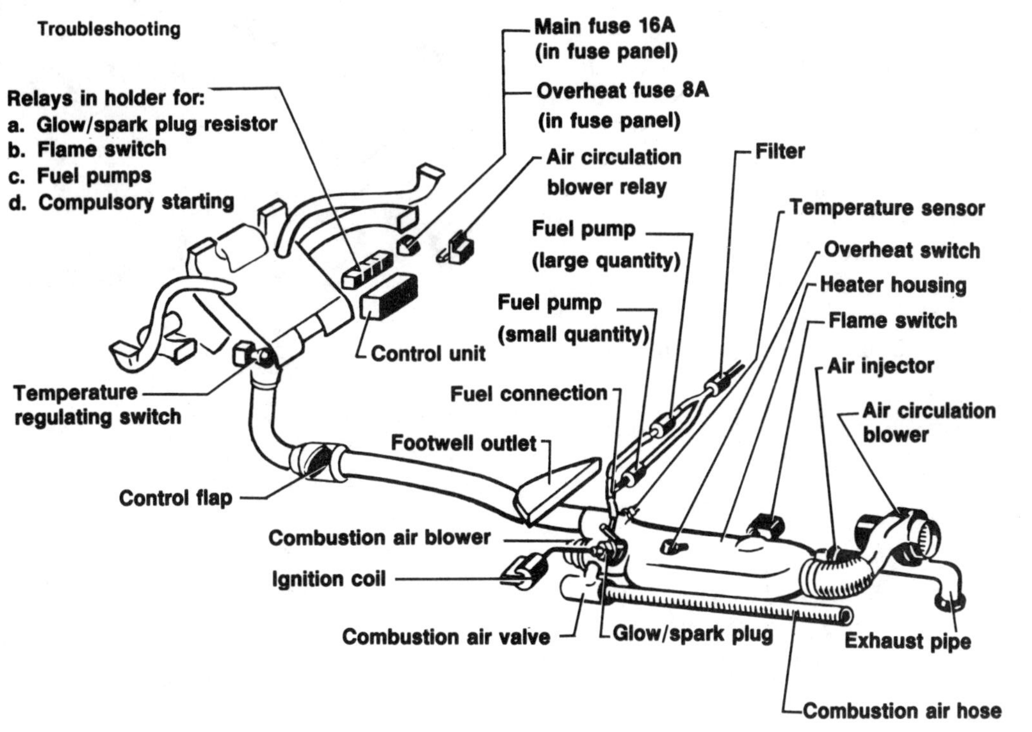

Troubleshooting

Relays in holder for:
a. Glow/spark plug resistor
b. Flame switch
c. Fuel pumps
d. Compulsory starting

Main fuse 16A (in fuse panel)
Overheat fuse 8A (in fuse panel)
Air circulation blower relay
Filter
Temperature sensor
Overheat switch
Heater housing
Flame switch
Air injector
Air circulation blower
Fuel pump (large quantity)
Fuel pump (small quantity)
Control unit
Fuel connection
Footwell outlet
Temperature regulating switch
Control flap
Combustion air blower
Ignition coil
Combustion air valve
Glow/spark plug
Exhaust pipe
Combustion air hose

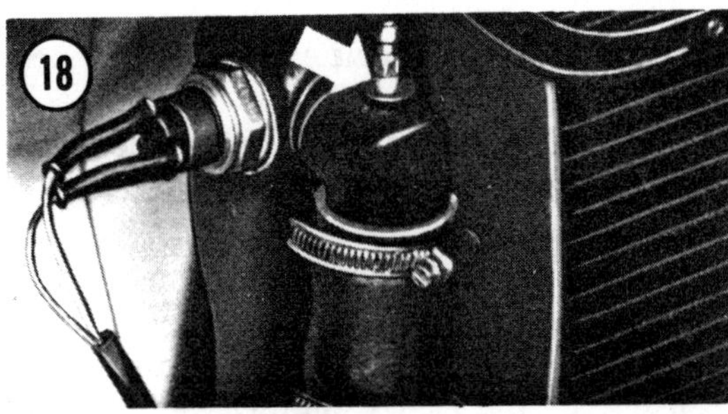

booster used with the AFC Vanagon is shown in **Figure 17**.

COOLING SYSTEM FLUSHING

The recommended coolant is a 50/50 mixture of water and ethylene glycol antifreeze. The coolant capacity is 16.9 quarts (16.0 liters). The radiator should be drained, flushed and refilled with fresh coolant every 2 years. Do not use a chemical flushing agent.

1. Coolant can stain concrete and harm plants. Park the vehicle over a gutter or similar area.
2. Place the heater temperature lever on the instrument panel in the WARM position.
3. Open the breather valve on the radiator (arrow, **Figure 18**).
3. Remove the expansion tank cap.
4. Disconnect the lower coolant hose from the water pump at the connection pipe (1, **Figure 19**).
5. Disconnect the center coolant hose from the water pump (2, **Figure 19**).
6. Disconnect the small hose between the water pump and cylinder head adapter.
7. Remove the thermostat as described in this section of the supplement. Reinstall the thermostat housing.
8. Connect a garden hose to the end of the small hose disconnected in Step 6. This does not have to be a positive fit as long as most of

the water enters the small hose. Run the water into the hose until clear water flows from the other hoses.

9. Insert the garden hose into the lower coolant hose disconnected in Step 4. Run water into the hose until clear water flows from the radiator. Repeat this step with the center coolant hose.

10. Drain and flush the coolant reservoir and the coolant expansion tank.

11. Install the thermostat. Reconnect all disconnected hoses.

12. Add the specified mix of antifreeze and water to the cooling system through the expansion tank until it remains full.

CAUTION

Remember that the cooling fan may switch on suddenly during Step 13 when the coolant warms up to approximately 200° F.

13. Start the engine and run at 2,500 rpm until coolant flowing from the breather valve contains no air bubbles. Close the breather valve.

14. Check the coolant level in the expansion tank. Top up, if necessary, and install expansion tank cap.

PRESSURE CHECK

If the cooling system requires frequent topping up, there is probably a leak somewhere in the system. Not only may coolant be lost, but the coolant recovery system cannot function properly without the correct pressure.

1. Remove the expansion tank cap.
2. Dip the cap in water and attach it to a cooling system pressure tester, using the adapters supplied with the tester.
3. Pump the pressure to 11-16 psi. If the cap fails to hold pressure in this range or if the pressure relief valve does not open, replace the cap.
4. Connect the pressure tester to the expansion tank neck.
5. Pump the system to approximately 14 psi. There should be no noticeable pressure drop in 30 seconds. If the pressure falls off, there is a leak which must be found and corrected.

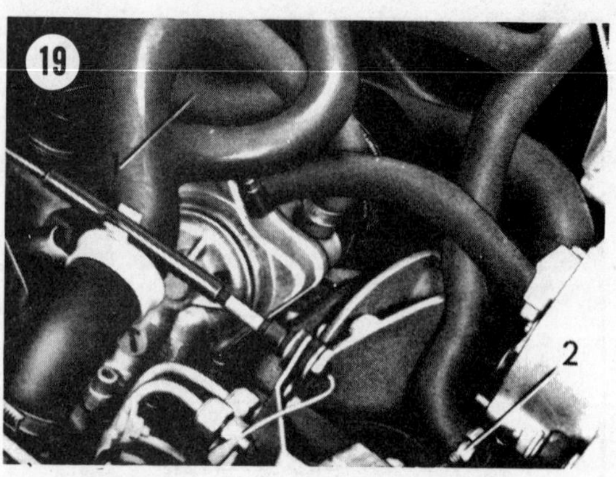

THERMOSTAT

The thermostat blocks coolant flow to the radiator when the engine is cold. As the engine warms up, the thermostat gradually opens, allowing coolant to circulate through the radiator. The thermostat should start to open at approximately 185° F (85° C) and reach a full open position at approximately 221° F (105° C). Check the thermostat when removed to determine its opening point; the heat range should be stamped on the thermostat flange.

Removal and Testing

1. Make sure the engine is cool. Disconnect the negative battery cable.
2. Place a clean container under the water pump housing. Remove the expansion tank cap and disconnect the lower coolant hose at the water pump. If the coolant which drains is clean, save it for reuse.
3. Remove the bolts holding the thermostat housing to the water pump. Remove the thermostat and seal from the housing.
4. Pour some of the coolant into a container that can be heated. Insert a 0.275 in. (7 mm) feeler gauge between the thermostat valve and its seat. Submerge the thermostat in this coolant and suspend a thermometer (**Figure 20**).

NOTE

Support the thermostat with wire so it does not touch the sides or bottom of the pan.

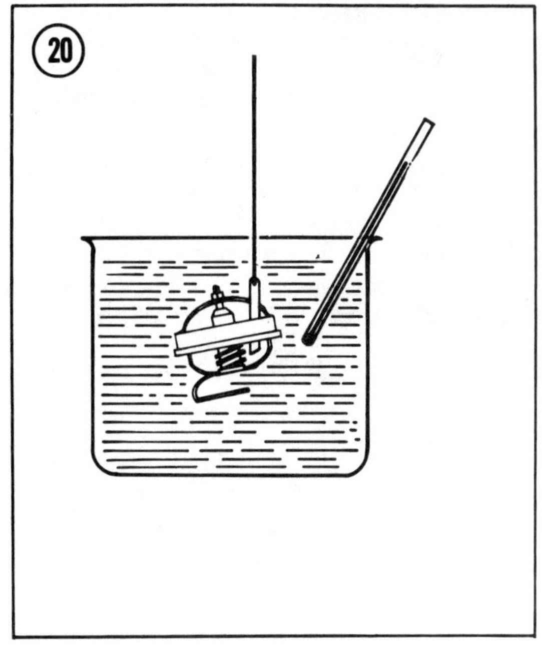

5. Heat the coolant and hold a slight tension on the feeler gauge.
6. When the valve opens and the feeler gauge slips out, read the thermometer. The temperature should be approximately 185° F (85° C).
7. If the thermostat opens at the wrong temperature or does not open at all, replace it.

Installation

1. If a new thermostat is being installed, test it as described in the preceding section.
2. Clean the mating surfaces on the thermostat and water pump housings with a putty knife to remove any contamination or other residue.
3. Install the thermostat in the housing. Install the housing seal.
4. Install the housing to the water pump. Tighten the housing screws to 7 ft.-lb. (10 N•m).
5. Reconnect the coolant hose to the water pump housing and tighten the hose clamp snugly.
6. Reinstall the drained coolant and install the expansion tank cap.
7. Reconnect the negative battery cable.
8. Start the engine and check for leaks.

WATER PUMP DRIVE BELT

Since drive belt tension affects engine cooling, it is important that it be properly adjusted. When correct, the belt should deflect about 3/16-3/8 in. (5-10 mm) when pressed midway between the crankshaft and water pump pulleys.

To adjust or replace the belt, hold a screwdriver in the pulley cutout to keep it from moving. Remove the 3 pulley retaining capscrews with washers and pulley cover plate. If installing a new belt, remove the old belt, install the new one and then the pulley cover plate. Tighten the cover plate capscrews to 14 ft.-lb. (20 N•m).

Belt tension is adjusted by varying the number of shims between the pulley halves. Decreasing the number tightens the belt; increasing the number loosens the belt. Store extra shims (if any) on the outside of the pulley cover plate.

Adjust belt tension carefully. If it is too loose, the engine can overheat. If too tight, belt life will be low and the water pump bearings will wear prematurely.

RADIATOR

Removal/Installation

Refer to **Figure 15** for this procedure.

CAUTION

Radiatiors may be manufactured with either brass or plastic end tanks. Use care in removing a hose from a plastic end tank fitting, as excessive pressure can crack or otherwise damage the plastic hose fitting.

1. Make sure the engine is cool enough to touch comfortably.
2. Coolant can stain concrete and harm plants. Park the vehicle over a gutter or similar area. Place a clean container under the radiator hose fittings.
3. Disconnect the hose at the breather valve. Disconnect the hose at the lower radiator fitting.
4. Remove the expansion tank cap to promote faster draining.
5. Disconnect the coolant fan motor plug.
6. Disconnect the 2 thermoswitch leads.

7. Remove the mounting nuts at the bottom of the radiator.
8. Loosen the upper and lower shroud mounting screws. Pull the shroud away from the radiator.
9. Remove the air duct from the radiator end tank.
10. Remove the upper radiator mounting nuts. Remove the radiator.
11. Installation is the reverse of removal. Tighten the lower shroud mounting fasteners to 11 ft.-lb. (15 N•m). Tighten all other fasteners to 7 ft.-lb. (10 N•m).

WATER PUMP

A water pump may warn of impending failure by making noise. If the seal is defective, coolant may leak through the bleed hole behind the pump pulley.

The water pump is a 2-piece unit, with a replaceable cover attached to the main pump body. The main body should not require service or replacement. The pump cover contains the hub, shaft and impeller. It is available as a separate replacement item if the water pump fails.

Removal/Installation

1. Drain the cooling system as described in this section of the supplement.
2. Remove the water pump pulley as described in this section of the supplement.
3. Disconnect the 3 coolant hoses from the water pump.
4. Remove the engine support-to-water pump housing bolt.
5. Remove the water pump mounting bolts. Lift the pump housing up and out of the engine compartment.
6. Check the block mounting pad and remove the large O-ring seal if it did not come off with the pump.
7. Installation is the reverse of removal. Use a new seal between the water pump and block; make sure it is properly seated. Tighten the support-to-housing bolt to 14 ft.-lb. (20 N•m). Tighten the pump mounting bolts to 16 ft.-lb. (22 N•m).

Pump Cover Replacement

1. Remove the pump-to-body screws.
2. Separate the pump from the body by tapping gently with a plastic mallet.
3. Clean any gasket residue from the pump body. Clean the O-ring groove.
4. Install a new gasket on the pump body with waterproof gasket sealant.
5. Position the cover to the body. Install and tighten the screws to 14 ft.-lb. (20 N•m).

THERMOSWITCH REPLACEMENT

Two thermoswitches are installed in the radiator end tank. The upper switch (Stage I) turns the cooling fan on at approximately 200-208° F (93-98° C) and off at approximately 190-200° F (88-93° C). The lower switch (Stage II) turns the cooling fan off at approximately 203-212° F (95-100° C) and on at approximately 212-221° F (100-105° C).

1. Drain the coolant as described in this supplement.
2. Disconnect the thermoswitch electrical lead.
3. Carefully unscrew the thermoswitch from the radiator end tank.
4. Installation is the reverse of removal. Be sure to use a new seal when installing the thermoswitch. Tighten the thermoswitch to 22 ft.-lb. (30 N•m).

ELECTRIC COOLING FAN

The 2-stage cooling fan is mounted inside the radiator shroud. When the coolant reaches approximately 200-208° F (93-98° C), the Stage I thermoswitch turns the fan on. At approximately 203-212° F (95-100° C), the Stage II thermoswitch turns the fan off. If coolant temperature exceeds this range, the Stage II thermoswitch will turn the fan on again.

Fan Motor Replacement

1. Disconnect the negative battery cable. Disconnect the electrical connector plug at the fan.
2. Unbolt the shroud from the radiator.
3. Remove the shroud and fan assembly.

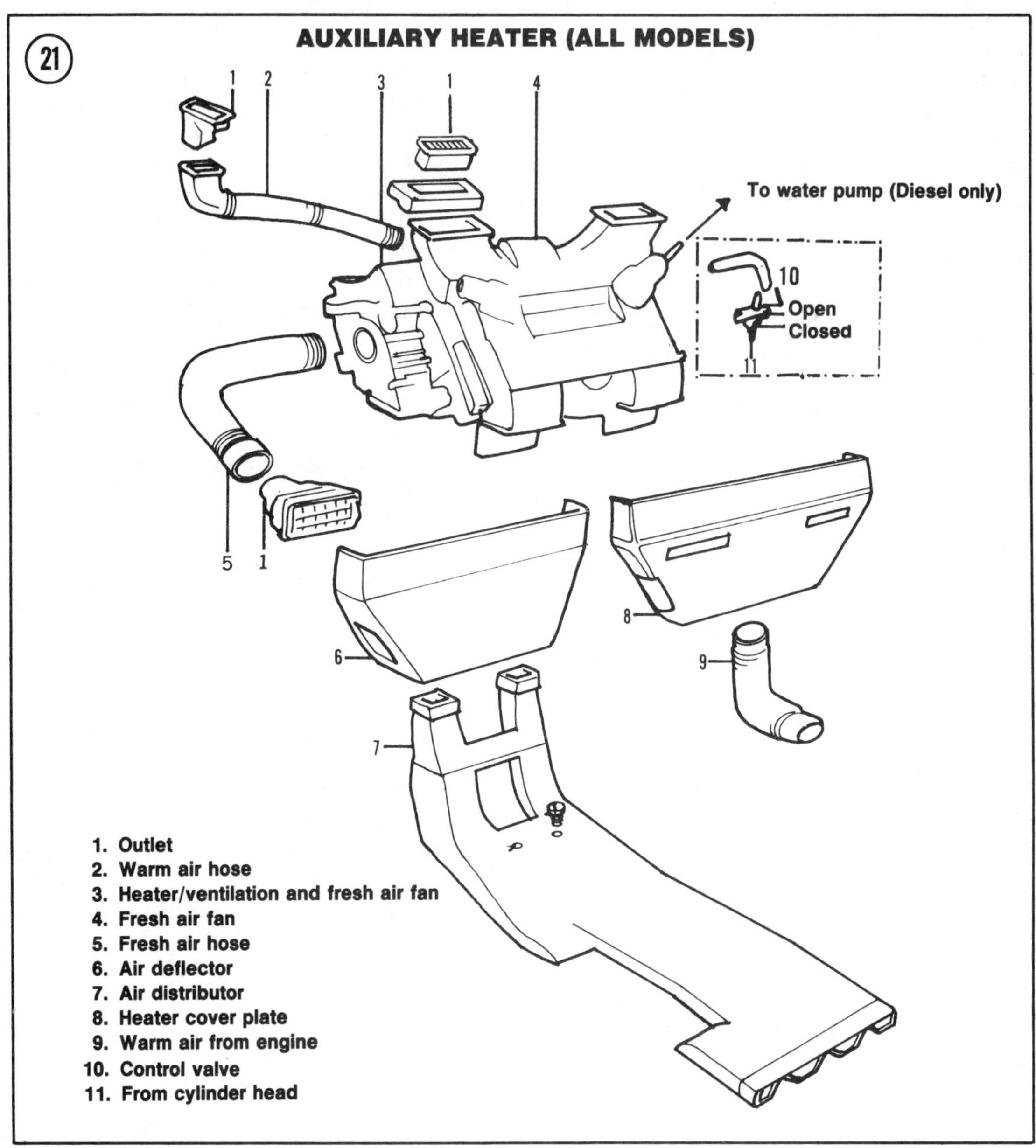

4. Remove the 3 nuts and washers from the rear of the fan motor. Separate the fan motor from the shroud.
5. Installation is the reverse of removal. Tighten the fan mounting nuts to 7 ft.-lb. (10 N•m).

HEATER

Heater and ventilation chamber design is modified for 1982. System operation, service and cable adjustment procedures remain essentially the same as earlier models. **Figure 21** shows the new design for both AFC and diesel vehicles.

An auxiliary heater similar to that used on AFC models is optional with the diesel Vanagon. While the system components, operation and service procedures remain essentially the same, the electrical circuitry has been changed. A wiring diagram for the auxiliary heater is included at the end of the book.

CHAPTER SIX

FUEL, EXHAUST AND EMISSION CONTROL SYSTEMS

EXHAUST GAS RECIRCULATION (EGR) SYSTEM

All 1981-on AFC Vanagons first sold in California are equipped with the modified EGR system shown in **Figure 22**.

EXHAUST SYSTEM (DIESEL ENGINE)

The exhaust system used with the diesel engine is shown in **Figure 23**. The exhaust system can be replaced without removing the engine. All system fasteners are torqued to 18 ft.-lb. (25 N•m) except the exhaust pipe to manifold flange nuts, which should be tightened to 14 ft.-lb. (20 N•m). Replace all self-locking nuts with new nuts when servicing the exhaust system.

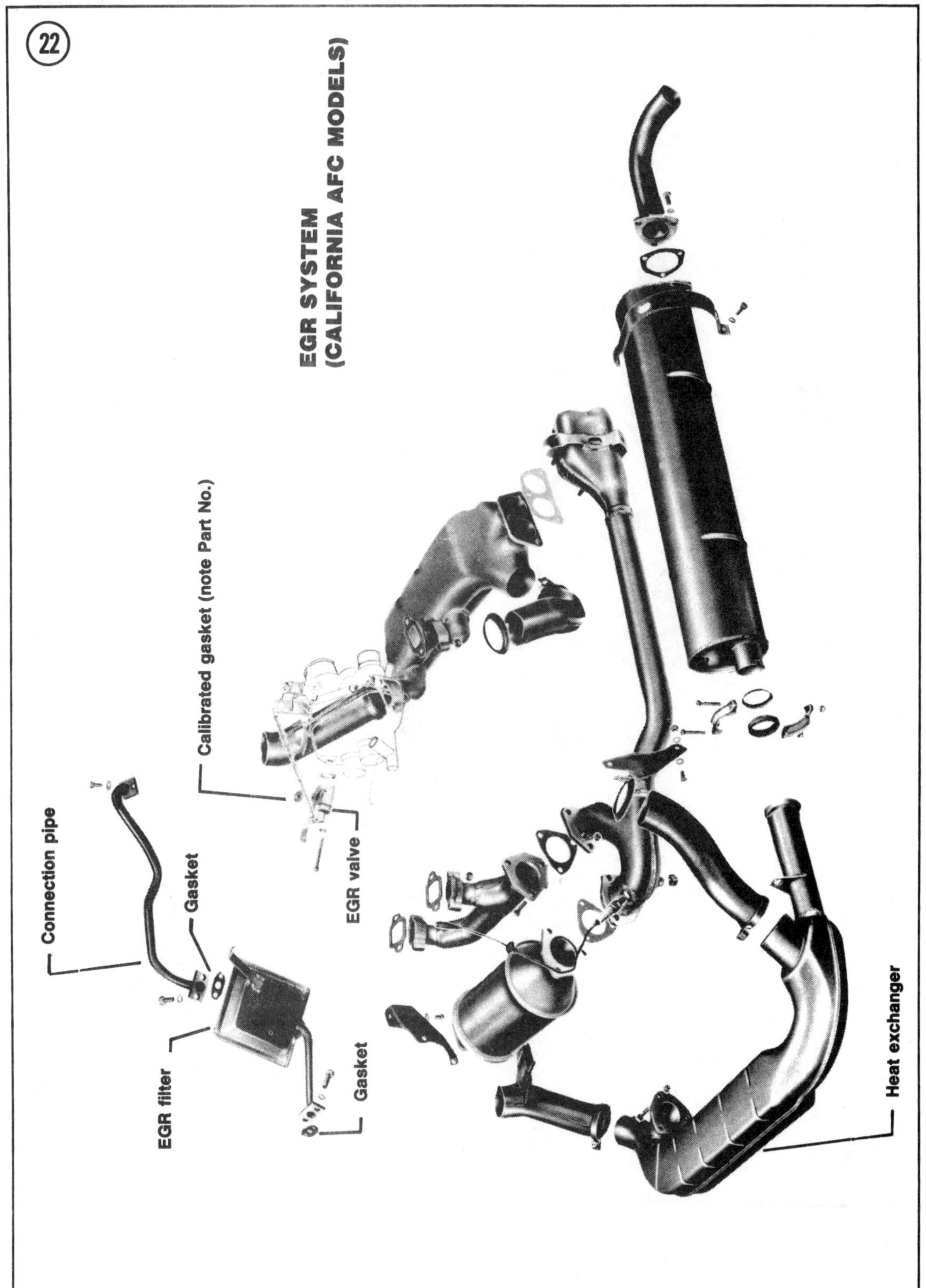
22
EGR SYSTEM
(CALIFORNIA AFC MODELS)
Connection pipe
Gasket
EGR filter
Gasket
Calibrated gasket (note Part No.)
EGR valve
Heat exchanger

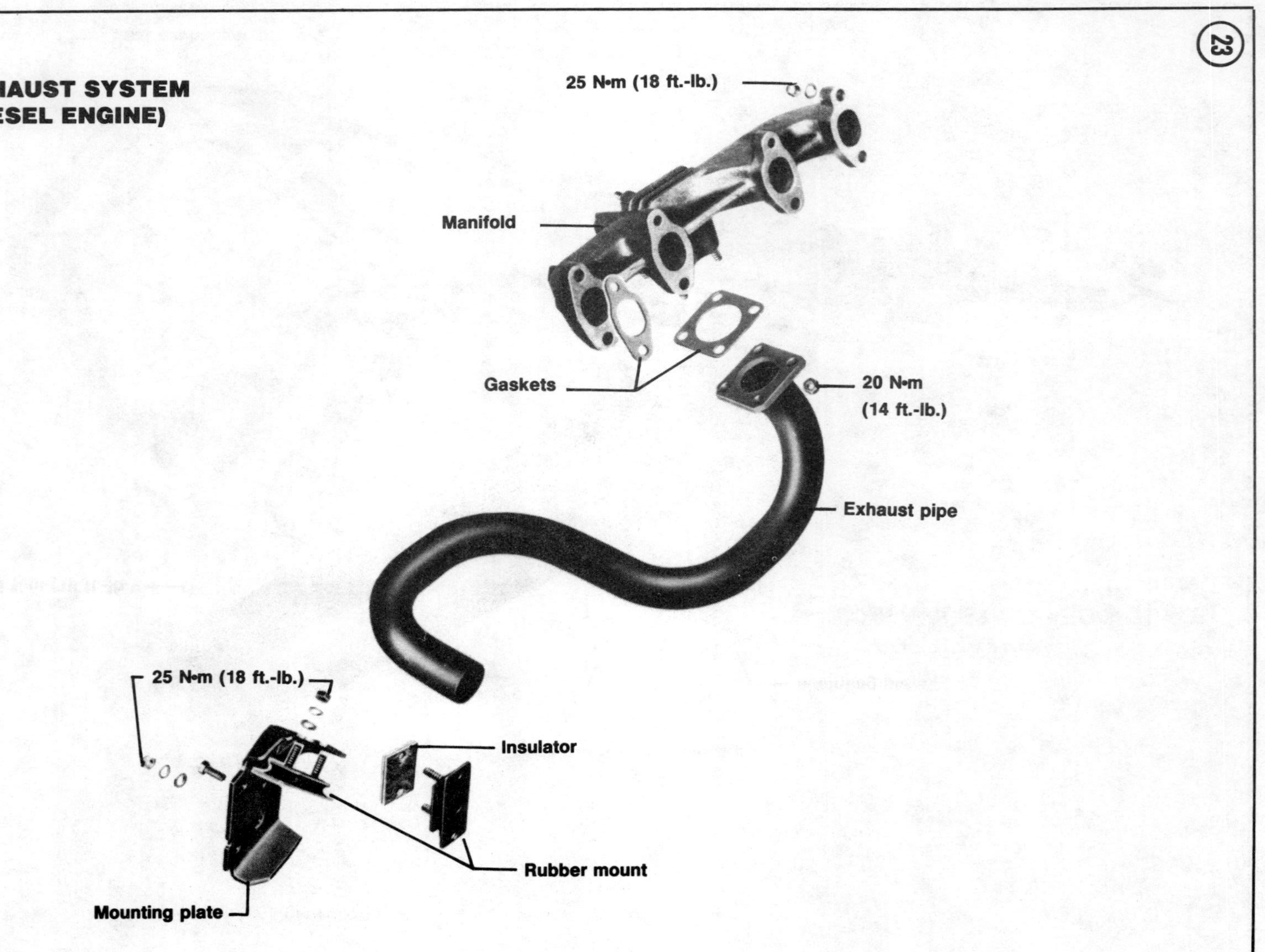
23
EXHAUST SYSTEM
(DIESEL ENGINE)
25 N•m (18 ft.-lb.)
Manifold
Gaskets
20 N•m
(14 ft.-lb.)
Exhaust pipe
25 N•m (18 ft.-lb.)
Insulator
Rubber mount
Mounting plate

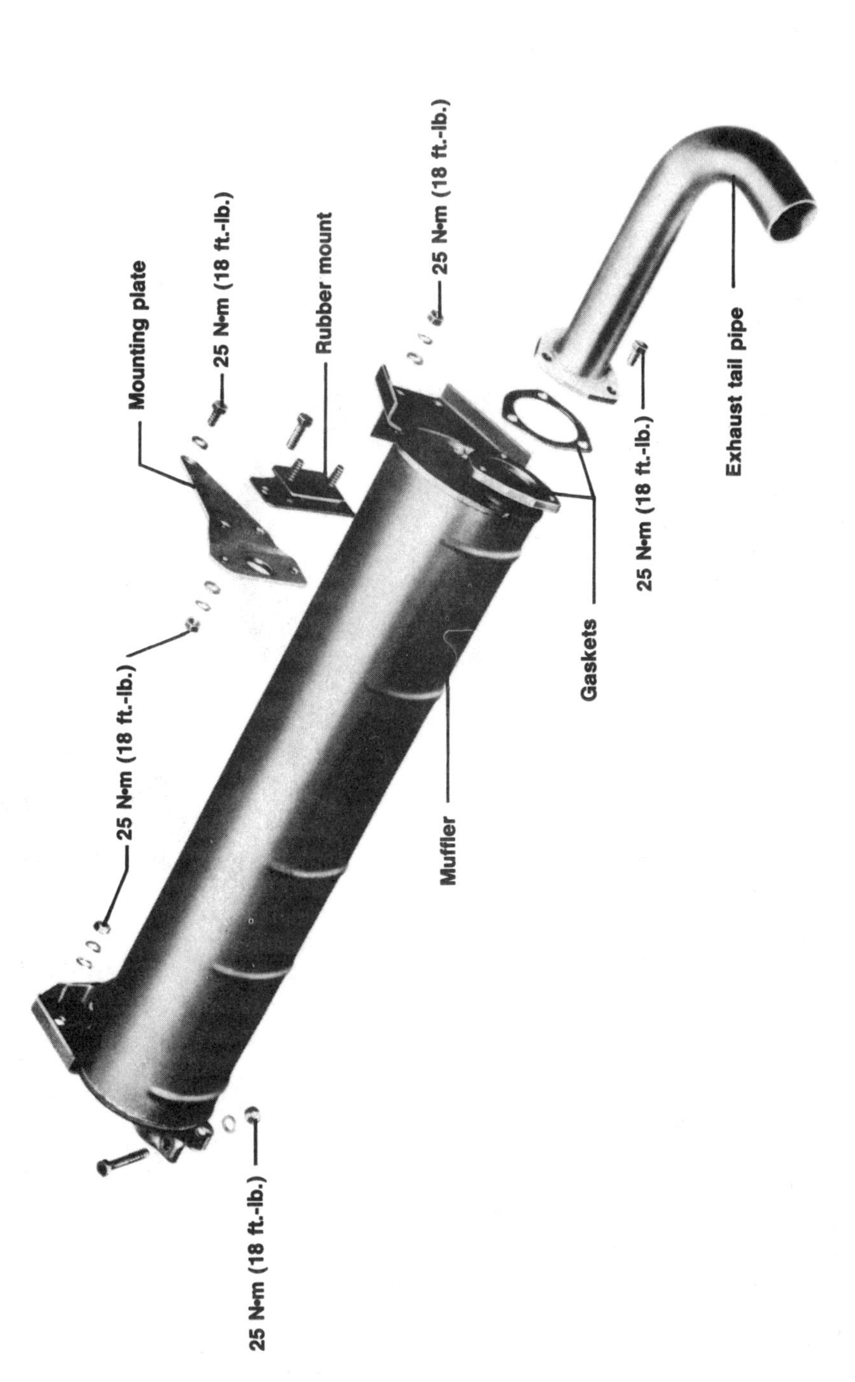
Mounting plate
25 N•m (18 ft.-lb.)
Rubber mount
25 N•m (18 ft.-lb.)
Exhaust tail pipe
25 N•m (18 ft.-lb.)
Gaskets
25 N•m (18 ft.-lb.)
Muffler
25 N•m (18 ft.-lb.)

CHAPTER EIGHT

CLUTCH, TRANSAXLE AND DRIVE AXLES

CLUTCH

The pressure plate spring fingers have been increased in length on the 9 in. (228 mm) clutch. As a result of this change, dimension a in **Figure 24** has decreased from 2 3/16 in. (55 mm) to 1 13/16 in. (46 mm).

The throw-out or release bearing installed in production with this new pressure plate has a 1 13/16 in. (46 mm) contact surface (**Figure 25**). To minimize possible problems in bearing selection, the older bearing with a contact surface of 2 3/16 in. (55 mm) is retained as the only replacement, since it will work with either pressure plate.

When an engine is exchanged, make sure the proper release bearing is used. Do not use a narrow contact surface bearing with the short-finger pressure plate.

MANUAL TRANSAXLE

Main Shaft Oil Seal Replacement

The service procedure in Chapter Eight of the basic book remains unchanged, but VW now specifies the use of seal installation tools part No. VW 244b and VW 454 as shown in **Figure 26**.

Shift Linkage Adjustment

A modified shift housing is used after chassis No. BH 25 137 155. Adjustment procedure remains the same as previous models, but a gap of 7/8 in. (22 mm) should exist at dimension a, **Figure 27**.

If 1st gear jams are encountered on vehicles up to chassis No. BH 25 137 155, recheck the adjustment. If the adjustment is correct (3/4 in. or 19 mm), install the new shift mechanism housing (VW part No. 251 711 107 B) and adjust dimension a, **Figure 27**, to 7/8 in. (22 mm).

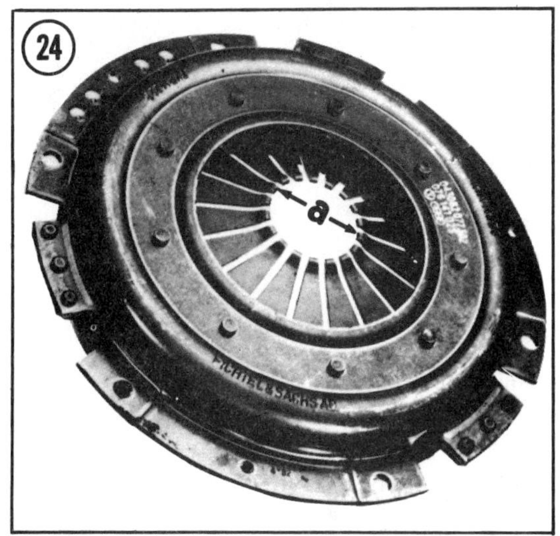
24
a
FICHTEL & SACHS AG

26
VW244b
VW 454

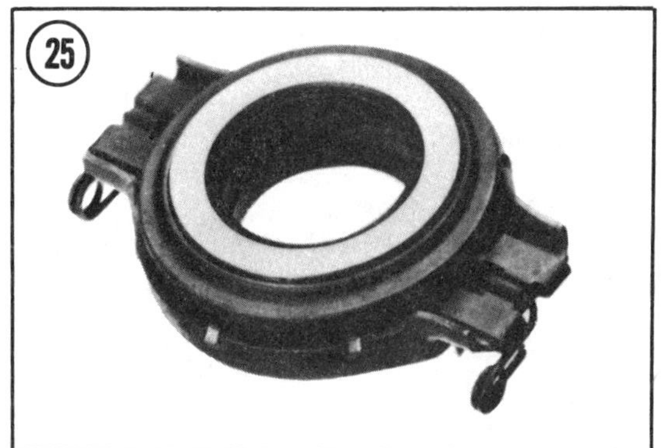
25

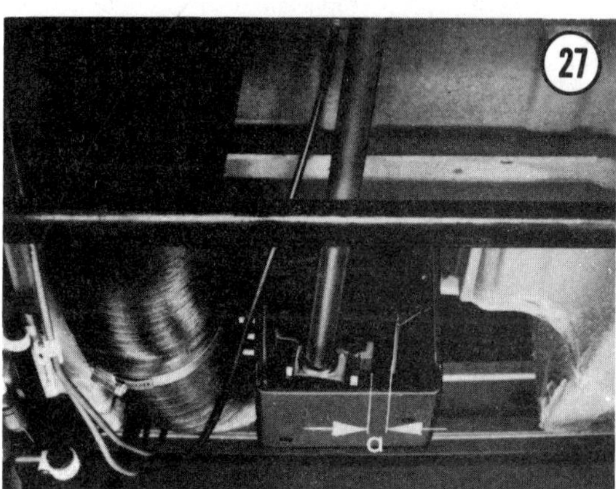
27
a

INDEX

V

W

SYMBOLS USED IN CURRENT FLOW DIAGRAMS

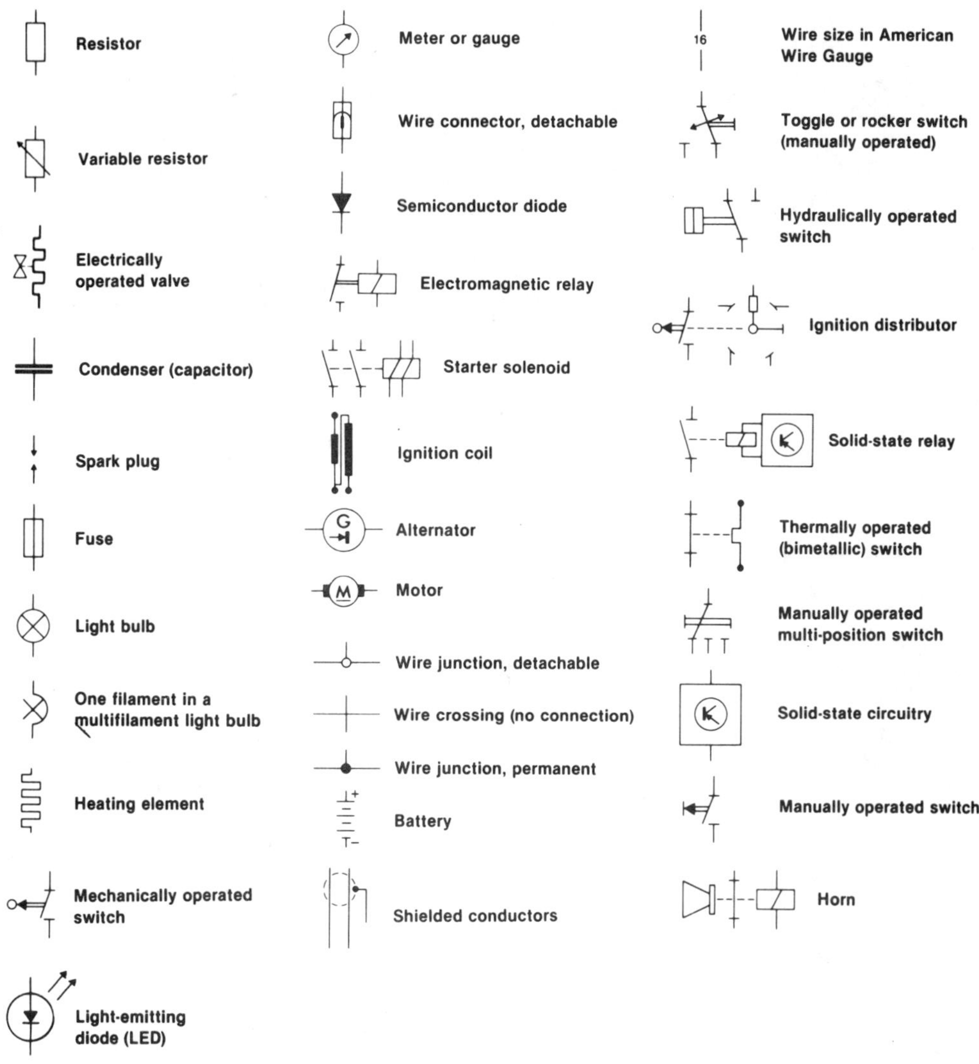

Color Code

Black — BK
Brown — BR
Clear — CL
Red — R
Yellow — Y
Green — G
Light Green — LT. G
Blue — BL
Violet — V
Gray — GY
White — W

Wire Connector Code

T1 — single
T2 — double
T3 — 3-point
T4 — 4-point
T6 — 6-point
T8 — 8-point
T12 — 12-point
T14 — 14-point

HOW TO READ WIRING DIAGRAMS

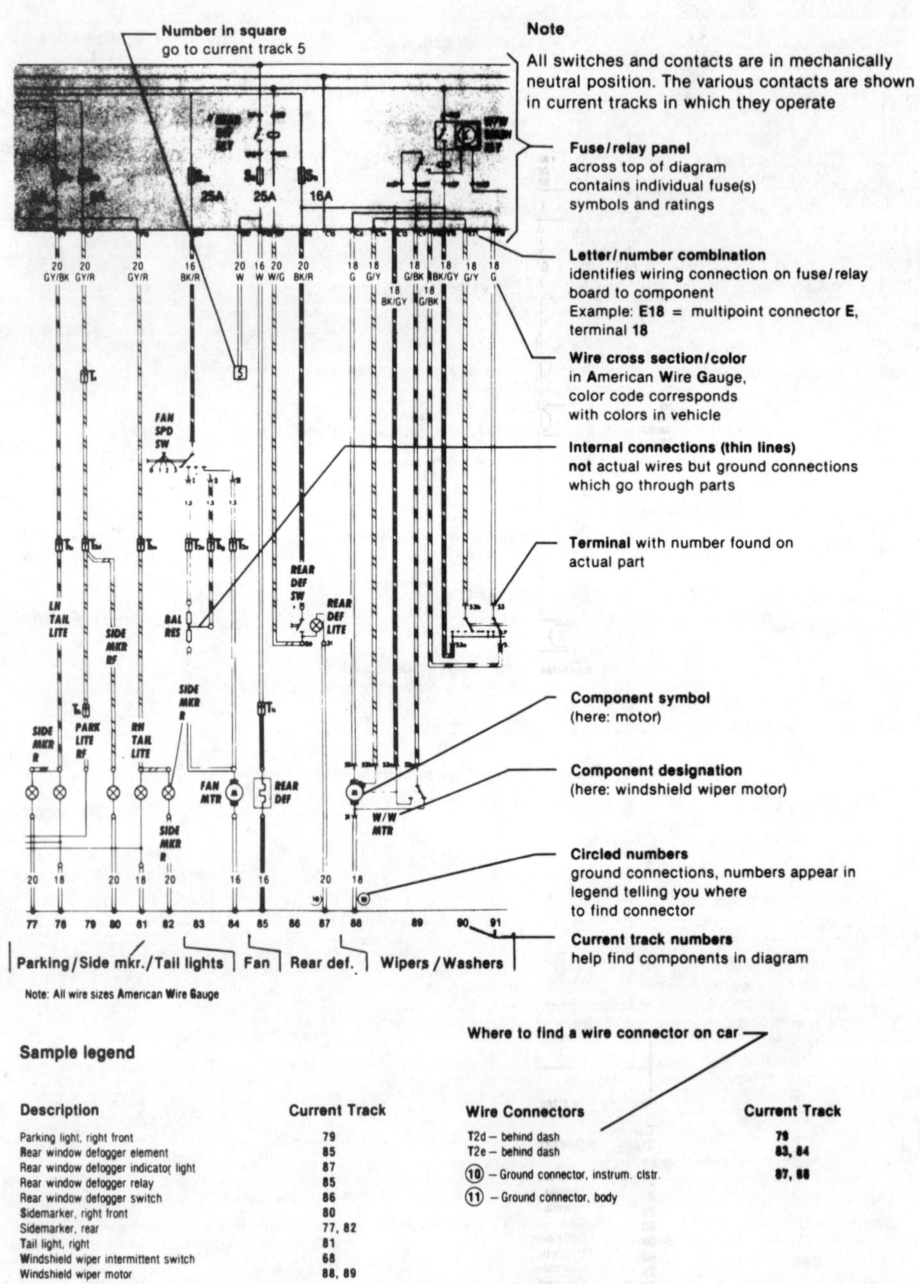

Note: All wire sizes American Wire Gauge

Where to find a wire connector on car

Sample legend

Description	Current Track
Parking light, right front	79
Rear window defogger element	85
Rear window defogger indicator light	87
Rear window defogger relay	85
Rear window defogger switch	86
Sidemarker, right front	80
Sidemarker, rear	77, 82
Tail light, right	81
Windshield wiper intermittent switch	68
Windshield wiper motor	88, 89

Wire Connectors	Current Track
T2d – behind dash	79
T2e – behind dash	83, 84
(10) – Ground connector, instrum. clstr.	87, 88
(11) – Ground connector, body	

1980-ON GASOLINE

(1 of 6)

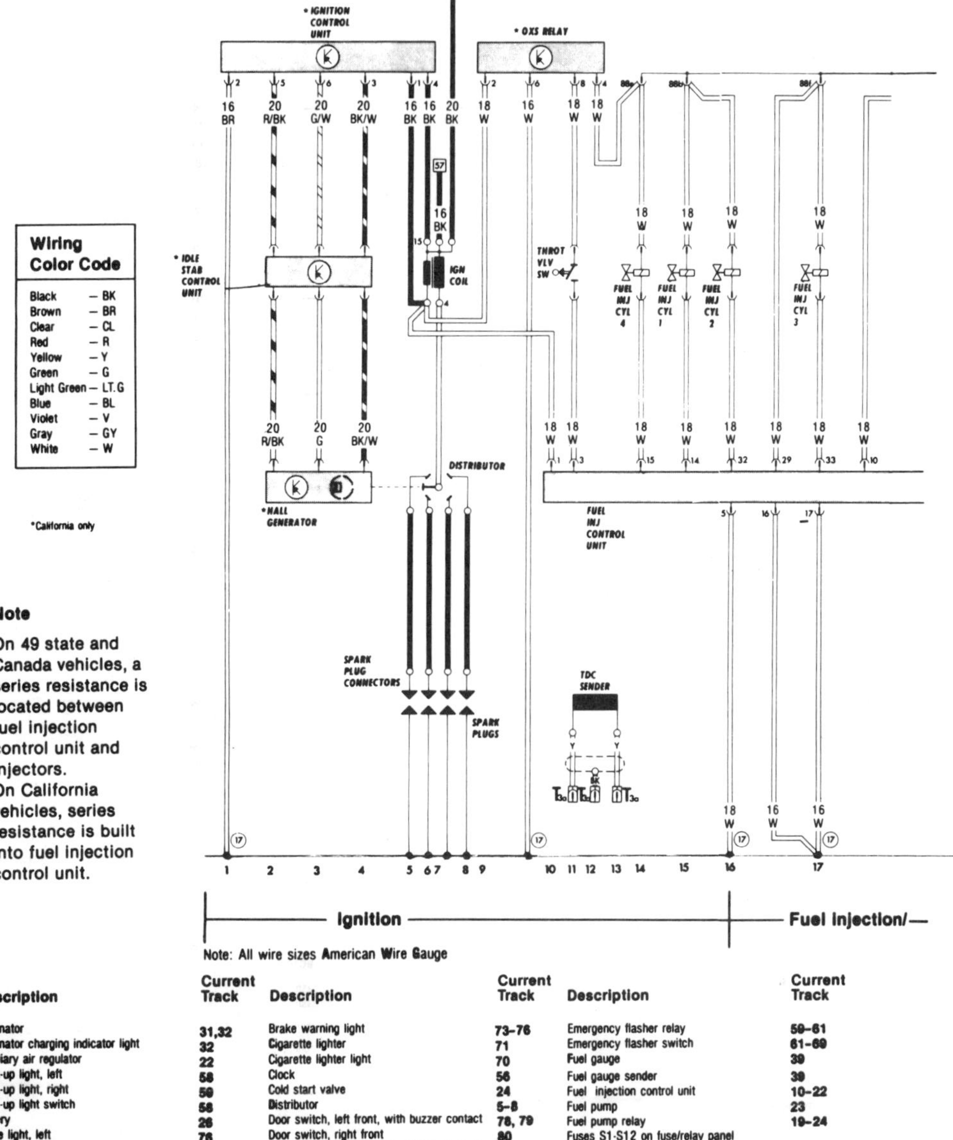

Note

On 49 state and Canada vehicles, a series resistance is located between fuel injection control unit and injectors. On California vehicles, series resistance is built into fuel injection control unit.

Note: All wire sizes American Wire Gauge

Description	Current Track	Description	Current Track	Description	Current Track
Alternator	31,32	Brake warning light	73-76	Emergency flasher relay	59-61
Alternator charging indicator light	32	Cigarette lighter	71	Emergency flasher switch	61-69
Auxiliary air regulator	22	Cigarette lighter light	70	Fuel gauge	39
Back-up light, left	58	Clock	56	Fuel gauge sender	39
Back-up light, right	59	Cold start valve	24	Fuel injection control unit	10-22
Back-up light switch	58	Distributor	5-8	Fuel pump	23
Battery	26	Door switch, left front, with buzzer contact	78, 79	Fuel pump relay	19-24
Brake light, left	76	Door switch, right front	80	Fuses S1-S12 on fuse/relay panel (under dash)	
Brake light, right	75	Elapsed mileage switch for OXS indicator*	33, 34		
Brake light switch	75, 76	Emergency flasher indicator light	67	Hall generator*	2-4

*California only

14

1980-ON GASOLINE

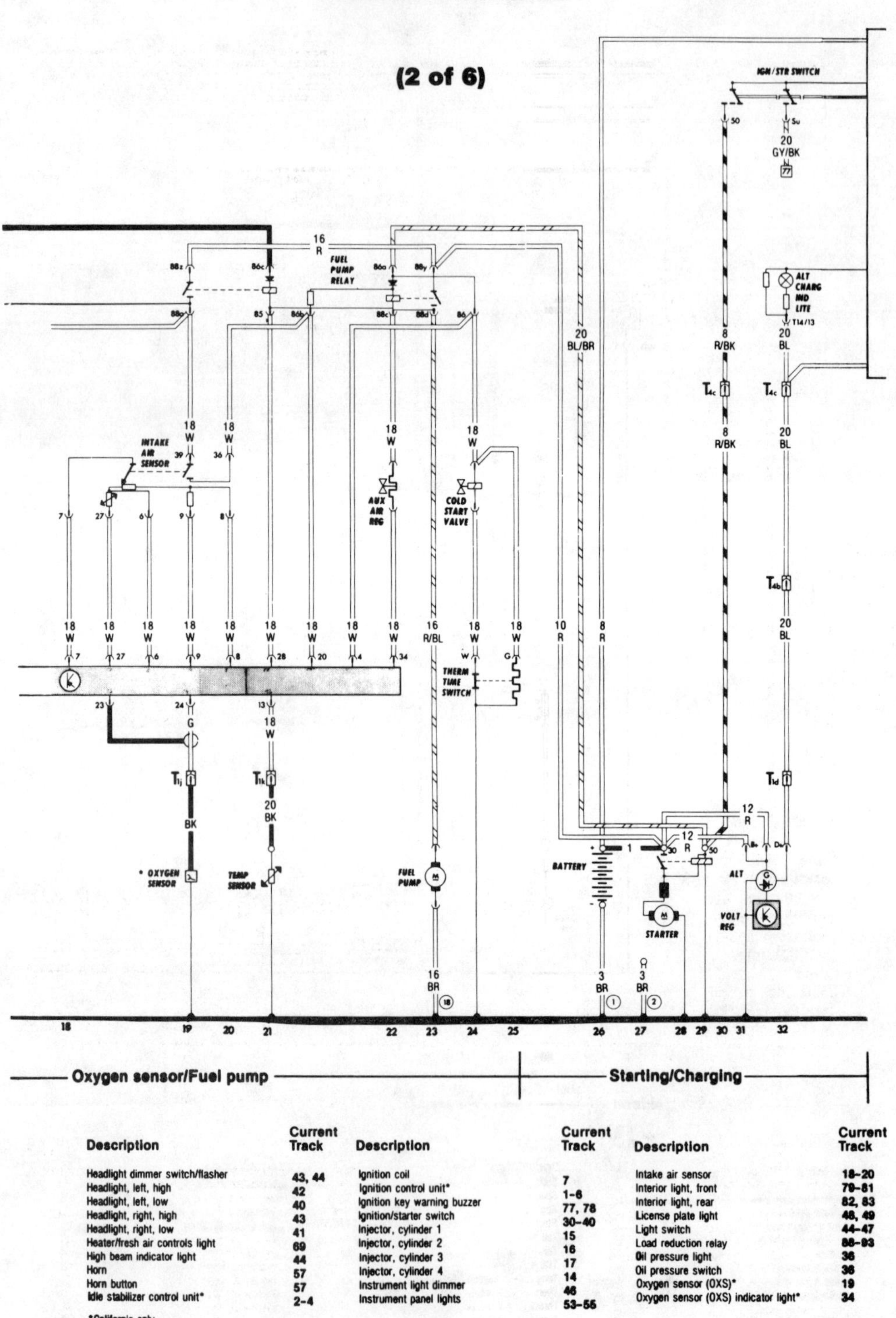

Description	Current Track	Description	Current Track	Description	Current Track
Headlight dimmer switch/flasher	43, 44	Ignition coil	7	Intake air sensor	18–20
Headlight, left, high	42	Ignition control unit*	1–6	Interior light, front	79–81
Headlight, left, low	40	Ignition key warning buzzer	77, 78	Interior light, rear	82, 83
Headlight, right, high	43	Ignition/starter switch	30–40	License plate light	48, 49
Headlight, right, low	41	Injector, cylinder 1	15	Light switch	44–47
Heater/fresh air controls light	69	Injector, cylinder 2	16	Load reduction relay	88–93
High beam indicator light	44	Injector, cylinder 3	17	Oil pressure light	36
Horn	57	Injector, cylinder 4	14	Oil pressure switch	36
Horn button	57	Instrument light dimmer	46	Oxygen sensor (OXS)*	19
Idle stabilizer control unit*	2–4	Instrument panel lights	53–55	Oxygen sensor (OXS) indicator light*	34

*California only

1980-ON GASOLINE

(3 of 6)

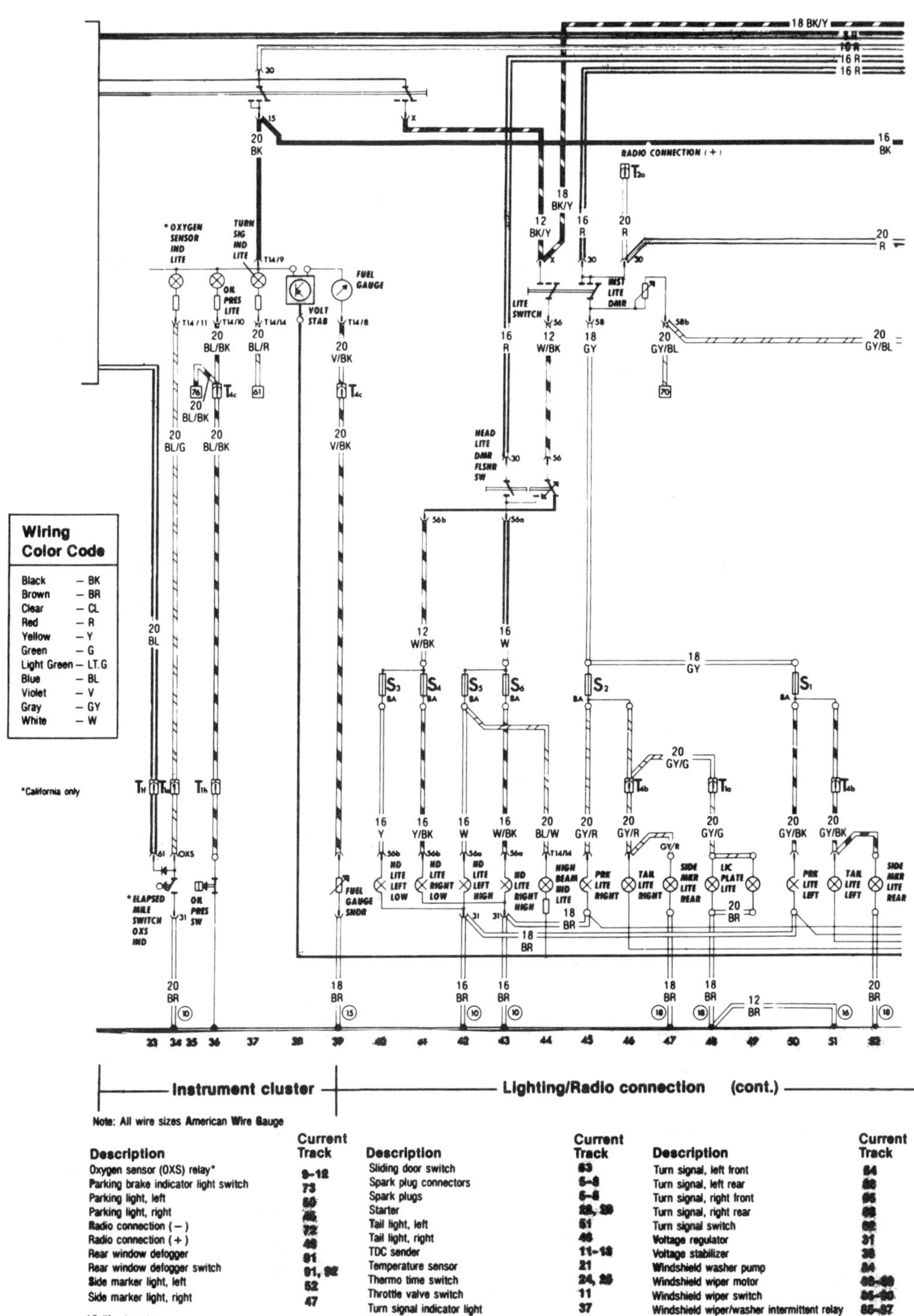

Note: All wire sizes American Wire Gauge

Description	Current Track	Description	Current Track	Description	Current Track
Oxygen sensor (OXS) relay*	9–12	Sliding door switch	63	Turn signal, left front	64
Parking brake indicator light switch	73	Spark plug connectors	5–8	Turn signal, left rear	68
Parking light, left	50	Spark plugs	5–8	Turn signal, right front	66
Parking light, right	45	Starter	28, 29	Turn signal, right rear	69
Radio connection (–)	72	Tail light, left	51	Turn signal switch	62
Radio connection (+)	46	Tail light, right	46	Voltage regulator	31
Rear window defogger	91	TDC sender	11–13	Voltage stabilizer	38
Rear window defogger switch	91, 92	Temperature sensor	21	Windshield washer pump	84
Side marker light, left	52	Thermo time switch	24, 25	Windshield wiper motor	88–90
Side marker light, right	47	Throttle valve switch	11	Windshield wiper switch	86–90
		Turn signal indicator light	37	Windshield wiper/washer intermittent relay	85–87

*California only

1980-ON GASOLINE

(4 of 6)

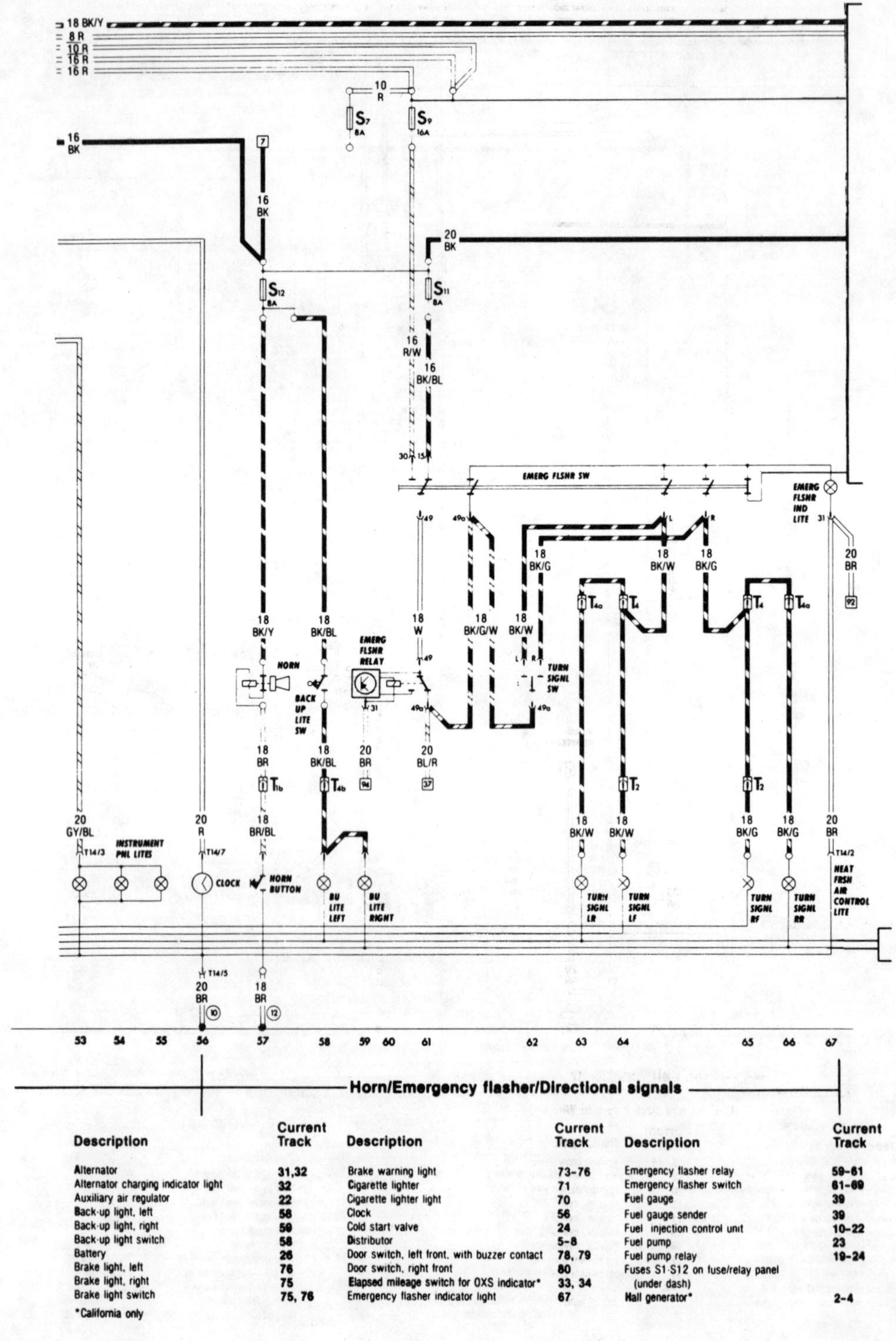

Horn/Emergency flasher/Directional signals

Description	Current Track	Description	Current Track	Description	Current Track
Alternator	31,32	Brake warning light	73-76	Emergency flasher relay	59-61
Alternator charging indicator light	32	Cigarette lighter	71	Emergency flasher switch	61-69
Auxiliary air regulator	22	Cigarette lighter light	70	Fuel gauge	39
Back-up light, left	58	Clock	56	Fuel gauge sender	39
Back-up light, right	59	Cold start valve	24	Fuel injection control unit	10-22
Back-up light switch	58	Distributor	5-8	Fuel pump	23
Battery	26	Door switch, left front, with buzzer contact	78, 79	Fuel pump relay	19-24
Brake light, left	76	Door switch, right front	80	Fuses S1-S12 on fuse/relay panel (under dash)	
Brake light, right	75	Elapsed mileage switch for OXS indicator*	33, 34		
Brake light switch	75, 76	Emergency flasher indicator light	67	Hall generator*	2-4

*California only

1980-ON GASOLINE

(5 of 6)

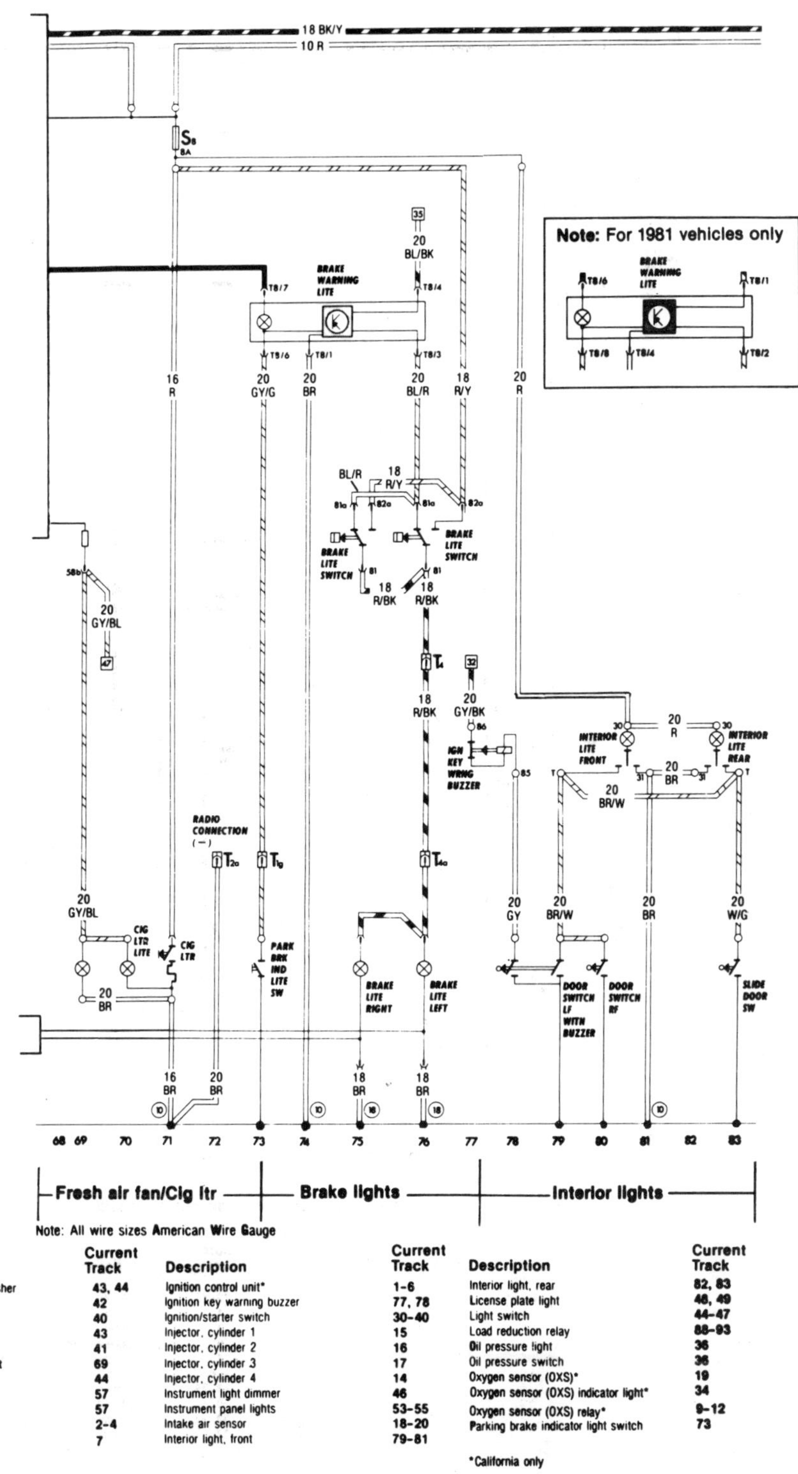

Note: All wire sizes American Wire Gauge

Description	Current Track	Description	Current Track	Description	Current Track
Headlight dimmer switch/flasher	43, 44	Ignition control unit*	1-6	Interior light, rear	82, 83
Headlight, left, high	42	Ignition key warning buzzer	77, 78	License plate light	48, 49
Headlight, left, low	40	Ignition/starter switch	30-40	Light switch	44-47
Headlight, right, high	43	Injector, cylinder 1	15	Load reduction relay	88-93
Headlight, right, low	41	Injector, cylinder 2	16	Oil pressure light	36
Heater/fresh air controls light	69	Injector, cylinder 3	17	Oil pressure switch	36
High beam indicator light	44	Injector, cylinder 4	14	Oxygen sensor (OXS)*	19
Horn	57	Instrument light dimmer	46	Oxygen sensor (OXS) indicator light*	34
Horn button	57	Instrument panel lights	53-55	Oxygen sensor (OXS) relay*	9-12
Idle stabilizer control unit*	2-4	Intake air sensor	18-20	Parking brake indicator light switch	73
Ignition coil	7	Interior light, front	79-81		

*California only

14

1980-ON GASOLINE

(6 of 6)

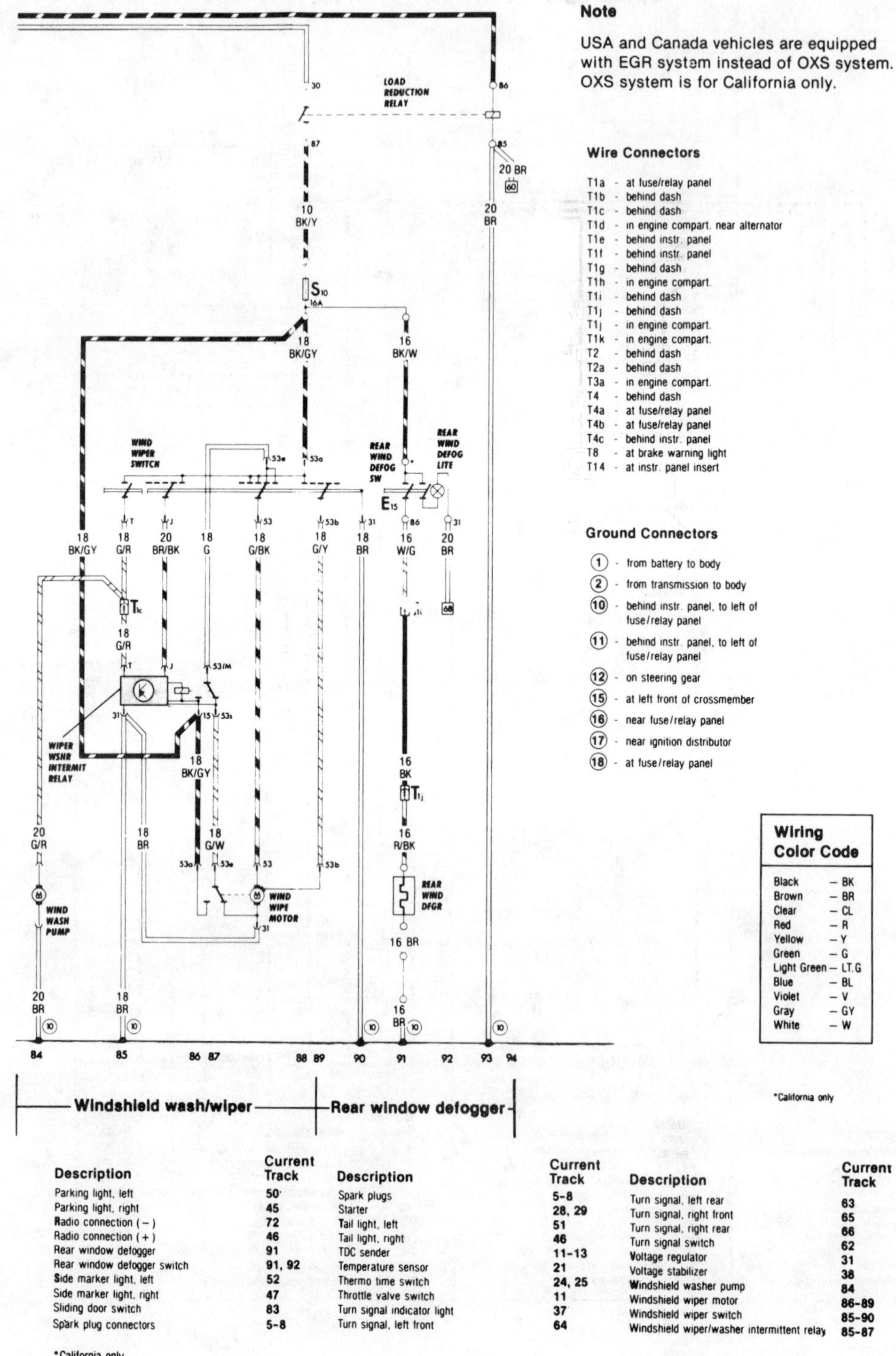

Note

USA and Canada vehicles are equipped with EGR system instead of OXS system. OXS system is for California only.

Wire Connectors

- T1a - at fuse/relay panel
- T1b - behind dash
- T1c - behind dash
- T1d - in engine compart. near alternator
- T1e - behind instr. panel
- T1f - behind instr. panel
- T1g - behind dash
- T1h - in engine compart.
- T1i - behind dash
- T1j - behind dash
- T1j - in engine compart.
- T1k - in engine compart.
- T2 - behind dash
- T2a - behind dash
- T3a - in engine compart.
- T4 - behind dash
- T4a - at fuse/relay panel
- T4b - at fuse/relay panel
- T4c - behind instr. panel
- T8 - at brake warning light
- T14 - at instr. panel insert

Ground Connectors

- (1) - from battery to body
- (2) - from transmission to body
- (10) - behind instr. panel, to left of fuse/relay panel
- (11) - behind instr. panel, to left of fuse/relay panel
- (12) - on steering gear
- (15) - at left front of crossmember
- (16) - near fuse/relay panel
- (17) - near ignition distributor
- (18) - at fuse/relay panel

Wiring Color Code

Color	Code
Black	BK
Brown	BR
Clear	CL
Red	R
Yellow	Y
Green	G
Light Green	LT.G
Blue	BL
Violet	V
Gray	GY
White	W

*California only

Description	Current Track	Description	Current Track	Description	Current Track
Parking light, left	50	Spark plugs	5-8	Turn signal, left rear	63
Parking light, right	45	Starter	28, 29	Turn signal, right front	65
Radio connection (−)	72	Tail light, left	51	Turn signal, right rear	66
Radio connection (+)	46	Tail light, right	46	Turn signal switch	62
Rear window defogger	91	TDC sender	11-13	Voltage regulator	31
Rear window defogger switch	91, 92	Temperature sensor	21	Voltage stabilizer	38
Side marker light, left	52	Thermo time switch	24, 25	Windshield washer pump	84
Side marker light, right	47	Throttle valve switch	11	Windshield wiper motor	86-89
Sliding door switch	83	Turn signal indicator light	37	Windshield wiper switch	85-90
Spark plug connectors	5-8	Turn signal, left front	64	Windshield wiper/washer intermittent relay	85-87

*California only

1980-1981 AUXILIARY HEATER

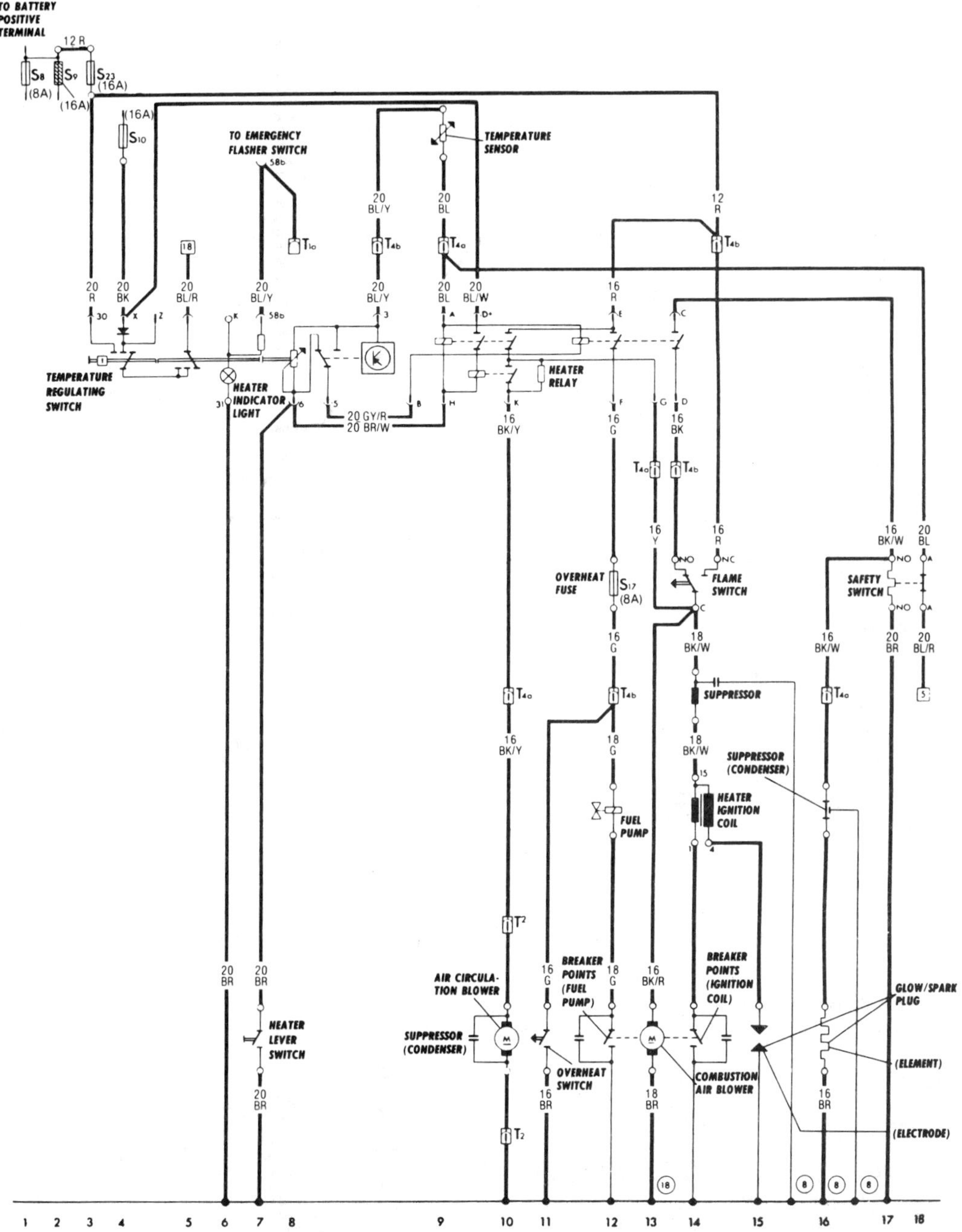

1980-ON GASOLINE

CAMPER WIRING

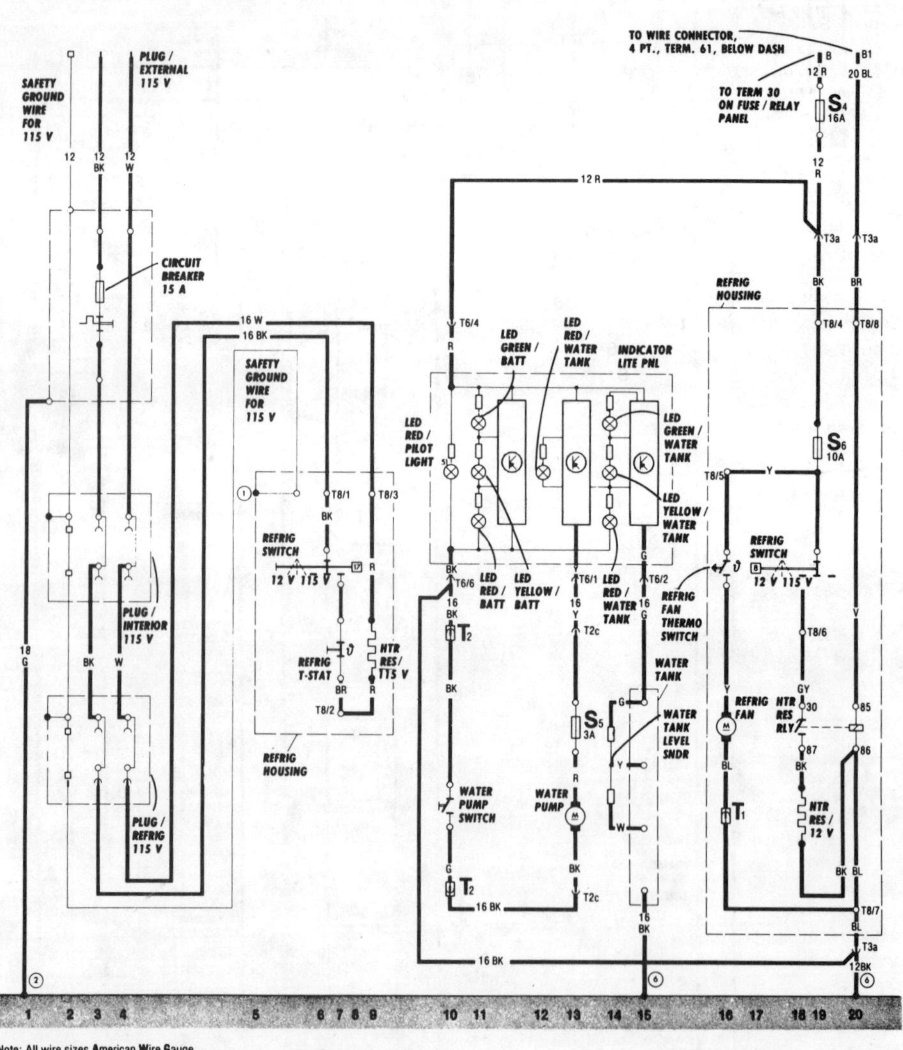

Note: All wire sizes American Wire Gauge

1980-ON GASOLINE

SEATBELT INTERLOCK SYSTEM

Wire connectors		Current Track
T1c	single, behind dash	3
T2a	double, under driver's seat	4
T3	3-point, behind dash	4, 6
T4	4-point, behind dash	8
T4a	4-point, in engine compartment	8

Wiring Color Code	
Black	– BK
Brown	– BR
Clear	– CL
Red	– R
Yellow	– Y
Green	– G
Light Green	– LT.G
Blue	– BL
Violet	– V
Gray	– GY
White	– W

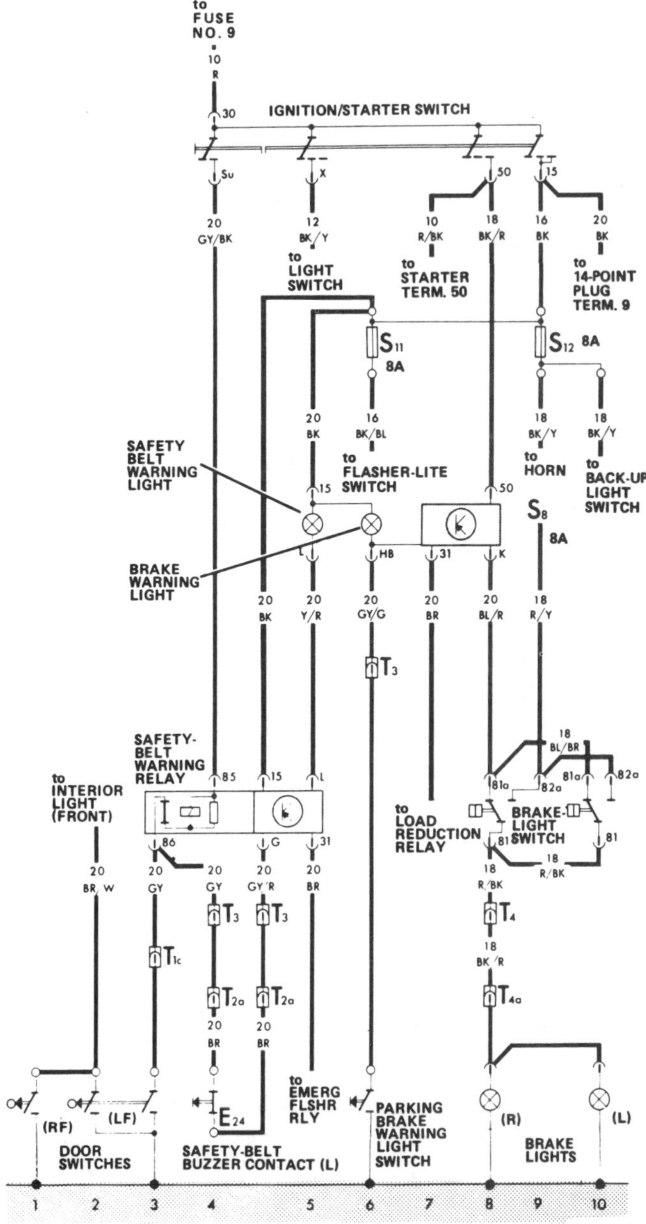

1982 GASOLINE

FRESH AIR FAN

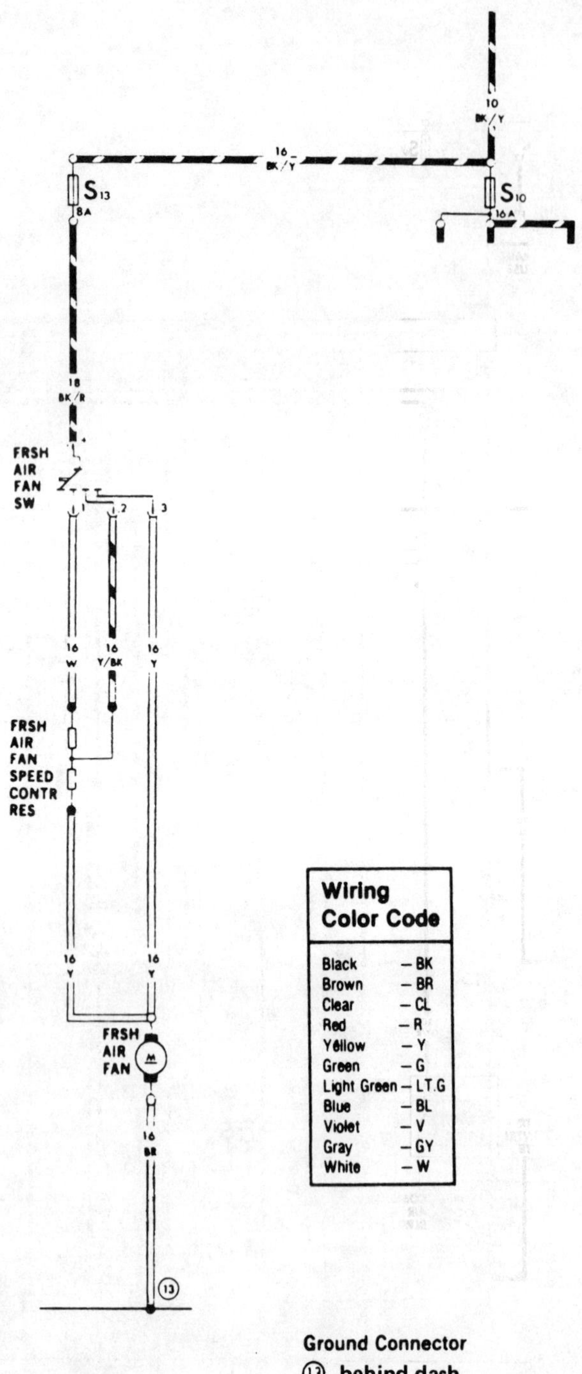

NOTE: All wire sizes American Wire Gauge

1982 AUXILIARY HEATER

(1 of 2)

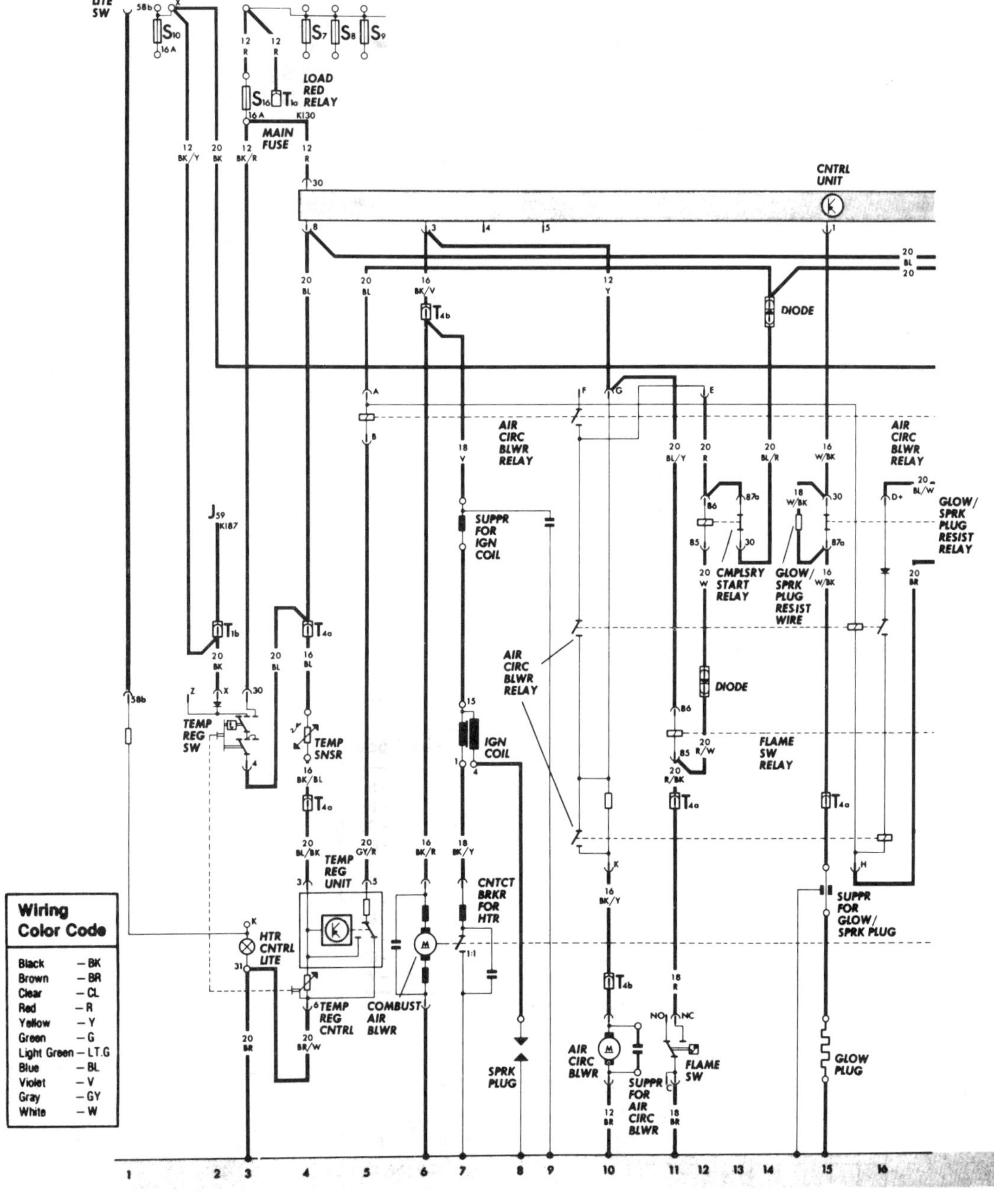

Note: All wire sizes American Wire Gauge

1982 AUXILIARY HEATER

(2 of 2)

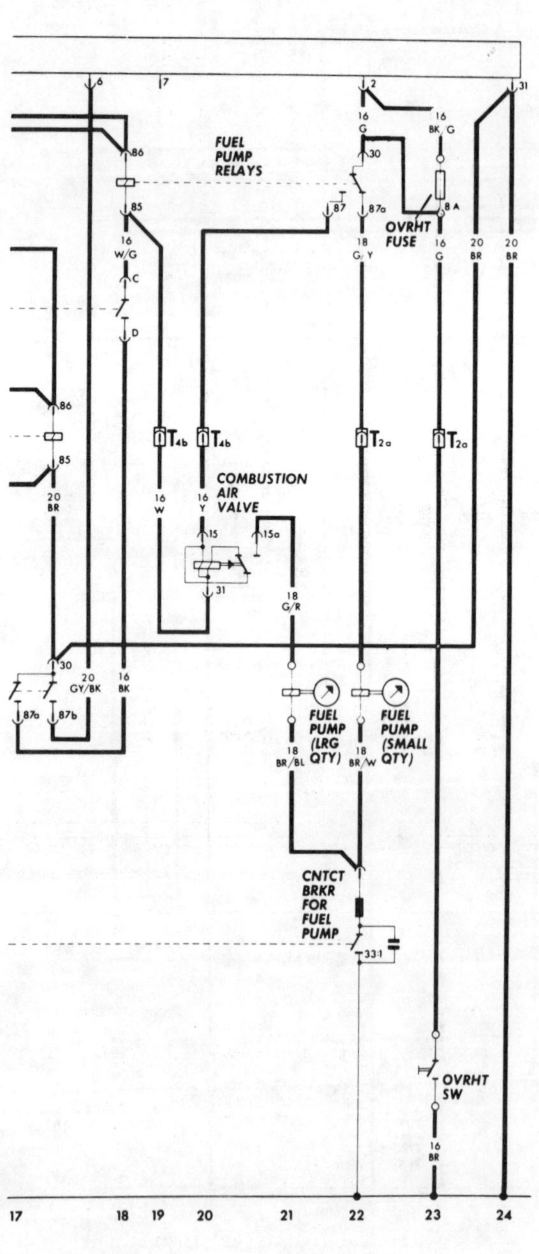

Description	Current Track
Air circulation blower	**10**
Air circulation blower relay	**5-18**
Combustion air blower	**6-22**
Combustion air valve	**20**
Compulsary start relay	**12-13**
Contact breaker for fuel pumps (in combustion air blower)	**22**
Contact breaker for heater (in combustion air blower)	**7**
Control unit	**4-24**
Diode (behind dash next to relay)	**12, 14**
Flame switch	**11**
Flame switch relay	**11-17**
Fuel pump (large quantity)	**22**
Fuel pump (small quantity)	**22**
Fuel pump relays	**18-22**
Fuse, main (16A)	**3**
Fuse, overheating (8A)	**23**
Fuses on fuse/relay panel	-
S7, 8, 9, 10	-
Glow plug	**15**
Glow/spark plug resistance wire	**15**
Glow/spark plug resistor relay	**15-17**
Heater control light	**3**
Ignition coil	**7**
Light switch	**1**
Load-reduction relay	**4**
Overheat switch	**23**
Spark plug	**8**
Suppressor for air circulation blower	**10**
Suppressor for glow/spark plug	**15**
Suppressor for ignition coil	**7-8**
Temperature regulator control	**4-5**
Temperature regulator switch	**1-3**
Temperature regulator unit	**4-5**
Temperature sensor	**4**

Wire Connectors

T1a -single, fuse relay panel
T1b -single, fuse relay panel
T2a -two point, behind dash, left
T4a -four point, behind dash, left
T4b -four point, behind dash, left

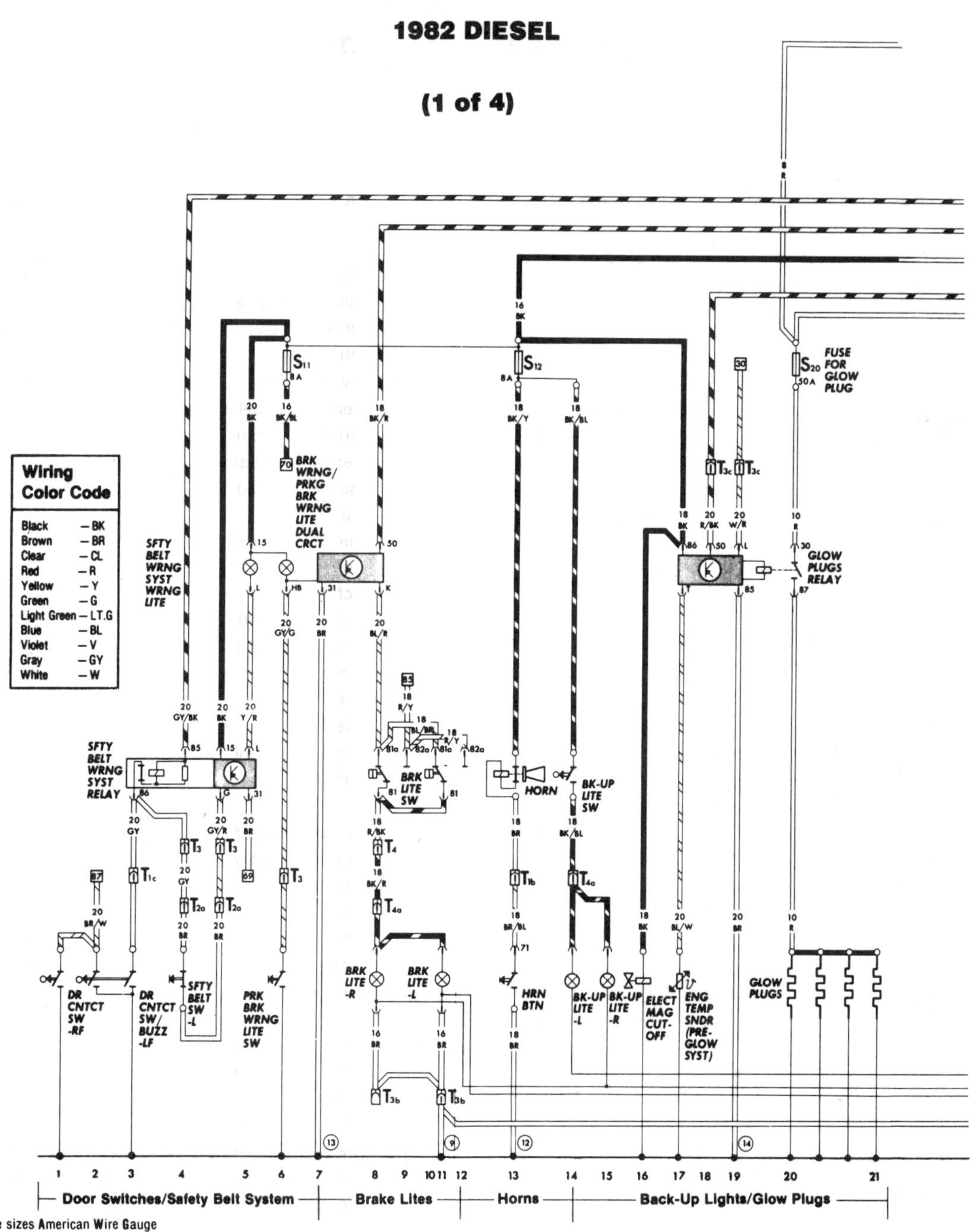

All wire sizes American Wire Gauge

Description	Current Track
Alternator	28,29
Alternator warning light	29
Back-up light, left	14
Back-up light, right	15
Back-up light switch	14
Battery	22
Brake light, left	11
Brake light, right	8
Brake light switch	8-12
Brake warning/parking brake warning light, dual circuit	6-8

Description	Current Track
Cigarette lighter	84
Cigarette lighter light	83
Clock	56
Coolant over-temperature warning light	36
Coolant temperature gauge	34
Coolant temperature gauge sender	34
Door contact switch/buzzer, front left	3
Door contact switch, front right	
Electro-magnetic cut-off	16

Description	Current Track
Emergency flasher relay	69-71
Emergency flasher switch	70-79
Emergency flasher warning light	79
Engine oil pressure switch	31
Engine oil pressure warning light	31
Engine temperature sender (pre-glow system)	17
Fresh air controls light	82
Fresh air fan	58
Fresh air fan resistor	57
Fresh air fan switch	57,58
Fuel gauge	33
Fuel gauge sender	33
Fuses, in fuse/relay panel (S-1 to S13)	

14

1982 DIESEL
(2 of 4)

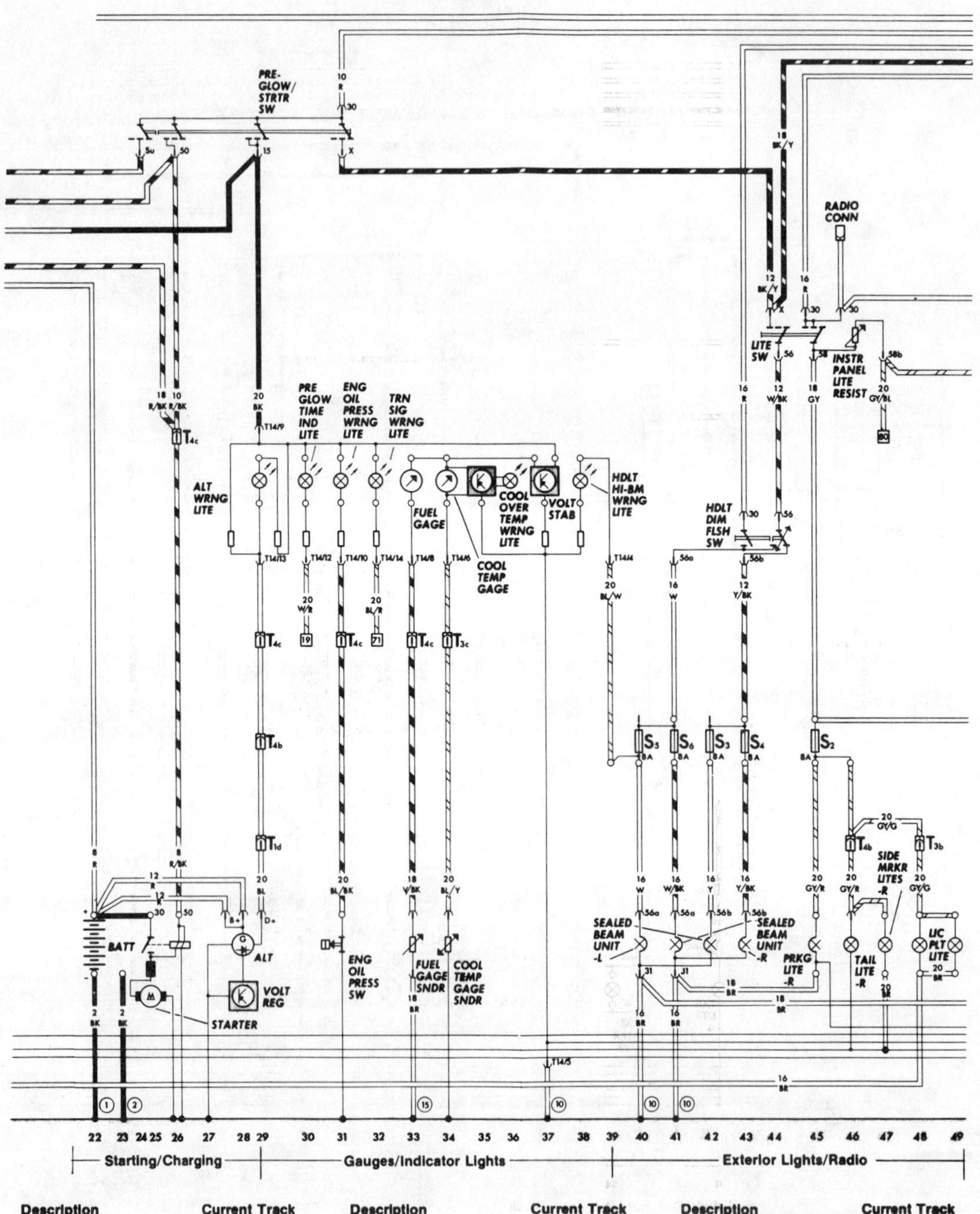

Description	Current Track
Fuse strip for glow plug, in engine compartment	20
Glow plugs	20,21
Glow plugs relay	17-20
Headlight dimmer and flasher switch	43-44
Headlight high-beam warning light	38
Horn	13
Horn button	13
Instrument panel light	53-55
Instrument panel light resistor	46
Interior light, front	86,87
Interior light, rear	88,89
License plate light	48,49

Description	Current Track
Light switch	44-47
Load reduction relay (X-contact)	65-68
Parking brake warning light switch	6
Parking light, left	50
Parking light, right	45
Pre-glow/starter switch	24-31
Pre-glow time indicator light	30
Radiator cooling fan	90
Radiator cooling fan relay for 2nd stage	91,92

Description	Current Track
Radiator cooling fan thermoswitch (switched on at 95°C/203°F)	90
Radiator cooling fan thermoswitch (switched on at 110°C/230°F)	92
Radio connectors	46,85
Rear-window defogger heating element	81
Rear-window defogger switch	81-83
Rear-window defogger switch light	82
Rear-window defogger warning light	81
Safety belt switch, left	4

1982 DIESEL

(3 of 4)

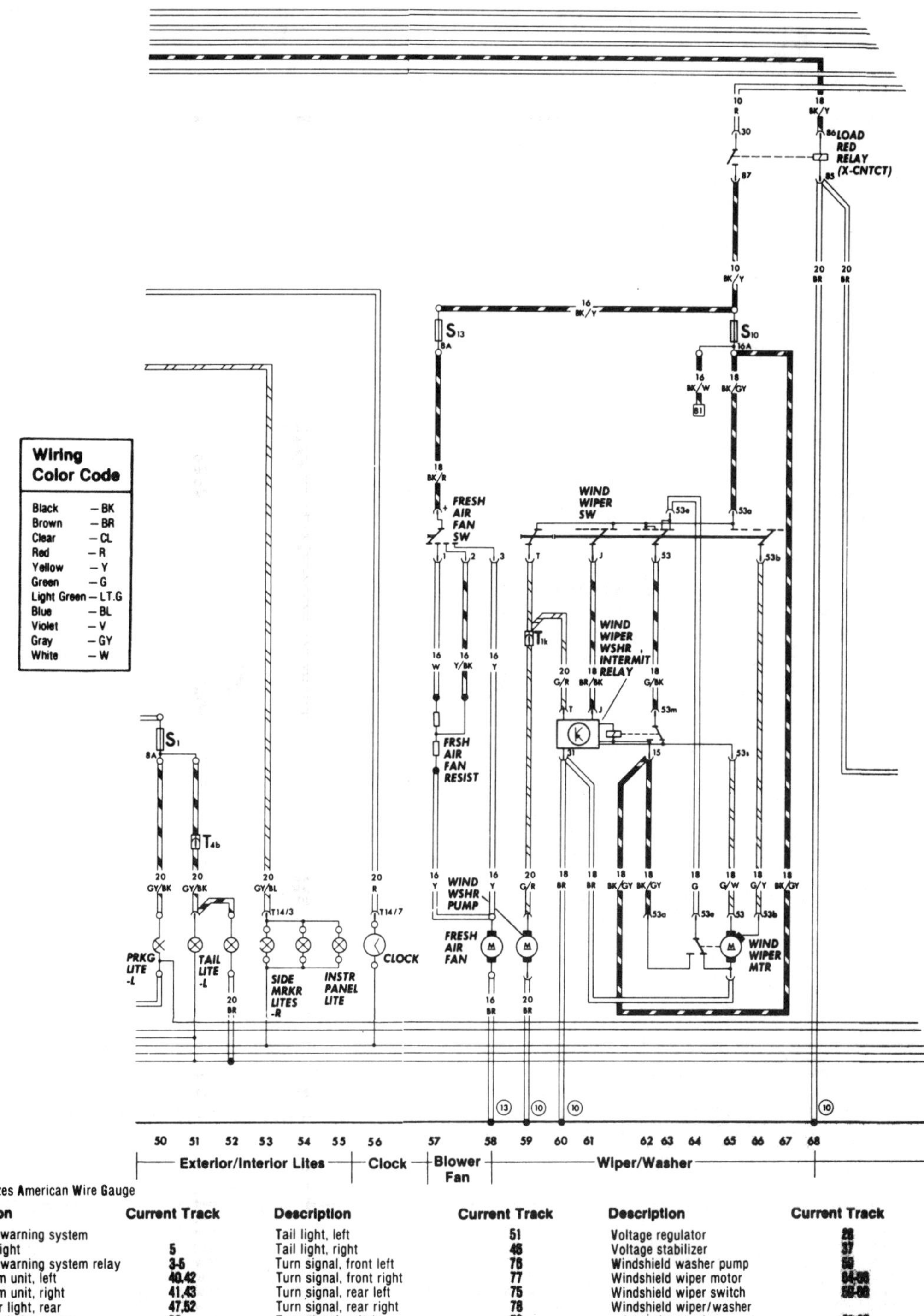

All wire sizes American Wire Gauge

Description	Current Track	Description	Current Track	Description	Current Track
Safety belt warning system warning light	5	Tail light, left	51	Voltage regulator	28
Safety belt warning system relay	3-5	Tail light, right	46	Voltage stabilizer	37
Sealed-beam unit, left	40,42	Turn signal, front left	76	Windshield washer pump	58
Sealed-beam unit, right	41,43	Turn signal, front right	77	Windshield wiper motor	64-66
Side-marker light, rear	47,52	Turn signal, rear left	75	Windshield wiper switch	58-66
Side-marker lights, rear	86	Turn signal, rear right	78	Windshield wiper/washer intermittent relay	60-63
Starter	24-26	Turn signal switch	73		
		Turn signal warning light	32		

1982 DIESEL

(4 of 4)

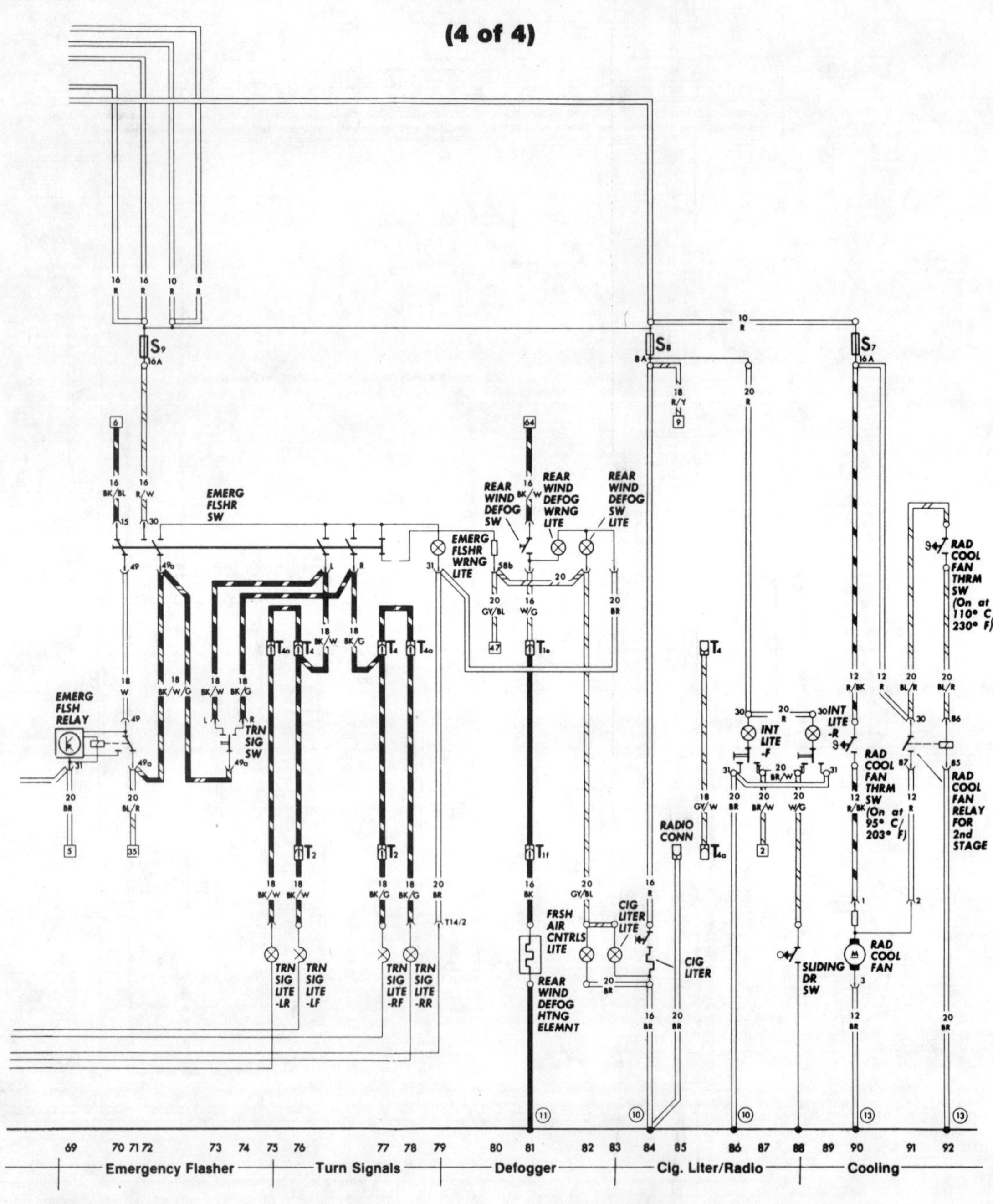

Wire Connectors

T1b	-single, behind dash
T1c	-single, behind dash
T1d	-single, in engine compartment next to alternator
T1e	-single, behind dash
T1f	-single, next to interior light rear, left
T1k	-single, behind dash
T2	-double, behind dash
T2a	-double, under driver's seat
T3	-three-point, behind dash
T3b	-three-point, in connection box
T3c	-three-point, behind dash
T4	-four-point, behind dash
T4a	-four-point, in connection box
T4b	-four point, in connection box
T4c	-four-point, behind dash
T14/	-fourteen point, on instrument cluster

Ground Connectors

(1)	-Battery ground strap, to body
(2)	-transmission/body
(9)	-in connection box
(10)	-behind dash, next to fuse/relay panel holder
(11)	-on rear lid
(12)	-on steering box
(13)	-behind fuse box
(14)	-in engine compartment, next to glowing-time relay
(15)	-on crossmember, front left